The Basque Country and Navarre

France • Spain

the Bradt Travel Guide

Murray Stewart

www.bradtguides.com

Bradt Travel Guides Ltd, UK
The Globe Pequot Press Inc, USA

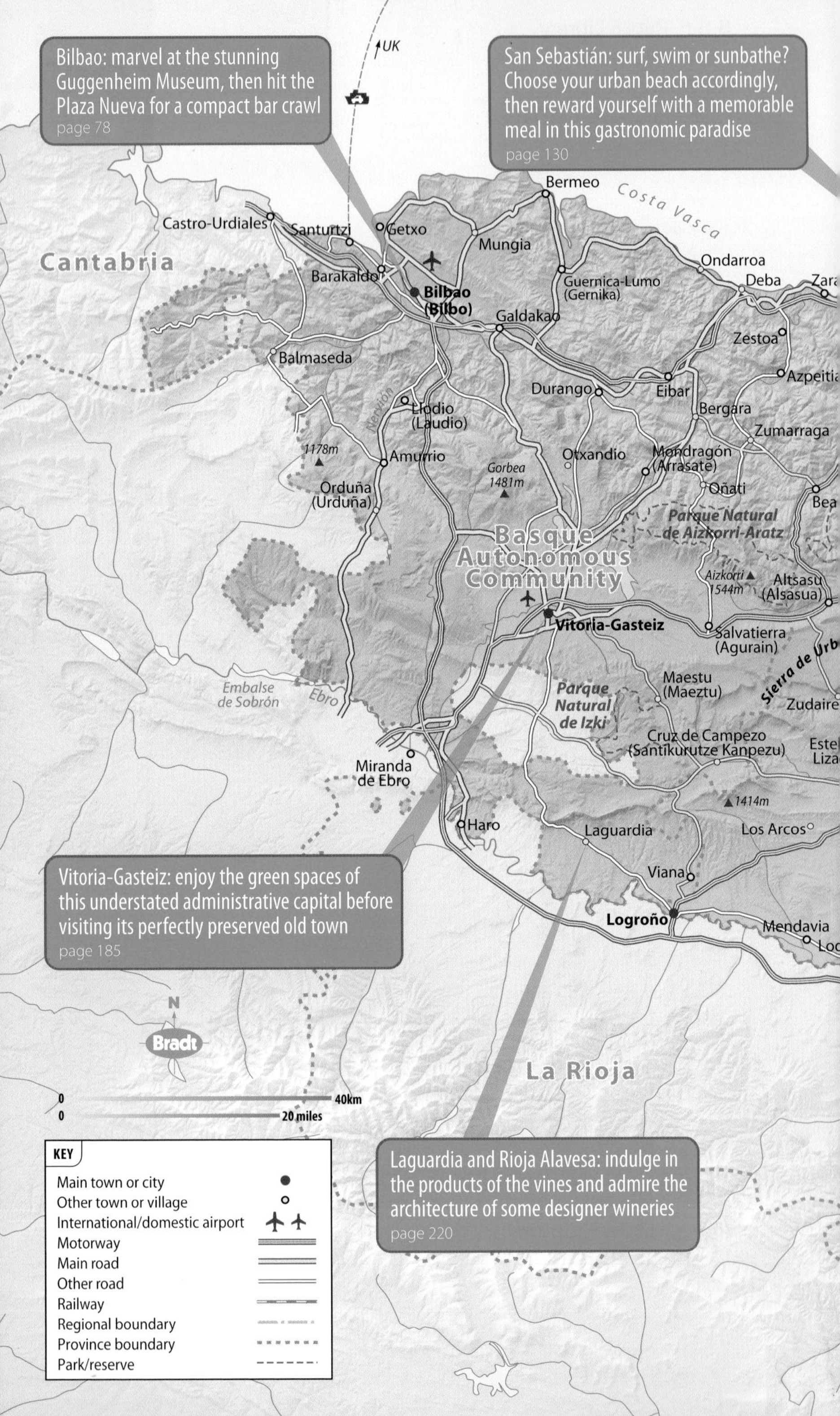

Bilbao: marvel at the stunning Guggenheim Museum, then hit the Plaza Nueva for a compact bar crawl
page 78
San Sebastián: surf, swim or sunbathe? Choose your urban beach accordingly, then reward yourself with a memorable meal in this gastronomic paradise
page 130
UK
Bermeo
Costa Vasca
Castro-Urdiales
Santurtzi
Getxo
Mungia
Cantabria
Barakaldo
Bilbao (Bilbo)
Guernica-Lumo (Gernika)
Ondarroa
Deba
Galdakao
Zestoa
Balmaseda
Eibar
Azpeiti
Durango
Nervión
Llodio (Laudio)
Bergara
Zumarraga
1178m
Amurrio
Otxandio
Mondragón (Arrasate)
Gorbea 1481m
Orduña (Urduña)
Oñati
Parque Natural de Aizkorri-Aratz
Basque Autonomous Community
Aizkorri 1544m
Altsasu (Alsasua)
Vitoria-Gasteiz
Salvatierra (Agurain)
Embalse de Sobrón
Ebro
Parque Natural de Izki
Maestu (Maeztu)
Zudaire
Cruz de Campezo (Santikurutze Kanpezu)
Miranda de Ebro
1414m
Haro
Laguardia
Los Arcos
Viana
Vitoria-Gasteiz: enjoy the green spaces of this understated administrative capital before visiting its perfectly preserved old town
page 185
Logroño
Mendavia
N
Bradt
La Rioja
0
40km
0
20 miles
KEY
Main town or city
Other town or village
International/domestic airport
Motorway
Main road
Other road
Railway
Regional boundary
Province boundary
Park/reserve
Laguardia and Rioja Alavesa: indulge in the products of the vines and admire the architecture of some designer wineries
page 220

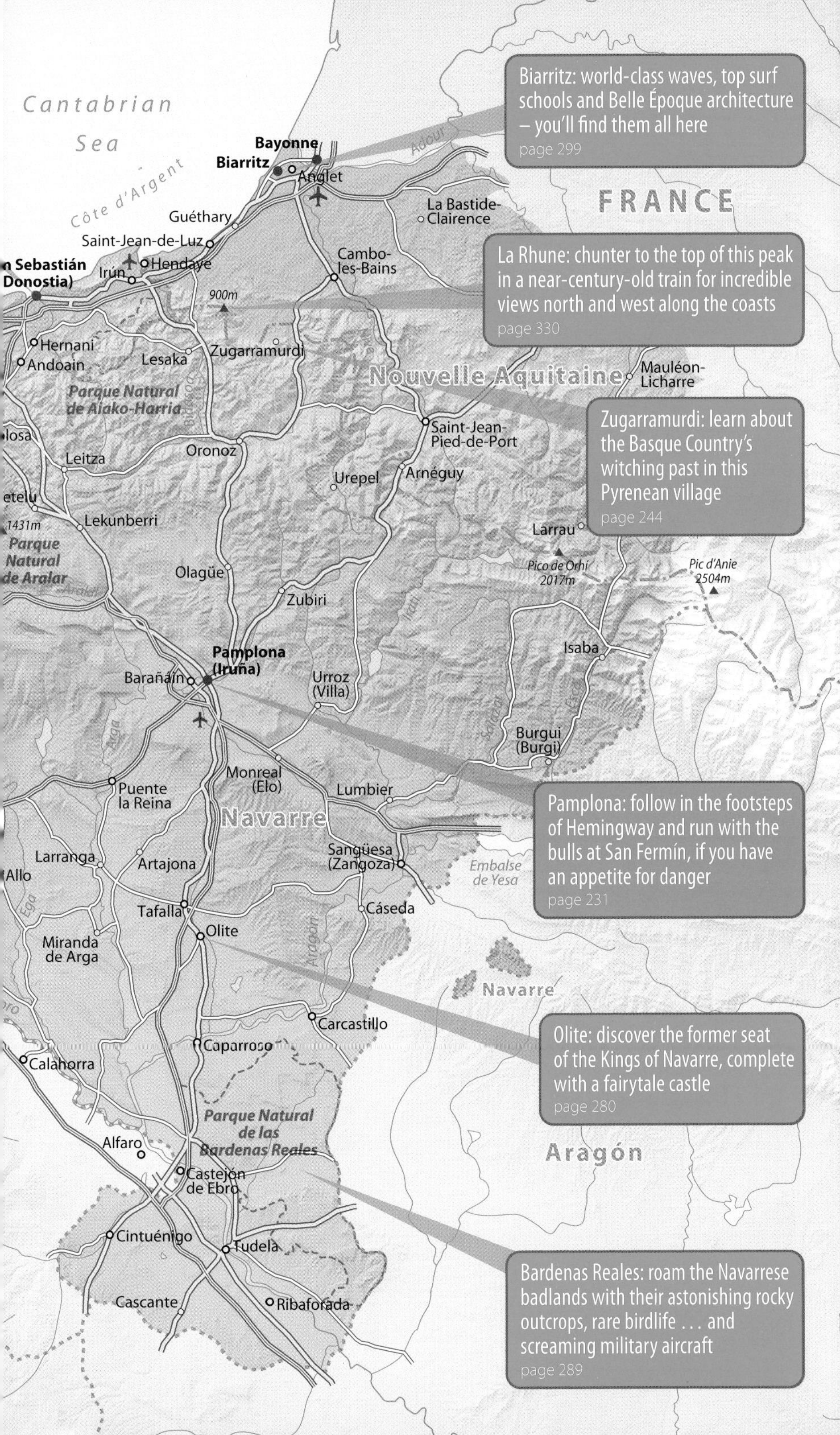

Cantabrian Sea
Côte d'Argent
FRANCE
Nouvelle Aquitaine
Navarre
Aragón
Bayonne
Biarritz
Anglet
Adour
Guéthary
Saint-Jean-de-Luz
Hendaye
Irún
San Sebastián (Donostia)
La Bastide-Clairence
Cambo-les-Bains
900m
Hernani
Andoain
Lesaka
Zugarramurdi
Parque Natural de Aiako-Harria
Bidasoa
Mauléon-Licharre
Saint-Jean-Pied-de-Port
Oronoz
Leitza
Arnéguy
Urepel
Larrau
Pico de Orhí 2017m
Pic d'Anie 2504m
Lekunberri
1431m
Parque Natural de Aralar
Olagüe
Zubiri
Irati
Isaba
Pamplona (Iruña)
Barañáin
Urroz (Villa)
Arga
Salazar
Esca
Burgui (Burgi)
Monreal (Elo)
Lumbier
Puente la Reina
Larraga
Artajona
Sangüesa (Zangoza)
Embalse de Yesa
Allo
Ega
Tafalla
Olite
Cáseda
Miranda de Arga
Aragón
Carcastillo
Caparroso
Calahorra
Parque Natural de las Bardenas Reales
Alfaro
Castejón de Ebro
Cintuénigo
Tudela
Cascante
Ribaforada
Biarritz: world-class waves, top surf schools and Belle Époque architecture – you'll find them all here
page 299
La Rhune: chunter to the top of this peak in a near-century-old train for incredible views north and west along the coasts
page 330
Zugarramurdi: learn about the Basque Country's witching past in this Pyrenean village
page 244
Pamplona: follow in the footsteps of Hemingway and run with the bulls at San Fermín, if you have an appetite for danger
page 231
Olite: discover the former seat of the Kings of Navarre, complete with a fairytale castle
page 280
Bardenas Reales: roam the Navarrese badlands with their astonishing rocky outcrops, rare birdlife … and screaming military aircraft
page 289

Basque Country Don’t miss...

Festivals

A speedy way to absorb local culture, the region’s calendar brims with colourful events. Pamplona’s San Fermín is a raucous summer celebration of Navarrese traditions

(M/S) page 239

Urban beach

Sea and city are separated by a beautiful beach: the famous La Concha, San Sebastián

(SS) page 151

Museums
Well-documented regional history juxtaposed with cutting-edge modernity: Bilbao's Guggenheim is a visual stunner and an emblem of a forward-facing people
(N/S) page 93

Take to the hills
In times of rain, the Salto de Nervión waterfall spectacularly tumbles into the gorge below (MMO/D)
page 214

Food
The Basque Country produces some of the world's best cuisine, accessible to all and enjoyed with ritual and ceremony, from *pintxo* bars to cider houses and gastronomic societies
(N/S) page 53

The Basque Country in colour

above Bilbao's Nervión River once brought ships right up to where the City Hall now stands (SS) page 76

left The Santuario de Nuestra Señora de Aránzazu is said to have been the site of a miracle and was the place where the first attempts were made to standardise Basque in written form (K/WC) page 162

below Vitoria-Gasteiz's Artium showcases contemporary art from the Basque Country and elsewhere in Spain (B) page 198

above Dating from the 10th century, the hermitage of San Juan de Gaztelugatxe has a colourful history that includes being sacked by Sir Francis Drake (MMO/D) page 115

above right Zerain's calcination furnaces are testament to Gipuzkoa's industrial past, which was often financed by British investors (MS) page 159

right Mutriku is one of several villages that punctuate the rugged Basque coast (s/S) page 184

below In typically Basque fashion, the gentle vineyards of Rioja Alavesa are boldly interrupted by the cutting-edge architecture of Santiago Calatrava's Ysios winery (SS) page 220

above Basque sculptor Eduardo Chillida's *Peine del Viento* ('Wind Comb') ushers the sea breezes into San Sebastián's bay (SS) page 144

left Jeff Koons's floral *Puppy* stands guard over the precious Guggenheim Museum in Bilbao (SR/S) page 91

below A replica of Picasso's iconic painting *Guernica* reminds visitors and inhabitants of the Civil War atrocity committed on the town (SS) page 120

AUTHOR

In 2009, with a new-found ambition to become a travel writer, **Murray Stewart** turned his back on a 20-year career in corporate restructuring that included receiving a House of Commons commendation for saving a Norfolk pea-processing factory. Drawing on visits to 56 countries, including periods teaching English in Chile and Mexico, as well as working as a consultant in Spain, he has since been published in national travel magazines as well as winning prizes for his online contributions. He jumped at the opportunity to write the Bradt guide to the Basque Country, an enigmatic region that for years had captured his interest. A self-confessed part-time 'pilgrim', Murray has walked the Camino de Santiago three times, raising thousands of pounds for charity in the process. He speaks French, Spanish and German. And thanks to this guide, he now talks a few words of Basque, too.

AUTHOR'S STORY

Walking alone guarantees time to think, time to create headspace. I had walked for weeks on the Camino de Santiago, through the French Basque Country and then across Navarre. My wanderings posed endless questions. Why these huge white-walled, red-shuttered houses that pepper the green Pyrenean foothills? Why this indecipherable language, full of 'x's and 'z's, written in a hostile-looking font?

In 2014, during three days in the city completing the purchase of a Spanish classic car, I had been smitten by San Sebastián. Here, in midwinter, was a city gearing up for a massive party, the *tamborrada*. In schoolyards, little children clothed in chefs' costumes were banging their tiny drums without a single concession to rhythm. On La Concha beach, a young sculptor carved a breathtaking masterpiece (a figure of a drummer) out of the wet sand, his contribution to the ensuing festival. Was this a city addicted to fun?

Bilbao seemed a harder sell, even with its gleaming Guggenheim. But I found a city of surprises: a characterful old quarter, an animated nightlife, an industrial heritage being polished up, a grand boulevard laid down like a red carpet to welcome its visitors. In Vitoria-Gasteiz, I watched a display of Basque sports, and pondered further. Who are these people who lift huge stones, who value their feet so little that they chop up logs wearing only training shoes? Cycling through Pamplona at San Fermín, my friend and I dodged the odd (fleetingly intact) glass which flew towards us out of the bars. Was this the Wild West? What was this raucous *fiesta* that had once entranced Ernest Hemingway? Here was somewhere truly foreign, yet so close to home. A strong and defiant culture, sometimes eyed suspiciously by outsiders but welcoming to all who respect it.

It was a pleasure to write this book, to uncover some of the area's mysteries, yet knowing that others remain unresolved, perhaps forever. Delve into all parts of this diverse region, walk the endless mountains, stroll the seaside promenades, surf the waves, embrace the culture, throw yourself into the festivals (some of the world's strangest), indulge in the food (some of the world's finest). My exhortation is simple: do what the locals do, and you are bound to be smitten by the Basque Country and Navarre.

PUBLISHER'S FOREWORD

Adrian Phillips, Managing Director

The Basque Country is a place of beaches and mountains, fabulous food and a passionate sense of identity that gives a richness of flavour to its festivals, music and sports. Murray Stewart is someone who can sympathise with such passionate self-identity – this is a man, after all, who gave up a well-paid corporate job to follow his dream of becoming a travel writer. We're very pleased he did. As it enters its second edition, this book continues to convey a love not only for the Basque Country but for the act of writing about it; it's more than useful – it's a pleasure to read.

Second edition published February 2019
First published 2016
Bradt Travel Guides Ltd
IDC House, The Vale, Chalfont St Peter, Bucks SL9 9RZ, England
www.bradtguides.com
Print edition published in the USA by The Globe Pequot Press Inc,
PO Box 480, Guilford, Connecticut 06437-0480

Project Manager: Heather Haynes
Cover research: Yoshimi Kanazawa

ISBN: 978 1 78477 624 4

British Library Cataloguing in Publication Data
A catalogue record for this book is available from the British Library

Photographs 4Corners Images: Gunter Grafenhain (GG/4CI), Reinhard Schmid (RS/4CI); Basquetour (B); Dreamstime.com: Lunamarina (L/D), Mikel Martinez De Osaba (MMO/D); www.flpa.co.uk: Otto Plantema, Minden Pictures (OP/FLPA); Shutterstock.com: Leonid Andronov (LA/S), Tono Balaguer (TB/S); Gael F (G/S), Alberto Loyo (AL/S), Rudy Mareel (RM/S), Miguel (M/S), Noradoa (N/S), Francisco Javier Gil Oriega (FJGO/S), Pecold (P/S), poliki (p/S), Quintanilla (Q/S), Santi Rodriguez (SR/S), sunsinger (s/S); Murray Stewart (MS); SuperStock (SS); Wikimedia Commons: Keto (K/WC)

Front cover Concha Bay and Isla de Santa Clara, Donostia-San Sebastián on Costa Vasca, Province of Gipuzkoa (GG/4CI); Monasterio Santa Maria la Real de Irache Monastery near Estella-Lizarra, Navarre (RS/4CI); Playing *pelota* in Tardets Sorholus, Pyrenees-Atlantiques, France (SS)
Back cover San Juan de Gaztelugatxe (MMO/D); Guggenheim Museum (RM/S)
Title page Wind comb sculpture in San Sebastian (SS); Plaza del Castillo, Pamplona (TB/S); Guggenheim Museum, Bilbao (SS)
Inside images page 73: San Anton Church, Bilbao (AL/S); page 225: Olite's Palacio Real (Q/S); page 297: Biarritz (G/S)

Maps David McCutcheon FBCart.S; colour relief base map by Geographx

Typeset by D & N Publishing, Baydon, Wiltshire
Production managed by Jellyfish Print Solutions; printed in India
Digital conversion by www.dataworks.co.in

Acknowledgements

The Basques and the Navarrese – and those who have adopted the territory as their own – are proud people, with much to be proud about. Their pride in what they have is matched only by their willingness to share it.

Among those who shared with me their culture, history and, most of all, their hospitality were Itziar Herrán Ocharan, Elixabete Arbe, Jagoba Martinez Bereziartua, Ainhoa Cordoba, Aner García Montero, Borja Irastorza, Itxaso Errabete, Ion Ubide Ibarguren, Brian Iñaki Xabier Cullen Bruneval, Mabel del Val Núñez, David Hosking, David Elexgaray, Natalia de Naverán Urrutia, Joseba Cerro Aguinagalde, Delia Vilchez Martínez, Iasmina Gorroño Elorriaga, Maria Padilla and Clara Navas. Jabier Muguruza assisted with the section on music. I would like to thank BasqueTour and all the individual tourist offices in the Basque Autonomous Community for their excellent support.

In France, Christiane Bonnat provided logistical support with excellent care and attention, and I would like to thank Tourisme Béarn/Pays Basque and all the tourist offices in the French Basque Country for their invaluable assistance.

At Bradt, a big thank you to Adrian Phillips and Rachel Fielding for trusting me with a new title and to Heather Haynes and Adrian Dixon for their editorial expertise.

Finally, to Sara Lister, my dear friend, for her support throughout.

FEEDBACK REQUEST AND UPDATES WEBSITE

At Bradt Travel Guides we're aware that guidebooks start to go out of date on the day they're published – and that you, our readers, are out there in the field doing research of your own. You'll find out before us when a fine new family-run hotel opens or a favourite restaurant changes hands and goes downhill. So why not write and tell us about your experiences? Contact us on 01753 893444 or **e** info@bradtguides.com. We will forward emails to the author who may post updates on the Bradt website at **w** bradtupdates.com/basque. Alternatively, you can add a review of the book to **w** bradtguides.com or Amazon.

Contents

LIST OF MAPS

HOW TO USE THE MAPS IN THIS GUIDE

KEYS AND SYMBOLS Maps include alphabetical keys covering the locations of those places to stay, eat or drink that are featured in the book. Note that regional maps may not show all hotels and restaurants in the area: other establishments may be located in towns shown on the map.

GRIDS AND GRID REFERENCES Several maps use gridlines to allow easy location of sites. Map grid references are listed in square brackets after the name of the place or site of interest in the text, with page number followed by grid number, eg: [78 B2].

Introduction

Whether you come to surf the waves off Biarritz or Zarautz, walk Navarre's northern mountains or its southern desert flatlands, marvel at the sparkling modernity of Bilbao's Guggenheim, admire the fairy-tale towers of Olite's historical palace or even plunge yourself into the heritage of Bizkaia province's industrial past, the Basque Country demands exploration. And if you choose to spend your stay revelling in the bars and restaurants of San Sebastián, blend into one or more of the strange festivals that punctuate a Basque or Navarrese summer, or simply stretch out on the pure sands of the coast, you'll find yourself rubbing shoulders with locals who cherish their downtime and know how to enjoy life.

The Basque Country means different things to different people. The edges are blurred. There is no Basque 'nation-state' and there never has been, apart from a tiny blink-and-miss-it period in the Middle Ages. 'Four plus three equals one' is the arithmetic favoured by Basque Nationalists, as they put together Bizkaia, Gipuzkoa and Álava before adding in the French Basque provinces of Labourd, Basse-Navarre and Soule, and completing the equation with Navarre to create the 'seven provinces'. This is their aspirational Basque Country. It's certainly complicated. Ask most citizens of Navarre whether their separate autonomous community is Basque, and for the majority the numbers above simply do not add up. Navarre may have a strong Basque feel in its northern valleys, but it nevertheless has an identity of its own, and south of Pamplona you are very much in Castillian Spain.

There may be no country or nation-state, but that in no way diminishes or dilutes what is certainly one of Europe's strongest identities. Basqueness is defined by a unique language, emphasised by a distinctive cuisine and some singular music, dance and sports. It's an identity that successfully rubbed along with the Roman Empire, survived the conflicts of the Middle Ages and later wars between France and Spain, absorbed immigrants during the Industrial Revolution, and was repressed and went underground during the dark years of Franco's dictatorship. Now it has re-emerged full of vigour.

Basque culture, language and traditions fluctuate in their strength north and south of the Pyrenees. In the diverse area covered by this book, *euskara* (the Basque language) can be heard regularly in the streets and bars of Getaria or Guernica, but rarely in Biarritz and hardly at all in Tudela in deep south Navarre. Making generalisations is therefore fraught with danger.

Mention 'the Basque Country' to many outsiders and you can sense the reaction of the listener before it's voiced. You know the association that's being made. Recent Basque history and its echoes of terrorism still sit like an unwanted ornament languishing on the mantelpiece, not yet packed away and consigned to the attic. The fact is that a permanent ceasefire has been in place since 2011; in 2017, weapons decommissioning began; in 2018, ETA announced its intention to disband itself. The horrors of the past will now surely never re-emerge. There are still live issues to be resolved, but differences of opinion over autonomy and independence now express themselves through impassioned dialogue and the ballot-box, no longer with bombs or bullets.

Two themes recur throughout this book, for which no apology is offered: food and pilgrimages. The region's near obsession with eating well ensures that every visitor will come away satisfied. *What* is eaten is of interest, but *how* it's eaten is equally important. Gastronomic societies, *pintxos*, wonderful grilled fish, a beef chop cooked over an open fire … endless creative ways to delight the taste buds, helped on the digestive journey by a glass of cider or the local wines. The people here rarely tolerate fools, and they certainly don't put up with any nonsense in the kitchen. Gastronomy is important here, which means that it's taken seriously and done *very* well.

Pilgrimages, of course, are of no interest to some visitors, but even if you never intend to set foot on the Basque or Navarrese sections of the Camino de Santiago, it's essential to understand how these age-old routes impact on the economy of the towns and villages along the way. Since the 1980s pilgrim numbers have soared and continue to do so, aided and abetted by books and films that have rekindled interest in what was originally a religious journey, but is now seen by many as something closer to a bucket-list 'must-do'. Hostels and restaurants continue to blossom, hosting and feeding the walkers, just as they did a thousand years ago. Make no mistake, some of these towns owe their good economic health and maybe their very existence to the pilgrims passing through.

Less solemn than any pilgrimage are the hundreds of festivals that cram the calendars of the Basque Country and Navarre throughout the year. Whether it's celebrating one of the many saints' days, fêting the pepper harvest in Espelette, watching young men try to break the neck of a (thankfully already dead) goose in Lekeitio or running with bulls in Pamplona, the festivals here serve the dual purpose of maintaining the region's culture and having fun.

Visitors to the area are growing in number as the raw edges of the recent past are rubbed smooth and the region's rejuvenation progresses. This book is divided into parts according to geography, but in truth the borders between them are of little import to visitors and the distances are short. A travel-writing cliché would be to claim that the Basque Country and Navarre are 'hidden treasures', but this wouldn't quite get at the truth. Rather, they are treasures that are as yet only partially uncovered. On your visit you are sure to enjoy uncovering them.

A NOTE ON PLACE NAMES

Given that the use of the Basque language varies greatly across the area covered in this book, it is difficult to be totally consistent when choosing which language (Spanish, French or Basque) to use when referring to place names. While you are likely to hear local people refer to 'Donostia' – the Basque name for San Sebastián – it would be very rare for someone to talk of Biarritz as 'Miarritze', its hardly used Basque alternative, and even rarer for someone in Navarre to speak of 'Tutera' as opposed to Tudela.

'Vizcaya' is the Spanish name for what we in English might refer to as 'Biscay' province, yet the official (and Basque) name is Bizkaia, and you are therefore very unlikely to see the name 'Vizcaya' when in the province itself. Adding to the confusion, the region is full of places that sport double-barrelled names – Vitoria-Gasteiz, Mauléon-Licharre – which could easily lead the visitor to conclude that the second part of the name is the Basque equivalent of the first. Not so: Vitoria-Gasteiz is Vitoria-Gasteiz, in any language.

The good news is that nearly every place is signposted in both Spanish and Basque, or French and Basque, depending on which side of the border you are, with only occasionally a bit of politically motivated spray-paint obliterating the Spanish or French version. In this book, we generally use the Spanish or French names, with the Basque equivalent in brackets where necessary. ('Bizkaia' is one exception – we use the Basque name, for the reason outlined above.) Tourist board maps generally use Spanish and French place-names, mindful no doubt that very few visitors will be Basque-speakers, and you are unlikely to find yourself in a place where only the Basque place name is recognised.

FOLLOW BRADT

For the latest news, special offers and competitions, subscribe to the Bradt newsletter via the website **w** bradtguides.com and follow Bradt on:

BradtTravelGuides
@BradtGuides
@bradtguides
bradtguides
bradtguides

Part One

GENERAL INFORMATION

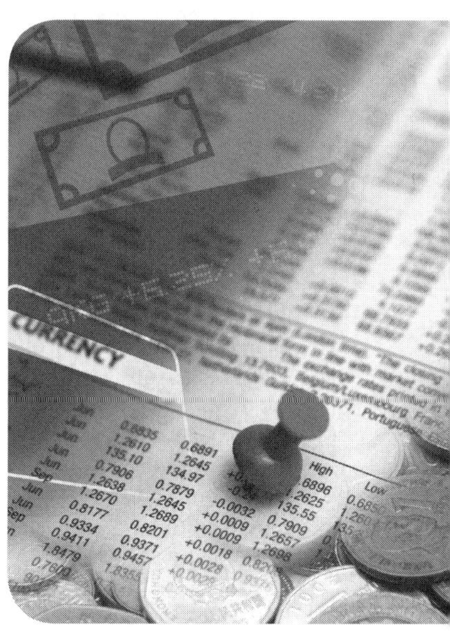

THE BASQUE COUNTRY (FRANCE AND SPAIN) AND NAVARRE AT A GLANCE

Location North-central Spain and southwest France
Size 20,747km^2
Climate Varied: oceanic with frequent rainfall around the Bay of Biscay, the inland French Basque Country and northern Navarre; warmer and drier in Álava; Mediterranean in central Navarre and semi-desert in southern Navarre
Status Gipuzkoa, Bizkaia and Álava together form the Basque Autonomous Community; the Chartered Community of Navarre is a separate autonomous community; Labourd, Basse-Navarre and Soule are all parts of the French *département* of Pyrénées-Atlantiques, within the Nouvelle-Aquitaine region
Population 3,087,000 (Basque Autonomous Community 2,189,000; Navarre 641,000; French Basque Provinces 277,000)
Life expectancy Spain: 80.2 (male), 86.1 (female); France: 79.0 (male), 85.6 (female)
Main towns Bilbao, Vitoria-Gasteiz, San Sebastián, Pamplona, Bayonne, Biarritz
Economy Basque Autonomous Community: industry based on metallurgy, manufacturing, tourism, service industries; Álava: winemaking; Navarre: winemaking, renewable energy, agriculture; France: some aviation-oriented industry, tourism and services, agriculture
GDP per capita Basque Autonomous Community €33,088; Navarre €30,914 (Spain €24,999); Aquitaine (includes French Basque Country) €35,000 (France €34,000)
Official languages Basque Autonomous Community: Spanish and Basque; Navarre: Spanish, Basque in the Basque-speaking parts; France: French
Religion Predominantly Roman Catholic
Currency Euro (€)
Exchange rate £1 = €0.88; US$1 = €1.12 (November 2018)
Airports Bilbao and Biarritz (both international); Vitoria-Gasteiz, Pamplona, San Sebastián (all domestic flights only)
International telephone code +34 (Spain), +33 (France)
Time GMT +1
Electrical voltage 220V (50Hz)
Weights and measures Metric
Flags Spain: red horizontal bands above and below broader yellow horizontal band; France: three vertical bands of equal width, from left to right blue, white and red; Basque flag (*ikurrina*): red background with white cross and green saltire; Navarre: red background with central shield
Public holidays 1 January, 6 January (Spain only), Maundy Thursday (Spain only, date variable), Good Friday (date variable), Easter Monday (date variable), 1 May, 8 May (France only), Ascension (France only, date variable), Whit Monday (France only, date variable), 14 July (France only), 15 August (Spain only), 12 October (Spain only), 1 November, 11 November (France only), 6 December (Spain only), 8 December (Spain only), 25 December

1

Background Information

GEOGRAPHY

With a combined area of some 20,700km^2, the Basque Country and Navarre occupy only as much space on the planet as the Principality of Wales, or slightly less than the state of New Jersey. In terms of pure geography, defining the Basque Country is relatively straightforward. Straddling two countries across the Pyrenean divide, the Basque Country occupies the coastal strip around the point where southwest France turns the corner around the Bay of Biscay and changes into the east–west coastal axis of north-central Spain.

South of the Pyrenees, the part of the Basque Country that falls within Spain consists of the Basque Autonomous Community's three distinct provinces of **Gipuzkoa (Guipúzcoa)**, **Bizkaia (Vizkaya)** and **Álava (Araba)**. Unlike their three French counterparts, each of these retains an important administrative significance. Inland, their landscape is often mountainous, with the hilly terrain extending close to the northern coast and the mountains dominating much of the interior of the provinces of Bizkaia and Gipuzkoa. Further inland still, the south of Álava province enjoys flatter countryside that lends itself more to viniculture and agriculture.

On the French side of the Pyrenean range, a mere 270,000 people inhabit the French Basque former provinces of **Labourd (Lapurdi)**, **Basse-Navarre (Behe Nafarroa)** and **Soule (Xiberoa)**, three names that are invisible on most modern maps. Nowadays these areas lack any individual or even collective identity immediately recognisable to outsiders. They form only a part of the larger French administrative *département* of Pyrénées-Atlantiques, which itself is a mere constituent of the *région* of Nouvelle-Aquitaine (formerly Aquitaine). Their Basque names largely long-consigned to history, even the French equivalents are scarcely prominent in the consciousness of most visitors to this corner of France. The principal towns – Biarritz, Saint-Jean-de-Luz and Bayonne – are much better known. To the west of the French Basque Country lies Béarn, still part of the Pyrénées-Atlantiques département, but distinctly non-Basque. To the north is the départment of Les Landes.

A fully autonomous community in its own right, landlocked **Navarre (Nafarroa)** accounts for half (10,400km^2) of the territory covered in this book, yet provides little more than a fifth of the total population. It lies to the east of the Basque Autonomous Community and its northern border with France is the high range of the western Pyrenees. Its own internal divide is both linguistic and geographical, between the Basque-speaking mountain- and valley-dwellers of the north and the Spanish-speaking inhabitants of its southern flatlands.

CITIES AND POPULATIONS As well as the French Basque towns mentioned above, all surprisingly modest in size (Bayonne (Baiona), the largest, can lay claim to only 49,000 inhabitants), the major population centres of the wider region are Bilbao

(Bilbo, 350,000), Vitoria-Gasteiz (245,000), San Sebastián (Donostia, 186,000) and – in Navarre – Pamplona (Iruña, 196,000). Adding in the inhabitants of their greater metropolitan areas, these four cities are home to nearly two-thirds of the three million people living in the entire territory.

Away from urban areas, with their industry and the housing for those whose labour feeds it, population density is low. Mountains and semi-desert do not make for populous communities and the Basque Country and northern Navarre have plenty of sparsely populated terrain, from the high Pyrenees bordering the north of Navarre to the modest hills at the eastern end of the Cordillera Cantábrica.

WATERS THAT FEED TWO SEAS The fate of the region's river waters demonstrates the territory's important geographical divide, that which separates the northern Atlantic (or oceanic) and southern Mediterranean zones. One of Spain's most important water courses, the **Ebro**, is the most significant river in the latter, arriving from its source in Cantabria, running from west to east along the southern borders of Álava and Navarre, gathering the waters of many tributaries and exiting the region long before emptying them into the Mediterranean Sea in Tarragona province.

In the rainy north, on the other hand, the river waters of the **Nive** and **Nivelle** make their way northwest to the Atlantic, while the **Adour** enters the French Basque Country and widens before discharging itself at Bayonne. Along the Spanish Basque coast, the narrow, south-to-north running valleys of Gipuzkoa and Bizkaia empty the waters of those provinces' rivers (Nervión, Oria, Oka and others) into the Bay of Biscay.

MOUNTAINS AND FORESTS, HIGH SIERRAS, CAVES AND GORGES Over 15 billion years ago the almighty collision of the then-island of Iberia into mainland Europe crumpled the landscape like a bonnet in a car crash, forcing the terrain upwards and creating the mountains that now characterise Bizkaia and Gipuzkoa, as well as the loftier Pyrenean peaks of northern Navarre. The Mesa de los Tres Reyes (2,424m) in northeast Navarre represents the region's highest point, but western Navarre is characterised by the craggy, imposing sierras of Andía and Urbasa, while the Spanish Basque provinces feature the massifs of Aizkorri (1,544m) in Gipuzkoa and Gorbea (1,480m) in Bizkaia and Álava.

In Bizkaia and Gipuzkoa, too, the hills running down steeply to the sea are flanked by populous valleys with a history of industrial exploitation. Despite having over 250km of coast, much of the Basque Country shoreline is not easily accessible, being defined by rocks and inlets. Nevertheless, there is still room for a succession of fine, sandy beaches scattered along the Basque coast from Anglet in northern Labourd to the western extremity of Bizkaia, beyond Bilbao.

The Atlantic climate in the region's north guarantees moderate seasonal variations in temperature, but it also means rain throughout the year, and plenty of it. Rain means trees, and the northern areas just inland are covered with deciduous species, particularly beech, oak, holm-oak and chestnut. More recent times have witnessed the commercial planting and harvesting of pine, as well as the introduction of eucalyptus.

Higher up and further inland, the mountains endure colder winters that force the livestock down to lower, warmer pastures during the inclement months. Heading south, by the time you reach Álava or southern Navarre, the landscape is a world removed from the hills and valleys of the north. As the land flattens into plains, agriculture seizes its chance. Passing through from north to south, the terrain is interrupted by the limestone caves of Sare and Urdax, La Verna further east and the spectacular gorges of Arbayún and Lumbier in east-central Navarre.

FLATLANDS IN THE NORTH AND SOUTH As you leave the Pyrenean range and traverse its southern foothills the land mellows out around the 'basin' of Pamplona, the capital of Navarre, and the natural vegetation begins to thin. Olives and vines appear, together with fields of wheat, and as the region heads towards its southern boundary marked by the Ebro, even paddy fields of rice. In Álava to the west, Vitoria-Gasteiz sits at an altitude of over 500m, yet in a flat plain bordered by the Sierra Cantabria to the south, beyond which lies the wine-producing subregion of Rioja Alavesa.

In the opposite direction, a descent of the northern slopes of the Pyrenees will eventually lead to the level terrain of northern Soule and Basse-Navarre, and finally the Adour River, which marks out the northernmost extremities of the Basque-speaking territories.

CLIMATE

Across the region as a whole, June, July and August are the driest months, and of these July and August are the warmest and sunniest. The Basque Country and northern Navarre are green for a reason, however, and that reason is rain. Rain usually falls on some days in every month, with December to March being the wettest. One peculiarity, particularly of the coastal region, is what's referred to as *sirimiri*, a persistent rain of tiny droplets that is much lighter than a drizzle – more refreshing than annoying. Winters along the coast are kept mild, thanks to the influence of the Gulf Stream.

Humidity is pleasantly low at all times of the year, with a slight increase in July and August, particularly in inland areas, but with nothing to deter the averagely tolerant visitor. Bear in mind that temperatures will be significantly lower if you are venturing into the Navarrese Pyrenees or other high places, and newcomers to the region should not underestimate the risks associated with winter trekking or hiking. On the highest peaks, snow can be found as late as June, but the lower ranges of Bizkaia and Gipuzkoa attract snowfall, too. In midwinter some mountain passes can be closed, or remain open but with compulsory use of snow chains on your vehicle.

In southern Navarre, where the climate has a more Mediterranean character, rainy days are fewer, temperatures will generally be 2–4°C higher than Pamplona, and the summer maximum in the Bardenas Reales desert area can reach 37°C.

Two other meteorological peculiarities: coastal regions, whether west- or north-facing, can be battered by high waves in winter, and sudden thunderstorms up in the Pyrenees are common, even in high summer.

FAUNA

BIRDS The region's river estuaries, inland wetlands and mountains of every shape and size guarantee that seasoned or amateur birdwatchers alike will find something of interest on a visit to the Basque Country, where nearly 350 avian species have been recorded. Nor does Navarre disappoint in this respect, with its topographical diversity – stretching from the high Pyrenees to the semi-desert of the Bardenas Reales – providing great bird-spotting opportunities. The apparent indifference of the locals to majestic, soaring vultures and eagles is a sure-fire sign that these birds are commonplace. More information about the sites described on the following pages, including precise locations, can be found within the individual chapter entries, or on the tourist board websites.

CLIMATE CHARTS

SAN SEBASTIÁN

Average minimum temperatures in °C

Jan	Feb	Mar	Apr	May	Jun	Jul	Aug	Sep	Oct	Nov	Dec
4	5	6	7	10	13	15	15	14	11	7	5

Average maximum temperatures in °C

Jan	Feb	Mar	Apr	May	Jun	Jul	Aug	Sep	Oct	Nov	Dec
11	12	14	15	18	21	24	24	23	19	14	12

Average sea temperatures in °C

Jan	Feb	Mar	Apr	May	Jun	Jul	Aug	Sep	Oct	Nov	Dec
13	12	12	13	15	18	21	22	20	18	15	13

Both air and sea temperatures for **Bilbao** and **Biarritz** will vary only slightly from the above.

PAMPLONA

Average minimum temperatures in °C

Jan	Feb	Mar	Apr	May	Jun	Jul	Aug	Sep	Oct	Nov	Dec
1	2	3	5	7	11	13	13	11	8	4	2

Average maximum temperatures in °C

Jan	Feb	Mar	Apr	May	Jun	Jul	Aug	Sep	Oct	Nov	Dec
8	10	13	14	18	23	26	26	24	18	12	9

TUDELA

Average minimum temperatures in °C

Jan	Feb	Mar	Apr	May	Jun	Jul	Aug	Sep	Oct	Nov	Dec
2	3	5	7	11	15	17	17	15	10	6	3

Average maximum temperatures in °C

Jan	Feb	Mar	Apr	May	Jun	Jul	Aug	Sep	Oct	Nov	Dec
10	12	16	18	23	27	31	30	26	20	13	10

Urdaibai (page 122) Situated at the mouth of the Oca River, close to Guernica, the Urdaibai Bird Centre is an enthusiastically run place for birdwatchers. It features observatories, excellent information and a live webcam allowing you to see exactly what's happening at any given time. If an unusual or interesting species arrives, you can be on to it straight away. Migrating ospreys stop here on their way to and from Scotland.

Txingudi (page 174) Just south of Hondarribia, this is a wetland centre popular with migratory species but also with many resident birds observable year-round.

Sierra Salvada Rock-breeding raptors and other smaller species are the draw here, thanks to the spectacular cliffs, which constitute their ideal environment. A highlight – in terms of both scenery and bird-spotting – is the Salto de Nervión waterfall (page 214) as it plunges 200m down into the valley.

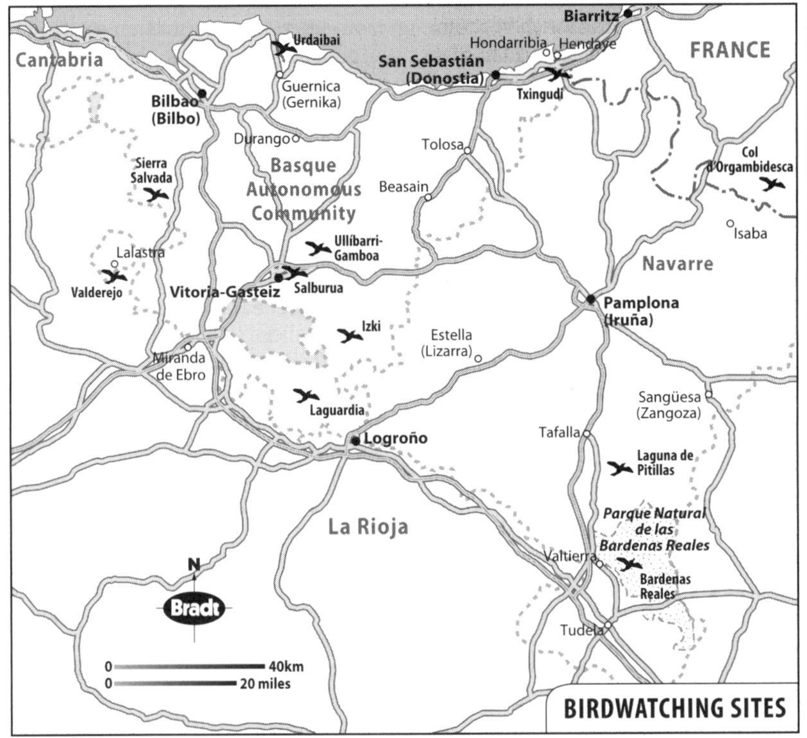

Salburua (page 199) On the outskirts of Vitoria-Gasteiz, an excellent and highly accessible wetland centre with observatories and well-defined circuits for walking and cycling.

Ullíbarri-Gamboa (page 202) Artificial reservoir just east of Vitoria-Gasteiz, with a circular cycle route and two observatories situated within its Mendixur Ornithological Park.

Lagunas de Laguardia (page 222) Four lakes – three natural and one artificial – within walking distance of Laguardia town. As well as the aquatic species, the surrounding Mediterranean vegetation attracts nesting from birds such as the short-toed lark and black-eared wheatear.

Izki (page 204) A natural park with areas of dense woodland scattered with limestone outcrops, Izki is another area rich in raptors. Woodpeckers are also a prized sighting.

Valderejo (see box, page 208) In the west of Álava province, rocky escarpments and the Purón River allow visitors to combine superb gorge-walking with easy spotting of vultures and eagles.

Laguna de Pitillas (page 287) This is a small *laguna* in the centre of Navarre which has an observatory and walking circuits. Over a hundred species have been recorded here.

Bardenas Reales (page 289) Stunning semi-desert scenery and unusual rock formations. Birds such as golden eagle seem undeterred by the military air force, which uses the area for target practice!

Col d'Orgambidesca High up in southwest Soule, this is a spot renowned for sighting migrating species. Mid-August until mid-November presents the best opportunities, with birdwatchers on the lookout for griffon and the rarer bearded vulture, as well as cranes, storks and pigeons, the last of these attracting a large number of hunters in October.

Other areas Visitors to either side of the **high Pyrenees** are likely to encounter vultures and other rock breeders, particularly in the valleys of **Belagua** and **Salazar**. In the France–Spain border-straddling **Irati Forest** (page 258), visitors may be rewarded with sightings of woodpeckers. Navarre's gorges, the **Arbayún** and **Lumbier** (page 263) and the hilltop town of **Gallipienzo** (page 285) are also locations where raptor – especially vulture – sightings are virtually guaranteed.

REPTILES AND AMPHIBIANS Those with an interest in reptiles will find several **snake species** such as the ladder snake (*Zamensis scalaris*), Montpellier snake (*Malpolon monspessulanus*) and Aesculapian snake (*Zamenis longissimus*), the last of these growing up to 2m and being one of Europe's longest.

Most of the region's snakes are not venomous, but there are two which definitely are, though sightings are rare and, like many snakes, they stay out of the way of humans and attack only when disturbed. The asp viper (*Vipera aspis*) grows to a maximum of 90cm, has a broad, triangular head, short dark stripes across its body and a bite which is painful, though rarely fatal and then only if left untreated. The Baskian viper, or Iberian cross adder (*Vipera seoanei*), usually brown in colour but with varied skin markings, is slightly smaller than the European one, and has a bite which requires medical attention but again is not fatal.

Two rare regional reptiles are the **European pond turtle** (*Emys orbicularis*) and the **Spanish pond turtle** (*Mauremys leprosa*), both of which are somewhat threatened with displacement by larger species of unwanted pet turtles discarded by their owners in ponds and rivers.

Also to be commonly found are the **slow worm** (*Anguis fragilis*) and the **Western three-toed skink** (*Chalcides striatus*), as well as **lizards** such as the European green (*Lacerta viridis*), Iberian wall (*Podarcis hispanica*) and common (*Zootoca vivipara*).

Salamanders, newts, frogs and toads all feature among the amphibians present here. The **fire salamander** (*Salamandra salamandra*) is black and yellow in colour and can grow to 16cm in length. Its preferred habitat is wooded, hilly areas. **Marbled newts** (*Triturus marmoratus*) are dark-bodied with green patterns and can grow up to 13cm. For those looking for an exclusive sighting, the small **Pyrenean brook newt** (*Calotriton asper*) is endemic to this mountain range, distinctive for its four fingers, five toes and lack of any crest.

Among the **toads and frogs** can be found the Iberian spadefoot (*Pelobates cultripes*), the common parsley frog (*Pelodytes punctatus*) and the aptly named agile frog (*Rana dalmatina*).

MAMMALS Neither a visit to the Basque Country nor a trip to Navarre will reward you with many mammal encounters. It's not that they're not present, just that they sensibly keep out of sight. Starting with the rarest, the last female **Pyrenean brown bear** was shot in 2004, although attempts have been made to introduce examples

LOOKING OUT FOR WHALES AND DOLPHINS

The above is the byline of ORCA, a clever play on words which sums up neatly the twin objectives of this marine mammal conservation charity that has been studying whales and dolphins in the Bay of Biscay since the 1990s.

If you're travelling to Bilbao or Santander on Brittany Ferries you may well encounter the workers or volunteers of ORCA onboard. They give excellent, informative presentations free of charge to passengers, raising awareness of the surprising number of species that might appear in the waters below. Dolphins are the most common, with pods of up to 200 mammals having been sighted in the recent past.

For those who want to focus more on these amazing giants of the ocean, there is the possibility to make a special trip, a 'Sea Safari' which gives you two nights on board, the benefit of the ORCA representatives' assistance with sightings and a few hours in Santander to look around. For more information on the charity, visit w orcaweb.org.uk or email anna.bunney@orcaweb.org.uk. If you fancy a safari, try w brittanyferries.com/whale.

of the species from Slovenia, with mixed results. The programme has not been universally popular, particularly among shepherds, as the bear is an omnivore and not averse to killing a few sheep when food is in short supply. It is thought that only around 20 bears live in the whole of the Pyrenean range, but only one in the Valle de Roncal in Navarre. Equally invisible is the **Iberian wolf**, systematically eliminated from most of Spain during the Franco dictatorship but with some reported sightings in the west of Bizkaia province. It is generally more easily seen in neighbouring Castile and León.

A little more common are **deer**, **beech marten**, **fox**, **red squirrel**, **European mink** and **European wildcat**, all present in various parts of the region. In the dense forests, **wild boar** are numerous but well concealed and much sought after during hunting season. The Bidasoa River harbours a population of **otters**.

Whales and dolphins Anyone crossing on the car ferry from the UK to northern Spain should keep their eyes peeled for the large pods of dolphins which play cat-and-mouse with the ship's bow – a quite spectacular show. Much rarer would be to see a whale or two, but you can increase your chances of a sighting, as well as your knowledge, by teaming up with ORCA, an organisation dedicated to cetacean conservation (see box, above).

Despite Basque sailors hunting the North Atlantic right whale to near-extinction many centuries ago, the Bay of Biscay is an excellent place to spot many species of cetaceans. Among those most frequently sighted amid these sometimes rough waters are killer whales, sperm whales, fin whales, beaked whales and pilot whales.

HISTORY

Whether from studying the scant available evidence of anthropology, archaeology or the Basque language, the only conclusion that can reasonably be drawn is that the precise origins and date of arrival of the people now known as the Basques are both unclear. Few peoples can claim such obscurity of origin.

Evidence, though somewhat patchy, shows that the Basque territories were certainly occupied around 250,000 years ago. Cave art from the Upper Palaeolithic period, such as can be found in the caves of Santimamiñe in Bizkaia or those of Istaritz in Basse-Navarre, provide more solid traces of human occupation in the Basque territories, but this dates back only 15,000 years, to around 13000BC. The ethnicity of the artists is not clear, however, and no-one can say with certainty that they were the ancestors of the present-day Basques.

The discovery and analysis of skull fragments from a Cro-Magnon man, dating back to around 9000BC, have been used by some to claim that the current inhabitants of the Basque Country have the same distinctive skull formation as their 11,000-year-old ancestors, and from that conclusion to assert that the Basques have been in continuous occupation of these lands to the west of the Pyrenees ever since then. Some commentators point out that this evidence is far too weak to form such bold conclusions with anything approaching certainty; some suspect that those assertions are being gladly adopted by those with some political axe to grind. (Of course, merely disputing such claims invites accusations of taking the opposite political stance.) Menhirs and dolmens attest to mountain-dwellers in the wider Aquitaine region around 5000BC, and Celtic people left traces here when they arrived in the 1st millennium BC. Without doubt, people did live here in ancient times, but were they Basques? No-one knows.

What's more, did they speak Basque, or even a language from which it derived? A study of a people's language and its connections to other tongues can often give strong evidence as to the origins of its speakers but, as is well known, *euskara* – the Basque language – is virtually without relation to any other. True, its undisputed status as a non-Indo-European language might suggest that the Basques *were* safely installed in their current homelands long before the Indo-European influx of peoples during the Bronze Age, but the counter-theory suggests that they were actually more likely to have been a part of those migrations and that their 'isolation' only commenced after they took up residence in their current corner of the European continent.

While the origins of the Basques will doubtless continue to interest historians and excite those who wish to establish them as the 'oldest and most original of European inhabitants', (or, to argue the opposite case), for the purposes of a travel guide and from the perspective of a curious visitor, it will have to be sufficient to leave the matter unresolved. Instead, we can be satisfied with what exists today: a unique and rich culture which has its origins somewhere in the mists of time. The Basques are certainly different, we just don't know from where the difference originates.

THE ROMAN PERIOD AND BARBARIAN INVASIONS It is only during the time of the Roman occupation that the first written evidence of the Basques' presence in their current location can be found. The Romans were the first to give these inhabitants a name, 'Vascones', from which *Vascos* in Spanish, *Basques* in French derive.

The mighty Roman Empire turned its attention to the Iberian Peninsula in the 3rd century BC, although it would take a further 200 years before their incursion was complete. But in respect of the area now covered by what are today deemed the seven Basque provinces, the conquest remained incomplete. Roman remains in southern and central Navarre (such as at Andelos), as well as those in Álava (for example, at Iruña-Veleia) bear testament to the extent of Roman occupation. No-one disputes that Pamplona, founded in 75BC, takes its name from Pompeii. But although the Roman-era walls at Bayonne and the remains at Saint-Jean-le-Vieux demonstrate Roman presence north of the Pyrenean divide, the inhabitants of the unwelcoming valleys and mountain regions of the Basque areas seem to have been left alone. As long as the Romans could protect their through routes crossing the mountains from south to north, control of the Pyrenees themselves and conquest of their inhabitants were not priorities – or else, were simply not worth the effort.

Today, the imprint of the Roman period is still evident in the agriculture in the southern part of the region. Vines and olive trees, introduced by the Romans, both remain an important part of the landscape in lower Navarre and Álava. In the north, the Roman routes allowed them to make use of some of the natural resources present: mines were established near Oiartzun in Gipuzkoa, for example, and their remains are still visible today.

Having waxed for nearly 500 years from 100BC, Roman influence in the region then began to wane, with unrest stirring from within the territories and invaders arriving from outside. From the north, the threat came from the Visigoths, who conquered the south of France before crossing the Pyrenees to occupy much of Spain, bringing with them their own brand of Christian beliefs. Roman authority was over, but the new invaders were not minded to establish proper control structures in its place and a period of sporadically troublesome coexistence ensued between Basque and Visigoth. Outbreaks of conflict and battles were common in the 6th and 7th centuries and the Basques resisted the spread of Christianity that was taking hold in the rest of Spain, retaining instead their many pagan beliefs. Additional threats were posed in the 6th century by the Franks, as they sought to extend their power base from central France towards the south and into Aquitaine. In AD507, the Frankish ruler Clovis defeated the Visigoths in battle, pushing them south of the Pyrenees. The occupants of the southern lands – including the Basques – resisted. But the early 8th century saw an event that would alter the course of Spain's history for centuries, diminishing the importance of any local skirmishes.

THE MIDDLE AGES

Conflict, unification, division and annexation In the year AD711, the Moors invaded Spain from the south, with the vestiges of the Visigoth tribes unable to repel them. Moorish conquerors pushed ever northward as the century progressed, taking over most of Spain before eventually being halted by Charlemagne's Frankish armies. The territories of the Basques were now under threat from both these forces. Allowing the Franks to cross their lands to subdue the Moors, the Basques then suffered as Charlemagne's forces razed Pamplona on their return journey northward. Basque revenge was swift and brutal, as in 778 they attacked and routed the Frankish rearguard under the command of Roland at Roncesvalles, high in the Pyrenees. Often cited as being the Basques' only military victory, it is incorrectly recorded in the renowned *Chanson de Roland* as being a Moorish triumph. With the Frankish threat temporarily quelled, the priority was then to deal with the Moors, who were continuing to press from the south. New alliances were necessary to meet this force, eventually resulting in the creation of the Kingdom of Pamplona (later to become the Kingdom of Navarre), with Íñigo Arista (790–851) as its first acknowledged monarch. Although Pamplona would be taken and retaken many times, the Moorish conquest would never reach as far as the northern coast. Despite using the Roman-built roads to cross the Pyrenees and fight the Franks, the Moors never properly subdued the Basque mountain-dwellers.

At the start of the 10th century the first pilgrimages began towards Santiago de Compostela, traversing what were often hostile and as yet un-Christianised Basque territories. By then an independent Duchy of Gascony had been established, with Sancho Menditarra as its duke: it was a region free from Frankish control and covered Labourd and Gipuzkoa; Moorish invaders had been repelled again at Pamplona. Foundations were inadvertently being put in place for a unified Basque territory, and this briefly came to pass under the rule of Sancho III of Pamplona (known as 'Sancho el Mayor' or 'Sancho el Grande', 999–1035), revered – for achieving this very feat – as Navarre's greatest king. Not only did the territories under his control include Bizkaia, Álava, Gipuzkoa, Gascony and Navarre (as far south as the Moorish stronghold of Tudela), but also parts of Aragón, Castile, La Rioja and even territories around Toulouse in southern France. With the rest of Spain under Muslim rule, this Kingdom of Navarre now stood firm as a bastion of Christianity against further Moorish expansion. Unique in the history of the Basques, this period of unification was nevertheless short-lived, and on Sancho el Mayor's death in 1035 these vast territories were divided between his sons. Nearly a thousand years later, this brief coming together of Basque territories still carries enormous significance in the minds of those who would one day seek to re-establish it.

The partition of Sancho el Mayor's great kingdom would divide the northern Basque lands from the southern territories, and also pave the way for the establishment of the separate kingdoms of Aragón and Castile, this latter incorporating for now both Gipuzkoa and Álava. Although Navarre regained both of them in the 12th century, they soon reverted to Castile once again, the loss of its coastline leaving Navarre permanently landlocked. In 1234, the succession to the Navarrese throne passed to the French house of Champagne, and with that it inched closer to France. Bizkaia staved off the threat of Castile more successfully than its two neighbours, being ruled at first by a succession of 'Lords of Biscay'. It was in this period that the tradition of the general assembly (*juntas generales*) of Guernica was established, each village sending its representative to meet under the famous oak tree, now an indelible symbol of Basque autonomy and political freedom. With the incumbent Lord required to swear to uphold the privileges of the Bizkaians, such as certain exemptions from taxation and military service, the cornerstones of Basque society were becoming entrenched. Even when Bizkaia and Castile came under common rule, from 1379, the Basque privileges were respected and the King of Castile had to journey to Guernica to honour them.

For the Basque provinces under Castilian control, charters known as *fueros* (see box, page 17) were granted to their towns (*villas*) to preserve their political autonomy, with the price being the allegiance of the townsfolk to the king. This system is still precious to the Basque psyche, and subsequent Basque history is a story of the *fueros*' diminishing status over the 800 years that followed.

The 200 years after Sancho el Mayor's death were also characterised by the struggles to free Spain from the Moors, with a significant blow being struck in 1212 at the Battle of Las Navas de Tolosa. For once, the rival forces of Castile, Aragón and Navarre united to defeat the Muslims, a success viewed as pivotal in the slow Christian march to reconquer Spain. (It would still take nearly 300 more years before Moorish Granada would succumb to the Catholic monarchs of Ferdinand and Isabella.)

Iparralde, an outpost of England North of the Pyrenees, the lineage of Duke Sancho Menditarra (page 11) had endured until the mid-11th century, but this Duchy of Gascony was gradually weakened by a decentralisation of power and eventually passed to the control of the more powerful Duchy of Aquitania (Aquitaine) in 1052. Basque influence had waned, the use of its language having retreated from the Bordeaux area back south to the Adour River, the northern boundary of the present-day Basque-speaking territories. Eleanor of Aquitaine's marriage to Henry Plantagenet in 1153 resulted in Henry becoming both Duke of Aquitaine and Gascony, and his subsequent succession to the throne of England brought the duchy under English control. Succeeding Henry as Duke, Richard the

Lionheart had to attack Bayonne to quell local disquiet at this English rule and, with the successful repression of further uprisings, most of the northern Basque lands were under English control by the start of the 14th century. For some locals, this would prove to be a time of prosperity and Bayonne's inhabitants would stay loyal to the English to the end of their rule. Basse-Navarre remained the exception to English rule, still under the control of the Kingdom of Navarre, away across the mountains to the south. It would take until 1449 before Soule was retaken for the French crown, with Labourd following a year later, thus ending 300 years of English dominance.

Anarchy in the south: the War of the Bands Back in the south, the experience of the latter Middle Ages in Bizkaia and Gipuzkoa was one of great unrest, mostly created from within, during a period known as the Bando Gerrak, or War of the Bands. After the Lordship of Bizkaia was partially subsumed under the Castilian crown in 1379, a series of blood feuds between noble families, already simmering, began to boil over. Each ruling over a compact area or one of the characteristic narrow valleys, various *jauntxoak* (chiefs) waged war against each other, settling old scores and taking refuge in the *casas torres* (tower-houses) that they built for their protection. (Although many were subsequently demolished, some of these distinctive buildings can still be seen in the Basque countryside today.) Among the family feuds, the conflict between the Oñacinos and the Gamboinos became the bloodiest, the two warring bands engaging with each other on several occasions and causing much slaughter both among themselves and others outside their clans. To counteract the anarchy, non-participants grouped together in *hermandades* (collectives for self-protection and peacekeeping) and organised themselves into settlements and towns with support from the crown. Nevertheless, it took until the 16th century before peace was fully restored.

Basque society and economy in the Middle Ages A singular feature of Basque society in the Middle Ages was the complete absence of the feudalism found elsewhere in Europe, with neither serfs nor forced labour. Rights of free assembly, equal rights of men and women before the law and the passing down of the family farm to the eldest offspring were all key features of the Basque social structure.

Although the Basques engaged in agriculture inland and fishing, whaling and shipbuilding along the coast, commerce provided an international aspect to economic activity. As early as the 14th century, Castile's wool exports were finding a route to northern Europe, particularly Flanders, through the ports of Bizkaia and Gipuzkoa; the English were employed as treaty partners to quell piracy and develop trade. In addition, the Basques' reputation as experts at both building and sailing ships would be put to use as Spain struck out to explore the New World.

Religion arrives late Despite France having been evangelised 800 years previously and Christian Navarre having complete control of the Basque territories – albeit briefly, in the 11th century – it was only in the 15th century that the Basques could be said to have been fully converted to the Christian faith. The boom time of the pilgrimages towards Santiago de Compostela, crossing both the Spanish Basque provinces and Navarre, helped to introduce the inhabitants to new ideas and philosophies and also necessitated the construction of monasteries and churches to support the pilgrims on their long journey westward. Additionally, the ships that set out to discover new territories took with them missionaries, exporting the ideology of the Jesuits, founded by a Basque, Ignatius of Loyola.

More turmoil as the nation-states emerge The end of the War of the Bands (page 13) may have heralded the diminution of internal conflicts, but plenty of trouble was already brewing outside the borders of the Basque territories, waiting to destabilise the status quo. Navarre, with territory on either side of the Pyrenean divide, was being eyed by France from the north and from the south by powerful Castile; its days as an independent kingdom were numbered. After previous attempts to carve it up had failed, and following years of conflict, Castilian troops finally took Pamplona in 1512 and the inevitable annexation soon followed. The Navarrese throne decamped north of the border and the Kingdom of Navarre was reduced to the territory more or less corresponding with present-day Basse-Navarre. Back in the south, the conquered part of Navarre would manage to hold on to many of its powers even under the new forced union with its Castilian master. Such autonomy was to persist, along with that of the Spanish Basque provinces, until the 19th century and the defeat of the Basques in the First Carlist War.

North of the border, the 16th-century threats to the French Basques were many and varied, with military attacks from the English, French and Spanish resulting in regular occupation and destruction of towns in Labourd. With forced translation of the *fors* (*fueros*) of Labourd and Soule into French and Béarnais respectively, the Basque language was also being weakened; religious wars resulted in Soule turning Protestant, putting it at loggerheads with its Catholic neighbour of Basse-Navarre. Although Spain had given up any attempts at annexing Basse-Navarre, the crowning of Henry IV of France and Navarre in 1589 led to its subsequent integration into France in 1620 and the end of Navarre as a kingdom. On a lighter note, the turbulent 16th century also saw the emergence of the first Basque university in the Gipuzkoan town of Oñati.

Despite attempts to reduce tensions through Franco-Spanish royal marriages, the 17th century witnessed the eruption of cross-border tensions between Spain and France into full-blown warfare, with the Basque Country's frontier location guaranteeing that its coastal towns would suffer attacks, sieges and destruction. Peace was finally established when the border between the two countries was delineated by the 1659 signing of the Treaty of the Pyrenees, followed by the marriage of Louis XIV of France to Princess Maria Theresa of Spain.

With an increasing thirst for centralised control in both Madrid and Paris, this was also a century in which the cherished autonomy of the Basques underwent further attack on both sides of the border. With Basse-Navarre's 1620 absorption into France, both it and Soule had been put under the control of neighbouring Béarn, against the will of the inhabitants, signalling a shift of power out of the Basque Country. This was not well received, and neither was the attempt by the king's appointed lackey to seize control of the traditionally communal grazing lands, leading to an uprising in Mauléon-Licharre. (The Château d'Andurain, page 358, in the town still bears the scars of the revolt.)

Of Jews, Moors, witches and inquisitors Although the existence of an Inquisition in Spain pre-dates the defeat of the Moors, it was after the 1492 *reconquista* of Spain that new concerns of both royalty and church resulted in an increase in its activities. Orders for the expulsion of Jews were given shortly afterwards and the Inquisition busied itself with flushing out those Christian converts who continued to clandestinely practise Judaism. Muslims would also soon become targets. At first, France tolerated Jews, though not without limiting their activities, but the Inquisition was not averse to monitoring their activities by planting spies in French Basque towns. Then, by a 1602 order of Henry IV, Jews were expelled from Labourd at short notice and, although some left the area completely, others cleverly resettled in Saint-Esprit, a stone's throw across the river from Bayonne, but importantly out of the Basque territories and just inside the department of Les Landes.

Riding on the waves of the Counter Reformation, other minorities were soon to be identified as ripe for persecution along with the Jews and Muslims. Protestants, gypsies and *cagots* (see box, page 245) were all hounded, before attention turned finally to the Basques and, in particular, those who were said to be engaging in witchcraft. At the start of the 17th century, suspicions existed that this was being widely practised, particularly in the French–Spanish borderlands. A series of interrogations, confessions and denunciations took place; once the Inquisition got wind of the matter, trials and executions followed, with the womenfolk of the Navarrese village of Zugarramurdi marked out for special persecution. (A visit to the village's excellent museum – page 244 – is highly recommended.) North of the border, dozens of supposed witches were burnt at the stake until the returning fishermen of Saint-Jean-de-Luz took violent exception to the fate being meted out to their womenfolk. The widespread witch-hunts were over.

THE 18TH CENTURY: A TIME OF TRADE AND INDUSTRY – AND A REVOLUTION

Old privileges lost, new opportunities taken In contrast to the preceding centuries of upheaval and conflict, the 18th century provided a calmer platform on which the Basque people could seek to exploit further their natural resources and maritime skills, developing trade with lands overseas. Today, vestiges of small-scale Bizkaian iron foundries from these times can be found, restored and operational, bearing witness to the industrial acceleration of the time. The heavily forested lands were decimated to serve increased shipbuilding, as the Basques played a full part in exporting to and importing from the New World. Although pepper and cocoa had probably arrived in the Basque Country by the 16th century, it was the cultivation of another New World import, corn, which was more instrumental in changing the agricultural landscape of the Basques.

A blow to Basque fishing was struck by the 1713 Treaty of Utrecht, which resulted in Britain acquiring former Basque rights in Newfoundland, in turn leading to the subsequent depopulation of fishing communities on the Basque coast. For French Basques, the complex treaty retained some limited rights to fish off Canadian shores, but provided nothing for their Spanish Basque counterparts. Part of the Basque coastal economy for centuries, fishing was now sorely diminished and new avenues had to be explored.

Often cited as a shining example of 18th-century Basque enterprise, the Real Compañía Guipuzcoana de Caracas was created in 1728 to explore the new opportunities being presented. Its initial target was the import of cocoa from Venezuela, and the directors cleverly included the Spanish crown as an investor, thus guaranteeing certain trading privileges. Taking advantage also of the Basque ports' exemption from Spanish customs duty (a special, historical favour ceded by Castilian kings), the company's burgeoning trading activities kick-started ancillaries such as shipbuilding and logistics along the Basque coast. Diversification took place, the cocoa being joined by imports of coffee, leather and tobacco. In the other direction went shiploads of Basque natural resources such as wood, as well as manufactured iron products. Navarre also benefited through the export of its wine and, eager to trade with everyone, the company became a true multi-national.

The French Revolution If the preceding centuries had seen an erosion of cherished rights and privileges, attacks on autonomy and a desire for centralised power by the mother states, for French Basques the situation was about to get a lot, lot worse with the French Revolution of 1789. The post-revolutionary parliament was from the outset hell-bent on getting rid of any regional privileges enjoyed by Basques or anyone else; indeed, they got rid of the regions themselves, instead replacing them with 83 departments and subsuming the three French Basque provinces into the new department of Basses-Pyrénées, along with Béarn. With the arrival of the new regime came the departure of Basque laws from France, including the unique inheritance rights of the oldest child and the common land rights – both cornerstones of the Basque societal structure. A process of eradicating all French regional languages began.

Owing to the unease caused by the radical ideas of the revolution, Spain and France went to war in 1792, with the latter forcibly taking San Sebastián, Bilbao and Pamplona, before peace was once again established in 1795 – at least for a while.

THE 19TH CENTURY: A TALE OF TWO BONAPARTES, THE DEMISE OF THE *FUEROS* AND THE BIRTH OF BASQUE NATIONALISM Napoleon's 1808 occupation of Spain and the imposition of his brother Joseph on the Spanish throne, at the expense of the incumbent Ferdinand VII, heralded a century of conflicts that would result in a seismic shift in the position previously enjoyed by the Basques in Spain. Much as the French Basques lost their privileges under their *fors* as a result of the French Revolution, so the Spanish Basques would see their ancient and dearly loved *fueros* disappear as a result of defeat in the two Carlist Wars fought in the 19th century.

Napoleon's expansionist ambitions in Spain were halted at the Battle of Vitoria in 1813, the French being defeated by the Duke of Wellington and his coalition forces. Ferdinand was restored to the Spanish throne, but a bitter dispute over his succession would eventually lead to further conflict and disaster for the Basques in Spain. Nor would it just be fought over succession. On the one hand, the anti-Carlist supporters of Ferdinand's daughter Isabella envied post-Revolutionary France and espoused a new era of liberalism, centralism, urbanism and secularism. In the other camp, those on the side of Carlos (Ferdinand's brother and the other claimant to succeed him) stood for a powerful monarchy, pro-Church conservatism, preservation of 'the old ways' and, most importantly for the Basques (and others, too), the continued existence of a high degree of regional autonomy. For the Basques, their precious *fueros* simply *had* to be maintained.

For six bloody, brutal years from 1833, the First Carlist War was fought in north-central and northeast Spain, with the Basque territories being centre stage. Carlist attempts to take Bilbao and Madrid were unsuccessful. With parts of Gipuzkoa and Navarre loyal to the anti-Carlists, Basque fought against Basque and massacres took place on both sides. Anti-Carlists burnt churches, showing their intent to weaken the power of the Church. In 1839, with the Carlists defeated, the war finally came to an end. The processes of diminishing the independence of Navarre and the Basque provinces continued, as well as the lessening of the Church's sway.

At the same time as the autonomy of the Carlist provinces was being dismantled, another change was taking place, one that would alter the landscape, this time quite literally. The Industrial Revolution arrived, and was to have a particularly strong impact on Bizkaia and Gipuzkoa. To take advantage of Bizkaia's natural resources, needed to feed Britain's voracious appetite for iron ore, ports were improved and the railway was introduced. Capital flooded in from northern Europe, funding the creation of infrastructure. Powerful local banks were created. Bilbao's economy was forged on the creation of huge steel works. By the end of the 19th century, over three-quarters of Spain's iron and steel were being made in Bizkaia.

THE *FUEROS*

At the very heart of the question of regional autonomy is the status of the *fueros* (or *fors*, in French). To diehard Basques and Navarrese, these are ancient statutes conferring on them certain rights and privileges, including exemption from military conscription, external taxation and political autonomy. The *fueros* were immutable and had something of a constitutional feel to them, so Spanish and French kings were obliged to honour them and respect them as confirmation of the Basques' political independence.

The interpretation of the *fueros* by those outside the region, less sympathetic to regional autonomy, is different. To those centralists, they were mere concessions of privilege by monarchs over the centuries and, importantly, could be withdrawn at any time. Much of the region's history has centred on the struggle to preserve the rights enjoyed under the *fueros*.

Large-scale industry would bring wealth to some Basques, but its arrival was at the expense of existing small family businesses. Foreign control and management were also imported, threatening the more rural way of life that was the cornerstone of Basque society and thus cherished by Carlist traditionalists. To provide labour for the mills and factories, immigrants arrived from elsewhere in Spain, thus diluting the 'Basqueness' of the population. Further weakening of Basque social structures occurred mid-century with the legalisation of secular marriage and the new freedom of religion. With so many fundamental changes afoot, it is unsurprising that the Basques' dissatisfaction continued to grow. It would result in the outbreak of another Carlist War in 1872.

Added to the power of the anti-Carlists in this new conflict were the vested interests of those benefiting from the industrialised era. Perhaps as a result, the Carlists were once again defeated, losing many of their remaining privileges in the process. But if the 19th century witnessed the dousing of the fires of Carlism and the partial extinction of the traditional ways of life, a new spark was about to be lit, one that would bring turmoil and strife for the next hundred years: Basque nationalism.

EARLY 20TH CENTURY: 'EUSKADI', CIVIL WAR AND DICTATORSHIP Stripped of their rights and privileges by military defeat, the Basque identity would soon start to reassert itself in adversity with the creation of the idea (though not the reality) of 'Euskadi' (an independent Basque state), a new flag (the *ikurrina*) and a political party (the PNV or Basque National Party) with an enduring rallying cry: *Jaungoikua eta lagizarra* or 'God and the old laws'. The architect behind this aspiration and its emblems was a Bizkaian, Sabino Arana (1865–1903; see box, page 18) whose tangible legacies were to long outlive both him and the uglier parts of his ideology.

When it arrived in 1931 with an anticlerical agenda and liberal character, the Second Spanish Republic was founded on beliefs that should have marked it out as clearly at odds with the pro-Church, conservative Basques. From its underground existence, forced upon it by the dictatorship of Primo de Rivera, the Basque Nationalists' PNV emerged re-energised under its leader José Aguirre, gaining supremacy in Bizkaia and Gipuzkoa and clamouring for a Statute of Autonomy. It would take the onset of the Spanish Civil War in 1936 before this would be granted, and then only as a means for the Republicans to secure Basque support against Franco and his fascists. (Navarre stayed outside the process.) But within a year of the outbreak of the Civil War, Guernica had been bombed from the air, Franco's troops had overrun the Basque provinces, the new Basque government had been exiled and the Basque Country in Spain was under Franco's control. Spanish Basques fled to the French Basque Country and the Americas; Basque children were evacuated to Britain and elsewhere. The backlash against what Franco called the 'traitor provinces' began immediately, manifesting itself in prison sentences and executions. By 1939 the war was over in every part of Spain and Franco's dictatorship had begun.

WORLD WAR II AND BEYOND The exile of the Basque political leadership gave them the chance to lobby abroad. Spain may have been neutral during World War II, but in many international eyes Franco's fascism was indelibly stamped with the same mark as Hitler's in Germany and Mussolini's in Italy. The assumption among Basques was that Franco's regime, internationally isolated and excluded from any post-war reconstruction cash, was unlikely to survive for long after the end of World War II; indeed, food rationing would not end until 1952. Ironically, it was communism – or rather the threat of it – that would save the dictator. In the early 1950s, with the USA seeking airbases in Spain to bolster its Cold War efforts, Franco was able to negotiate both economic aid and diplomatic recognition in return. Basques were dismayed by Spain's coming in from the cold, aghast at the Americans' perceived 'betrayal'. The situation was soon compounded by Spain's subsequent admission to the United Nations in 1955. Some fervour disappeared from the Basque nationalist cause, the PNV being seen by some as being too moderate, too soft to push the hard-line agenda.

Factions were created within the group, and the splinter in the Basque nationalist ranks soon led to the foundation of a new vehicle for change, Euskadi Ta Askatasuna (ETA, 'The Basque Country and Freedom'). Determined to promote the still-outlawed Basque language, its primary objective was to push for full independence and, unlike the PNV, its members were prepared to engage in violence to achieve it. To the outside world, ETA would become inextricably linked with the Basque Country

SABINO ARANA: HERO, VILLAIN OR BOTH?

Given the fiery passion for asserting their identity, it would seem appropriate that there should be a national figure, a hero to form a focus for the Basque cause. Although he died at the age of only 38, Sabino Arana certainly left some lasting pegs on which the garb of Basque nationalism still hangs. One of these is the green-red-white *ikurrina* flag, now adopted as the official flag of Euskadi and which can be seen fluttering from balconies or imprinted on T-shirts. The political party that he founded has lasted too, being the most significant in Euskadi, and currently still holding the most seats in the Basque Parliament – which it has done throughout nearly all of its existence.

But although some Basque nationalists would embrace him as a hero, his writings and pronouncements would certainly find no favour with Spaniards and be considered unpalatable by many outside observers. A significant number of Basque nationalists, too, would distance themselves from his more extreme views, while remaining grateful for the catalyst he provided to nationalism at the turn of the century and the legacy that he left. He was a firm believer of the racial superiority of the Basque over the Spaniard, resented the influx of immigrants to Bizkaia during the industrial era and was vehemently opposed to intermarriage of Basque and non-Basque, which he viewed as corrupting the 'purity' of the race.

for decades to come; it still is, despite a ceasefire and weapons decommissioning. The emergence of ETA, with an agenda being driven by youth rather than the PNV old guard, signified a movement to the left among some Basque nationalists, capturing the global revolutionary spirit of the 1960s. Sabino Arana's definition of a Basque, based on genetics and implying a racial superiority, was ditched in favour of one simply requiring a 'Basque' to be someone who speaks the language.

Although ETA's stated willingness to use violence amounted to little at first, the position had changed by the end of the 1960s. A policy of direct action that avoided casualties changed to calculated, targeted killings, often aimed at the police or military, but claiming civilian lives too. Madrid's responses to the attacks would at times bring the imposition of martial law, together with arrests and trials that did not always follow proper legal process. Claims of police torture of detainees were often made. In the meantime, the French Basque Country provided a safe haven for ETA activists, allowing them to plan their attacks in relative safety. Aside from such violent episodes and the turbulent politics of the time, the 1960s also saw the standardisation of the Basque language, harmonising the linguistic differences which until then had existed between the seven provinces and even between adjoining valleys. An overarching arts movement that incorporated everything from music and sculpture to literature was in train, too, promoting Basque culture and anchoring it ever more firmly in a period of severe repression and adversity.

Franco died in 1975. Freed after over 35 years of dictatorship, Spain had to quickly navigate its way through a transition to democracy, satisfying the competing claims of regional separatists while avoiding the real danger of a right-wing coup.

The Basque Country post-Franco In the Spanish Basque Country and Catalonia the dictator's death was celebrated. Spain's changeover from dictatorship to democracy would not bring a halt to the ETA killings, however, nor did it see any immediate end to the Spanish government's repression of the Basques, although by the end of 1977 all political prisoners had been released.

In 1978, a new constitution for Spain was created. A key clause, and one that has become particularly important in the light of Catalonia's current push for independence, affirms the 'indissoluble unity' of Spain. For the Basques, too, it was a clause that created a significant barrier to any meaningful talk of an independent nation. The constitution was ratified across Spain, though not in the Spanish Basque provinces. Nevertheless, it took effect. Navarre, with a different history and with much of its territory culturally 'non-Basque', chose its own path, declining to be joined to the Basque Autonomous Community (BAC) and becoming a separate community of its own. Both the BAC and Navarre gained a higher degree of autonomy under their subsequently enacted statutes of autonomy than anywhere else in Spain, including Catalonia. But for many Basques, it was still not enough.

The years immediately following the new constitution and the statutes of autonomy were the bloodiest in the history of ETA, with many assassinations. They also witnessed a new twist in the retaliation by the Spanish state. As well as the imprisonments without trial and torture, kidnappings and assassinations of ETA activists took place by a sinister group known as GAL (Grupos Antiterroristas de Liberación), believed by many to have been sponsored by the Madrid government, or at least those close to it. Since the initial release of prisoners in 1977, further arrests have taken place, with those convicted being consigned to far-flung prisons in Tenerife or Seville, well away from the Basque Country.

Throughout the 1980s and 1990s, violence persisted and the final and shocking tally amounts to over 820 killings attributed to ETA, while the police and the Guardia

Civil have been responsible for around 200 deaths. GAL, in its short existence from 1983 to 1987, killed 27. Towards the end of the 1990s and beyond, ceasefires were announced then broken; political parties associated with ETA were banned, but reinvented themselves with new names, only to be banned again. Negotiations for peace began and then were terminated. Mass street demonstrations against violence took place: the cause for independence did not fade, but any appetite for pursuing it through shootings, kidnappings or car bombs, only ever favoured by a small minority, had been swamped by a huge majority that was clearly sick and tired of the killings. Infamously, the false implication of ETA in the 2004 Madrid train bombings is generally thought to have cost José Aznar and his Partido Popular the Spanish general election, which took place three days later.

In 2011, ETA announced a permanent cessation of its armed struggle. A decommissioning of weapons began with much fanfare in 2017, but although overseen by an international commission, its work was not recognised by the Spanish government. Finally, in May 2018, ETA announced that it would disband itself, a decision that had been expected for some time.

HISTORICAL TIMELINE

c250000BC	First traces of human habitation in the region can be traced (Palaeolithic period)
c4000–3000BC	Dolmens, primarily to be found in Navarre and Álava, demonstrate the presence of pastoral people (Neolithic period)
900BC	People of Celtic and Indo-European stock arrive in Navarre from north of the Pyrenees
2nd century BC	Romans arrive in Navarre, settling mainly in the south and introducing cereal farming and viniculture
75BC	Founding of Pamplona by the Romans
56BC	Aquitaine (incorporating most of the present-day French Basque Country) is occupied by Julius Caesar
AD400–500	Decline of the Roman Empire, invasion of Visigoths from the north
711	Arrival of Moorish invaders on the Iberian Peninsula
778	Charlemagne's Frankish troops defeated by the Basques at Roncesvalles
824	Íñigo Arista rules as the first 'King of Pamplona'
c900	First pilgrimages to Santiago de Compostela
1004–35	The seven Basque provinces are united – briefly, for the only time in history – under Sancho III ('Sancho el Grandé'), who is proclaimed 'King of Spain'
1153	The marriage of Eleanor of Aquitaine to Henry Plantagenet results in the provinces of Labourd and Soule coming under English rule
1200	Navarre loses its access to the coast
1234	The succession of the throne of Navarre passes to the Counts of Champagne, beginning the line of French Kings of Navarre
1300	Bilbao gets its charter
14th–16th centuries	'War of the Bands', a succession of blood feuds, settling of old scores and family rivalries take place, mainly south of the Pyrenees. Rival bands subsequently join forces to fight against the *villas*, and the chartered towns are created and given privileges by the Navarre and Castile monarchs to diminish the powers of the nobility.
15th century	More than 80% of the iron brought into England emanates from Gipuzkoa and Bizkaia, as the Basques exploit their natural

	resources of iron ore and charcoal for their own benefit, as well as using their strategic location to export to northern Europe
1450	Labourd reverts to France at the end of the Hundred Years War
1468	Aragón and Castile unite with the marriage of Ferdinand and Isabella, a union that lays the foundation for the creation of modern Spain. Navarre's position is severely weakened.
1491	Birth of Ignacio de Loyola, who in 1540 will found the Company of Jesus (Jesuits)
1492	The fall of Granada to the Catholic armies signals the end of 780 years of Muslim rule of Al-Andalus (effectively, most of the Iberian Peninsula). Expulsion of the Jews in Spain by royal decree.
16th century	Advances in shipbuilding allow Basque sailors to extend their whale-hunting activities, reaching the northwest Atlantic
1512	Navarre is conquered by Castile, though Basse-Navarre remains an independent kingdom north of the Pyrenees
End 16th century	Recession badly affects the Basque iron ore trade. Corn imported from the New World is cultivated and in part replaces dependence on wheat.
1589	Henry IV is crowned in France and eventually brings Labourd, Basse-Navarre and Soule under common control
1620	The integration of Basse-Navarre into France finally heralds the end of the Kingdom of Navarre
1659	The Treaty of the Pyrenees is signed by Louis XIV and Philip IV, delineating the frontiers of the kingdoms of Spain and France
1728	The Real Compañía Guipuzcoana de Caracas is created in San Sebastián, the first Spanish company with shareholders. The company acquires the monopoly on the Venezuelan cocoa trade. The king's shareholding ensures trading preferences are granted to the company.
1765	The Royal Basque Society is founded during the Age of Enlightenment
1789	The French Revolution leads to the abolition of feudal rights and the repression of regional languages north of the Pyrenees
1790	Soule, Basse-Navarre and Labourd provinces are joined to Béarn, forming the new French *département* of Basses-Pyrénées
1808	Start of the Spanish War of Independence. Napoleon I arrives in Bayonne to receive the abdication of the Spanish monarchy in favour of his brother Joseph.
1813	The Battle of Vitoria sees the defeat of the French forces by the Duke of Wellington and his allies, heralding the decline of Napoleon's power
1833	Start of the First Carlist War. Despite the opposition of the French government, the French Basques support the Carlists, who are also supported by the Basques south of the Pyrenees. Against them, Navarre takes the anti-Carlist side.
1839	End of the First Carlist War, with Basques on the losing side
1853	Marriage of Napoleon III to Eugénie. In the following years, seaside tourism develops in Biarritz and San Sebastián, helped in the former case by the arrival in Bayonne of the railway (1862) and the building in both towns of second homes by the aristocracy.

1856	The Treaty of Bayonne newly establishes the French–Spanish border
1863	Seeking room for expansion, San Sebastián demolishes its city walls and plans the construction of suburbs
1872–76	Second Carlist War, with the Basques again defeated
1890–1900	Football is first introduced into the Basque Country from England, accelerating the significance of sport for the masses
1890	First labour dispute in Spain breaks out, in the Bizkaian mines
1894	The *ikurrina* (Basque flag) makes its first appearance, designed by a native of Abando, Sabino Arana, who then founds the Basque National Party (PNV) in 1895
1900	Bilbao develops industrially, while San Sebastián continues to flourish as a leisure resort. Vitoria establishes itself as a military and religious stronghold.
1911	Founding of the Basque Artists' Association heralds a renaissance of Basque culture
1914	First *ikastola* (Basque-language school) founded
1919	Basque Language Academy founded, promoting Basque language and reinforcing the cultural renaissance
1920	Population of Bilbao reaches 101,000 (1877: 32,000); San Sebastián 68,000 (1877: 21,000)
1931	Second Spanish Republic proclaimed in April
1936	Approval of the Statute of Autonomy for the Spanish Basque Provinces (excluding Navarre). Victory of leftist parties in the Spanish elections leads to subsequent military reaction of Nationalist forces, led by General Franco, and the start of the Spanish Civil War. The Basque Country in Spain shows divided loyalties, with the military uprising successful immediately in Álava and Navarre, while Gipuzkoa and Bizkaia support the Republican cause, motivated by their own independence agenda.
1937	Allied to Franco, the German Condor Division and Italian Air Force perpetrate aerial bombardment on the Basque towns of Otxandio, Durango, Elorrio and – most infamously – Guernica, killing hundreds. More perish as Francoist forces advance. The war is swiftly ended in the Basque Country, while preserving Basque heavy industry, allowing Franco to exploit it in his power struggle elsewhere in Spain.
1939	End of the Spanish Civil War, with Franco's Nationalists victorious. Start of 36 years of dictatorship, repression of left-wing activity and the Basque language and culture in Spain. Basque government exiled first in France and the USA.
1952	End of rationing
1955	International recognition of Franco's regime as Spain admitted to the United Nations. Franco considered by the West as a bastion against the advance of communism. This heralds the end of Spain's international isolation but comes as a blow to Basques.
1956	Founding of the co-operative movement in Mondragón, Gipuzkoa, based on humanist principles. Co-operatives become hugely significant in the Basque Country economy.
1959	Founding of ETA (Euskadi Ta Askatasuna), a Basque separatist organisation with revolutionary ideology and prepared to commit acts of violence against the regime. North of the border,

	an equivalent organisation – Enbata – is created in France. The Franco regime becomes receptive to overseas investment, leading to further economic growth in Spain.
1960s	New industrialisation of the Basque Country takes place, with people arriving from elsewhere in Spain to provide the workforce. The Basque cultural movement begins.
1968	First killings committed by ETA
1975	The death of Franco coincides with a deep economic recession, affecting heavy industry and causing industrial disputes. Transition towards democracy begins, with many new political parties created. The two issues are the traditional division between left and right and the party's stance on Basque nationalism. Basque is recognised as an official language in Spain.
1977	Basque University set up
1978	Amnesty is declared for Basque political prisoners. A new Spanish constitution is created, but not supported by Basques.
1978–80	ETA killings reach their peak
1979	Statute of Autonomy approved and the Basque Autonomous Community (Bizkaia, Gipuzkoa and Álava) created. Navarre refuses to join them, preferring to become a separate autonomous community.
1980	Sitting of the first Basque Parliament, with Basque nationalists in power
1983	Torture and extrajudicial killings by extreme right-wing GAL organisation take place in retaliation against ETA suspects. Actions continue sporadically until 1987.
1997	The murder by ETA of a Bizkaian councillor brings a strong reaction from Spaniards and Basques, with millions protesting on the streets against the killing
2005	'Peace' talks with ETA are authorised by the Spanish Parliament, on condition that the former lays down its arms
2006	'Permanent' ceasefire announced by ETA in March, but an attack at Madrid airport in December, which claims two victims, brings it to an end
2009	For the first time in its history, the majority in the Basque Parliament is not held by Basque nationalists; for the three years until 2012, a non-nationalist coalition takes charge
2010	Announcement of another ETA ceasefire is met by understandable scepticism
2011	October sees the announcement by ETA of a cessation of its armed struggle, accompanied by a commitment to laying down its weapons
2012	Basque nationalists regain the majority in the Basque Parliament after the regional elections
2015	General elections in Spain see the rise of newly created political parties, in particular the left-wing populist Podemos, which takes around 25% of the vote in the three BAC provinces and Navarre. In France, the rise of the right-wing Fronte Nationale is less marked in the southwest than in the country as a whole.
2017	Amid much fanfare, decommissioning of ETA weapons begins
2018	ETA announces that it will disband

GOVERNMENT AND POLITICS

Modern-day Spain is divided into 17 autonomous communities, each of which contains a number of provinces. The Basque Autonomous Community (BAC) consists of the three provinces of Bizkaia, Álava and Gipuzkoa. Navarre is an autonomous community in its own right, and also a province. North of the Pyrenees, the three former Basque provinces of Labourd, Basse-Navarre and Soule together form part of Département 64, Pyrénées-Atlantiques (which also includes non-Basque Béarn), and which is itself one of the five departments of the larger French *région* of Nouvelle-Aquitaine.

In terms of politics specific to the French Basques, there is precious little support north of the border for the idea of an independent, seven-province Basque state. In the 1960s, the Enbata political movement was created in France with exactly that objective. Calls were made to have a statute of autonomy, mirroring the position of the BAC in the south; under the tenure of President Mitterrand there was talk of official recognition for the Basque language as well as the resurrection of the Pays-Basque as a separate French department composed of the three former Basque provinces, but neither of these notions came to fruition.

In the south, the parliament of the BAC in Vitoria-Gasteiz wields wide-ranging autonomous powers under the 1979 Statute of Autonomy and is made up of 25 representatives from each of the three provinces of Álava, Bizkaia and Gipuzkoa. Since the creation of the BAC, the PNV (Basque Nationalist Party) has been the predominant political party, only briefly ceding power to a socialist coalition between 2009 and 2012 before once again forming a minority government. Currently it holds 28 of the 75 parliamentary seats and governs with support of the PSE-EE Basque socialists. EH Bildu is a leftist, pro-independence, coalition party, the second most significant in the BAC with 18 seats. (It also has a presence in Navarre, polling 14% of the votes in the 2015 parliamentary election.) In the September 2016 elections, the populist Elkarrekin Podemos leftist alliance won 11 of the 75 seats in the BAC, making it the third most important party.

Navarre has its own government, ruled since the May 2015 elections by a leftist four-party coalition. It is also invested with wide-ranging powers and, like the BAC but unlike other Spanish autonomous communities, these powers include the collection of taxes.

In both the BAC and Navarre, regional parliamentary elections occur every four years, but on different cycles. These took place in the BAC in late 2016 and the Navarre parliament is up for re-election in May 2019. Each parliament elects a president, known in the BAC as the *lehendakari.*

Following a major corruption scandal that reached its conclusion in mid-2018, Spanish president Mariano Rajoy was forced out of office after the Basques of the PNV turned against him in a no-confidence vote tabled by the PSOE socialist opposition. It was the first successful no-confidence vote in Spanish history. In recent years, a seismic shift has affected Spanish politics, with the rise of two new populist political parties. On the left of the political spectrum, Podemos ('We Can') was only founded in 2014 but now attracts around 20% support from the Spanish electorate; in the parliament of the Basque Autonomous Community Podemos, with its junior allies, holds 11 of the 75 seats. In Navarre, they hold seven of the 50 parliamentary seats. The second of the new populist parties lies on the centre-right of the political continuum: Ciudadanos ('Citizens') party has less of a following in the Basque Autonomous Community or Navarre.

ECONOMY

Subject to different governmental regimes, and with different natural resources driving their economic evolution, in economic terms it is impossible to generalise meaningfully about the Basque Country and Navarre as a whole. The Basque Country in Spain remains one of the wealthiest regions in the country, along with Catalonia and the capital, Madrid. The recession of 2008, which devastated Spain's economy, heavily reliant as it was on property construction in the south of the country, only had an impact much later in the industrial north. But as time went on the Basque Autonomous Community and Navarre did inevitably suffer. Unemployment rates in Spain have now fallen in recent years as the economy has once again shown growth. The Basque Autonomous Community and Navarre are wealthy regions, something reflected in their 11% rate of jobless being significantly lower than the Spanish 17% average. Gipuzkoa and Bizkaia are still the two most expensive provinces in Spain for real estate, higher even than Madrid.

By contrast to the industrial past of its southern counterpart, the extreme southwest of France, while having some pockets of industry such as a branch of global giant Dassault Aviation in Biarritz, has an economy largely based on services, tourism and agriculture. Despite the elegance of some of the coastal resorts, the region as a whole is not a wealthy one, though unemployment rates in recent years for the Pyrénées-Atlantiques département have been lower than the French national average. It is appropriate to remember that the combined population of Labourd, Basse-Navarre and Soule is a mere 270,000, without any massive population centres to attract large industries.

TOURIST ECONOMY In terms of tourism, France continues to be the leading tourist destination in the world, with in excess of 85 million visitors annually. Spain welcomes around 70 million visitors every year, but while Catalonia was the most popular regional choice for visitors to Spain, by contrast the Basque Country and Navarre were nowhere to be seen in the 'top ten' Spanish visitor destinations. Nevertheless, perhaps with the boost created in part from San Sebastián's 2016 City of Culture status and the interest in the Camino de Santiago, the number of English-speaking visitors – particularly from the USA – has shown a healthy increase.

PEOPLE

Globally, there are estimated to be an astonishing 18 million people of Basque descent, six times more than the current population of the region itself. Much of the spread of the Basques around the world can be attributed to the fishing and whaling traditions, with a significant number of descendants in New Brunswick and Newfoundland in eastern Canada. Today, more than eight million people in South and Central America can claim Basque origins. In particular, many citizens

BIOLOGY AND THE BASQUE DIFFERENCE

It is not just a strong and vibrant culture which differentiates the Basques from their neighbours – it's literally 'in the blood.' Not only do they have the highest frequency of blood-type 'O' of any people in Europe (and the lowest frequency of blood-type 'B'), they also have the highest global occurrence of Rh-negative blood – two or three times that of other European peoples.

LEARNING BASQUE: MAKE THE 'TX' SOUND YOUR BEST FRIEND

You may be slightly disconcerted by Euskara, the Basque language. A few words, imported in modern times from other tongues, may have a welcome familiarity about them, but they are the exception. For the most part, trying to decipher the meaning of Basque words will be impossible, forcing you to revert to your Spanish, French or English.

But if you're going to pull out just one sound from the bewildering mass of 'x's and 'z's and the preponderance of 'j's that flood the Basque vocabulary, then you would do well to master the 'tx' sound, pronounced like the 'ch' in the English word 'church'. Why? Well, it seems to appear in a lot of Basque words that are associated with fun.

First of all, you need to get involved in a ***txikiteo***, which in Anglo-Saxon cultures we might crudely classify as a pub crawl. But here, it's certainly not about drinking as much as you can, more a chance to bar-hop with a group of good friends, enjoying their company, feasting on ***pintxos*** (there goes another useful 'tx' word, meaning 'tapas') and, yes, having a beer or a glass of wine. You might even have a glass of the local white, ***txakoli***, to liven up your evening. If you're in one of the renowned Basque cider-houses, wait to hear the owner call '***txotx***' (two 'tx's for the price of one there), summoning you to top up your glass. To accompany your chosen drink you could choose to chew on a ***txistorra***, the spicy sausage which is a regional speciality, or nibble some ***txangurro donostiarra***, the spider-crab that is a San Sebastián delicacy.

Pinned to the wall of a particularly good bar might be a ***txapela***, the broad Basque beret. (The tiny stub in the centre of the beret is called a ***txortena***, by the way.) Awarded to competition winners, the *txapela* can signify that the person wearing it is a ***txapeldun*** (literally 'He who wears the hat', but taken to mean 'champion') and its presence on the wall usually signifies that the bar has won an award for its *pintxos* at some point or another. Finally, should you be lucky to have some musical accompaniment during your Basque Country stay, listen out for the ***txalaparta*** (like a giant wooden xylophone) or the ***txistu*** (a small Basque flute).

of Argentina, Chile and Mexico trace their roots to the Basques, their ancestors having left at various times to work as shepherds, farmers and miners.

There are about 60,000 people of Basque ancestry in the USA. Many reside in Boise, Idaho, Nevada and other places in the American West. The University of Nevada at Reno has a very active Basque Studies department, producing many English-language publications on Basque history and culture.

In terms of character, the Basques have a reputation for industriousness and innovation, as well as having a love of independence and freedom. Some also characterise them as being forthright, direct and determined – and stubborn! If a Basque gives you his word, it is said to be his bond.

LANGUAGE

Euskara, sometimes written as 'Euskera', the Basque language, defines and delineates the Basque identity. Spoken north and south of the Pyrenees, the degree to which it shares the linguistic space with French or Castilian (Spanish) in different parts of the territory can be used as an unofficial 'barometer of Basqueness'.

Whereas just over a third of the inhabitants of the Basque Autonomous Community (BAC) know the language (and perhaps only half of those use it regularly in preference to Spanish), only one-quarter of French Basques speak it and that figure drops to around 10% in Navarre, where it is spoken mainly in the north. Nor is Euskara even officially recognised throughout the territory. Although it ranks equally with Spanish in the BAC and northern Navarre, it enjoys no official status at all in France or in southern Navarre, and its standing in central Navarre is unclear. In total, there are fewer than one million Basque speakers, with virtually no-one now speaking it as their exclusive language.

With no proven deep-rooted linguistic ties to other tongues, Basque stands alone in almost splendid isolation and, as such, its historic origins have been the subject of much study, many claims, some wild conjecture and a fair degree of hyperbole. Studies that seek to relate it to Caucasian, Finno-Hungaric or Iberian languages have been inconclusive. A link to the ancient tongue of Aquitaine in France is generally accepted, and it is also substantiated that Euskara is a pre-Indo-European language. But at various times, and perhaps with a Basque nationalist agenda, some academics and others have laid claim to Euskara as having been the language of the *whole* Iberian Peninsula before Roman times, or even more fancifully, that it was the language spoken by Adam and Eve.

Although some written evidence of Basque has been traced back to the early Middle Ages, Bernart Etxepare's 1545 *Linguae Vasconum Primitiae* (a book of love poems) is acknowledged as the first Basque-language book, appearing some 25 years before the first translation of the New Testament into Basque. As the language was fragmented into different dialects and with significant variations in vocabulary, much of which resulted from the isolating geography of the mountainous and valleyed terrain, work was done only in the 1960s to bring about a standardisation of written Basque. And with much success, resulting in an accepted form which has undoubtedly helped the survival of the language and aided the wider development of Basque culture. It now holds sway in administrative and public life in the BAC. But in the spoken tongue, many dialects and subdialects still exist, with the language of Soule differing significantly from that of Bizkaia.

But more than the mysteries of its origins or the complexities of its structure and pronunciation, the most incredible aspect of Euskara is its survival and the way in which, unlike many threatened minority languages, it is now flourishing. Over the centuries the language has withstood a number of challenges, direct and indirect, intentional and unintentional. In the wake of the French Revolution, the French state sought through legislation to destroy the many regional French languages – and with great success. South of the border, of course, the language was prohibited in the Franco years, becoming a symbol of resistance that exceeded its importance as a vehicle of communication. Although those who were caught speaking it were punished, nevertheless it was taught, learned and spoken in private throughout the dictatorship. The influx of immigrants at various times, arriving from other parts of Spain to work in the factories and industries of Bizkaia and Gipuzkoa, diluted the density of Basque speakers in those areas.

For career advancement in public service positions in the BAC, speaking Basque is essential. The health of the language is under some threat in France. In Navarre, some eye it with suspicion, seeing it as a tool being used to bring about the eventual absorption of Navarre into a future, independent Basque state. However, given its ability to survive a hostile history, it seems clear that it will continue to be the benchmark of Basque culture and identity for many years to come.

RELIGION

The predominant religion either side of the Pyrenees is Catholicism, as is obvious from the many religious festivals and saints' days celebrated throughout the year. Churches on either side of the mountain divide are not packed to the rafters come Sundays, but masses are still reasonably well attended and the religious element of most of the festivals is respected. However, the teachings of Catholicism on matters such as contraception and same-sex marriage are largely ignored, especially by the young. Religion in the Basque Country follows a similar profile to other parts of western Europe, a story of declining interest, particularly among the younger generation. Little more than 50% of Basques now claim any religious adherence.

In Spain, the Church was strongly allied to Franco during and after the Civil War, partly due to the threat posed to religion by communism and partly because, at the inception of the Republic in the early 1930s, a great number of churches were destroyed, atrocities were committed and religious adherents were persecuted. However, religion was always a cornerstone of the Basque nationalist movement and during the Civil War the Church in the Basque Country was more supportive of Republicanism than it was in many other parts of Spain. Indeed, some Basque priests were condemned to death by the Franco dictatorship.

EDUCATION

Important to the future survival of the Basque language is the question of education. Key to the future of Euskara are the *ikastolak*, the schools in which lessons are taught mainly or wholly in the language. Since the end of Franco's dictatorship, during which public use of the Basque language was prohibited, the Basque Autonomous Community has held autonomous powers in respect of education and parents can choose how their children are educated from four different state-funded 'models'. Just over half of them currently choose to have all instruction given in Basque. Very, very few (less than 1%) select the model that is based on all lessons being given in Spanish. Slightly more than a quarter of children take lessons in Spanish, but with Basque as a compulsory subject, while the rest are educated partly in Spanish and partly in Basque.

In France, there are 30 privately funded *ikastolak*, including some secondary education establishments in the form of three colleges and a *lycée*. In total they educate a relatively small number of children and students, around 3,500.

The Universidad del País Vasco (University of the Basque Country), with campuses around Bilbao, in San Sebastián, Eibar and Vitoria, offers nearly half of its degree courses in Basque to its 45,000 students. It is the only public university in the BAC. The Catholic Universidad de Deusto was founded by the Jesuits in Bilbao in 1886 and now also has a campus in San Sebastián, while the Mondragón Unibertsitatea (Mondragón University) is a not-for-profit university with faculties across the BAC. It was established only in 1997 and forms part of the Mondragón Corporation, based on the co-operative movement.

CULTURE

LITERATURE Basque literature – or at least, literature written in the Basque language – is hardly plentiful, its translations into English even less so. A slow start to Basque as a written language has meant that the profile of any Basque literature outside of the territory itself has remained fairly subdued.

THE *LAUBURU* OR BASQUE CROSS

Although it is not exclusive to the Basque Country and Navarre, the distinctive *lauburu* is very common in the region and can be seen on the walls of houses, carved on to furniture, engraved on tombstones and also printed on to countless T-shirts, mugs and other souvenirs. It makes for a very popular tattoo, as well. It is found in nearby Asturias and Galicia, as well as in India and Iran among other places, and also has very strong Celtic connections.

True to form for this enigmatic region, its significance is something of a mystery and open to many interpretations. In appearance it is similar to a swastika, except that the four arms – or 'heads' – are curved rather than angular. (Use of another symbol, the *euskal orratza*, was abandoned after World War II due to its Nazi connotations.) The heads can face to the right, in which case the *lauburu* is said to be a good luck symbol, representing creation and life. If the heads face to the left, as is often found on tombstones, then it is said to signify bad luck and death. Some theories hold that the heads themselves represent the four seasons, others that they symbolise the four states of mankind: mental, physical, emotional and perceptual. A third school of thought asserts that the *lauburu* is simply a version of the Christian cross. Whatever the meaning, it has become an established symbol of the Basque Country and Navarre.

Although the first Basque-language book was written over 450 years ago, a strong oral tradition, the lack of standardisation of the language and, very recently, its harsh repression during the Franco years, has meant that Basque-language literature has not kept pace with those of other tongues. Only five novels were written in the 19th century, although the emergence of Basque nationalism at the beginning of the 20th century brought with it the belief that literature was a tool to help promote the future proposed Basque nation. The contemporaneous establishment of the first literary festivals undoubtedly lent some impetus to literary production and it was also at this time that the first *ikastolak* – schools where instruction was given in Basque – appeared. Euskaltzaindia, the Royal Academy of the Basque Language, was established in 1918.

The move to industrialisation in the Basque Country, with mass immigration of non-Basque-speaking workers from elsewhere in Spain, served to weaken the language somewhat, leaving it categorised by urbanites as the 'rural language' and somewhat backward. Spanish became dominant in the newly industrialised areas.

The effects of the Spanish Civil War are evident in the fact that only one novel in Basque was published in the region during the conflict (1936–39). After the war, two significant demographic effects influenced the literary output. First, many Basques fled into exile, allowing literature to emanate from the USA and elsewhere; secondly, back in the Basque Country itself, the language and therefore Basque-language literature were repressed under Franco, a situation that would continue to some degree until his death in 1975. Nevertheless, Durango hosted the first Basque book fair in 1965, an event that still flourishes to this day. The 1960s also saw the creation of Basque publishing houses and the emergence of allegorical literature, commenting obliquely on the repressive regime, appearing suitably disguised to slip under the radar of censorship.

After the new Spanish Constitution was ratified in 1978, Basque became an official language in the Basque Autonomous Community and in parts of Navarre, paving the way for bilingual education. Two significant figures of literature, Bernardo Atxaga and Koldo Izagirre, were born in the 1950s. Prizewinning Atxaga is perhaps the best-known Basque author, and the writer with the most books available in English translation. His *Obabakoak* is a book of short stories, available in English and providing a good introduction to his output. Some of his works deal with the core Basque political conflicts, such as in *The Accordionist's Son* (2007). Izagirre addresses issues arising from the Civil War but, moving into the 1990s and into the new millennium, more contemporary topics became the focus of Basque writers' literary output.

Significant Basque writers expressing themselves in Spanish are Pío Baroja (1872–1956) and Miguel Unamuno (1864–1936). Writing in English, Basque-American Robert Laxalt (1923–2001), based in Nevada, became an important voice of the diaspora. In his novel *Sweet Promised Land* he addresses the thoughts and feelings of émigrés towards their distant Basque homeland.

A few suggestions of Basque works of fiction, translated into English, are listed on page 375.

MUSIC Any music with Basque-language lyrics is inevitably going to be hampered in gaining universal recognition outside of the Basque-speaking territory itself. On the world stage, classical composer **Maurice Ravel**, born in Ciboure, and Navarrese tenor **Julián Gayarre** (page 263) both enjoyed the international limelight in their day, but while Ravel's pieces live on to be enjoyed (*Bolero* being the best known), Gayarre's powerful voice is uncaptured by any recording and only contemporary reviews bear witness to his reputation. In any event, neither of their careers depended on any audience appreciation of the Basque language.

For visitors and casual music fans, catching the *bertsolari* in full voice, enjoying the enchanting sound of the *txalaparta* or marvelling at the richness of a Basque choir will prove the easiest ways of experiencing something characteristically Basque. Festivals and performances, advertised through posters or via the tourist offices (though not always adequately, and sometimes only in Basque!) will be the best chance for visitors to enjoy traditional Basque music. For aficionados, a history of more modern Basque music is given below.

The first Basque literature was only written in the mid-16th century, testament to the power and longevity of the oral tradition in Basque society. Music has played its part in that tradition, particularly through singing, with Basque ballads passed down from generation to generation only by word of mouth. Visitors to the Basque regions today should look out for ***bertsolari***, the distinctive 'head-to-head' singing contests that can be seen at festivals in the Basque-speaking regions. Even if the words mean nothing to you, you can appreciate that you're witnessing something unique, as contestants make up their lyrics on the spot and belt them out to the assembled audience.

Choirs and *bertsolari* both certainly demonstrate a very strong a cappella tradition in Basque music, but that's not to say that Basque musical traditions are devoid of instruments. Many of those used are universal, with nothing particularly Basque about them, but there are several that are very specific to Basque traditional music. The ***txalaparta*** is certainly one such, a chunky wooden xylophone-like instrument that is played simultaneously by two musicians. Equally characteristic is the ***alboka***, a clarinet that demands a particular breathing technique to ensure its mastery. A ***txistu*** is another instrument that frequently appears at festivals,

EIGHT BASQUE SURNAMES

Premiered in Spain in March 2014, *Ocho Apellidos Vascos* (*Eight Basque Surnames*) quickly became the most watched Spanish film, in Spain, of all time. Although it is available with English subtitles, the decision to release it to the Anglophonic audience with the seriously unimaginative name of *Spanish Affair* is hardly likely to have had you rushing to the box office. But for those who persevere, the film itself is a delight, succeeding in being a love story, an excellent comedy and, most importantly, a thoughtful and courageous insight into Basque and Spanish perceptions and misconceptions of each other. Some excellent acting performances have been recognised with awards.

Ignoring the (Sevillian) boy-meets-and-pursues-(Basque) girl romantic plot, the film cleverly manages to gently poke fun at the Basque language, the common Basque female haircut (a rather severe fringe), a Basque penchant for facial piercings and Basque machismo, but also mercilessly teases Sevillians' supposedly high opinion of their own attractiveness, their perceived obsession with ostentatious pomp and ceremony and their mistaken belief that the Basque Country is a dangerous place stuffed full of terrorists and political extremists.

Undoubtedly some watchers will have taken offence at these generalisations, but most Basques seem to have taken it with good humour, recognising that there is some truth in their quirks and foibles, albeit exaggerated by the director in the interests of making a good film.

Watching with subtitles detracts only a tiny bit from the enjoyment of seeing *Ochos Apellidos Vascos*, and although the film gets better the more you know about Basque and Spanish culture, it is well worth seeking out as a piece of standalone cinema. And the title? Early Basque nationalist Sabino Arana declared that to be a true Basque, all four of your grandparents *and* those of your spouse had to have Basque surnames.

As a follow-up film, the Catalans became the subject of *Apellidos Catalanes*, released in 2015. Let's hope they found it funny in Barcelona.

a three-holed flute that can be played one-handedly. The ***trikiti*** is a diatonic button accordion. Drums, tambourines and horns are also popular. Although the pipes are sometimes associated with the Basque Country, their use is more common in Rioja Alavesa and Navarre. For those with an appetite to learn more about these and other instruments, a visit to the museum in Oiartzun (page 170) is a must.

But it is words and language that are intrinsic to Basque identity, and music played a significant part in the wider cultural revival that took place in the early 1960s, at a time when Basque culture and language were still repressed. Since then, music has been a vehicle for important social and political comment, as well as simply providing the soundtrack for people intent on having a whole lot of fun. A key figure from the early 1960s was **Mixel Labéguerie**, a doctor from Bayonne who is now recognised as the first Basque singer of the modern era and who controversially promoted the use of the Spanish guitar in a Basque music culture firmly wedded to a cappella. A songwriter (and politician), much of his focus was on preserving and promoting Basque identity. Following on from Labéguerie, **Ez dok Amaiaru** was a collective not just of musicians but of artists, dancers, poets and writers. From 1965, they drew on influences from abroad but with the stated objective of modernising the existing Basque songbook as well as creating an environment in which others were liberated to translate international songs into

Basque. This was part of the wider Basque cultural renaissance, part of a movement that also included sculpture, notably the work of Chillida and Oteiza.

The 1970s saw a shift in Basque musical expression, as it sought to share in the optimism that followed the death of Franco and the move towards democracy. Music festivals appeared and Basque record labels such as Elkar were founded. Basque-language songs became engrained in the consciousness of the citizens.

Not everything, however, was laden with political or social messages, and the improvised verses of the *bertsolari* and the setting of pre-war poetry to music also found favour. At the end of the 1970s, influences from the UK and the USA gained further footholds. As the 1970s turned into the 1980s, the birth of so-called **Rock Radical Vasco** (Radical Basque Rock, or 'RRV') took place, a movement loose enough to encompass styles such as punk, heavy metal, blues and even reggae. **Eburri** and **Niko Etxart** are largely unknown internationally, but were key to the development of Basque rock, while elsewhere the 'pomp-rock' of English bands such as Genesis and the folk music of groups such as Fairport Convention influenced the sounds of the Basque Country, particularly south of the Pyrenees. The emergence of punk in the UK also had its impact on a Basque society that at this time had a strong anti-establishment groundswell. RRV employed Spanish as the main language, rather than Basque, though some groups such as **Zerama** proved an exception.

At the end of the 1980s, the Rock Radical Vasco movement lost its impetus, with heavy rock in particular coming more to the fore. The emergence of popular groups such as **Negu Gorriak** and **Esan Ozenki** heralded the demise of RRV and the beginning of something new: importantly, Basque language was once more in the musical limelight, though several groups chose to sing in English, taking their influences primarily from the USA. This was also a time of increased diversity of style, with anything from punk to folk to hip-hop finding a ready audience. On the heavy rock scene, **Su Ta Gar** was a group with a major fan base and an influence on later bands. Some of this influence remains to this day. Another characteristic of this period was the increasing prominence of the *trikitixa* accordion, with its traditional sound being incorporated into rock groups. **Joseba Tapia** and **Kepa Junkera** were pioneers in this respect. In this genre, traditional Basque songs were played side by side with rhythms from Cuba and elsewhere.

Basque music post-2000 has not been immune to the seismic shifts in the music industry, with record labels disappearing in the face of downloadable content. In musical terms, the previously undeveloped genre of pop music has emerged as a strong force in the Basque Country, with **Ken Zazpi** being the most popular artist.

Despite increased diversity in Basque-based music in recent years, the electric guitar remains the mainstay of the music scene, in line with rest of the world, and **Berri Txarrak** is one of the biggest bands to have dominated the scene. Despite this predominance, fusion music is still popular, with the sounds of the traditional *alboka*, *txalaparta* and *trikitixa* instruments all being blended into more contemporary styles by **Ibon Koteron**, **Oreka TX** and **Iker Goenaga** respectively. A capella also lives on, outside the purely traditional, with all-female group **Amaren Alabak**.

A network of late-night venues, known as the **Kafe Antzokia**, focus on Basque culture and are often a good choice if you want to hear some modern Basque music (see page 88 for the Bilbao venue). For traditional sounds, including *bertsolari* and unusual Basque instruments, a visit to a festival or two is strongly recommended, as some form of musical accompaniment is virtually guaranteed.

DANCE Basque culture embraces a wide variety of dances, in many cases differing from each other only slightly. Festivals rarely pass by without a display by the local dance group, usually dressed immaculately in predominantly white costumes, contrasted perhaps with colourful sashes and berets in red or blue. Perhaps the most celebrated dance is the *aurresku*, performed as a welcome and often as a mark of respect to visiting dignitaries. While many of the dances are similar, there are nevertheless some that stand out. One such is the *kaixarranka*, performed with great ceremony in Lekeitio, where a man dances on a wooden chest carried by six others (page 126). Whether the marching of the enigmatic *joaldunak* in northern Navarre counts as a dance is open to debate, but there is no doubt that it is worth seeing, should you get the opportunity (see box, page 247). Navarre is also known for its sword dances; some variants 'arm' the participants with wooden batons.

Attending a festival is certainly the most accessible way of seeing a performance. Aficionados might enjoy the Bizkaiko Dantzari Eguna (Dance Day; w dantzarieguna.net), which takes place in mid-May each year, at a different venue in Bizkaia province. For something more cosmopolitan, Biarritz celebrates dance with an annual festival each summer (page 306) – and it's fully participatory!

ARCHITECTURE Even if you have little or no interest in architecture, you will still be occasionally slapped in the face by it when confronted by some of the extraordinary buildings during your visit to this region, particularly in the cities south of the Pyrenees. You could surely describe this part of the world as a 'land of architectural juxtaposition' and, whether the architect is actually Basque or merely commissioned by Basques, you could not accuse the design here of being created by shrinking violets. Sometimes they seem to fly in the face of convention.

Bilbao's spectacular Frank Gehry-designed **Guggenheim** is, of course, the headline act and universally acclaimed, but those with a taste for the bold and innovative will also admire the city's **airport**, designed by Santiago Calatrava, and also the 'scooped-out' **Azkuna Zentroa** (formerly the Alhóndiga, by Frenchman Philippe Starck), the city's former wine warehouse now turned over to leisure pursuits and featuring a glass-bottomed swimming pool. For anyone brought up to watch football in grim, concrete venues, a restorative visit to the city's visually arresting **San Mamés** stadium is recommended; even from the outside, it is stunning.

San Sebastián's **Kursaal** is an acquired taste and it took a while for the city's inhabitants to learn to love this cultural centre, the work of Navarrese architect Rafael Moneo. The juxtaposition of the two parts of the same city's **San Telmo Museum** are also a challenge on the eye, until you understand that the modern building's steel-plated exterior is a work in progress, with Mother Nature being left to complete it.

Some of the best creative minds from the Basque Country and elsewhere conspired to put together the **Sanctuary of Arantzazu** in Gipuzkoa. Even if you find its exterior a bit gloomy, the fascinating story of its construction and decoration, together with its stunning rural setting, make it a must-see.

Vitoria-Gasteiz has its **Artium**, the modern art museum, and further south in the Rioja Alavesa region are the modern designs of the ultra-chic wineries which contrast so brazenly with the gentle vineyard landscapes.

In France, it seems to be a question of preserving past glories, a successful operation in respect of the 1930s casino building and the **Musée de la Mer** in Biarritz, where the elegant, beautifully maintained villas are also a fitting tribute to the town's heyday.

SCULPTURE Even if you don't go looking for it in one of the region's museums, at some point during your stay you will almost certainly be confronted by an impressive piece of sculpture. South of the border, sculpture is the most prominent and easily accessible art form, with many works displayed outdoors, making an encounter inevitable. A long history of working with wood and stone, then with iron in the subsequent industrial age, has resulted in this Basque passion for sculpture.

Facing off across the bay of La Concha in San Sebastián are works by the two dominant figures of Basque sculpture, **Jorge de Oteiza** (1908–2003) and **Eduardo Chillida** (1924–2002). Below Monte Urgull and facing westward out across the bay is Oteiza's *Construcción vacía* (*Empty Construction*), while at the foot of Monte Igueldo on the bay's western side are the three steel structures of Chillida's famed *Peine del Viento* (Wind Comb). It is acknowledged that the two luminaries did not always see eye to eye throughout their careers, but happily they had reconciled their differences before Chillida's death.

Oteiza's other prominent works include the enigmatic 14 'apostles' at Arantzazu (page 162) and his architecturally futuristic museum (page 242) is located just outside Pamplona.

Chillida's works can be found abroad, with installations in Paris, Berlin, Washington and Dallas; some of his pieces have fetched multimillion-dollar prices in art auctions. His plans for a piece to be displayed in the town centre of Whitehaven in Cumbria, England had to be abandoned, however, when over 80% of the locals voted against it! Nearer to home, the Museo Chillida Leku (w museochillidaleku.com) in Hernani, Gipuzkoa was shut for financial reasons, but may be open again by the time this book is published. In any event, fans can enjoy his symbolic *Our Father's House,* on open display in Guernica (page 120).

SPORT

If you wondered why the region's obsession with food isn't obviously reflected in burgeoning waistlines, then sport probably provides the answer. Rain or shine, it won't be long before you encounter an octogenarian walking between villages, a wafer-thin cyclist pounding up a seemingly impossibly steep mountain road, a runner enjoying the seafront promenade in San Sebastián or two young schoolboys vigorously practising their *pelota* on the village *frontón*. If food is an obsession, then happily so is sport. And while eagerly sharing in the global passion for the world's most popular sports, the Basques have their own particular ones, too.

For mass spectator sports, north of the border it is rugby that provides the focal point for spectators, while to the south football holds sway.

FOOTBALL While the oval ball rules the Basque Country north of the Pyrenees, south of the national boundary it's football that grabs the attention of the sporting population. To many outsiders looking in, Spanish football begins and ends with Real Madrid and FC Barcelona. But the Basque people have a proud tradition of contributing to the world's favourite ball game, and its links to the UK are surprisingly strong.

Athletic Bilbao – or Athletic Club, to give it its correct name – is historically the region's most successful team, having won La Liga eight times and enjoying huge success in the Copa del Rey, or Spanish Cup. The club have never been relegated. The players are, and always have been, exclusively Basque in origin, another example of the Basques fiercely protecting their identity amid the cosmopolitan mishmash that is modern-day football. But despite their rigorous adherence to picking only Basque players, their managerial history has embraced those of many nationalities, including Hungarians, French, Argentinians and Serbs. At the forefront of Athletic's managerial history, however, are the English, who have provided no fewer than nine coaches or managers over the years. Indeed, it was a combination of British miners and steel and shipyard workers who introduced the sport to Bilbao at the end of the 19th century, and Spanish students returning from Britain who founded Athletic Club in 1898, hence the English spelling of their name, rather than the Spanish: 'Athletic', not 'Atlético'.

San Sebastián's team is **Real Sociedad**, fierce local rivals to Athletic, twice winners of La Liga and one-time Cup winners. In the past they too employed only Basque players, but the signing of Irishman John Aldridge in 1989 signalled an end to this policy. They list revered sculptor Eduardo Chillida among their former goalkeepers. 'La Real', as they are known, have also frequently looked beyond regional boundaries for managerial guidance over the years, using the services of a Uruguayan, a Frenchman, an Austrian, a Welshman (John Toshack) and most recently a Scotsman (David Moyes) to steer them to varying degrees of success.

The third major city in the Basque Autonomous Community, Vitoria-Gasteiz, can scarcely compete with the other two in terms of footballing glory. Their team, **Deportivo Alavés**, have spent more time than they would choose playing in the second tier of Spanish league football. Now back in the top flight, they had their moment in the spotlight in 2001. In their debut participation in European competition, in a game still remembered for its end-to-end entertainment, they succumbed by four goals to five to Liverpool, in the final of the UEFA Cup.

And what about **Eibar**, tiny, tiny Eibar? With a stadium which holds little more than 6,000 spectators, this industrial town surely cannot support a team in La Liga for any length of time, can it? Sure enough, and despite winning their final game of the 2014–15 season, Eibar finished in 18th place and seemed doomed to be relegated back to Spain's second tier after only one season. But salvation reared its head in the shape of the taxman, for rivals Elche had not stumped up their fiscal dues and were relegated instead, granting tiny Eibar another tilt at glory among footballing giants such as Barcelona and Real Madrid. And as of 2019, they retained their place in the elite La Liga.

In Navarre, Pamplona's team is **Osasuna** (Club Atlético Osasuna), whose peak was a fourth-place finish in the top division in 2006, with a semi-final in the UEFA Cup the following season.

France's Basque heartlands have never had a great football tradition, with neither Bayonne nor Biarritz having achieved any footballing feats of great note. If you want to make a sporting friend north of the western Pyrenees, you need to be able to talk about the oval ball. Rugby is king in southwest France.

RUGBY Flying the flag for rugby union in the French Basque Country, both Biarritz Olympique and Aviron Bayonnais are professional teams who have enjoyed their share of glory although, at time of publication, their fortunes have taken something of a dip in terms of trophies. Their fans, however, remain as loyal and passionate as ever. For a few seasons now, Biarritz have been bottom-feeders in the second tier of French rugby: a sobering loss of face for the five-times French champions who even contested the final of the Coupe d'Europe as recently as 2010. In 2018, they were even threatened with demotion to the *third* tier, due to financial problems. Bayonne were briefly back in the top flight in the 2017–18 season, but returned to the ProD2 (second division). The resumption of local derby games with Biarritz at the lower level is of little consolation to either club.

While the Basque contribution to rugby may at first glance seem to merge seamlessly into the wider French game, the strength of the Basque character still sometimes stands out. The most cherished son of Basque rugby is Imanol

Harinordoquy, born and raised in the Pays Basque and established as one of France's all-time most popular and respected forwards. In a hard man's game, Harinordoquy was the hard man's hard man and a very proud Basque. After a poor run of form and exclusion from the French national team, some disrespectful English commentators – unable to pronounce his Basque surname – lazily renamed him 'Harry Ordinary', a feeble joke which backfired spectacularly in the 2011 Rugby World Cup quarter-finals when France beat England, and 'Harry Ordinary' duly picked up the man-of-the-match award.

Although rugby in the Basque Country is a game mainly played north of the Pyrenees, it has nevertheless sometimes spilled over on to the Spanish side, with both Biarritz and Bayonne having played big games at the Stadio Anoeta in San Sebastián. Of the 12 teams playing in the División de Honor, Spain's highest level of rugby, four are based in the Basque Country. The region's developing interest in rugby was recognised when Bilbao was made host city for the two European rugby finals in May 2018, played in the San Mamés stadium.

PELOTA Of the sports that have strong regional connections to the Basque-speaking region, *pelota* is the convenient catch-all term for a furiously fast sport that appears in some 22 (14 official) variations on both sides of the border. Not that it is restricted to the region, being popular in one form or another in Latin America, the USA and elsewhere. *Pelota* – or *pelote*, in French – simply means 'ball' – in this case made of wound rubber bound with cotton and covered in leather. Historically, the sport derived from games in ancient Greece and Rome, from which court/racquet sports such as real tennis and squash could also be said to have developed over the centuries. Nearly every village from Bizkaia in the west to Soule in the east, and Bayonne in northern Labourd to Tudela in southern Navarre, seems to have an outdoor *pelota* court – a *frontón* (*fronton* in France), often slap-bang in the village centre and varying in dimensions. Some have a *trinquet*, which is an indoor venue. The differences in the various games centre around the way in which the ball is projected (bare hand, basket, bat), the numbers of players involved and the type of court on which the contest takes place. Some exponents of pelota play professionally and a good living can be earned from the sport in the USA. Most of the official variants are 'men only'. Below are some of the major variants, but if you want to know their many rules, the website of the International Federation of Basque Pelota (w fipv.net) explains more.

Pelota mano (à main nue) As the name suggests, this game is played bare-handed, without the use of bat or basket. And yes, it does hurt. Normally played one against one, or by two teams of two players, it can take place outdoors or indoors, on a court with one, two or three walls.

Grand chistera* and *cesta punta The *chistera* is a handmade curved basket used by the players to propel the ball against the walls of the court. *Grand chistera* is played by two teams of three, but its popularity has been usurped by *cesta punta*, which has similar rules, but with teams of two, and whose scaled-down court, using the indoor *jai-alai* three-walled court, makes it more exciting to watch. The ball can travel at nearly 300km per hour.

Pala corta* and *pala Two slightly different games played by teams of two, using wooden bats as the mode of ball propulsion. In the *pala corta* version, a short (*corta*) bat is used.

Xare Using a wooden ring strung with a net, the ball is thrown as hard as possible, rather than hit.

Rebot Played by teams of five per side, on the traditional open *frontón* with a wall at one end only. A smaller version of the *chistera* is used for propelling the ball.

***HERRI KIROLAK/FORCE BASQUE* (BASQUE TRADITIONAL SPORTS)** Given the area's strong maritime and rural traditions, it is perhaps no wonder that in times past manual workers developed a certain competitive streak. Various tasks have evolved and survived in a variety of Basque sports which, without an understanding of their origins, might look seriously strange to an outsider who hasn't seen an episode or two of the *World's Strongest Man* TV series.

These odd-looking activities are taken seriously, however – seriously enough for the Basque government to have identified and listed no fewer than 18 of them in 2006, with the intention of ensuring their preservation. The most popular of these pursuits can be seen during the summer months, when they either form part of some of the major festivals or appear grouped together as standalone demonstrations of *herri kirolak* or *Force Basque*. The most common ones are:

***Harri jasotzea* (stone-lifting)** Very commonly performed, this involves the lifting on to the shoulders of round, square or cylindrical granite stones of up to an incredible 300kg in weight.

***Aizkolari* (log-chopping)** Using an axe, the competitors go head-to-head, each standing on a log with legs apart and trying to chop through the log as quickly as possible, bringing the axe down each time on the gap between their feet. Exhausting to watch, and given that they don't appear to wear protective footwear, nerve-wracking even for the spectators.

***Orka joko/Andartza* (cart game)** Involves lifting up the back of a cart, weighing around 350kg, and completing as many rotations as possible, with the front of the cart fixed to the ground.

Other sports on the list, more familiar to non-Basques, include arm-wrestling and donkey races.

TRAINERAS The Basque maritime tradition flexes its muscles, not in chopping logs or lifting stones, but in the *traineras*, which culminate in grand finals being held annually in La Concha bay in San Sebastián every September. Different explanations of the origins of these fiercely contested rowing competitions exist, the most common being that whenever a whale was spotted offshore in the Bay of Biscay, the boat that arrived first and planted its harpoon went home with the considerable spoils. Others say that the races originate from the necessity for the fishing-boats to get their catch back to port and market before their competitors. Whatever the truth (perhaps a bit of each has contributed), races now take place along the northern coast during the summer, sometimes point-to-point, sometimes in a circuit round a buoy until the best eight boats have established their right to contest the final. These races attract big crowds and generate a party atmosphere.

Crews consist of 12 rowers and a helmsman, with teams representing the coastal towns of Gipuzkoa and Bizkaia. The boats are now glass-fibre rather than traditional wood. In 2015, Orio – who are usually one of the stronger teams – incorporated a head-to-head race with Cambridge University as part of their training schedule.

2

Practical Information

WHEN TO VISIT

A number of factors determine the best time to visit the Basque Country and Navarre. In terms of climate (page 5), no months can be guaranteed as being totally rain-free. July and August may be the warmest, but they are also the most popular, with the latter being particularly awash with visitors, mainly locals and tourists from other parts of Spain. Prices for accommodation in those months can be significantly higher, especially on the coast; roads are busy, parking spaces in resort towns harder to find. Visitors who enjoy the 'buzz' of busy resorts or who intend to spend time on the wonderful beaches will enjoy being here in the peak of summer, and can also benefit from the many *fiestas* that are unsurprisingly organised to coincide with the locals' downtime. June and September bookend the Spanish holidays, making these months very pleasant for those who like to escape the crowds or who baulk at paying higher accommodation prices; such visitors should also avoid Easter week, though again this is a lively and educational time to be in Spain, slightly less so in France.

If you are determined to visit a specific town or area at a specific time, check the relevant tourist office website to see whether your visit coincides with a local festival: this may be exactly what you want, but if it's not then you may wish to reconsider your dates to avoid higher prices or non-availability of accommodation. Some hoteliers report that the peak season is getting longer each year as the region becomes more popular.

Expert surfers brave the waves right across the calendar, undeterred by the weather even in winter, though summer, with its warmer and calmer waters, is a much better time for beginners. If your main priority is to visit museums and other indoor, city-based attractions, then winter is naturally cheaper for accommodation, but colder and wetter. For anyone determined to take advantage of the wonderful walking opportunities, winter is less than ideal, and hillwalking during this season has safety implications. Snow can linger in the higher mountains until late spring or beyond.

All other things being equal, the 'shoulder seasons' of May/June and September would be the best times to visit, with a good chance of pleasant weather but without the crowds of high summer.

HIGHLIGHTS

SAN SEBASTIÁN Surf, swim or sunbathe? Choose your urban beach accordingly, then reward yourself with a memorable meal in this gastronomic paradise. Promenade around the bay, admire the Belle Époque elegance of the buildings, enjoy the atmospheric Old Town, or shop at the many boutiques (page 130).

BILBAO Walk the banks of the Nervión River, marvelling at the city's urban regeneration, symbolised by the stunning Guggenheim Museum, then hit the bars of the Plaza Nueva for a compact bar crawl and some *pintxo* sampling. Perhaps take in a match at San Mamés stadium (page 78).

VITORIA-GASTEIZ Enjoy the green spaces of this understated administrative capital on foot or by bike before visiting its perfectly preserved Old Town (page 185).

LAGUARDIA AND RIOJA ALAVESA Indulge in the products of the vines, admiring the architecture of some designer wineries, and walk the narrow, atmospheric streets of beautiful Laguardia (see box, page 215).

TO BE A PILGRIM Join the devout and the curious as they walk the ancient pilgrim trails towards Santiago de Compostela. (See boxes, page 66, 182 and 204.) Or, go further off the beaten path on the Camino Ignaciano (see box, page 166).

TAKE THE TRAIN UP A MOUNTAIN Grind your way to the top of La Rhune in a near-century-old train, catch the incredible views north and west along the coasts, then walk back down and visit nearby Sare or Ainhoa, officially two of France's most beautiful villages (see box, page 331).

VISIT SPAIN'S SEMI-DESERT Roam the Navarrese badlands of the Bardenas Reales (star of many a film set), with their astonishing rocky outcrops, rare birdlife … and screaming military aircraft (page 289).

RUN WITH THE BULLS AT SAN FERMÍN Follow in the footsteps of Hemingway, party hard in Pamplona and outpace the *toros*, if you have an appetite for danger (see box, page 239).

LEARN TO SURF IN BIARRITZ Or almost anywhere along the coast. World-class waves, top surf schools, renowned board-makers – you'll find them all in the Basque Country (page 68).

WATCH THE BIRDIE Choose from the wetlands of the Urdaibai, the *lagunas* near Laguardia or Pitillas, or the craggy cliffs of the Pyrenees to see some avian wonders (page 5).

SUGGESTED ITINERARIES

The Basque Country, both French and Spanish, and Navarre are compact regions and a decent road network allows speedy travel between the major towns and cities. Away from the motorways, pottering around rural Rioja Alavesa, the back roads of peaceful Soule or the high parts of northern Navarre will take longer on the narrower, winding or mountain roads. Despite their diminutive size, the Basque Country and Navarre could still provide a lifetime of holidays for the inquisitive. Rushing through this beautiful part of north-central Spain and southwest France will deny a wealth of treasures to the impatient visitor. Depending on your particular interests and assuming that your time and budget are not limitless, it makes more sense to choose an area covered by this guide and delve into it in more detail, or follow a theme and pursue it. With the mix of languages and landscapes, the richness of cuisine and fascinating character of the people, travelling 'slowly' is strongly recommended.

The following itineraries are devised to take in the major recognised sights of historic and cultural interest, and can be adapted whether you arrive in Bilbao or Biarritz. Each of these itineraries could last for a couple of days or a week, though the former would be a needless rush. For the wine tour, the latter is absolutely essential!

URBAN BEACHES Combine some time in Biarritz (page 299) with a stay in San Sebastián (page 130), making the most of the beaches while having all the facilities of town and city right on your doorstep. Two urban Belle Époque beauties vying for your attention, with swish restaurants, beaches, museums and, above all, the good life to pamper you.

WINE TOUR Head to Álava's southern extremities to find the Rioja Alavesa region, adorned with designer wineries, basing yourself for a few days in Laguardia (page 220). Then drive east to Olite in Navarre (little more than an hour away) to sample its excellent wines (page 280). If you're a hardcore wine-buff, you could then head north on a 2-hour drive to Irouléguy (page 345) to sample its product, made on a tiny scale, before completing your tour with a glass or two of *txakoli* in the buzzing bars of Getaria (page 179), again a mere 2 hours to the west. Allow plenty of recovery time between tastings – or take a designated driver.

FAR FROM THE CROWDS Base yourself in the gorgeous Baztán Valley with its picture-perfect villages, visiting Zugarramurdi (page 244) and Urdax (page 246) before border-hopping into France to Sare (page 332), Ainhoa (page 334) and a train trip up La Rhune (page 330). Enjoy some seaside downtime too, at Hendaye (page 326) or Saint-Jean-de-Luz (page 320), less than an hour away. As an alternative, sleepy Soule (page 355) is a peaceful destination, almost oblivious to tourism.

EASTERN NAVARRE – FROM HIGH MOUNTAINS TO DESERT Enjoy Navarre's topographical extremes, descending from the French border at the top of the Belagua Valley down to the spectacular gorges of Arbayún and Lumbier (page 263) and then delving into the 'deep south' to the desert of Bardenas Reales (page 289).

A TALE OF FOUR CITIES Keeping the car engine running, city-lovers could drive San Sebastián–Bilbao–Vitoria-Gasteiz–Pamplona in less than 3 hours. Not that you *should* hurry, but everything urban here is comfortably within reach, meaning you could visit all four diverse cities and their sites *and* stay relaxed, all within a few days.

SURFING THE BASQUE COUNTRY Surfers could cruise the coast in that battered VW camper-van, trying out the French Basque waves of Anglet, Biarritz, Saint-Jean-de-Luz and Hendaye (page 329), before crossing the border and surfing San Sebastián, Zarautz and Mundaka's famed left-hander (page 117).

PILGRIM TOURISM From Saint-Jean-Pied-de-Port to Santiago de Compostela is a four- or five-week walk for most people. But doing the sections through Navarre or across the Basque Autonomous Community takes a lot less time. This is the ultimate in 'slow travel'. Beginners might prefer to start at Roncesvalles (page 252), thus avoiding any really steep sections, while experienced pilgrims might tackle the ups and downs of the 'Way of the North', starting in Irun. For something 'new' and away from the pilgrim crowds, try the Camino Ignaciano (see box, page 166), which starts in Azpeitia and heads towards Catalonia.

TOURIST INFORMATION

Official sources of tourist information for the various subregions are given below. These are all comprehensive, with an English-language option, and are particularly useful if you are searching for festival dates or other live events taking place during your stay. Tourist offices across the region are plentiful, well signposted and they have plenty of information available in English in hard copy. Many of them also have their own websites, often translated into English. All the offices in the principal cities and towns possess information for their wider provinces, but not much 'crosses the border': don't expect to find lots of information available on Soule at the Bilbao office, for example, or vice versa.

Bizkaia, Gipuzkoa and Álava w tourism.euskadi.eus/en/

French Basque Country w bearn-basquecountry.com

Navarre w turismo.navarra.es/eng/home/

SPANISH AND FRENCH TOURIST OFFICES ABROAD In the age of electronic information and government cutbacks, requests for brochures by telephone or by personal visit without prior appointment are not encouraged by many of the French and Spanish tourist offices located abroad. Brochures for the Spanish Basque provinces and Navarre can be ordered from the Spanish Tourist Board website, w spain.info, or obtained by email for download. The French Tourist Board's official website is w france.fr/en.

MAPS The best general-purpose map covering the entire region detailed in this guidebook is Michelin map number 573 'España Norte' in its 'Regional España' series (1:250,000). Despite the title, it also includes the French Basque Country. For something more detailed on the Spanish side, IGN (Instituto Geográfico Nacional) publishes a series of very reasonably priced 1:25,000 and 1:50,000 scale maps which each cover parts of the Basque Country and Navarre (indeed, this series is available for all regions of Spain). Michelin's 1:150,000 map series covers nearly all of the region.

These maps are available in the Basque Country from Elkar outlets (page 63) or from Stanfords bookshop in London if you want to get them in advance of your visit.

TOUR OPERATORS

INTERNATIONAL

General

Classic Journeys ☎ 1 800 200 3887; e moreinfo@classicjourneys.com; w classicjourneys.com. US-based company offering walking adventures in the Basque Pyrenees.

Travel Editions ☎ 00 44 (0)20 7251 0045; e tours@traveleditions.co.uk; w traveleditions.co.uk. Specialising in rail & walking holidays to both the French & Spanish Basque Country.

Specialist

Basque MTB m 00 34 (0)662 61 44 70; e doug@basquemtb.com; w basquemtb.com. British/Basque-run company based in Santesteban (Navarre) & Hondarribia (Gipuzkoa), offering coastal & Pyrenean mountain biking adventures as well as bike skills holidays.

Bike Basque m 00 33 (0)695 94 82 37; e x.lopez@bikebasque.co.uk; w bikebasque.co.uk. Organises cycling 'camps' covering some less-visited places in the region.

Bikecation ☎ 00 44 (0)1435 884368; e email@bikecation.co.uk; w bikecation.co.uk. UK-based company offering road biking trips in the Basque Country.

Inn Travel ☎ 00 44 (0)1653 617001; e inntravel@inntravel.co.uk; w inntravel.co.uk. Walking holidays that include the Basque Country.

IN THE BASQUE COUNTRY/NAVARRE

General

Fresco Tours Colón de Larreategui, 26–7 C, 48009 Bilbao; m 0034 944 24 89 89; e info@frescotours.com; w frescotours.com. Based in Bilbao, walking & cultural tours in the region along the Camino de Santiago.

Specialist

Adore Basque ☎ 00 34 (0)943 05 35 61; m 637 97 87 48; e info@adorebasque.com; w adorebasque.com. City tours, & cultural & gastronomic tours in the region.

Basque MTB See opposite

Basque-Ways e david@basque-ways.com; w basque-ways.com. David Elexgaray speaks perfect English, has a deep knowledge of Basque history & culture, & can do accompanied trips to museums & longer trips as required.

Green Euskadi ☎ 00 34 (0)945 25 15 16; e info@greeneuskadi.com; w greeneuskadi.com. Small, local company focusing on sustainable tours.

Kabi m 00 34 (0)671 94 67 30; e info@kabi-travels.com; w kabi-travels.com. Kabi is an exclusive agency, & company founder Edurne Pasaban was the first woman to climb the 14 mountains of over 8,000m in the world. Guided trekking trips to the mountains & skiing.

On Foot in Spain m 00 34 (0)686 99 40 62; e info@onfootinspain.com; w onfootinspain.com. Camino de Santiago & Basque Country tours.

Pyrenean Experience Iaulin Borda, Ameztia, Ituren, Navarre; ☎ 00 44 (0)121 711 3428; e langadventures@hotmail.com; w pyreneanexperience.com; see ad, 2nd colour section. Spanish lessons, guided & self-guided walking tours & Basque cultural immersion in a house party atmosphere.

RED TAPE

SHORT STAYS Citizens of the UK, Ireland and other EU countries do not at present need a visa to visit either France or Spain. A valid passport or national identity card is sufficient. There is no 90-day limit on the length of stay, though there are certain limitations imposed on citizens of some of the countries that have recently joined the EU. After the UK leaves the European Union, documentation requirements for UK citizens may change. Check before travelling.

Citizens of the USA, Canada, Australia and New Zealand and certain other countries can visit France or Spain as tourists for up to 90 days with a valid passport, and have no need of a visa.

Citizens of other countries visiting France or Spain will need to obtain a Schengen visa, valid for up to 90 days, which involves showing that you have sufficient funds and the necessary travel insurance. You should apply well in advance. Note that possession of a Schengen visa allows the holder to travel throughout the 26 Schengen countries during the period for which the visa is valid. Schengen visas cannot be extended.

To ensure that you are up to date with any changing requirements, those visiting France should check the 'Coming to France' section of the French Ministry of Foreign Affairs website (w diplomatie.gouv.fr). Those visiting Spain should visit the website of their nearest Spanish embassy or consulate for updates.

LONGER STAYS Even if staying beyond 90 days, citizens of the UK, Ireland and other EU countries have no need for a visa, nor do they need a residence card (*carte de séjour* in France or *tarjeta de residencia* in Spain), provided that they are living and working legally in either France or Spain.

Citizens of the USA who wish to stay in **Spain** beyond the 90-day period may apply for an extension, but should do so from outside the country and may be required to supply proof of funds. Citizens of non-EU countries who wish to stay in Spain longer than 90 days will need to obtain the correct visa before departure, contacting the Spanish consulate in their own country well in advance of departure to fully understand the process.

Citizens of the USA, Canada, Australia and New Zealand and certain other countries who wish to stay in **France** for longer than 90 days should also contact their nearest French embassy/consulate long in advance of their trip, as the procedure can be very lengthy, and it is not possible to extend visas from inside France.

Those who hold a **long-term visa** will need to obtain a *carte de séjour* from the office of the mayor (*mairie*) within eight days of their arrival in France. Those in a similar situation in Spain will need to get a *tarjeta de residencia* from the local office of the Oficina de Extranjeros.

GETTING THERE AND AWAY

BY AIR Whether accessing the region through France or Spain, the ever-increasing tentacles of budget air travel allow the visitor direct flights, principally through Biarritz or Bilbao, from London and a few regional UK airports. Not all flights are operated daily. Given that new flights regularly appear or are removed, it's a good idea to check the airport websites (as well as the airline websites listed, see below) or a site such as w skyscanner.com in case an airport near you has suddenly acquired a connection to the region. Note that the flight schedules of budget airlines can be reduced, or suspended, in winter.

For those arriving on long-haul flights from the USA, Canada or elsewhere, it will almost certainly be necessary to fly first to either Madrid or Barcelona (or even London) and connect to Bilbao, San Sebastián, Vitoria-Gasteiz or Pamplona (for the Spanish provinces), or alternatively fly to Paris and connect to Biarritz for the French Basque Country.

Scheduled airlines

✈ **Air France** w airfrance.com. Arriving in Paris on the French national carrier from worldwide destinations allows access to onward flights to Biarritz, but note that it may be necessary to change airports in Paris.

✈ **British Airways** w ba.com. Flies directly to Bilbao from London Heathrow. Some flights code-share with Iberia, which is part of the same corporate group.

✈ **easyJet** w easyjet.com. Direct flights to Bilbao from London Stansted, Bristol, Manchester & Edinburgh, & to Biarritz from London Gatwick & Luton.

✈ **Flybe** w flybe.com. Direct flights to Biarritz from Birmingham.

✈ **Iberia/Air Nostrum (Iberia Regional)** w iberia.com, w airnostrum.com. Iberia is the Spanish national carrier, while Air Nostrum is a regional franchise operator. Between them, it's possible to fly from some UK regional airports to Madrid, allowing connections through to Spanish regional airports such as Pamplona or San Sebastián. Will often require more than 1 change of planes, however, & the cost can sometimes be prohibitive.

✈ **Ryanair** w ryanair.com. Direct flights to Biarritz from London Stansted & Dublin.

✈ **Vueling** w vueling.com. Direct flights from London Gatwick and Heathrow to Bilbao & (via Madrid) to San Sebastián.

Airports In addition to the two airports covered below, other airports in the region are San Sebastián, Pamplona and Vitoria-Gasteiz. At present none of these airports service international destinations, but could be of interest to those visitors who are coming long-haul and arriving at either Madrid or Barcelona, from where a connecting flight can be picked up.

Bilbao Airport Bilbao's designer Loiu Airport is only 20 minutes from the city, with excellent, cheap bus connections to central Bilbao as well as a direct bus service to San Sebastián. For full details, see page 77.

Biarritz Airport Aéroport de Biarritz Pays Basque (previously Biarritz-Anglet-Bayonne Airport) is a mere 10 minutes by bus or taxi from Biarritz town centre. Buses also go directly to Bayonne, Anglet, Bidart, Saint-Jean-de-Luz, Hendaye, Pamplona and San Sebastián. For full details, see page 300.

BY BOAT For those wishing to take their own vehicles to the Basque Country, there are direct ferries from the UK to Bilbao. Sailing to Santander, in the neighbouring province of Cantabria, is another option with a drive of only around an hour to reach western Bizkaia province. Schedules vary according to season, as do prices, and while they are not cheap, could make sense for a party or family of four, taking into account that you won't have to pay for car hire when you arrive.

Ferry companies **Brittany Ferries** (☏ 00 44 (0)330 159 7000; e reservations@brittanyferries.com; w brittanyferries.com) sail to Bilbao from Portsmouth and Plymouth in the UK, with a journey time of around 24 hours. Foot passengers are no longer accepted on the direct routes to or from Bilbao, though those travelling without a vehicle could sail to Santander in Cantabria and take the bus from there. Santander bus station is 2 minutes' walk from the ferry terminal. Ferries also sail to Santander from Cork in the Republic of Ireland.

BY TRAIN Travelling to the Basque Country from abroad by train is fine if you have time to spend and cash to burn. Much money has been invested in the initial stages of a high-speed network between France and Bilbao, and progress has accelerated in the last few years. It is unlikely that this will materialise very soon, however, and maybe not within the life of this edition. From London it is of course perfectly possible to get to Biarritz with SNCF, the French national rail network, but your journey will route you via Paris – with a change of station – and take at least 7 hours. Flying is usually cheaper and quicker, but if you're determined to take to the rails, try w raileurope-world.com for schedules and fares.

BY BUS Buses do connect London Victoria Coach Station with cities as far away as Bilbao, Vitoria-Gasteiz and elsewhere, but there are only rarely cost savings to be had over flights or train journeys, and roughly 22 hours on a coach, however comfortable that coach might be, is too much for many people (w alsa.com/en/web/bus/home).

HEALTH *with Dr Felicity Nicholson*

There are no serious health issues to worry about, and no endemic diseases. Insect bites are perhaps the biggest risk in rural areas so it is worth taking an insect repellent. It is wise to be up to date with the standard UK vaccinations including diphtheria, tetanus and polio which comes as an all-in-one vaccination (Revaxis), and which lasts for ten years.

If you do have an accident or fall ill, the level of healthcare is on a par with much of the rest of Europe. Residents of EU countries including the UK and Ireland should obtain a **European Health Insurance Card (EHIC)** before travelling, as this covers the costs of any standard medical treatment you may require. This is available in the UK by calling ☏ 0845 606 2030, or online at w ehic.org.uk. (Note, however, that after the UK leaves the European Union, UK citizens may not be entitled to an EHIC certificate.) Everyone, including holders of an EHIC, should also take out travel insurance that includes medical costs, as the EHIC doesn't cover all eventualities, such as repatriation to your home country following an accident.

In a medical emergency in either Spain or France, you should dial ☎ 112 to call for an ambulance.

TRAVEL CLINICS AND HEALTH INFORMATION A full list of current travel clinic websites worldwide is available at w istm.org. For other journey preparation information, consult w nathnac.org/ds/map_world.aspx (UK) or w wwwnc.cdc.gov/travel/ (US). Information about various medications may be found on w netdoctor.co.uk/travel. All advice found online should be used in conjunction with expert advice received prior to or during travel.

SAFETY

Of course, anything can happen, anywhere in the world, but the good news is that both Spain and France enjoy lower crime rates than, for example, the UK or the USA. All the Spanish Basque provinces have much lower crime rates than either Madrid or Barcelona, which according to official statistics are Spain's crime 'danger areas'. Here you won't be plagued by bag-snatchers or pickpockets as you might be in the more famous tourist hot spots. Navarre's crime rate is also lower than the Spanish average. In France, the *département* of Pyrénées-Atlantiques (which includes the three former Basque provinces) has a crime rate which is lower than the French average. In general, there are no specific safety concerns for visitors to the Basque Country or Navarre and, if common sense is applied, it is perfectly reasonable to expect a trouble-free visit.

For anyone worried about the activities of ETA, the armed organisation that once used violent tactics to fight for Basque independence, it officially declared a 'definitive cessation to its armed activities' in October 2011, and no violent incidents have occurred since then. Indeed, they announced a decommissioning of weapons in 2017, followed by a 2018 declaration that they were to disband themselves. If you are puzzled by the black-and-white banners hanging from balconies, particularly in Gipuzkoa and Bizkaia, imploring '*Euskal presoak Euskal Herrira*' and accompanied by a map of the 'seven Basque provinces' then this translates as '[Bring] the Basque Prisoners back to Euskal Herria' and refers to the many convicted Basque prisoners who are pointedly being made to serve their sentences in places as far away as Seville or Tenerife.

Of course, both France and Spain have been subject to terrorist attacks from so-called Islamist groups in recent years, but to date these have not directly affected the Basque Country or Navarre.

SEASIDE SAFETY Anyone used to bathing in the mellow Mediterranean or dipping in the calmness of the Caribbean will need to remember that a visit to the Basque coast will involve exposure to a real, live (and lively) ocean. Take appropriate precautions at all times.

The waves here may be ideal for surfing, but they command respect from everyone. Having said that, millions of people every year swim, paddle and surf very safely in the region's waters, and many of the beaches are supervised in high season, with warning flags in place to advise when swimming is prohibited. Novice surfers are strongly advised to take lessons from a reputable school, not only to receive training on how to surf, but to learn the local peculiarities of the waves, rocks and sandbanks that can determine the safety or otherwise of surfing conditions. In high season there can be real conflict between surfers and swimmers and it is important to understand that certain areas of some busy beaches are reserved for one group or the other. If in doubt, ask the lifeguard before entering the water and obey any instructions given.

WOMEN TRAVELLERS

In general, female travellers to the Basque Country and Navarre should not experience any hassle, even if travelling alone. Although normal common sense should be applied, the Basque male has a reputation of being rather 'backward at coming forward' when it comes to making approaches to the opposite sex, to the extent that some Basque women complain that the menfolk are far too slow to make a move! This bodes well for female visitors seeking a hassle-free trip. Certainly, the stereotypical characterising of some Mediterranean males as testosterone-fuelled and pushy lotharios would rarely apply to Basques.

SENIOR TRAVELLERS

Seniors command respect throughout the region and you can expect to be welcomed and be treated with courtesy. Always be prepared to enquire about discounts for travel and museum entrance tickets, as these are often more widely available than they are advertised.

TRAVELLERS WITH DISABILITIES

General guidance on travelling abroad for disabled people is provided by the UK Foreign and Commonwealth Office (w gov.uk/guidance/foreign-travel-for-disabled-people). As members of the European Union, both France and Spain are subject to the many regulations in place to facilitate access to new buildings.

The tourist offices are always good sources of information and sometimes have specific publications on accessible sites and destinations, in English, for those with less mobility. For example, an *Accessible Tourism* booklet is published south of the Pyrenees, listing accessible hotels, restaurants and museums and available at most tourist offices. In France, the Pays Basque/Béarn Tourism website has a special *Personnes Handicapées* section, translated into English, with useful information on accessible restaurants, accommodation, beaches, transport and visitor attractions (w bearn-basquecountry.com).

If booking accommodation, especially in more rural establishments, do check in advance about any potential access difficulties. Some of the websites of organisations such as Nekatur (w nekatur.net) or Casas Rurales Navarra (w casasruralesnavarra.com) allow you to apply a filter to show accommodation suitable for those with access difficulties.

Help is often available in high season for those wishing to access beaches; in France, under a scheme called 'Handiplage', special equipment and trained staff (in high season) are on hand at certain beaches including in Biarritz (Plage de la Milady), Anglet (Plage due VVF) and Hendaye (Plage des Deux Jumeaux). The tourist offices have more details.

ETHNIC MINORITY TRAVELLERS

Although the Basque Country and Navarre are hardly a heady cosmopolitan mix on the scale of London or Paris, it would be wrong to believe that those you're rubbing shoulders with on your visit are a homogenous mass. Both France and

Spain have colonial histories which ensure that there are many residents of the former whose origins are West or North African, and inhabitants of the latter who come from Latin America. Drawn to the area in times of booming industry, many Bizkaian residents in particular come from other parts of Spain.

Certain singularities exist, such as a strong Muslim population in Navarre's second-largest town, Tudela, or the noticeable presence of West African fishermen in the ports of Gipuzkoa. In the Spanish Basque Country, many of the discount bazaars are operated by those of Chinese ethnicity. In general, the ethnic mix in the region is sufficiently integrated to ensure that visitors of different ethnicities should not experience any hostility.

GAY AND LESBIAN TRAVELLERS

Same-sex marriage is legal in both France and Spain. Gay-friendly bars can be found in the region's major cities and a few are listed in the relevant chapters. In Spain, there is a focus on the *bar de ambiente*, a bar that welcomes everyone; often these are the coolest places for people to hang out, regardless of their sexuality or gender orientation. A Bilbao-based monthly LGBT magazine, *Blue* (**w** revistablue.com) is widely distributed in hard copy via the city's tourist office, hotels and libraries as well as being available online, though it is only in Spanish.

TRAVELLING WITH KIDS

Family life in both Spain and France is much treasured, arguably more so than in Anglophone countries. There are no particular issues for visitors to be aware of: children are welcome almost everywhere and can often be seen playing out on the streets until late at night. Special attention should be paid by parents to the advice given on page 46.

WHAT TO TAKE

Almost everything is available in the region, so there are no special requirements as to what to bring, other than two-pin adaptors to accommodate all those devices and chargers we have to carry around with us these days. The electricity supply in France and Spain is 220V. What clothing you bring will depend on the time of year of your visit, and whether you are intending to loll around on beaches or hike the high Pyrenees. A waterproof and a compact umbrella are good ideas, whatever the season. Photocopies of passports (kept separately) are advisable, together with any prescription drugs. In respect of the latter, it is surprising what French and Spanish pharmacies are legally allowed to dish out over the counter and without prescriptions, so it is always worth asking if your supplies run out.

MONEY

The euro is the currency on both sides of the border. There are sufficient banks in both France and Spain to mean that accessing your funds is rarely a problem. Most ATMs (cashpoints) are furnished with multilingual instructions and every reasonably sized town has at least one. It is rare that they are not compatible with British or other international bank cards. On-screen instructions are often available in English.

> **PRICES IN THIS GUIDE**
>
> Unless otherwise stated in the text, prices in this guide are quoted in euros, the currency for both Spain and France. The exchange rates for sterling and US dollars at the date of publication are given on the inside front cover of this book and on page 2.

CHANGING MONEY There is rarely any need to visit a bank for actual counter service if your visit here is purely for leisure. That said, banks in Spain usually operate on weekdays only from around 08.30 in the morning but close around 14.00, and in France from 08.30 or 09.00 and close around 16.00, sometimes staying open until 17.30. Rural branches sometimes close at lunchtime.

You could of course bring all your spending money with you in euros, but carting large quantities of cash around is questionable practice: although crime-rates are low, there's always the risk of losing it. With cash machines in all major towns, there's no need to come armed with enough cash to sustain you during your entire stay. Instead, bring a reasonable quantity of cash with you, and use ATMs when you need to withdraw more (although your bank will charge you a nominal fee). A prepaid euro cash card is a good idea, as the exchange rates are usually competitive; no transaction fee is levied for ATM withdrawals from some, but not all French and Spanish banks. These cards can also often now be used as debit cards.

CARDS AND TRAVELLERS' CHEQUES Credit cards such as Visa and Mastercard are accepted by nearly all hotels and major restaurants, together with petrol stations and shops. Diners Club and American Express should be acceptable in most hotels, less so in restaurants. Bars both north and south of the Pyrenees generally deal in cash and rural guesthouses are sometimes not geared up to accept plastic money of any sort – check when making your booking. Travellers' cheques, once the globetrotter's friend, are largely a thing of the past, and nowadays are likely to cause more trouble than they are worth.

COSTS AND BUDGETING

Guide prices in euros are given below for items commonly purchased. The prices relate to items purchased in convenience stores in an average-sized town. You could certainly pay a bit less if visiting a large supermarket, and just as easily pay double in a seafront grocer's in a resort town. Overall, Spain is around 10% cheaper than France for day-to-day costs. For information on tipping, see page 53.

	Spain	France
Bottle of water (1 litre)	€0.30	€0.40
Bottle of beer (500ml)	€0.70	€0.80
Loaf of bread	€0.80	€0.85
Postcard	€0.50	€0.50
Litre of petrol	€1.20	€1.45

Based on two people sharing costs and a room, and excluding any car hire costs, below is a rough guide per person to daily budgeting for accommodation, transport, food and entertainment, in high season.

BASIC If you're a backpacker or simply counting the euros, then you should be able to get by on around €50 per person per day. This assumes using hostels with dormitory accommodation or campsites, breakfasting in a bar, gorging on a three-course *menú del día*, sniffing out the free attractions or simply enjoying the beaches or mountains, walking or making use of public transport, and taking a modest meal in the evening (or a couple of *pintxos*) and a glass of wine.

COMFORTABLE Staying in a modest two-star hotel, *casa rural* or *pensión* with a breakfast *in situ* or at a nearby bar, visiting a museum or two, enjoying a lunchtime *menú del día* and having an evening restaurant meal should cost you around €70 per person.

RELAXED Choosing between hotels of two-stars plus, rather than working 'down to a price', taking breakfast in the hotel, visiting two or more museums, ordering a lunchtime *menú del día*, having a couple of *pintxos* in the evening *and* a restaurant meal plus a bottle of wine should come to around €90 per person.

LUXURY Staying in three-star-plus establishments with breakfast, with two good meals with wine per day at high-quality restaurants, museum trips and perhaps a guided city tour will put your spend at about €110 per person.

NO LIMITS You could spend a small fortune here, if you have one. The five-star or four-star beachfront hotels in San Sebastián and Biarritz, together with the Michelin-starred restaurants, would put a deep dent in your riches.

GETTING AROUND

For maximum flexibility, use of a car is advisable, and almost essential if you are visiting the remoter outposts of this region. If you are based in one place, however, and taking into consideration fuel prices, motorway tolls, parking costs and scarcity of spaces, making use of public transport for some trips while you are in the region is worth considering and often the extra cost is negligible, especially if you are travelling as a couple or on your own.

BY CAR Unless you are bringing your own vehicle, a self-drive hire car is recommended (see opposite). All you need is a UK, other national or international driving licence, a passport and a credit card. Vehicles can be picked up and returned at airports or in city centres. In the Spanish Basque Country and Navarre, the roads vary from excellent motorways to single-track roads. The numbering system for all roads was revised in 2004, so maps printed before that date will only serve to confuse. Motorways (*autopistas*) are designated with the prefix 'A' or 'E' followed by the road number. Where the motorway is a toll road (*autopista de peaje*), this is indicated on maps by the prefix 'AP' and the road number. Moving down the pecking order, dual carriageways (*autovías*) carry the prefix 'E' and the road number. National highways (*carreteras nacionales*) are marked with an 'N' or 'CN' followed by the road number. Lesser routes are signed with the prefix of the province in which they are located (eg: 'BI', 'GI', 'A' and 'NA' for Bizkaia, Gipuzkoa, Álava and Navarre respectively), and the number. Using toll roads can be expensive and involves taking a ticket on entering and paying on exit. For an example of how tolls can add to your cost, the hour's stretch between San Sebastián and Bilbao can be €13. Payment can be by cash or card.

In the French Basque Country, the bad news is that tolls are payable on the motorways, but the good news is that once you're away from the coast, there *are* no motorways. Enjoy the winding mountain roads and country lanes and be thankful that they cost nothing.

Different rules apply for driving in both France and Spain, so preparation is required if bringing your own vehicle. As well as having your licence and all necessary vehicle documents, be sure to fit headlight beam converters and carry a warning triangle, high-visibility vests (inside the car, not in the boot), spare bulbs, first-aid kit and a plate or sticker identifying the nationality of your vehicle. These are legal requirements, as is carrying an approved breathalyser when driving in France. For full details, the UK Government website w gov.uk/driving-abroad is a good starting point.

Many towns and villages have linguistic variants to their names. Most signposts with place names are written in both Spanish and Basque, or French and Basque, depending on which side of the border you find yourself. One annoyance is that occasionally the Spanish or French name will be spray-painted out by someone with a political point to make.

Fuel stations are not usually self-service in Spain, so you may have to wait for the helpful attendant to appear. The exceptions are motorway service stations, where it's usually do-it-yourself.

Car hire Car-hire agencies can be found at Biarritz and Bilbao international airports, the domestic airports in Pamplona and San Sebastián and at offices in the city centres. All the usual international companies are represented in the region and the websites of some are listed below. There are few reliable local alternatives. If you are arriving by plane, it's always worth checking the car-rental partner on the airline's website, or simply enter 'car rental' into a search engine to find a site that does the research for you – often this will get you a cheaper deal than using the sites listed below. If you are worried about paying over the odds for insurance, and are likely to hire a car abroad more than once in a 12-month period, consider buying an annual 'car hire excess insurance' policy that protects your excess before you leave home. Typically, an annual policy will cost you the same as a week's cover provided by the car-hire company.

- **Avis** w avis.com
- **Budget** w budget.com
- **Dollar** w dollar.com
- **Europcar** w europcar.com
- **Hertz** w hertz.com
- **Sixt** w sixt.com
- **Thrifty** w thrifty.com

BY TRAIN RENFE in Spain and SNCF in France are the national rail networks relevant to this region. In the Spanish Basque Country, the FEVE company which once operated the coastal narrow-gauge line was merged with the main RENFE organisation in 2012. Euskotren operates trains from Hendaye in France to San Sebastián, from San Sebastián to Bilbao and towns in-between, leaving RENFE to connect the region's major cities with other Spanish cities and towns. In France, the rail network in the Basque Country covers the coast between Bayonne and Hendaye, as well as the solitary inland line that connects Bayonne with Saint-Jean-Pied-de-Port at the base of the Pyrenees.

Fares given in this book are *indicative* single fares: booking several weeks in advance, which is possible online, can bring the cost down quite considerably. On some routes, there is a choice of fast or slower trains, which can also affect the price quite considerably.

BY BUS Bus is still a major mode of transport in France and even more so in Spain for travelling between towns and villages, and it should certainly not be dismissed out of hand as a useful way of getting around. In some cases, it is surprisingly faster than the train (for example, San Sebastián to Bilbao) and for reliability, cost and comfort, it often can't be faulted. The major bus companies run smart, intercity coaches in the Spanish Basque Country and Navarre, while the coastal service in France which joins Bayonne and Hendaye – and points in-between – is also efficient, regular and user-friendly. While many smaller towns in the region, especially in Soule or northern Navarre, still retain bus services, these might operate only once or twice per day, so relying on them will result in you spending much of your holiday hanging around.

Bus company services in Spain are thankfully far more reliable than their sometimes temperamental websites. South of the Pyrenees there are too many bus companies to list but some useful websites for bus stations and networks are given below, for both north and south.

For transport around the region's towns and cities, rather than between them, see the relevant chapter.

w **donostiasansebastian.com/autobuses.html** Useful information, in Spanish only, about buses to & from the city, the towns around Gipuzkoa, other Spanish cities & beyond.

w **estaciondeautobusesdepamplona.com** As most of Navarre's buses begin & end in the capital, Pamplona's bus station website is a useful resource, though currently without any English-language option.

w **termibus.es** Now with an English-language option, Bilbao's bus station website shows live departures & also allows you to click through to many of the bus operators' own sites.

w **transports64.fr** Bus network website for north of the border. 'Department 64' includes the whole French Basque Country, though this website does not have an English-language option.

w **vitoria-gasteiz.org** Vitoria's municipality site contains information & timetables for all buses to, from & around the city. In English.

ACCOMMODATION

Outside of Easter week, July and August, accommodation is plentiful and the full range of options is available from camping and pensions to five-star luxury hotels, though the latter are really only present in the super-chic locations of Biarritz and San Sebastián. Many small and medium-sized hotels are owner-managed, which usually guarantees some personal care and attention. Prices south of the Pyrenees, whether in Navarre or in the Basque Autonomous Community, are generally cheaper than in France, though accommodation in San Sebastián and elsewhere along the coast is pricier. Pamplona's prices during the San Fermín festival are a shock to the system, and if you're visiting any location when there's a festival planned, advanced booking is advised. At peak periods establishments may occasionally specify a requirement for a minimum booking period of two or three nights. In most hotels in France or Spain, breakfast is not included in the price. In the cities, hotel car parking is rarely free of charge.

HOTEL PRICE CODES

Price codes indicate the cost, in euros, for a double room, per night excluding breakfast.

€€€€€	€220+
€€€€	€140–220
€€€	€ 90–140
€€	€ 60–90
€	below €60

Of particular interest to those who either seek their own space on a self-catering basis, or who wish to rub shoulders with locals, is the chance to stay in a ***casa rural*** or ***agroturismo*** establishment south of the Pyrenees. Here you will either stay in a room in a large house on a basis similar to the familiar 'bed and breakfast' option, or rent the entire house for self-catering. Where the listing states '*habitaciones*' you will be engaging in the former; where it states '*casa entera*' you will be engaging in the latter. In Navarre, most properties of this type are only available for renting as a whole house, but it's worth looking around for those that offer individual rooms. Addresses for umbrella organisations for this type of accommodation are given below, and they represent very good value, though breakfast is often at a moderate extra charge. Quite often, these establishments are in beautifully converted farmhouses whose previous agricultural function has passed into history. If visiting in winter, check that they have heating!

In France, staying in what is effectively a **bed and breakfast** through the *Gîtes de France* organisation is also a cost-effective and more personal option than staying in a large hotel. This same organisation will also rent you whole houses north of the border.

For **campers**, there are many, many sites along the coast, both north and south of the Pyrenees, but fewer inland. Note that 'wild camping' is strictly prohibited in Spain, but although the legal position in France is a bit misty, it is generally permitted. It is best to ask the landowner first, if you can track them down, and don't light any fires.

TIPPING Unlike in some countries, tipping is not mandatory in Spanish or French hotels, though a coin or two to the hotel porter or for the person who cleans your hotel room will be appreciated.

USEFUL ADDRESSES

Camping France w campingfrance.com/uk. A website with English-language option, listing nearly 160 sites in the Pyrénées-Atlantiques department.

Campings Euskadi w campingseuskadi.com. The official Euskadi camping federation website, in English, with full details of the sites in Biscay & Gipuzkoa – & the one site in Álava.

Campings Navarra w campingsnavarra.com. Useful site, in English, of the Navarre Camping Association, with details of Navarre's 20 or so campsites.

Casas Rurales Navarra w casasruralesnavarra.com. Rooms in houses, as well as whole houses to rent, in Navarre, at good prices. Website in Spanish only. Also lists some rural hotels & campsites.

Gîtes de France 0871 277 0399 (UK); w gites-de-france.com. Comprehensive site, in English, for those who are looking for whole properties to rent for weekends, whole weeks or parts of weeks, with many properties in the French Basque region. Also has a number of bed & breakfasts available to book per night.

Nekatur w nekatur.net. An excellent resource offering rooms & whole houses to rent, by the day or week, in Bizkaia, Gipuzkoa & Álava. They are often very good value. Website in English. Note that they also run a discount card scheme, giving you reductions on the cost of subsequent stays & some visitor attractions: each establishment should carry details.

EATING AND DRINKING

FOOD There is a saying that, for a Basque, the first priority is food and the second priority is 'What's for dinner?' When one Basque suggests to another 'Let's go walking on the mountain on Sunday,' the likely reply is not 'Which mountain?' but 'What food shall we take?' or 'Which restaurant are we eating at afterwards?' When

RESTAURANT PRICE CODES

Price codes indicate (in euros) the cost of a typical main course only, per person, without drinks.

€€€€€	€25+
€€€€	€20–25
€€€	€15–20
€€	€10–15
€	below €10

reading a regional newspaper, it is not unusual to see a solemn announcement like this: 'The Guild of the Beasain Black Pudding will hold its Annual Assembly tomorrow' (author translation).

It is impossible to overstate the importance of eating when talking about the Basque culture and there is no apology for the number of times the content of this book turns to food, eating, chocolate, ham or seafood. Food here is a religion.

Quality is everything: every Basque has an opinion on where to find the best cheese, ham, seafood and *chuletón* (beef chop). Moreover, they will be very happy to discuss it at great length with each other and anyone prepared to listen. Good cuisine is universal: the people eat like kings and the kings (if there were any left) would eat like the people. This obsession with food does not mean that they gorge themselves irrespective of the consequences. You won't see many overweight Basques, something which is partially due to a diet that is healthy – in both senses of the word – and partially due to their active lifestyle and love of sport.

What strikes the visitor is not just *what* the Basques eat, but also *how*, *when* and *where* they eat. The 'what' is usually straightforward, as cuisine is based on fresh seasonal ingredients, largely unadulterated, taken from the sea or brought down from the mountains. Simplicity is key. There is no need to spoil a decent piece of hake or sea bream with an elaborate sauce: in fact, some view such adornments with suspicion. Some fresh hake? Simply cook it with some oil and garlic and it will be deemed quite sufficient. A nice beef chop? Grill it and serve it on a plate, often without any vegetables to distract from the flavour.

Of course, although the freshness of ingredients is the most important factor, another strand to the region's cuisine has developed in recent years. The rise of *nueva cocina vasca* (new Basque cuisine) demonstrates a highly creative and innovative approach that combines Basque traditions and recipes with the elevation of cooking to the status of kitchen art. Most evident in the higher-end restaurants, this cuisine comes at a price, but its quality and the value that it still represents is underlined by the accolades frequently heaped upon the region's top chefs. This is a region that glitters with Michelin stars.

Below are some culinary specialities to look out for during your stay.

Meat

Chuletón *or* chuleta Unless you're a vegetarian, it would be a shame to visit the Basque Country without sampling at least one *chuletón*, a magnificent beef chop cooked *a la plancha*. It's often priced on the menu by weight, and sometimes a restaurant will stipulate that a minimum of two people order it. Be aware that the local preference is to leave it rare in the middle, but most restaurants will be more than happy to cook it for a bit longer to satisfy the taste of foreigners. If ordering a *chuletón*, arrive hungry and be prepared to leave bloated, as they don't skimp on portions.

Axoa de veau Not everyone is happy eating veal, but if you are, then this speciality from north of the border comprises shoulder meat chopped together with onions and seasoned with the famed Espelette pepper, though it has several variations.

Txistorra Many visitors will be familiar with *chorizo*, but these thin, spicy pork sausages are often available as *pintxos* or served in crusty rolls – like a hot dog, but infinitely tastier.

Chorizo de Pamplona Neither Navarre nor any of the Basque provinces can claim any monopoly on *chorizo*, the great spicy Spanish sausage, but Pamplona produces its own variation that is thicker and has a finer texture than most.

Ham Bayonne is justly renowned for its ham, protected by an IGP (*indication géographique protégée*) which, although it guarantees a certain quality, does not mean that the pork actually comes from Bayonne, or even from the Basque Country! A ham that's allowed to call itself a Bayonne ham will be stamped with the *lauburu* (Basque cross) emblem (see box, page 29), but to get something high-quality from pigs reared in the (Basque) open air, it's worth seeking out the products of a producer such as Oteiza (page 347). In the southern Basque provinces, no self-respecting bar will be without some ham on its premises, even if it's in a simple sandwich. Usually, however, there will be a dozen of them hanging from the ceiling.

Poulet Basque Made with peppers and tomatoes, this is a tasty chicken stew popular in the French Basque Country. South of the border, some locals explain away the general lack of chicken on menus, saying that it is not considered special enough to eat when dining out.

Palombe In October, migrating pigeons are trapped in nets or shot by hunters around the border areas, especially near the town of Etxalar. When *palombe* or *paloma* pops up on the menu around this time of year, as it often does, it's pigeon that you're being offered.

Fish and seafood Although not all the produce of the sea you find here is fished off the Basque coast (some comes from Galicia and elsewhere), the demand for freshness ensures that the quality is invariably high. As well as those specialities listed below, look out for fresh *rape* (monkfish) and *rodaballo* (turbot).

Anchoas Anchovies are fished from around April and start to appear on menus shortly afterwards, lasting until around the end of July. Getaria in Gipuzkoa is a major centre of anchovy fishing. Outside the fishing season, they can be found in tins and jars.

Besugo *(sea bream)* Most often offered *al horno* (oven-baked) and truly delicious. Very popular in the Gipuzkoan coastal town of Orio.

Merluza *('merlu' in French)* Hake is definitely one of the treats awaiting visitors to the Basque coastline. Usually cooked simply in oil and garlic, it can appear on the daily menus of even the less expensive restaurants but will also take top billing in some of the best ones. Particularly prized are the *kototxa* (hake cheeks), rated by local gourmets as a delicacy.

Bacalao *(salt cod)* Although cod is a big part of the cuisine here (in some towns there are whole shops dedicated to it), it is rarely *fresh* cod that ends up on your plate. Salt cod, desalted and rehydrated, is the main ingredient. It appears in one of the region's favourite recipes, *bacalao al pil-pil*, cooked with olive oil, garlic and an optional pinch of chilli pepper.

Marmitako A traditional recipe delivers this rich tuna and potato stew, which is at its best in summer, the season for catching *bonito* (albacore tuna), which is the dish's main ingredient.

Txangurro *(spider-crab)* Most often encountered as an ingredient in carefully crafted *pintxos*, this is another coastal must-have. Look out also for *txangurro a la Donostiarra*, a San Sebastián recipe with crab, brandy and vegetables, said to have been invented especially for 19th-century Spanish royalty, who were too squeamish to eat crab straight from the shell.

Txipirones *(baby squid)* Usually served '*en su tinta*' (in its ink), these are another mainstay of midday *menús del día* along the coast.

Cheeses Three delicious cheeses, all produced from unpasteurised ewe's milk, are worth seeking out across the Basque Country and Navarre.

Idiazábal Although this cheese is named after a Gipuzkoan village, it is also produced in other parts of that province and in northern Navarre. Often served with *membrillo*, a quince jelly.

Ossau-Iraty North of the Pyrenees, this cheese makes frequent appearances on restaurant menus, accompanied by the delicious black cherry jam from Itxassou village. Along with the better-known Roquefort, it is the only French sheep's milk cheese to enjoy AOC (*appellation d'origine controlée*) status.

Roncal From the northeast Navarrese valley of Roncal, Roncal cheese received its official denomination in 1981. It is highly recommended with a glass of Navarre red wine.

Vegetables Here, as is common with other parts of Spain, you can never assume that any dish you order in a restaurant will arrive with an entourage of vegetables on the plate. It's simply not part of the culture. Often, if you want vegetables to form part of your meal, you have to order them separately as a starter course, or ask the waiter to find out what (if anything) will turn up with your meat or fish. That's not to say that vegetables don't exist here: people are very proud of what is grown on their allotments. The region of La Ribera in southern Navarre, where the climate is virtually Mediterranean, has for many centuries harnessed the waters of the River Ebro to cultivate highly rated produce that features prominently on menus. Depending on the season, artichokes, white asparagus and *pochas* (beans) are worth pursuing.

Alubias de Tolosa From the former capital of Gipuzkoa, these black/purple beans form the base for many recipes. In poorer times, beans were a staple of the region's diet and are now making something of a comeback as people become more health-conscious.

Desserts and chocolate The sweet-of-tooth will suffer no disappointment on a visit to the Basque Country and Navarre. Pastry shops can be found in most major towns in the region and there are plenty of places devoted to chocolate, too, especially in Bayonne.

Goxua A fairly recent arrival to the Basque dining table, this is now a renowned, typically Alavese dessert. It consists of whipped cream, light sponge and sweet caramelised custard.

Gâteau Basque Found mainly in the French Basque Country (south of the Pyrenees, it's known as *pastel vasco*), this delicious pastry comes filled with either black cherry jam or cream. Opinion is divided on which is tastier and which of the many bakers produces the best. Try as many as possible has to be the advice.

Vegetarian food If arriving from a country that is well attuned to catering for vegetarians, you will find your options a bit limited here. Even an innocent-looking salad may turn up with tuna mixed in. If there are no vegetarian options available among the main courses, study the starters carefully, as seasonal vegetables will often feature. It's not an ideal situation, but better than going hungry. The higher-end restaurants will generally be able to cater to vegetarians, and overall the

TXAKOLI – THE BASQUE CHAMPAGNE?

Not many people outside of the Basque Country will have heard of *txakoli* (pronounced *cha-ko-lee*) unless they've visited the region. You could even call it the Basque champagne, as it's a light, white wine, with a very slight sparkle sometimes accentuated by it being poured into the glass from a height to give it some oxygen on its descent. But unlike champagne, *txakoli* is not a special occasion drink – far from it – and you'll see the bars of Gipuzkoa in particular full of customers sipping this favoured tipple as they meet for an early evening gossip and a couple of tasty *pintxos*. Delightful and popular it may be, but most of the bottles, produced around Getaria on the coast west of San Sebastián, never make it out of the Basque Country, which explains why it remains virtually unknown elsewhere. There is some appetite for it among the Basque diaspora in the USA; some restaurants in Catalonia and elsewhere in Spain include it on their wine lists and a tiny amount is exported to other parts of Europe. (In London, in 2018, I discovered a bottle in a well-known specialist chain of off-licences, wrongly labelled as coming from Catalonia!) But by and large the Basques drink it all themselves.

Unless you're a wine-buff you may not have heard of *hondarribi zuri* or *hondarribi beltza*, the main grapes used for *txakoli* production. Having been in severe decline for many years, the viniculture in Gipuzkoa and Biscaya has been revived due in no short measure to the granting of Denominación de Origen status at the end of the 1980s. Some growers now also produce red *txakoli*, and an increasing number of wineries are exploiting the limited opportunities to plant more vines. Growers admit that a bigger export demand will only be created for their product if visitors returning from holiday start to ask for it when they get home. Its popularity in the Basque bars proves that it is certainly not a luxury drink, nor is it expensive, but it may still be some time before it reaches your local pub or supermarket shelves at home. So, don't pass up the opportunity to wash down an anchovy or two with a glass of delicious *txakoli* during your stay.

WINE IN THE BASQUE COUNTRY AND NAVARRE

With so much wine sloshing around the world, mention of the Basque Country in connection with the precious liquid may not immediately ring a bell with the amateur wine-drinker. But wine there is, on both sides of the Pyrenees. In the provinces of the Basque Autonomous Community, but especially in Gipuzkoa, the focus is firmly on *txakoli* (see box, page 57) the region's white wine, light and with just a hint of sparkle. In Álava, some wines can legitimately but confusingly label themselves 'Rioja', as the neighbouring administrative region of La Rioja is not the only one permitted by the DO (*denominación de origen*) regulations to use the 'Rioja' name on its wines. Rioja Alavesa (page 215), as this Basque region is known, prides itself on its reds, some of whose producers are firmly established names both at home and abroad. Navarre has a small piece of Rioja's DO too, though it has also become increasingly well known in recent years for wine produced and marketed under its own *denominación*. North of the Pyrenees, the French Basque Country can lay claim to its own *appellation*, but its name – Irouléguy – is not one that is usually recognised by anyone other than a true wine expert.

While the consumption of *txakoli* and Irouléguy mainly takes place close to the places of their respective production, the wines of Rioja Alavesa and the rosés and reds from Navarre now have a firm foothold in export markets. Although production of wines was nothing new, it was only the late-20th-century introduction of grapes such as tempranillo, cabernet sauvignon and merlot – to bolster the ubiquitous garnacha – that transformed Navarrese wines from workaday bulk wines into something worth sitting up for and taking notice of. A diversity of climate and soil means that Navarre is responsible for oaked reds, fruity rosés and even the renowned *moscatel* dessert wine from Corella in deep south La Ribera.

situation is improving. A few vegetarian/vegetarian-friendly places are listed in this guide.

Ethnic food With so much excellent indigenous food around, the penetration of cuisines from other parts of the globe is perhaps less than you might find elsewhere in Europe. If you look hard, you can usually find Chinese, Japanese, Italian and occasionally Indian establishments in the cities. For overall choice of cuisine from outside the territory, compact Biarritz is probably the most cosmopolitan town, perhaps not surprising given that it has been exposed to foreign visitors for longer than most.

DRINK Basque peculiarities extend to drink as well. Wine is an important part of the scene on both sides of the Pyrenees (page 345 and the box, above).

Neither Spain nor France are countries that connoisseurs would strongly associate with **beer** in the same way as they might with Belgium or Germany. While the big breweries of France and Spain have churned out their Kronenbourg (France), San Miguel and Damm (both Spain) for decades, there are now strong signs that a taste for craft beer has emerged on both sides of the Pyrenees. It is no longer impossible to find something just a bit out of the ordinary, at least in bottle form. In Navarre, **Naparbier** is a name to look out for, with their ZZ+ Amber Ale being a tasty brew.

The beers of pioneering **Pagoa** (page 170) and **Baias** are becoming more common in the Basque Autonomous Community and **Akerbeltz** from Ascain and the not-so-Basque-sounding **Bob's Beer** from Hasparren represent the best of Basque brewing in the French Basque provinces. Indications are that craft beer is definitely making its mark in the area, as elsewhere in France and Spain. Be aware that some apparently Basque craft beers (not those mentioned above) are actually brewed as far away as Strasbourg!

Cider and its drinking rituals (see box, page 155) have a much longer pedigree here than craft beer, and a meal at a *sagardotegia* (cider-house) makes for an interesting experience that has its roots firmly in the Basque farmhouses of yesteryear.

Patxaran is the area's best-known spirit, emanating from Navarre and usually taken after mealtimes as a *digestif.* Although produced commercially, it is also made by many at home by soaking sloe berries in an anise-flavoured spirit. **Izarra** is a liqueur originally made in Bayonne from a Basque recipe, with up to 16 herbs in its composition.

WHEN TO EAT Those coming to the region from other cultures will need to adjust their body clock to Basque mealtimes and restaurant opening hours. In **Spain**, there is no problem finding a city bar with coffee and a bite to eat for breakfast from 07.00, with *tortilla*, croissant or *tostada* (toast) being the favourite offerings at this time of day. Be warned that lunch and dinner happen a great deal later than in other countries. Lunch will rarely be available before 13.00, and 13.30 or even 14.00 is more usual. (But you can always rely on a heaped bar counter of *pintxos* to fend off mid-morning hunger: they start appearing from the kitchen from early morning.) Restaurants will open for dinner at 20.30 or 21.00 and service will be over by 23.00 or even 22.30.

In **France**, while most hotels provide breakfast, many bars offer no food at all in the early hours, but if that is the case then they usually won't object to you bringing in a *croissant* or two from the nearest bakery to go with your early morning coffee. Lunch in France is taken slightly earlier than in Spain, perhaps around 13.00, as is dinner, served from 20.00 or even 19.30 if you strike it lucky. Note that the time 'window' for evening dining can be short in France, especially in off-season, when service may finish at 21.00 or 21.30.

Down by the coast, where the restaurant trade is fully accustomed to visitors, the chances of eating outside of the standard hours is increased. Along the pilgrim routes, it's sometimes possible to find filling, three-course menus being served at any reasonable time of day. Restaurateurs recognise that a tired, hungry pilgrim finishing his or her day's walking at 15.00 is not going to wait until 20.00 to be fed.

WHERE TO EAT AND DRINK For the visitor to the Spanish Basque Country, the novelty of bar-hopping and grazing on *pintxos* may be too hard to resist. Be aware that you can soon rack up a decent-sized bill by eating in this fashion, enjoying a gastronomic journey through a variety of savouries, all carefully crafted and beautifully presented. The alternative is to wait until the standard restaurants open and dine 'normally' on a sit-down meal. Many of the locals choose to do both, though years of experience means that they know when to stop the grazing and start the 'proper' eating. In-between a *pintxo* and a full meal, many bars offer *raciones* ('portions') of certain dishes and *media raciones* ('half-portions') for those who are less hungry. These are basically bigger helpings of some of the more popular *pintxos*, and are usually indicated on a blackboard or on the menu.

In France, the options of eating *pintxos* or *raciones* are rarely available, perhaps only in Biarritz.

GASTRONOMIC SOCIETIES

A slightly haunted-looking face stares out from a poster on the wall. I expect to see the words 'Wanted: $5,000 reward' written above the man's head, but he is no criminal, and this is no police station. I am in Tolosa, in one of the town's best *txokos*, the renowned, private gastronomic societies that still stitch together the tight Basque social fabric south of the Pyrenees. The man on the poster, Antxon, is applying to join this *txoko*, and the poster is the existing members' opportunity to agree or otherwise to his joining.

One single thumbs-down, and his application will fail. Perhaps that explains the trepidation etched on his face. Or perhaps he's afraid of the hefty joining fee (€2,500). *Txokos* date back to the 19th century, but their exact origins are unclear. San Sebastián is undoubtedly where they started, but the 'how?' and 'why?' provoke different answers. Some believe that the menfolk invented the *txoko* in order to avoid the restricted opening hours of bars. Others credit fishermen with their invention, claiming that weeks of isolation at sea, followed by shore-time with their womenfolk was too big a contrast to handle, leading to the search for some private, male-only space ashore. For others, however, the *txoko* was a response to the city's overcrowding: a pleasant evening could hardly be spent in cramped little houses, nor in public bars and cider-houses full of occupying soldiers. Basement space was available, however, an ideal subterranean opportunity for male get-togethers. And although some concessions have been made in recent years, somewhat grudgingly, towards letting in the ladies, in most cases they are still merely guests, not members. *Txokos* are a last bastion of maleness.

Here in Tolosa, the open-plan *txoko* kitchen is beautifully fitted with professional-standard equipment. Four middle-aged to elderly men are busy creating artistic *pintxos*. At the serving-hatch, I am presented with a tower of *perretxico* mushrooms, neatly skewered with a cocktail stick and nestling on Idiazabal cheese shavings. Members take great pride in cooking in full view of everyone and serving up the results of their labour to their own *cuadrilla*, their group of friends.

Common to all of these societies is the trust between the members, each of whom has his own key. Ingredients used are recorded (as are any dents made in the wine stock) and paid for each time the member cooks.

For decades, some have predicted the demise of these societies. In a time of economic hardship, convincing new members to join can be difficult, while the gender imbalance of the membership was at odds with 20th-century thinking, never mind 21st. But with an estimated 1,000 societies still in existence, it seems that they remain a bastion of Basqueness.

Thankfully, the fast-food and take-away culture barely has a hold in either the north or south of the region, though in larger towns you might find a kebab shop or burger joint. But who needs that sort of fare when you've got *pintxos*?

HOW TO EAT This is not advice on table manners, but understanding a few of the quirks and rituals of the region will hopefully eliminate the potential for confusion and allow you to enjoy the experience of eating out in the Basque Country.

Gastronomic societies (see box, above) are really only of curiosity value to most visitors as they are effectively private clubs, but if you are well in with a local who is a member, you may be lucky enough to be invited and get an insight into what goes on in these fine and very Basque institutions. For members, the cooking, cost and eating are all shared experiences: traditionally, though less so nowadays, they were 'men only' dining clubs.

Accessible to all are the ***sagardotegiak*** (cider-houses; see box, page 155) found around the region but with a very high concentration in the towns just south of San Sebastián, such as Astigarraga and Hernani. They usually serve up a fixed menu, cider (of course) and a whole lot of fun, particularly if you visit in a large group intent on having a good time.

For those not accustomed to being faced with a bar counter dripping with delicacies, the whole ***pintxos*** (Basque tapas) thing can be daunting. Do I just help myself? (As a beginner, best to ask the bartender first.) When do I pay? (At the end.) How does the barman know how many *pintxos* you've had? (He doesn't, the whole thing's done on trust. Not a system to be abused.) You will note in the better bars the plaques on the walls proclaiming their accolades ('Best *pintxo* in Álava, 2018', etc), which signify the quality of their kitchen and also remind you that food is taken very seriously here.

Much of the principle behind enjoying food here is **sharing** it. Hence a weekend walk into the mountains will often be undertaken in a big group of family or friends, accompanied by a picnic or a **barbecue** in good weather, maybe reserving a long table at a restaurant for an even longer lunch.

A recent phenomenon that emerged from the 2008 economic crisis in Spain is the ***pintxo pote***. Faced with dwindling numbers of customers (who were staying at home to save money), bar owners hit upon the idea of offering their *pintxos* for very little money on one night of the week. At the beginning, revellers could pick up a *pintxo* and a drink for a trifling €1 in participating bars, and although the price has now edged up to €2 or €2.50 in many places, it is still enormously popular, very good value and still going strong. (Even though the economy has recovered slowly, it's 'fingers crossed' that *pintxo pote* is now part of the social structure.) Typically *pintxo pote* night is Thursday in most towns, and not all *pintxos* or all drinks are included in this bargain deal, but it is a great angle on a pub crawl. On the relevant night, groups of friends – known as ***cuadrillas*** – can be seen moving from bar to bar, taking a drink and a bite in each until they run out of energy. The correct name for this bar-hopping is a ***txikiteo***, and while it is certainly not unique to the Basque Country and Navarre, it does happen at a fast pace here. A bar that is empty one minute can be filled in a blink of an eye by the sudden arrival of a noisy *cuadrilla* or two … and equally can be empty again as soon as they move on.

In some towns, mainly in Gipuzkoa and Bizkaia, you will sometimes come across a ***herriko taberna***, or 'Basque bar' as they are sometimes called. There is no reason why you as a visitor can't drink in here, though they are often favoured by Basque nationalists and have a political edge to them. Wearing the Spanish flag draped around your shoulders or expressing political opinions in these bars would both be bad ideas.

Tipping The service charge in a Spanish or French restaurant is already in the price, whether or not it is stated on the bill. Aside from that, a tip should be given if you are particularly pleased with the service that has been provided, but would never exceed 10%. Less than that is certainly acceptable. If you do choose to leave something in a restaurant, then anything less than a solitary euro could be perceived as a bit of an insult, so if you're going to tip, make it worthwhile. In bars, rounding up a bill is quite normal.

PUBLIC HOLIDAYS AND FESTIVALS

As well as the holidays mentioned in the box below, it is worth remembering that there is a tendency (a welcome one, perhaps!) to create a 'bridge' (*puente* in Spanish, *pont* in French) when a public holiday falls either on a Tuesday or Thursday.

PUBLIC HOLIDAYS ACROSS THE BASQUE COUNTRY AND NAVARRE

Date	English name	Spanish name	French name
1 January	New Year's Day	Año Nuevo	Jour de l'an
6 January	Epiphany	Día de Reyes	not a holiday in France
19 March	St Joseph's Day	San José (not in Basque Autonomous Community)	not a holiday in France
March/April	Maundy Thursday	Jueves Santo	not a holiday in France
March/April	Good Friday	Viernes Santo	not a holiday in France
March/April	Easter Monday	Lunes de Pascua	Lundi de Pâques
1 May	Labour Day	Día del Trabajador	Fête du travail
8 May	VE Day	not a holiday in Spain	Fête de la victoire (Armistice)
39 days after Easter Sunday	Ascension	not a holiday in Spain	Ascension
50 days after Easter	Whit Monday	not a holiday in Spain	Pentecôte (not universally recognised)
14 July	Bastille Day	not a holiday in Spain	Fête nationale
15 August	Assumption	Asunción	Assomption de Marie
12 October	National Day	Fiesta Nacional de España	not a holiday in France
25 October		Euskadi Eguna (not in Navarre)	not a holiday in France
1 November	All Saints' Day	Día de Todos los Santos	Toussaint
11 November	Armistice Day	not a holiday in Spain	Armistice de 1918
6 December	National holiday	National holiday	not a holiday in France
8 December	Immaculate Conception	Inmaculada Concepción	not a holiday in France
25 December	Christmas Day	Navidad	Nöel

This means that many people 'declare' the Monday or Friday to be a holiday too, taking a day off their annual entitlement and creating a long weekend. Happy days. In addition to the above, there are many local holidays that are particular to individual towns and villages.

FESTIVALS Both in France and Spain, the festivals enjoyed by the local people are an excellent way to engage with the locals and to participate in their colourful culture. The number of festivals held in the summer months is extraordinary. A document obtained for the purposes of writing the first edition of this book showed no fewer than 291 *fiestas patronales* (local fiestas dedicated to saints or virgins) scheduled for Navarre alone, just between the months of June and October. (Remember: Navarre's population numbers a trifling 640,000!) The same schedule also included an additional 187 carnivals, sports- and food-related festivals and other events in Navarre, throughout the calendar year.

Right across the region, August is a particularly busy time for festivals, with events coinciding with the shut-down of factories and businesses. As it is impossible to list all the events taking place annually, the best advice is to use the tourist office websites in advance of your stay or visit the offices in person. A website with an English-language option that can prove useful for the Spanish side is w fiestas.net, which allows you to search 'what's on' by province. In high season, you will almost certainly find something being celebrated in the vicinity. Some of the best-known or downright peculiar festivals are highlighted or described in greater detail in the following chapters; the region covered by this guidebook plays host to everything from world-famous events such as San Fermín and its bull-running in Pamplona to fiestas celebrated in the smallest of mountain villages. Note that restaurants will be shut on both Christmas and New Year's Day; many also close early on Christmas Eve.

SHOPPING

While not really competing as one of the world's great shopping destinations, the area covered by this guide can still offer enough opportunities to treat yourself or fill your suitcase with gifts for your nearest and dearest, particularly if they like food and wine. Individual specialist shops are listed throughout this book, but here are some suggestions of things that you might buy during your stay. For those who want to browse fashion outlets, San Sebastián and Biarritz offer the region's best choice of owner-managed, one-off boutiques.

GENERAL SOUVENIRS If you are allergic to souvenir shops, then this is a region that will endear itself to you. In the old quarters of Bilbao and San Sebastián, prime locations (you would think) for the peddling of tourist rubbish, you will find very little indeed. True, a town like Espelette in Labourd embraces its opportunities for selling souvenirs, but even there the shopping is relaxed and the products are of decent quality. You can find a genuine Elosegui Basque beret from Tolosa to put on your head (will it look good when you're back home?), but if you want a T-shirt, try a Basque-themed one from Kukuxumusu, a Pamplona firm whose well-known products are sold across Spain and display a self-deprecating sense of humour.

BOOKSHOPS The most important publisher and bookseller is **Elkar** (w elkar.eus), with several branches across five of the 'seven provinces'. Addresses of some of these are given in the relevant chapters, and they stock a good range of books in

Basque and Spanish. They also stock some English-language books, including some Bradt guidebooks.

CHEESE If your baggage allowance is enough to smuggle back a whole Idiazábal or Ossau-Iraty cheese, take the opportunity to do so.

CHOCOLATE The Spanish Inquisition and its persecution of minorities in the Iberian Peninsula was responsible for the Jews and their chocolate-making expertise ending up in southwest France, and in Bayonne in particular. There are some excellent chocolatiers huddled together, almost all in one street, in Labourd's principal town, making life very easy for the sweet-toothed shopper (page 317). High-quality chocolate, often with a price to match, can also be found in many other towns north and south of the border.

ESPADRILLES Although French-made espadrilles have had to move from mass production to niche fashionwear to meet the challenge of Far East imports, this gives the homemade footwear something of a cachet that can be lacking in the more basic styles. If you're not visiting Mauléon-Licharre (page 357), the spiritual home of the French espadrille, then search out a fashionable brand such as Pare-Gabia, available from shops in Biarritz, for example (page 305).

LINEN Basque linen has a distinctive look, featuring bold, colourful stripes. From a rather rough and ready beginning – it was originally used by herdsmen to keep insects off their cattle – Basque linen has evolved into a high-end product these days and its patterns are easy on the eye, adorning a range of products from pencil-cases to tablecloths. Not everything you see in the outlets is linen, as cheaper cotton has intervened in recent times, and certainly not everything is made in the Basque Country any longer. Look out for the brand Ona Tiss, made in Saint-Palais, for something of genuine Basque manufacture. Other good-quality products are those carrying the Jean Vier or Les Tissages de Luz names, though these are not manufactured so locally. Biarritz, Sare, Espelette and other towns in Labourd have shops stocking the linen.

WINE Assuming you can carry it home safely, the low-volume production wines of the region make for distinctive gifts for oenophile friends. Irouléguy (page 345) and *txakoli* (see box, page 57) are mercifully much easier to quaff than they are to pronounce and, given their general scarcity outside their area of origin, they may raise an interested eyebrow or two from their recipients. Wines of Navarre and Rioja Alavesa are more readily available abroad, but are also excellent souvenirs.

SIGHTSEEING AND ENTERTAINMENT

For those who like to visit museums and historical sights, the low admission charges on both sides of the border will be very welcome indeed. On top of that, some attractions have days on which admission is free and tourist offices have a variety of passes and discounts available. (These are indicated in the chapters that follow, but you should always make the tourist offices your first stop, as new offers arrive and old ones become obsolete.) Don't plan to make Monday your 'museum day': many museums and visitor attractions in both France and Spain stay shut on this day of the week.

Although the provision of English-language information at the region's visitor attractions is not yet ubiquitous, the big cities (Bilbao, San Sebastián, Vitoria-Gasteiz and Pamplona) are now well geared up to receive English-speakers, as is Biarritz, given its long association with visitors from Great Britain and elsewhere. The majority of foreign visitors to the Spanish Basque provinces still come from France, so you may occasionally find that English is only the *fourth* language, after Spanish, Basque and French. There is not quite yet the critical mass of Anglophone visitors to justify the wholesale translation of museum wall panels or to have English-speaking museum guides hanging around on the off-chance of someone turning up.

Most of the time, however, English-language information of some sort *is* available, often by way of excellent audio guides, leaflets or returnable booklets. Audio-visual displays can often be shown in a variety of languages, so don't be afraid to ask at the relevant ticket office. If guided tours are offered at tourist attractions or by tourist offices, it is always best to telephone in advance wherever possible to ensure that an English-speaking guide will be available.

Whether in the French or Spanish Basque Countries or Navarre, the locals are rightly proud of their regions and very keen to promote them, making the effort to arrange assistance for foreigners whenever possible.

BEACHES Fantastic beaches are one of the highlights of the region, especially for families. In high season locals and visitors occupy every patch of available sand and even in winter the coastal delights of the beaches are a well-used resource. The only surprise is that the sands of Ereaga and Arrigunaga in Getxo, near Bilbao, make up the only Blue Flag beaches in the Basque Country, either north or south of the border. Other individual beaches are detailed in the appropriate chapters. Waters are generally clear and the main beaches are manned by lifeguards from June to September in daylight hours. The only hazards are the strong swell and ocean waves, and occasionally overeager surfers (page 46).

EVENING ENTERTAINMENT A few days' stay will be enough for you to adjust to the rhythm of the area you've chosen to visit. Naturally the big cities will offer most to those who like to extend their late nights into early mornings, while you're not likely to encounter the wild side of life in rural Soule or the Pyrenean valleys of Navarre. Wherever you are, people of all ages can be seen out on the streets and squares of cities and towns until much later than you would find in northern Europe, for example. Bars exude a relaxed ambience, often lively but rarely rowdy. The best time of day to spot a worse-for-wear local may be at 06.00 – not midnight – as they stagger home. Weekend discos will sometimes not open until nearly midnight and then close at dawn. For many people, a bit of bar-hopping with some *pintxos*, or an extended, relaxed evening meal in a restaurant, will be a pleasant enough way to pass an evening. Festivals, of course, are a chance for everyone to stay out longer and indulge a little bit more.

SPORTS AND OTHER ACTIVITIES

CYCLING Cycling is a veritable passion in both the Basque Country and Navarre, with the roads full of amateur riders eager to take on the many mountain challenges or simply to turn the pedals and enjoy some of Europe's best roads, pleasantly untroubled by a glut of vehicle traffic. Some very fine cyclists have been spawned in this region, the most prominent being Miguel Indurain, a five-time Tour de France winner who hailed from just outside Pamplona. British cycling fans will recognise the sterling efforts of Mikel Nieve and Mikel Landa, the two able, Basque lieutenants of Chris Froome, who were instrumental in securing the Kenyan-born Briton his 2017 Tour de France victory.

THE CAMINO DE SANTIAGO

From the Middle Ages to the present day, the various paths of the Camino de Santiago have lured pilgrims from around the world to travel on foot, on horseback and, in later years, by bicycle to Santiago de Compostela in Galicia.

Most pilgrims are Spanish or French, but occasionally new trends emerge. A middle-aged German comedian's decision to suspend his career and walk the route prompted a wave of German pilgrims in 2010; a book about the pilgrimage by a Korean girl saw a huge influx of Asian pilgrims; and the recent increase in Anglophonic walkers can be partially attributed to the film *The Way*, first screened in 2010.

A pilgrimage should start from your own doorstep, so perhaps talking about different, established 'starting-points' such as Saint-Jean-Pied-de-Port or Roncesvalles is meaningless. But the various *caminos* inject a huge, welcome shot of economic activity into the midst of the towns that line the 'official' way-marked routes, guaranteeing thousands of visitors annually. As a result, hostels and restaurants thrive, servicing the transient pilgrims. Of course, the walkers are only here today and gone tomorrow, many of them looking to spend as little as possible on a dormitory bed and a simple pilgrims' menu. Nevertheless, the benefits of having a pilgrimage route passing by have not gone unnoticed. Now also being marketed is the Camino Ignaciano, which traces the 16th-century footsteps of St Ignatius of Loyola, the founder of the Jesuits, from Azpeitia in Gipuzkoa all the way to Catalonia (see box, page 166).

The Basque Country and Navarre offer several pilgrimages. The Camino Francés ('The French Way') is still the most popular route to Santiago and includes a stretch from Roncesvalles down through Pamplona and across Navarre. (Before reaching the Pyrenees, there is excellent walking on the GR65 path through the French Basque Country, effectively a precursor to the Camino Francés.)

The **Camino del Norte** ('The Way of the North') from Irun follows a tortuously hilly trail via San Sebastián and Bilbao before exiting the Basque Country at Koboron, keeping walkers close to the sea at times. The **Camino Interior** ('Inland Route') again starts in Irun and heads south to reach Vitoria-Gasteiz and beyond, before leaving Álava province just beyond Zambrana.

Walking the *camino* trails will certainly introduce you to some of the best landscapes offered by this region. And despite claims that the whole thing has turned into a commercial circus, it remains a wonderful way of spending a holiday: fitness, fresh air, camaraderie, cuisine, history and culture as you pass slowly through. There's still joy in having your *credencial* (pilgrim passport) stamped nightly in hostels, and a huge sense of achievement collecting your pilgrim certificate in Santiago de Compostela. Having now walked the *camino* three times, I can assure you that it is still an item that should be put on – and ticked off – that bucket list.

Planning a camino *is beyond the scope of this guidebook. For detailed information on the routes, there are myriad books and planning websites, some of which are detailed on page 376.*

For those who have no desire to grind their way up a mountain, there is a Vía Verde ('Greenway') network in Spain, using the disused railway lines to allow a gentle introduction to the countryside. A dedicated website (**w** viasverdes.

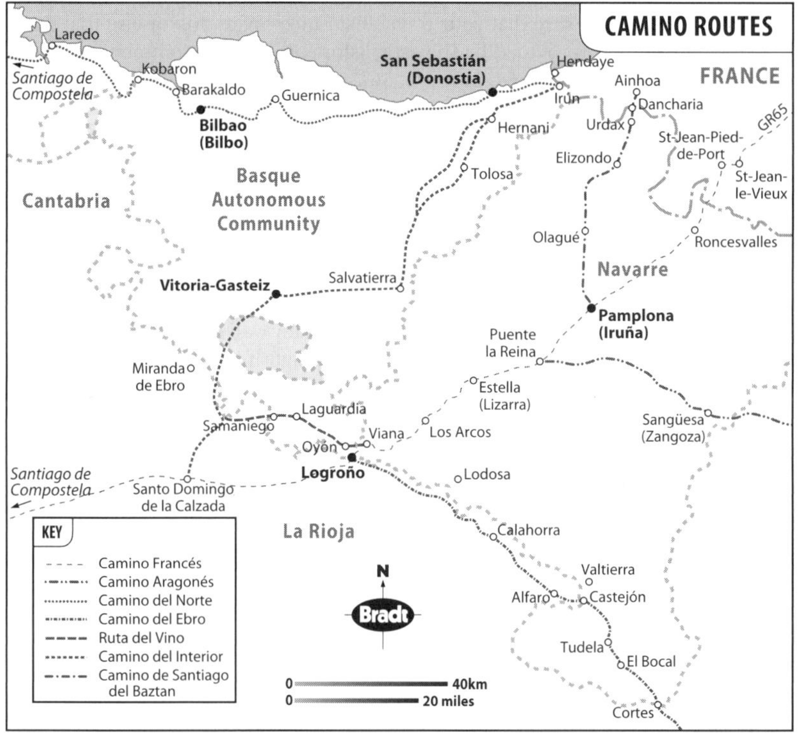

com) details all such routes, including the ten or so in the region covered by this guidebook. The route along the Bidasoa Valley is detailed on page 255. You can also hire mountain bikes at a few places in the region (pages 252 and 260).

GOLF Although you can find golf courses sporadically dotted around the Spanish Basque provinces and Navarre, lovers of the game would be advised to head straight for the coastal area around Anglet, Biarritz and the Atlantic coast stretching down to the Spanish border. Here you'll find a long-established golfing tradition dating back to the late 19th century, as well as the region's best choice of top-class courses. Among these are the oldest, the **Golf de Biarritz le Phare** (2 Av Edith Cavell, Biarritz; ☎ 0559 03 71 80; e info@golfbiarritz.com; w golfbiarritz.com), created for the pleasure of the British as far back as 1888. Also of interest in this area is the modern **Centre International d'Entrainement Golf d'Ilbarritz (Ilbarritz International Golf Training Centre)** (Av du Château, Bidart; ☎ 0559 43 81 30; e info@ilbarritz.com; w golfilbarritz.com), offering a series of improvement courses on a huge site 5 minutes south of Biarritz. Full details of all courses in this coastal region are detailed on the tourist board website (w tourisme64.com).

HORSERIDING For those who prefer to see the landscape from horseback, Navarre and the French provinces in particular provide excellent opportunities. The tourist office websites (page 42) list establishments offering everything from a 1-hour excursion to a seven-day long-distance trek. Prices are usually very reasonable, so it's just a question of overcoming any language difficulties, ensuring that you are below any weight limit (usually 80kg), checking that you will be provided with a riding hat and making sure that your travel insurance covers you or else that there is adequate insurance provided by the establishment. A few recommended places can be found on pages 243, 264, 291, 345, 362 and 364.

WALKING Walkers could happily spend a lifetime or two feasting on the crumpled landscape of the Pyrenees, pre-Pyrenees, natural parks, coastline, pilgrim routes and even the city landscapes of the Basque Country and Navarre. Seventeen fairly short walks are documented in detail in this edition, but this can barely touch the wealth of opportunities presented by a varied and often undulating countryside.

In addition to the walks detailed in this guidebook, many local tourist offices and their websites have free, downloadable walking routes, or else hard-copy walking leaflets available for a moderate cost. One issue for many walkers may be the problem of language, as while some routes are available in English translation, most are not and it would be foolish to set off on serious hillwalking with inadequate instructions unless you are satisfied that the waymarking is up to date. Sometimes it is, sometimes it isn't, with consequences which can be frustrating at best and disastrous at worst.

French walking routes and waymarking in general seem to be better maintained than their counterparts south of the Pyrenees. A high proportion of the routes on the southern side of the border are linear rather than circular, meaning that a retracing of steps is required. Easier to navigate, but a bit repetitive when your holiday time is precious.

SURFING Since surfers first made an appearance on the Basque Country coast in the 1950s, it has developed into an excellent surfing destination. It took a while

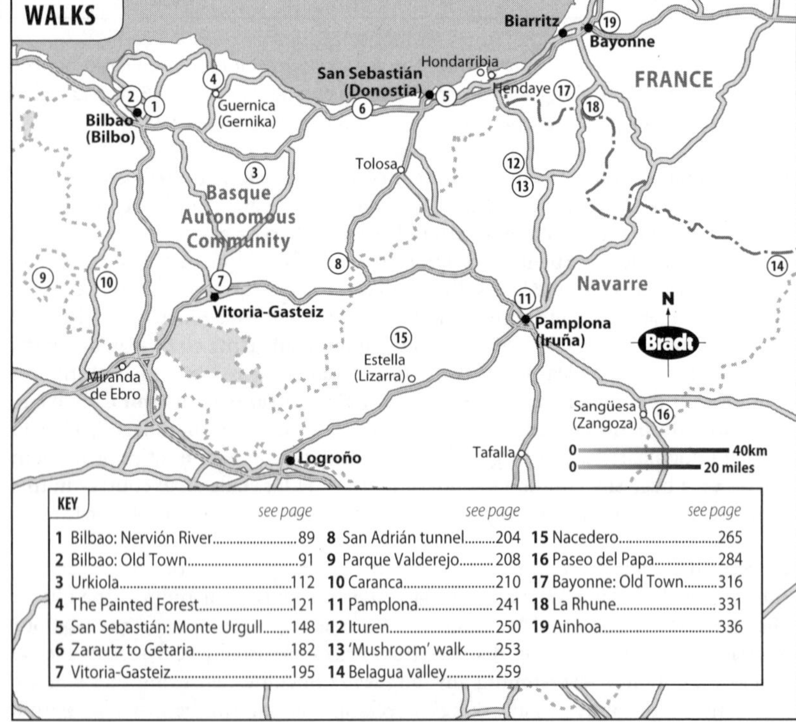

for the major competitions to arrive, but surfing is now a big industry on both sides of the border, with schools, camps and surfboard-makers all set up to service the beginner and the experts who visit year-round, seeking to master the waves rolling in on the Atlantic. While some tips are given here, this guidebook cannot profess to provide expert advice. Conditions change, sandbanks shift and the coastline features many rocks, some invisible at high tide. The best advice is to find a good, well-established surf school if you want to learn. Experienced surfers will already know the ropes if visiting a surf spot unfamiliar to them, but one site worth checking out is w wannasurf.com, with ratings of all the various surf spots across the world, including 27 on the north-facing Basque coastline and no fewer than 32 on the French Basque coast.

Winter is the surfing season for advanced and expert surfers: in summer, the sea can be flat, too flat for thrill-seekers, but the calmer, warmer waters then present opportunities for beginners to practise their technique. Summer season welcomes surfers and would-be surfers from all over the world, but they have to compete for space with swimmers and paddlers. In the colder months, when the sea temperature can be as low as 11°C, the hardy locals are more prominent. Lessons at some schools are available all year round.

For those seeking **lessons**, these are most cost-effective if you take them as part of a group, either with strangers or friends. In France, count on paying around €40 for a 1½-hour introductory lesson; a course of five lessons spread across a week will cost around €180. Once across the border, prices drop considerably and five lessons taken in a group can cost as little as €110. Private individual lessons will be much more expensive, probably around €80 for 1½ hours in France and €65 in Spain. Many schools will accept pupils from the age of six to those in their 70s, so age is no barrier at either end of the scale. Equipment hire (wetsuit and board) and insurance should be included in the prices, and most established schools will provide lessons in English, though you obviously need to check this in advance. For experienced surfers, most schools will be able to hire out equipment to you, though any decent school should check your expertise before doing so.

Detailed **information** can be found in the publications available, in English, from any of the coastal tourist offices. These include listings of all schools, surf camps, surf-friendly accommodation, tips on safety, the surfing 'code of conduct' and equipment guides. Local surfers use international websites to monitor conditions, but for beginners the various factors that need to be taken into account to determine the conditions (wave height, wave period, wind direction, tides, etc) are a bit bewildering; far better to start surfing with a reputable school, who will determine your level, provide the necessary equipment, sell you insurance (advisable), teach you the surfers' etiquette and – of course – teach you how to surf. Crucially, locals also know the currents. Webcams are also used to scan many of the beaches. Experienced surfers will always take advice from the locals before entering the water.

For those who want to see top surfers in action but prefer to stay dry themselves, the **competitions** across the world, sometimes including a few hosted in the Basque Country (on both sides of the border), are scheduled in the diary of the WSL (World Surf League; w worldsurfleague.com).

Surfing the French Basque Coast The French Basque Coast may have welcomed surfing to Europe from California only 60 years ago, but from its humble one-man beginnings in 1956 the sport has grown exponentially. By the end of the summer of 1957, the coast had four surfers; in 1959, the first surf club was established. Biarritz and Anglet began to host big international events in the 1980s and they remain on the competition calendar, with the Plage Côte des Basques (Biarritz) and the Chambre d'Amour (Anglet) being the favourite venues. Nowadays, the short 30km of French Basque coastline from Anglet in the north to Hendaye by the border with Spain is home to over 40 surf schools. On offer are surf spots ideal for novices, such as the bay at Hendaye, as well as legendary waves for kamikaze surfers such as Belharra, rated among the world's biggest, and the ominously named Avalanche.

Surfing the Basque Country in Gipuzkoa and Bizkaia In **San Sebastián**, the beach that gets the best swell is undoubtedly Zurriola, but if the waters get too lively then the other two shore beaches of La Concha and Ondarreta are put to use. Indeed, winter conditions can be such that Zurriola beach is completely closed, along with the Kursaal Bridge and the Paseo Nuevo, the road that circumnavigates Monte Urgull. (Have a look for videos on the internet, and be prepared to be awestruck by the size of the breaking winter waves!) Zurriola is manned by lifeguards from June through to September, and they have their work cut out during this high season. La Concha has no surfing in summer.

Moving west from San Sebastián, **Zarautz** is famous for its surfing and for some it lays claim to being the spiritual home of the sport in the Spanish Basque Country.

Next west is **Zumaia**, then **Deba**, before you reach Bizkaia province and **Mundaka,** famous for its left-hander, which controversially disappeared for a while, but is once again rated as one of the world's best waves. The town now no longer hosts the top international competitions, as waves have proved to be a bit inconsistent, but Spanish and provincial competitions take place here regularly and there is a good choice of schools. **Bakio** has surf schools and consistent waves and the area just east of Bilbao between **Gorliz** and **Getxo** is full of surf spots, with **Sopela** popular with day trippers from Bilbao.

MEDIA AND COMMUNICATIONS

TELEPHONE To telephone anywhere in **Spain** from the UK, dial 00 (international), then 34 (Spain country code), then the relevant nine-figure number; for **France**, dial 00 (international) then 33 (France country code) and then dial the number excluding the initial '0'. If dialling a Spanish or French mobile phone from the UK, dial 00 then 34 or 33 (Spain or France, as appropriate), then the number excluding its first '0'. To dial the UK from either Spain or France, dial 00 (international), then 44 (UK country code), then the town code minus the initial '0', then the number itself. From the USA, dial 011 then 34 (for Spain) or 33 (for France) then the number itself, once again excluding the initial '0' for France. When dialling mobiles to either country, exclude any initial '0' prefixed to the number. French mobile phone numbers begin with either 06 or 07; while in Spain they start with 6 or 7. A local SIM on a pay-as-you-go basis is a good idea if you are staying a while.

Emergency telephone numbers If in any doubt, the pan-European 112 number is the best bet in an emergency. See the inside front cover for further details of emergency numbers in Spain and France.

INTERNET CAFÉS/WI-FI While the age of the internet café is not quite over, the availability of free Wi-Fi has certainly seen their number decline here, as elsewhere. Some of the few that remain are listed in the relevant chapters. Nearly all hotels right across the region now offer free Wi-Fi, to such an extent that it is a bit of a shock if they *don't* provide it. Where it may not be provided is in some of the more remote *casas rurales* or *gîtes*, but this is something you can check in advance of booking through the umbrella organisation websites listed on page 53. Even most campsites now have some kind of Wi-Fi facility, even if it's in the campsite bar or reception. In most decent-sized towns, you will not have to work too hard to find a café or bar with Wi-Fi coverage, though be prepared to ask, as they don't all advertise the fact. In some cities municipal Wi-Fi is now available and this is detailed in the appropriate chapter. Even some smaller towns offer this, particularly inside the tourist office itself. Libraries are another good place to access the internet, if you're really stuck.

POST Postal rates are very reasonable for postcards and letters to other parts of Europe, costing less than a euro from either France or Spain. Postcards take only a few days to reach most European destinations. Outside of Spanish post office opening hours, you can buy stamps from many tobacconists.

NEWSPAPERS If you speak Spanish or French, you'll find that many bars have copies of at least one newspaper to digest while you enjoy your morning coffee. South of the Pyrenees the most frequent papers are *El Diario Vasco* and *El Correo* in the Basque Autonomous Community and the *Diario de Navarra* in Navarre. In France, you might find a copy of the regional *Sud-Ouest* on the bar counters. UK daily papers and the occasional *International New York Times* or *Financial Times* can be found in Bilbao, San Sebastián, Pamplona and Biarritz, but only with difficulty elsewhere unless there is a significant Anglophonic, expat community. The most likely outlets in the major cities are detailed in the relevant chapters.

TELEVISION AND RADIO EITB (Euskal Irrati Telebista) is the local provider of television and radio broadcasting south of the Pyrenees, with programmes in Basque (channel ETB1) and Spanish (ETB2). Through ETBsat, programmes are available on the internet, aimed at reaching the diaspora in the Americas and elsewhere and as such are often in Spanish. In addition, they have five radio stations, one in Basque, one in Spanish, two music channels and one focused on Álava province.

Close to the Spanish/French border you may have the choice of picking up both countries' broadcasting networks. For those looking for English-language channels, you may have to book into a fairly upmarket hotel to find them – usually CNN or BBC World – via satellite.

CULTURAL ETIQUETTE

Particularly south of the Pyrenees, the Basques and Navarrese are tactile people and recognising this helps to ensure that no misunderstandings take place. (In truth, this propensity for non-verbal communication is shared with many Spaniards.) It's not unusual, even when holding a brief conversation with a complete stranger, for physical contact to take place. This is largely alien to many English-speaking cultures, and can sometimes cause discomfort or confusion among visitors. Nothing should be read into it, and it usually just involves a light touch on the arm, for example when someone is giving directions on the street. Greeting people is slightly more complex: to kiss, or not to kiss, that is the question. Men meeting each other will shake hands. With a man and a woman meeting for the first time, a handshake is enough, but the woman may put her face slightly forward for a quick brush of cheeks, in which case the man should accept and also repeat the greeting on the other cheek. If in any doubt, the safe option is always to just stick to a handshake: local people generally appreciate that those from some other cultures are slightly more formal than they are.

Finally, some visitors to Spain and particularly France complain about 'surly service' in shops, bars and restaurants. My advice is to ensure that you greet the shopkeeper, bartender or waiter with a heartfelt '*Buenos días/Buenas tardes/Bonjour/Bon soir*' as appropriate, as soon as you enter the establishment. Accompany your greeting with a beaming smile: it costs nothing and should guarantee good service; to fail to do so is considered rude … and that rudeness could be reciprocated!

BUYING PROPERTY

The property market in the Basque Country south of the Pyrenees is a different world from that of the concrete *costas* of Andalucía and elsewhere, where the economic crisis of 2008 and beyond brought dwindling demand face to face with chronic oversupply and rich pickings for anyone brave enough to spot the bottom of the market. Property prices have shown some decline in the Basque areas, but not to the same extent as elsewhere in Spain. Most people in the Basque Country live in apartments and, while you can pick up a three-bedroom flat for less than €100,000, this is most likely to be in somewhere unfashionable and away from the coast. Bear in mind that coastal property here attracts huge price tags, with some stretches of seafront real estate in San Sebastián being the costliest property per square metre in the whole of Spain. While northern European property buyers may not have swarmed to the area in the past, plenty of Spaniards have invested in second homes in the Basque Country and helped to keep prices high. It is no surprise to learn that in and around Pamplona, property costs more than elsewhere in Navarre, with bargains still to be found in less populated areas, especially if you are a DIY guru. At present, international buyers make up a tiny percentage of total buyers in Bizkaia, Gipuzkoa, Álava and Navarre when compared with somewhere like Málaga or Almería in southern Spain.

North of the border, a similar situation exists in the French Basque coastal areas, where Biarritz, Saint-Jean-de-Luz and other resorts have long been on the radar of second-home purchasers. Around 30% of houses in Biarritz are second homes, and it ranks in France's top 15% of the most expensive towns in which to buy property. Away from the seashore, property in Bayonne would be around one-third less expensive. If you've set your heart on a big Basque farmhouse somewhere super-picturesque like Ascain or Sare, expect to pay a lot, but if you are content with peaceful, unfashionable Soule, you might be pleasantly surprised by the price of a detached house with a bit of land.

This guidebook does not give property buying advice, but as when buying property elsewhere in the world, it is necessary to have a good understanding of the French or Spanish system, which may be quite different from what you are used to, before putting pen to paper or parting with any money. The details of a couple of books on property purchasing in France and Spain are referenced on page 376.

Part Two

THE BASQUE AUTONOMOUS COMMUNITY

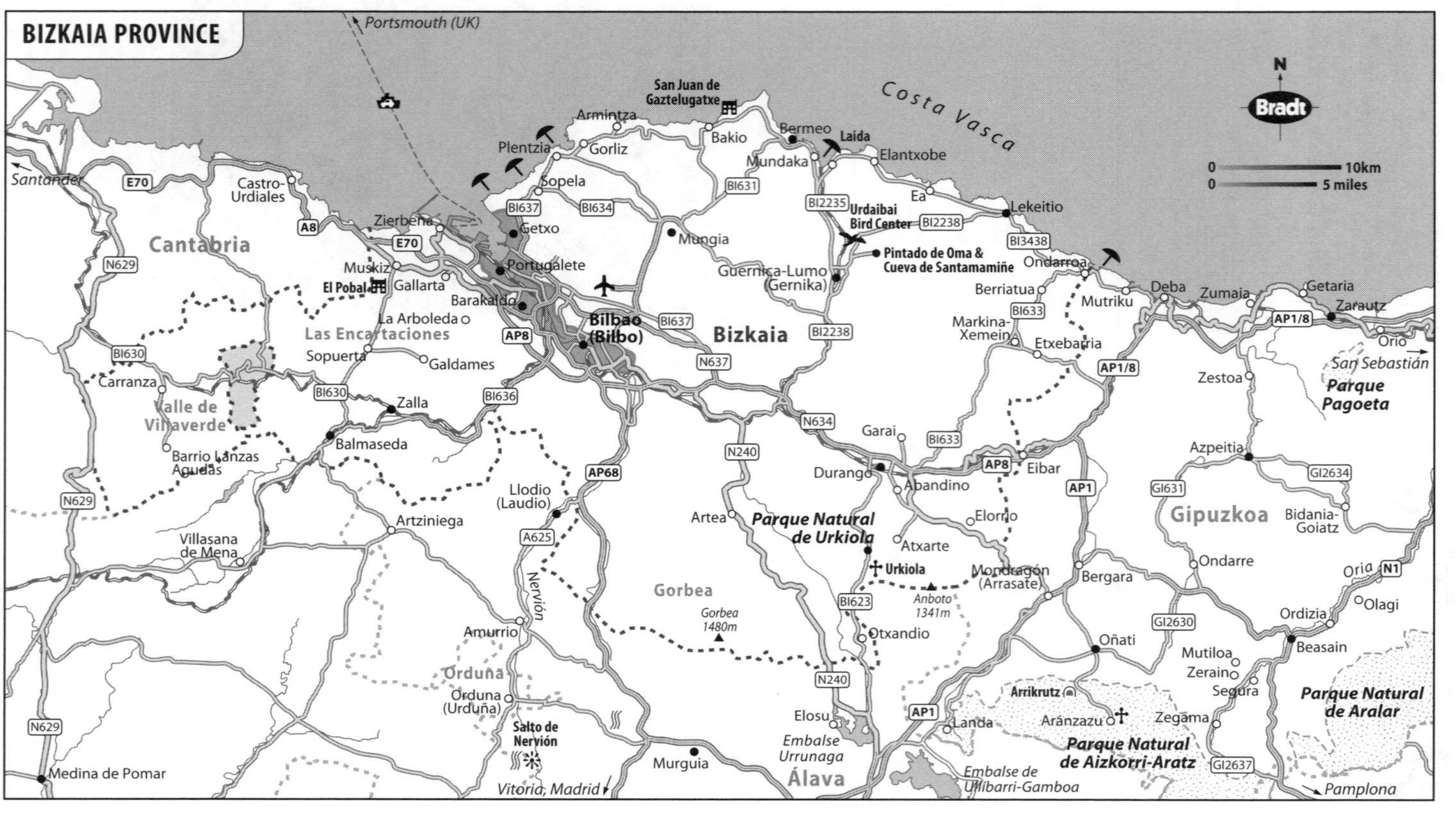

BIZKAIA PROVINCE
Portsmouth (UK)
Costa Vasca
N
Bradt
0 10km
0 5 miles
Santander
E70
Castro-Urdiales
A8
Cantabria
N629
Zierbena
E70
Muskiz
El Pobal
Gallarta
Armintza
Plentzia
Gorliz
Sopela
BI637
BI634
Getxo
Portugalete
Barakaldo
La Arboleda
Las Encartaciones
Sopuerta
Galdames
AP8
Bilbao (Bilbo)
BI637
BI630
Carranza
Valle de Villaverde
BI630
Zalla
BI636
Balmaseda
Barrio Lanzas Agudas
N629
San Juan de Gaztelugatxe
Bakio
BI631
Mungia
Bermeo
Laida
Mundaka
Elantxobe
Ea
BI2235
Urdaibai Bird Center
BI2238
Pintado de Oma & Cueva de Santamamiñe
Guernica-Lumo (Gernika)
BI2238
Bizkaia
N637
Lekeitio
BI3438
Ondarroa
Berriatua
BI633
Markina-Xemein
Etxebarria
Mutriku
Deba
Zumaia
Getaria
Zarautz
AP1/8
Orio
San Sebastián
Parque Pagoeta
AP1/8
Zestoa
N634
Garai
BI633
N240
Durango
Abandino
AP8
Eibar
AP1
Azpeitia
GI2634
GI631
Gipuzkoa
Bidania-Goiatz
AP68
Llodio (Laudio)
Artziniega
A625
Villasana de Mena
Nervión
Artea
Parque Natural de Urkiola
Elorrio
Atxarte
Urkiola
Mondragón (Arrasate)
Anboto 1341m
Bergara
Ondarre
Oria
N1
Olagi
Gorbea
Gorbea 1480m
BI623
Otxandio
GI2630
Ordizia
Oñati
Beasain
Amurrio
Orduna
Orduna (Urduña)
N240
Mutiloa
Zerain
Segura
Arrikrutz
Aránzazu
Zegama
Parque Natural de Aralar
N629
Salto de Nervión
Elosu
AP1
Landa
Embalse Urrunaga
Parque Natural de Aizkorri-Aratz
Medina de Pomar
Vitoria, Madrid
Murguia
Álava
Embalse de Ullíbarri-Gamboa
GI2637
Pamplona

3

Bilbao (Bilbo) and Bizkaia Province

Driving through Bizkaia (in English, 'Biscay') province along the motorway south of Bilbao and looking down on the concrete outskirts of the Basque Country's only really big city, you might be tempted to keep the foot on the accelerator pedal. Forty years ago, that would have been wise. Here is a place with a tough background; a city shaped by its industrial history, with all the battle scars to prove it. There's something hugely masculine about Bilbao, but ignoring the city simply because it lacks the obviously seductive qualities of San Sebastián would be a massive mistake; this giant is a solid testament to urban reinvention. Some places look better from a distance than at close quarters, but Bilbao is not one of them; once you are in the heart of the city, pleasant surprises await.

Of course, Bilbao is also capital of Bizkaia province. Out of the city, nearby Getxo provides a pleasant seaside distraction with its promenade and beaches, as do Sopela, Gorliz and Plentzia a little further east: playgrounds for the city-dwellers and easily accessible by public transport. The Puente Bizkaia, the UNESCO Heritage Transporter Bridge, joins Getxo to Portugalete across the river estuary. Further afield, a day trip west of the greater Bilbao conurbation first introduces you to the ravaged former mining area around Gallarta – unattractive, yet fascinating – before leading you on to Balmaseda, a pleasant town famous for its Passion Play. Deeper still into the interior await the quaint villages and lush countryside of the Encartaciones region, craggy and karstic. Choosing an eastward direction from Bilbao and a succession of fishing villages, now largely given over to tourism, dot the coastline as it heads towards Gipuzkoa and San Sebastián. Guernica, a place steeped in tragedy and at the very core of Basqueness, demands an inland diversion for the culturally and historically curious, while the Urdaibai estuary will satisfy ardent birdwatchers. Where the Guernika estuary becomes the sea, Mundaka is revered by surfers for its left-hand wave. To the south, nature lovers and walkers will revel in the jagged mountains and dense forests that decorate the natural parks of Gorbea and Urkiola.

HISTORY

For over 700 years, the tides of commerce and industry brought to Bilbao the ebbs and flows of population and prosperity. Although there was a small settlement here before the year AD1300, it was then that the city received its charter, and from that point onward its access to the sea allowed it first to prosper as a trading port, then to exploit its proximity to natural resources such as iron and charcoal to spawn heavy industries, finance them with a healthy banking sector, people them with immigrants and send their products across the seas to the markets of northern Europe and beyond.

Habitation in what is now Bizkaia province can be traced back to the mists of the Palaeolithic period, evidenced by the paintings in the caves of Santimamiñe (page 122) and even beyond. Some evidence of Roman settlement has been unearthed near Guernica, but the exact relationship between Basque and Roman is unclear: conquered and conqueror, or peaceful co-habitants?

By the early Middle Ages, the land that is now Bizkaia was under the control of the Kingdom of Pamplona, which was constantly warring with powerful Castile. As a result of these conflicts, and Castile's victory, the 11th century saw the appearance of the very first Lord of Bizkaia, and he and his successors governed the territory, subject to them swearing to defend the *fueros* (the ancient rights and privileges of the Basques and Navarrese). Bilbao's charter was granted by the then Lord of Bizkaia, Don Diego López de Haro, and other Bizkaian towns were also similarly 'chartered' around the same time. Commercial activity increased and the area prospered gradually. Bilbao became the port town for Castile, with wool exported to Flanders and other goods heading to northern Europe. Taking the honour previously held by Bermeo, Bilbao became Bizkaia's capital in 1602. Once independent, the town of Durango was absorbed into Bizkaia in the 17th century, as was Encartaciones to the west.

During the Carlist Wars of the mid-19th century, Bilbao resisted three sieges by the anti-Carlists, but the city's support for what proved to be the losing side resulted in the cutting of its preciously guarded independence.

But it was the mid-to-late 19th century and the Industrial Revolution that provided the catalyst for Bilbao's next seismic change. Greedy for iron, northern Europe turned to the hills around Bilbao to feed its frenzy, with Britain in particular providing finance and human resource to facilitate the exploitation of Bizkaia's ore. At one time, late in the 19th century, two-thirds of Britain's iron ore originated in Bilbao. The city prospered again – the railway arrived in 1857, the first banks were established, along with a stock exchange, and football was introduced by the English. Industries sprang up along the Nervión River, including, in 1902, the emblematic iron and steel conglomerate Altos Hornos de Bizkaia, which in much later years would employ 13,000 people. From 1880 the city's population multiplied sevenfold in 20 years, reaching 80,000 by the turn of the century.

Bizkaia supported the Republicans during the Civil War, and paid the price. Betrayed to the Nationalists by the engineer who had orchestrated Bilbao's defensive strategy, the city was taken by Franco's forces in 1937. Bizkaia lost its right to self-rule and had to wait until the dictator's death, when democracy was restored to Spain as a whole, to reassert itself.

Bilbao and its surroundings suffered in the 1980s as part of a global industrial decline, exacerbated by regional factors, but it has since sought to reinvent itself as a service economy. The 'Guggenheim effect' is held up as the flagship project in this process – which is not yet complete – but Bilbaoinos can also point to their swanky airport, swish metro system, the Azkuna Zentroa (formerly Alhóndiga) venue, the new 'superport' and the cleaned-up banks of the Nervión River. The '*botxo*' – the 'hole', as then-polluted Bilbao was once derisively called – is thankfully no longer a suitable nickname.

Not a city to be left behind when it comes to partying, Bilbao takes nine days out in late August for its *Aste Nagusia* or 'Big Week' which follows on after those of San Sebastián and Vitoria. Many concerts and events are free. A Basquefest (**w** basquefest.com) is held to coincide with Easter celebrations, involving food, sport and much more. July is the time for BBK Live, a music festival with top-name acts. On 21 December, pre-Christmas frenzy takes hold with San Tomás when hundreds of market stalls offer their wares. Music and dance accompany the crowds around Plaza Nueva and El Arenal. Book hotels and restaurants well in advance if visiting at these times.

GETTING THERE AND AWAY

BY AIR Bilbao's chic-looking Loiu Airport (w aeropuertodebilbao.net/en) lies around 12km northeast of the city. From the UK, it is serviced by British Airways (Heathrow), easyJet (London Stansted, Edinburgh, Bristol and Manchester), and Vueling and Iberia (London Gatwick). From the Republic of Ireland, Aer Lingus connects Bilbao with Dublin. Domestic flights go to a variety of places such as Madrid, Barcelona, Valencia and Tenerife, while other direct international destinations include Paris, Frankfurt, Brussels, Istanbul and Warsaw. For airline details, see page 44.

To get to and from the airport by **public transport**, the number 3247 bus service runs from the city between 05.25 and 21.55, every 15 minutes, and from the airport from 06.15 to midnight at the same frequency. One-way fares doubled suddenly in 2018, but still cost a modest €3, and are available from a kiosk at the far end of the Arrivals area. (An adjacent machine sells tickets for airport buses directly to San Sebastián (departs hourly, €17) and other destinations such as Eibar, Zarautz, etc.) The bus from the airport to Bilbao makes four stops in town, including Plaza Moyua for metro connections, before reaching the main Termibus bus terminal (see below). Journey time is around 25 minutes. The bus company website w bizkaia.eus is in Spanish and Basque only. For connections to most other cities, take the airport bus to the Termibus and connect from there.

A **taxi to the city** will take 15 minutes and should cost €22–25. Between 22.00 and 07.00, all taxis are about 10% more. (See page 82 for contact details.)

The airport Arrivals hall has a helpful, manned information kiosk (🕘 09.00–21.00 daily), plus an excellent multilingual touch screen on the outside, allowing access to details of bus timetables, official taxi fares, nearby hotels, etc, when the office is closed.

BY SEA If you prefer a more leisurely journey to Bilbao from the UK and are bringing your own car, you can avoid a long drive through France, as Brittany Ferries sail directly to Bilbao from Portsmouth. For contact details, see page 45.

BY CAR By road, Bilbao is a 4-hour drive north from Madrid and nearly 6 hours northwest from Barcelona. San Sebastián is just over 1 hour to the east along the AP-8 motorway. To the south lies Vitoria, less than an hour away via the AP-68, while Pamplona is 1 hour 45 minutes to the southeast, initially using the same road.

BY BUS Bilbao's medium- and long-distance bus station is the jauntily named **Termibus** (w termibus.es, a good website with English-language option), reached by taking the metro to San Mamés station, or by tram to the stop of the same name. All major Spanish cities are served, including San Sebastián (shown as 'Donostia' on the timetables; 1hr 20mins; from €6.50), Madrid (5hrs) and Barcelona (8hrs), and local buses to many towns in Bizkaia also terminate here. You can even get the occasional bus to London, Porto or Paris, if you're a glutton for long-distance punishment. At the time of writing, Bilbao was following the lead of Pamplona and San Sebastián and digging deep to create a new, underground bus station, on the existing site. Completion is due for 2019. Detailed timetables are on the website. For towns around the metropolitan area of Bilbao, the bus service is operated by Bizkaibus (w bizkaia.eus). Their services are good value and efficient, but their website unwieldy and without any English-language information. Local buses leave from other places in the city, including Plaza Moyúa, Termibus and Calle Bailén, depending on the destination.

BY TRAIN Bilbao is served by three different rail networks, with three corresponding train stations in the city centre. **RENFE**, the intercity network, operates from Abando station [83 B1], with trains to long-distance destinations such as Madrid, Barcelona and La Coruña. The **FEVE** (in reality now part of RENFE) terminal is the ornate Santander (La Concordia) station [83 B2] next door to Abando, with three trains daily to/from Santander (€8.90), one to/from León (€25.60) and trains virtually every half-hour to and from Balmaseda (€2.95). Atxuri station [83 D4/E4] has lost some of its importance in recent years as the San Sebastián trains now depart from the station at Casco Viejo [83 D1], but travellers still use it to shuttle to and from Bermeo, Guernica and Mundaka. **Euskotren** (w euskotren.eus, no English-language option) is the network serving San Sebastián from Casco Viejo (2hrs 30mins; €6.30 – the bus is quicker), stopping at Durango, Eibar, Deba, Zumaia and Zarautz, among others. (At San Sebastián, you can then connect for Hendaye and Irun.) Atxuri also serves as the eastern terminal for Bilbao's tram line.

GETTING AROUND

Outside of Bilbao, a car is advisable for covering the ground around Bizkaia as efficiently as possible (for rental-car companies, see page 51). Nevertheless, for those with time to spare, the public transport is reliable, frequent and cost-effective, though being reliant on it reduces flexibility and makes reaching some of the rural attractions difficult, if not occasionally impossible. For bus and train options around the province, see page 77.

TOURIST INFORMATION

Details of Bilbao's tourist offices are given on page 82. Most towns of any size in Bizkaia province have their own websites and tourist offices; details are given in the relevant sections of this chapter. The information given is usually comprehensive, but sometimes available only in Spanish and Basque. Staff generally speak some English, so getting information is usually easy, and the availability of information in English is constantly improving.

BILBAO

The undisputed urban giant in the Basque territories, Bilbao is a smart, innovative, lively city, which has emerged from a difficult past with a strong identity. The inhabitants have a reputation in the rest of the Basque Country for being proud, maybe a bit *too* proud, but they can laugh at themselves as well. And they have plenty to be proud of. By night, it's a city full of life, but it's not in a hurry to wake up, especially on Sunday mornings – a great time for a stroll if you're hankering after some tranquillity.

The excellent public transport keeps vehicle traffic to a minimum and encourages a relaxed ambience. The largely pedestrianised old quarter (Casco Viejo) and some traffic-free streets in the newer city extensions contribute to this too, while a promenade down the considerable length of the elegant (and elegantly named) Parisian-style boulevard, the Gran Vía Don Diego López de Haro, is an unfailingly grand experience.

While the Casco Viejo is certainly the quarter that pulls in many visitors, it is still essentially a central meeting point for locals, day and night. West across the river by Abando station, Ensanche is now the financial and commercial district, having originally been created in the late 19th century to accommodate a burgeoning population; as part of the much more recent regeneration, the area north of Ensanche around the Guggenheim has been smartened up considerably to welcome the resultant influx of visitors. South across the river from the Casco Viejo, the adjoining areas of Bilbao la Vieja and San Francisco are ethnically diverse quarters that have perhaps seen better days, but are now being regenerated and certainly have a buzz all of their own, with just a hint of the Bohemian thrown into the mix. On Sundays, they are great places to hunt out inexpensive world cuisines.

For information on getting to Bilbao, see page 77.

GETTING AROUND Although Bilbao is surrounded by hills, its city centre is flat and reasonably compact. With help from the Nervión River, the wide Gran Vía and a few landmarks, it is easy to find your way around. It is also very safe by medium-sized city standards. To the question 'How do I get around?' the answer is: walk, if possible. However, Bilbao has a good bus system, trams, an underground train network and overland trains to the nearby towns, so there are plenty of alternatives to wearing out the shoe leather. If you are staying a few days and intending to visit several museums, it's worth considering buying a **Bilbao Bizkaia Card** (w bilbaobizkaiacard.com), available from the tourist office for 24/48/72 hours and costing €10/15/20 respectively. This gives unlimited use of tram, metro and bus services, as well as the funicular, and deals and discounts on shopping, selected restaurants and even some accommodation. It also allows you to skip some museum queues, though no longer covers museum admission charges (the price of the card has been reduced accordingly). Another flexible option is to buy a ***barik*** for €3. This is a prepaid travel card that can be used (almost exclusively in Bizkaia) on trains, metro, bus, airport bus and tram, as well as the funicular and even the Puente Bizkaia in Portugalete (page 99). On purchase, you also have to buy a minimum of €5 of credit; you simply swipe it as you get on your chosen transport and, before it expires, you top it up again (€5). The advantage is that it then makes all journeys significantly cheaper. The *barik* and subsequent credits can be obtained from Abando station, the tourist office and many tobacconists. It can also be recharged at tram stops and metro and train stations.

By metro Bilbao's three underground lines run north to south, two on the north side of the river estuary and one on the south. The trains run between 06.00 and 23.00, but at weekends the service operates late (all night on Saturday). Tickets are obtainable from machines at the stations. Information is given in English. Depending on how many zones your journey crosses, tickets cost €1.60–1.90 for a single, depending on distance, and double the price for a return. Or buy a *barik* (see above) if you're staying here a while or planning on doing a lot of travel. More information in English can be found at w metrobilbao.eus. The metro was finished in 1995, having been partially designed by Sir Norman Foster, the renowned British architect. Although the stations themselves are functional rather than aesthetic, the transparent accesses from the street are discreet: in a less-than-creative piece of

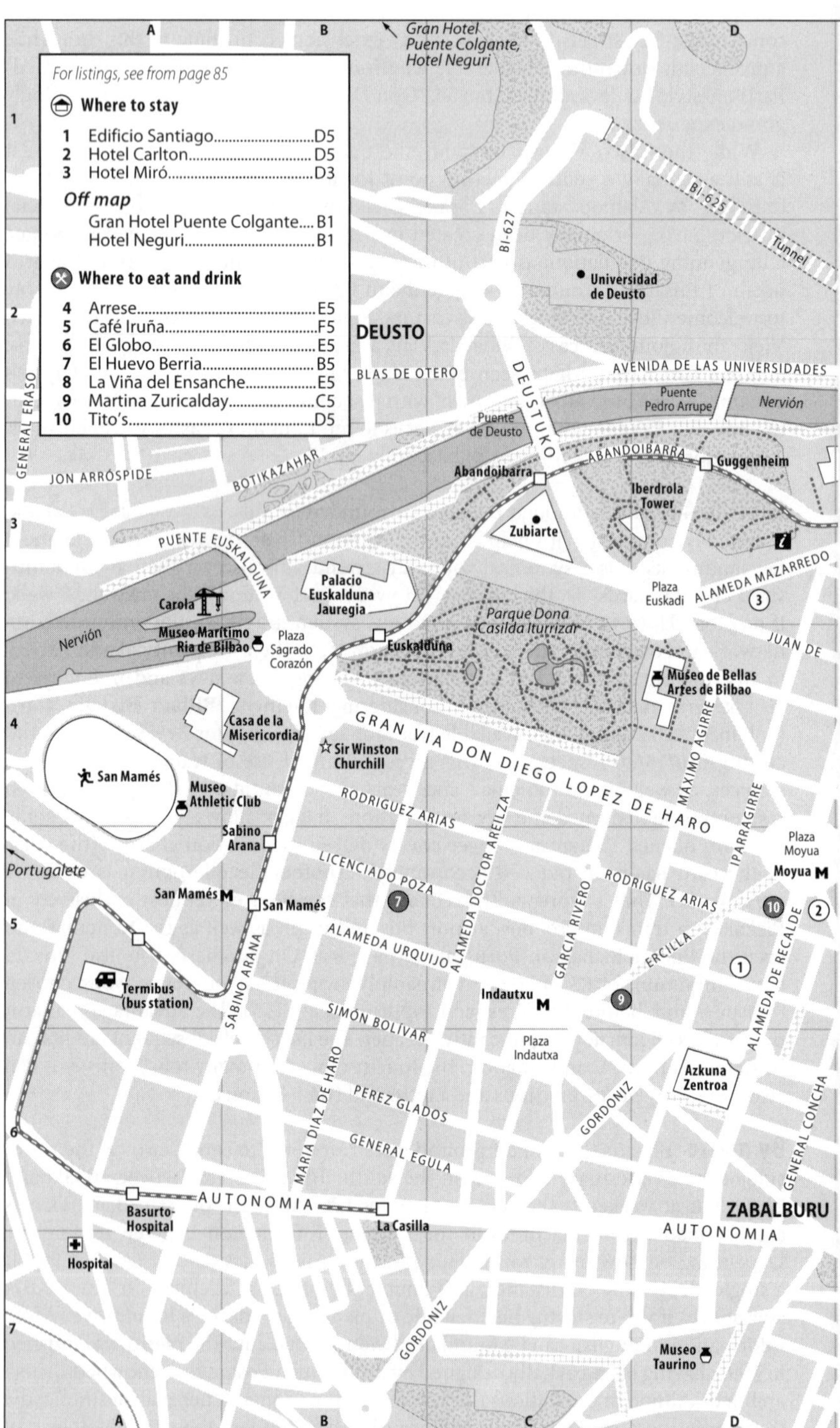

For listings, see from page 85
Where to stay
1 Edificio Santiago....D5
2 Hotel Carlton....D5
3 Hotel Miró....D3
Off map
Gran Hotel Puente Colgante....B1
Hotel Neguri....B1
Where to eat and drink
4 Arrese....E5
5 Café Iruña....F5
6 El Globo....E5
7 El Huevo Berria....B5
8 La Viña del Ensanche....E5
9 Martina Zuricalday....C5
10 Tito's....D5
Gran Hotel Puente Colgante, Hotel Neguri
Portugalete
DEUSTO
ZABALBURU
Universidad de Deusto
Guggenheim
Iberdrola Tower
Zubiarte
Abandoibarra
Palacio Euskalduna Jauregia
Carola
Museo Marítimo Ria de Bilbao
Plaza Sagrado Corazón
Euskalduna
Parque Dona Casilda Iturrizar
Plaza Euskadi
Museo de Bellas Artes de Bilbao
Casa de la Misericordia
Sir Winston Churchill
San Mamés
Museo Athletic Club
Sabino Arana
San Mamés
Termibus (bus station)
Indautxu
Plaza Indautxa
Azkuna Zentroa
Plaza Moyua
Moyua
Basurto-Hospital
La Casilla
Hospital
Museo Taurino
Puente de Deusto
Puente Pedro Arrupe
Nervión
BI-627
BI-625
Tunnel
AVENIDA DE LAS UNIVERSIDADES
BLAS DE OTERO
DEUSTUKO
ABANDOIBARRA
BOTIKAZAHAR
JON ARRÓSPIDE
GENERAL ERASO
PUENTE EUSKALDUNA
ALAMEDA MAZARREDO
JUAN DE
GRAN VIA DON DIEGO LOPEZ DE HARO
RODRIGUEZ ARIAS
LICENCIADO POZA
ALAMEDA DOCTOR AREILZA
GARCIA RIVERO
MÁXIMO AGIRRE
IPARRAGIRRE
ALAMEDA URQUIJO
ERCILLA
ALAMEDA DE RECALDE
SABINO ARANA
SIMÓN BOLÍVAR
MARIA DIAZ DE HARO
PEREZ GLADOS
GENERAL EGULA
GORDONIZ
GENERAL CONCHA
AUTONOMIA

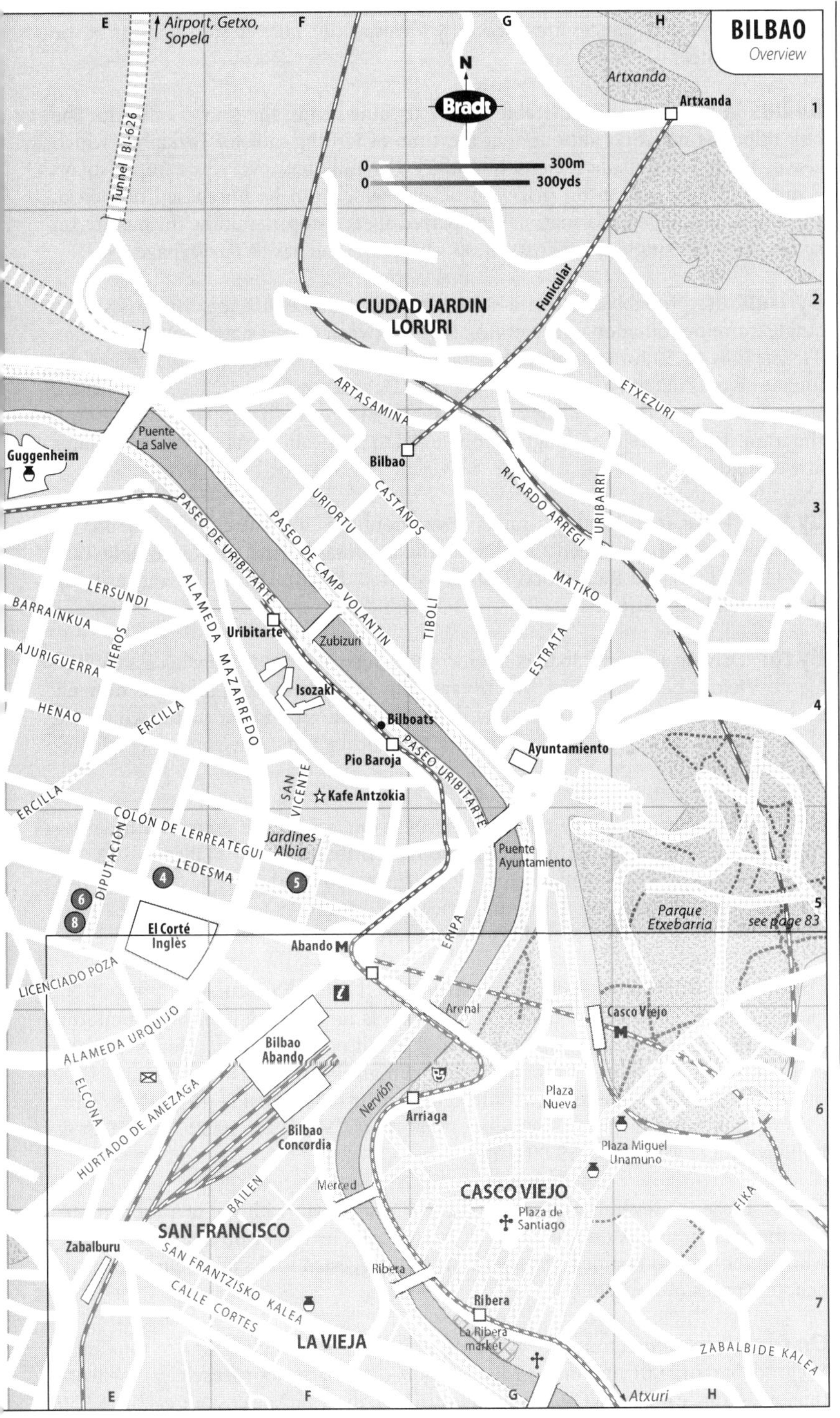

BILBAO
Overview
300m
300yds
Airport, Getxo, Sopela
Tunnel BI-626
Artxanda
Artxanda
CIUDAD JARDIN LORURI
Funicular
ARTASAMINA
ETXEZURI
Bilbao
Guggenheim
Puente La Salve
CASTAÑOS
URIORTU
RICARDO ARREGI
URIBARRI
PASEO DE URIBITARTE
PASEO DE CAMP VOLANTIN
MATIKO
TIBOLI
LERSUNDI
BARRAINKUA
ALAMEDA MAZARREDO
Uribitarte
Zubizuri
ESTRATA
AJURIGUERRA
HEROS
Isozaki
HENAO
ERCILLA
Bilboats
PASEO URIBITARTE
Pio Baroja
Ayuntamiento
ERCILLA
SAN VICENTE
Kafe Antzokia
COLÓN DE LERREATEGUI
Jardines Albia
DIPUTACIÓN
LEDESMA
Puente Ayuntamiento
Parque Etxebarria
see page 83
El Corté Inglès
Abando
ERIPA
LICENCIADO POZA
Arenal
Casco Viejo
ALAMEDA URQUIJO
Bilbao Abando
ELCONA
Nervión
Arriaga
Plaza Nueva
HURTADO DE AMEZAGA
Bilbao Concordia
Plaza Miguel Unamuno
BAILEN
Merced
CASCO VIEJO
Plaza de Santiago
FIKA
SAN FRANCISCO
Zabalburu
SAN FRANTZISKO KALEA
Ribera
CALLE CORTES
Ribera
La Ribera market
LA VIEJA
ZABALBIDE KALEA
Atxuri

'Spanglish', these entrances are known by locals as the '*fosteritos*', in honour of the British architect.

By bus A bus map and timetable can be obtained from the tourist office for the city Bilbobus network, although, at the time of writing, not for Bizkaibus which serves the towns outside the city boundary. For Bilbobus, every bus stop displays a map and information on prices of tickets, which can be purchased on board. Electronic passenger information is displayed at each stop, heralding the bus arrival times. An adult single ticket costs €1.30, cheaper if you have a *barik* (page 79).

By tram It's probably a bit of a stretch to call it a network, but Bilbao's smart, single tramline runs along the Nervión River between Atxuri station and La Casilla. Tickets cost €1.50 for a single ticket, but if you have a *barik* (page 79), then each journey works out at virtually half that price. Tickets must be purchased in advance from machines at the tram stops and must be validated at the stop before boarding the tram. The service runs roughly from 06.00 to 22.45 but starts an hour or so later at weekends.

By taxi There are several taxi ranks throughout the city centre, including one by Abando station. If you need to call one, the two main firms are **Radio Tele Taxi** (944 10 21 21) and **Radio Taxi Bilbao** (944 44 88 88). Generally, you can't flag them down in the street.

By car Driving around Bilbao is not recommended and not usually necessary. The Casco Viejo is pedestrianised. While car traffic is rarely heavy, parking is difficult and expensive, whether on the street or in the underground car parks, which are clearly signposted. Fines for infractions of parking rules can run to a holiday-spoiling €200.

By bicycle There are cycle paths by the Nervión, which are shared with daring rollerbladers. Bikes can be hired from **Tourné Bilbao** [83 C1] (Villarias 1; 944 24 94 65; e info@tournebilbao.com; w tournebilbao.com). Various types of bike are available, including tandems, and prices are around €8 for 2 hours, or €20 per whole day. This company also offers some interesting guided tours around the city.

TOURIST INFORMATION **Bilbao Turismo** [83 C1] (Plaza Circular 1; 944 79 57 60; w bilbaoturismo.net; 09.00–21.00 daily) is housed in a handsome building beside Abando, the main train station, and is full of information. This is also the place to obtain the Bilbao Bizkaia Card, which gives transport and museum entry privileges (page 79). There is an additional tourist office outside the Guggenheim (Alameda Mazarredo 66; Sep–Jun 10.00–19.00 Mon–Sat, 10.00–15.00 Sun & holidays, Jul & Aug 10.00–19.00 daily).

Tours There are several ways of getting to know Bilbao with the help of a guide, whether real or audio, on foot, by bike (see above), by bus or on a boat. For those who prefer unaccompanied trips on foot, two suggested walks are included in this chapter (pages 89 and 91).

On foot Two guided tours are available at weekends in English, one to the Casco Viejo (departs 10.00) and one to 'Modern Bilbao' (departs noon), each leaving from the tourist office on Plaza Circular and lasting 90 minutes. The cost for each is €4.50

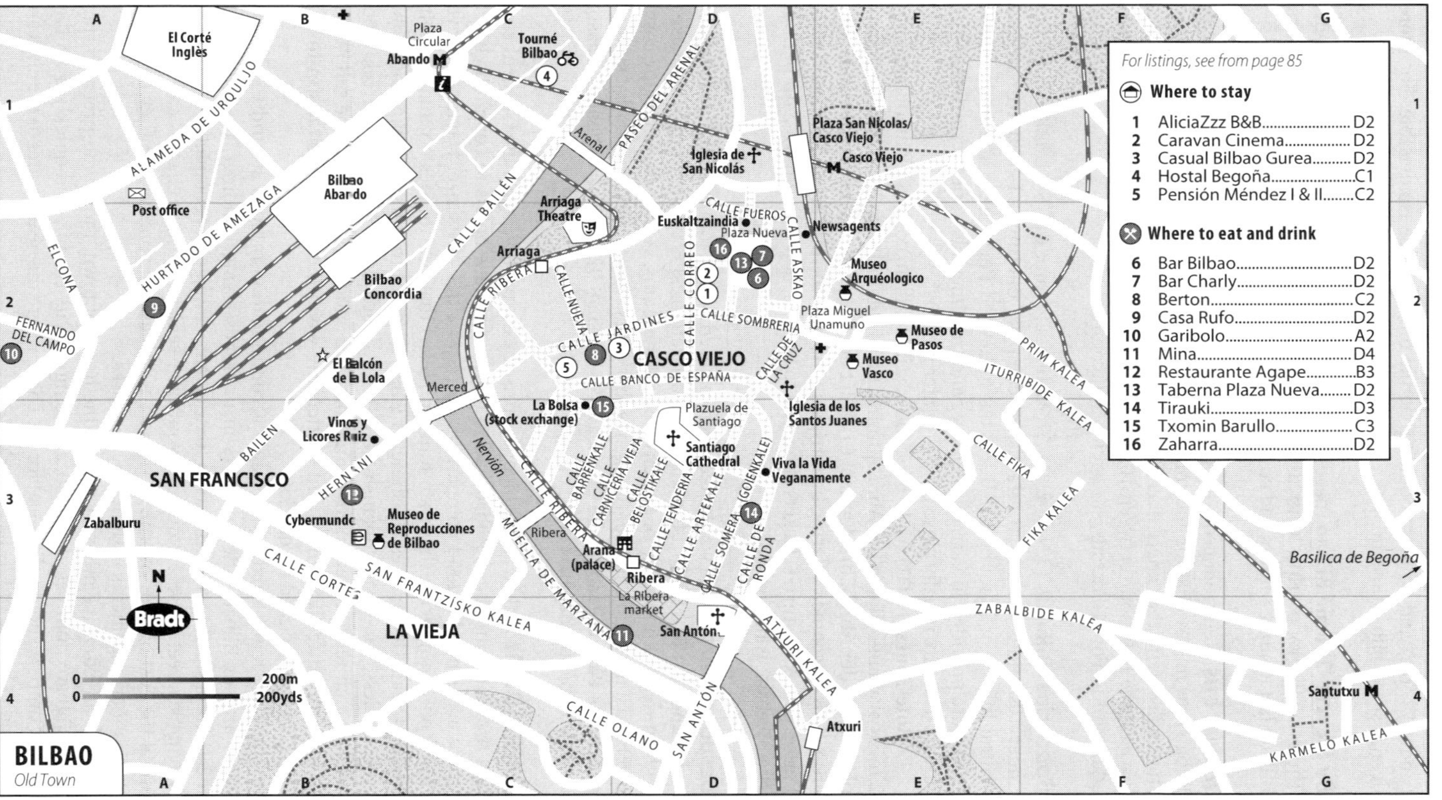

BILBAO
Old Town
For listings, see from page 85
Where to stay
1 AliciaZzz B&B....D2
2 Caravan Cinema....D2
3 Casual Bilbao Gurea....D2
4 Hostal Begoña....C1
5 Pensión Méndez I & II....C2
Where to eat and drink
6 Bar Bilbao....D2
7 Bar Charly....D2
8 Berton....C2
9 Casa Rufo....D2
10 Garibolo....A2
11 Mina....D4
12 Restaurante Agape....B3
13 Taberna Plaza Nueva....D2
14 Tirauki....D3
15 Txomin Barullo....C3
16 Zaharra....D2
CASCO VIEJO
SAN FRANCISCO
LA VIEJA
El Corté Inglès
Post office
Abando
Plaza Circular
Tourné Bilbao
Bilbao Abando
Bilbao Concordia
El Balcón de la Lola
Vinos y Licores Ruiz
Cybermundo
Museo de Reproducciones de Bilbao
Zabalburu
Arriaga
Arriaga Theatre
Arenal
Merced
Nervión
Ribera
La Bolsa (stock exchange)
Arana (palace)
Ribera
La Ribera market
San Antón
Santiago Cathedral
Plazuela de Santiago
Iglesia de los Santos Juanes
Viva la Vida Veganamente
Museo Vasco
Museo de Pasos
Museo Arqueológico
Plaza Miguel Unamuno
Newsagents
Euskaltzaindia
Plaza Nueva
Iglesia de San Nicolás
Plaza San Nicolás/Casco Viejo
Casco Viejo
Atxuri
Santutxu
Basilica de Begoña
ALAMEDA DE URQUIJO
HURTADO DE AMEZAGA
FERNANDO DEL CAMPO
ELCONA
BAILEN
CALLE BAILEN
HERNANI
CALLE CORTES
SAN FRANTZÍSKO KALEA
MUELLA DE MARZANA
CALLE OLANO
SAN ANTON
CALLE RIBERA
PASEO DEL ARENAL
CALLE NUEVA
CALLE JARDINES
CALLE BANCO DE ESPAÑA
CALLE CORREO
CALLE SOMBRERIA
CALLE FUEROS
CALLE ASKAO
CALLE DE LA CRUZ
CALLE BARRENKALE
CALLE CARNICERIA VIEJA
CALLE BELOSTIKALE
CALLE TENDERIA
CALLE ARTEKALE
CALLE SOMERA
(GOIENKALE)
CALLE DE RONDA
ATXURI KALEA
ZABALBIDE KALEA
ITURRIBIDE KALEA
PRIM KALEA
CALLE FIKA
FIKA KALEA
KARMELO KALEA
0 200m
0 200yds
Bradt
N

(under 7s free) and advance booking via the tourist office is advisable. For more details, see **w** bilbaoturismo.net.

By bicycle **Tourné Bilbao** (page 82) offer tours with an English-speaking guide. These small-group trips, with a good reputation, cover known and unknown Bilbao, last around 3 hours and cost €32.

Tourist bus Reintroduced for 2018, the hop-on, hop-off open-top bus tour of Bilbao now makes 11 stops and could be done in an hour. Making the most of those stops will extend the experience. The departure point is the Guggenheim and buses leave on the half-hour between 10.30 and 17.30, more often in high season (€16/8 adult/child). For full details, see **w** city-tour.com/en.

Boat trips **Bilboats** (☎ 946 42 41 57; **w** bilboats.com; €13/9/1 adults/seniors & under 10s/under 4s) are an established company offering a 1-hour trip around central Bilbao, or 2 hours (€19/12/1) out to beyond Portugalete and back. Audio guides are provided in various languages and the timetable varies according to the season. They are usually closed in the winter months.

El Bote Tours (**m** 605 01 43 65; **e** tours@elbotebilbao.com; **w** elbotebilbao.com; 2 tours available: 'Bahía del Abra', 40mins, €13/1 adult/under 3s, or 'Ría de Bilbao' plus 'Bahía del Abra', 2hrs 40mins; €19/12/1 adults/seniors & under 10s/under 3s) are a 2018 newcomer, offering boat trips up the Nervión and around Bilbao, Getxo, Portugalete & Santurtzi. Tickets allow you to hop-on, hop-off within a 24hr period. Their website is in English.

Bespoke tours If you would like a personalised guided tour of the city, **Mabel del Val Núñez** (**m** 610 98 28 14; **e** mabeldelval@yahoo.es) is a fluent English-speaker with in-depth knowledge of the city and its museums. A half-day city tour costs €180 and a museum trip €80. An agency that offers similar services – and at similar prices – is **Paso a Paso** (Calle Egaña 17; ☎ 944 15 38 92; **e** info@bilbaopasoapaso.com; **w** bilbaopasoapaso.com).

WHERE TO STAY Taken a little bit by surprise by the positive effect the Guggenheim had on visitor numbers, Bilbao had to build a few new hotels to cope. The hotel prices are generally good compared with other cities of its size. Having one eye firmly on commerce rather than tourism means that Bilbao does not have its fair share of really top-end establishments when it comes to tourist accommodation. Nevertheless, the major Spanish hotel chains such as NH, Silken, Barceló and Melia are all represented in town and there are options right across the full range of budgets. At festival times, and particularly when there are trade fairs in town, things can get booked up quickly.

There are many small, good-value accommodation options around the Casco Viejo area of Bilbao, often upstairs in unprepossessing buildings, their elevated locations protecting their clients to some extent – though not completely – from the inevitable street noise. If you have your own vehicle, parking charges can quickly spiral the cost of your overnight stay: it's worth asking your hotel if they have any discount arrangements with nearby car parks.

With an extensive metro system to the north of town, those who prefer to stay out of Bilbao's confines can do so, accessing the city cheaply and quickly from the coast. Campers should also head for the coast, where the nearest sites to the city can be found at Sopela or Gorliz (Elexalde).

In Bilbao

Upmarket

Hotel Miró [80 D3] (50 rooms) Alameda Mazarredo 77; 946 61 18 80; e reservas@mirohotelbilbao.com; w mirohotelbilbao.com. Much praised & with justification. If you can't take your eyes off the Guggenheim, you don't have to: just beg for a room here that overlooks it. Stylish, chic & tasteful, the hotel has a private spa, massage service (both extra cost) & small fitness centre. Bikes for hire. Rooms feature TV, AC & free Wi-Fi. **€€€€**

Mid range

AliciaZzz B&B [83 D2] (6 rooms) Calle Sombrerería 1; 946 79 21 98; e info@aliciazzz.com; w aliciazzz.com. Free Wi-Fi &, unusually, b/fast is included. Close to the action in the Casco Viejo, an Alice In Wonderland theme permeates. Popular & advanced booking is essential. Good value. **€€€**

Caravan Cinema [83 D2] (5 rooms) Calle Correo 11; 688 86 09 07; e info@caravan-cinema.com; w caravan-cinema.com. Modern chic in an old building with original brickwork & wooden columns. Retro furniture from the 1960s & 1970s. Each room is themed on a big name from Spanish cinema. Centrally located for the Casco Viejo, double glazing keeps the noise at bay. It has gained a good reputation since its 2014 opening. Free Wi-Fi, coffee, flat-screen TV & AC. Cheap b/fast. Parking arranged (extra cost). **€€€**

Edificio Santiago [80 D5] (35 apts) Poza Licenciado 12; 944 70 39 20; e reservas@edificiosantiago.com; w edificiosantiago.com. Centrally located 1- & 2-bedroomed apartments, all with spacious living area & kitchen. The 7-storey building features a terrace, small gym & restaurant. It could do with a lick of paint in places, but it's a good self-catering option. Parking can be arranged on request. **€€€**

Hotel Carlton [80 C3] (142 rooms) Federico Moyua 2; 944 16 22 00; e carlton@aranzazu-hoteles.com; w hotelcarlton.es. Part of a (small) chain, but with plenty of elegant character in its generously proportioned public spaces. It is so elegant, in fact, that the hotel was briefly used for the home of the wholly unofficial 'Basque Government' during the Civil War. Rooms are spacious & have AC, TV. There's a modest gym, free Wi-Fi throughout & a terrace, restaurant & cocktail bar. Parking is on-site, but needs reserving & is expensive – as is b/fast. Very close to Moyua metro station. Friendly, professional staff. **€€€**

Budget

Casual Bilbao Gurea [83 D2] (22 rooms) Bidebarrieta 14; 944 16 32 99; e casualbilbaogurea@casualhoteles.com; w casualhoteles.com. Central location, stylish artwork on the walls. Upstairs, with no lift. Free Wi-Fi. Cycle hire available. **€€**

Hostal Begoña [83 C1] (17 rooms) Calle Amistad 2; 944 23 01 34; e info@actioturis.com; w actioturis.com. Located out of the Old Town but only 2mins' walk away across the bridge & close to Abando station. TV, free Wi-Fi, computer terminal & heating. Has own parking (needs reserving). Trpls & family rooms available. Obliging staff. **€€**

Shoestring

Pensión Méndez I & II [83 C2] (24 rooms) Santa María 13; 944 16 03 64; e comercial@pensionmendez.com; w pensionmendez.com. 2 pensions under the same ownership & on different floors of the same building. Some with private baths, some with shared. Street-side rooms are noisier, some have balconies. All with TV, free Wi-Fi. A basic, budget option, well-established & family run. **€** (shared bathroom), **€€** (en suite)

Out of town: Portugalete, Getxo and Sopela

If you're likely to be bar-hopping or clubbing until the wee small hours, staying out of town is not really the best option. Unless, of course, like some *bilbaoinos*, you intend to catch the night bus, metro or tough it out until dawn. But if you want to trade the urban daytime bustle for an evening of seaside relaxation (Getxo), or simply a change of scene (Portugalete), there are out-of-town options, easily accessible by metro & sometimes offering better value.

Hotel Neguri (10 rooms) Av Algorta 14, Neguri, Getxo; 944 91 05 09; e hotelneguri@hotelneguri.com; w hotelneguri.com. Only 200m from Neguri metro station & a 10min walk from Ereaga beach. Wooden floors give character in this small, family-run, friendly hotel. TV, free Wi-Fi & heating. No AC, but you can usually rely on a sea

BILBAO'S BEST

Bilbao may have to acknowledge that San Sebastián bears the title of 'culinary king,' but visitors to the Basque Country's biggest city will not be disappointed with what it has to offer in terms of food. Currently, the most fêted chef in town is **Eneko Atxa**, young and local and proud of the three Michelin stars awarded to his **Azurmendi** restaurant (Barrio Legina, Larrabetzu; 944 55 83 59; w azurmendi.restaurant/en; €€€€€). In truth, Azurmendi is a little drive out of the city, perched on a hill top in the town of Larrabetzu near the airport. Out of town, but well worth the trip. Food is crafted, sculpted, beautifully presented; enjoy your 'welcome picnic' then choose from two elaborate tasting menus. Accept the option of wine pairings, or simply select your own from the wine list. Vegans and vegetarians can be catered for; nobody need miss out.

As you would expect from a restaurant of this quality, this is not a budget experience, so the best advice is to give yourselves plenty of time to relax and enjoy your meal. Consider it as 'art-as-food' and it will seem good value for a gastronomic experience of a lifetime, with top-notch service to match. Most diners here would recommend around 3 hours to get the most out of their Azurmendi visit. And take a taxi!

breeze. B/fast often included in the quoted rates, but check. Free car parking. **€€€**

Gran Hotel Puente Colgante (74 rooms) Calle de Doña María Díaz de Haro 2, Portugalete; 944 01 48 00; e info@granhotelpuentecolgante.com; w granhotelpuentecolgante.com. The hotel website 'dares you to sleep under a bridge', which is not *too* daunting, as this grand old riverside building does provide you with a roof & walls, too. Overlooks the famous 'hanging bridge'. Easily & cheaply reached from Bilbao by metro or train (take the train, rather than the metro, to Portugalete if you have heavy luggage). Popular with Brits just off the ferry from England. Rooms have free Wi-Fi, safe & minibar. Restaurant on-site. Can organise excursions. **€€**

WHERE TO EAT AND DRINK

Pintxos For hardened *pintxos* aficionados visiting Bilbao, the Casco Viejo is the city's obvious 'go-to' destination. Here, bars are crammed into a compact area, with the customers usually crammed in, too. Forget any thoughts of a quiet evening out. Given their sheer density, sampling a variety of bars and their delicacies requires very little physical effort on the part of the visitor, and a short-distance bar crawl is virtually unavoidable.

The very richest pickings in the Casco Viejo are to be had inside the **Plaza Nueva**, where establishments piled high with plates of mouthwatering savouries rub up alongside one another. It's unusual to have a bad experience, but if you find a morsel or a bar that's not to your taste, just move on to the next bar, which is probably right next door.

Away from the Casco Viejo, two other streets stand out as pleasant places for some serious grazing and nibbling. Pedestrianised **Calle Ledesma** wedges about a dozen bars of decent quality into the small section between Calle Berastegui and Alameda Mazarredo. In **Calle García Rivero**, a similar number of high-quality establishments jostle for custom, often packed and spilling on to the street. On football match days, flags fly from all of them, tempting in fans on the way to the stadium. Bar Okela, Gaztandegi and El Huevo Frito are perhaps the pick of the crop on this tiny street.

Below is a selection of *pintxos* bars, both in the Casco Viejo and elsewhere, that should find favour with most people. Undoubtedly, you will find others. Prices vary little from bar to bar, usually hovering around the €2 mark, more for specialities.

Bar Bilbao [83 D2] Plaza Nueva 6. One of the oldest & best, with over 100 years of offering up great snacks. The website has a pictorial guide, so swot up & sound knowledgeable on your arrival. This bar has a great tiled interior, Belle Époque style.

Bar Charly [83 D2] Plaza Nueva 8. Another Old Town favourite, famed for its *rabas* (squid). Also caters for vegetarian *pintxo*-hunters & serves up a *plato del dia.*

Berton [83 C2] Jardines 8. Just away from the main tourist scramble, this is a pleasant bar with mouthwatering morsels. The *brocheta de pulpo y langostino* (octopus & langoustine skewer) is a favourite.

El Globo [81 E5] Diputación 8. Popular with a well-heeled older crowd at lunchtime, they clearly know what they're doing. Ask for a *txangurro gratinado* (crab gratin), if you can make yourself heard above the excited chatter. Busy, with a capital 'B'.

El Huevo Berria [80 B5] Calle Licenciado Poza 65. A bit out of town, on the corner with Calle María Díaz de Haro. A great selection, innovative & high-quality. They even manage to shoehorn baby squid (complete with ink) into a croquette. Good cider, too.

La Viña del Ensanche [81 E5] Diputación 10. An after-work favourite for locals, with chorizo & hams to the fore, all served from a counter said to be hewn from a single tree. Local legend has it that the new monarchs of Spain used to come here to taste the ham – you should do the same, though there's plenty more on offer.

Taberna Plaza Nueva [83 D2] Plaza Nueva 9. This place has been run by 2 brothers for over 20 years & is constantly reinventing its already creative delicacies. Around Easter week, they create a new *pintxo* for each of the 9 *cofradías* (religious brotherhoods) in the city, each snack identified by a little figurine dressed in robe & hood. At carnival time, similar ingenuity is deployed. The *txistorra* (spicy sausage) with chocolate sounds unlikely to please, but is delicious.

Tirauki [83 D3] Somera 12. A bar with something of a hipster feel, but more importantly a range of vegan *pintxos*. Good quality, too.

Tito's Bar [80 D5] Alameda de Recalde 42. A tiny, eclectic little bar which once vied with Reims next door for the title of 'best *tortilla* in town'. Usually has 6 different flavours on offer – the chorizo one has some real zing to it.

Zaharra [83 D2] Plaza Nueva 2. Newish & trendy, with customers as smart as the chic décor, but its food stacks up with the best around.

Restaurants When you're tired of propping up *pintxos* bars, cheap-to-chic restaurants – with the added luxury of tables and chairs – abound. Bilbao has some Michelin-starred restaurants that are priced lower than Paris or London, so if you want that once-in-a-lifetime splurge, you could do it here without breaking the bank.

Casa Rufo [83 D2] Hurtado de Amezaga 5; 944 43 21 72; w casarufo.com; 13.30–16.00 & 20.30–23.00 Mon–Sat. In a relatively unvisited part of town, the modest frontage of a former grocery store conceals an atmospheric dining room with tiled floors & old-world charm. What's more, the food's top-notch, with *chuletón* a particular speciality & cod dishes also prominent. €€€€€

Mina [83 D4] Muelle Martzana; 944 79 59 38; w restaurantemina.es; 14.00–15.30 & 21.00–22.30, daily. Nov–May closed Sun evenings. Close to the La Ribera market, this tiny Michelin-starred place needs advance booking. The name reminds us that once there were mines in the heart of the city. The cuisine is contemporary, tasting menus are available. €€€€€

Restaurante Agape [83 B3] Calle Hernani 13; 944 16 05 06; w restauranteagape.com; 13.00–16.00 Mon–Sat, also 21.00–23.00 Thu–Sat. Agape is rightly renowned for its quality lunches. Pricewise, they're an absolute steal: €13.50 for the *menú del día* (incl wine & bread), voted as one of the top 20 in Spain! Evening menus are a bit pricier. Reservations are recommended for evenings & Thu, Fri & Sat lunchtimes. €€€

Txomin Barullo [83 C3] Barrenkale 40; 944 15 27 88; lunch & dinner, daily. Handsome wood-panelled dining room with a bewildering range of menus, 1 for each day of the week. Mon lunch is the cheapest; Sat evenings the priciest. Vegetarian options. €–€€€

Café Iruña [81 F5] Berastegui 4; 944 23 70 21; w cafeirunabilbao.net; 07.00–01.00 Mon–Fri, 09.00–01.00 Sat, noon–01.00 Sun (kitchen 13.00–16.00 & 20.00–23.00 daily). A stunning tiled interior, worth the visit on its own. This 100-year-old establishment endears itself further to its many admirers with prices for *pintxos* lower than those in the Casco Viejo, with no drop in quality. The restaurant section is as pretty as the bar, with reasonably priced menus to boot. Summer terrace & Wi-Fi. €€

Garibolo [83 A2] Calle Fernandez del Campo 7; 944 22 32 55; w garibolo.com; 13.00–16.00 daily, also 21.00–23.00 Fri & Sat. Vegetarians & vegans have little choice in Bilbao. This place, which has mixed reviews, may well be one of the few veggie options in town. Good-value *menú del día*. €€

Bakeries In the unlikely event that your regular mealtimes in Bilbao have left you hungry, a visit to either of these renowned bakeries should sort you out with a quick fix.

Arrese [81 E5] Gran Vía Don Diego López de Haro 24; w arrese.biz; 09.00–21.00 Mon–Sat, 09.00–15.00 & 17.00–21.00 Sun. Dating back to 1852, this ornate shop carries itself like an elegant lady & definitely belongs on Bilbao's grandest boulevard. The fancy interior is awash with tasty cakes & more; try the *pastel vasco*, despite its hefty price tag, or the *palmera de chocolate*, another local favourite. Look out for other branches in town.

Martina Zuricalday [80 C5] Ercilla 43; w martinazuricalday.com; daily. Bilbao's most famous pastry is the *bollo de mantequilla*, & this is where to try it, in Bilbao's oldest bakery (since 1830). A sort of bun filled with sweet butter, it looks bland but tastes sublime. Go on Tue, when everything's half price.

NIGHTLIFE

If you are really sure that you want to stay out beyond the generously late bar-closing hours, then Bilbao can certainly oblige with all-night dancing or just a chilling venue for a drink.

☆ **El Balcón de la Lola** [83 B2] Bailén 10; 23.00–06.00 Fri & Sat. Famously gay-friendly, in truth this is a cool hangout for everyone & recognised as one of the best dance venues in the city. Its exterior is unpromising, but let's face it, the fun is all on the inside. Don't turn up before midnight, though. Occasional live music.

☆ **Kafe Antzokia** [81 F4] Plaza San Vicente; 944 24 46 25; w kafeantzokia.eus. Check website for events/opening times. A late-night venue with a bit of Basque attitude. In reality, this combines being a concert venue, dance hall & also a good-value place for lunch (13.30–15.30 Mon–Fri, 14.00–16.00 Sat; €€). Don't expect traditional Basque music, more hardcore rock, though it also hosts blues & other more international concerts. Entrance fees vary according to who's playing – check the website.

☆ **Sir Winston Churchill** [80 B4] Sabino Arana 1; 944 27 78 73; w sirwinstonchurchill.es; 16.00–02.30 Sun–Thu, 16.00–04.00 Fri & Sat. A highly commended, late-night place for a gin & tonic or a swish cocktail.

SHOPPING

Poking around the Casco Viejo is fun, made more so by the lack of vehicles and the number of small shops geared towards everyday living. You can find a genuine Basque beret or a decent copy of one. A few tacky souvenir shops make up the picture. The Gran Vía is the place to go for big-name fashion brands, should you need them, and is also the home of a branch of El Corte Inglés [81 E5], Spain's top department store.

Vinos y Licores Ruiz [83 B3] Hernani 8; ☎ 944 16 22 61; ⏲ 09.45–13.30 & 17.00–20.00 Mon–Fri, 10.00–13.30 Sat. Established for 70 years, this is a well-stocked wine shop with over 1,000 wines, beers & spirits at all price ranges.

Viva la Vida Veganamente [83 D3] Somera 17; ☎ 944 34 53 07; ⏲ 11.00–14.30 & 18.00–20.00 Tue & Wed, 11.00–14.30 & 18.00–22.00 Thu–Sat. In a land of committed carnivores, a vegetarian shop/caféteria tends to stand out. Here you will find organic pasta, tofu, b/fast cereals, snacks, pizzas & even vegan chorizo.

OTHER PRACTICALITIES

Hospital Bilbao's massive hospital complex, in the southwest of the city, is the **Hospital Universitario Basurto** [80 A7] (Av de Montevideo 18; ☎ 944 00 60 00), accessible by tram or by train lines B1, R3, R3a or R4 from La Concordia station (page 78), in each case getting off at the Hospital/Basurto stop.

Pharmacies You're never far from a pharmacy in the city centre – just look for the flashing cross sign. In the Casco Viejo there's one located right next to the Museo Vasco in the Plaza Miguel Unamuno [83 E2], and another at Gran Vía de López de Haro 8.

Post office Bilbao's main post office [83 A1] is located at Alameda del Urquijo 19 (⏲ 08.30–20.30 Mon–Fri, 09.30–13.00 Sat).

Internet/Wi-Fi Free, unlimited municipal Wi-Fi is available in many public places in the city, such as at the Arenal and Plaza Indautxu. The network is simply called Bilbao Wi-Fi and no password is necessary. As Wi-Fi availability increases, so the number of internet cafés dwindles: Calle San Francisco is currently the best bet if you don't have your own device – try **Cybermundo** [83 B3] (Calle San Francisco 16; ⏲ 10.00–23.00 daily).

Foreign newspapers Foreign press is very difficult to source in Bilbao, except for the *Financial Times* and *The Wall Street Journal*, which can both be found in the kiosks on the Gran Vía. Occasionally you may find *The Times* or *The Daily Telegraph* here, too.

WHAT TO SEE AND DO

A walk along the river to the Old Quarter (45mins, easy) This walk takes you along the city centre section of the Nervión River, through what was previously the heart of some of Bilbao's heavy industry, allowing you to get a feel for the incredible reinvention of the city, before entering the Casco Viejo (Old Quarter). It is a city walk, all paved underfoot, and flat.

To reach the start of the walk, you can stroll or take the tram to the **Plaza Sagrado Corazón** roundabout [80 B4] at the western end of the **Gran Vía Don Diego López de Haro**, the grand boulevard that is home to department stores, banks and some very expensive real estate. To get a street like this named after you, you have to found a city, which is what Don Diego did in 1300. Although there was a settlement here before then, in his capacity as Lord of Bizkaia Don Diego granted it some trading and tax privileges that set it on its way to prosperity. The roundabout, however, is dominated by an obelisk with a bronze statue of Jesus – not to be confused with Don Diego.

San Mamés [80 A4], the stadium of Athletic Club de Bilbao, is the stunning newish white edifice visible a few hundred metres to the west. Known to fans as 'The Cathedral', it was opened in 2013 to replace the existing one, which could no longer cope with the number of fans eager to see their beloved team. It now houses a football museum (page 94). In between the Plaza Sagrado Corazón roundabout and the stadium stands the **Casa de la Misericordia (House of Mercy)** [80 A4], now an old people's home. Its chapel is said to contain the remains of St Mammes, a child martyr thrown to the lions. It is from this connection that the stadium takes its name and the team takes its nickname, 'Los Leones' ('The Lions'). On the northwest side of the roundabout, down some steps, is the **Museo Marítimo Ria de Bilbao (Maritime Museum)** [80 B4] (page 95) and on the northeast side is the huge, modern **Palacio Euskalduna Jauregia** [80 B3]. A large concert hall and conference centre, it opened in 1999 on the site formerly occupied by a shipbuilding company, closed in the 1980s, from which the centre takes its name.

Cross the road, and keeping the Palacio Euskalduna Jauregia on your left, note the rather controversial mishmash of materials, colours and styles as you follow around three sides of this building and take the path down to the river. Turn right and, with the river now always on your left-hand side, head along the riverside towards the town. On the opposite bank, the architecture is unexceptional, but it is worth remembering that until very recently the ground on which you are now walking was a centre for heavy industry such as shipbuilding and ancillary trades. (A visit to the Maritime Museum is highly recommended to fully comprehend the transformation.) To your right, you will soon pass a building that appears from some angles to resemble a bullring, but is in fact only the **Zubiarte** shopping centre [80 C3], full of familiar brand names.

Passing under the bridge, the **Puente de Deusto** [80 C2], before you reach the by-now-visible Guggenheim, on the opposite bank the two buildings of the **Universidad de Deusto (University of Deusto)** [80 C2] are prominent. The university was founded by the Jesuits in 1886, making it Spain's oldest private university, but it was used as a military base during the Civil War before reverting to its academic role in 1940. To your right there are more modern university buildings and the lofty **Iberdrola** skyscraper [80 D3], the headquarters of a major energy company. If you keep your eyes to the ground about 100m before the Guggenheim, you'll come across a large plaque embedded in the pavement, etched with a poem, celebrating how the English brought football to the Basque Country:

A CRANE CALLED CAROLA

Surely there is absolutely nothing to link a beautiful Basque woman to a large, ugly crane?

Outside the Maritime Museum in Bilbao stands Carola, the last crane from the era when ships and shipbuilding dominated a riverfront landscape now given firmly over to leisure. Why Carola? In the days when the bridges across the Nervión were less numerous, legend has it that a stunning woman called Carola used to take a boat daily across the river to go to work, providing a welcome distraction for the shipyard workers. To get a better view of this Basque beauty, the labourers used to down tools and climb up the crane, thus seriously reducing their productivity.

Desperate to find a solution to this problem, the shipyard owner approached the young lady and offered to provide her with a car to take her to work, upstream and far away from the lusty gaze of his employees. But Carola politely declined the kind offer, continuing to be the workers' pin-up and now honoured with the preservation of the crane that bears her name.

The Pitch of the English

Here is where the English played, here on a field by the river.
At that time, there was just a little pitch and a scrapyard.
Sometimes the ball fell into the water, and if they couldn't reach it
They threw stones to bring it to the bank. And a ripple was created,
Little waves which turned into bigger ones.
And like this, Athletic played in Lamiako, then Jolaseta, then finally at San Mamés.
One wave, then another wave, then another.
(*Kirmin Uribe*, author translation)

Looking up to the right as you come at last to the spectacular structure of the **Guggenheim** [81 E3], you will see the back of the giant, flower-covered ***Puppy* by Jeff Koons**, which stands guard at the museum's main entrance. Citizens of Bilbao have a favourite joke: they point at the structure and say 'How do you like Jeff's *Puppy*?' and then point to the Guggenheim itself and ask, 'And how do you like the kennel we built for him?' Note also how, rather unusually, architect Frank Gehry chose to build some of the Guggenheim's structure under the pre-existing bridge.

Look across the river and up to the grassy slopes, and you may do a double take at this point when you see a flock of sheep grazing on the hillside, an odd juxtaposition so close to a major city.

Coming into sight now is the **Zubizuri pedestrian bridge** [81 F4], the swirly affair to the east of the Guggenheim, designed by **Santiago Calatrava**, who was also responsible for Bilbao's futuristic airport. You'll notice that a concrete walkway has been added to the southern end of the white structure, put there by the municipality to make access more user-friendly. This appendage enraged Calatrava, who threatened the municipality with legal action for 'ruining *my* bridge', but the case eventually petered out. By the side of the bridge are what might be described as Bilbao's 'Twin Towers', actually called the **Isozaki Atea** [81 F4] development, designed by Japanese architect Isozaki. His brief was to keep part of the original structure of the old bonded warehouse, a brief he has certainly achieved though the result is somewhat bizarre (the façade on the other side of the development has also been retained). These are the Basque Country's tallest residential developments, at 83m.

Continuing along the walkway and with the impressive **Ayuntamiento** (Town Hall) building [81 G4] across the river, this is where we climb the steps on to the bridge of the same name and leave the river. You can now cross the bridge to enter the **Casco Viejo**, or turn right to return to the **Plaza Circular** [83 C1] and the eastern end of the Gran Vía Don Diego López de Haro.

A walk through Bilbao's Old Town (45mins, easy) This walk through the Old Town includes the original seven streets ('Siete Calles') that once made up Bilbao. It is all paved underfoot and completely flat.

We start the walk at the eastern end of the **Puente del Arenal** [83 C1], in the Arenal area, so-called because it used to be a beach (*arena* is Spanish for sand). At one time it was a port area but, as ships got bigger and the port moved further towards the sea, it became a place of leisure. Assuming you've just crossed the bridge from the west, to your right is the solid 1890 structure of the **Teatro Arriaga (Arriaga Theatre)** [83 C2] and to the left is the Rococo **Iglesia de San Nicolás (St Nicholas Church)** [83 D1], which took 13 years to build and was consecrated in 1756. Appropriately, St Nicholas is the patron saint of mariners. From the front of the church, take the Calle Fueros right into the **Plaza Nueva** [83 D2], the favourite meeting-point of locals and stuffed full of bars. Take time to do a complete circuit of this square, trying (not too hard) to resist the temptingly laden bar counters and their appealing *pintxos*. The Plaza Nueva and surroundings were completed between 1831 and 1851, and indeed much of the 'Old Town' is not actually that old. It is also now the home of **Euskaltzaindia** (Royal Academy of the Basque Language) [83 D2], the organisation tasked with continuing the work of standardising the diverse Basque language. Exit the square under the arches by the Café Bilbao, turning immediately left up Calle Libertad to reach **Plaza Miguel Unamuno** [83 E2]. Here you'll find two museums, the **Museo Arquéologico (Archaeology Museum)** [83 E2] and the **Museo Vasco (Basque Museum)** [83 E2] (see opposite). The steps to the left of the former lead you up to the **Basílica de Begoña (Begoña Basilica)** [83 G3], but are not part of this walk, and the statue in the middle of the square is (of course) of señor Unamuno himself. A Bilbao-born intellectual, poet, essayist and playwright, he initially supported Franco's uprising but changed his position rapidly and was removed from his job as Rector of Salamanca University for opposing Francoists. He died soon afterwards. Now exit the square down the **Calle de la Cruz**, opened at the end of the 15th century, and which was formerly the site of the Convent of the Cross. After 100m you come across the house where José Antonio Aguirre Ikube was born. 'Prime Minister' of the Basque Country between 1936 and 1960, he spent much time in exile and died in Paris. Next to his house is the **Iglesia de los Santos Juanes (Church of St John and St John)** [83 D2], in Classical style and built in 1622. (To the right, though not on this walk, a wall plaque in **Calle Banco de España** [83 D2] marks a house as a one-time dwelling of Simón Bolívar, the great liberator of South American peoples.) Now take a sharp left down Goienkale, which soon becomes **Somera** [83 D3], one of Bilbao's original seven medieval streets but now very popular as a night-time haunt of the young. At the end of the street, already visible is the **Iglesia de San Antón (Church of St Anthony the Great)** [83 D4], a 15th/16th-century creation, from where proclamations used to be read down to the masses mingling in the then market square. Turning right at the end of Somera, on your left next to the church is the renovated **La Ribera market** [83 D4], and opposite it is a Basque beret shop, in case you want to join the locals with some quality headgear. We pass the end of some of the other original seven streets: first, **Artekale** [83 D3], 'the midpoint between two bridges'; then **Calle de la Tendería** [83 D3], also known as Santiago, which joins the former gate with the church of that name; next up is **Belostikale** [83 D3], also known as Pesquería due to the many fish shops once located there; at this end is a Renaissance palace, the **Arana** [83 D3], from the 16th century. A few hundred metres up Belostikale, we turn left into **Cantón Echevarría Camarón** [83 D3], crossing **Calle Carnicería Vieja**, once home of many meat merchants in times gone by. Then right up **Barrenkale** [83 C3], another of the seven streets; in Basque, the name refers to 'the lower street'. Reaching the end of Barrenkale, we turn left then right in front of **La Bolsa (Stock Exchange)** [83 C3]. Looking up the **Calle del Perro** ('Dog Street'), this is the only point in the Old Town from which you can see the Virgen de Begoña, high up on the hill. Her nickname, in Basque, means 'Mum' and so beloved was she that the footballers of Athletic Bilbao used to visit her to seek success before the season began. The hill on which she stands also used to be the site of the Altos Hornos de Bizkaia, the huge ironworks that employed thousands in its heyday: all that remains now, not visible from here, is a solitary chimney. Proceeding up the Calle del Perro, you reach the **fountain**, the second oldest in Bilbao. Although the animals on this fountain are clearly lions, the locals (who of course had never seen lions) mistook them for dogs and the street was duly misnamed. Taking a right at the fountain brings us to the **Plazuela de Santiago** (Done Jakue Plazatxoa) [83 D3], with its 14th-/15th-century **cathedral**, the focal point in the city for pilgrims on the northern route to Santiago de Compostela. Note the saint's emblem, the scallop shell, above the main entrance. It was formerly just a modest church, but when they decided that they should have a cathedral to match the town's growth, they put a façade on to the church to make it more cathedral-like. Pass down the **Carrera Santiago** (Done Jakue Karrera) and, having done a complete circuit of the cathedral, proceed down the **Calle Correo**, which will return you to your starting point. Alternatively, if you are looking to catch the metro, take Calle de la Cruz and you will arrive at the **Casco Viejo station** [83 D1].

Museums Visitors sometimes overlook the fact that, when it comes to museums, Bilbao is not a one-trick pony. Sure, none of the more established museums can hold a candle to the Guggenheim in terms of striking exterior or international fame, but they are increasingly gearing up to showcase the history of the city. Whether seafaring, football, fine arts or something more religious takes your fancy, you will find it here.

Museo Guggenheim Bilbao (Guggenheim Museum Bilbao) [81 E3] (Av Abandoibarra 2; ☎ 944 35 90 80; w guggenheim-bilbao.eus; ⏲ 10.00–20.00 Tue–Sun, Jul–Aug daily; €10–16/6–7.50/free adults/seniors & students/children (under 12s), prices vary according to date; ticket office closes 30mins before closing time; tickets can be reserved online & collected at a machine, allowing you to avoid the queue; 1hr guided tours in English, free with admission ticket, take place at 12.30 Tue–Fri, 17.00 Sat & Sun (30min express tour at 17.00 Tue–Fri, 12.30 & 13.30 Sat & Sun), but with a min 8 people, so turn up 30mins before (no reservations allowed) & hope that there are enough to make up the numbers; if not, there is an audio guide, updated for the temporary exhibitions showing at the time, plus multilingual panels) So much has been written about the unique building that single-handedly put Bilbao on to the tourist map. Bilbao arguably took a huge gamble, paying handsomely for the right to site the Guggenheim Bilbao, but no-one would argue that it hasn't been a huge commercial success if you take into account the benefits accrued by the wider city. The fact that this space-age museum was built on the site of a brick factory only emphasises how it wrested the city from its industrial past and placed it, almost prematurely, into the 21st century when it opened in October 1997. There's simply so much of interest about the Frank Gehry-designed, titanium- and glass-clad building, even before you set foot inside. Over 100 exhibitions have been hosted here since its opening, and the surprise for some is that there is little space given up to permanent displays or indeed to exhibitions of Basque works. Indeed, although Basque sculptors Oteiza and Chillida have featured in the past, at the time of writing they were conspicuous only by their absence. Nevertheless, the prestige of being in the Guggenheim Bilbao ensures that some fine temporary displays pass through, and the permanent exhibits, particularly those outside the building, are interesting, innovative and at times laced with humour. The giant puppy dog, covered with flowers, by Jeff Koons will bring a wide smile to anyone's face. On the river side of the museum, Nakaya's jets of steam will turn your head.

Museo Vasco (Basque Museum) [83 E2] (Plaza Miguel de Unamuno; ☎ 944 15 54 23; w euskal-museoa.eus; ⏲ 10.00–19.00 Mon & Wed–Fri, 10.00–13.30 & 16.00–19.00 Sat, 10.00–14.00 Sun; €3/1.50/free adults/students/under 12s & over

65s, free to all on Thu) Housed in a former Jesuit school, this attractive building with interior courtyard has also served as a police HQ in its past life. English-language information is provided mainly by A4 sheets in front of the exhibits, with the panel displays in Spanish and Basque only. The content replicates at least in part the more comprehensive information given in San Sebastián's San Telmo Museum (page 147), so if you've already been there, this might disappoint. Nevertheless, the essentials of history and economy – the wool trade, whaling, chocolate, shepherding and fishing – are all covered. Perhaps of most interest is the room used by the Bilbao Consulate, which administered the maritime trade and the activities taking place on the estuary all the way down to Portugalete. From a later era, there are parts of the trunks of various trees from Guernica. A relief model of the whole of Bizkaia graphically demonstrates how mountainous the province is: the effect of this topography is that the Basque language varies from valley to valley, not only in terms of accent but with different words, too.

Museo Athletic Club [80 A4] (Located inside the San Mamés stadium, entrance between gates 19 & 20; 944 66 11 00; Mar–Oct 10.00–20.00 Tue–Sun, Nov–Feb 10.00–19.00 Tue–Sun; museum & stadium tour €14/5/free adults/under 14s/under 6s, museum only €10/3/free adults/under 14s/under 6s) The fact that the Barcelona Football Club museum is the second most visited museum in Spain (after the Prado) must serve as some inspiration to this excellent testimonial to Bilbao's own unique and much-loved sports team. Only opened in 2017, this fully embraces technology and is a must for those who love the round-ball game. All the connections with England's contribution to football in Bilbao are duly celebrated and most importantly of all, the information is translated and videos are subtitled for the benefit of Anglophones. Football fans could comfortably spend 2 hours here, especially if they include the stadium tour which will be conducted by an English-speaking guide. The stadium itself was opened only in 2013, but this is a club where tradition is deeply rooted and given ultimate respect. The club is a true club, with 47,000 *socios* (members), so there are no distant, foreign owners. Surely, that makes a difference? All members known from the inception of the club are listed on a particularly impressive panel: you can search for a relative, if you think they might be numbered among the 100,000 or so recorded here. With a commitment to culinary excellence, local Michelin-star chefs cook up their wonders on match day at ten eating stations around the ground. What better evidence of how important this team is to its locality?

Museo de Reproducciones de Bilbao (Reproductions Museum) [83 B3] (Calle de San Francisco 14; w bilbokoberreginenmuseoa.eus; 10.00–13.30 & 16.00–19.00 Tue–Sat, 10.00–14.00 Sun; €3/1.50/free adults/students/seniors & under 10s, free to all on Thu) Resulting from a late 19th-century fad to reproduce artworks at a time when not everyone could afford the European *grand tour* to see the real things, this museum of plaster casts occupies a Neo-Gothic church that was renovated to house what is effectively a collection of copies from other European museums in London, Rome, Florence and other cities. The church was built in the 1890s from funds provided by the wife of one of the founders of the BBVA bank. Previously, the museum was in the Abando district. English-language information is sparse, though there is a pamphlet available.

Museo de Bellas Artes de Bilbao (Museum of Fine Art) [80 D4] (Museo Plaza 2; w museobilbao.com; 10.00–20.00 Wed–Mon; €9/7/free adults/students, under 25s & seniors/under 12s & disabled; access to permanent collections free

18.00–20.00; audio guides €3) A collection of over 10,000 pieces – not all on show *at once* – fuels the displays at Bilbao's Museum of Fine Art. Spanning all periods from Romanesque and Gothic through to contemporary, including Basque sculpture and painting, the works are displayed in far more traditional spaces than the Guggenheim Bilbao's exhibits and with a higher proportion of permanent displays. English-language information is provided by way of audio guides and information panels, and there are reading spaces that contain reference books for those who crave more detail. Many familiar names are represented, including Goya, El Greco, Bellotto, Velázquez and Gauguin; among the Basques, sculptors Oteiza and Chillida feature, though their exhibits are not as impressive in this indoor setting as when they are braving the elements outside. The last of the 33 galleries houses works by lesser-known Basque artists such as Badiola, Bados and Goenaga. The museum is fully accessible to those with reduced mobility and there is a café and museum shop.

Museo Arqueológico/Arkeologi Museoa (Archaeological Museum) [83 E2] (Escaleras de Mallona 2; ☎ 944 04 09 90; w euskalmuseoak.com; ⏲ 10.00–14.00 & 16.00–19.30 Tue–Sat, 10.30–14.00 Sun; €3/1.50/free adults/under 26s, seniors & disabled/under 12s, free to all on Fri) Housed on the site of the former railway station, this modest museum for archaeology fans has permanent exhibits to take the visitor on a journey from the Palaeolithic era through the ages to modern times. English-language information is by way of a brochure, to be returned at the end of the visit, as the panels are only in Spanish and Basque, but if you have an Android phone you can download a free app at the entrance. To follow the exhibits chronologically, start on the second floor and work downward. Contrary to what might be fancifully claimed elsewhere, the archaeological evidence gathered at the museum points to most of the Basque Country being fully subjected to Roman rule. Visual displays show the role the tower-houses of the Middle Ages played in collecting taxes, and explain the 'War of the Bands' and how the *villas* (towns) were given rights of exemption from direct taxes by the Lords of Bizkaia, effectively making them tax-free zones, but giving the inhabitants the rights to collect tolls and taxes from anyone passing through. Only part of what was collected had to be paid up to the Lords, so these rights made the *villas* attractive places to live, but resulted in the huge conflict between the bands – who saw their powers being diminished – and the *villas*. Anyone working the land outside of the villas had to pay direct taxes to the Lords, who – of course – owned the land.

The museum also stores a large number of archaeological remains still waiting for cleaning and examination.

Museo Marítimo Ria de Bilbao (Maritime Museum) [80 B4] (Muelle Ramón de la Sota 1; ☎ 946 08 55 00; w museomaritimobilbao.eus; ⏲ winter 10.00–18.00 Tue–Fri, 10.00–20.00 Sat, Sun & hols, summer 10.00–20.00 Tue–Sun; €6/3.50/free adults/students & seniors, free to all on Tue, between Sep & Jun) Even if maritime museums do not 'float your boat', an understanding of Bilbao's maritime history is essential to get any real appreciation of the city's history and development. This museum is quite specific to Bilbao and you will learn how the river was straightened, widened and deepened over time to allow the clear passage of vessels down to the city centre, which is some 10km from the coast. Such has been the manipulation of the Nervión that Barakaldo, once on the right bank, is now on the left; work is still continuing, the intention being to transform the current river peninsula into an island. (Concerns over flooding have delayed the project, but the famous Basque determination will ensure that it happens!) A visit to this museum will also give you a great insight into Bilbao's ability to reinvent itself. English-language information is provided by the leaflet that you are given with your ticket, occasional wall panels, video presentations and information boards that are kept in wooden boxes on the floor. There are displays of model ships, methods of fishing, a huge glass panel that shows many of the dock-based activities (the information for which is upstairs) and a life-size replica of the *falua*, a wooden boat used by the Consulate, the body that historically controlled river trade on the Nervión. The displays are innovative, in particular a widescreen video (with English text) that relates the development of the city and is cleverly enhanced by a scale model that lights up as the relevant section of the city is discussed on the screen. Up on the first floor a map shows the trade routes in and out of Bilbao across the ages, and there is a gallery dedicated to ship design. In the dry dock outside the museum, various vessels are available for inspection, including a customs vessel and a round-the-world yacht, but the most interesting of which is the *gabarra*, a flat boat on which the Athletic Bilbao footballers sailed down the river estuary from Portugalete when they last won a trophy in 1984. (In 2015, it was again primed for action, but sadly they lost the cup final to Barcelona.) On the river itself, tall ships visit every year and, when in town, can be visited as part of the museum entrance fee.

Museo de Pasos (Museum of Religious Floats) [83 E2] (Iturribide 3; ☎ 944 15 04 33; w museodepasosbilbao.com; ⌚ 11.00–13.00 & 17.00–19.30 Tue–Fri, 11.00–14.00 & 17.00–20.00 Sat, 11.00–14.00 Sun, also closed for 2 weeks around Semana Santa (Holy Week); €2/free adults/seniors & children) A museum of religious images, however ornate, is a difficult sell, perhaps, unless you're a real religious fanatic, but scratching below the surface shows that there's more to the displays than just wonderfully crafted images of a bleeding Christ. The museum is housed in a former wine warehouse. It is largely a visual experience, as the English-language information almost begins and ends with a dry leaflet that details the history of each of the nine *cofradías* which are attached to the various churches of Bilbao. But if you've never seen the processional floats used every day during Holy Week as an expression of faith, you can marvel at the work that goes into creating these representations of scenes from the Passion. Perhaps the surprising fact is that nearly all of the brotherhoods and processional floats are quite recent, most being from the 20th century, and new ones are still being commissioned. Only one brotherhood, the Cofradía de la Santa Vera Cruz, is really old, dating from 1553, unlike in southern Spain, where the brotherhoods are older and the processions are better attended. Nowadays many of the floats are carried on wheels rather than on shoulders during the processions, although the traditional shoulder-carrying is making a return. Photographs on display show that the sinister pointed hoods worn by those participating in Bilbao's processions were unknown in the region until around 1940, when influences from southern Spain introduced them in place of the formal dark lounge suits worn previously. Incredibly, the cost of a new float, funded by the brotherhoods, can be more than €100,000. The museum's raised walkway allows visitors to see the displays from above as well as below. What is not obvious to the casual visitor is the humour subtly associated with some of the *pasos*. Many of the human models who posed for the creators were well-known local characters, and the artists didn't miss the opportunity to poke some fun, entertaining spectators who would recognise the human models from the perfectly replicated facial features. For example, the model for Christ in the *paso* called *Los Azotes* (1955) was the local policeman, so great satisfaction must have

JOHN ADAMS

Halfway down the Gran Vía you'll find the bust of John Adams, the very first Vice President of the USA, its second President (succeeding George Washington) and the founder of the American Constitution. Having visited the Basque Country, he was clearly an admirer of what he found, stating in 1787: 'This extraordinary people have preserved their ancient language, genius, laws, government, and manners without innovation longer than any other nation of Europe'.

been derived from seeing his nearly naked replica getting soundly whipped. In *Ecce Homo* (1944), the model was a gypsy from Granada who posed readily, accepting his 'modelling fee' of two sacks of potatoes. In *Coronación de las Espinas* (1745), a young boy can be seen using his hand to cover up a hole in his trousers.

Of course, the best place to see these elaborate artworks is in the streets as part of the actual Semana Santa (Holy Week) processions, with the biggest ones being on Good Friday, but if you don't get the opportunity, then the modest entrance fee here is well spent.

Museo Taurino (Bullfighting Museum) [80 D7] (Martín Agüero 1; ☎ 944 46 86 98; w plazatorosbilbao.com; ⏲ Mar–Oct 10.00–13.30 & 16.00–18.00 Mon–Thu, 10.00–13.30 Fri, Nov–Feb 10.00–13.30 Mon–Fri; €3) One for aficionados, this little-visited museum is hidden away inside the Plaza de Toros, the bullring built in 1962 to replace the wooden structure that burnt down the previous year. There is no English-language information, so unless you speak Spanish or Basque the experience is a purely visual one. Having said that, there is a certain pomp about the exhibition hall, displaying the clothes of the toreadors, the tools of their trade, a model of the previous wooden bullring (far more beautiful than the present edifice) and iconic bullfighting posters from times gone by. You can step into the *capilla* (chapel) where the bullfighters say their prayers before 'battle' commences. Bullfighting in Bilbao now only takes place over nine days in August, coinciding with Bilbao's festival, and the rest of the year the bullring makes do with concerts, corporate events and the hosting of festivals.

Other sights

Mercado de la Ribera (Ribera Market) [83 D4] (⏲ 08.00–15.00 Mon & Sat, 08.00–14.30 & 17.00–20.00 Tue–Fri) Bilbao's main market is a beautifully bright, revamped affair spread over two floors with excellent fresh fish, meat and vegetables at attractive prices. Enhancing any visit, the ground floor houses a pleasant modern space to take a drink or snack – chic and trendy. Its 1930s exterior architecture has a distinctive maritime theme, and the handsome building is sometimes lit up at night.

Plaza Nueva flea market [83 D2] Except for during Holy Week and other festivals, a small flea market takes place every Sunday morning in the Plaza Nueva. Although it starts around 09.00, it takes a further hour to look lively. Most of the stalls are focused on books, with a few English titles, though you might find an interesting collectable or a caged bird, too. If nothing else, it gives the locals an excuse (not that they need one) to meet up for an early-morning *txakoli* or beer and contrasts nicely with the square's more raucous ambience the night before. By around 14.00 the market is virtually over.

Azkuna Zentroa [80 D6] (Plaza Arriquibar 4; **w** azkunazentroa.eus; ⌚ 07.00–23.00 Mon–Thu, 07.00–midnight Fri, 08.30–midnight Sat, 08.30–23.00 Sun) Until recently known as the Alhóndiga, here again the Basques' ability to surprise you architecturally strikes powerfully. Behind the attractive exterior of Bilbao's huge former wine warehouse, the interior has been stripped out and creatively refitted to house a variety of cultural and leisure activities that stretch across six floors. As well as a cinema, gym and two swimming pools, you'll find a terrace restaurant, cooking school and exhibition spaces. As a minimum, you should at least walk through the ground floor, admiring the astonishing collection of 43 columns – each different in style – that hold up the ceiling. At the information point you can pick up an English-language brochure with general information about the centre, as well as a detailed leaflet about the columns themselves. The Azkuna Zentroa (Alhóndiga) was mooted as a possible venue for the Guggenheim Museum, but didn't find favour with Frank Gehry. If you fancy a swim, bear in mind that the pool's transparent bottom allows people to watch your efforts from the ground floor, far below. It's always busy with aqua-aerobics classes and lap-swimmers, and the facilities are first class.

Funicular de Artxanda [83 F3/H1] (Plaza Funicular; ⌚ 07.15–22.00 Mon–Sat, 08.15–22.00 Sun, extended by 1hr Jun–Sep; €1.75/0.31/free adults/under 12s/under 6s) Bilbao's funicular railway, although a hundred years old in 2015, has nothing of the quaintness provided by the wooden carriages of San Sebastián's version. Although it does attract tourists who want to enjoy the spectacular views from the summit, your fellow passengers are more likely to be locals making their way home from work or from the shops. This is primarily a mode of transport, not a novelty. Fully refurbished in 1983, it takes 3 minutes to ascend 225m. Turning left when you exit the station, you will first see the giant *Huella Dactilar* (*Fingerprint*) sculpture by Juan José Novella, in memory of Spanish Civil War victims. The funicular station and its surroundings were actually bombarded in 1936. You can then enjoy a great panorama out over the city and the mountain backdrops from the pleasant park area, but don't forget to check the view from the other side, too, allowing you to gaze out at Calatrava's space-age airport building in the near distance.

AROUND BILBAO

PORTUGALETE A short metro or train ride away from Bilbao will take you to Portugalete, which despite a couple of quaint old streets that plunge you down to the west bank of the Nervión River, a brightly painted tourist office, handsome Neoclassical town hall and an industry museum, can't really escape from the fact that it has one real attraction: its UNESCO World Heritage Site Transporter Bridge, the Puente Bizkaia. For a speedy appreciation of the town's main points of interest, there is an English-language information board on the riverbank, next to the statue of 19th-century industrialist Víctor Chávarri, located between the tourist office and the bridge.

Tourist information Situated 400m upstream from the bridge, the tourist office (Paseo de la Canilla; ☎ 944 72 93 14; **w** portugalete.com; ⌚ Nov–mid-Mar 10.00–14.00 & 16.00–18.00 Mon–Fri, 10.00–14.00 Sat & Sun, mid-Mar–30 Jun & 11 Sep–31 Oct 10.00–14.00 & 17.00–19.00 Mon–Sat, 10.00–14.00 Sun, Jul–10 Sep 10.00–15.00 & 16.00–19.00 daily) is situated in a handsome but gaudily painted 19th-century building, formerly a railway station that fell into disuse in 1925.

Puente Bizkaia (Puente Colgante) (w puente-colgante.com; ⌚ continuous service in daylight hours, year-round; €1.65 per passenger to cross in the transporter car, cars €3.20, €10/8 for pedestrians with/without audio guide to do the 'catwalk') Linking Portugalete to Getxo on the other bank of the Nervión, and opened in 1893, this (literally) towering feat of engineering celebrated its 125th anniversary in 2018. It serves as a huge reminder of the estuary's industrial age, but it's more important to realise that it still carries an average of over 16,000 passengers and 1,200 vehicles every day. The bridge became a victim of the Spanish Civil War: having already suffered damage from bombing raids, on 17 June 1937 it was sacrificed by Republican engineers who destroyed it with explosives as Nationalist troops advanced on the city. Ironically, five days later, the battle for Bilbao was over as Franco's troops took the city. The debris was dredged to ensure continued access for ships servicing Bilbao's blast furnace and other vital industries upstream and reconstruction led to the reopening of the bridge in 1941. For those who are unafraid of heights, you can pay a hefty fee to do the so-called 'catwalk', taking a lift to the top and walking across the structure, feeling the vibrations of the transporter car as it passes below. A couple of hundred metres upriver, you have the option of taking a boat back across the water for the same nominal fee, if one transporter bridge trip is enough for you.

GETXO AND THE BEACHES At the other end of the bridge lies the Las Arenas quarter of Getxo, a town of over 80,000 that serves both as a suburb of Bilbao and as a summer getaway for the many citizens who want to make the most of its handful of beaches. Let's be honest, the beaches that you'll find here are not the Cantabrian coast's finest, and even some of Getxo's citizens will readily admit that Sopela just a few metro stations further east has better sands and cleaner sea. But Getxo still enjoys its long promenade that attracts joggers and snoggers, cyclists, dog-walkers and rollerbladers as well as those just taking a casual stroll. Of the beaches, the one nearest the bridge is small and the least attractive, while the next one to the east, Ereaga, is perhaps the best.

If you choose to stroll the promenade eastward from the bridge, there are a number of smart mansions to admire, each accompanied by an English-language signboard giving information about their architecture and former inhabitants, adding some interest to your walk. Architectural influences are mainly eclectic, English and regionalist in style. Getxo is still referred to by some locals as 'posh' or the 'town of the management', compared with 'poor' Portugalete on the other bank. For walkers, a bracing coastal hike from Getxo to Plentzia is a possibility; from there, you can catch the metro back to Bilbao.

SOPELA, PLENTZIA, GORLIZ AND THE COSTA DE URIBE Continuing along the coast eastwards from Getxo, visitors will find further settlements which are both commuter towns and playgrounds for the population of Bilbao. First is **Sopela**, whose beaches exposed head-on to the ocean make it a year-round surfers' paradise. In summer the sands are packed, so arrive early, choosing between Barinatxe beach with few facilities and the longer Arriatera which has more surf schools and cafés. From the cliffs above, you can see the distinctive *flysch*, the layered sedimentary rock formations that characterise this coastline. Sopela town and its metro station are 1km inland, but a shuttle bus operates in high season. Next comes **Plentzia**, a town with a well-preserved little centre and a small museum close to its church. One curiosity is its experimentation with underwater wine storage (page 100). Beaches here and at adjoining **Gorliz** benefit from being housed in a sheltered bay, ensuring safer swimming for youngsters. The attraction of tiny **Armintza** is not a beach but rather its minuscule fishing port and the backdrop of forested mountains. There is usually some activity around the harbour, with a few bars and restaurants offering people-watching opportunities. Further east comes **Bakio** with a new *txakoli* museum and a chance to visit a nearby winery and taste this singular Basque wine. Inland lies **Mungia** with an excellent hotel (see Palacio Urgoiti, below). All of the above towns can offer accommodation close to the airport, if you don't want to venture into Bilbao.

Where to stay and eat

Palacio Urgoiti Hotel-Golf (43 rooms) Calle Arritugane, Bilbao-Mungia; 946 74 68 68; e info@palaciourgoiti.com; w palaciourgoiti.com. Incredibly, this beautiful building was deconstructed stone-by-stone on its original site & rebuilt here. With a smart restaurant, pitch-&-putt (both open to non-residents) & a swimming pool, this is a luxury option but at affordable prices. Stylish décor, international TV channels, free Wi-Fi. The rooms are all spacious, but there are superior options too, & also suites. **€€€**

Hotel Modus Vivendi (15 rooms) Sipiri 32, Getxo; 946 76 70 77; e info@hotelmodusvivendi.com; w hotelmodusvivendi.com. A brand-new building, bright & functional. Satellite TV, free Wi-Fi. 1 room suitable for the less mobile. Gym, sauna, spacious lounge & bar. Friendly staff, decent b/fast & a few mins' walk from the metro. **€€**

Camping Sopelana Calle Atxabiribil 30, Sopela; 946 76 19 81; e recepcion@campingsopelana.com; w campingsopelana.com. The closest site to Bilbao, open year-round, near the beach & has pool, kids' pool, jacuzzi & shop to service the occupants of its 150 pitches (€35). Cabins for up to 6 people are also available here (€120). The site is 15mins' walk from Sopela metro station. **€**

Restaurante Harria At the Palacio Urgoiti Hotel-Golf (see above); 13.00–15.30 & 20.00–22.30 daily. Sophisticated cuisine, in elegant surroundings. It comes at a price, but is beautifully presented. **€€€€**

What to see and do

Txakolingunea (Wine Museum) (Basigoko Bide Nagusia 3, Bakio; 946 02 85 13; w bizkaikoa.bizkaia.eus/txakolingunea; Easter, Jul & Aug 10.00–15.00 & 16.00–19.00 daily, May, Jun & Sep 10.00–14.00 & 16.00–18.00 Mon–Sat, 10.00–15.00 Sun, other months 10.00–14.00 Tue–Sun; €3.50/1.75 adults/under 26s & over 60s, including tasting; other options (with more wine!) & *pintxos* are available, too) A brand-new space dedicated to the Basque Country's fresh, lively wine. Two English-language films introduce the wine and Bakio town to you, there are touch-screen information boards and, of course, a tasting from the town's four wineries. The **Bakio Tourist Office** is on the ground floor, with the same hours.

Crusoe Treasure Cellar (Areatza Iribidea, Plentzia; 944 01 50 40; w underwaterwine.com) Inspired by the surprisingly well-preserved taste of wine rescued from nearby shipwrecks, an experiment is underway here to store wine under the ocean. Divers are used to deposit the wine then 'rescue' it as and when it is required. To find out if it is working … well, it costs €100 per bottle. Housed in a sea container at the border between Plentzia and Gorliz, contact this company in advance to take a boat trip, learning about the process, enjoying some onboard tapas (and wine, of course). The storage is 20m down, and has spawned an artificial reef which attracts hundreds of fish species.

Doniene Gorrondona Winery (Gibelorratzagako San Pelaio 1, Bakio; 946 19 47 95; e gorrondona@donienegorrondona.com; w donienegorrondona.com) Prices, including tasting and a bottle to take away, from €15.50. A couple of days' notice of your visit is advisable. A few hundred metres up the hill from the Wine Museum (see above), you can continue your tasting at the town's largest winery.

Genial, English-speaking owner Andoni will answer all your questions about *txakoli* and a tasting of the wine or the grappa he also makes is a good way to end the tour. Upstairs is a small museum.

Izenaduba Basoa (Basque Mythology Interpretation Centre) (Caserio Landetxo Goikoa Baserria; 946 74 00 61; w izenaduba.com; Jun–Sep 09.00–18.00 daily; €9.80/8/free adults/under 14s/under 2s; phone ahead to ensure there's an English-speaker available) A chance to meet some of the Basque Country's famous & infamous legendary, mythical creatures (see box, page 363). In a fun and child-friendly environment, with a maze and a host of monsters, your English-speaking guide will introduce you to witches and one-eyed ogres. For the adults, you can step inside the ancient restored farmhouse (*baserri*) to learn the importance of these massive dwellings.

WEST OF BILBAO: LAS ENCARTACIONES (ENKARTERRI)

West of Bilbao, Las Encartaciones is a little-visited area, a region of irregular terrain and mixed history. Its coastal strip is short, squeezing in the international car ferry terminal at Zierbena and the nearby La Arena beach, but has little else of interest before it runs out at the western border with the autonomous community of Cantabria. And Bizkaia's neighbour has a peculiar part to play in inland Encartaciones, too, as the Cantabrian enclave of Villa de Villaverde carves the area almost in two, dividing the eastern part of Encartaciones from its west. Bilbao may have enjoyed a big makeover in terms of its urban regeneration, but the eastern section of Encartaciones, immediately to the west of the city, has also had to recover from the scars of its own industrial past. **Gallarta** is the mining town that literally disappeared, an incredible story that is well documented in the town museum. On the other hand, next-door **La Arboleda** is the town that survived, to re-emerge as a popular centre for Bizkaians making the most of a rugged landscape that draws in hill-runners, cyclists and walkers who arrive in droves at weekends and holidays to test their fitness. At **Galdames**, classic car enthusiasts will discover a most unlikely site for some automotive gems. **Balmaseda** is a handsome enough town, known to all Basques for its phenomenal passion play during Easter week, when the whole population either participates in or watches the re-enactment of the last days of Jesus Christ – both gruesome and captivating.

Western Encartaciones is a different story, less troubled by industrial history, more given to rural peace and with the caves at **Pozalagua** as the standout visitor attraction. To its south, the roads peter out into dead ends, confronted by mountains that rise to over 1,300m in places – a place of true solitude.

EASTERN ENCARTACIONES

Tourist information There are tourist offices in both **Balmaseda** (Calle Martín Mendia 2; 946 80 29 76; w visitenkarterri.com; winter 10.00–14.00 & 16.00–19.00 Mon–Fri, 10.00–14.00 w/ends & holidays, summer 09.00–14.00 & 16.00–19.00 Mon–Sat, 09.00–14.00 Sun & holidays) and **Sopuerta** (Plaza Carmen Quintana Zabala 6; 946 10 40 28; w sopuerta.biz/es; 10.00–14.00 Tue–Sat). From mid-June to mid-September, a tourist information point also operates at **La Arena beach**.

Getting there and away While many of the towns in the area are served by bus (and a few by train), visitors really need the flexibility offered by a car to explore all of Encartaciones.

Where to stay

Hotel Convento San Roque (21 rooms) Campo de las Monjas 2, Balmaseda; 946 10 22 68; e info@hotelsanroque.es; w puntuanhoteles.com. A characterful hotel, with the original wooden staircase retained from its 17th-century days as a convent. For lovers of old stone & modern comforts, this is the place, though it gets mixed reviews. Parking is free, as is Wi-Fi. B/fast included in high season. **€€**

Hotel Ibarra (14 rooms) Barrio Llantada 11, Zalla; 946 39 17 01; e info@ibarrazalla.com; w hotelibarrazalla.com. This tastefully renovated hotel is set off the main road (a little traffic noise intrudes – ask for a quiet room) & has TV, free Wi-Fi & heating. Terraces & garden. B/fast available, no restaurant but owner will recommend nearby establishments. **€€**

Hotel Kaia (7 rooms) Calle El Puerto 19, Bajo, Zierbena; 946 36 63 74; e bittor78@hotmail.com; w hotelkaiarural.com. Down towards the port, this well-run hotel is handy for those getting on or off the ferry to England – it's 5mins from the terminal. Heating, TV & free Wi-Fi (public areas). English is spoken. **€€**

Where to eat and drink

La Fabrica de Juan Playa la Arena, Zierbena; 946 36 53 61; w lafabricadejuan.biz; 13.00–16.00 Mon–Thu, 13.00–23.00 Fri & Sat. On the beach, a favoured location & popular, with good à-la-carte choices & competitive lunchtime menus. **€€€**

Restaurant Convento San Roque See *Hotel Convento San Roque* (above). The *menú del día* at this smart, courtyard restaurant in a former convent is not quite budget, but represents excellent value, while the à la carte is extensive. If you don't have room for dessert, try to squeeze down a *sorbete de Bizkaiko txakoli* (Bizkaian txakoli sorbet) – a light, refreshing way to end a meal. Vegetarian menu on request. **€€€**

Zierbenako Batzokia See *Hotel Kaia* (above); lunch only Wed–Mon, 20.30–23.00 Fri & Sat, closed Tue & 3 weeks in Feb. Run by a charming, talented young couple, this is a smart dining room popular with local lunchers. Competitive *menú del día* featuring fresh fish & seafood, plus more expensive (but still good value) menus & à la carte. **€€€**

Gallarta There's nothing beautiful about Gallarta, yet it is truly remarkable for two distinct but intricately related stories. Although iron ore had been mined in this area for centuries, from the late 19th century the insatiable appetite of the Industrial Revolution in northern Europe ensured that Gallarta and its neighbours were a frenzied hive of mining activity, with over 200 active opencast mines extracting iron ore from the surrounding hillsides for export. Nothing exceptional, but in 1958, as a scramble took place for future deposits, a huge vein of iron ore was discovered in the mountain directly beneath the houses of Gallarta. Little by little, the town of 7,000 and the mountain on which it sat were dismantled and the iron ore extracted. In 1986, the last house was bulldozed. In 1993, the mine was closed. The second part of this story is written thanks to the passion of an ex-miner, Carmelo Uriarte, who gathered together the remnants of this huge industry – now, like Uriarte himself, redundant – and determined to preserve it in a museum. Manned by staff and volunteers and precariously funded by a foundation with some government support, the museum remains open.

Museo de la Minería del País Vasco (Basque Mining Museum) (Barrio Campodiego; 946 36 36 82; e informacion@museominero.net; w museominero.net; 09.00–14.00 & 16.00–19.00 Tue–Fri, 11.00–14.00 & 16.00–19.00 Sat & holidays, 11.00–14.30 Sun; €3/2/free adults/students, seniors & under 12s/under 8s; to reach Gallarta by public transport, take train C2 from Abando (departs every 30mins or so) & walk (20mins), or catch the 3336 bus from Bilbao Abando station, asking for the 'El Minero' bus stop) The lust for raw material to satisfy the appetite

LA PASIONARIA, GALLARTA'S FAMOUS DAUGHTER

Cometh the hour, cometh the woman. Dolores Ibárruri was born in Gallarta in 1895. She's suitably name-checked in the town's mining museum, and the famous battle-cry of this communist activist – *'No pasarán'* ('They shall not pass') – was an oft-repeated rallying call during the Spanish Civil War. Among her many claims to fame, her colourful life involved periods in prison, periods in exile, giving birth to six children (five of whom died before her), having an asteroid named after her, being elected as a Member of Parliament (twice, with a 41-year gap in-between), setting out on a daring attempt to rescue starving children of imprisoned miners and standing alongside strikers and evicted tenants.

An impassioned speaker, she is recognised as one of the great orators of the 20th century. Also known as 'La Pasionaria' ('The Passion Flower'), she died in 1989. A statue of her, dedicated to British members of the International Brigade who fought against Franco in the Spanish Civil War, stands on Custom House Quay in Glasgow.

of the 19th-20th-century Industrial Revolution created a golden age of opencast mining in and around the area west of Bilbao. Nothing illustrates Gallarta's strange story better than the scale model of the area that greets you as you enter this museum. It features a 'lid' on the model of the mountain, dotted with tiny houses, which you can simply lift off to demonstrate how the town was removed and the mountain was gradually turned into a huge hole, visible across the road from the museum. There is enough English-language information here to make sense of the exhibits, with a leaflet, laminated sheets and even an unpromising but ultimately informative cartoon to enhance your experience, but the most striking impact is made by the old photos of the miners and their 'mining assistants', who were often children as young as nine years old. Up until 1849, when the law was changed, anyone could stake a claim to mine the ore, but after that the lands were put under the control of landowners who rented out the mining rights. The working conditions in the late 19th century and early 20th century were truly appalling, graphically illustrated in the museum, and the mine-owners would deduct board and lodging (provided in ramshackle, lice-ridden bunkhouses without sanitation) from the workers' wages, often leaving them with nothing. Disease was rife, accidents plentiful and the old hospital, now a sort of community centre, dominates the ridge across from the museum. The collections both inside and outside are extensive and volunteers can be seen renovating tools and equipment found in the nearby hills. There's information too about a famous daughter of Gallarta, Dolores Ibárruri, also known as 'La Pasionaria', a socialist activist who spent time in exile in Russia (see box, above). Apart from the information at the museum, English translations of which are improving all the time, with advanced notice you might be able to get a guided tour of the museum and the surroundings from Kevin Young (**m** 637 56 41 34; **e** kev_ortu@hotmail.com).

La Arboleda With only 30 houses but nine restaurants, La Arboleda's current priorities are clear. Weekends bring walkers and cyclists, but for the casual visitor the main interest is the chance to see the old miners' wooden sleeping quarters, now tarted up and inhabited by rather more well-to-do residents. A neat town square and a couple of recently built golf courses complete a peaceful picture of reinvention, part of the ironing-out of the wrinkles caused by the surrounding area's industrial past. The town is reached on the same bus line as the Mining Museum (page 102). Of the restaurants, **Leon XIII** (☎ 946 36 43 05; w restauranteleonxiii.com; €€€), with its traditional Basque cooking, is one of the best.

Muskiz Continuing on the industrial theme, the village of Muskiz lies 8km west of Gallarta along the N-634. It is marked by being the home of a giant, ugly oil refinery, but for visitors the point of interest, La Ferrería de El Pobal, is situated 4km to the south.

La Ferrería de El Pobal (Barrio El Pobal, on the BI-2701 4km south of Muskiz; m 629 27 15 16; e elpobal@bizkaia.eus; w bizkaikoa.bizkaia.eus; ⌚ 15 Apr–15 Oct 10.00–14.00 & 16.00–19.00 Tue–Sat, 10.00–14.00 Sun, 16 Oct–14 Apr 10.00–14.00 Tue–Sun; guided or unguided tours €3.50/2.25/free adults/under 26s & seniors/under 12s, €2 extra on Sat with forge demonstration) Originally built in the 16th century by the powerful Salazar family, this is a fully functional iron foundry, with preserved mallet and vertical wheel, a flour mill and a quaint 13th-century bridge, all bought by Bizkaia's council for loving restoration. No traces from the 16th century remain, as the foundry underwent many changes over the years, before it ceased to operate commercially as recently as 1965. Nevertheless, some parts of the forge, such as the stone bellows, date from the mid-18th century and are still in use. The guided tour, which lasts an hour, starts with an explanation using a scale model of the complex, allowing you to understand the whole process of producing ingots from iron ore and charcoal, both sourced locally. Although you can visit unaccompanied, a guided tour is recommended; to ensure that you get one in English, phone a couple of days ahead, and if you can visit on a Saturday you will see the forge in operation and the blacksmith at work.

Sopuerta/Abellaneda Further south down the BI-2701 and you'll bypass Sopuerta before reaching Abellaneda and its museum.

The **Museo de las Encartaciones** (at the roundabout on the BI-2701, Barrio Abellaneda, Sopuerta; ☎ 946 50 44 88; w enkarterrimuseoa.eus; ⌚ Oct–Jun 10.00–14.00 & 16.00–18.00 Tue–Sat, 10.00–14.00 Sun, Jul–Sep 10.00–14.00 & 17.00–19.00 Tue–Sat, 10.00–14.00 Sun; admission free) is a well-presented ethnographic museum in the former Casa de Juntas (council meeting house), dating from the 16th century, though it seems clear that meetings of representatives from the surrounding districts were taking place at this spot from at least the 14th century. When the Encartaciones *juntas* were abolished by royal edict in 1806, the meeting house fell into disrepair. Now fully renovated and reinvented as a museum, it is a handsome building, with its permanent exhibitions tracing the history of this little-known region through from prehistoric times to the present day.

Galdames There are few places on earth less likely to boast the world's biggest private collection of Rolls-Royce cars than a medieval tower, on a hill above a lush valley in rural Bizkaia province. The **Museo de Coches Antiguos y Clásicos (Antique and Classic Car Museum)** (Barrio Concejuelo – from the BI-3631, at the 33km marker, follow the signs for Torre Loizaga; ☎ 946 80 29 76; m 649 41 20 01; e info@torreloizaga.com; w torreloizaga.com; ⌚ 10.00–15.00 Sun & national holidays only; €7/4/free adults/children & seniors/under 12s) has every single model of Rolls-Royce made 'until the Germans bought the company' (as the owner puts it) – 45 in total. It's an incongruous setting – four hangars in the grounds of a rebuilt medieval castle. It's difficult to decide which is the most impressive, the cars themselves (80 in total, including some models of other makes), the castle (rebuilt from ruins) or the setting, overlooking a bucolic landscape. The original owner, Miguel de la Vía, was an industrialist, musician, artist and general bon viveur who, having restored the castle from its ruined state, began to collect the cars to give the property some useful purpose. The Rolls-Royces include a Phantom IV, one of only 18 ever built; the list of buyers of this model included the Shah of Iran and General Franco, who bought three.

As well as the Rollers, there's a Ferrari Testarossa, Lamborghini Countach, E-type Jaguar, a stunning Hispano-Suiza and an Italian Isoto Fraschini, among others. The oldest exhibit is from 1898, an Allen Runabout, previously owned by Formula 1 driver Sir Stirling Moss.

The castle itself can be admired from the outside, though not visited, as it is reserved for functions and conferences. The views are great and you might encounter the Torre's other collection, a slower form of transport: a drove of 30 donkeys who wander aimlessly around the grounds.

Balmaseda (Valmaseda) Even if you're not here for the town's biggest event, the Semana Santa, Balmaseda represents a worthwhile stop for anyone in the area. Balmaseda was Bizkaia's first fortified town, founded in 1199. Although it was already on the pilgrimage route, it subsequently gained importance due to its location on the south–north trade road between Castile and the coast. To today's

BALMASEDA'S PASSION PLAY

A relentless drumbeat, growing nearer and nearer, gradually begins to hush the crowd. They've already witnessed the suicide of Judas Iscariot as he hanged himself from a nearby tree, his limp body cut down and carried off. A sense of shock, at least for those witnessing it for the first time, lingers in the air. Now the crowd's heads turn to the right, alerted by a doubling of the volume, to see that the drummers have turned the corner and entered the square. Roman soldiers, two dozen of them, expressionless, helmeted, march to the deathly beat, the crowd now fully quietened. The soldiers, barelegged beneath their short tunics, line up in front of the convent. Soon Jesus will arrive to be tried before Pontius Pilate, who despite finding him not guilty, will condemn him to death. The gathered citizens of Balmaseda, together with visitors from far and wide, will watch the placing of the crown of thorns, then Jesus being soundly whipped before he sets off around town, staggering under the weight of the cross on his way to his place of execution. A gruesome end, indeed, to a day laden with solemnity and grief.

Visitors to Balmaseda at Easter week might have to pinch themselves as a reminder that the scene unfolding before them is realistic, yes, but not real; that Jesus is in actuality being played by the local bank manager, turned amateur actor for the day, and that Pilate is perhaps being portrayed by a manual labourer or civil servant from this small, Bizkaian town. This living Passion traces its origins back to the 19th century, though it may have been played out long before that. Now, the townsfolk of Balmaseda throw themselves into it with great enthusiasm, aware that although there are many other towns in the Basque Country and beyond re-enacting this very play, there are few places whose citizens perform it with the same intensity.

visitor it offers a couple of museums, a medieval bridge, a 15th-century church and a classy hotel and restaurant. The town's other three churches have now been found alternative roles, but you can also admire the imposing houses of the so-called *indianos*, townsfolk who left Balmaseda (and other parts of the Basque Country) for the Americas before returning to invest their new-found wealth in rather ostentatious dwellings. On Saturday mornings there is a fairly low-key market, which brings a little extra vibrancy to town. Balmaseda also has a solar calendar clock: if you stand in the middle when the sun is shining, your shadow tells you the time at any hour of day. Just outside Balmaseda is Boinas La Encartada (Beret Museum), the now-closed factory that for over a hundred years made the distinctive Basque headgear.

See page 101 for details of the tourist office at Balmaseda.

Getting there and away From Bilbao Concordia station, **trains** operate regularly – at least hourly – to Balmaseda (w renfe.com; 50mins; €2.95). **Buses** run every 30 minutes to and from Bilbao's Termibus depot with Bizkaibus (w termibus.es; 50mins; €2.50).

What to see and do

Pasión Viviente de Balmaseda (Balmaseda Passion Play) (w viacrucisbalmaseda.com, website in Basque/Spanish only; ⌚ Maundy Thu (Last Supper), Easter Fri (Judgement & Crucifixion); free to watch around town, but tickets for seats can be booked for the Last Supper (€3) or for a grandstand, front-row seat to see Pontius Pilate passing judgement for €15 – recommended; tickets can be booked online) If you're in the Basque Country at Easter, this should not be missed. The re-enactment of the last days of Christ involves hundreds of townsfolk, all dutifully clad in period costume, performing the Easter story from the Last Supper through to the gruesome crucifixion itself (see box, page 105). If you don't happen to be there at Easter, there is always the Learning Centre (page 107).

Iglesia San Severino (San Severino Church) (At the junction of Virgen de Gracia & El Castillo, town centre) A Gothic church with an 18th-century Baroque reworking of its exterior, San Severino dominates what was originally Balmaseda's marketplace. Much of the styling influences come from Burgos Cathedral, which is hardly surprising given that the town is on what was once the main trade route from Burgos to the coast. For those with a keen interest in the architecture, there is detailed information available in the church or from the tourist office. St Severin himself is celebrated on 23 October with a festival, and the town is also famous for its *putxeras* cooking competition.

Museo de Historia de Balmaseda (History Museum) (Calle Martín Mendia 27; m 657 79 58 06; ⌚ Oct–May 10.00–14.00 Tue–Sat, Jun–Sep 10.00–13.30 & 17.00–19.30 Tue–Fri, 10.00–14.00 Sat, Sun & holidays; €1) Located in a former church, the Iglesia de San Juan del Moral, Balmaseda's history museum hosts a mixture of original town documents, art, artefacts and pictures of local nobility inside the former San Juan del Moral church building.

Boinas La Encartada Museoa (Beret Museum) (Barrio El Penueco 11 – just out of town on the BI-636 towards Burgos; ☎ 946 80 07 78; w bizkaikoa.bizkaia.eus/laencartada; ⌚ mid-Oct–mid-Apr 10.00–14.00 Tue–Fri, 10.30–19.00 Sat, 11.00–15.00 Sun, mid-Apr–mid-Oct 10.00–14.00 & 16.00–19.00 Tue–Fri, 10.30–19.00 Sat,

PUTXERA ('RAILWAY STEW')

Balmaseda is said to be the birthplace of the *putxera*, or 'railway stew', so-called because train drivers in the steam age used the steam from their trains to heat up their food during long journeys. Traditionally the dishes contained a variety of red beans, onions, chorizo, bacon and other ingredients, according to availability.

The *putxera* itself is actually the name given to the large metal pot, supported within an outer metal container, in which the dish is cooked. A letterbox-style opening at the base of the container was where charcoal was introduced and through which air was blown through with a pair of bellows to regulate the heat. They can still be seen in use on the feast day of San Severino, and sometimes at other Balmaseda festivals.

11.00–15.00 Sun; €5.50/3.25/free adults/under 26s & seniors/under 12s, free to all on Fri) While part of this is a museum, it would be more accurately described as a perfectly preserved factory, founded in 1892 by a Basque returnee from Mexico. All the machinery is intact, much of it supplied here for the factory's opening by a firm in Oldham, Lancashire. At its peak (no pun intended – berets don't have peaks) the factory employed around 130 people and produced a daily average of 400 *txapelas* (berets), until it hit hard times and closed in 1992. All visits take the form of a guided tour in English, which starts with a short video and continues with your guide explaining the whole process of making the distinctive headgear, from washing the wool to packing the finished product. Although the factory is closed, there is still activity, as the turbine that once used hydraulic power to generate electricity and run the whole factory now produces electricity which is contributed to Iberola, the Spanish electricity giant. The factory director's house has also been preserved and can be visited, though the houses provided for the workers are derelict. The only current manufacturer of *txapelas* in the Basque Country is in Tolosa, Gipuzkoa.

Puente Viejo (Medieval Bridge) The three-arch bridge across the Cadagua River is a distinctive landmark, notable for the steep slope of the roadways up towards the middle. The slope was designed to slow down weary travellers, allowing the locals to collect the taxes as the wayfarers passed across.

Centro de Interpretación de la Pasión de Balmaseda (Passion Play Learning Centre) (Iglesia Convento de Santa Clara, Calle Campo de las Monjas 2; ☎ 946 80 14 38; w balmaseda.eus; ⌚ 10.00–14.00 Tue–Sun, Jul & Aug 10.00–14.00 & 17.30–19.30 Fri; €1) The centre can give you some idea of Balmaseda's famous 'living passion', though not a whiff of the incredible atmosphere generated at the live happenings in Holy Week. It contains a permanent exhibition of clothing and everything pertaining to the play.

WEST ENCARTACIONES: THE KARRANTZA VALLEY

Certainly far removed from the juxtaposition of industry and nature in the eastern half of the Encartaciones, the Karrantza Valley is a beautiful, tranquil part of Bizkaia that is still unknown even to some of Bilbao's residents, despite the city's proximity. Having escaped the ravages of industrial exploitation, this is an area made for rural relaxation, though with a few other sights worthy of a visit. With the neighbouring provinces of Cantabria and Burgos nuzzling up close, you're far more likely to hear Spanish spoken here than Basque.

WHERE TO STAY Follow the Lanzasagudas sign south on the BI-4625 for 5km to find **Casa Rural Gailurretan** (6 rooms; Barrio Lanzasagudas; 946 80 66 67; e gailurretan@gailurretan.com; w gailurretan.com; €€). The road trickles out just beyond this *casa rural*, leaving just the twittering of birds, animal bells and an occasional tractor roar to disturb you. Rooms have bright décor, bathrooms, heating and free Wi-Fi. There is a communal TV in the lounge. The restaurant can provide dinner and breakfast if required (b/fast €6), and there is a swimming pool for summer use. A few waymarked walks leave from right outside the property.

WHERE TO EAT AND DRINK **Casa Garras** (Barrio Concha 6, Karrantza; 946 80 62 80; 09.00–midnight daily; €€€) has a boisterous bar below and a much-revered restaurant up above. The cuisine fuses Basque favourites with *nouvelle* twists; don't be put off by the slightly laboured menu translations into English – the food is delicious. It gets packed with locals, so book early.

WHAT TO SEE AND DO

Cueva de Pozalagua (Barrio de Ranero, Valle de Carranza; m 649 81 16 73; w karrantza.org; Apr–mid-Oct 11.00–20.00, mid-Oct–31 Mar 11.00–18.00 w/ends & holidays only, but daily at Easter & 15 Jun–15 Sep (except Mon); €7/4/free adults/children, students & seniors/under 8s; audio guides provided in English & all trips – around 45mins – are with a guide, who might be able to speak English; the cave is also partially adapted for wheelchair visits) This cave was only discovered in 1957, as a result of mineral mining that took place in this area. Sadly, the mining continued for a further 18 years after the cave's discovery and the explosives used in mining the dolomite resulted in significant destruction: one area, known as 'the cemetery', shows where the stalactites have been broken off by the explosions. Nevertheless, the stalactites, stalagmites and pillars that adorn the 125m of the cave are truly astonishing. Whether you are an expert or not, of particular interest is the vast amount of so-called 'eccentric' stalactites that spread out almost horizontally at times like tree roots, rather than just dropping vertically in the conventional fashion. The dominant colours in the cave are white and orange, and some of the columns are around 300,000 years old. If you have a torch and an extra layer of clothing, you are encouraged to bring them, though note that no cameras are permitted. There is another, bigger cave nearby, but as access is via a 60m vertical chimney, it can't be visited. Access along most of the cave's walkways is possible for those with lesser mobility.

Parque Natural de Armañón and Learning Centre (Opposite the Pozagua cave entrance, accessible by taking the BI-4769 from the BI-630; w karrantza.org; 10.00–14.00 & 16.00–18.00 daily; admission free) Around 100m from the cave ticket office is this centre, providing an English-language handout with some information about the landscape, flora, fauna and human activity in this park. Some fun for the young: a large movement-activated screen allows you to wave your arms and 'fly' (virtually) over the park as the film advances in response to your movement. During the era of mineral extraction, this building was the 'crushing station' and, by taking the elevator down, you can see where the minerals departed by aerial tramway to the *barrio* of La Concha, far below.

A number of walks depart from the centre, allowing you to explore some of the 3,000ha of the Armañón natural park, which is rugged terrain and home to a number of modest peaks of up to 850m in height. The presence of over 200 caves has been recorded beneath the park.

Karpin Abentura (Biáñez Auzoa 37; ☎ 946 10 70 66; w karpinabentura.com; ⌚ 1 Jul–15 Sep 11.00–19.00 daily, 16 Sep–mid-Oct & 1 Apr–30 Jun 11.00–19.00 w/ends only, mid-Oct–31 Mar 11.00–17.00 w/ends only, also opens daily during Easter & Christmas holidays; €9/7/6/free adults/seniors/under 14s/under 4s) This is one for the children: a small zoo with the added attraction of some fairly full-sized dinosaurs who will happily roar at your dear offspring. As for real animals, rather than convincing models, you will find crocodiles, panthers, lynx, pumas as well as less exotic species. There is a picnic area, café, children's play areas, a shop and a restaurant.

INLAND FROM BILBAO: DURANGO AND AROUND

DURANGO A handy base for anyone who intends to spend time exploring the nearby Parque Natural de Urkiola and not without interest of its own, Durango is a staunchly Basque town with a noisy history whose citizens formerly enjoyed a reputation for their skills in metalwork. Surrounded by mountains, Durango is a place of some size (28,000 inhabitants) with fairly industrial outskirts. The centre has now undergone careful restoration, but the cruelties of history have bestowed Durango with a double misfortune. Although it received aerial bombardment from German and Italian aircraft during the Spanish Civil War, one month before nearby Guernica, nevertheless it is the latter town on which world attention and sympathy have focused ever since. Around 340 citizens of Durango died as a result of the atrocity – the town was targeted because of its reputation for Republicanism – but Picasso's famous painting of Guernica has ensured that, outside of the Basque Country, the atrocity perpetrated on Durango's citizens has passed into obscurity.

On a much happier note, the town comes to life on Thursday, which is *pintxo pote* night (page 61). This is when people gather to bar-hop up and down Goienkalea and the surrounding streets, often with their children in tow. The atmosphere is truly convivial and prices are low. Durango's indoor market is open daily, except Sundays, but is at its liveliest on Saturday mornings, when some outdoor stalls are erected. At the southern end of Kalebarria, a sculpture of a bull and a man reminds people that bull-running used to be a daily occurrence in town, until being banned during the Civil War. Now it only takes place during the two weekends of the town's San Fausto festival in October.

Getting there and away Durango's train station and bus stops are very central. **Euskotren** serves both Bilbao (40mins; €3.40) and San Sebastián (2hrs; €6.30), with services roughly every half-hour from 06.30 until 21.30. Buses run to Bilbao (40mins; €4.65) and nearby Elorrio around five times per day, with a reduced service on Sundays. The service to San Sebastián is only twice per day (2hrs; €7.00). For more information, see w pesa.net (website in English).

Tourist information The tourist office (Kurutziaga 38; ☎ 946 03 39 38; w turismodurango.net; ⌚ 10.00–14.30 & 16.00–18.30 Mon, Thu & Fri, 10.00–14.30 Tue, Wed, Sat & Sun) should be your first port of call, as from there you can pick up an excellent map and audio guide in English (€1) for a walk around town.

The 75-minute, self-guided tour starts right outside the office itself. This walk covers the points of most interest, and there is now also a second audio guide available to accompany a new tour, which concentrates on the 1937 bombing.

Where to stay

Gran Hotel Durango (68 rooms) Gasteiz Bidea 2; 946 21 75 80; e reservas@granhoteldurango.com; w granhoteldurango.com. A fine building just 2mins' walk from the centre of town. Rooms are spacious, & fixtures & fittings modern. TV, free Wi-Fi, AC. Outdoor pool in summer. Spa with steam-room, gym, massage (all extra cost). Multilingual staff. **€€€**

Garaiko Landetxea (8 rooms) San Miguel 10, Garai; 944 65 60 03; e info@garaikolandetxea.com; w garaikolandetxea.com. Away from Durango town, this is a newish, stylish *casa rural*. Garai village is beautifully swept and kept, the hotel is gorgeous, & the views, with mountains on both sides, even more so. Garai has a couple of restaurants, churches & a *frontón*, & would make an excellent rural base for those who like walking. Rooms have TV, free Wi-Fi & heating. The b/fasts are excellent, while the owners are charming & can organise trips all over the Basque Country. It is situated next to the *frontón*. To find it from Durango, take the N-634 signposted San Sebastián, then BI-633 towards Markina Xemein, then at a further roundabout take a left on to BI-3341 to Garai. The *casa* is at the entrance to town, by a small church. **€€**

Juego Bolos (9 rooms) San Agustinalde 2; 946 21 54 88; e info@juegobolos.com; w juegobolos.com. A simple, clean, budget pension in the heart of the town. All rooms have a balcony & free Wi-Fi, TV & private bathroom. **€**

Where to eat and drink

Finding a midweek lunch for around €12 is never a problem in a working town such as Durango. *Pintxos* options are also good, for a town this size.

Kobika San Ignacio Auzunea 8; 946 81 00 03; 09.00–17.00 Tue–Fri (20.00–01.00 (Thu & Fri only), 14.00–17.30 & 21.00–01.00 Sat & Sun. A good 5min walk from the centre, in an unpromising apartment building, this place has won national awards for its *pintxos*, best sampled on Thu evenings. Menus range from *menú del día* to gastronomic fare, with excellent desserts. **€€€**

Barria Kalebarria 1; 946 03 03 41; lunch & dinner Tue–Sat. Informal & earthy, a good selection of hearty *raciones* in a typical Basque bar with a special ambience. **€€**

Shopping Ideal for anyone planning a picnic is **Saltsan Delicatessen** (Kurutziaga 40; 946 20 04 27; w saltsan.com; 09.00–14.30 & 17.00–19.30 Tue–Fri, 09.00–14.30 Sat & Sun). This shop sells some upmarket wines, but the real treats are the fine freshly prepared foods to take away, including delicious sun-dried tomatoes.

San Fausto Festival Durango's San Fausto celebration takes place in the middle of October, right at the end of the summer festival season. The timing allows locals to claim that this makes it better than the rest. Two specialities of San Fausto are the *zezenak dira*, a sort of 'bull-running lite' which starts at the ungodly hour of 07.00, and the *reparto de artopillak*, which is the handing out of small cakes by the municipal authorities. Over-indulgence in the latter is not advised in advance of participation in the former.

What to see and do Undoubtedly the best way to get to know Durango is to grab an audio guide and a map from the tourist office (page 109) and show yourself around town. Spots to look out for include **Plaza Ezkurdi**, a large, modern square which has some attractive houses. Nearby, the **Basilica de Santa María (Basilica of St Mary)** sports a wide, unusual wooden portico which covered the town's previous marketplace. The church was severely damaged in the 1937 bombing. A little way south, the **town hall** (Barrenkale 17) dates back to the 16th century and was rebuilt in the 1940s, also having suffered bomb damage. Its frontage sports paintings in Rococo style.

Museo de Arte y Historia (Museum of Art and History) (San Agustinalde 16; ⏲ 11.00–13.30 & 16.30–20.00 Tue–Fri, 11.00–14.00 & 17.00–20.00 Sat, 11.00–14.00 Sun) A majestic Baroque palace, the free entrance might lure you in to look at the model of 15th-century Durango, but there is little else of interest, particularly if you don't speak Spanish or Basque. The tourist office and its website have some limited information about the exhibits on display.

Museo Kurutzesantu (Kurutziaga Cross Museum) (Kurutziaga 38) Now sharing the building with the tourist office, and with the same hours, this museum houses a remarkable 15th- or maybe 16th-century carved Gothic cross, showing Flemish influences and depicting both Old and New Testament scenes representing almost the whole Bible story. Close examination reveals depictions from the Book of Genesis and the 12 apostles, as well as the Crucifixion. It is believed that the cross is linked to the so-called 'Durango Heresy', a 15th-century movement that radically proposed the communal ownership of property. Needless to say, this was not well received by the civil or ecclesiastical authorities (who were the property owners) and the movement was brutally suppressed by the Spanish Inquisition. Copies of this cross can be found in both Bilbao and Madrid. Formerly the cross was out in the street but, as can be seen from the photos in the museum, it incurred substantial Civil War damage in 1937. It also survived a terrorist attack in 1981 and was given its own museum space in 2009. There is information about the cross in English, available on site, including via the touch screens.

Espacio para la Memoria (Space for Remembrance) (Kurutziaga) A surprisingly modest memorial to those who died in the 1937 bombing, this consists of a large stone surrounded by carvings that bear the names of places that were of special significance during the Civil War. Three local battles are remembered – Intxorta, Saibigain and Santamañazar – and Barcelona is name-checked, being the city to which many Durango citizens decamped to continue the struggle against Franco after Bizkaia had fallen. On one carving, in Basque, the inscription next to an open book translates as 'We must do all we can for those who love liberty'. Another, on a stone plinth bearing another book – this time closed – has the inscription 'That my name may never be erased from history'. The memorial was inaugurated in 2013.

What to see and do nearby

Parque Natural de Urkiola Directly south of Durango, the BI-623 winds its way steeply skywards and enters the Parque Natural de Urkiola, a beautiful region of pine and beech forests and imposing rocky mountain tops that reach their zenith at the peak of Anboto (1,331m). At the top of the Urkiola Pass, the Toki Alai Visitors' Centre is the place to pick up information and also the starting point for a number of walks. On the opposite side of the road stands the Santuario de Antonios, a big, bold, in-your-face building inaugurated by the Bishop of Vitoria as recently as 1933. Both the exterior grey stone and the interior with its giant mural are impressive rather than pretty, but from the sanctuary car park you should walk the short distance to the 'three stone crosses' that overlook the spectacular cliffs to the south and east. On a clear day, they say that the beach of Laida is visible at

CIRCULAR WALK FROM ATXARTE TO URKIOLA

Distance: 9.5km; time: 3hrs; difficulty: easy/moderate. Parking is usually available, by either of two old quarry buildings at Atxarte. To reach Atxarte, turn right off the N636 after Abadino (coming from Durango), continue for 2km then take the right-hand fork. Terrain underfoot is nearly all concrete and good, wide paths. Refreshments and food are available at the halfway point.

After parking your car, continue up the road in the same direction, soon reaching a signboard which indicates Atxarte and shows the *zona de escalera*, or 'climbing area'. The surrounding cliffs offer the adventurous a number of climbing opportunities (see opposite). To your right on the rock, see the memorial plaque for Joxe Miguel Barandiaran, a much-revered student of Basque mythology and cave paintings. After a further 100m, the road splits and you follow the left fork, signed for Txakurzulo which is 5.4km away; the right fork is the one you will come down on your return. Shortly you arrive at a further signpost, but you continue straight ahead on the concrete for Txakurzulo. At a further fork in the road, take the left fork and continue your climb. Urkiola, your destination, was the last part of the Basque Country to receive Christianity, but this is also an area steeped in pagan legend and myth. For example, Mari, the 'top dog' of all Basque gods (and note Mari is a 'she') is said to have her main cave on Anboto, a nearby and much-revered mountain. You cross a cattle grid before the road flattens and then crosses a wide stream and does a U-turn. Soon you can enjoy the views of the sheer rock faces that entice those climbers to the area. Untzillatx, Aitz Txiki, and Alluitz are among the most impressive, with the highest rising to over 1,000m. Eventually you reach a signpost. Down to your right is the next step of your circular walk, but to see the three crosses and sanctuary, turn off the main path and follow the sign for Urkiola, which is a 1km climb away. You will first reach the three crosses up to your left, in front of which you will find an orientation table allowing identification of the surrounding craggy peaks. A further 500m past the crosses is the sanctuary (page 111) and the **Lagunetxea bar/restaurant** (usually ⌚ 11.00–18.00 Mon & Wed–Fri, 10.00–20.00 Sat, Sun & hols). There are two more bars down on the main road, 200m away, plus a bus route which has a very infrequent service to Durango or Vitoria if you don't want to walk back. Otherwise, retrace your steps to beyond the three crosses and descend back to the signpost to Atxarte which is now a little over 2km away. The downward path is steeper than the ascent, but is straightforward as it descends through the woods towards Atxarte. Soon you reach the broad stream, its rough bridge and the fork where you started your ascent. The car park is down to your left.

the mouth of the Urdaibai River. An orientation table by the crosses helps you to identify the surrounding peaks. There are a couple of restaurants on the main road at the top of the pass.

If you are heading back down towards Durango or have originally approached the pass from the south, you'll find the scenery to be almost alpine, with the chalet-style farmhouses and glut of forested slopes. Hairpin after hairpin challenges your driving skills until the beautiful scenery comes to a temporary halt with the appearance of some huge quarrying enterprises heralding your proximity to Durango itself.

At the top of the Urkiola Pass, the **Parque Natural de Urkiola Centro de Interpretación Toki Alai** (park learning centre) (☎ 946 81 41 55; e espacios.naturales.protegidos@bizkaia.net; w urkiola.net; ⏲ winter 10.30–14.30 & 15.30–17.30 daily, summer 10.00–14.00 & 16.00–18.00 daily) has permanent exhibitions, audio-visual presentations and the opportunity to watch a vulture colony through a video camera. For walkers, the website above contains many routes of various lengths and difficulty levels, detailed in English, starting both from the centre and also from Atxarte. If you would like the services of a professional guide, you could try **Inguru Abentura** (☎ 635 74 89 48; e info@inguruabentura.com; w inguruabentura.com), who can provide an English-speaker with a bit of notice. Time spent with a guide gives you a great opportunity to learn more about Basque culture. As well as walks, they can organise more technical climbs.

ELORRIO Another Basque surprise awaits those who venture into Elorrio. If you've just driven through Durango's functional and industrial outskirts, the uninitiated would not bet on finding such an ornate, intact town centre so close by, featuring an undeniably fine selection of churches, as well as 24 'palaces', built by wealthy merchants between the 16th and 19th centuries. That description, however, fits Elorrio. The town is a place to take a wander, marvelling at the palaces, admiring the nine stone crosses, delicately engraved and erected in the 16th century, and, if you have time, visiting the necropolis at Argiñeta just outside the town boundary: it is one of the most celebrated funerary Basque monuments.

Tourist information Elorrio's tourist office (Calle Berrio Otxoa 15; ☎ 946 82 01 64; w visitelorrio.com; ⏲ 10.30–14.00 & 14.30–17.00 Tue–Fri, 10.00–14.30 & 16.00–18.00 Sat & hols, 10.00–14.30 Sun) provides a free English-language audio guide and a map, which allows you to find all the points of interest around town. When the tourist office is closed, you can collect it from the local police station! The tourist office website offers various trails around town and excellent background information to enhance your visit.

GORBEA Gorbea as a region provides an alternative playground for the inhabitants of nearby Bilbao, a mountainous retreat rather than a coastal one. The region also carries the name of the highest summit, at 1,480m, though aesthetically it can't really compare with the stunning craggy peaks and landscapes that surround it. On sunny days, city folk crowd the many picnic areas and walkers take to the hills.

Otxandio (Otchandiano) Although in many ways Otxandio is a rather unexceptional town, it nevertheless has a strong Basque nationalist feel to it, for which it suffered heavily during the Civil War. Of interest here is the quaint 19th-century bowling alley, beautifully arched as it flanks the main square, a quaint old *frontón* with an uneven floor that would surely produce a bounce or two, a fountain dedicated to the Roman god Vulcan, and a memorial to those killed in the Spanish Civil War, with a striking mural and a list of the names of the dead. Otxandio was targeted for aerial bombing, even before Durango and Guernica. For anyone intending to spend time in the Gorbea to the west, this is a traditional town which could serve as a useful base.

Where to stay Just 1km outside Artea and 20km north of Otxandio, **Casa Rural Madariaga** (6 rooms; Madariaga 9, Artea; ☎ 615 73 96 18; e reservas@casamadariaga.com; **€€**) is a beautifully renovated family farmhouse with a peaceful position and commanding views over the Gorbea countryside. It is handily placed for Urkiola Natural Park, too (page 111). Rooms have TV, free Wi-Fi and heating. Ask for Room 3, the only one with a balcony. The *casa* can provide basic, good-value evening meals and breakfast on request. There is a communal lounge with fireplace. Charming Maider runs the house, which has been passed down through the generations.

THE COAST EAST OF BILBAO

East of Bilbao, a pleasant day's drive lets you pick and choose from a collection of fishing villages, each of which has its own attractions. Taking first the inland road through Mungia to emerge at coastal Bakio, then meandering along the coast to Ondarroa at Bizkaia province's eastern end is a total distance of around 130km. Along the way, pristine beaches quickly let you shake off the memory of the rather industry-ravaged waterfront of the Nervión riverscape around Bilbao. The Urdaibai estuary is an excellent focal point for nature lovers with its biosphere reserve that stretches from west of Bermeo to east of Ea and covers the whole Oka River estuary, as well as south to Mendata and beyond. It is a diverse area of towering cliffs and atmospheric marshlands which provide shelter for many species of birds. Tracing the estuary inland takes you to Guernica, a special place embedded in the Basque soul, synonymous with the Spanish Civil War and Pablo Picasso's famous painting, yet now looking firmly forward and accentuating the positive with its thought-provoking Peace Museum. Continuing east, the quaint village of Elantxobe tumbles down the valley, almost into the ocean. Beyond the eastern reaches of the biosphere reserve, Lekeitio is an important fishing town, with some festive traditions that are seriously unusual, even by Basque standards. Finally, the flocks of seagulls over Ondarroa – the last major settlement before the coast reaches neighbouring Gipuzkoa province – tell you that it owes its importance to fishing, not tourism. The towns, villages and sights of interest along this coastal stretch – with an essential inland diversion to Guernica – are listed below from west to east, starting at Bakio and ending at Lekeitio.

GETTING THERE AND AWAY

By car Driving time along the coast is around 2 hours from Bilbao via Bermeo to Lekeitio, but this allows no time for stops. You could truncate your Bizkaian coastal trip at Lekeitio, returning to Bilbao by the quicker inland route or continue eastward to San Sebastián.

By bus and train For those without a car, frequent bus services with **Bizkaibus** (w bizkaia.net) link Bilbao to all of the towns listed below, while Bermeo, Mundaka and Guernica can also be reached by rail with **Euskotren** (w euskotren.es).

GUIDED TOURS If you need the services of a guide for your visit to Urdaibai, or indeed elsewhere in the Basque Country, English-speaking **David Elexgaray** (e david@basque-ways.com; w basque-ways.com) is a native of the area and has an in-depth knowledge of history, culture, birdwatching and a lot more.

BAKIO With its wide beach, Bakio is a surfer's heaven and is geared up for those seeking to catch a wave. If you're not surfing, there's not much other activity in town, but if you need a first coffee-break on your coastal trip, then grab a seafront spot and watch those waves.

SAN JUAN DE GAZTELUGATXE (signposted off the BI-3101 6km east of Bakio; the island is accessible at all times; hermitage Jul & Aug only 11.00–18.00 Tue–Sat, 11.00–15.00 Sun, reserved for those celebrating mass only on 24 Jun, 31 Jul, 29 Aug & 30 Dec; admission free) This renowned hermitage, on the site of a former castle, is spectacularly perched on a photogenic islet linked to the land by a narrow bridge. The islet is bashed by the sea, as evidenced by the presence of two spectacular rock arches. Dating from the 10th century, the hermitage is dedicated to St John the Baptist (San Juan) and its colourful history includes being sacked by Francis Drake and destroyed by various fires, most recently in 1978. It is accessible by a path and a climb of some 240 steps to the summit. Having climbed the steps, you can expend any remaining energy by ringing the bell (three times) and making a wish. Following the clear signs from the main coastal road, park on the left immediately after the turn-off, from where it is a 5-minute walk to the viewpoint or a full 40 minutes to make the steep descent then ascent to the hermitage – allow 90 minutes for the round trip. It is hard work, but that does not deter the throngs in summer, so it is best visited early in the morning. Its recent connection with *Game of Thrones* has accelerated its popularity even further.

BERMEO Between 1476 and 1602 Bermeo was the Bizkaian provincial capital, way more significant than Bilbao, and though such importance is long gone, as a town of 17,000 inhabitants it still has enough interest to detain the day tripper. Many of the attractions are maritime-related, which is unsurprising given that the town has drawn its livelihood from the sea since it was founded more than 700 years ago. A local quirk in Bermeo is that the locals address each other as '*txo*', a reference to the historic name for a crewman on the fishing-boats. On 22 July, all the fishing-boats set off in procession to the village of Elantxobe, stopping off to reaffirm their territorial claim to Izaro island … by tossing a roof tile on to the shore.

Tourist information

(Lamera; 946 17 91 54; w bermeo.eus; winter 10.00–14.00 & 16.00–19.00 Mon–Sat, 10.00–14.00 Sun & holidays, summer 10.00–19.00 Mon–Fri, 10.00–14.00 & 16.00–19.00 Sat, 10.00–14.00 Sun) is just to the west of the horseshoe-shaped old harbour. Both train and bus stations are less than 2 minutes' walk west from there.

Where to stay and eat nearby

Goiena Casa Rural (5 rooms) Emerando auzoa, Bakio Bidea 7, Mungia; m 630 93 41 34; e info@casaruralgoiena.com; w casaruralgoiena.com. Tucked away off the main BI-2101 road, 13km southwest of Bermeo & overlooking a forested valley, this is a classic, well-kept inland *casa rural* with stone-tiled floors & a smell of polished wood. TV, heating, good free Wi-Fi & spacious rooms. Best of all are the welcoming hosts, Karmele & Joseba, who speak a little English. **€€**

Almiketxu Almike auzoa 8, Bermeo; 946 88 09 25; w almiketxu.com; 14.00–16.30 & 20.30–22.30 Tue–Sun. A kilometre southwest of Bermeo town, this characterful place comes highly recommended, serving up excellent fish & meat including *chuletón*, both sold by the kilo (or part thereof!), plus a good wine list. Charming Francisco is a former *pelota* player who has spent time in the USA & speaks good English. He has some stories to tell. **€€€**

What to see and do

Ballenero Aita Guria (Aita Guria Whaling Ship) (Located in front of the tourist office; 946 17 91 21; Easter–end Oct) Renovated fairly recently, following storm damage, a visit to this reconstruction of a 17th-century whaling ship is recommended. Whaling was big business for the Basques for many centuries, first off their own shores, then further west along the Cantabrian coast and finally with long-distance hunting expeditions to Newfoundland and Greenland as whale stocks thinned out – due to the hunting, of course. Multilingual notices allow visitors to find out about the life aboard a whaling ship and the hunting of the great mammals. The reconstruction is based on a fishing vessel, so is not quite full-scale; just as well, as a crew of up to 60 men lived on board. Guided visits in Spanish, if pre-arranged.

Museo del Pescador (Fishing Museum) (Torre de Ercilla; ☎ 946 17 11 71; 🕘 10.00–14.00 & 16.00–19.00 Tue–Sat, 10.00–14.00 Sun; €3.50/1.75 adults/under 26s & seniors) Continuing with the maritime theme, this small fishing museum is housed in a 15th-century tower-house on the northern side of the old harbour. If you've already visited one or more of the sea-related museums along the coast, you'll not find much new here: the exhibits cover whaling, fishing and the *trainera* rowing-boats. Some of the panel displays are translated into English, and further information is provided by way of a brief leaflet. The museum also shows four videos on small and large screens, covering subjects such as whaling, and on request the museum staff will change the subtitles to English. The most interesting is a series of testimonies from local women who once worked as net-menders and fish-filleters.

Apart from the above, the other Bermeo attractions are the sculptures of celebrated Bermeo-born artist, Nestor Basterretxea, whose works can be seen in the town's main square. His 12 pieces, representing figures from Basque mythology, are arranged as a circle at the square's western end.

MUNDAKA Just 3km further on from Bermeo, Mundaka is a much smaller, neater, picturesque fishing port without too much in the way of overdevelopment and a pleasant beach at the southern end of town. For surfers, the town's holy grail is its left-handed wave, considered by many to be the best in Europe. At one time, this wave mysteriously disappeared, the blame being laid variously at the feet of ecologists, shipbuilders and academics, whose activities were said to be disrupting the Oka River estuary and corrupting the sandbanks. Happily, the breaker has re-emerged. A small market sets up beside the harbour on Tuesday mornings.

Tourist information Mundaka's tourist office can be found on Calle de Joseba Deunaren (☎ 946 17 72 01; **w** mundakaturismo.com; 🕘 winter 10.30–14.30 Wed–Mon, summer 10.30–14.00 & 16.00–19.00 daily) and has free internet access.

MUNDAKA'S BRITISH CONNECTIONS

Famous among surfers for its wave, said to be the best left-hander in Europe, Mundaka is less known for its links with the UK. More than one school of thought exists as to the origins of the town's name, but one theory has it that it is an adaptation of the Latin '*munda aqua*', meaning 'clear water' and bestowed on the town in the 11th century by an exiled Scottish princess and her companions who favoured it over the muddy tidal water of the nearby Urdaibai estuary. More readily tangible than this legend is the British connection to the Palacio de Larrinaga, situated on Goiko Kalea. The architectural influences of this neo-Baroque building may be French, but the family who had it built in the 19th century owned and ran a shipping company based in Liverpool. The elegant town hall, situated in the main square, owes its construction in part to a donation from this same family.

Where to stay and eat

Apartamentos Mundaka (14 apts) Lorategi Kalea 1; 946 02 84 00; e info@apartamentosmundaka.com; w apartamentosmundaka.com. No rustic charm here, but spotless, bright beachfront apartments for self-caterers. Friendly staff, free Wi-Fi, cable TV, heating & private parking (extra cost). Ask for a room away from the main road. Off-season rates are very attractive. **€€€**

Atalaya Hotel (13 rooms) Itxaropen 1; 946 17 70 00; e reservas@atalayahotel.es; w atalayahotel.es. This hotel has a quaint, old-time seaside air with traditional glass galleries. Some rooms have sea or estuary views (room 32 has both), some have balconies. TV, heating, sauna, free Wi-Fi & parking. Excellent buffet b/fast – don't hesitate to ask for bacon & eggs! **€€€**

Atxarre Antzora 24, Ibarrangaru (Laida beach); 946 27 66 79; w atxarre.net; 09.00–23.00 daily. Across the water from Mundaka (so a boat trip or drive around the estuary), in a great location matched by super food & friendly staff. A lively vibe in high season. €€€

What to see and do

Mundaka beach In high season, Mundaka's own beach can become rammed, but a **boat shuttle** (m 622 22 29 19; w urdaiferry.com; 1 Jun–30 Sep 10.00–20.00 daily, Oct–May w/ends & holidays only; €2.80/4.50 single/return) takes you from the harbour across the estuary to the more expansive sands of **Laida** (page 123), where there are also a few bars and restaurants, including Atxarre (see above).

If you have been overcome by the urge to surf Mundaka's left-handed wave, head to **Mundakasurfshop** (Paseo Txorrokopunta 10; 946 17 72 29; m 656 79 80 56; e info@mundakasurfshop.com; w mundakasurfshop.com; closed early Nov–20 Dec & 15 Jan–1 Mar), where a five-day beginner's course costs from around €130. You can also rent kayaks and stand-up paddles from here.

Ekoetxea Urdaibai (Basque Biodiversity Centre) (Barrio San Bartolomé, 3km south of Mundaka, off the main BI-2235 Mundaka/Guernica road; 946 87 04 02; w ekoetxea.eus; Sep–Jun 10.00–19.00 Tue–Sun, Jul & Aug 10.00–20.00 Tue–Sun; €3/1/free adults/students & seniors/children) With great views out over the estuary, this centre challenges you to understand biodiversity, starting with the observation that the human being is biodiverse. The views and café make this a worthwhile stop.

GUERNICA-LUMO (GERNIKA) Guernica's symbolic oak tree, the Gernikako Arbola, ensures that the town will always hold a special place in the Basque psyche and soul, having come to represent the rights of the Basques as a whole, and stands as an emblem of their freedom. It was under the tree that the meetings of the General Assembly of Bizkaia took place, with the earliest reference stretching back to the 14th century; here, local chiefs swore to defend Basque freedoms, resolved local disputes and determined taxation levels. In times gone by, the Kings of Castile would swear allegiance to the Basque *fueros* – the laws and privileges – beneath its shady branches. In terms of international profile, the town is seemingly destined to be remembered for its use as a cruel 'experiment' by the Luftwaffe's Condor Legion in 1937, during the Spanish Civil War. Hitler supplied planes in support of General Franco, and in the process of bombing the town for 4 hours on 26 April killed hundreds of citizens, in a rehearsal for his own aerial bombardment tactics in World War II. Over 85% of the town was destroyed in the bombing, though this and almost everything else about it was immediately, and for many years after, denied or disputed by the perpetrators. Even the very *fact* of the bombing was refuted, with Francoists blaming the town's destruction on retreating Basque Republicans. It took Germany until 1997 to admit their involvement and apologise for it, something that the Spanish army

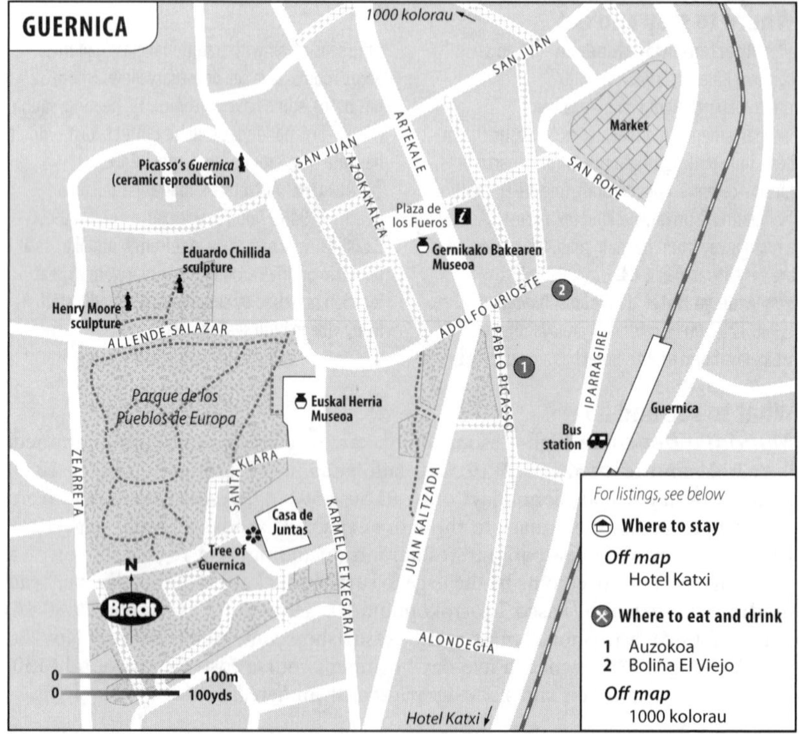

has yet to do. Although this tragedy and Pablo Picasso's famous painting has given Guernica a certain infamy, the current town of 17,000 inhabitants is now turned towards the future. Once at loggerheads over territorial matters, Guernica and neighbouring Lumo became as one in the late 19th century, giving rise to its official double-barrelled name. Visitors who wish to immerse themselves in Basque history should certainly not miss a visit to the town, with the museum, Assembly House and tree being essential must-sees. If you are staying in or near the town, then there are other attractions, listed on the following pages, which deserve time.

Tourist information The tourist office (Artekale 8; 946 25 58 92; e turismo@gernika-lumo.net; w gernika-lumo.net; 10.00–14.00 & 16.00–19.00 Mon–Sat, 10.00–14.00 Sun, Jul & Aug 10.00–19.00 Mon–Sat, 10.00 Sun) provides information and a 'global ticket' that gives discounts on entrance fees to the Peace Museum and Euskal Herria Museum. Ask here about the 'Pintxo Route' voucher (see opposite).

Where to stay nearby *Map, above*

With nowhere exceptional in town, most visitors will choose to stay in one of the nearby coastal towns, or at least out of the town centre. A good option is **Hotel Katxi** (9 rooms; Barrio Andra Mari, Morga; **€€€**). With free car parking, an excellent well-established restaurant (closed Sun afternoon & Mon; **€€€**) and air conditioning, free Wi-Fi, garden and sun terrace, this well-run hotel with English-speaking staff might tempt you to forego the sea air. A few kilometres west of Guernica, Morga is a quiet town.

Where to eat and drink *Map, opposite*

Guernica is perhaps a place to take a lunch rather than stay overnight or take dinner. However, for five years, the tourist office has teamed up with local bars to offer discounted *pintxos* on the 'Pintxo Route'. You pay a meagre €8.80 in exchange for a voucher that entitles you to no fewer than eight *pintxos* in 15 participating bars. You then just pay for your drinks as you visit. Buy the voucher at the tourist office.

1000 kolorau Plaza San Juan Ibarra 9; 946 25 76 19; 11.00–23.00 Fri–Sun, 11.00–17.00 Mon, Wed & Thu. A friendly, flexible place, popular & with tasty, well-priced *pintxos*, main dishes & delicious desserts. Enjoyable. €€

Boliña El Viejo Adolfo Urioste 1; 946 25 10 15; closed Sun & Tue evening. An old traditional-style bar, with traditional-style customers. Recommended for its lunchtime *menú del día*, basic Basque cuisine at a good price. €€

Auzokoa Pablo Picasso 5; 946 25 16 66. No meals, *pintxos* only, but they're generally reckoned by some to be the best in town.

What to see and do

Guernica Market '*Lunes gerniques, golperik ez*' translates as 'Not a lot of work gets done on Mondays in Guernica'. This local saying might be partially an exaggeration, but the arrival of the town's market on a Monday morning generates something of a holiday atmosphere. It is an event aimed squarely at townsfolk and traders from Guernica and the surrounding villages, rather than at tourists. Although rarely a riot of colour, it is nevertheless important for locals to meet and exchange gossip. On the last Monday in October, a special market is held, with cheese-making competitions and other events, drawing in visitors in their thousands.

Gernikako Bakearen Museoa (Guernica Peace Museum) (Plaza de los Fueros; 946 27 02 13; w www.museodelapaz.org; Mar–Sep 10.00–19.00 Tue–Sat, 10.00–14.00 Sun, Oct–Feb 10.00–14.00 & 16.00–18.00 Tue–Sat, 10.00–14.00 Sun; €6/free adults/under 12s) Using the bombing of the town as a platform for something more constructive, the Peace Museum seeks to look forward and encourages its visitors to consider wider issues such as 'What is peace?' with an exhibit containing definitions of the concept by Gandhi and the Dalai Lama, among others. English speakers can collect a laminated booklet from reception, with detailed information corresponding to the museum's wall panels, but there are also a number of videos with either subtitles or English-language options. As well as an eyewitness account of the fateful day in 1937, there are exhibits illustrating the characteristics of the town beforehand, the extent of the damage caused and the historical context of the Spanish Civil War. Franco's plan was to crush the Basque resistance quickly, and the use of his allies' air forces was key to how he achieved his objective. The war was ended in the Basque Country long before it finished elsewhere. The museum also covers the reconstruction of Guernica town after the bombing, before moving on to deal with the more recent violence of ETA and GAL (page 19). There are also occasional temporary exhibitions. A thought-provoking museum, the exhibits are well laid out and a visit is strongly recommended.

Casa de Juntas and Gernikako Arbola (Assembly House of Guernica and the Tree of Guernica) (Allende Salazar; 946 25 11 38; summer 10.00–14.00 & 16.00–19.00; winter 10.00–14.00 & 16.00–18.00) Guernica's Assembly House is an important symbol for the Basque people. Since the Middle Ages, the General Assembly has been the highest governing authority in the territory. In the **Room of the Stained Glass Window** a small screen shows three short videos about the tree and the Assembly House – these are better and more up to date than the information provided by the large-screen video which is also available on request.

Perhaps the most impressive part of the Casa de Juntas is the 19th-century **Assembly Room**. A truly magnificent forum, surely this is exactly the kind of place where important decisions *should* be taken? The altar in the apse and the fonts show that the building was conceived as a place where both political and religious functions could be performed. Pictures of various lords of Bizkaia stare down from the walls, duly consigned to history, but this elegant room today remains the venue for a number of assemblies, even though much of Bizkaia's business is now carried out in Bilbao. A further wall painting shows King Ferdinand receiving the lords of Bizkaia, who duly show their respect by kissing his hand. As a contrast, in 1981, when the visiting King Juan Carlos was perceived as showing a lack of respect to the Tree of Guernica, Basque Nationalists reacted by vociferously singing a nationalist song in this very chamber.

Understanding the historic importance of the **Gernikako Arbola (Tree of Guernica)** is essential to appreciating it: as the current incumbent tree was only planted in 2015, anyone expecting a gnarled old monster which imbues gravitas to this hugely important setting will probably be disappointed. As part compensation, part of the trunk of one of its predecessors has been preserved a few metres away, thus providing a more suitable location for the endless groups of visiting schoolchildren to take their selfies. However, it is the symbolism of the oak tree, rather than the object itself, which is significant.

Euskal Herria Museoa (Museum of the Basque Country) (Allende Salazar 5; ☎ 946 25 54 51; **w** bizkaikoa.bizkaia.eus; ⌚ 10.00–14.00 & 16.00–19.00 Tue–Sat, 10.30–14.30 Sun, Jul & Aug, also open 10.00–14.00 Mon; €3/1.50 adults/students & seniors, free to all on Sat) Although the ground- and first-floor exhibits are a little bit dry (covering such topics as physical environment and political structure), it all perks up a bit on the upper floors where you can use interactive screens and audio to watch and listen to traditional dance and music from the Basque Country, as well as finding out about folklore and mythology. A hand-held 'point-and-shoot' audio device allows English speakers to activate useful commentary as they view the exhibits.

Parque de los Pueblos de Europa (Park of the Peoples of Europe) (Calle Zearreta) Guernica's central park is most notable for two **sculptures**. The title of the piece by Eduardo Chillida, *Gure aitaren etxea* (*Our Father's House*) was taken from a famous poem and it references the need to defend the Basque Country. (Rather sadly, it now seems a favourite target for Guernica's less artistically gifted graffiti artists.) Henry Moore's 20-tonne bronze sculpture entitled *Large Figure in a Shelter*, with its obvious gaps, provokes the thought that 'shelter' is not entirely foolproof, an apt choice for Guernica with its tragic 20th-century history.

***Picasso's* Guernica** (Pedro de Elijalde Kalea 2; ⌚ free access at all times) Underneath this actual-size reproduction of Picasso's famous painting, the inscription written in Basque translates as 'Bring *Guernica* back to Guernica', a reference to the fact that the original of Pablo Picasso's work is currently displayed in the Reina Sofia Museum in Madrid. For many years it remained in New York, with the artist insisting that it should stay there until democracy was restored to Spain. It finally came back in 1981.

AROUND GUERNICA A short drive from Guernica, a pleasant day's outing could involve a walk through the painted forest, then a visit to the neighbouring caves

A WALK IN THE PAINTED FOREST

Distance: 5km; time: 2hrs; difficulty: easy.
This circular walk takes you up through pine and eucalyptus forest, presenting you with views over the peaceful Basondo and Oma valleys, the chance to see Agustín Ibarrola's tree paintings and a look at some traditional farmhouses (caseríos) on the way back. Depending on how much time you spend looking at the artwork on the trees, the walk should take around 2 hours. Walking is on good paths on the outward section, returning on tarmac by the side of a quiet road. Some short, steepish ascents and descents are involved.

From the parking area at the Lezika Restaurant, walk back to the road and follow the wooden sign for Bosque Pintado (2.8km) and Oma (3.8km) up the path which turns quickly from tarmac to concrete. Go 50m up the track, and you can see behind you, beyond the restaurant, the structure of the former chapel that now houses the 3D projection of the Santimamiñe caves. The path quickly levels off, becoming gravel. Soon your view down to the left includes the road that will be your return route after the forest visit. The path now continues uphill, with pine and eucalyptus trees on either side. After you've walked around 1.5km, at a fork, keep to the wider path that leads to the right, then ignore a further path that heads left into the trees. Further on, at a junction, take the left, again marked Bosque Pintado and Oma. You are now 1km from the painted forest. After a slight descent, at a clearing in the forest with a crossroads of four paths, take the left turn, descending and again following the Bosque Pintado sign, now only 250m away. You'll soon see the colour of the first painting, a yellow diamond painted across two trees, but giving the appearance of one single painting. On the ground, look out for the directional pointers which guide you to look around and fully appreciate the works (some are behind you!). The idea now is to simply wander around for as long as you choose, looking at the work from various angles and gaining different perspectives. For some of the paintings, it is necessary to line up a number of trees in your eye-line, to make the image complete. When you've had your fill of painted trees, continue down, following the same direction as you entered the painted forest. At the end of the forest, you turn right down a well-marked path, signed for Oma (700m) and Basondo (2.9km), zigzagging down to reach the road, when you turn left after passing through a turnstile. After 300m you come across a typical farmhouse (*caserío*) on your right, somewhat dilapidated. After passing two more *caseríos*, a stone bridge on your right crosses the stream. Cross the bridge and follow the stream for a few metres to make out the colours of further artworks in the garden of the artist's house. Retrace your steps now, back across the stone bridge and continue along the road. You now follow the road back to your starting point, first in the Oma Valley then, after a steep climb, passing into the Basondo Valley.

of Santimamiñe, a UNESCO World Heritage Site, before a *costera* (a 'coastal'), which is a potter in your car along the coast, stopping in the seaside villages for refreshment and a relaxed look-see, or a dip in the sea.

Bosque Pintado de Oma (Painted Forest of Oma) (Basondo Auzoa, Kortezubi; 944 65 16 57, 60; free access) To reach the start point for the painted forest and the Santimamiñe caves, take the BI-2238 from Guernica for just under 3km, passing through Idokiliz village and turning right on to the BI-4244. Parking is at the Lezika restaurant car park. Artwork on trees, an example of 'land art', is an unusual attraction, admittedly, but combined with an opportunity to take a pleasant walk (see box, page 121) among pine forests and eucalyptus and ending at a local restaurant, it is a well-balanced way to spend a morning. In 1982, Agustín Ibarrola began to paint his figures in the forest, first in white, before progressing through red and black to other colours. He finished in the year 2000, leaving a legacy of painted trees. His gift to visitors provides a colourful focal point to a pleasant walk. In total, there are over 40 figures, with enigmatic titles such as *Invitation to a Kiss* or *A Curve is Not Equal to the Section of a Circle*. An English-language leaflet, listing the titles to all the works, is available from the information centre at the mouth of the Santimamiñe cave, or from tourist offices along the coast.

Cueva de Santimamiñe (Address, directions, parking & contact details as for the Bosque Pintado – see page 121; **w** santamamine.com; note that advanced reservations are required for guided tours; information centre ⏲ 15 Apr–14 Oct & Easter 10.00–14.00 & 15.00–19.00, 15 Oct–14 Apr 09.30–15.30; guided tours 15 Apr–14 Oct & Easter 10.00, 11.00, noon, 13.00, 15.30, 17.00 & 17.30 daily, 15 Oct–14 Apr 10.00, 11.00, noon & 13.00 Tue–Sun; €5/3/free adults/under 26s & seniors/under 12s) Although there is a 3D show and a visit to see the 'archaeologists' area', the actual cave can no longer be visited for, after years of being trampled over, it is now protected. The show explains the formation of the cave and details the 14,000-year-old artwork that was found inside, which depicts deer, bison, goats, horses and even a bear. You'll need to phone a few days in advance to book a time to see the English-language version of the show.

Urdaibai Bird Center (Orueta 7, Gautegiz Arteaga, on the BI-2238, around 10km north of Guernica, where it is signposted to the left; ☎ 946 25 11 57; **e** urdaibai@birdcenter.org; **w** birdcenter.org; ⏲ Nov–Mar 11.00–17.00 Fri–Sun & holidays, Apr–Jun 11.00–16.00 Tue–Fri, 11.00–19.00 Sat, Sun & holidays, Jul & Aug 11.00–19.00 daily, Sep & Oct 11.00–14.00 Tue–Fri, 11.00–19.00 Sat, Sun & holidays; €5/2/free adults/under 12s/under 5s) Possibly *the* best place to see birds in the Basque Country, with over 290 species recorded, the Urdaibai Bird Center, only opened in 2012, is a well-designed, carefully thought-out high-tech enterprise with passionate management and easy-to-understand displays. There are two hides outside, which can be visited when the centre itself is closed, but the real highlight is an indoor viewing area with apparatus that allows you to find birds out in the wetlands while your chosen field of view is projected on to a huge screen. This allows you to discuss with your friends what you're seeing through the viewfinder, while they watch it on the screen. The centre is involved in a number of projects worldwide with organisations and schools and also has a residential research facility. Migratory routes are clearly shown on display panels and the effect of wind and weather is discussed on a video. Audio guides in English are provided, but there is usually an English-speaking member of the highly motivated team to answer any questions arising. Of particular interest to British visitors will be the ospreys, breeding of which the centre is trying to encourage. At present they are transitory, just passing through in spring and autumn, but chicks are brought from Scotland and released once acclimatised. Ospreys or not, the best time to visit is either of those two seasons, though there are plenty of resident birds and at any time of year there is always something to see. If you want a bit of advance information, the centre's website shows live footage of the wetlands. Recommended.

Mendata Mountain Biking Centre (Barrio Elexalde, on the BI-3122, 11km southeast of Guernica; 946 25 72 04; w mendata.eus; Apr–Oct 10.00–14.00 & 17.00–19.30 Wed–Sun, Nov–Mar 10.00–14.00 Wed–Sun; €8 per day, including helmet but not insurance; €20 deposit required) This hilltop centre has 15 mountain bikes to hire and a map with routes around the area. A certain level of fitness is required as the gradients around here are challenging, to say the least. It is not always manned during the stated opening hours, so ringing ahead is advisable.

LAIDA Heading north up the eastern side of the estuary, after visiting the painted forest and the Santimamiñe cave, you soon reach **Laida**, a popular beach with a car park that struggles to cope on warm (and therefore busy) summer days. If your plan is for a day's sunbathing here on the spotless sands, it is worth noting that you can get here by bus from Guernica, or by the ferry which shuttles passengers to and from Mundaka (page 116). Three cafés serve beachgoers here. A little further on is the beach at **Laga**, smaller and with very basic facilities, but frequented by surfers as well as sun-lovers.

ELANTXOBE After the inland trip down the estuary to Guernica, the next coastal stop is the village of Elantxobe, a collection of houses that seem to be eagerly queueing up to fall into the sea. It is worth a photo stop to capture the neat harbour from the car park up above, but when you see how far the zigzag path has to descend to get you down to the water, you might decide just to enjoy the views from above. You're not advised, especially in summer, to try to access the tiny harbour area by car. Up above you may also note the turntable on the road, used by the buses: that's how tight the space is here. Things get even tighter on 22 July every year, when crowds gather as the mayor of Bermeo and his fellow townsfolk arrive by boat, commemorating his town's historic victory over Elantxobe in a territorial dispute over the island of Izaro. Nowadays, he is received by the mayor of Elantxobe, granted control of the town for a few hours and hosted with a few drinks, before jumping back in his boat to return home, stopping at Mundaka, which was also involved in the dispute, to remind them also who's boss.

EA The last little settlement on your recommended coastal trip from Guernica, you would hardly guess from the main road that there's a beach in town. But there is: after turning sharp right when entering town from the west, and parking your car, just cross the main road and head down the narrow street opposite the bar to reach the *frontón* and a tiny, sheltered stretch of sand.

LEKEITIO A gentle sense of purpose permeates Lekeitio, with its diminishing fishing fleet and three beaches. The town flies the international Cittaslow ('Slow City') flag, with a development plan based on fiercely protecting its heritage, both tangible and intangible. The huge Gothic structure of the Santa María de la Asunción church seems out of scale with its surroundings, particularly with the narrow, cobbled streets of the fishermen's quarter. In summer, particularly August, bed spaces can be hard to find and parking spaces likewise as visitors flock to make the most of the golden sands and safe swimming. Lekeitio certainly has some peculiar heritage worth preserving, with two utterly strange festivals. Human settlement has been traced as far back as 30000BC, evidenced by remains found in the Lumentza cave on the forested hill that rises behind the church, and which is topped with three crosses. Another town that benefited from trade with northern Europe, especially Flanders and England, Lekeitio gained its charter in 1325 from María Díaz de Haro, the 'first lady' of Bizkaia. The town walls were erected shortly afterwards and the wooden houses of the town were destroyed twice by fire, once in the 15th century and once in the 16th.

Fishing has always been important here. Whaling took precedence in the Middle Ages, and custom dictated that, from the proceeds of the sale of a whale's tongue, two-thirds were used to repair the quays while the other third went to the church. Whales gave way to bream as the main catch but, as stocks of those also diminished, Lekeitio's nets are these days more likely to bring back hake, red mullet and anchovy in season.

Tourist information Lekeitio's tourist office can be found on Independentzia Enparantza (☎ 946 84 40 17; **e** turismo@lekeitio.eus; **w** lekeitio.org; ⏰ Easter, Jul & Aug 10.00–15.00 & 16.00–19.00 daily, 2nd half Jun & 1st half Sep 10.00–14.00 & 16.00–18.00 Mon–Sat, 10.00–14.00 Sun, other months 10.00–14.00 Tue–Sun). From the office, pick up your audio guide in English (€3), with accompanying map showing 25 points of interest, allowing you to undertake a self-guided tour around the compact town centre. Included on the route are the church, several old palaces, the harbour, lighthouse and the city wall. At the harbour entrance, Lekeitio has its very own island, Garraitz ('Rough Crag'), accessible on foot at low tide. In town, just across from the Hotel Palacio Oxangoiti, was the boundary between the town's two quarters, the fishermen's quarter and the craftsmen's quarter. In honour of this meeting-point, where gossip of dubious veracity was often exchanged, the bar opposite is called Guzermendi, which translates from the Basque as 'Mountain of Lies'.

Where to stay

Hotel Palacio Oxangoiti (7 rooms) Gamarra 2; ☎ 944 65 05 55; **e** hotel@oxangoiti.net; **w** oxangoiti.net. Creaky wooden floors, wooden beams & a rather grand lobby in this centrally located 17th-century former palace house. Old-world charm right in the heart of the port area. TV, free Wi-Fi & heating. **€€€**

Hotel Zubieta (23 rooms) Calle Atea; ☎ 946 84 30 30; **e** hotelzubieta@hotelzubieta.com; **w** hotelzubieta.com. Set on the outskirts of town, in attractive gardens, a smart professionally run & stylishly decorated 3-star. Rooms are bright, with TV & free Wi-Fi. No AC, but that's rarely a problem near the coast. Larger deluxe rooms & suites are also available. **€€€**

Where to eat and drink You can *pintxo* yourself to your heart's content along the front of the harbour, where a string of bars provide useful outdoor space for people- and boat-watching. But for sit-down meals, you are better moving off the seafront. **Egaña** (Antiguako Ama 2; ☎ 946 84 01 03; **w** eganarestaurante.com; ⏰ 13.00–15.30 & 21.00–23.00 Mon–Sat, 13.00–15.30 Sun; **€€€**) has a spacious, wood-panelled dining room, and the welcoming owner of this 50-year-old family business serves up traditional Basque favourites sourced from sea and mountain. Monkfish, cooked simply in oil and with a slice of garlic, is one of the delights. Another option is **Lumentza** (Buenaventura, Zaparain 3; ☎ 946 84 15 01; ⏰ noon–midnight Tue–Sun; **€€**), which features a flexible menu with *pintxos*, main meals, homemade desserts and a lively bar at weekends.

What to see and do The self-guided audio tour provided by the tourist office is recommended but, if you choose not to indulge, the following sights can of course be visited without audio accompaniment.

Iglesia Santa María de la Asunción (Church of the Assumption) (Calle Abaroa; ⌚ 08.00–noon & 17.00–19.30 Mon–Fri) Given its monstrous size, you couldn't miss it, even if you wanted to. An information leaflet in English is available in the church, which is open for weekday visits though, as it is staffed by volunteers, this can be somewhat unreliable. Started in the 15th century and finished in the 16th century, the buoyant trade and whaling industry allowed Lekeitio to fund this fairly ostentatious church. The high Gothic-Flemish altarpiece is possibly by Flemish artists, though the creators' actual identities are unknown. After those in Seville and Toledo, it is considered to be the third largest in the whole of Spain. As you enter the church, on your left against the wall is the coffin of one of the town's famous sons, Íñigo de Artieta, a ship-owner, sailor and part-time corsair. The church was extended (the section behind the altarpiece) in the late 1800s, thanks to the generosity of a rich local family who also improved the town's services by introducing street lighting and water provision.

Santa Catalina Lighthouse (On the coast, west of the town centre; ⌚ 11.30, 13.00, 16.30 & 18.00 Wed–Sat, 11.30 & 13.00 Sun; €6/4.50 adults/under 12s & seniors) The first – and only one – of the Spanish Basque coast's 15 lighthouses to be opened to the public, this is an innovative exhibition with audio guides in English provided. Children will particularly enjoy the virtual ride: you are seated in a mocked-up fishing-boat that rocks about as a widescreen video gives the impression of taking you around the coast, encountering dolphins and even surviving a storm (capes are provided – you can get slightly wet!). Tiny tots might be a bit frightened by the storm, however. Back outside, views along the coast are great from this vantage point, and there is a café and a small shop.

Walk along the Lea River A walking path has been developed along the banks of the Lea River, which flows into the sea at Lekeitio. In total the walk is 23km long, ending at Munitibar, a good 8 hours of trekking, but the advantage is that there are several points along the route where you can hop on a bus to return to Lekeitio if you've had enough or the weather turns sour. In summer it can get crowded, but the walk is well marked, the ground is even and there are several villages with

THE LEGEND OF AITXITXA MAKURRA

Due to set sail from Lekeitio harbour one day, the captain of a fishing-boat suffered a heart attack. As he was being attended to, a man dressed in black walked by and instructed one of the crew as to what he had to do to save the captain's life. Following the advice carefully, the man duly saved his skipper. The dark stranger told the captain that he should from now on devote his life to healing the sick … but that he should keep an eye on his roof. If he should ever see grass growing through it, he should say 'goodbye' to his family and make his way down to Isuntza beach. Having lived to the ripe old age of 90, and having spent his days as instructed, tending to the sick, one day the captain saw grass poking through his roof. He bid farewell to his family and went to the beach, where he found the stranger, still in black. He told the captain that he was Death and that the seaman's time had come. Touching him, the captain turned to stone. Now, when Lekeitio suffers from a storm, a large stone appears and the locals say that this is 'Aitxitxa Makurra' – the 'stooped grandfather', the man who Death turned into stone.

restaurants, bus stops and points of interest along the way. The tourist office (page 124) has a map and leaflet which make the walk easy to follow, and they will be happy to help you with planning. As the walk is linear, it makes sense to take the bus from Lekeitio to your chosen starting point then walk back, generally and gently downhill with the flow of the river. Along the way, you'll have the chance to see (2km upriver from Lekeitio) the distinctive coloured boats used in the Goose Festival, the old tidal mill (by the bridge that divides Lekeitio and Mendexa) and perhaps some interesting species of birds and mammals along the way. And even if you don't see or visit any of those, the river valley is nevertheless a beautiful environment for a stroll.

Beaches Lekeitio's beaches have quality certificates and get busy in high season. For watersports, **Ur Lekeitio** (Txatxo Kaia 5, Bajo; ☎ 946 24 35 86; **m** 656 79 96 46; **e** info@urlekeitio.com; **w** urlekeitio.com; 🕘 Apr–Oct 10.30–13.30 & 17.00–20.30 Mon–Fri, 10.00–14.00 & 16.30–20.30 Sat & Sun) is an established company renting kayaks, canoes and stand-up paddles. Their prices vary according to group size.

The nearest beach to town is **Isuntza**, a well-protected wide piece of sand, some of which remains visible at high tide and which curries favour with families. In high season, volunteers are available to assist those with lesser mobility to access the sand. On the other side of the river estuary is another tiny piece of sand.

Also visible from town, **Karraspio** is very much the surfers' choice, though it actually belongs to the neighbouring municipality of Mendexa.

Festivals Taking place on 29 June and the two following days, the festival of **San Pedro (St Peter)** is most famous for the *kaixarranka* dance, unique to the town, when eight sailors hold a wooden chest on which a further seaman dances in honour of St Peter. Inside the chest is kept safe the money of the fishermen's guild, to be passed over from the outgoing to the incoming secretary. The tradition originates from the 15th century, and the festival is made all the more colourful by the local people all donning traditional dress. In the afternoon of 29 June there is more dancing in the square, performed – unusually for the Basque Country – only by the women.

Among the strangest of the Basque festivals, **San Antolines (Goose Festival)** is Lekeitio's big party and a great time to be in town, unless you happen to be a goose. Over 60 numbered boats take part, each one with a crew, of which one member is designated to grab the neck of a dead goose which is suspended over the harbour by a rope. Once he grabs it, he hangs on for dear life, trying to break its neck while a group of men pull the rope up and down, trying to dislodge the man who is entangled with the goose. The winner is the one who breaks the neck, having survived the most number of pulls on the rope. Needless to say, a lot of drinking is involved, too. San Antolines takes place between 1 and 8 September, with the Goose Festival frivolities usually taking place on 5 September.

ONDARROA On the Bizkaia/Gipuzkoa border, this is principally a working town whose energy derives from its industrious fishing-port. Tourist attractions are thin on the ground – the beach most favoured by its inhabitants is actually just across the border in Mutriku – but the fish market can be lively when the boats return. Their catch depends on the season, with anchovies, sardines and many more. A tradition still maintained is that the fleet sound their horns to signify what sort of fish they have caught. In this day of mobile phones, it is all strictly unnecessary but previous attempts to dispense with the custom met with fierce resistance.

Where to eat and drink

Ondarroako Batzokia Artabide 36, Behea; 946 83 26 65; closed Tue, & 2nd half Aug. With views down over the port from on high, a traditional wooden-panelled dining room stuffed with locals, cheap weekday lunch menu & super-fresh fish from the harbour. A great place to nourish yourself if you're in town. €€€

MARKINA-XEMEIN A traditional Basque town, whose claim to fame derives from that most Basque of sports, *pelota*. Less well known, its hermitage is a curious construction.

Where to stay nearby

Hotel Antsotegi (15 rooms) Antsotegi Erota 15, Erxebarria; 946 16 91 00; e antsotegi@antsotegi.com; w antsotegi.com. An interesting building, once a foundry & mill, now restored in wood & stone & put into great use as a smart rural hotel. Run by 3 brothers, whose father was in the first group of Basques to summit Everest, it boasts a popular restaurant, houses a small bar & has ample terrace space for summer use. A number of walking options pass by, right outside. Free Wi-Fi. 1 of the brothers organises a range of outdoor activities, including bungee-jumping. B/fast inc. **€€€**

What to see and do

Ermita de San Miguel de Arretxinaga (Arretxinaga Hiribidea 24; open access, admission free) A six-sided hermitage may be a bit unusual, but you will certainly be more astonished by its contents. At the confluence of two rivers, it seems that this was always a special location, and with the arrival of Christianity in the Basque Country, a hermit duly took up residence on this spot. Nevertheless, it was much later – around 1740 – when this hermitage was actually constructed. The curiosity awaiting those who enter is the presence of three giant stones, each leaning against the other. They are entirely natural, deposited here 40 million years ago, and offer the impression almost of a mini Stonehenge inside a chapel. Well worth the short diversion from the town centre.

Iglesia de Santa Maria de la Asunciôn y Cementerio (Xemein Hiribidea 25; although the church is sometimes closed, the cemetery is accessible) If in town, pop your head into Markina's church, replete with three naves and an impressive altarpiece. The building appears as wide as it is long, but the cemetery next door tells a more interesting story, perhaps. The tradition of burying locals *inside* the church was banned in the early 19th century, but then reintroduced briefly. Around the cemetery is the evidence of the compromise that was reached between those who wanted their dead interred inside and thus honoured, and those who insisted partially on grounds of hygiene on burial outside the building. A mock cloister was constructed, giving shelter to the deceased, and you can still see the graves.

Pilotaren Unibertsitatea (University of Pelota) Not *exactly* a university, yet over 1,000 players of the *festa punta* form of *pelota* have 'graduated' from here to the professional jai-alai circuit in the United States – not bad for a town of 5,000. That US pro circuit collapsed a few years back, but the game and its university are still central to this quiet town. Now, the most important days in Markina's sporting calendar are 16 July and then in December, when finals take place. On other dates, it's certainly worth dropping by to see if anyone's practising this superfast ball game. You might even ask to try your own nascent skills.

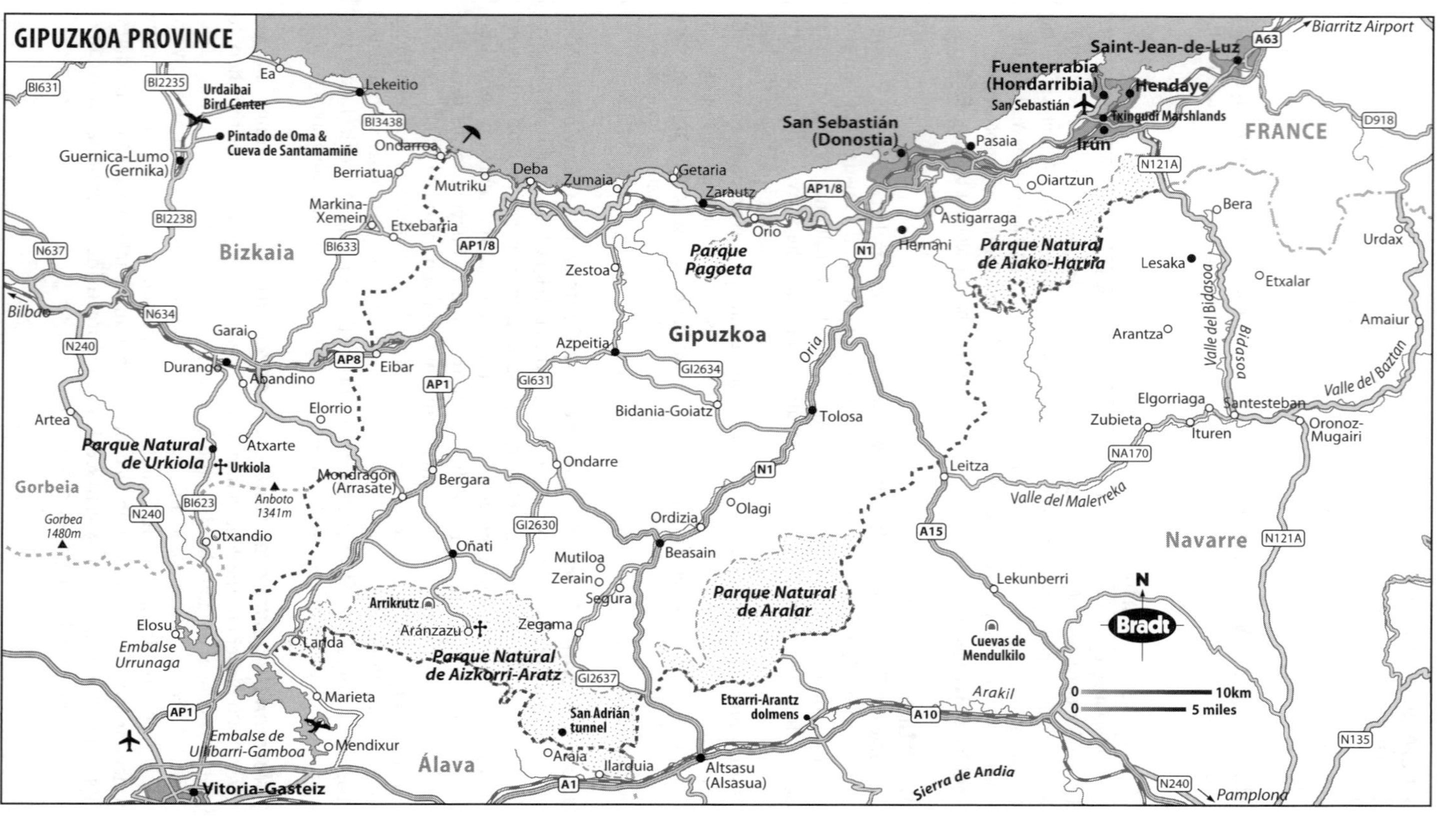
GIPUZKOA PROVINCE
Biarritz Airport
A63
D918
FRANCE
Saint-Jean-de-Luz
Hendaye
Txingudi Marshlands
Fuenterrabia (Hondarribia)
San Sebastián
Irún
N121A
Urdax
Amaiur
Valle del Baztan
Oronoz-Mugairi
Etxalar
Bera
Bidasoa
Santesteban
Valle del Bidasoa
Lesaka
Arantza
Elgorriaga
Ituren
Zubieta
NA170
Navarre
N121A
N135
Pamplona
N240
10km
5 miles
Bradt
N
Valle del Malerreka
Oiartzun
Parque Natural de Aiako-Harria
Pasaia
Astigarraga
Hernani
San Sebastián (Donostia)
Leitza
Lekunberri
A15
Cuevas de Mendukilo
Arakil
A10
Sierra de Andia
N1
AP1/8
Tolosa
Oria
Orio
Zarautz
Getaria
Parque Pagoeta
Gipuzkoa
GI2634
Olagi
Parque Natural de Aralar
Etxarri-Arantz dolmens
Altsasu (Alsasua)
Bidania-Goiatz
Ordizia
Beasain
Zumaia
Zestoa
Azpeitia
Ondarre
Mutiloa
Zerain
Segura
GI2637
San Adrián tunnel
Ilarduia
Araia
A1
Deba
GI631
GI2630
Zegama
Parque Natural de Aizkorri-Aratz
Mutriku
AP1/8
Oñati
Aránzazu
Álava
Lekeitio
BI3438
Ondarroa
Etxebarria
AP1
Bergara
Arrikrutz
Berriatua
Markina-Xemein
BI633
Eibar
AP8
Elorrio
Mondragón (Arrasate)
Landa
Marieta
Mendixur
Ea
Urdaibai Bird Center
Pintado de Oma & Cueva de Santamamiñe
Bizkaia
Abandino
Atxarte
Anboto 1341m
Urkiola
Otxandio
Embalse de Ullibarri-Gamboa
Vitoria-Gasteiz
BI2235
BI2238
Garai
Durango
Parque Natural de Urkiola
BI623
AP1
Guernica-Lumo (Gernika)
N634
N240
Elosu
Embalse Urrunaga
BI631
N637
N240
Artea
Gorbeia
Gorbea 1480m
Bilbao

4

San Sebastián (Donostia) and Gipuzkoa Province

Spain's smallest province, Gipuzkoa, squeezes the most out of its short coastline, green and hilly interior and the rushing rivers that pour down from the mountains to the sea. If 'Basqueness' is measured by language, then Gipuzkoa comfortably carries off the trophy, with nearly half of the 720,000 inhabitants speaking Euskara – a higher percentage than in Bizkaia, Álava, Navarre or anywhere in the French Basque territory.

For first-time visitors, it is the province's capital city that tends to provide the lure for the wider area. If you wanted a shortcut to designing the ideal city, then cloning San Sebastián would be an excellent way to start. Cradled in a perfectly shaped bay, it boasts a quartet of beaches waiting to welcome everyone from lazy sunbather to adrenaline-pumping surfer. Gorgeous stretches of sand right on the doorstep might be enough for some cities to rest on their laurels, but San Sebastián doesn't stop there, comfortably accepting its accolades as a global gastronomic giant and its frequent appearances in most 'world's best cities' lists, and rejoicing in the vibrancy of its festivals, which stretch from the chic internationalism of its annual film festival and its well-established jazz festival to the unbridled raucousness of January's *tamborrada*. And all the while it basks in the elegance of its Belle Époque buildings. Here, above all, is a city seemingly entirely happy in its own skin, and while it is certainly accepting of the many, many visitors who flock here from Spain and further afield, it draws its true strength from simply being a very fine host to its own citizens throughout the year.

It is understandable, then, if first-time visitors to the region refuse to tear themselves away to explore the lesser-known Gipuzkoan hinterland that lies to the south, or to meander along the surrounding coast to find the treasures that lie to the east and west. But treasures there are outside the city boundaries, and taking only a slight diversion from the beaten tracks will reveal them. This is a region of charming coastal resorts on a smaller scale than the provincial capital, natural parks and mountainous terrain, lively markets that have endured for centuries, fiercely preserved festivals and traditions, churches, tower-houses and forts. And almost everywhere visitors can enjoy outstanding gastronomy and characterful lodgings.

Gipuzkoa is not without its scars. Across the centuries, the waters of the province's rivers have been harnessed for power, industries have grown up in the valleys and apartment blocks (too) hastily erected to house the workers. But inland forays will reveal a depth of history, a richness of nature and, most importantly, a strong, unbowed and very-much-alive Basque culture that will be here for centuries to come.

SAN SEBASTIÁN

HISTORY Although human settlement in the area is evidenced from over 20,000 years ago, the documented history of San Sebastián could reasonably be described as 'quiet' until around the Middle Ages. When the Romans arrived in the area, they found this coastal region occupied by the Varduli tribe, but whether these people were of Celtic or Aquitanian origin is not clear.

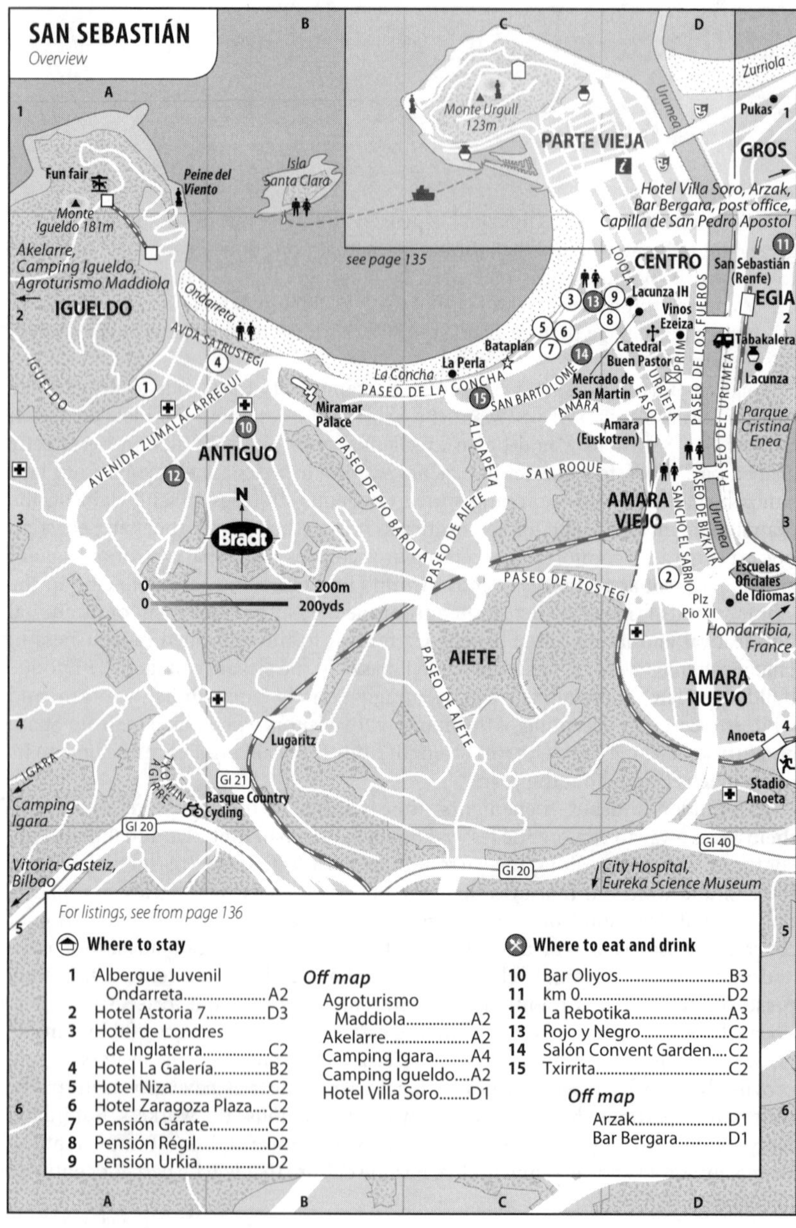

Even at the beginning of the 11th century, San Sebastián – insofar as it then existed – was still merely a monastery with a few surrounding houses, falling under the jurisdiction of Leyre (page 267) in present-day Navarre. The founding of the city really dates to 1180, when Sancho the Wise, the then King of Navarre, granted it its charter and triggered the development of the area now known as the Parte Vieja. (The monastery had been situated across La Concha bay, near the location of today's Miramar Palace.)

But by the year 1200, the area had been vanquished by powerful, expansionist Castile, and Navarre was deprived of its valuable coastal access. The march of the Moors ever northward had caused tensions between Castile and Navarre: as the Castilians were pushed out of their own land, so they sought to gain territory from neighbouring Navarre. It was from the end of the 12th century that San Sebastián had really begun to take shape, with an influx of people from Gascony, in what is now France. The incomers were encouraged to settle in San Sebastián and, as the entrance to the port at Bayonne had been silted up, hindering the inhabitants of that town's maritime exports, they needed little further incentive to relocate to the Gipuzkoan coast, just around the corner. As well as the flourishing commerce, fishing and whaling also became increasingly important during this period, though the town's commercial port would only be constructed in 1450.

A further important influence on San Sebastián's development was its position on the northern route of the Camino de Santiago, which had guaranteed a steady passage of pilgrims through the town since the early Middle Ages, bringing the citizens into contact with foreigners and their diverse ideas. Having lost its route to the sea in 1200, Navarre had peacefully regained it again, from Castile in 1265. As petty family feuds and squabbles erupted into virtual civil war in Bilbao, Bermeo and other towns to the west – a period known as the Bando Gerrak, or War of the Bands – once again, San Sebastián and its inhabitants kept their heads down, historically speaking. When peace finally came to its western neighbours, San Sebastián became part of Gipuzkoa for the first time, rather than Navarre.

Destroyed by a huge fire in 1489, the city was then wisely rebuilt in stone, rather than wood. With the subsequent fall of the independent Kingdom of Navarre in 1512, once again to powerful Castile, newly drawn boundaries put the town perilously close to the front line between Spain and France: the beefed-up city walls built at that time evidenced an expectation of coming wars and instability, from which San Sebastián in its precarious geographical position could no longer hide. King Felipe IV granted it city status in 1662. In ensuing centuries, the town would be conquered by the French in 1721 and 1808, and then besieged, stormed and finally taken in 1813 by a combination of British and Portuguese troops who forced the garrisoned French to surrender. The victors then engaged in a frenzied orgy of pillage and slaughter, culminating in the city being ravaged by a fire that left standing only one street, now named after the date of the assault, 31 de Agosto. The tragedy is still commemorated each year.

The city was then rebuilt from scratch, still within the confines of the existing walls. Although it continued to suffer from the occasional attack during the 19th century, this was the period that would shape the current city. In 1817, the Plaza de la Constitución was built along with other grand edifices such as the (then) city hall, and the previously compact San Sebastián began to expand inland and spread alongside La Concha beach. With the patronage of Queen Isabel II, who visited the city for medical reasons, San Sebastián became fashionable as a destination for the 'who's who' of Spain. In 1854, it assumed the role of Gipuzkoan capital, superseding Tolosa, and nine years later felt confident enough to demolish its city walls and continue its expansion. In the late 19th and early 20th centuries, and with further development of

Parisian-style buildings, the opening of a casino and the considerable ambassadorial campaigning of María Cristina, the King's widow, San Sebastián's status as seaside resort and liberal town of leisure and pleasures was confirmed. Further reinforcement of its new-found desirability came with Spain's neutrality in World War I, with wealthy European citizens looking to invest both time and money in a 'safe' destination away from the conflict. Beautiful, elegant San Sebastián clearly fitted the bill.

San Sebastián's fortunes took a turn for the worse in the Spanish Civil War, with Franco's Nationalists executing hundreds of inhabitants after taking control of the city, the perceived capital of the pro-Republican so-called 'traitor province' of Gipuzkoa. Post-war recession was followed by a period of burgeoning industrial growth and an influx of jobseekers from the rest of Spain, resulting in the erection of suburban housing estates, for better or worse. In recent years, the city has had a good share of makeovers, maintaining its elegant façades and upgrading its tourist services, but above all, providing the infrastructure to complement its setting, allowing the inhabitants to live their day-to-day lives. San Sebastián was given the chance to showcase itself in 2016, when it assumed the role of European Capital of Culture. Since then, visitor numbers have continued to increase.

GETTING THERE AND AWAY

By air The nearest **international airport** is Biarritz, 40km to the northeast, while Bilbao lies 100km to the west (see page 77 for flight and access details). Both of these airports have direct bus links to San Sebastián (Biarritz: see w pesa.net and w alsa.es; 45mins–1hr; €7–10; Bilbao: w pesa.net; departing almost hourly, 75mins; about €17). At the time of writing, **San Sebastián's own airport** (w aena.es) caters only for domestic flights to Madrid and Barcelona, with services provided by Iberia, Vueling and Air Nostrum (for airline details, see page 44). Located some 22km to the east, near Hondarribia, the airport is easily reached from San Sebastián, either by car or by taking the direct hourly E 21, E 20 or E 27 bus service (w ekialdebus.eus; 25mins; €2), which operates between roughly 07.00 and 20.00. Buses leave San Sebastián from the Plaza Gipuzkoa [135 F4], and hours of operation and frequency are more restricted at weekends and on holidays. Full details of all airport bus lines, including services to Irun and Hondarribia, can be found on the San Sebastián airport website.

By car San Sebastián is reached, from west or east, by exiting the E-5 motorway where signposted. From Bilbao, a car journey takes around 70 minutes; from Biarritz, about 45 minutes. To the south, Pamplona is an hour away on the A-15.

By train San Sebastián has two train stations. **RENFE** (w renfe.com), the national Spanish network, operates from the rather scruffy main station [130 D2] on the east side of the Urumea River, with services to major cities such as Madrid (5–7hrs; €50), Barcelona (6hrs; €40) and Pamplona (1hr 45mins; €6), as well as regional trains to nearby inland towns such as Tolosa and Ordizia. (It's also possible to get to Irun, for Hendaye, with RENFE from here, but the services are few and far between compared with those of Euskotren.) From the Estación de Amara, west of the river, [130 D3], **Euskotren** (w euskotren.eus), sometimes referred to as the 'Metro', will take you eastward to Hendaye (30mins; €2.55) or westward to Bilbao (a painful 2hrs 30mins; €6.30). A promised high-speed connection is under construction, due for completion in … well, sometime. For Bilbao, the bus is currently much quicker, although the train is inexpensive and certainly worth considering for reaching interim stops such as Zarautz, Zumaia or Deba. Euskotren trains from San Sebastián to both east and west depart at least every hour.

By bus San Sebastián is now well served from its brand-new bus station, a 'reward' to itself for being crowned European Capital of Culture in 2016. (The predecessor was a rather embarrassing glorified bus stop.) Next to the RENFE train station, the newcomer is hidden underground, with a smart café which offers free, open Wi-Fi. There are frequent services to Bilbao (1hr 20mins; €6.55), Madrid (5hrs 30mins; €35), Pamplona (1hr 10mins; €7.80) and Vitoria-Gasteiz (1hr 15mins; €6), as well as occasionally to international destinations such as London with **Alsa** (w alsa.es). There is also a service to Irun/Hendaye/Saint-Jean-de-Luz/Biarritz and Bayonne) with **Pesa** (w pesa.net) or **Ouibus** (w ouibus.com) to Biarritz Airport (1hr 5mins; €7). If you like really long bus trips, **Bilmanbus** (w bilmanbus.es) can take you to Alicante, plus loads of other far-flung destinations within Spain.

ORIENTATION San Sebastián is arranged in part around the famous La Concha bay, the entrance to which is guarded on its west side by Monte Igueldo and on its east by Monte Urgull. Beneath the latter's steep southern slope is the Parte Vieja, or Old Town, which is separated from the district of Gros and Zurriola beach by the mouth of the Urumea River. In the middle of La Concha bay sits Santa Clara Island, protecting La Concha and Ondarreta beaches from the often wild seas. For most visitors, and certainly for first-timers, a stay in San Sebastián is likely to focus heavily on the Old Town for atmosphere, food, drink and sights, together with time on one or more of the beaches in periods of favourable weather. Gros and Egia, lying east of the river, are both developing as popular alternatives to the Old Town for a good night out. The Centro (Zentroa) district, south of the Old Town, is home to some hotels, pensions and good shopping; as you continue further south, the outlying districts become more residential and hold less of interest for visitors.

GETTING AROUND

On foot Beautiful San Sebastián is begging to be walked around and most visitors will gleefully take the opportunity to do so. Despite hilly surroundings, the centre itself is flat and compact: poking around the Old Town on foot or breathing in the sea air as you stroll along the pedestrianised Paseo de la Concha is your best way of pretending that you're a local. Just don't get knocked over by one of the many cyclists and joggers who use the latter for their morning exercise. In summer, it happens quite frequently to the unsuspecting.

Delightfully, the narrow streets of the Old Town are mainly pedestrianised, encouraging you to zigzag from bar to bar.

By bicycle San Sebastián has around 30km of flattish city cycle paths, while the hilly surroundings can challenge the more ambitious. If you fancy hiring a bike, whether to pedal along the coast or take on a mountain climb, several options are available. Note that some hotels advertise bike hire, too.

Basque Country Cycling [130 A4] Txomin Aguirre Ibilbidea 12; 943 53 71 34; e info@basquecountrycycling.com; w basquecountrycycling.com; 09.30–18.00 Mon–Fri. Not the cheapest, but highly rated BCC rent out top-of-the-range bikes of all styles, together with helmets. They also suggest a variety of cycle routes & offer guided tours. A delivery service is available, so their out-of-town location is not a hindrance.

Bici Rent Donosti [135 G2] Av Zurriola 22; 943 27 11 73; m 639 01 60 13; e info@bicirentdonosti.es; w bicirentdonosti.es. Cheaper than most. Rents out both bicycles & scooters.

DISCOUNT CARDS

For those who intend to make frequent use of the city bus, the **San Sebastián Card** is worth considering. This discount card is valid for ten days and its price of either €9 or €16 includes six or 12 bus journeys as well as numerous discounts in museums, attractions, shops, restaurants, boat trips and on some souvenir merchandise. If you are extending your visit to other towns in Gipuzkoa province, and perhaps travelling to Bilbao or Vitoria-Gasteiz by public transport, the **Basque Card** is another option. Also valid for ten days, this costs either €26 or €41 and offers transport credit of €20/35 respectively on the Dbus, Lurraldebus and Euskotren networks as well as the other discounts mentioned above. The cards can be bought at the tourist office and full details can be found at w sansebastianturismo.com/en/offers.

By bus There is a fairly extensive, efficient and regular network of buses within the city, operated by the company **Dbus** (w dbus.eus), which run from around 07.30 until 22.30. From midnight, the same company operates the appropriately named Gautxori ('Owl') night bus service, which runs until 04.00. The main bus 'hub' is on the Alameda del Boulevard, by the tourist office, with other services departing from the streets nearby. Although the Dbus website is multilingual and comprehensive, it would not win many prizes for being user-friendly. Single-journey tickets can be bought on board and cost €1.75. For journeys to the outlying suburbs, and to towns in the immediate surrounding area and beyond, there are many services operated by **Lurralde Bus** and **Ekialdebus** (w lurraldebus.eus & w ekialdebus.eus, both in Spanish & Basque only). If you're intending to travel around the city and/or the province, consider getting the appropriate card (see box, above).

By taxi Taxis need to be summoned by phone or picked up at one of the 20 taxi ranks around town. Flagging them down on the street is not permitted. All taxis operate with a meter and charges increase between the hours of 22.00 and 06.00. Vehicles suitable for those with limited mobility can be ordered from **Taxidonosti** (☎ 943 46 46 46; w taxidonosti.com, website in English), or **Vallina Teletaxi** (☎ 943 40 40 40).

Car hire All the major rental agencies are represented in the city, including:

Avis Av Pío Baroja 15; ☎ 943 46 15 56; w avis.com

Europcar Plaza Irun 6, Centro Commercial Arco; ☎ 943 32 23 04; w europcar.com

TOURIST INFORMATION The main tourist office [135 E3] (Alameda del Boulevard 8; ☎ 943 48 11 66; e sansebastianturismo@donostia.org; w sansebastianturismo.com; ⊕ summer 09.00–19.00 Mon–Sat, 10.00–14.00 Sun & holidays; there is also a compact, new office beside the bus station; ⊕ 09.00–18.00 Mon–Sat, 10.00–14.00 Sun) is situated just west of the Puente del Kursaal and has efficient, multilingual staff who have maps and endless information to share. They can also book guided walking tours for visitors, cookery courses, cider house visits and other events, either at the office or directly via their website, which is comprehensive, well-maintained and multilingual. If you're in town for a few days, or doing a whirlwind tour of museums, make sure to ask for details of the **San Sebastián Card** (see box, above) and any special offers that coincide with your visit.

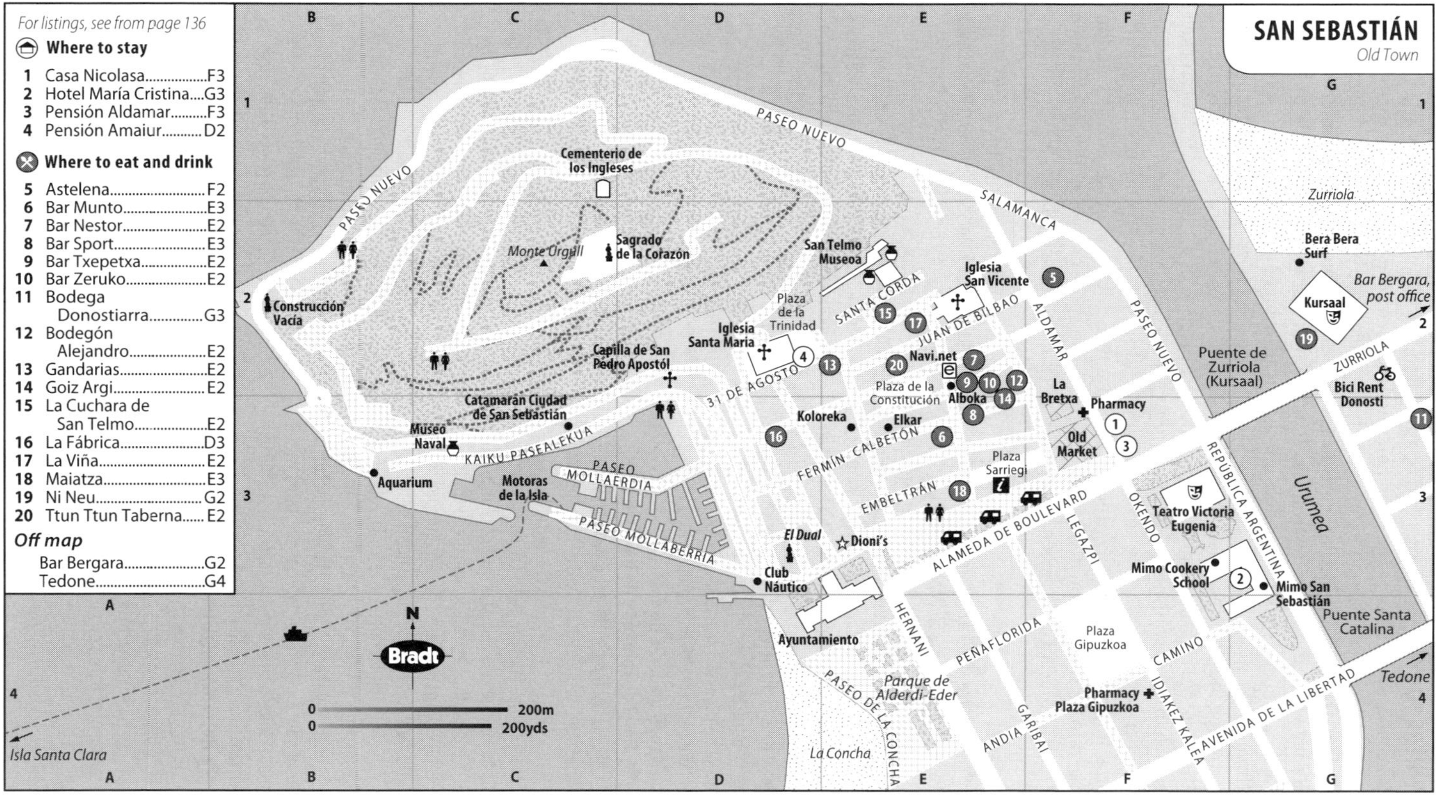

SAN SEBASTIÁN

Old Town

For listings, see from page 136

Where to stay

1 Casa Nicolasa........F3
2 Hotel María Cristina....G3
3 Pensión Aldamar........F3
4 Pensión Amaiur........D2

Where to eat and drink

5 Astelena........F2
6 Bar Munto........E3
7 Bar Nestor........E2
8 Bar Sport........E3
9 Bar Txepetxa........E2
10 Bar Zeruko........E2
11 Bodega Donostiarra........G3
12 Bodegón Alejandro........E2
13 Gandarias........E2
14 Goiz Argi........E2
15 La Cuchara de San Telmo........E2
16 La Fábrica........D3
17 La Viña........E2
18 Maiatza........E3
19 Ni Neu........G2
20 Ttun Ttun Taberna...... E2

Off map

Bar Bergara........G2
Tedone........G4

Paseo Nuevo
Cementerio de los Ingleses
Monte Urgull
Sagrado de la Corazón
Construcción Vacía
Capilla de San Pedro Apostól
Catamarán Ciudad de San Sebastián
Museo Naval
Aquarium
Kaiku Pasealekua
Paseo Mollaerdia
Motoras de la Isla
Paseo Mollaberria
Club Náutico
El Dual
Dioni's
Ayuntamiento
San Telmo Museoa
Plaza de la Trinidad
Iglesia Santa María
Santa Corda
31 de Agosto
Koloreka
Elkar
Fermín Calbetón
Embeltrán
Iglesia San Vicente
Juan de Bilbao
Navi.net
Plaza de la Constitución
Alboka
Aldamar
Salamanca
La Bretxa
Pharmacy
Old Market
Plaza Sarriegi
Alameda de Boulevard
Hernani
Paseo de la Concha
Parque de Alderdi-Eder
La Concha
Peñaflorida
Andia
Garibai
Legazpi
Okendo
Plaza Gipuzkoa
Pharmacy Plaza Gipuzkoa
Idiakez Kalea
Camino
Avenida de la Libertad
Teatro Victoria Eugenia
República Argentina
Mimo Cookery School
Mimo San Sebastián
Puente Santa Catalina
Urumea
Puente de Zurriola (Kursaal)
Zurriola
Bera Bera Surf
Kursaal
Bar Bergara, post office
Bici Rent Donosti
Tedone
Isla Santa Clara
Bradt
N
0 200m
0 200yds

WHERE TO STAY By Basque and Spanish standards, San Sebastián is an expensive place to stay. The full range from parsimonious camping to wallet-emptying luxury is available in and around town, but hotel prices can be gently shocking in high season and eyebrow-raising even in the off-season. During the summer months, Easter week and major festivals such as the film festival, it's advisable to book as far in advance as possible. Prices are significantly higher at these times, sometimes three times more than in the low season. Location is an important factor when choosing lodgings, as noise can be an issue if you are seeking a good night's rest. In the Parte Vieja, which conversely is the best place to be if you don't want to travel far when you've finished a late-night *pintxos* crawl, you may be kept awake by other revellers. Note that many small pensions and hostels in the Old Town are on the first floor or above, often without a lift, so unsuitable for some guests. If you don't need to be right in town, do consider options in some of the smaller inland towns (page 153), especially where there are good public transport links.

Luxury

Akelarre [130 A2] (22 rooms & suites) Paseo Padre Orcalaga 56, Monte Igueldo; 943 311 208; e info@akelarre.net; w akelarre.net. Now vying with the Hotel María Cristina as *the* place to stay, a new boutique hotel in a great location west of the town. Only recently opened, this is a 5-star establishment. Small, exclusive & expensive (at least b/fast is included in the lofty prices!) service is tip-top & the Michelin-star restaurant is a big attraction. Sauna & hammam, fitness centre, indoor pool. Free Wi-Fi. Bedrooms feature great views over the sea. **€€€€€**

Hotel de Londres y de Inglaterra [130 C2] (182 rooms) Zubieta Kalea 2; 943 44 07 70; e reservas@hlondres.com; w hlondres.com. Overlooking La Concha beach, a notch down in luxury & price from the María Cristina (see below). Its advantage over its 5-star rival, of course, is that it overlooks the bay, rather than the river. This century-old *grande dame* has bright rooms & suites with views (city or sea) from balcony or terrace (some with sun-loungers), free Wi-Fi, coffee/tea-making facilities, large TV with international channels, minibar & AC. Hotel facilities include restaurant & old-world-style bar decorated with model ships & huge windows overlooking the bay. Private parking at extra charge. **€€€€€**

Hotel María Cristina [135 G3] (136 rooms) Paseo República Argentina 4; 943 43 76 00; e reservations.hmc@luxurycollection.com; w hotel-mariacristina.com. A grand statement of Belle Époque opulence that oozes period characteristics, while still finding space for top-class facilities & some modern touches. An elegant portrait of Queen María Cristina herself awaits you from behind reception, giving gravitas to this genuine 5-star establishment. Rooms range all the way up to a Royal Suite, but the beds in even the 'ordinary' ones are big enough to get lost in. All rooms come with free Wi-Fi, satellite TV, minibar & AC. Ideal for those without a budgetary limit, including the stars of screen who stay here (& presumably outshine the hotel chandeliers) during the town's annual film festival. **€€€€€**

Upmarket

Casa Nicolasa [135 F3] (11 rooms) Aldamar 4; 943 43 01 43; e pension@pensioncasanicolasa.com. Stylish & high-quality, refurbished décor with bright & spacious rooms. Old Town is just a few steps away, free Wi-Fi, heating, AC, TV & private bathroom. Balcony rooms are extra. Free coffee/tea. In high season, a min booking of 3 or even 4 nights upwards may be required, but excellent prices off-season. **€€€€**

Hotel Astoria 7 [130 D3] (102 rooms) Sagrada Familia 1; 943 44 50 00; e info@astoria7hotel.com; w astoria7hotel.com. Away from the beach & Old Town action, though well connected by bus. A large, new & popular (though, despite its cinema theme, slightly characterless) establishment. Connecting rooms & sofa beds, so a family option. Free Wi-Fi. Fitness room, decent ground-floor cafeteria & restaurant. Sometimes specifies a 2-night min stay at peak times. **€€€€**

Hotel La Galería [130 B2] (23 rooms) Infanta Cristina 1; 943 31 75 59; e hotel@hotellagaleria.com; w hotellagaleria.com. An impressive copy of a 19th-century French building, this is surprisingly good value. 20mins' walk west from the Old Town, this would suit those who seek peace & quiet. Sea-view rooms are €20 extra. Rooms have AC & TV. Free parking, but limited places, so arrive early. **€€€€**

Hotel Niza [130 C2] (40 rooms) Zubieta 56; 943 42 66 63; e reservas@hotelniza.com; w hotelniza.com. Not the plushest option, but it belongs to the Chillida family, so plenty of originals crafted by the famous sculptor are on display. All rooms with private bathrooms, TV & free Wi-Fi. Sea-view rooms lack AC, but just open the window & catch the breeze; street-side rooms do have AC. A room here with a bay view is good value compared with others. The bar/cafeteria needs an upgrade to be of consistent style & standard, but the basement restaurant has a good reputation. **€€€€**

Hotel Villa Soro [130 D1] (25 rooms) Av Ategorrieta 61; 944 58 05 60; e info@villasoro.com; w villasoro.es. An elegant boutique hotel set in 2 classical buildings away from the hustle & bustle but right on a bus route or a mere 15mins' walk from the city centre. Friendly, multilingual staff. Rooms have TV, AC & safe. Free Wi-Fi, free parking (a rare bonus), gym, free bicycles & beach towels. Airport transfers arranged. **€€€€**

Hotel Zaragoza Plaza [130 C2] (29 rooms) Plaza de Zaragoza 3; 943 45 21 03; w hotelzaragozaplaza.com. Good location, a warm welcome, free Wi-Fi, discount parking. Coffee machine in rooms. No fancy frills, sometimes a little overpriced but check the off-season rates. **€€€€**

Mid range

Pensión Aldamar [135 F3] (10 rooms) Calle Aldamar 2; 944 58 03 43; e pension@pensionaldamar.com; w pensionaldamar.com. A welcoming statue in the lobby points you upstairs to a swish, refurbished guesthouse, run efficiently by friendly staff. Under the same ownership as the next-door Casa Nicolasa, though slightly cheaper. Central location. Rooms feature TV, safe, fan, heating & tasteful, Basque-themed artwork. Some have a balcony; all have free Wi-Fi, coffee & tea. B/fast available (extra cost). Ask for a quiet room. **€€€**

Pensión Amaiur [135 D2] (11 rooms) 31 de Agosto 44; 943 42 96 54; e info@pensionamaiur.com; w pensionamaiur.com. This pension is bang in the heart of the action & boasts a wonky staircase that could be disorientating after a few too many wines. Some rooms have balcony, some shared bathrooms; all have TV & free Wi-Fi. Street-side rooms can be noisy in high season, so ask for a room at the back. Different prices reflect different quality of rooms, but this often offers comparatively good value. **€€€**

Pensión Gárate [130 C2] (9 rooms) 1st Floor, San Martín 54; 943 47 36 43; w pensiongarate.com. 5mins' walk away from the Parte Vieja, this is a modernised pension with friendly staff. All rooms have TV & free Wi-Fi; some have AC, some have a balcony. Nicely & recently renovated. Ask for discounts if staying more than 2 nights. **€€€**

Pensión Régil [130 D2] (10 rooms) Easo 9; 943 42 71 43; e pensionregil@pensionregil.com; w pensionregil.com. Not refurbished, so the décor is a little tired, but rooms have TV & private bathrooms. Pleasant management & very good value for its central location. **€€€**

Pensión Urkia [130 D2] (8 rooms) Urbieta 12; 943 42 44 26; e pensionurkia@gmail.com; w pensionurkia.com. All rooms have TV, private bath, microwave, fridge. Some have balcony, but some are interior rooms without much natural light, so ask the right questions when reserving. Free coffee/tea offered. Free Wi-Fi, plus computer for those without a laptop. Off-season, this is one of the cheapest options in town, & way better than acceptable at this price. Despite the lift, it's not suitable for visitors with limited mobility. **€€€**

Budget

Agroturismo Maddiola [130 A2] (6 rooms, 3 apts) m 652 70 31 28; e info@agroturismomaddiola.com; w agroturismomaddiola.com. This beautifully appointed, recently built house on a hilltop is a great option if you don't need to be right in town. Although the bus network doesn't *quite* reach here, phone the owners & they'll come and pick you up. If driving, it's clearly signposted. Free sauna, hot tub, Wi-Fi. Massages available. A roaring fire is a winter bonus. Interesting animals, including alpaca & pot-bellied pigs to entertain youngsters. B/fast available (extra cost). A very popular choice, so book well in advance. **€€**

Shoestring

Albergue Juvenil Ondarreta [130 A2] (96 beds, mainly in dormitories) Paseo Igeldo 25; 943 31 02 68; e ondarreta@donostia.eus. No need to be young, or even a member of the Youth Hostelling Association. In a high-price town, this is a spotless, low-cost, mainly dormitory option, west of centre in Ondarreta district. It is reached by Dbus no 16, which stops right outside. It pulls in a mixture of surfers, passing pilgrims & bargain-hunters. Limited number of family rooms, too. Kitchen facilities. Friendly staff. €

Camping

Camping Igara [130 A4] Camino de Igara; 943 37 42 87; e info@campingigara.com; w campingigara.com. A little bit nearer town than Igueldo, though not serviced by the bus network. Created only in 2014, it has been constantly developed, offering tent pitches, 11 static cabins accommodating 2–6 people, plus facilities for motorhomes & caravans. It has Wi-Fi (payable on-site), restaurant, saunas, hot tub & a large swimming pool. €

Camping Igueldo [130 A2] Paseo Padre Orkolaga 69; 943 21 45 02; e info@campingigueldo.com; w campingigueldo.net. Located about 6km from town, this is a pleasant campsite in leafy surroundings, reached by Dbus no 16 from the city, stopping outside the site (takes 30mins). Supermarket, bar/restaurant, laundry, children's playground, free Wi-Fi throughout. Price include car, caravan/tent with water & electricity. Fully equipped bungalows (2–5 people) also available. Open all year. €

WHERE TO EAT AND DRINK San Sebastián is internationally renowned for its culinary scene, with a plethora of Michelin-star-awarded restaurants. But flexibility is the order of the day here, and if you can't stretch to the big names in top-end cuisine, then there are still endless opportunities to feast on great food. A *pintxo* crawl is a fantastic way of filling up while seeing the Old Town area and drinking in the atmosphere, though your appreciation of the surrounding Neoclassical architecture may diminish as the accompanying *copas* of wine or your other chosen tipple take effect. A staple *pintxo* in town, offered by many bars, is the *gilda*, essentially a simple skewer of anchovy and pepper, bookended by a couple of juicy olives, drenched in olive oil and served on bread. It's not the most artistic or inventive offering in a star-studded culinary cast, but it's delicious and much treasured by the natives. In truth, hunting delicious snacks in San Sebastián is like shooting fish in a bucket, at least in the Old Town area: there's a bar on every corner, and plenty more in-between. For a more relaxed experience than *pintxo* hunting, a sit-down meal in one of the many restaurants rarely disappoints: food is taken seriously here and reputations are dearly cherished. For those on a budget, look out for some cracking lunchtime set menus.

The restaurants that line the harbour area serve up lunchtime *menús del día* for around €20, including wine and bread, but fancier fare is found elsewhere. The fish is no longer landed in the harbour here, but will come from the towns east or west along the coast: the quality, however, will almost invariably be good.

Pintxos

The following are a few of the most celebrated venues in the Old Town & elsewhere, but everyone will find their own favourite so don't hesitate to visit the many others. You can't avoid them!

Bar Bergara [130 D1] General Artetxe 8; 943 27 50 26; w pinchosbergara.es. OK, so it's not a restaurant, but the array of *pintxos* here is so tempting they could easily take the place of a meal. It has a bright, almost garish interior but is in its 3rd generation of family ownership & 1 of the best in the Gros district.

Bar Munto [135 E3] Fermín Calbetón 17. *Bola del mar* or *bola del bosque*? The former is *chipirones* (squid) in ink with a Japanese sauce, the latter a round mushroom ball with mushroom sauce. Plenty of other choices & friendly service. Restaurant on-site as well.

Bar Nestor [135 E2] Pescadería 11. Choice of dishes here is nearly as limited as the number of tables at this family-run, popular spot. To join in with the local ritual, pre-order the *tortilla*. It works like this: first, arrive at 19.30, give the barman your name and tell him you want *tortilla*. Only 16 slices are available. Secondly, make sure you're back at the bar at 20.00, when the *tortilla* is brought in from the kitchen. The barman calls your name and you claim your prize. If you're late, forget it. The *tortilla* is very good, but the procedure is even better. Peppers are also a speciality here.

Bar Oliyos [130 B3] Escolta Real 4. Over in the Antiguo district of the city, with good prices, excellent *pintxos* and a complete lack of pretentiousness. A good choice.

Bar Sport [135 E3] Fermín Calbetón 10. The name is all that is dull about this place, its counter bedecked with mouthwatering temptations that might include foie gras or savoury crepes. Vegetarian options are usually on display, too & everything is served with a bit of tongue-in-cheek mock chaos.

Bar Txepetxa [135 E2] Pescadería 5. How many ways can you serve anchovies? If you like them, this is your little piece of heaven. If you don't, & it's anchovy season, best head elsewhere. Inexpensive & popular.

Bar Zeruko [135 E2] Pescadería 10; 943 42 34 51; closed Sun eve & all day Mon. Innovation at its best, with a great selection of creative, artistic hot & cold *pintxos*. Can't decide? Try the sharing menu for €36. Otherwise it's €2–4 per mini delight, & don't be surprised if someone's *pintxo* choice starts to emit a little smoke – it's all part of the fun.

Bodega Donostiarra [135 G3] Peña y Goñi 13; 943 21 15 59; w bodegadonostiarra.com; 09.30–23.00 Mon–Thu, 09.30–midnight Fri & Sat. A popular place, worth reserving if you can, though many tables are on a first-come, first-served basis, so rock up early at mealtimes. Ask for an Indurain, named in honour of the famous Navarran cyclist (page 65), which is pepper, *bonito* (tuna), anchovy & an olive, or try a freshly made-to-order omelette. Full meals are very good value indeed.

Gandarias [135 E2] 31 de Agosto 23; w restaurantegandarias.com. Takes its wines as seriously as its food – & that's very seriously indeed. Sensational mushrooms in garlic sauce with a slice of *serrano* ham, the *tarta de txangurro* (giant crab tart) & *solomillo* (tenderloin) are equal contenders for the 'tastiest morsel' winner here. Wines by the glass, unusually, include some surprising offerings from South Africa & Mallorca.

Goiz Argi [135 E2] Fermín Calbetón 4. Embracing technology with a large screen outside, showing you the menu then a video of the prep work going on in the kitchen. *Brocheta de gambas* (prawn skewer) is a recommended order here.

km 0 [130 D2] Duque de Mandas 35, Egia; 943 56 17 51; w veganvegetariankm0.com; 10.00–17.00 & 19.00–midnight Tue–Sat, 10.00–17.00 Sun & hols. A rarity: a vegan/vegetarian *pintxos* bar/restaurant in the Basque Country, with gluten-free & organic options, too. In the Egia district, east of the river, the bonus is that the quality is good. Wash it all down with an organic wine or two. Prices are reasonable, the ambience convivial. Half-menus are offered here, too: ideal if you're only half-hungry.

La Cuchara de San Telmo [135 E2] 31 de Agusto 28, off Plaza de Valle Lersundi. A real favourite of many a tourist & local, which means it is often packed. Try to arrive early (around midday or evenings at 17.00) to grab some floor space; otherwise, keep your elbows tucked in. Everything from goat's cheese to duck ravioli & foie gras.

La Rebotika [130 A3] Av Zarautz 6, Antiguo; 943 21 89 06; w larebotika.es; closed Sun pm & all day Mon. For those staying in Antiguo district, this is an excellent choice for grilled specialities, both meals & *pintxos*. Also cocktails.

La Viña [135 E2] 31 de Agosto 3; 943 42 74 95. Much-vaunted cheesecake & delicious *pintxos*, but if you have a bigger appetite that needs satisfying quickly, they also serve seafood & fish *cazuelas* (stews). Popular & lively.

Rojo y Negro [130 C2] San Martzial 52; w barrojoynegro.es. Bright interior with stone walls, good coffee, decent choice of *tortillas* & other *pintxos*, including a *pintxo del día*. Also does main meals. Away from the *parte vieja*, a pleasant place for a relaxing, good-value b/fast.

Cider house

While the spiritual home of the *sagardotegia* (cider house) may be in the nearby towns of Astigarraga & Hernani, there are now a handful in San Sebastián itself.

Txirrita [130 C2] San Bartolomé Kalea 32; 943 46 76 38; w txirritasagardotegia.com; 13.00–15.30 & 20.30–23.00 Tue–Sat. Once a bit rough-&-ready, this dark, atmospheric cellar has now been smartened up to give the full cider-house menu, but also offers a lighter alternative with *pintxos*. A handy alternative if you don't want to travel out to the cider heartland of Astigarraga (page 154). €€€

Restaurants

Arzak [130 D1] Av Alcalde José Elósequi 273; 943 27 84 65; w arzak.info; 13.30–16.30 &

20.45–23.30 Tue–Sat. For many, this will be way above budget. But 3 Michelin stars do not come cheap, nor does being one of the top restaurants in the world. Over 100 years of family ownership, & with one of the region's most celebrated chefs, it has certainly earned its stripes. €€€€€

Bodegón Alejandro [135 E2] Fermín Calbetón 4; 943 42 71 58; w bodegonalejandro.com; 13.00–15.30 & 20.30–22.30 Wed–Sat, 13.00–15.30 Sun. Fine, imaginative Basque dining, towards the top end in quality but not in price, a favourite with locals in the know. Tasting menu available. Immaculate service, too. €€€€

Astelena [135 F2] Euskal Herria 3; 943 42 58 67; w restauranteastelena.com; 13.30–15.00 Tue–Sun, 20.00–23.00 Thu–Sat, closed evening Sun, all day Mon. Don't judge a book by its cover. Viewed from outside, not much would tempt you inside this place. The dining room is functional & smart, the clientele professional & well-heeled. The food is excellent. The *menú trabajo*, available for w/day lunch & evenings Thu, is genuine value for 3 courses & includes wine. Budget? No. Value for money? Definitely. €€€

La Fábrica [135 D3] Puerto 17; 943 43 21 10; w restaurantelafabrica.es; 12.30–16.00 & 19.30–23.30 Mon–Fri, 12.30–16.00 & 20.00–23.00 Sat & Sun. W/day menus are a very good price/quality ratio; tasting menus are available, with or without a drink included. They cater for children too. Good range of choices. €€€

Ni Neu [135 G2] Av de la Zurriola 1; 943 31 00 62; w restaurantenineu.com; 10.00–20.00 Sun, Tue & Wed, 10.00–23.00 Thu–Sat, closed Mon. Excellent, modern restaurant with top-quality food & a reasonable price. Staff are young, polite & efficient. The menus are tremendous value & the atmosphere is often lively. Position yourself strategically to watch the sunset. Vegetarian options available. €€€

Tedone [135 G4] Corta Kalea 10, Gros; 943 27 35 61; w www.tedone.eu; 13.00–15.30 & 20.15–23.00 daily. A vegetarian restaurant with organic ingredients in lively & up-&-coming Gros. Tucked down a side street, it also offers at least 1 fish dish & the occasional meat option, making it ideal for 'mixed' groups. €€€

Salón Convent Garden [130 C2] Manterola Kalea 15; 943 42 95 89; w conventgardensansebastian.com; 13.30–15.30 Tue–Fri, also 19.00–23.00 Thu & Fri, noon–16.00 & 19.00–23.30 Sat, noon–16.00 Sun. Carved out of the crypt that once sat below a former convent, this building now houses 2 characterful dining-rooms & a music venue that hosts events at w/ends. Vegetarian options, exceptional w/day lunchtime value. €€–€€€

Ttun Ttun Taberna [135 E2] San Jerónimo 25; 943 42 68 82; 11.00–02.00 Sun–Thu, 11.00–03.00 Fri & Sat. The service is gruff & the décor super-basic, but this place offers a cheap 3-course *menú del día* in the midst of the Old Town. The price includes a half-bottle of (just) passable house wine. Don't expect fine cuisine & you'll be happy. Popular with local tradesmen. The place for a good-value lunch, rather than a special evening meal. €€

Maiatza [135 E3] Embeltran 1; 943 43 06 00; 09.00–23.00 Sun, 07.30–20.00 Mon–Thu, 07.30–23.30 Fri, 08.30–23.45 Sat. Popular, tiny venue for a b/fast pastry, good coffee, splendid lunch or dinner at very reasonable prices. Cheesecake here is a top pick & the salads are a good choice if you want something between a *pintxo* & a full menu. Open daily with non-stop kitchen service at w/ends from dawn until nearly midnight. Free Wi-Fi. €

NIGHTLIFE For anyone with normal levels of energy, the closure of the *pintxo* bars at around 01.00 will probably be enough. But if you want to party longer, San Sebastián will not bat an eyelid. The venues below should satisfy most people.

☆ **Bataplán** [130 C2] Paseo de la Concha; 943 47 36 01; w bataplandisco.com. This club has survived the vagaries of fashion for 35 years, so it must be good enough. In summer, the outdoor terrace is the place to be seen, & it is frequented by movie stars during the film festival. The support DJs generally kick off around midnight, so don't bet on an early night.

☆ **Dioni's** [135 E3] Igentea 2; 943 42 97 46; w dionisbar.com; noon–03.00 Sun–Thu, noon–04.00 Fri & Sat. On the edge of the Old Town, a gay-friendly lounge with cool music, sofas & decent cocktail choices. Daytime *pintxos* are also worth sampling.

SHOPPING Tacky souvenirs are thankfully thin on the ground in San Sebastián, but there are a number of places where you can find something of some quality to remind you of your stay. For mouthwatering markets, see page 148.

Alboka [135 E2] Plaza de la Constitución 8; 943 42 63 00; w albokaartesania.com; Jul–Sep 10.30–20.30 daily, Oct–Jun 10.30–13.30 & 16.00–20.00 daily. Here's a good place to get something superior to a tacky souvenir. Ceramics, Basque berets, puppets & key rings, all good quality & relatively tasteful, are packed into this outlet on the square. Most of them are made in the Basque regions. Don't mention the word 'souvenir' to the owner, she'll get justifiably upset. These are *handicrafts*. Got it?

Elkar [135 E3] Fermín Calbetón 30; 943 42 26 96; w elkar.com. There are 2 branches of this bookshop on the same street. This one is mostly dedicated to travel, with plenty of local guidebooks, & even some English-language fiction.

Koloreka [135 E3] San Jerónimo 19; m 645 70 35 39; w koloreka.com; Easter–Sep noon–20.00 daily, low season Sat only. Sells some excellent Basque-themed artwork depicting city scenes. There are plans to open every day in low season. Recommended for a pictorial & tasteful souvenir of your visit.

Mimo [135 G3] República Argentina 4; 943 42 11 43. Runs tours & cooking classes (page 143) but, at the front of the Hotel María Cristina, they also operate this gourmet food shop selling fine wines & delicacies in a bright environment.

Vinos Ezeiza [130 D2] Calle Prim 16; 943 46 68 14; w vinosezeiza.com; Jul–Sep 08.30–19.45 Mon–Sat, other months also closes Sat pm. At this established place by the side of the post office, you'll find a €250 bottle of Rioja, but there's plenty of inexpensive options here too, as well as free & friendly expert advice, homemade *patxaran* & cheeses from Idiazábal. Even if you're not buying, poke around the fascinating museum-like interior: this family-run shop's been here for 110 years – as have some of the bottles, perhaps. Staff speak enough English to sell you something.

OTHER PRACTICALITIES

Post office [130 D2] (Calle Urdaneta 7; 08.30–20.30 Mon–Fri, 09.30–13.00 Sat) There's another branch in the Gros neighbourhood [130 D1] (corner of Paseo Colón/Claudio Luzuriaga) with the same opening hours.

Public toilets The city is well equipped with public conveniences. For locations, see map, page 135.

Hospital The city hospital, the Hospital Universitario Donostia [130 D5] (Doktor Begiristain 115 943 00 70 00; w osakidetza.euskadi.net) is located to the south of town.

Pharmacies The **Farmacia Plaza Gipuzkoa** [135 F4] is open 24/7, every day of the year. Other pharmacies can be found at the corner of Calle Mayor and Calle Nagusia, at the side of La Bretxa market [135 F3] and plenty more across the city centre.

Internet/Wi-Fi Many cafés and bars now offer free Wi-Fi, as does the Dbus city bus network. You can also help yourself to 30 minutes' free Wi-Fi in the tourist office and other public buildings, although it is not always reliable. The occasional internet café still exists in the Old Town and elsewhere for those without their own devices, with a dependable outlet being **Navi.net** [135 E2] (close to the corner of Kalea Narrika/Arrandegi; 10.00–22.00 daily).

Foreign newspapers British and many other international newspapers are usually available from the street stall on the corner of Avenida de la Libertad and

Kalea Loiola, sometimes even on the actual day of publication, and also from the large newsagents situated immediately behind La Bretxa, a market turned shopping mall.

ACTIVITIES

Swimming With four beaches, swimming is popular and is a year-round activity, though winter dips are reserved for the very hardy. Conditions vary and it's essential to take your cue from the locals.

Swimming at **Zurriola** [135 G1] increases the chances of getting wiped out by a surfer, and is a no-no in rough weather, while **La Concha** [130 C2] is gently sloping, usually well protected from the waves and thus good for children. Lifeguards are normally on duty from Easter until the end of September and each beach has showers and toilets. Strong swimmers can strike out from **Ondarreta beach** [130 B2] to **Santa Clara Island**, which also hosts beach number four with a seasonal café, visitable in summer and usable only at low tide. Boat trips (see opposite) will ferry less confident swimmers back and forward in season. (See page 151 for more beach details.)

Surfing Whether you're an expert surfer or just a wannabe, the place to head to before catching a wave is Avenida de Zurriola, which runs along the back of **Zurriola beach** [135 G1]. Here you'll find a cluster of surf schools and shops, well established and with all the expertise to advise and make your experience a safe one. Theoretically, surfing takes place all year, but the conditions range from flat-calm to 'beach closed'. If the waves are too big at Zurriola, the schools will walk their clients across the Zurriola (Kursaal) Bridge and enjoy the more protected waters of La Concha [130 C2].

Winter is the favoured surf season for the brave, but there's always the chance the waves will be too high; in summer, when it's warmer, there is a chance of the water being too flat, but this is a popular time for novices. Two of the better-known schools at Zurriola beach are the following:

Bera Bera Surf [135 G2] Zurriola 2; m 662 96 72 76; e surf@berabera.com; w beraberasurf.com. Well established & with good facilities. Open all year – even if the office is closed, they will have something going on.

Pukas [130 D1] Zurriola 24; ☎ 943 32 60 35; e surfeskola@pukassurf.com; w pukassurf.com. Pukas has been making its own boards for 40 years & running schools for over 30. It has a well-stocked shop, equipment hire & lessons.

LANGUAGE SCHOOLS If you need an excuse to extend your stay in San Sebastián, then brushing up on your Basque or Spanish might provide it. Language schools are readily available, some offering homestays and other accommodation options, or even combining language courses with surfing lessons.

Escuelas Oficiales de Idiomas del País Vasco (EOII) [130 D3] Paseo de Bizkaia 22; ☎ 943 28 63 12; e info@eoidonheo.org; w eoidonheo.org. Offering courses in Basque & Spanish in San Sebastián & elsewhere in the Basque Country.

Lacunza IH San Sebastián [130 D2] Camino de Mundaiz 8; ☎ 943 32 66 80; e info@lacunza.com; w lacunza.com. Based next to Cristina Enea Park, this school with 18 classrooms, cinema & library offers lessons in Spanish.

WHAT TO SEE AND DO If you're in the city for three days or more, it's worth considering the San Sebastián Card, saving you money on museum entrance (see box, page 134).

Guided tours

Walking tours For a quick introduction to San Sebastián's many highlights, whether historical or gastronomic, a couple of excellent, bilingual and reasonably priced walking tours around town are available through the tourist office. These generally last a couple of hours, cost from €10 (under 12s free) and run all year long at weekends, daily between May and September. Full details are available on the tourist board website, w sansebastianturismo.com.

Follow Me 943 84 50 03; m 685 75 76 01; w justfollowme.com. A private company whose tours cost more, but whose guides share their in-depth city knowledge with passion – & in excellent English.

Mimo [135 G3] Okendo 1; 943 42 11 43; w mimofood.com; 09.00–18.00 daily. Catering for individuals or groups, this is a high-end operation with super-enthusiastic staff & a great reputation. Offering everything from their gastronomic shop (page 141) through to '*pintxo*-hunting' tours – accompanied by an expert guide – to wine-tasting & cooking masterclasses in a state-of-the-art kitchen in the basement of the Hotel María Cristina [135 G3]. Highly rated, a combination of expertise & fun.

Bus tours San Sebastián's centre is flat and ideal for walking. If you are pushed for time or unable (or simply unwilling) to walk, you can take a bus tour, which comes with multilingual commentary options piped through headphones. You can hop on and off at will, minimising the strain on your shoe leather. The tours are organised by **San Sebastián City Tours** and tickets can be booked online (w sansebastian.city-tour.com; €12/6/free adults /under 12s/under 5s), or enquire via the tourist office. It runs daily in high season; see website for full schedule. The same company also runs a 'mini train' service (€5/3 adults/children), trundling around the city highlights, running daily in high season but only at weekends in low season. See website for full details.

Boat trips As you would expect, San Sebastián makes good use of its seaside location by offering a number of water-based excursions, principally during the summer months (Jun–Oct). A ferry operated by **Motoras de la Isla** (w motorasdelaisla.com; €6.50) operates between the harbour and Santa Clara Island, while **Catamarán Ciudad San Sebastián** runs catamaran cruises from the harbour (m 607 20 11 55; w ciudadsansebastian.com; (spring–autumn; €11).

On the waterfront: San Sebastián's coastline from west to east A walk from west to east along the seafront, starting from Monte Igueldo, promenading along the elegant sweep of La Concha bay, entering the charismatic Old Town from the west and then exiting it to cross the Urumea River to reach Zurriola beach and watch the surfers, would be a wonderful way to experience the best of the city. You could stretch this out over a couple of days to give yourself time to visit the museums listed on page 145. And make sure that you give yourself some downtime in the Old Town itself (page 146) to enjoy the bars and restaurants, blending in with the noisy, chattering throngs of locals. The attractions below are listed in west-to-east order.

Monte Igueldo [130 A2] (At the western end of Ondarreta beach; w monteigueldo.es) Towering above the western end of Ondarreta beach, the summit of Monte Igueldo can either be accessed by the quaint, antiquated funicular railway (€3.15/2.35 return adults/under 7s; 10.00 daily, closing times vary each month – see w monteigueldo.es) that runs up its eastern slope, or on foot/by car, when an entrance fee of €2.30 is charged. The funicular is pure time warp, with wooden seats and rattling carriages. Funicular up and a walk down is a good combination. On a clear day the views from the top are well worth the modest fee; looking down on the town, Santa Clara Island and the beaches, you'll feel you're in an aeroplane. Any reluctant offspring can be tempted by the promise of the seasonal amusement park at the summit. It, too, is a step back in time, with a House of Horrors, dodgem cars and a primitive but hair-raising roller coaster. The panoramas out over the bay and also to the west are exceptional; if you're not already impressed by the city's location before you reach the top of Monte Igueldo, you certainly will be by the time you leave. An ugly, modern hotel at the top only slightly spoils the otherwise olde worlde ambience.

Peine del Viento *(The Wind Comb)* [130 A1] One of Basque sculptor Eduardo Chillida's most renowned works, this city icon can be found beyond the western end of Ondarreta beach. Three steel sculptures are twisted into shapes designed to 'comb' the prevailing wind as it approaches the city from the west. With the sculpture in constant battle with the elements, it may appear from its rusted appearance that the weather is winning, but in fact the pieces were intentionally left outside before even being installed as Chillida wanted nature to 'complete' his masterpiece by weathering it. Each of the three pieces weighs over 13 tonnes. The one facing the rock represents the past, the one facing upwards and out to sea represents the future, and the one you can touch represents the present. In wild weather, a nearby underground tunnel (not part of Chillida's creation) funnels the incoming waves, forcing water upwards through a series of holes in the ground and creating a geyser effect.

Miramar Palace [130 B2] Marking the divide between La Concha and Ondarreta beaches, this was the site of El Antiguo Monastery, which was just about the sum total of San Sebastián back in the 12th century. Miramar was acquired for María Cristina and inaugurated in 1893. Yet it was actually an earlier queen, Isabel II, who first frequented San Sebastián, making it her resort of choice. Isabel had been advised by her medics to visit the north of Spain as she suffered from psoriasis and the learned doctors felt that the waters would be beneficial for her skin. Following the tradition set by Isabel, María Cristina continued to visit San Sebastián as her preferred resort. Old photos show that she would descend from the palace and enter the sea in a wagon, pulled by oxen. Obviously it would be too undignified for the queen to don a swimsuit and be ogled by all and sundry, especially as there was then a prison at the west end of Ondarreta beach. It was said by the locals that only the violent, the dangerous and royalty would swim in the sea. The construction of the palace itself is notable for the use of its brickwork, a distinctly British influence, as well as the ubiquitous local stone. The tunnel underneath the palace gardens was built to accommodate the city tram line and now hosts the main road that runs along the seafront. Nowadays the building itself is home to a music school, but the Miramar Parkea gardens are a public park (🕘 Apr–Sep 08.00–21.00, Oct–Mar 08.00–19.30, daily) as the site was bought by the municipal government in 1972. In the unlikely event that you tire of walking along the seafront between Antiguo and the city centre, there is a parallel road that runs east from the Miramar and which offers good views down over La Concha beach.

Club Náutico [135 D3] Forming part of the sea wall at the eastern end of La Concha beach, and easily identifiable due to its partially successful attempts to look like a ship, the white building in front of the City Hall is San Sebastián's Club

Náutico (Yacht Club). Although a private club, it occasionally hosts summer discos that are open to the public.

Ayuntamiento (City Hall) [135 E4] At the very eastern (Old Town) end of La Concha stands the elegant Belle Époque City Hall, completed in 1887 and built originally as a casino. A 1924 prohibition on gambling thwarted its original purpose. In front of it is the beautiful park of **Alderdi-Eder** designed by the designer of the gardens at Versailles. The stumpy tamarind trees were a present from Napoleon III to the city. When Napoleon chose his Spanish bride-to-be, she agreed to the nuptials on the condition that she could continue to spend her summers in San Sebastián. Realising that it would be unacceptable for a proud Frenchman to leave his native country regularly in this way, instead he scouted France's Atlantic coast and located Biarritz as a San Sebastián lookalike. There he duly built her, in 1854, a fine palace, the Villa Eugenia, now the Hôtel du Palais (page 304), and the couple spent their summers there instead.

El Dual [135 D3] San Sebastián commemorates its victims of the Spanish Civil War with this hole-studded sculpture next to the City Hall. Franco's troops took the city on 13 September 1936. Although an estimated 40,000 inhabitants had fled in the days prior to its capture, recriminations started almost straight away, beginning with executions on the very spot where the memorial now stands. In total, more than 400 citizens were shot in the days, weeks and months that followed.

Capilla de San Pedro Apóstol [130 D2] Along the north side of the fishing harbour, set flush with the multi-storey houses and fish restaurants, is this church, which is used only by fishermen – of which, in San Sebastián, there are now precious few. A plaque on the wall in Basque and Spanish notes that it was here that the first state school of fishing was created in 1912 by the Gipuzkoan Oceanographers' Association.

Museo Naval [135 C3] (Kaiku Pasealekua 24; ☎ 943 43 00 51; w untzimuseoa.eus; ⏲ 10.00–14.00 & 16.00–19.00 Tue–Sat, 11.00–14.00 Sun; €3/1.50/free adults/students & seniors/under 14s, free to all on Thu) Home to many temporary maritime-related exhibitions that change once per year. English-language information is usually now available for the displays, which will always centre on a maritime theme such as whaling or the Basque contribution to the New World, shipwrecks or the changing role of San Sebastián as a port. The aquarium (see below) has displays with English translations that will also give you an overview of the city's many past maritime activities.

Aquarium [135 B3] (Plaza de Carlos Blasco Imaz 1; ☎ 943 44 00 99; w aquariumss.com; ⏲ 1 Oct–Easter 10.00–19.00 Mon–Fri, 10.00–20.00 Sat & Sun, Easter–30 Jun & Sep 10.00–20.00 Mon–Fri, 10.00–21.00 Sat & Sun; Jul & Aug 10.00–21.00 daily; for other months, consult website; €13.00/9.00/free adults/students & seniors/under 4s) With many permanent exhibitions and English-language information boards and audio guides, this is a better bet than the Naval Museum (see above) for anyone wishing to get clued up on the maritime history of the Basques. The exhibition includes a timeline of their seafaring exploits from the 1st to the 21st centuries, including fishing and whaling. It reveals how San Sebastián's harbour – previously known as La Jarana – has declined in importance and its activities have changed from fishing to tourism. Whale-hunting goes back to the 6th century, and the last whale caught off the Basque coast was in distant 1901. Scale models demonstrate the different types of commercial fishing – *seine*, trap, gillnet, etc. Another display covers the story of the emblematic *trainera* rowing regattas, the finals of which are vigorously contested each September in La Concha bay. Female crews have taken part in these important contests since 2008. The last section of the aquarium is the 30 aquatic tanks and walk-through tunnel stuffed with adhesive starfish, huge waving lobsters, menacing sharks and giant rays. This is a great place to take the children if the weather turns bad. Watching the divers feed the sharks and rays (noon Tue, Thu & Sat) is sure to be a highlight. There are panoramic views from the café/restaurant, which can be visited separately from the aquarium.

Monte Urgull and Cementerio de los Ingleses [135 C1/2] (see box, page 148) Monte Urgull on the east side of the bay faces off against Monte Igueldo on the west, with Isla Santa Clara and the often wild ocean in-between. Urgull makes for a pleasant climb and, for extra interest, sports a castle, cemetery and, at the western end of its base, an emblematic sculpture. The hilltop castle, Castillo de la Mota, has existed here in some form or other since the 12th century, but is now fairly unimpressive in its current creation. The ravages of war and weather have claimed its presumably more useful predecessors, which provided some protection from various invaders. The sculpture at the foot of the mount on its western side is the ***Construcción vacía* (*Empty Construction*)** [135 B2] by Jorge de Orteiza, who died aged 94 in 2013 and whose work is also well evidenced in the monastery at Aránzazu (page 162). Also of note here is the Cementerio de los Ingleses, burial ground for British soldiers who perished in the Carlist wars. The cemetery looks more like a rockfall, though the individual burial places are clearly visible, as is a mass grave, above which is proclaimed: 'Honour to those known only to God'.

Old Town (Parte Vieja) Old by name it may be, but the city's so-called Old Town was not the first part to be settled by inhabitants. Until the 12th century, San Sebastián was merely a monastery, standing on the bulge where the Miramar Palace now sits, with only a few primitive dwellings surrounding it. The 'Old' here refers to the part that existed within the city walls before they were demolished in 1863.

Calle 31 de Agosto From the harbour area, you now enter the Old Town area through two gates, marking your arrival into the Parte Vieja itself. This puts you on to 31 de Agosto, the only street to have survived the disastrous fire of 1813. Shortly before reaching the Iglesia Santa María, on your right is one of the Basque Country's famous gastronomic societies (see box, page 60). The name of this one, Gaztelupe, means 'below the castle', a reference to Monte Urgull up above. This street also delights in some of the city's best *pintxos* venues (page 138).

Iglesia Santa María [135 D2] (🕘 10.00–13.30 & 16.00–19.00 daily; €3) The current church is the third to grace this site, the previous ones being victims of the fires that were all too commonplace in the days of wooden constructions. This 18th-century Baroque successor is notable for the ship emblem and the crown that adorn the top of the wall above the main door. The ship represents the Real Compañía Guipuzcoana de Caracas, a hugely significant trading company whose founders gifted the Spanish king a shareholding, in return for which they were granted generous commercial rights. At a certain point in history, the two church towers were under renovation, so the crown and the company's ship emblem were the highest points on the church – pure sacrilege, yet evidence of the extraordinary importance once bestowed on the New World traders. Behind the church is the original square of San Sebastián, Plaza Trinidad, now a five-a-side football pitch next to which is that bastion of Basqueness, the *frontón*, where you will quite often find a couple of youngsters honing their *pelota* skills. This square is also used as a stage for performances during the celebrated Jazzaldia jazz festival, held annually. On the north side of the court, high up in the rock, is the city's most prestigious gastronomic society, the only one to employ a professional chef. Originally part of the castle fortifications, it also once served time as a prison. On the south side of the square, you can see the exposed, distinctive narrow bricks on what is now the oldest house in the city, which escaped the destruction by fire in 1813. With your back to the door of the church, you can look down the long, narrow street towards the Catedral Buen Pastor.

San Telmo Museoa (San Telmo Museum) [135 E2] (Plaza de Zuloaga 1; 943 48 15 80; w santelmomuseoa.eus; 10.00–20.00 Tue–Sun, closed Christmas Day, New Year's Day & 20 Jan; €6/3/free adults/students & seniors/under 18s, free to all on Tue) The structure of this eye-catching museum is a curiosity in itself, with what appears to be a bolt-on extension to the original sandstone edifice, a 16th-century convent. The walls of this new section are made of metal, with small holes drilled in it to let plants grow through the plates, mirroring the natural vegetation on the steep rock behind. Birds also nest between the metal part and the stone walls behind. Since an extensive renovation in 2010, the San Telmo Museum has billed itself as a 'Museum of Basque Society and Citizenship', and lays claim to over 26,000 exhibits. The permanent exhibition is inside the former convent, while the new building hosts temporary displays. Although the information boards are only in Spanish and Basque, the excellent and free English-language audio handsets guide you seamlessly and concisely through the history of the Basque people from the earliest evidence of human habitation until the modern day.

The museum tour starts in the cloisters, where the renovation work uncovered some forgotten wall paintings from the 16th century. These can be seen where the walls join the ceiling. Most of the wall space, however, is now bedecked with giant canvases by the Catalan muralist Josep Maria Sert, commissioned after the conversion of the convent into a museum and depicting some historic achievements of the Basque people, including feats by traders, explorers, shipbuilders and the Jesuits. This part of the museum is equipped with multilingual touch-screen information, though the lighting is poor.

The linear journey through history begins in the next room and continues in a series of further rooms on the ground and first floors. Whaling, fishing, agriculture and rural life are all covered in some detail, as well as music, dance, and rituals surrounding births, marriages and deaths. For many, the most interesting section may be that describing the industrialisation of the Basque Country and the shifting demographics that resulted from it, as well as the impact of the Civil War, the repression of the Basques and increased industrialisation under Franco, and the years since his death.

There are also two rooms dedicated to fine art from the 15th to 19th centuries, with works by El Greco, Rubens and Tintoretto, but also later works by Basque artists such as Oteiza and Chillida.

For anyone interested in Basque history, this museum is a must.

Iglesia San Vicente [135 E2] This was built as both a church and a defensive bastion, as evidenced by the slit windows through which rifles could be fired to repel invaders. It was once part of the city walls, which have long since been dismantled.

A WALK UP MONTE URGULL

You can get spectacular views from Monte Igueldo, at the western end of La Concha bay – and it has the advantage of being accessible by funicular railway. This walk, however, takes you up San Sebastián's other significant bump, Monte Urgull, with views down over the city, along the bay and across to the Isla de Santa Clara. It starts and finishes in the Parte Vieja. Steep at times, it is nevertheless nearly always paved underfoot and therefore fairly easy.

Taking the road marked Plaza de la Trinidad, to the right of the Iglesia Santa María, you then turn left in front of the *pelota* court and proceed up the Pasaia Eugenia Goya. Continue up the steps, turning right in front of the Gastronomiazako Euskal Andre Artea, the only gastronomic society with a professional chef, and continue up the steep road, which will take you – eventually – to the summit of Monte Urgull. You can soon drink in views of the city, both over the Gros area to the east, the Parte Vieja directly below and the suburbs beyond. La Concha and Ondarreta beaches look spectacular on calm and stormy days alike. A few (sadly vandalised) signboards provide some pictorial information on the vegetation around you on Monte Urgull. Continue upwards and the arched interior courtyard of the former convent – now the San Telmo Museum – comes into view immediately below, as does Zurriola beach to the east. You soon reach the Baluarte del Mirador (Mirador Bastion), which you can access by doubling back slightly after going through an archway. From the easternmost point, you can see the tiny figures of the surfers who nearly always frequent Zurriola and appreciate the breakwaters put in place to protect the city from the wild winter waves. Looking now to the south, the distinctive slit windows of the Iglesia de San Vicente can be seen across the square, evidencing its defensive purpose in times gone by. Retracing your

Plaza de la Constitución [135 E3] At one end of the Plaza de la Constitución is the **old city hall**, in use as such until the 1940s and one of the first buildings to be rebuilt after the 1813 fire. Neoclassical in style, it features imposing Corinthian columns. The most notable features of the square are the **numbered apartments** on the other three sides. Each apartment is two windows wide and the square was used for public events such as dances and bullfights. Ordinary citizens would go to the city hall and apply for a ticket that would give them access to watch the chosen event from inside the private apartment to which their ticket number corresponded. No fee was charged for this, though the spectators would perhaps bring food for their hosts, who would watch from one window while their 'guests' would watch from the other.

La Bretxa and the Old Market [135 F3] (Bd Zumardia; ⌚ 08.00–21.00 Mon–Sat) It's ironic that in a town filled with high-quality fast food – you never wait long for a *pintxo* – the only branch of a well-known hamburger chain should be slotted shamefully into San Sebastián's former market building. Facing on to the Alameda del Boulevard, the other occupants of the handsome *mercado* building are fashion chains of no particular interest for visitors. All is not lost, however, for those in search of something more authentic: directly behind the *mercado* is the old fish market building, and descending into the basement will bring you to a host of fish stalls, butchers, fruit and veg vendors and the chance to buy some local products such as cider and honey. The upstairs space is currently not put to great use, but down in the basement is the old market clock, with English-language signage

steps, you briefly continue around the circumference of the hill before doubling back after 50m, following the signpost for the Batería del Gobernador. At the next corner take the right-hand fork, continuing upwards. Reaching the Batería del Gobernador (Governor's Battery) you are rewarded with another signboard. Take the steps up to the right towards the castle. While unexceptional in itself, it was clearly of enormous strategic importance. A few cannons remain and the structure is intact. At the top, a new exhibition is being created with photographs and audio-visual displays. After admiring the statue of Jesus – which does not really compare at close quarters with the one in Rio de Janeiro, whatever people might try to tell you – you can now proceed out of the north side down some rather uneven steps, then join the tarmac heading downward and eastward, with the sea now temporarily on your left side. After a few hundred metres, you come to the sign for the Cementerio de los Ingleses (English Cemetery). You can now retrace your steps, following the signs for Batería de las Damas (Ladies' Battery), which allows you great views over the mouth of the bay to Monte Igueldo. Shortly afterwards, a bend in the road leads you to a flat area where you can see the battering that the northern side of the Isla de Santa Clara takes from the sea: it does a good job in protecting La Concha beach from the worst of the weather.

Choosing to complete your circuit at high level, you ignore the sign 'Salida Paseo Nuevo', which leads downward, and you can now look down on the aquarium, leisure port and former fishing harbour. Continuing above the harbour and ignoring the steep steps down, the road will return you gently to the Calle de Nuestra Señora del Coro, entering the Parte Vieja on the western side of the Iglesia de Santa María where you began.

explaining how, in times gone by, fish was bid for in a kind of auction. The market used to form part of the city walls, and its name, La Bretxa (The Breach), refers to it being the spot where troops broke through in one of the many city sieges. Outside, on the western side of the building, is a statue of a drummer with the words of San Sebastián's song, exhorting the citizens to overcome the disasters that have befallen them over the years, composed by local musician Raimundo Sarriegi Etxeberria.

Beyond the Old Town: eastward along the seafront If you wish to continue the walk towards the east after exiting the Old Town, there are three points of interest – one west of, one east of and one over the Urumea River, before you reach the waves of Zurriola beach.

Teatro Victoria Eugenia [135 F3] (Paseo República Argentina 2) Generally only viewable from the outside, unless you're going to a show, the interior is spectacular if you get a chance to peek inside this 900-seater auditorium. Built in 1912, this was the venue for the city's renowned film festival before the construction of the Kursaal across the river.

Puente de Zurriola (Zurriola Bridge) [135 G2] Also referred to as the Kursaal Bridge, this bridge spanning the Urumea River is an ornate, early 20th-century creation, with the Victoria Eugenia Theatre at its western end and the Kursaal to the east. Being the bridge nearest to the sea, it takes quite a battering when the waves are high, and this has resulted in it being strengthened since its original construction in

1915. In times of bad weather, it can even be closed to pedestrians and traffic. The lighthouse-like street lamps add some quirky character.

Kursaal [135 G2] The Kursaal is one current venue for the San Sebastián film festival, which it now shares with the rejuvenated Tabakalera (see below). It draws the beautiful people to town as one of the main events in the city's calendar. Constructed after full consultation with the citizens of the city, it is said that the negative feedback received for its radical design was then roundly ignored. That said, the rather austere building has now become accepted by the townsfolk. Viewable from the outside, or inside if you're attending an event.

Beyond the Old Town: away from the seafront After exiting the Old Town, you could take a break from the shore to head briefly inland to the city's 'new' cathedral, before crossing the river via the María Cristina Bridge to find some green space and the new cultural centre.

Mercado de San Martin (San Martín Market) [130 D2] (Urbieta 9; ⌚ 08.00–20.00 Mon–Sat) Is it a market, or is it an early-evening nightspot? Depends on when you visit. In the large building which houses some chain stores lurks a bustling morning market. But visit on a Thursday evening from 19.00 to 22.00 and you'll find stallholders turned *pintxo*-makers, the whole event usually accompanied by live music. All the culinary delicacies on offer at that time are made in-house and offered with a drink for €2.50 – they call it '*gastro pote*'. This is where the locals come to avoid the touristy *parte vieja*. All very civilised, all a lot of fun.

Catedral Buen Pastor (Cathedral of the Good Shepherd) [130 D2] (⌚ 08.00–12.30 & 17.00–20.00 daily; admission free) Just about visible from the main door of the Iglesia Santa María (page 146), the cathedral's location was chosen to provide a visual link between the old and new town churches. This Neo-Gothic sandstone church was consecrated in 1897 after nearly a decade of construction. Built to meet the needs of the town as it expanded rapidly outside the former walled area, this is the largest in Gipuzkoa and can accommodate 4,000 people. The church organ is the biggest ever built in Spain – it has nearly 10,000 pipes.

Parque Cristina Enea [130 D2] (Paseo del Duque de Mandas 66; ☎ 943 45 35 28; **w** cristinaenea.eus; ⌚ summer 08.00–21.00, winter 08.00–19.00 daily; admission free) If you're looking for a green space away from the sea, you can thank the Duque (Duke) de Mandas, who donated this park (and his library of nearly 20,000 books) to the municipality. It has a wide variety of trees and plants and many locals enjoy a Sunday morning stroll here, admiring the water features and the small population of strutting peacocks. The highest point of the park does not provide the panoramic views you might expect, but the renovated palace on the summit is home to the Cristina Enea Foundation, which holds temporary exhibitions on the theme of environmental protection.

Tabakalera [130 D2] (Paseo del Duque de Mandas 52; ☎ 943 01 13 11; **w** tabakalera.eu; free admission to building, cost of performances/films, etc, varies) San Sebastián's former cigarette factory is now being put to healthier use, reopening in 2016 as the International Contemporary Cultural Centre. Its English-language website allows you to view the range of performances, films and exhibitions should you fancy some culture time. Even if you're not attending an event, take advantage of the relaxed ambience and take the lift to the top floor for a great view of the city (less strenuous than climbing Monte Urgull or Igueldo). Then take the stairs down, perhaps stumbling across a fashion show or workshop, maybe even some live music on one of the floors. At the bottom, a chic café awaits. The content is still developing and the focus is perhaps on locals, but it is certainly worth a visit. Parts of the city's film festival have now moved here and a number of cultural institutions have relocated.

Beyond the Old Town: further afield

Eureka! Zientzia Museoa (Eureka Museum of Science) [130 D5] (Paseo Mikeletegi 43; 943 01 24 78; w eurekamuseoa.es; see website for opening hours, which vary according to season, closed Christmas Day & New Year's Day; €10/€7 adults/students & seniors, under 4s free; some exhibits cost extra; south of the city centre, take bus 28, 31 or 35 – ask the driver for the Polyclínica stop, after which it's a 2min walk) With a planetarium plus flight, roller coaster and F1 car simulators among the many interactive displays, this is a museum orientated towards younger visitors. There is multilingual signage in the museum itself, but the planetarium shows tend to be either in Spanish or Basque. In recent times, a new *Animalia* section has been created, focusing on animals and their ecosystems. The museum is well laid out and, while it is no different from many other science museums across the globe, it would probably entertain children for a couple of hours on a wet afternoon.

Beaches

La Concha [130 C2] San Sebastián's sandy icon is the best known of its beaches, and it still enjoys some vestiges of its Belle Époque cachet. The beach slopes gently, and in most weathers it is a very safe place to swim. Its wide stretch of sand disappears completely at high tide. In the middle is the **La Perla** spa (943 45 88 56; w la-perla.net), much used year-round and open to all. It contains a gym, a pool with a variety of water jets and offers various massages and treatments, as well as having a restaurant. In summer, you will see the *toldos*, wooden poles driven into plots of sand just to the east of La Perla and covered with a cloth roof and walls to form beach tents. These tiny patches of sand are in great demand by locals, but to secure one they have to enter a ballot through the city hall and if they're lucky the plot will be theirs for the season. The overall area allocated to this system has decreased over the years, and there is an air of exclusivity about La Concha as a result. Standing on the beach in front of La Perla spa, notice the metal fixings on either side of the ground-floor windows. These are where boards are slotted in to protect the windows from the waves in stormy conditions. A few metres to the west is another ornate building on the beach, seemingly mimicking La Perla, but on a smaller scale. This is a private, male-only swimming club. In the centre of the building, at the top, are the emblems of the united Spain: the lions of León, the castle of Castile, the chains of Navarre and the vertical stripes for Catalonia and Aragón.

Ondarreta [130 B2] Frequently less busy than its famous neighbour, Ondarreta has an altogether more neighbourhood feel to it. More steeply sloping, it is nearer to Santa Clara Island, a popular target for strong swimmers in good conditions. Even in winter and at high tide there is always some sand on Ondarreta left uncovered by the sea, unlike La Concha.

Zurriola [135 G1] This beach is a surfers' heaven at the city's eastern end. Arrive here on almost any day and there will be a steady stream of surfers proceeding like

SAN SEBASTIÁN FESTIVALS

San Sebastián steps up a gear during its many festivals, moving seamlessly from leisure town to hedonistic frenzy. The main events are outlined below, but there is nearly always something happening and the tourist office website is well worth monitoring in the run-up to your visit. The **Tamborrada** takes place every year on 20 January and is definitely not a time for those seeking the quiet life, with the streets awash with citizens dressed as chefs and soldiers furiously beating on their barrel drums. The tradition may have originated from the townsfolk mocking the retreating French soldiers (who were defeated in the city in 1813) by banging on pans with sticks and spoons, but no-one can be absolutely sure. Nowadays, the festival is driven by the energy of local gastronomic societies and social clubs, plus thousands of costumed children who set off at noon from the city hall, banging their own drums. The **Caldereros ('Boilermakers') Festival** takes its origins from the visit of a Hungarian carnival group back in 1884. Its success has waxed and waned ever since (and it was banned in the late 1960s for political reasons), but the event is now firmly fixed in the calendar for the first Saturday in February. Immediately following this comes **Iñudes and Artzaiak**, which began in 1885 and relates loosely to the religious festival of the Día de la Candelaria (Candlemas), with much dressing up as shepherds and nursemaids, waving of baby dolls, music and dancing. The **San Sebastián Jazz Festival** (or 'Jazzaldia') has been going for over 50 years now, with performances taking place all over the city, notably in the tiny Plaza Trinidad in the Old Town, at the *Peine del Viento* sculpture and also on the beach at Zurriola. It is held every July and some of the events are free.

Semana Grande ('Big Week' – the clue is in the title) always starts and ends on a Saturday and its eight days of fun always include 15 August, the Feast of the Assumption. Its history tracks back to the mid-19th century, when it was created to coincide with the city's emergence as a resort. As well as theatre and musical performances, highlights include a funfair and an international fireworks competition.

The second and third Sundays of September see the finals of the ***traineras***, the rowing regattas that set off from La Concha beach. The best eight teams from along the coast fiercely contest these much-loved events, with each club bringing its own band and displaying its own team colours.

More refined than most of the above is the **San Sebastián Film Festival**, established in 1953. Celeb-spotting is a sport in itself at this September event and actors who have graced the festival in years gone by include Orson Welles, Elizabeth Taylor, Harrison Ford, Matt Damon and Sophia Loren, as well as directors such as Luis Buñuel, Pedro Almodóvar and Francis Ford Coppola. The event is now staged primarily in the Kursaal, though part of it has since relocated to the revamped Tabakalera (page 150).

Near the end of the year comes the fair of **Santo Tomás**, a centuries-old event famed for the *txistorra*, a type of spicy sausage. Much, though by no means all, of the action takes place in the Plaza de la Constitución, where societies and schools set up stalls to sell *pintxos*, *talos* and *txistorra*-based treats. Santo Tomás takes place on 21 December. A pig is fatted for months prior to the fair and presented to the winner of a public raffle, the highlight of the event.

ants to and from the water. Behind, on Avenida de Zurriola, are the surf schools and shops that nurture them.

Isla Santa Clara (Santa Clara Island) [130 B1] Home to a tiny stretch of sand – the only south-facing one on the entire Basque coast – Santa Clara is reachable in summer by swimmers or via the boats that depart from the city harbour (page 143). In high season, the intrepid are rewarded by the presence of a beach bar and reassuring lifeguards. If you still have energy left after your swim, the hilltop has picnic tables. Santa Clara's main function is to act as an inadvertent buffer to the fierce waves sweeping in from the northwest.

San Sebastian: other city districts

Gros [130 D1] Originally an area of small workshops and craftsmen, in more recent times the Gros area has undergone development and is now trendy and fashionable. Down the main Gran Vía, which arrives at the beach about halfway along the Paseo de Zurriola, there are a variety of unexceptional shops servicing the surrounding apartment blocks. Although largely residential and commercial, it can provide some respite for bar-crawlers when the Parte Vieja is too rammed with revellers. However, even here can get busy during peak season. For the finest watering holes, the cross-streets of Gran Vía – particularly the eastern end of Zabaleta – are the best bet and on Thursday, many of these are willing participants in the *pintxo pote* scheme (page 61), where a snack and drink can be secured for a painless €2.50. The western end of Gros (nearer the river) has more upmarket bars, with more elaborate *pintxos*, but they are not usually part of *pintxo pote*: a few of these can be found in the *Where to eat and drink* listings on page 138.

Antiguo [130 B3] Unlike the Parte Vieja, Antiguo is the real deal when it comes to being genuinely old. A 15-minute walk west of the town centre, it was here that the monastery of San Sebastián el Antiguo ('the Old') was located in the 12th century, though not much evidence of an ancient settlement can be found today. Industry was developed here in the mid-19th century, but nowadays the area is a hotchpotch of commerce and residential buildings, without any real tourist interest. If you're looking for an authentic bar in this part of town, try **Bar Oliyos** (page 139).

Centro (Zentroa) [130 D2] On the west side of the Urumea River, just south of the tourist office, this is a commercial district where shoppers will bump into familiar retail names. As part of the urban expansion after the city walls came down, it's not as claustrophobic as the Parte Vieja, but has less character: a pleasant enough place for a stroll, or to visit the San Martín Market.

INLAND FROM SAN SEBASTIÁN

Much as you may probably have fallen in love with the city after a few days, dragging yourself off San Sebastián's beach or out of the *pintxos* bars will bring its own rewards. Climb in the car or hop on a bus or train and head into the interior of Gipuzkoa with its valleys of rivers descending from the mountains of Aralar and Aizkorri to the south. For some visitors, a minor shock or two is in store before they find the real attractions of Gipuzkoa's hinterland. The Oria River, which stretches from the border with Álava to Orio on the coast, has the noisy neighbour of the busy N-1 motorway for company. A curious mixture of still thriving industry and lush green mountains, the valley is a bit despoiled by development that took place in the latter part of the

20th century. Close to the road, four-storey apartment blocks thrust themselves skywards in places where you might reasonably be expecting quaint cottages and peaceful villages. While initially unattractive, the further south you go, the more rural the setting becomes. Industry disappears in favour of more pastoral activities. Moving west, the rivers of first Urola and then Deba are the other two watercourses that divide up the Gipuzkoan mountain ranges. Such divisions traditionally resulted in limited communications and linguistic differences between the inhabitants of one valley and the next. This historic sense of isolation has been considerably alleviated by improved east-to-west roads and modern transport. The following trip starts south from San Sebastián, picking out the major points of interest, moving west and looping back to the city. In a car, in a couple of days, you could visit most of the sights described here, but although distances are not severe, the roads further inland are more challenging and a more leisurely approach is recommended.

ASTIGARRAGA AND THE ORIA VALLEY An interesting inland excursion could begin with a cider-house visit, before joining the Oria Valley and heading upstream to take in quirky Tolosa and the venerated market at Ordizia, before entering Goierri and the upper river valley.

Getting there and away

By train Trains from San Sebastián's RENFE station (page 132) will take you to either Tolosa (5 per day; 20mins; €4), or Ordizia (4 per day; 35mins; €5).

By car Astigarraga is 15 minutes south of San Sebastián on the GI-41, Tolosa is reached in 30 minutes via the A-1 or A-1/A-15 and Ordizia in 10 minutes more, by the same routes.

By bus The A1 and A2 buses regularly link San Sebastián to Astigarraga (w autobusesareizaga.com; 20mins; €3). For Tolosa or Ordizia, buses connect frequently to San Sebastián (w lurraldebus.eus or w pesa.net; 30mins & 55mins; €2.50 & €4.50 respectively), and Bilbao (2hrs 15mins & 2hrs; €12.30 and €9.15 respectively).

Astigarraga If you're a fan of cider or simply want to begin to understand the importance of the drink to local culture, a visit to the capital of Basque cider just south of San Sebastián should satisfy both your thirst and your curiosity (and if you want to indulge in more than one glass, the frequent Lurraldebus service A1 or A2 from Calle Okendo in San Sebastián takes about 20 minutes to reach the town). Astigarraga is a small town with 19 *sagardotegiak* – cider-houses – and also home to a cider museum. You can arrange a 'package' involving a museum visit and a meal at one of the cider-houses either through the tourist office in San Sebastián or directly via the museum. The town celebrates its favourite tipple each year with a full-blown festival on St Anne's feast day, 26 July, while the last Sunday in September is reserved for the harvest festival. The Sagardo Berriaren Eguna, or 'new cider day', is another (this time, private) party held in mid-January. Some traditionalists claim that Astigarraga has become a bit too commercialised in recent years, selling its soul and losing its connection with the very essence of what the cider-houses were all about: a meeting place where good conversation would flow more than the cider itself. Stag parties at the wrong end of the boisterous scale can occasionally mar the enjoyment, so for a more authentic experience you could try a lunchtime visit or somewhere a bit more family friendly, where the behaviour of the customers is still respectful of the traditions. The website w sagardoarenlurraldea.eus advises on which cider-houses offer children's menus, giving a clue as to where might suit your needs (see box, below). The nearby town of Hernani is also known for its cider-houses.

Sagardoetxea (Basque Cider Museum) (Kale Nagusia 48; ☎ 943 55 05 75; e info@sagardoarenlurraldea.eus; w sagardoarenlurraldea.eus; ⌚ summer 11.00–13.30 & 16.00–19.30 Tue–Sat, 11.00–13.30 Sun & holidays; €4/2/free adults/under 17s/under 9s; visit is by self-guided or guided tour, including a tasting; although the enthusiastic staff will always try to oblige with a tour, calling in advance is advisable; tickets can be booked online) The Cider Museum is modern and takes you through the history of the drink, annual apple and cider cycle, the various types of apple and the town's inevitable associated parties. Once carried on Basque ships and quaffed by sailors to fight off scurvy, in recent years cider has gained a bit of cachet and become popular in restaurants. Apple growers in Astigarraga jealously guard their secrets: you won't find the variety of the fruit stated on the bottle labels!

Tolosa Once the capital of Gipuzkoa, Tolosa's top status derived from it being at the confluence of the main routes from France, Navarre and Castile. However, once the Spanish royalty discovered sea bathing in the 19th century and started to favour San Sebastián as a result, Tolosa's importance began to wane and its exalted status was lost. In those days, the locals profited to the max by levying tolls on anyone passing through; nowadays, visitors to town encounter no such hardship, but can instead wander the attractive Old Town with its churches and palaces, take a tour around the puppet museum, visit the markets or eat like a local – which is eating very well indeed. In a town of only 19,000 inhabitants, there are around 40 gastronomic societies and, while these are private, they are evidence of the importance of food in these parts. For market-lovers, a Saturday trip to Tolosa provides rich rewards, with three to choose from.

Tolosa's **carnival** is its biggest annual bash, held a week before Ash Wednesday. Beware: if you're in town that day, make sure that you're in fancy dress, because they take their fun seriously here and someone may well plonk a silly hat on your

BASQUE CIDER-HOUSES

When you hear the call '*txotx*' (pronounced 'chotch') today in the cider-house, it's an invitation to all diners to come and refill their glasses. While you stand a few feet away, glass tilted at a 45-degree angle, your host turns on the tap fixed to the giant wooden barrel which contains hundreds of litres of the revered apple nectar. With a bit of luck, some of the stream that squirts from the tap will land in your glass. And hopefully, your feet will stay dry. Protocol dictates that only about two centimetres of cider is taken at a time: more than that and the delicate aromas are lost in the glass and the experience diminished. Not to worry, as another cry of '*txotx*' will not be far away.

Before the age of the tap, wooden 'toothpicks' known as '*txotxa*' were inserted into the barrel and when you fancied a drink, you simply pulled out your *txotxa* and out flowed the liquid. Nowadays, in-between filling your boots (almost literally, if your host's aim is poor), you tuck into the standard cider-house menu, consisting of cod *tortilla*, followed by fried cod with peppers, then a generous helping of *chuletón* (beef chop) and cheese with walnuts and quince jelly. If you stay sober long enough, you should be able to discern the subtle differences between the various ciders on offer.

head. Capturing that sense of frivolity on a weekly basis, townsfolk gather every last Saturday of each month to sing traditional Basque songs in a thoroughfare whose nickname translates as 'silly street'. To join in, or more likely just to listen, be at the corner of Arostegieta Kalea and María Luisa Aguirre Plaza at high noon.

Tourist information The tourist office (Plaza de Santa María 1; 943 69 74 13; w tolosaldea.eus; Easter, Jul & Aug 10.00–14.00 & 15.00–19.00 daily, rest of the year 11.00–14.00 & 16.00–18.00 Tue–Sat, 10.00–14.00 Sun) has a multilingual website, helpful staff and brochures. There is English-language information on the town's markets, sculptures and monuments. It also organises guided tours (see below).

Where to stay Tolosa offers surprisingly thin pickings on the accommodation front, so better to get out of town to find something acceptable.

Hotel Iriarte Jauregia (19 rooms) Eliz Bailara 8, Bidania-Goiatz; 943 68 12 34; e info@iriartejauregia.com; w iriartejauregia.com. An elegant & tasteful mansion-style hotel that is well worth the 11km drive west of Tolosa. A restored 17th-century palace, the hotel & its beautiful gardens enjoy an elevated position. Rooms have TV, A/C, heating & free Wi-Fi. English-speaking hosts & friendly & attentive staff. The Bailara restaurant has a deserved top-drawer reputation, gained from its short fine dining menu & respectful service. The only problem might be finding it: signposted off the GI-2634, in the village of Bidania-Goiatz, between Tolosa & Azpeitia. **€€€€**

Casa Rural Korteta (6 rooms) Barrio San Esteban 70; m 639 48 98 33; e info@agroturismokorteta.com; w agroturismokorteta.com. Pleasant rural house just 3km west of Tolosa, built from traditional stone & wood. Large rooms, central heating. Good-value, well-priced b/fast. Use of kitchen at small extra cost. Free parking & Wi-Fi. May stipulate a min stay in high season. **€€**

Where to eat and drink

Casa Julián Santa Clara 6, Tolosa; 943 67 14 17; w casajulianmg.com; 13.15–15.30 Sun–Thu, 13.15–15.30 & 20.45–22.30 Fri & Sat. An atmospheric place to try *chuletón* (beef chop), accompanied by peppers & all cooked to perfection on an open fire right in front of you. The menu consists of 5 pages of wines & half a page of food. Basically, it's *chuletón* or nothing. There are no vegetarian options here, but it's a carnival for carnivores. The atmosphere verges on the boisterous. The owner himself can often be found smoking a fat Cuban cigar in the lobby. Recommended. **€€€€**

What to see and do

Guided tours Recommended guided tours of the old quarter are available all year, but you should give at least 24 hours' notice to secure one in English. Tours cost a bargain €3 and last about an hour. Full details can be found on the town's tourist office website (see above).

Markets Saturday's markets take place between 08.30 and 13.30, so arrive early to see them at their best. The **Zerkausia** market next to the river is the most traditional, with high-quality seasonal products brought in by local farmers, perhaps the best place to pick up some of the region's famous *alubia* beans, cheese, honey or cider, plus excellent bread. In one corner, a busy stall cooks up a very limited selection of excellent, weekly-changing *pintxos*. Slow food at its best, wash it down with an early-morning glass of wine. **Verdura Plaza** is the home of flower and plant vendors, while in **Euskal Herria Plaza**, where you'll also find the Puppet Museum, there is yet another market, where chorizo sellers rub shoulders with stallholders flogging non-traditional, ubiquitous manufactured tat of dubious quality.

Topic (Puppet Museum) (Plaza de Euskal Herria 1; 943 65 04 14; w topictolosa.com; 11.00–13.00 & 16.00–19.00 Tue–Fri, 10.00–14.00 & 15.00–19.00 w/ends & holidays, hours may be extended in summer; €4/3/free adults/children/infants) Beyond the façade of the one-time justice building and former jail lies Tolosa's puppet museum, now sharing the space with a small theatre. In fact, the building is almost entirely new: only the façade is original. Less spooky than some museums of its ilk (is that puppet staring at me?), if you've never thought much about puppets before, then this is a good place to start. Tolosa's puppet tradition came from a local enthusiast who started a collection over 30 years ago, though the museum itself is only five years old. The city continues to host a renowned international puppet festival which takes place every November.

The puppets themselves are grouped together according to the various characters they represent: good puppets in one section, for example, bad puppets in another. You can admire shadow puppets, glove puppets, string puppets and rod puppets as well as other unusual genres from all across the world. Discover also how some of Spain's artistic luminaries such as Joan Miró and Federico García Lorca contributed to the world of puppetry. Both the young and not so young can take the opportunity to play with some of the exhibits. On the first floor, the museum gives exhibition space to temporary displays. The museum is fully accessible for those with limited mobility and there are information leaflets in English. A number of videos, accompanied by music, help bring some animation to the displays.

GKo (Graffiti Art Gallery) (Calle Nagusia 24; 943 67 01 51; w gko-gallery.com; 10.00–13.00 & 17.00–20.30 Sat, 17.00–20.30 Tue–Fri) Tolosa's very own street graffiti artist has (literally) set up shop, selling his wares. His work is an acquired taste, but it's certainly interesting and quirky. Exhibitions here change regularly.

Goierri Continuing southward up the Oria Valley, you pass imperceptibly from the region of Tolosaldea into that of Goierri (whose name translates as 'highlands'). The fast-flowing river water has fed the valley's industry, which is juxtaposed with faint vestiges of history and rugged natural landscapes. Every little town and even village seems to contain a large factory or warehouse, sometimes more than one. The region's ability to grimly hang on to industrial production has helped to preserve its inhabitants and thus its culture. Whereas in other parts of Europe a greater drift of youngsters to the cities has left decaying or dying settlements, here the array of new apartment blocks is testament to the fact that the residents of these valley towns have stayed put (to some extent, at least), with employment prospects to keep them here. Agriculture and the economic importance of the farmsteads may have declined in terms of livestock, but out here on the hills you'll still find shepherds tending their flocks. Goierri lets you enjoy the products of artisanal cheese and cider producers, and for accommodation options you can take advantage of the seamless conversion of many of the imposing farmhouses into cheap-as-chips tourist accommodation or restaurants. With youngsters not quite so tempted to leave, the Basque culture and language have thrived and family units have stayed strong in Goierri.

Ordizia On a Wednesday morning Ordizia is an absolute must for market-lovers and people-watchers. Some say that the market has lost a bit of its authenticity in recent years, but as a visitor you're likely to be delighted and enthralled at the quality of the rustic products – and entertained by the lively characters selling them. With over 500 years of history behind it, it could reasonably be described as 'well established'. The original charter to hold the weekly Wednesday market was granted as part of a rebuilding exercise after a disastrous fire which destroyed the town in 1512. All the interesting action takes place in the main square, and the stalls are covered by a stone roof which is supported by huge stone columns which look like escapees from ancient Athens or Rome. Get there by 08.00, grab a table at one of the cafés on the square and people-watch as the stallholders painstakingly set out their stalls of prized cheeses, immaculate vegetables and jars of honey. Towards lunchtime, the market starts to wind down and the vendors retire to chew the fat in the local bars and restaurants. At certain times of the year, special markets take place, such as the shepherds' market, held on the Wednesday after Semana Santa (Holy Week). This coincides with the transhumance and is nowadays one of the few occasions when live animals can be seen at the market, as the shepherds drive their herds of sheep through town up to the summer mountain pastures. September is the month for the town's famous cheese auction while in October, the attention turns to the serious and valuable subject of mushrooms, 'hunted' in the surrounding countryside and brought to market in many varieties. Details of other special markets, including one at Christmas, can be found on the town's website, w delikatuz.com, although at the time of writing it was only in Spanish or Basque.

Ordizia is also on the inland Camino de Santiago route that wends its way down from Irun and is the birthplace of the explorer and Augustinian friar Andrés de Urdaneta, credited for achieving the second successful circumnavigation of the globe after fellow Basque Juan Sebastián Elkano (page 181) and celebrated for bringing Christianity to the Philippines.

Despite the rustic impression given by its market, don't be fooled into thinking that this area is a rural backwater or industrial has-been. A major private university has its engineering faculty in town and the heavy industry in nearby Beasain includes bus- and train-manufacturing enterprises, the latter being responsible for the manufacture of the trams now running in Edinburgh and Birmingham.

Tourist information (Santa Maria 24; 943 88 22 90; Easter, Jul & Aug 10.00–13.00 & 16.00–19.00 daily, 10.00–14.00 Sat & Sun; other months 09.00–13.00 Mon–Fri, 10.00–14.00 Sat & Sun) Housed in a building with the D'elikatuz interpretation centre (see opposite).

Where to stay Given the way that industry has hemmed in the original town centres and now rubs up close to the countryside, it's preferable to choose rural options when deciding where to stay. Prices here are very reasonable.

Agroturismo Sidrería Olagi (4 rooms) Urrutibera Berria, Altzaga; 943 88 77 26; e olagi.altzaga@gmail.com; w nekatur.net/olagi. English-speaking hosts welcome you to a handsome, rustic house in the country, around 4km northeast of Ordizia. A real bargain; the HB prices are attractive too. What's more, there's a working cider factory on-site. May stipulate a min stay in high season. **€**

Ondarre Baserria (6 rooms, 2 apts) Beheko Arrabal, Segura; 943 80 16 64; e ondarresegura@gmail.com; w nekatur.net/ondarre. An *agroturismo* in a restored 16th-century building with adjoining cheese factory, next to the Oria River & with views to the mountains. Wood-burning stove, heating, free Wi-Fi. Large communal area with TV. May stipulate a min stay in high season. **€**

Where to eat and drink

Ostatu de Mutiloa Herriko Plaza, Mutiloa; 943 80 11 66; w mutiloa.eus; 10.00–22.00 Sun & Tue–Thu, 10.00–midnight Fri & Sat. Evening meals only Fri & Sat. Some 15mins' drive southwest of Ordizia, a small, innovative bar/restaurant in the main square of a minuscule town, well off the beaten track. Restored stone walls & a tiled floor suggest simplicity, but the food quality is excellent, with the 3-course lunchtime menu a true bargain. Some English is spoken. This is a local favourite. Excellent fish dishes, seasonal vegetables. €€€€

Pias Taberna Nagusia 42, Ordizia; 943 88 00 16; 08.00–20.00 Mon, Tue & Thu–Sat, 07.00–15.00 Wed, 08.00–14.00 Sun. A mere minute from Ordizia's market square, an excellent place for a coffee/snack, with a selection of high-quality *pintxos*, plus *bocadillos* & a few main courses. €€

What to see and do

D'elikatuz (D'elikatuz Gastronomy Museum) (Santa María 24; 943 88 22 90; w delikatuz.com; see tourist information, opposite; €3.20) Within the same building as the tourist office, this centre focuses not just on gastronomy, but on local history as well. Although the information on the walls is only in Spanish and Basque, English-speaking visitors can use the laminated leaflets that explain the exhibits, allowing them to do self-guided tours. A touch-screen facility shows visitors the highlights of each of the 18 Goierri villages. Upstairs, there is an explanation of the region's history, plus excellent audio-visual presentations about the importance of Ordizia's market. The video also clearly shows the traditional almond shape of the original town, something that is difficult to discern when driving into the present-day version, with its many modern blocks of apartments. Two important periods of Ordizia's history are emphasised: first the 13th century, when it was a staging post on the wool route from the Basque Country to Flanders; secondly, the 17th century, when the area produced iron for transportation through Basque coastal ports such as Pasaia for export to northern Europe.

The on-site shop sells a decent range of edible products and handicrafts, for those hunting souvenirs.

Ondarre cheese factory (See *Ondarre Baserria*, opposite, for details; short visit (40mins) €6 including tasting, long visit (90mins) €12; English is spoken) If you are a fan of the region's famous and delicious DO Idiazábal cheese, then this is a tiny award-winning, artisanal producer where you can indulge. You can even say hello to some of their 100 sheep. A bidder at Ordizia's famous September auction once paid €13,000 for a single prize-winning cheese produced here, but all is not *quite* what it seems. By tradition, the winning bidder at the public auction actually donates the money to charity and gains some good PR for themselves in so doing. For the Ondarre cheese factory, prestige was the only benefit: not only did they not receive the €13,000, but when you see the size of the place, you will realise that production can't be increased beyond the 14 cheeses made here every two days, and market forces mean that prices can't be raised to take advantage of their success. At the Ordizia cheese-making competition, around 60 producers take part, their products assessed using four of the judges' five senses. (Presumably you can't '*hear*' a cheese!) Sheep's milk is the staple ingredient. A video here shows visitors the manufacturing process from start to finish.

Zerain A real attempt is being made to turn tiny Zerain's industrial heritage into a tourist attraction. At various times, iron, lead and silver have been mined here, starting in the 11th century and stepping up in 1512 when King Ferdinand granted exploitation rights to a local family. New facilities were created in the 20th century to cope with the demands of the Industrial Revolution, but no mining activity takes place here any more.

Tourist information The tourist office (Herriko Plaza; ☎ 943 80 15 05; e turismobulegoa@zerain.com; w zerain.com; ⊕ Easter–end Sep 10.30–13.30 & 15.30–18.30 Mon–Fri, 11.00–14.00 & 16.00–19.00 Sat & Sun, other months 11.00–14.00 daily) has information in English and English-speaking staff. Here you'll find information and maps on the surrounding area's many walking trails, some of which feature information panels on subjects as diverse as iron production, mushrooms and woodpeckers. There is also a small ethnographical museum with good audio-visual features and a shop selling local food products and Basque handicrafts.

Where to stay and eat In a tranquil setting just north of the village, at **Oiharte Sagardotegia** (6 rooms; Irukarate-gain Auzoa; ☎ 943 50 10 13; m 680 17 12 91; e sagardotegia@oiharte.com; w oiharte.com; **€€**) the silence is interrupted only in the evening when the cider flows. The cider cycle and the process can be demonstrated to you before you sit down to dine on the time-honoured cider-house set menu. While traditionally this was offered from January to April, modern storage techniques allow the cider to now be at its best all year round. The rooms are beautifully renovated and have heating, which is essential in winter. There is a cheap breakfast too.

What to see and do

Centro del Visitante Aizpitta (The Aizpitta Learning Centre and the Iron Mountain) (Aizpea Auzoa; ☎ 943 80 15 05; ⊕ Nov–Mar 10.30–13.30 & 15.30–18.30 Mon–Fri, 11.00–14.00 & 16.00–19.00 Sat, Sun & hols; hours can vary – it is advisable to contact the tourist office in advance) This centre offers a chance to see the well-preserved 20th-century calcination furnaces, overhead cable system, coal stores and loading bays, as well as to take a walk into a mine tunnel itself. Over 200 galleries were created inside the mountain searching for ore after exhaustion of the surface mineral, but only one tunnel is safe today. The vestiges of foreign involvement are also visible, with the remnants of both the English- and German-built railways, which in recent centuries transported the iron. Indoors, the learning centre has an excellent audio-visual presentation, in English, and further information on laminated leaflets for visitors to peruse.

THE DEBA VALLEY

Oñati Showing a commendable Basque brevity of expression, the name of this delightful, unspoilt little town translates as 'place of many hills'. Apart from the topography of the Aizkorri mountain range to the south, Oñati was also once dubbed 'the Basque Toledo' in recognition of its collection of elegant buildings. It's not an epithet that it is eager to give up and, combined with a visit to the sanctuary of nearby Aránzazu and perhaps to the caves at Arrikrutz, a wander around town will more than reward the visitor. If you can arrange a guided visit, all the better. To the visitor, Oñati presents two distinct faces, each one visible to the exclusion of the other, depending on where you are. At ground level, wandering past the university, the town hall, the churches, down the pedestrian streets or across the generously proportioned square, you encounter an extraordinarily handsome town with elegant buildings, all proudly preserved. Children play happily in the streets while parents enjoy a quiet drink at one of the bars. All around are points of interest, tracing the town's religious, cultural and industrial history. Up on the hill stands the old tower-house of the counts of Ibarra, now a luxury hotel (see opposite). From above, the town – which appears so pretty at eye level – is slightly sullied. Its still-healthy industrial output – the one remaining chocolate factory, machine tool manufacturers and belching chimneys – conspire to spoil the vista slightly.

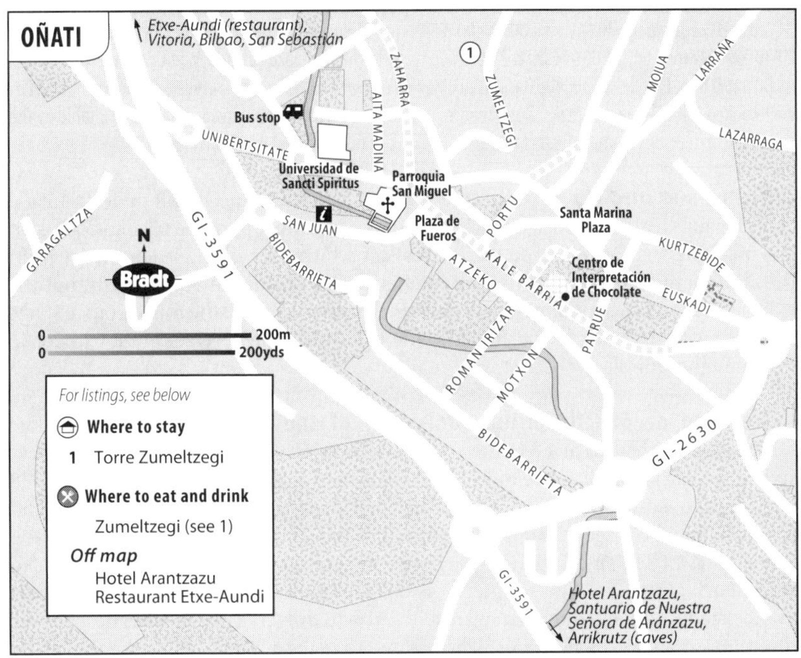

During the Middle Ages (14th to 18th centuries) the town saw the tired old saga of blood feuds, with two clans battling for supremacy. With that all resolved, Oñati remained independent, under the authority of the counts until it finally became part of Gipuzkoa in 1845. As well as beautiful buildings, Oñati has its share of idiosyncrasies, such as the townsfolk's nickname (see box, page 163) and their own distinctive regional accent, which is distinctly Bizkaian rather than Gipuzkoan.

Corpus Christi is the town's principal festival, celebrated in May or June.

Tourist information The tourist office (San Juan 14; ☎ 943 78 34 53; e turismo@onati.eus; w onatiturismo.eus; ⏰ Jan–Apr & Oct–Dec 10.00–14.00 & 16.00–18.00 Tue–Sun, May 10.00–14.00 & 16.00–18.00 Tue–Fri, 09.30–14.00 & 15.30–19.00 Sat & Sun, Jun–Sep 09.30–14.00 & 15.30–19.00 daily) is housed in a former mill, which can be seen working – just ask at the desk and they'll crank it up for you. More importantly, guided tours of the town are available, though at least a day's notice is required.

Where to stay *Map, above*

Torre Zumeltzegi (12 rooms) Calle Zumeltzegi; ☎ 943 54 00 00; e contacto@hoteltorrezumeltzegi.com; w hoteltorrezumeltzegi.com. High above the town, this place is not difficult to see, but a little tricky to find on foot. Formerly the home of the all-powerful counts of Ibarra, the interior has been gutted to produce a chic, ultra-modern hotel. TV with international channels, free Wi-Fi & AC. Grab a room on the 4th floor for the best view of the town. The staff are friendly & speak English, & the restaurant is excellent (page 162). **€€€**

Where to eat and drink *Map, above*

Restaurant Etxe-Aundi Torre Auzoa 9; ☎ 943 78 19 56; w etxeaundi.com. The huge portions are top quality. Lunch or dinner, service is good, which it has to be, as this place is popular. Lunch is good value, dinner more expensive. Booking is advisable. €€€

Zumeltzegi (page 161) 13.00–15.00 & 20.30–22.30 Mon–Fri, 14.00–16.00 & 21.00–23.00 Sat & Sun. Excellent nouvelle Basque cuisine, well-cooked & high-quality steaks. Don't ignore the *goxua*, a delicious creamy dessert. €€€

Hotel Arantzazu 943 78 13 13. Right next to the Aránzazu sanctuary, with wonderful views down into the gorge. Serves a decent *menú del día* for €15, including wine & bread. Take a table by the window. It also has rooms (**€€**). €€

What to see and do If you're not taking a guided tour, Oñati's pedestrianised centre is an ideal place to stroll around unaccompanied, perhaps taking a drink in the spacious square (Plaza de los Fueros) off which everything leads. Apart from the church, most of the buildings are to be admired from the outside only, but the experience is a pleasant one nonetheless. Pick up a map from the tourist office (page 161). Start at the church and finish at the Centro de Interpretación de Chocolate for a naughty nibble.

Universidad de Sancti Spíritus (University of the Holy Spirit) (Unibertsitate Hiribidea) Of greatest pride to the townsfolk here is the 16th-century Renaissance-style university building, the oldest in the Basque Country. It was founded in 1548 and is still used for the study of law. The exterior of the university building – and that's all that you'll see without a guided visit – is decorated with carvings depicting the labours of Hercules, its design chosen to remind students that they ought to work hard to achieve. Also of interest is the depiction of women on the upper part of the façade: after all, only men were allowed into university in those times, but the founder was a wealthy humanist who wanted to make a point. Inside the university is a small chapel with a disproportionately huge altarpiece and a hallway with intricate and unusual Arabian-style woodwork. (Unusual, as of course the Moorish conquest never made it this far, although its influence clearly did.)

Parroquia de San Miguel (Church of St Michael) (Plaza de los Fueros) The church of San Miguel is one of only three in Europe that can trumpet the fact that a river runs underneath it. (For the record, the others are in Cambridge and Hungary.) Short of building land, two bridges were constructed over the water to ingeniously solve the problem. The crypt holds the tombs of the counts of Ibarra, and materials from Andalucía, over 1,000km to the south, were brought to build the mausoleum.

For the lovers of the macabre, the gruesome torture of Oñati's saint, Miguel de Aozaraza, who was beheaded in Japan in 1637, is depicted in the church.

Opposite the church, the former convent building is now in dual use as a school and the town's theatre.

Centro de Interpretación del Chocolate (Chocolate Learning Centre) (Kale Barria 29; Sep–Jul 10.30–13.30 & 17.00–20.00 Mon–Thu, 10.30–13.30 & 17.00–19.00 Fri, 10.30–13.30 Sat; Aug 10.30–14.00 daily, also 18.00–19.15 Tue & Thu.) What is now a small shop was once the site of Orbea, one of several chocolate manufacturers that played a large part in the town's history. Only one manufacturer remains, on the outskirts of the town, but the history of chocolate is recorded here through displays of various chocolate-related artefacts, if you're interested. And of course you can taste and buy, if you're not.

Santuario de Nuestra Señora de Aránzazu (Arantzazu) (Well signposted from Oñati; 943 71 89 11 or 943 79 64 63; 09.00–20.00 daily; admission free; guided visits €2 in English, by reservation, preferably with a day's notice; a bus connects Oñati with the sanctuary, Sun only, 15mins, €0.70) Some 9km to the south of Oñati and 750m above sea level sits the Sanctuary of Aránzazu, a site of great importance to the Basques and an example of bold Basque architectural style. But first, the legend. The original sanctuary, it is said, was built on the site of a hawthorn bush where a local shepherd discovered an image of the Virgin Mary in 1468. The site duly became a place of pilgrimage. The Virgin was also credited with bringing about peace between two sets of warring clans, and for ending a period of drought that happily coincided with her discovery. On his way to Jerusalem in 1522 St Ignatius of Loyola stopped here, but the history of the sanctuary is subsequently punctuated by a series of fires, the last of which was started by troops fighting the Carlists in 1834 and completely destroyed the building. Construction on the new basilica began in 1950. A competition was held to decide on the design, for which style was not the only consideration when deciding the winner. Some of the leading Basque and Spanish artists were involved in the project, apparently with enormous artistic licence to do as they pleased: Chillida made the iron doors, which access the church, Oteiza the 14 'apostles', while the somewhat funky paintings in the crypt are by Nestor Basterretxea, who apparently created and installed them without any

A TOWN OF FROGS AND CHOCOLATE

Oñati is a small town that many will whizz past on their way to the Santuario de Nuestra Señora at Aránzazu. But while the town centre is pleasant, with its large and well-used square, an ancient university and some handsome streets and churches, it is chocolate and frogs that set it apart from many of its neighbours.

The surviving chocolate factory is an important local employer, set in a large, modern construction of no architectural interest whatsoever. However, it serves as a reminder of the part that chocolate has played in the history of the town. The university, or more specifically the Faculty of Medicine, came up with the idea of covering bitter, unpalatable medicines with chocolate to try to make them more acceptable. Cocoa was brought to the town and at its peak there were ten chocolate factories in the town centre. Now there is only one, but housed in the building of one of the defunct ones is the chocolate learning centre (see opposite), showing the history of chocolate, how it connected the Basque Country with the outside world and gave the name 'chocolate town' to Oñati.

Oñati no longer bears that nickname, but another one, given this time to its citizens, endures. The townspeople refer to any type of frog as '*txantxiku*', a word not used anywhere else in the Basque Country; this has also become the nickname for the inhabitants of Oñati. Look closely around town in the shops and houses and you'll encounter many frog logos and other references to the *txantxiku*.

But why? Well, the answer depends on who you ask, as there are various versions. The most popular is that one of the counts who ruled the town had a black-and-white tiled floor at the entrance to his tower-house. He became incensed when his subjects dragged their muddy boots across his nice, clean, white tiles. He decreed that, in future, they should only stand on the black tiles when visiting. The sarcastic peasants responded by hopping across the entrance, landing only on the black squares and avoiding the white ones. The count saw this and started to call them *txantxiku*, or frogs – a name that has stuck with them to the present day.

consultation with the resident Franciscans. His depiction of Christ, looking for all the world like an angry cartoon superhero, is particularly unusual. For the interior of the church, Lucio Muñoz, who won the 1961 competition to design it, drew his inspiration for the enormous wooden altarpiece from the sheer cliffs that line the valley on the approach to the sanctuary. The image of the Virgin, as discovered in 1468, but actually dating from the 13th century, perches diminutively in the centre of the giant masterpiece. But most controversial of all are Oteiza's 14 figures above the church entrance. Are they apostles, and if so, why 14, not 12? Various theories abound but enquiries of the sculptor, Oteiza, produced different explanations at different times of asking. Once he claimed that they were actually oarsmen from the *trainera* (rowing team) in his home town of Orio; then when asked why there were 14, he replied – presumably tongue-in-cheek – that there was no room for any more in the limited space provided; when asked a third time, he said that they were politicians. It seems that the mystery will never be solved.

Aránzazu also holds particular significance for Basque culture, specifically the language, for it was here that successful attempts were made to standardise a language that relied primarily on an oral tradition, which, due to the mountainous geography, differed from valley to valley. Both before the Civil War and again in the 1960s, conventions for representatives of all seven Basque provinces were held here to carry out the standardisation work.

On Sundays, Aránzazu and its car park can get packed as Basques descend on the sanctuary to celebrate mass. Pilgrimages from Oñati take place on 28 March and 9 September, the latter being the day of Our Lady of Aránzazu. In high season (June–September), English-speaking guides can be found to show you around the sanctuary and explain the history and construction.

Otherwise, information is available in English from the tourist office, situated between the car park and the basilica. Above the car park is a learning centre that provides information on **Aizkorri–Arratz Natural Park**, which was designated as such in 2006 and has a summit, Aizurri, of over 1,500m. Information on walks into the park, some of which start from the sanctuary, can be obtained here, though sadly not in English. Although the centre itself has no English-language information, the excellent audio-visual displays give a visual overview of the landscape and the life of the shepherds who still inhabit the high grounds in summer.

Near Aránzazu If you want to see something almost unique, visit the shepherds' school 2km back down the road towards Oñati. **Gomiztegi Baserria** (943 25 10 08; e info@gomiztegi.com; w gomiztegi.com) is one of only two shepherd schools in the world. Students flock here to learn the art of shepherding. Courses last for six months, a combination of classroom work and practical lessons in the field, covering essential skills like dog control. Each student has to complete a 16-week 'placement' and produce a project at the end of the course. Visitors are welcome, although there is no guarantee that the sole English speaker will be present! If so, he is happy to give a free tour of his premises, explaining the cheese-making process, introducing you to the sheep and showing you the milking process. Cheese produced here carries the Idiazabal mark and visitors can purchase it along with some sheep-related souvenirs.

Arrikrutz (Oñati Caves) (signposted off the GI-3591 between Oñati & Aránzazu; 943 08 20 00; e arrikrutz@oinati.org; w onati.eus; Mar, Apr & Oct–Dec 10.00–14.00 & 15.30–17.30 Tue–Fri, 09.30–14.30 Sat & Sun, May–Jun 10.00–14.00 & 15.30–17.30 Tue–Fri, 09.30–14.30 & 15.30–19.00 Sat & Sun, Jul & Aug 09.30–14.30

& 15.30–19.00 daily, Sep 09.30–14.30 & 15.30–19.00 Tue–Sat, €9/6/free adults/under 16s & seniors/under 5s; contact in advance for visits in English) Opened in 2007, this is part of nearly 15km of limestone caves, with only 500m open to public. A 1-hour visit lets you see stalactites, stalagmites and columns, as well as a replica of a complete cave lion skeleton that was found here in 1966. These creatures were believed to grow up to 3.5m in length, much bigger than an African lion. Traces of panthers have also been found here. Speleologists and researchers worked for years at Arrikrutz before an artificial tunnel was created to facilitate visitor access. Outside the caves, the surrounding cliffs are hugely impressive and are home to a large colony of vultures, some of which can usually be spotted soaring high above.

VALLEY OF UROLA Between the valleys of the Oria to the east and the Deba to the west, central Gipuzkoa's third major river wends its way down to the coast and empties into the sea at Zumaia. Halfway down the valley is the main attraction, the town of Azpeitia, with the celebrated Sanctuary of Loyola and a very worthwhile railway museum. Zestoa and its caves are another interesting diversion in this area.

Azpeitia The town itself is of little interest: the sanctuary and the railway museum being the two attractions here which make a visit well worthwhile.

Getting there and away Azpeitia is 40 minutes' drive from San Sebastián (via the AP-8 then the GI-631) and 55 minutes from Bilbao (on the AP-8 then the GI-2634). From San Sebastián, both **Lurraldebus** (943 41 52 08; w lurraldebus.eus) and **La Guipuzcoana** (943 85 11 59; w laguipuzcoana.eus) operate a frequent service to Azpeitia with a stop outside the sanctuary before it reaches the town centre (1hr; €4.50).

Where to stay and eat Slap-bang next to the sanctuary, **Hotel Arrupe** (50 rooms; 943 02 50 26; e hotelarrupe@sjloyola.org; w hotelarrupe.org; **€€**) was formerly the Jesuit spiritual centre, which has now moved across the road. Rooms have a certain monastic simplicity about them, though worldly luxuries like TV, free Wi-Fi and central heating are still present. It is a little removed from the town centre, if you're looking for any nightlife action. **Jai-Alai** (Urrestilla bidea; 943 81 22 71; 10.00–16.00 Sun–Thu, 10.00–23.00 Fri & Sat; **€€€**) is popular with corporate groups, but don't be put off. It offers welcoming hosts and excellent food with Basque cuisine such as wild boar stew, plus fresh hake and cod dishes.

What to see and do

Santuario de Loyola (Sanctuary of Loyola/Tower-House) (w santuariodeloyola.org; Sep–May 10.00–13.00 & 15.30–19.00, Jun–Aug 10.00–13.30 & 15.30–19.30, daily; €4/3/free adults/seniors, students & under 18s/children; audio-visual guides in 12 languages are available for visiting the tower-house) Driving into town up the Valley of Urola, there is nothing to prepare you for what you are about to see. Suddenly your eyes, inured to a melange of rushing river waters, towering hills, modern industrial units and six-storey apartment blocks on the edge of modest towns, are opened wide by the appearance of this enormous Baroque-styled grey edifice, a sanctuary designed as a mini Vatican. It does not initially smite you with its beauty, just its size and the very fact that it is here – exactly where you would least expect it.

Although on-site information about the Italians who designed the building and the Basques who constructed it is somewhat lacking, the helpful, multilingual staff at the tourist office (in a narrow office to the side of the building) will provide additional details.

The sanctuary has an ornate ceiling inside, and if you catch part of a weekend mass you will be able to hear the organ, its pipes looking like a collection of exhaust-pipes on a Ferrari. However, the more interesting building actually lies within, invisible from the outside. The actual purpose of the sanctuary building was to protect and preserve the 15th-century tower-house, the solid, impressive fortresslike structure where Ignatius was born as Íñigo López de Loyola in 1491. And you have to admit that they did a good job, even if the construction work did take over a hundred years.

The lower stone part of the tower-house, with walls 2m thick, was built without windows for defensive purposes; the upper part is brick. The tower-house was reconstructed in 1460 by Ignatius's grandfather on his return from exile. Azpeitia is the spiritual headquarters of the Jesuits and on 31 July, the feast day of St Ignatius, thousands flock here to commemorate his death.

Museo Vasco del Ferrocarril (Basque Railway Museum) (Julián Elorza 8; 943 15 06 77; w bemfundazioa.org; 10.00–13.30 & 15.00–18.30 Tue–Fri, 10.30–14.00

CAMINO IGNACIANO

w *caminoignaciano.org*

Clearly noting the commercial success and profile that the various caminos de Santiago have brought to the regions through which they pass, there is now a big push to develop the Camino Ignaciano into something similar. Born in 1491, Ignatius was wounded in the defence of Pamplona in 1521 and, during his recovery in the family house in Azpeitia, he decided to dedicate his life to God. Ignatius vowed that he would make a pilgrimage to Jerusalem once he had recovered from his injuries. Starting out from the family home, he reached Manresa, near Barcelona, around 675km away, where he then spent a year in a cave, producing his famous Book of Spiritual Exercises and founding the Society of Jesus (the Jesuits).

The route tracing his steps starts at the front door of the sanctuary in Azpeitia and reaches Aránzazu via the 'La Antigua' hermitage and thus this part is known as the Route of the Three Temples. As a pilgrimage, the Ignaciano is still in a period of relative infancy, but there are already a number of companies that can offer support for pilgrims, such as transporting your backpack, picking you up to transfer you to accommodation in places where there is none on the route itself, or even organising the entire trip for you. With the 500th anniversary of Ignatius's walk arriving in 2021, you can expect pilgrim numbers to steadily increase; in any case, it is already attracting more and more walkers, particularly from Germany, Australia and the USA. At present it retains a more religious ambience than its more celebrated Santiago brother, though this may change in future. If your motivation for a pilgrimage is religious or to find some headspace for spiritual thought, you might find this preferable to the more crowded Santiago routes. For anyone interested in walking the Basque part of the Ignaciano, the stretch between Azpeitia and Aránzazu is a mere 45km – two days' trek – before it crosses into Álava (another 80km), exiting the Basque provinces and traversing La Rioja to enter Navarre. More information can be found on the website above.

& 16.00–19.30 Sat, 10.30–14.00 Sun & holidays; steam train runs only at 12.30 & 18.00 Sat & 12.30 Sun; visit €3/free adults/under 16s; with steam train ride €6/free adults/under 4s) Azpeitia's railway museum is fashioned from the disused station, and exhibits an impressive collection of rail transport and associated paraphernalia gathered inside the engine repair shed and adjoining power station. There is plenty to engage the interest of British visitors here, with engines manufactured in Glasgow, Newcastle, Bristol and Bedford. Inside the station building itself and probably of less general interest is a collection of railway uniforms, some dating back to 1849. On the top floor are station clocks and pocket watches. Every Friday, the clocks are all faithfully wound up to keep them in (nearly) perfect time. Although the information in this part of the museum is only bilingual (Spanish/Basque), the trains, housed in and around the old engine repair shop, are accompanied by information signs in English. The curators are extremely enthusiastic and may take you for a 50m ride on a swish, stylish tram from 1940s Zaragoza, or set in motion a dazzling array of machine tools in an adjoining workshop, a fine performance of whirring parts and trundling, circling pulleys. The museum is also the residence of the oldest working-order Stephenson steam train anywhere in the world.

On Saturdays (12.30 & 18.00) and Sundays (12.30 only), and daily in high season, visitors can hop on board the 100-year-old Manchester-built ***Aurrera***, a steam train that will chug you down the valley for 5km to Lasao in the princely time of around 45 minutes, and then all the way back again. The route is part of the original line that connected the town of Zumarraga and coastal Zumaia, a service that ran for 60 years and closed in 1986. The museum is located on the north side of Azpeitia.

Ekain berri (cave paintings) (Portal Kalea 1, Zestoa; 943 86 88 11; e info@ekainberri.com; w ekainberri.com; ticket office 10.00–13.30 & 15.00–17.30 Mon–Fri, 10.00–13.30 & 15.00–18.30 Sat, Sun & holidays; €6/5/free adults/students, children & seniors/infants) The fourth main centre of interest in this area is the 15,000-year-old cave paintings in Zestoa. You cannot actually visit them, but ingeniously the local people have created an almost exact replica of the caves and their paintings about 600m away from the originals. This was a necessary measure in order to prevent a repeat of the damage caused by visitors to other cave paintings elsewhere in the Basque Country. The paintings are mainly of horses and bison, with a deer and a couple of bears, too. An innovative video, screened from underwater and demonstrating the primitive art of making fire, adds to the experience. There are audio guides in English and further English-language information is available on laminates in the learning centre, which is a short walk away.

To visit, you have to go to the tourist office in the very centre of **Zestoa** (Portale Kalea 1; 943 86 88 11; w zestoaturismo.net), parking your car in the car park (signposted) just down towards the river. You are then given a ticket and make the 25-minute walk along the river to what looks like a massive nuclear bunker. Inside here are the meticulously replicated caves and reconstructed paintings: the whole thing took around nine years to create, and the chosen few to have seen the original paintings testify that the replicas are excellent.

There is also a workshop where staff supervise children in the making of bows and arrows before taking them out into the woods to hunt targets. It's all safe and a bit of fun for children between six and 14 years old, though the staff report that the parents usually enjoy it more than their children.

EAST TO FRANCE

From San Sebastián to the border with France is little more than half an hour's drive, a blink of an eye on the motorway. Once you're east of quirky little Pasaia, much of the coast is beach-free and devoid of interest – and indeed inaccessible by car – until you reach handsome Hondarribia on the Bidasoa River and Hendaye in France across the estuary. Inland attractions in this border region include the Aiako-Harria Natural Park, some 13km south of the motorway. The largest town here is Irun, a useful transport hub and commercial centre due to its border location. On Saturday mornings it attracts French visitors bargain hunting at its vibrant market, and its bridge is the starting point for two routes of the Camino de Santiago in Spain, one that initially hugs the coast while the other plunges inland through Oiartzun and Astigarraga.

PASAIA Only around 4km from the centre of San Sebastián, the scruffy outskirts of Pasaia might prompt you to pass hurriedly by. Don't! Four distinct settlements cluster around the mouth of the Oiart River estuary here, together making up the Pasaia municipality. Most of the points of interest are concentrated in Pasai Donibane and Pasai San Pedro, down towards the sea, and pay homage to the region's maritime history. Boatbuilding, fishing and whaling all once brought prosperity to the town and the estuary is still home to a busy industrial port. For visitors, pedestrianised **Pasai Donibane** on the estuary's east side has a quaint yet rough-round-the-edges feel, with a pleasant square overlooking the estuary and a number of good options for lunch. Whether arriving by car, bus or on foot (there's an excellent coastal walk

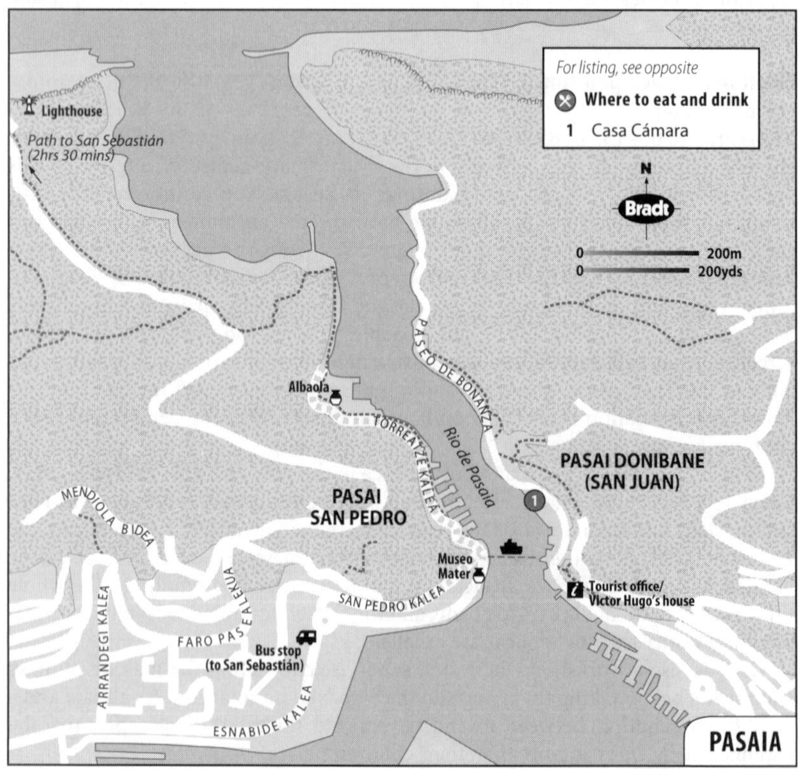

from San Sebastián – see below), you should start – and park your car, if driving – in **Pasai San Pedro** on the west side of the estuary, visit its points of interest and then use the dirt-cheap passenger boat to cross the estuary to Pasai Donibane.

Getting there and away Take the E 08 or E 09 **bus** from Okendo Kalea in central San Sebastián to Pasai San Pedro. For the active, there is an excellent 2-hour **coastal walk** from the eastern end of Zurriola beach in San Sebastián to Pasai San Pedro. The frequent bus services will whisk you back again, avoiding any need to retrace your steps.

Where to eat and drink *Map, opposite*

Casa Cámara (San Juan 79; 943 52 36 99; w casacamara.com; 13.30–15.30 & 20.30–22.30 Tue–Sat, 13.30–15.30 Sun; €€€) has been run by one family for well over a century. It makes a great spot for lunch, and serves particularly good fish. It's not a bargain, but if you've come across the water, you deserve the best in town. You can choose your lobster from the cage.

What to see and do

Pasai San Pedro Well down the estuary from the port, those with a maritime interest can satisfy their passion at two sites before crossing the estuary. The **Albaola (Sea Factory of the Basques)** (Ondartxo Ibilbidea 1, Pasai San Pedro; 943 39 24 26; w albaola.com; mid-May–mid-Sep 10.00–14.00 & 15.00–19.00, mid-Sep–mid-May 10.00–14.00 & 15.00–18.00; €7/5 adults/under 18s, students & everyone between 18.00 & 19.00) is where old boats are restored and boatbuilding skills are preserved. The *San Juan* whaling ship, originally built in Pasaia in 1563 and discovered on the ocean floor off Canada in 1978, was recently reconstructed here as part of the project celebrating San Sebastián's status as European City of Culture in 2016. Pasaia was at one time Europe's biggest whaling port. There is also a ship-modelling workshop and occasional events and performances.

The **Museo Mater** (m 619 81 42 25; w matermuseoa.com; Jul & Aug 11.00–14.00 & 16.00–19.00 Tue–Sat, 11.00–14.00 Sun; other months (closed Jan & Feb) 16.00–19.00 Thu & Fri, 11.00–14.00 & 16.00–19.00 Sat, 11.00–14.00 Sun; €7/5 adults/children, including tuna & *txakoli* tasting) was once an anchovy- and sardine-fishing boat. Nowadays the 33m-long *Mater* enjoys a quieter existence most of the time in its new role as a museum. It also offers various excursions around Pasaia, workshops on fish-canning, as well as eco-activities. These other activities explain the rather limited museum opening times. You will need good Spanish to get the most out of a visit here.

Pasai Donibane Linking Pasai San Pedro on the estuary's west side to Pasai Donibane on the east is a **boat service** (m 630 44 88 13; w turismopasaia.com), which shuttles back and forth constantly from 06.00 until 23.00, taking less than a minute and costing a non-whopping €0.80. Donibane ('San Juan' in Spanish) is a little treasure, buried away at the northern end of the estuary after you've passed by all the industrial detritus. With its quaint houses, narrow streets and clothes drying from the balconies around the large square, it makes a pleasant lunch spot and is popular on sunny weekends. **Victor Hugo's former house** – the famous Frenchman lived here for a short time in 1843 – is now a museum and doubles up as the tourist office. Pilgrims have to cross the water from Pasai Donibane on their way to Santiago, and the pilot boat buzzes around purposefully, guiding large ships out through the narrow channel to the open sea. At the San Juan boarding point, take time to look at the shrine giving thanks for the victory over Charlemagne's army at Roncesvalles. By appointment, the same boat company offers boat tours around the estuary, exploring maritime-related points of interest.

OIARTZUN Oiartzun is a medium-sized town, featuring a few attractive houses and a pleasant square, but it is primarily a convenient centre for those wishing to go walking in the nearby Aiako-Harria Natural Park. Oiartzun's tourist office opens only at Easter and July/August, but information can be found at nearby Errenteria, 3km away along the GI-2134. Walking routes are available from there. Oiartzun is the site of a museum of Basque traditional music (see below).

Tourist information The tourist office for the immediate area is now in Errenteria (Madalen 3, Errenteria; 943 49 45 21; e turismoa@oarsoaldea.eus; w oarsoaldea-turismoa.eus; 10.00–14.00 & 16.00–18.00 Tue–Sat, 10.00–14.00 Sun, Jul, Aug & Easter week 09.00–14.00 & 16.00–19.00 daily).

Where to stay and eat

Casa Malkorra (8 rooms) Gurutze Bidea 33, Oiartzun; 943 49 50 30; w casamalkorra.com. Only opened in 2017, the location, management & high standards make this an excellent alternative to staying in nearby, pricey San Sebastián. Get a room that looks down the valley, not on to the road. Included in the price is a superb b/fast & an hour in the spa bath/sauna. Seasonal swimming pool is free. The Casa Malkorra also has a restaurant (lunch & dinner Tue–Sat, lunch Sun; €€€–€€€€). Food that feels like a Michelin star should be shining on it. Not cheap, but great value for elaborate, straight-from-the-heart cuisine of a high standard. W/day menu is a superb price/quality ratio, w/ends are, however, expensive. **€€€**

What to see and do

Soinuenea (Basque Music Museum) (Tornola Kalea 6; 943 49 35 78; w soinuenea.eus; 10.00–14.00 & 15.00–18.00 Tue–Sat; €3 with audio guide; guided tours are available in English for groups of more than 5, advance notice required) A huge collection of Basque musical instruments is available for inspection, together with others from around the world, grouped together in 'families' so that the relationships between them can be seen. Juan Mari Beltran, a renowned Basque musician, is the man responsible for the collection. The audio guide allows visitors to listen to each of the instruments as they look.

About four times per year the museum holds concerts, which are advertised on the website. To find the museum, take the GI-2134 from Errenteria towards Hondarribia, then turn right at Oiartzun on to the GI-3420 towards Arditurri. The museum's blue sign is on the right after 2km.

Pagoa Cerveceria (Artesanal Brewery) (Ergoien Auzoa, Oiartzun; 619 42 11 53; e pagoabeer@pagoa.eus; w pagoabeer.eus; Mon–Sat, by prior arrangement; €10/5/free adults/under 12s/under 6s, min 4 persons) Your host at this craft brewery, Joxe Anjel Arbelaitz, was at the forefront of craft brewing in the Iberian Peninsula. His 1998 introduction of his excellent Pagoa brand was not only the first craft beer in the Basque Country, but the first in Spain. Currently Pagoa produce a stout, pilsner and red ale, reaching around 40,000 litres per year. Joxe was assisted in the project by his friend and illustrious Basque writer Bernardo Atxaga. A visit here will be entertaining: Joxe speaks good English and is rightly proud of his creations. You taste all three beers and Joxe will serve up a complimentary plate of meat and cheese to accompany the brews. Behind the serving area, which closely resembles an English pub, is a 500-capacity hall where weekend concerts take place – mainly heavy-metal tribute bands – to the delight of locals. See the separate website w pagoa.eus for upcoming musical events.

Kapitain Etxea/Jantzarien Zentroa (Costume Museum) (Kapitainenea Kalea, Errenteria; 943 44 96 92, or contact the tourist office (see opposite); 11.00–14.00 & 17.00–20.00 Mon–Sat, noon–14.00 Sun & hols; €5/3 guided (Spanish only)/self-guided visit, under 5s free) Set up in a handsome 17th-century house in Errenteria town centre and staffed by volunteers, this museum spreads itself over three floors, detailing the evolution of Basque costumes from the area and exhibiting a few items from elsewhere in Europe. A short film introduces the visit. Many of the exhibits are original, donations from families and friends of the local traditional dance troupe who came up with the idea of a museum. For children, they can marvel at the Errenteria *gigantes* called Maialen and Xanti. Each of these two wicker figures is 4m tall and are now 'retired' from their role in the town's big fiestas. Youngsters can also open a wardrobe on the third floor and try on a few period costumes (these are copies, of course!). The building itself is one of the oldest in the town, which suffered from three savage fires between the 15th and 17th centuries.

Aiako-Harria Natural Park (best accessed from Oiartzun, then continue up the GI-3420 towards Lesaka; park just before reaching the tunnel) Known as 'Peñas de Aya' in Spanish, this natural park is shared by Gipuzkoa with neighbouring Navarre and is the birthplace of the three significant rivers of Oiartzun, Bidasoa and Urumea. Planted conifers together with oak and beech trees dominate Aiako-Harria, which spreads out over nearly 7,000ha and is covered by a network of well-waymarked trails. The park reaches its maximum height with the summit of Erroilbilde at 837m, with two other peaks of almost equal stature. The Aiako-Harria granite massif is over 250 million years old. For anyone interested in the geology of the park and its formation, there is a nearby geological interpretation centre/museum, **Oiartzungo Ikasgune Geologikora** (Poligono Pagoaldea 41–42, Barrio Ergoien, Oiartzun; 943 26 05 93; year-round 09.30–14.00 & 16.00–18.00 Tue–Fri, 10.00–14.00 & 16.00–18.00 Sat; €3) Within the park's boundaries, points of interest include the disused mines of **Arditurri** (943 49 45 21; w arditurri.com; tours in English only for groups of 10 persons+), a 100m-high waterfall where the Aitzondo stream takes a plunge, and a large number of scattered prehistoric dolmens and burial mounds. Nature lovers can track elusive wild boar, deer and even wildcat, and horticulturists can be on the lookout for two unusual species, the garland flower (*Daphne cneorum*) and the snowbell (*Soldanella villosa*), which add colour to the landscape when in flower. For avian fans, the cliffs within the park provide nesting places for raptors such as vultures.

FUENTERRABIA (HONDARRIBIA) The first staging post on the Spanish Basque coast, if you're arriving from France, and the last if you're leaving Spain, this now welcoming town faces out across the Bidasoa estuary, proud to have resisted at least nine military blockades in its long history. Nowadays, far from seeking to repel any Gallic invaders, Hondarribia happily ushers in visitors from France, who account for around 60% of the town's tourists. They come by car or boat it across the river mouth to wander the Casco Viejo, which wears a casual ambience almost entirely unblemished by any tacky seaside bars or souvenir shops. At the top of the hill, the former castle is now a *parador*, one of the best-patronised establishments of the state-run hotel chain (though one of the priciest, too). For a dose of fun, Hondarribia invites everyone down to its marina quarter, formerly the fishing port, where the wide pedestrian street is flanked by busy bars and restaurants. Locals

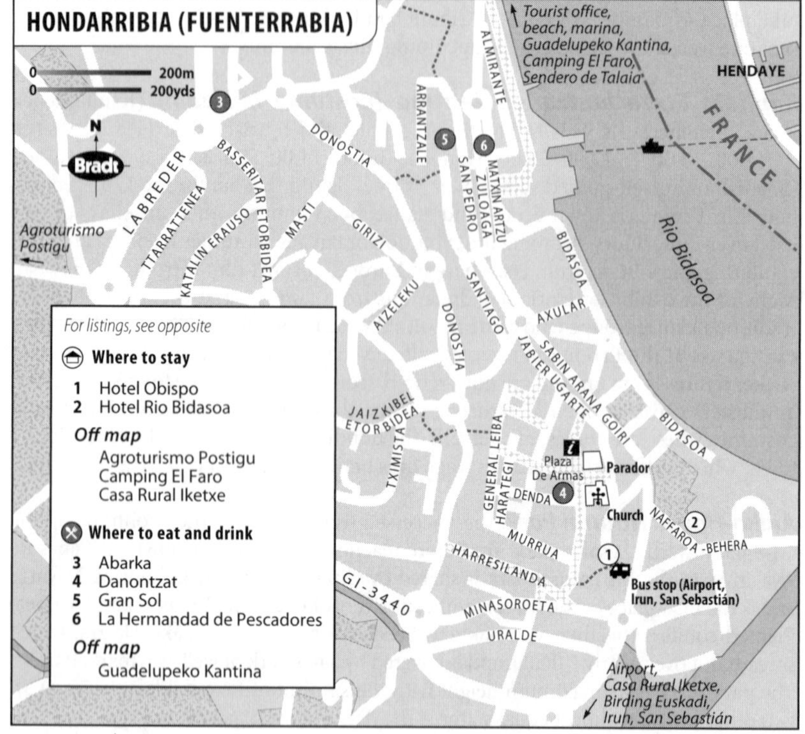

compare their *pintxos* very favourably with those of San Sebastián along the coast, and some bars display their awards proudly to prove their point. Beyond the town lies the now relocated fishing harbour, home to an active fleet that leaves for sea on the Sunday and returns on the Friday. Further west still, a couple of kilometres from town, some multi-storey 1970s apartment blocks detract little from the pristine beach, which is well protected from the waves and popular in high summer.

Getting there and away

By bus The e 20 and e 21 bus services connect Hondarribia with San Sebastián's Gipuzkoa Plaza, via the airport. Buses operate almost hourly on weekdays and with only slightly less frequency at weekends (Ekialde Bus; 943 64 13 01; w ekialdebus.eus). Bus e 25 is the one to catch for Irun's train stations, and also calls at the airport. There are several stops around town, but both of the above can be boarded at Sabin Arana Kalea 3.

By train Although Hondarribia itself has no train station, neighbouring Irun is a major junction with two stations. The **RENFE** network serves inland Gipuzkoa, as well as Pamplona, Vitoria-Gasteiz, Madrid, Barcelona and destinations in France. **Euskotren**'s terminal is a few steps away from RENFE's and has frequent services to San Sebastián, Bilbao and many points in-between.

By air The proximity of the airport (officially, it is the airport of San Sebastián) to Hondarribia may make it seem attractive, but it only has domestic services to Madrid and Barcelona (page 132).

Tourist information The tourist office (Arma Plaza 9; 943 64 54 00; w bidasoaturismo.com; Jul & Aug 09.30–19.30 daily, spring & autumn 10.00–19.00 Mon–Sat, 10.00– 14.00 Sun, winter 10.00–18.00 Mon–Sat, 10.00–14.00 Sun) is opposite the *parador*. In high season, there is a further office down in the leisure port. The staff speak English, however, and have plenty of information to hand.

Where to stay *Map, opposite*

Hotel Obispo (16 rooms) Plaza del Obispo; 943 64 54 00; e recepcion@hotelobispo.com; w hotelobispo.com. Set in the old part of town, beautifully renovated with preserved old stone & wooden beams, spotless & with all mod cons. Ask for a room with a view out over the estuary – you could be the first to warn of any latter-day French incursions. B/fast inc. Obispo is not cheap, so search their website for the often-available discounts. **€€€€**

Hotel Río Bidasoa (42 rooms) Nafarroa Behera; 943 64 54 08; e reservas@hotelriobidasoa.com; w hotelriobidasoa.com. A gentle stroll from the Casco Viejo, this is a pleasant enough hotel in a peaceful part of town, with no particular character but with a decent restaurant, garden area, seasonal outdoor pool, free Wi-Fi & free parking. Rooms are spacious, with international channel TV & heating. **€€€€**

Agroturismo Postigu (6 rooms) Semisarga Auzoa; 943 64 32 70; e postiguavr@gmail.com; w nekatur.net/postigu. Set in rural bliss a few mins' drive from Hondarribia town. Run by a spirited septuagenarian, the rooms are not huge, but have TV & heating. Some sport a balcony & all are en suite & complete with TV. Go to sleep to the bleating of sheep & wake to a chorus of birdsong. A communal kitchen is available. Excellent value. **€€**

Casa Rural Iketxe (5 rooms) Barrio Arkoll 61; 943 64 43 91; w nekatur.net/iketxe. Fatima speaks good English & Patxi cracks the jokes. Add them together & you have truly delightful hosts. Out of town, but well worth the effort. B/fasts are included & the food is excellent; a freshly baked cake might be conjured seemingly from nowhere. Rooms are spacious with free Wi-Fi, the setting is isolated but wonderful & 2 restaurants are within easy walking distance. Recommended. **€€**

Camping El Faro Higer bidea 58 (next to the lighthouse, 3km north of town); 943 64 10 08; e faro@campingeuskadi.com; w campingeuskadi.com/en/faro. Well-maintained site with seasonal swimming pool, shop, games room & Wi-Fi zone. Swimming in the sea possible. Tent pitches, bungalows, caravans welcome. 2 on-site restaurants (1 seasonal). **€**

Where to eat and drink *Map, opposite*

Abarka Basseritar Etorbidea 36; 943 64 19 91; w restabarka.com; 13.00–15.00 & 20.00–23.00 Tue–Sat, 13.00–15.00 Sun. A bit out of the centre, but worth the trip. The enthusiastic owner serves top-quality fish & meat dishes from the grill. Not cheap, but merits the expense. Divine monkfish, cooked simply with garlic. **€€€€€**

La Hermandad de Pescadores Zuloaga kalea 12; 943 64 27 38. In a 14th-century building that was once a store for fishermen's equipment, here the waitresses sport traditional outfits, adding to the ambience. Since a Japanese magazine declared this to be the home of 'the best fish soup anywhere', it has regularly filled up with Japanese taking pictures & eating fish soup. But it is good, so reservation is recommended. **€€€**

Danontzat Denda Kalea 6; 943 64 65 97; noon–23.00 Thu–Mon, 18.30–23.00 Wed. Away from the heaving masses of the marina district, this is *pintxos* served in a chic setting in the Old Town. There's a proper, civilised menu, too, & you can book in advance. Mussels in tempura are a good choice here, among the *pintxos*, *raciones* & full meals. **€€**

Gran Sol San Pedro 63–65; 943 64 70 75; w bargransol.com; 13.00–15.30 Tue–Sun, 21.00–23.00 Fri & Sat only. A bar & restaurant. For *pintxos*, check out the numerous awards above the bar. Some say this place is on the slide, but if it is, it still has a long way to fall & nobody's told the gleeful crowds permanently jostling for position at the bar. A little system operates here: ask for the English-language menu, go to the bar, place your order & pay, leaving your name, which they call when your choice is ready. If you don't hear it at first, they reach for the tannoy, which is loud enough to drown out the chattering throng outside. Each *pintxo* has a name, & the *jaizkibel* – a mushroom stuffed with cheese mousse, ham and aioli – simply has to be recommended. Not cheap, but you're not exactly slumming it here. Next door is their restaurant, with fish & meat favourites. Recommended. €€

Guadelupeko Kantina Barrio Montaña 27; 943 64 12 11; 09.30–19.00 Sun, 11.00–19.00 Mon & Thu, 11.00–21.00 Fri & Sat, 11.00–16.30 Tue, closed Wed. Shared tables, good, rustic cuisine & time-warp prices provide a pleasant surprise. Service can be abrupt at times, but bite your lip – it's cheap. 5km out of town on the GI-3440, next to the Guadelupe sanctuary. Popular & busy, so reservation required. W/day menus are a real bargain. €€

What to see and do

Casco Viejo (Old Town) Plenty of impressive, balconied buildings flank the cobbled, atmospheric streets, though the only real standout is the magnificent *parador*, which was at one time the chateau of Carlos I of Spain (Carlos V of Germany), the 16th-century ruler of the Holy Roman Empire.

Sendero de Talaia More coast-hugging initially than the Camino de Santiago, which also passes by the town, this waymarked path can take you all the way to Pasai Donibane (page 169), if you have the legs for 6 hours' walking (21km), or even San Sebastián if you can manage a further 2 hours. The scenery is good, but there are virtually no bars or restaurants along this coastal path, so come armed with your own sustenance. This route, the GR 121, starts from the El Faro restaurant next to the lighthouse northwest of town. No bicycles allowed!

Birding Euskadi (Parque Ecológico de Plaiaundi) (Pierre Loti Ibilbidea; 943 61 93 89; spring/summer 10.00–14.00 & 16.00–19.00, autumn/winter 10.00–13.00 & 15.30–17.30, daily). Second only to the Urdaibai Reserve, Txingudi is considered to be the next best spot for birdwatching in the coastal Basque Country. Of the five areas around the coast and the Bidasoa estuary that make up Txingudi, the best area and hence the one with the most facilities is here at Plaiaundi, which consists of 24ha of rejuvenated marshland, with a visitor centre ('Txingudi Ekoetxea') where entrance is free and binoculars are provided. Here you can observe the lagoon and its birdlife, though there is no English-language information. Nevertheless, laminated cards will help you identify the species, which are mainly migratory. There are five bird hides and 2km of walking routes with information panels. September through to November is considered to be the best time to visit, though the centre is open every day except public holidays. Among the over 250 species identified here, there are occasionally ospreys in passage between Scotland and Africa.

Monte Jaizkibel A short drive out of town on the GI-3440 west of town, or a strenuous walk along the Camino de Santiago, takes you to this 547m high point from where you can get a great panorama of the estuary towns and over to the Aiako-Harria Natural Park, which stretches upwards into Navarre. For cyclists who wish to tick a peak off their list, this is a climb in the annual Clásica de San Sebastián cycling race.

WEST OF SAN SEBASTIÁN

Heading west of San Sebastián introduces the visitor to a succession of seaside resorts with coastal delights on a smaller scale than the regional capital. Before Gipuzkoa province reaches its western boundary, there are four principal towns, each with their own characters, quirks, claims to fame and points of interest. They may share a coastline, but each protects its identity, and a healthy rivalry comes to the boil when their rowing teams (*traineras*) compete each year for maritime supremacy in the regional finals. A rather hurried day trip by car from San Sebastián would allow you time to visit all of these towns, but if you're relying on public transport or simply want a more relaxed itinerary, it would be better to be more selective or to spend a night or two along the way. Surfers certainly linger longer on this coast (all summer if they can get away with it) and you should do the same if you want to enjoy any beach time. Accommodation-wise, average prices remain a bit higher than you might expect. Moving slightly inland or out of the towns and using some of the smaller *casas rurales*/*agroturismos* will ease the financial burden. Getaria is the most compact and has some great overnight options.

GETTING THERE AND AWAY

By train Euskotren services from San Sebastián Amara station stop at Orio, Zarautz (two stops) and Zumaia, but there's no station (or, for that matter, any track!) at Getaria. Frequency is half-hourly at peak times and, to give an example of the cost, a single fare to Zumaia (the westernmost of the towns) takes 40 minutes and is a meagre €2.55.

By bus Lurraldebus (w lurraldebus.eus) connects all the towns, including railway-less Getaria, with San Sebastián. San Sebastián–Zumaia is 45 minutes by the motorway, 1 hour via the N-634.

ORIO Orio's historic centre features houses in various styles – Baroque, Renaissance, Gothic – and if you're on your way to lunch at delightful Katxina (and you probably should be – see below), there are a few 'ponderables' here to help you work up an appetite, such as a stiff walk up and down the Kale Nagusia. Orio's historical claim to having caught the last whale in 1901 may be disputed by some of its neighbours, but it doesn't stop the townspeople celebrating the event, albeit only every five years, on 14 May (next due in 2021). They even have a song about the occasion.

Where to stay and eat

Casa Rural Mailan (5 rooms) Arratola 18, Aia; 943 39 08 45; e contacto@casaruralmailan.com; w casaruralmailan.com. In Aia village & located just behind Orio train station, 5km east of Zarautz, this is an excellent value, bright & spacious house with river & mountain views, though its presence near the main road & railway detract somewhat from any real rural pretensions. Still, it's a bargain. All rooms are en suite, with free Wi-Fi. The house has various rooms at different prices & an apartment. **€€€**

Katxina San Martín Bailara, Orio; 943 83 14 07; w katxina.com; 13.30–15.30 & 20.30–22.00, closed Thu &, in winter, Sun evening. You may have tasted better fish, but it's doubtful. The owner uses a Cuban charcoal to cook his dishes. The result is sensational *besugo a la parrilla* (grilled sea bream), though the *rape* (monkfish) runs it close. Meat lovers can savour a beef chop, but vegetarians will be disappointed. They do their own *txakoli* as well. English-language menu available. Reserve as far ahead as possible. Recommended. Price varies according to market. **€€€€€**

What to see and do From the east, after passing the **Ermita de San Martín** on the hill, which is also where the whale lookouts were once sited, the Camino de Santiago enters town down the sharp incline of the Kale Nagusia, where inside a restored 'palace' at number 17 you'll find the tourist office and the Done Jakue

Bidearen (Way of St James) Learning Centre (see below), and an array of well-preserved 16th- and 17th-century houses, many with handsome coats of arms, each one accompanied by a helpful explanatory plaque in English. Many houses carry the initials 'IHS' above their door, standing for 'Iesus Hominum Salvator', Latin for 'Jesus, Saviour of Men' and indicating the once-strong influence of the Jesuits on this locality.

The beaches here are handsome, great for sunbathing or strolling, though far from ideal for swimming due to the large swell. Orio is also the birthplace of the renowned sculptor **Jorge Oteiza**, though the memorial by the church barely does justice to the man who created the famous and controversial 14 Apostles at the Aránzazu sanctuary (page 162). In the third week of July, Orio celebrates a sea bream festival, drawing in visitors from all over the Basque Country to enjoy the fish, which are grilled by local chefs in the town square. Its rowing team is one of the most feared, having won over 30 'flags', presented to the winners of the *trainera* rowing contests in San Sebastián's September finals.

Done Jakue Bidearen (Way of St James Learning Centre) (Kale Nagusia 17; ☎ 943 83 55 65; w turismo.orio.eus; 🕘 15 Jun–13 Sep 10.00–14.00 & 16.00–20.00 Mon–Sat, 10.00–14.00 Sun, 15 Sep–14 Jun 09.30–13.00 Tue, 09.30–13.00 & 16.00–19.00 Wed–Sat, 10.00–14.00 Sun; €0.50/0.20/free adults/children & seniors/pilgrims) Sharing this former palace with the tourist office, pilgrims and would-be pilgrims can glean some basic information here about the caminos de Santiago on their routes through the Basque Country.

Kayaking Kayaking on the Oria River is possible with **Begi-Bistan** (m 657 79 46 77; e info@begi-bistan.com; w begi-bistan.com; 🕘 Feb–Nov). Life jackets are provided, but you'll still have to be able to swim. The prices depend on the size of your group. They can also organise walking and boat trips to see the *flysch* (page 182).

ZARAUTZ It may have had more success in days gone by, pulling in the rich and famous, but no-one can deny Zarautz its permanent claim to fame, namely the longest beach in the Spanish Basque Country. Yes, the town has lost some of its post-war élan, but you can't argue with the statistics: the population of around 23,000 booms in summer, mainly with Spanish tourists, and it's a very popular place for surfing.

In truth, the long promenade here is a peculiar combination, with a collection of sculptures that draw your gaze from the purely functional apartment blocks that form the front line along the beach. There is a fine walk that takes you from the west end of town up the hill to Getaria, then back by the usually bracing coastal road, admiring the waves (see box, page 182). The Camino de Santiago rolls through Zarautz, but for non-pilgrims accommodation prices remain fairly high in summer. There are not too many buildings left of historic interest, but some good eateries and a lively enough bar scene are centred around the Plaza Barren.

Tourist information The tourist office (Nafarroa Kalea 3; ☎ 943 83 09 90; w turismozarautz.com; 🕘 mid-Jun–mid-Sep 09.00–20.00 daily, mid-Mar–mid-Jun & mid-Sep–end Oct 09.30–13.30 & 15.30–19.30 Mon–Fri, 10.00–14.00 & 16.00–19.30 Sat, 10.00–14.00 Sun, other months 09.30–13.30 & 15.30–19.00 Mon–Fri, 10.00–14.00 Sat) lies towards the western end of the beach, and one block back. The very helpful multilingual staff can provide details of walking routes.

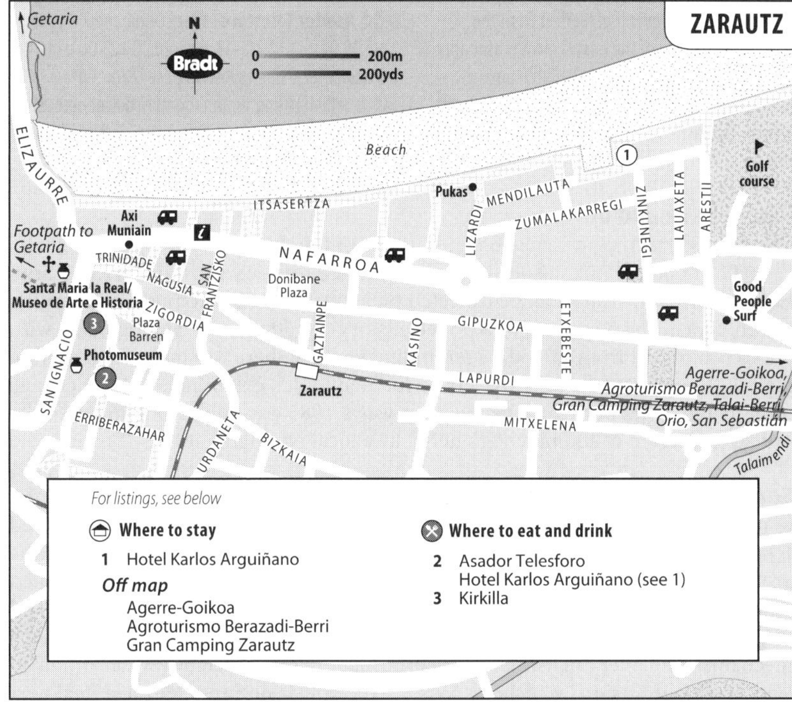

Where to stay *Map, above*

Hotel Karlos Arguiñano (12 rooms) Mendilauta 13; 943 13 00 00; e kahotel@karlosnet.com; w hotelka.com. Not cheap, but set in a beautiful seafront building & with excellent food on hand. Watch the sunsets from the terrace. Friendly staff, owner is a TV celebrity chef who is revered in town for keeping Zarautz in the limelight over the 20 years of his TV show. A peculiarity is the statue of him (he's still alive), with visitors queuing up to have their photos taken with it. **€€€€**

Agroturismo Berazadi-Berri (6 rooms) Talai-Mendi; 943 83 34 94; e berazadi723@gmail.com; w berazadiberri.es. On top of the hill at the east end of town, next to the campsite. Modest but friendly, with restaurant & sun terrace below. Rooms are smaller than some, but more than adequate. Free Wi-Fi. B/fast available at extra cost. **€€**

Agerre-Goikoa (6 rooms) Talaimendi Auzoa; 943 83 32 48; e agerregoikoa@gmail.com; w nekatur.net/agerregoikoa. Just off the roundabout to the east of Zarautz, this is a good-value option. The beach is 400m away. Rooms with TV & heating. Use of kitchen for a little extra charge, allowing self-catering if desired. 2-night min stay in high season. Apartments also available. **€**

Gran Camping Zarautz Monte Talaimendi; 943 83 12 38; e info@grancampingzarautz.com; w grancampingzarautz.com. This well-established site with a 50-year track record lies 2km east of Zarautz, off the N-634, enjoying sea views from its lofty perch. Shop, bar & restaurant. Wi-Fi available. Open all year, it gets crowded in peak season. A long hike up the hill for surfers. **€**

Where to eat and drink *Map, above*

Hotel Karlos Arguiñano (see above) With a celeb chef & sea views, backed up with a great tasting menu, you can't go too far wrong. A less formal bar/cafeteria churning out high-quality *pintxos*, with a slight price premium over other establishments, & there's a terrace to watch the waves. **€€€€**

Kirkilla Santa Marina 12; 943 13 19 82; w kirkilla.com; 13.00–15.30 & 20.30–23.00, closed Mon & Sun evening. Modest from the outside, this is one of the best & most reasonably priced restaurants in Zarautz. Reliable but innovative Basque dishes, & a good-value *menú del día*. The tasting menu is well worth the extra stretch. €€€

Asador Telesforo Plaza Donibane 7; 943 83 09 01; 12.30–13.30 & 20.30–23.00 daily. Popular local due to lowish prices & decent fare in a usually bustling dining room. Fish & generously proportioned salads are good choices here. Some English spoken. €€

What to see and do

Photomuseum (San Ignacio 11; 943 13 09 06; w photomuseum.name; 10.00–14.00 & 17.00–20.00 Tue–Sun; €6/3/free adult/under18/under13) A brief English-language leaflet can be collected on arrival at the Photomuseum, detailing the contents, which amount to a potted history of 150 years of photography, with photo equipment from early days reminding you that there was indeed a life before digital. The ground floor is the home for temporary exhibitions, which change roughly ten times per year. The museum was a 1983 creation, owing much to the private collection of equipment gathered by a local photographer.

Santa Maria la Real (Art and History Museum) (Elizaurre 1; 943 83 52 81; w menosca.com; 10.00–14.00 & 16.30–18.30 Tue–Sat, 16.30–18.30 Sun, closed 1 Jan–mid-Feb; €2/free adults/children) Housed in a 15th-century belltower, the ground floor displays human skeletons unearthed in the area, and is accompanied by a video in English, while the upper floors detail the history of Zarautz and display some artworks. The most striking (pardon the pun) exhibit is the giant clock mechanism. Further English-language information is provided by way of laminated leaflets. The admission fee includes a visit to the **Iglesia de Santa María la Real** next door, a mainly 15th-century building with a defensive structure befitting of its time.

Parque Pagoeta Exit Zarautz east on the N-634 towards Orio and take the GI-2631 signposted towards Aia. After 3.5km, the entrance to the park and the Iturran Learning Centre/Museum is on your left. Entrance is free, unless you want to visit the museum, but as its information is only Basque/Spanish, you may decide not to pay the nominal charge. The park has a number of pleasant circular walks among the beech and oak trees, and the information centre can provide maps for circuits that take in the botanical gardens (at their best in spring) and the forge. The botanical gardens are divided into different zones, depending on whether they are north- or south-facing. Plants are identified by their Latin names, so keen botanists will be satisfied. Dating partially from the 15th century and partially from the 18th, the forge can be visited at any time (to view the exterior) or on Sundays at 11.00 when free access is given to enter both the forge and the working mill downstream. The manner in which the natural contours and water flows were harnessed to provide power is interesting, and there are no fewer than three mills here. Even without detailed information, the park's waymarking is clear enough.

Talai Berri (Talaimendi Auzoa 728; 943 13 27 50; e info@talaiberri.com; w talaiberri.com) Located at the very top of the hill east of Zarautz, this is a fifth-generation winery, one of the few to produce both white *and* red *txakoli*. Visits for those in groups of five or more cost €10 per person and can be carried out in English, with notice and on request. The winery building itself is of interest, having been built personally by the owner, and 12ha of vineyard surround it; 70% of the production is sold inside the Basque Country, with only 18% exported, nearly all of which goes to the USA. (The remaining production services the restaurant market in Catalonia and the rest of Spain.) The winery features a terrace with great views down over the vineyards.

Surfing Zarautz probably has the best claim to being the 'spiritual' centre of surfing in the Spanish Basque Country. A number of surf schools dot the promenade and the main thoroughfare (Nafarroa Kalea, or N-634). Lessons, board hire and all sorts of equipment can be had from the companies listed below. Foreign surf camps also appear in town in season, somewhat antagonising the local schools, especially as the new regulations being introduced at the time of writing seem likely to limit the numbers of surfers in the waters in years to come.

Axi Muniain Trinidad Kalea 1; 943 83 56 48; m 655 72 12 40; e axisurfschool@gmail.com. Described as master of the XXXL-wave, you can take lessons from champion surfer Axi all year round.

Good People Surf Nafarroa 64; 943 53 66 27; e info@goodpeoplesurf.com; w zarautzsurfcamp.com. Between Jun & Sep they run surf camps based at the Talaimendi campsite.

Pukas Lizardi 9; 943 89 06 36; e zarautz@pukassurfeskola.com; w pukassurf.com. Right on the promenade, this school was founded by a pioneering group of surfers in the 1970s & is now a well-renowned establishment that even makes its own boards. Also with a school on Malkorbe beach in Getaria, same telephone number.

GETARIA Getaria is the prettiest of the towns along this stretch of coast, with its fishing giving it a sense of purpose, its narrow pedestrianised Kale Nagusia (main street) funnelling locals and visitors into a compact commercial hub with some high-quality bars and food-orientated shops. The town's two famous sons, Elkano and Balenciaga, bestow it with some extra bragging rights to lord it over nearby Orio and Zarautz. Getaria is the acknowledged Basque centre of the anchovy and, from the start of April, these delicious little fish are the preferred catch for some of the town's 17 fishing-boats. Wash them down with *txakoli*, as Getaria is renowned as a centre of production for the young, white wine. There are two beaches to boot, one wild child for wave-watching (Gaztetape), one calmer one for safe swimming (Malkorbe). The Gothic church at the coast end of Kale Nagusia is highly unusual in that its floor slopes quite sharply upwards towards the altar. All in all, these make a decent list of attractions for a town of a mere 2,800 inhabitants. You will also see a large number of West African faces around town: fishing-boat owners today need to look to Senegal and elsewhere to find crew willing to take on the arduous life at sea.

Where to stay *Map, page 180*

Hotel Itxas-Gain (16 rooms) San Roke 1; 943 14 10 35; e info@hotelitxasgain.com; w hotelitxasgain.com. Much better inside than out; ask for one of the more expensive top-floor rooms enjoying balcony views over the beach. Some rooms have a spa bath. Heating, free Wi-Fi. Pleasant outdoor terrace for summer b/fasts. **€€€**

Hotel Saiaz-Getaria (17 rooms) San Roke 25–27; 943 14 01 43; e info@saiazgetaria.com; w saiazgetaria.com. Beautifully renovated building offering tasteful rooms, including suites, some overlooking the wave-battered beach. All have AC, heating, free Wi-Fi, TV with international channels. **€€€**

Katrapona (8 rooms) Katrapona 4; 943 14 04 09; e info@katrapona.com; w katrapona.com. 6 rooms have excellent views out over the harbour, or beyond to the beach, or even both; number 2 is a good choice. Formerly a gastronomic society, this renovated building has polished floors, exposed stone & wooden beams, & a charming owner. Built in 1901, it was also once in use as a place where fish brought in by the fishermen were 'brined' to preserve them. Free Wi-Fi. B/fast available. **€€€**

Agroturismo Usategi (6 rooms) Akerregi Auzoa 32; 943 14 04 07; e usotegi@hotmail.com; w nekatur.net/usotegi. To find this place, take the

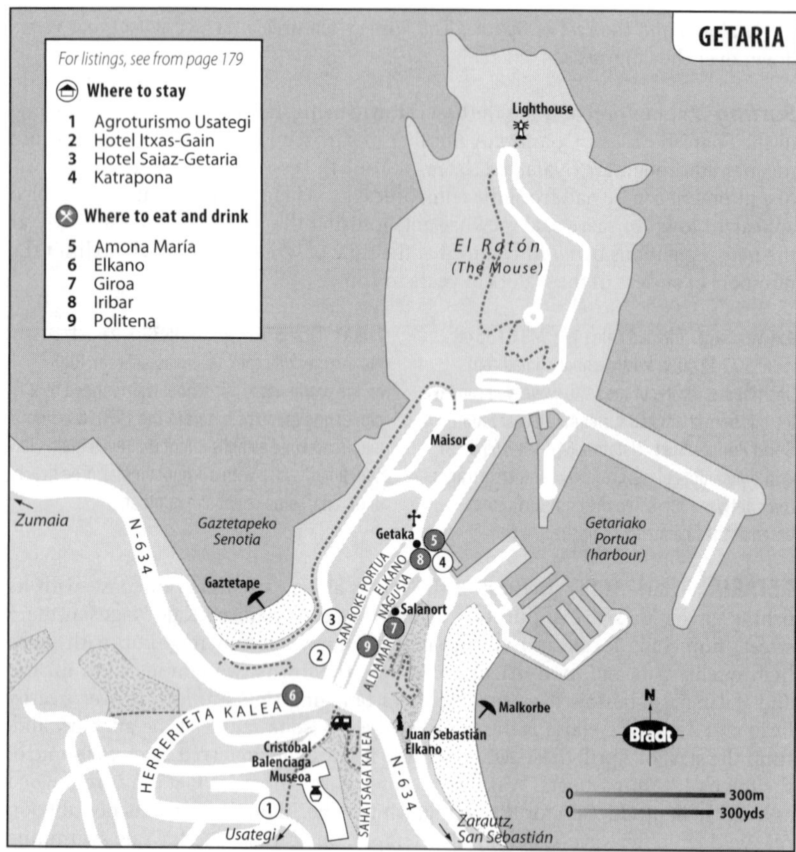

inland road (GI-3391) opposite the Elkano statue, signposted Meaga, in the middle of Getaria & follow it for 2km, then follow the sign off to the right. If you want tranquillity at a decent price, this is the venue. Huge rooms with heating & TV in a tasteful new building, plus views to the distant sea. Also has 2 self-catering rooms, ideal for families. A cock crowing or a harvesting tractor – you're right in the vineyards – are the only possible interruptions to the peace here. B/fast at a modest extra cost. **€€**

Where to eat and drink *Map, above*

Kale Nagusia ('Main Street') has a number of houses with signboards detailing (in English) the histories of their former occupants and a few lively bars with creative *pintxos*, the standouts being **Politena** at number 9 and **Giroa** at number 20, both trusty specialists in churning out creative, artistic *pintxos*, as well as full menus. **Salanort** (w salanort.com) at number 22 and **Getaka** (w getaka.es) at number 35 are shops with a great selection of local wine and delicatessen products, if you want a gastronomic souvenir.

Elkano Herrerieta Kalea 2; 943 14 00 24; w restauranteelkano.com; 20.30–22.30 Mon, 13.15–15.30 & 20.30–22.30 Wed–Sat, 13.15–15.30 Sun. Now probably the town's top table, this prominent place combines super-fresh fish (sold by the kilo) with artistic touches, a great choice of *txakolis* & even artisan beers. **€€€€–€€€€€**

Iribar Nagusia; 943 14 04 06. Old-fashioned dining room, attentive service, excellent food. Everything on the plate looks as though it has been crafted in an artist's studio. And it tastes delicious, with plenty of goodies straight off the barbecue. Go for the oxtail, lamb or the turbot, red sea bream or other fish. €€€

Amona María Katrapona Plaza 2; 943 14 04 05; w amonamaria.com. With views down over the fishing-boats, this is a cross between a wine bar & a delicatessen, showcasing Basque dishes. No coffee or tea available, but delicious *tiramisús* & desserts to indulge in with a glass of *txakoli*. €€

What to see and do

Maisor (Edificio Astillero, Portua; 943 14 09 93; w maisor.com) A small shop in Getaria's port area, the proprietors of Maisor now prepare and conserve delicious anchovies, rather than catching them as their ancestors once did. You can watch a video (in English) demonstrating the production process and even prepare and label your very own jar of anchovies to take home. While the products may seem a bit expensive, you'll soon understand how labour-intensive the process is. And once you taste them, that recently created gap in your wallet will seem totally insignificant.

Monuments to Juan Sebastián Elkano Not one, not two, but three: that's how many statues there are to the local lad who became the first man to circumnavigate the globe. Although Ferdinand Magellan is sometimes credited with this feat, it was none other than Getaria's Elkano who returned home in 1522 from the three-year trip with only 17 other survivors. Magellan? Well, the poor man was killed in the Philippines halfway round and possibly eaten by cannibals, which rather denies him the claim to fame. Two of the Elkano monuments are actually on the main road as you pass through, with the larger of them listing the names of the intrepid sailors who made it home. The third lies at the bottom of the main street.

Cristóbal Balenciaga Museoa (Aldamar Parkea 6; 943 00 88 40; w cristobalbalenciagamuseoa.com; Jun & Sep 10.00–19.00 Tue–Sun, Jul & Aug 10.00–19.00 daily, Oct & Mar–May 10.00–17.00 Tue–Fri, 10.00–19.00 Sat & Sun, Nov–Feb 10.00–15.00 Tue–Fri, 10.00–17.00 Sat & Sun; €10/7/free adults/under 18s & seniors/under 9s) On the landward side of the main road, directly opposite the white statue to Elkano, is this fashion museum, which resembles the Guggenheim and for non-fashion fans is almost as interesting for its space-age exterior as for its contents. For fashionistas, however, the relatively high entrance price is fully justified. A number of temporary exhibitions are usually in place, which might show how he made clothes for clients in the performing arts or provide an insight into the world of haute couture.

El Ratón de Getaria (The Mouse of Getaria) At one time an island, this mountainous promontory is now a mere peninsula and pushes out into the sea, protecting Getaria's port and eastern beach from the Atlantic Ocean's worst excesses. Getaria's famous rodent – yes, it does look like a mouse – also provides the setting for a short, pleasant walk on tarmac and paved paths, which takes you to the remains of the whale lookout at the top of the hill. On the way you'll pass a number of carved faces in the rock (the work of a local resident), the **lighthouse** and even an old road-roller dating from 1931 and curiously deposited halfway up. The route is easy to navigate: from the western end of the harbour, follow the sign that says 'San Anton Parkea', walking on a road that is always closed to traffic, and just keep heading upwards. On the return, you take a narrower path that leads you to the water fountain you passed on your ascent.

ZARAUTZ TO GETARIA: HILLSIDE AND COAST

Distance: 7km; time: 2hrs 15mins; difficulty: mainly easy underfoot, steep ascent at the start then level. Refreshments in Getaria at the halfway stage.

A short walk that ascends steeply out of Zarautz through txakoli vineyards and follows a section of the Camino de Santiago, giving great views over Zarautz, Getaria and the sea. At halfway, you have the chance to visit Getaria (page 179) before taking the coastal path back, retracing your steps or even hopping on a bus.

From the Santa María la Real church at the west end of Zarautz, head inland for 100m, passing the retirement home (marked 'Zaharren Egoitza') before taking the tarmac path up to the right, following the yellow Camino de Santiago signs. Once you've gone another 40m, veer right up a rough-cobbled track, following the sign that says 'Getaria, 3.7km'. The yellow *camino* arrows will be your companion until you reach Getaria. After a few hundred metres you'll enjoy a view over the urban sprawl of Zarautz and the much more appealing mountains beyond. Continuing to climb, you begin to pass through the vineyards that produce the region's *txakoli* wine (see box, page 57). At a crossroads, follow the sign to Getaria, now 3.4km distant. At this point, on the hill to your left, you'll notice a strange edifice that looks like a bullring, but is in fact an abandoned viewpoint that may be restored in the future: not currently worth the detour. Pass the Santarba winery and a few metres further on there is a drinking water tap, handy if you're running low. Continue uphill, leaving the Allene farmhouse to your left, until you reach a crossroads where you take the signpost marked for Zumaia. Continue to climb, always with the sea to your right. Reaching a crest where the path levels off, you have your first sight of your destination, Getaria, with its busy fishing port and the unmistakable 'Mouse of Getaria' rock that juts out into the sea beyond. Continue along the wide level path, ignoring paths off to the left or right. After a few hundred metres, the track becomes a wide tarmac road, but with negligible traffic. From here, looking down to Getaria, you can see how the 'Mouse' protects the town's eastern beach

ZUMAIA Zumaia is the major starting point for excursions to see the Geopark (see below), a coastal park where the spectacular geological formations and colours of the *flysch* (rock strata) make a fascinating backdrop for boat trips and walking. In 2009, this area was declared a biotope, which means it is protected for its geological significance and much visited by scientists; it is also part of the Global Geoparks Network.

A somewhat quirkier claim to fame is the white San Telmo church that looks out defiantly over the ocean. It was the setting for some wedding shots in the outrageously funny 2014 film *Ochos apellidos vascos* (literally 'Eight Basque Surnames'; see box, page 31), and now welcomes visitors for photoshoots.

Tourist information At the eastern end of the town centre and the junction of Zumaia's two rivers, the tourist office (Kantauri Plaza 13; 943 14 33 96; w zumaia.eus/tourism) has all the information on boat trips to see the Geopark, although tickets can also be bought online (see below). They also issue an excellent leaflet in English covering hikes in and around town, with a passable map. The Geopark's own website offers maps and narratives of several walks, and although the details are mainly in Basque at present, the walks are generally waymarked and easy to follow.

Geopark (w geoparkea.eus) At present, only one of the many boat trip options has an English-language audio guide (90mins; €17), but the rock formations along

from the massive waves that rush in from the west, while its western beach takes a hammering. Continue along the tarmac, flanked by the massive houses, some of them now wineries, some guesthouses, all surrounded by further vineyards. At the end of the road, at a junction, take the right-hand fork downhill, following the by now familiar yellow arrows. As you descend, the port and the squiggle-shaped roof of the modern Balenciaga Museum are apparent. After 500m on the main – though usually quiet – road, it's a relief to take a sharp right down a narrow, rocky path, just before the power cables that cross above the road. You are now heading directly towards the town, a brief departure from the Camino de Santiago. Coming to a junction of paths, continue straight ahead towards the 'Mouse', with a modern U-shaped apartment block down to your right. A few hundred metres further, a gravel track bears down to your right and you should follow it: you have once again picked up the Camino de Santiago. Taking a right at the road junction, then an immediate left down some steps, you enter into Getaria. The mass of the Balenciaga building to your right is yet another example of the innovative architecture found in the Basque Country. Now in front of you is the white statue of Elkano and, silhouetted against the sky to your right, is another monument to the town's favourite son (page 181). A walk around town is recommended and, if you have the energy, you could do a circuit of the 'Mouse' itself (page 181).

To return to Zarautz, you now follow the flat path that runs between the sea and the busy road. This is a popular track for joggers and walkers, and coming the other way you may meet some 'cheating' pilgrims who didn't fancy the hilly route you've just walked. Spare a thought for them: they are still over 700km from Santiago de Compostela, while you only have 3km to your destination, Zarautz. Apart from the crashing waves and some interesting rock formations at low tide, there is not too much of interest to see on your return route, so you can always consider taking the twice-hourly bus that departs from the stop in front of the white Elkano statue.

the coastline are stunning and even non-geologists will be interested to learn how the amazing formations were created by the collision of Iberia (which was then an island) with mainland Europe many millions of years ago. This low-speed clash of land masses was responsible for the creation of the Pyrenees. Tickets are best booked through the website w geoparkea.eus, the tourist office in Zumaia (see opposite), or in Deba or Mutriku tourist offices, well in advance in high season. The boat has a capacity for around 40, and all excursions are subject to favourable weather/sea conditions. As a free alternative, if you want to go about 1km out of town on foot to see some of the rocks, ask for directions at the Zumaia tourist office. And if you want to take the 14km coastal path to Deba, this provides a chance to see further formations. The website also now features a downloadable 'Route of the Viewpoints', ideal for car drivers who want to see the Geopark landscapes in a hurry.

Walking One of the best and most convenient of the walks around Zumaia is the 'Geological Walk' (1hr 40mins; 4km), which runs along the coast west of town, climbing Talaimendi hill, and then follows the clifftop before bringing you to a wonderful vantage point over the *flysch* rock formations at Algorri point. As well as the alternating layers of hard and softer rock, deposited on the sea bed and now forming an incredible rock platform that at times looks manmade, geologists have also found asteroid particles here among rocks that are over 60 million years old.

CRISTÓBAL BALENCIAGA: 'HIS CLOTHES MADE THEM BEAUTIFUL'

Sara Lister

The shape and style of the 19th-century Aldamar Palace contrasts sharply with the new, juxtaposed, angular entrance to the museum that bears the name of Getaria's famous couturier, Cristóbal Balenciaga. The stark contrast between the two buildings inadvertently mirrors the differences between his creations at the very start of his career and in later years. Inside, the visitor can trace the progression in style and shape, from the lavishly embroidered early masterpieces from the first haute couture collection in 1917, drawing on historical influences, to the elegant designs of simplicity and minimalism for which he became so famous at the height of his career.

The collection in the museum is set out with style and thought, giving visitors the opportunity to wander at their own pace through the exhibits, arranged in such a way to let them imagine they are in an exclusive shopping street where only window-shopping is allowed. However, if you are curious to know more about the exhibits on display or learn more about the pioneering tailoring techniques for which Balenciaga was so famous, you can pause and absorb the content of the information panels or listen to your audio guide.

Cristóbal Balenciaga was born in the fishing village of Getaria in 1895, the son of a seamstress. Accompanying his mother as she worked for the important families of the area, he observed the fine clothes of the Basque aristocracy, ordered from the fashion houses of London and Paris. By 22 years of age he had opened his first haute couture atelier in San Sebastián. During his career of over 50 years, he gained an international reputation, specifically pioneering the idea that the clothes he designed should balance both the aesthetic and practical needs of the women who would be wearing them. Iconic designs of the 1950s such as the 'sack', 'baby doll' and 'tunic' dress were all designs of Balenciaga. Among his customers were international celebrities such as the Duchess of Windsor and Gloria Guinness. During his lifetime he became a cult couturier, attracting critical acclaim from all quarters. Memorably, Christian Dior described Balenciaga as the conductor of the orchestra of haute couture, the other couturiers merely being 'the musicians following the instructions he gave'. When he died in 1972, a longstanding client provided the perfect sign-off to this star of Basque haute couture: 'Women did not have to be perfect or even beautiful to wear his clothes. His clothes made them beautiful.'

FURTHER WEST: DEBA AND MUTRIKU

Before Gipuzkoa reaches its western border with Bizkaia, the coastal road passes first through **Deba** and **Mutriku**. Deba's main beach is deep and long, but devoid of cafés or restaurants. At one end the Deba River enters the ocean after a final couple of twists and turns; at the other, you can take a short walk to the smaller, narrow Laparri beach which reveals the black rock formations characteristic of this coast. Mutriku's buildings tumble down the steep hillside towards the sea, culminating in a surprisingly large leisure port. West of town, and before reaching Ondarroa – across the 'border' with Bizkaia – you can turn off at the sign for Saturrarán where you'll find a pleasant stretch of sand with few facilities but some rocky intrusions that could provide good crab-hunting grounds for children.

5

Vitoria-Gasteiz and Álava (Araba) Province

Álava's extensive borders with Burgos to the west and La Rioja to the south and the resultant centuries of rubbing shoulders with the inhabitants of those non-Basque provinces have certainly had their effect: it's a province that feels less obviously Basque than its northern neighbours of Gipuzkoa or Bizkaia. Álava lies on an alluvial plain, framed on three sides by mountains and with its southern edge rimmed by the River Ebro. The main A-1 road connecting Irun with Madrid cuts an east-to-west swathe across the province, hurrying traffic to and from the national capital. At nearly 3,000km^2 Álava is larger than the other two constituents of the Basque Autonomous Community (BAC), but with around 325,000 inhabitants it is much less populous. The capital of Álava, and indeed of the whole BAC, is Vitoria-Gasteiz. As the city accounts for three-quarters of Álava's population, the remainder of the province has a slow-paced feel.

Meanwhile, Rioja Alavesa, below the imperious peaks of the Sierra de Cantabria range, is a region that seems at times almost empty of any Basqueness, geographically and culturally. Wine is the lure here, the well-ordered rows of vines drawing many, many visitors from across the globe to sample the precious liquid and admire the stunning landscape that nurtures it. Elsewhere, Añana and its surroundings to the west of Vitoria favour the traveller who wants to combine some walking with a few really worthwhile attractions and no-frills but welcoming accommodation. Here, for example, you will find the Roman remains of Iruña-Veleia and the shimmering salt pans of Salinas de Añana village. East of Vitoria, the less developed regions of Montaña Alavesa and Llanada Alavesa are even more tranquil and rural in character. Finally, and shared with Bizkaia province to the north, Gorbeia is a lush, tree-rich Natural Park which spreads out over 20,000ha, a popular retreat for the city-dwellers of Vitoria to its south and Bilbao to its north. While it has a few museums, Mother Nature with its mountains and waterfalls is Queen here.

VITORIA-GASTEIZ

Understated, under-visited and hardly a household name: here's a well-organised city with a great quality of life, getting on quietly with its day-to-day business, enjoying its weekends and counting down the days to its vibrant festivals. And when it comes to those, Vitoria's inhabitants can surely compete with all comers in any 'letting your hair down' tournament. Vitoria was officially named 'European Green Capital, 2012', and its environmental credentials are much in evidence as you wander around the city, from its green belt and six parks to its cycle paths,

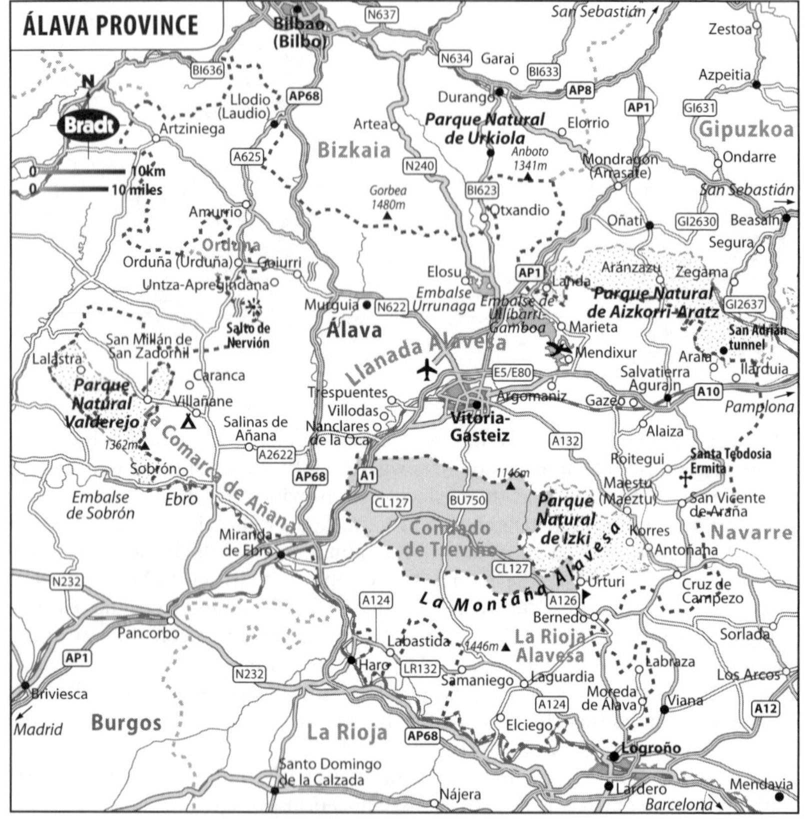

pedestrianised Old Town streets and nearby wetlands – a haven for birdlife. Indeed, Vitoria was the very first Spanish city to sport a bicycle path, and each citizen has over 40m^2 of green space. Mountains are present on the horizon on three sides, and that green belt will extend to over 1,000km^2 when the plan, devised in the 1990s and constantly evolving, is complete. No-one can say that the city doesn't make the most of this accolade. Not only do the inhabitants talk the talk, but they walk the walk too. And run, speed-skate and cycle their way around town (so much so that they have banned the use of bicycles in the Old Town, not that many people take any notice, of course). Using Vitoria's green belt, you could cycle all the way around the city's perimeter, a distance of 30km.

As an additional welcome to visitors, all of Vitoria's official buildings and museums are adapted for those of lesser mobility, including a rolling walkway that takes people gently up to the preserved Old Town. One standout feature of the Old Town is the series of 13 colourful murals that decorate the end walls of houses, each depicting a scene relevant to the history or culture of the city. The website **w** muralismopublico.com gives their locations and a short introduction to the significance of each of them. Designed by local and international artists, and painted by them and city volunteers with the permission of the town council, they add a splash of modernity and funkiness to a city that embraces both while cherishing and respecting its rich history. An itinerary, known as the Itinerário Murallistico Vitoria-Gasteiz, will take you around them all. On a more sombre note, the former Bank of Spain building in Lehendakari Aguirre Kalea has been fully renovated and by mid-2019 was due to open as the Central Memoriál de las Victimas del Terrorismo (Central Memorial of the Victims of Terrorism).

Vitoria's Centro Histórico (Old Town) surprises many visitors from elsewhere in Spain with its intactness, and is certainly full of points of interest: a cathedral under renovation (but nevertheless visitable, and infinitely more interesting as a result of the works in progress); old city walls; palaces with stories to tell. When it comes to partying, the inhabitants do indeed hit it pretty hard, particularly during Vitoria's Virgen Blanca fiesta week in August, and the four days in April devoted to San Prudencio, Álava's patron saint. The latter is an excellent time to witness Basque traditional sports such as wood-chopping and stone-lifting (page 37).

It's a tough job to compete when you've got Bilbao and San Sebastián as your nearest rivals. After all, not many cities have a household-name museum, and not every city can stretch itself out behind a world-class urban beach. Nevertheless, no-one can deny that Vitoria-Gasteiz is making a good fist of it.

The 2016 publication of *El Silencio de la Ciudad Blanca*, a novel set in the city, has drawn many curious visitors to Vitoria to identify the locations mentioned in the book. It was one of the year's best-selling books in Spain.

Culturally, Vitoria and Álava province are less overtly Basque than their northern rivals (though it might be wise not to mention it), with the language of the city streets being predominantly Spanish. You'll certainly see fewer banners of political protest hanging from the balconies here. For industry, two international industrial giants, namely Mercedes and Michelin, as well as their suppliers, provide significant employment to the town.

HISTORY Despite some claims that Vitoria was founded in the 8th century in its present location as *Victoriacum*, the evidence for this is unclear. Certainly a settlement had been in existence on this site since the early Middle Ages, but any association with the name *Victoriacum* is open to dispute. A common and understandable mistake made by visitors nowadays is to think that 'Gasteiz' is the Basque alternative name for the Spanish-sounding 'Vitoria', but the double-barrelled designation is in fact the correct one. Gasteiz is the early name of the small settlement located where the cathedral now stands, but when the King of Navarre, Sancho the Wise, conquered Gasteiz in 1181, he marked his success by calling it 'Nueva Victoria' ('New Victory'). It seems that the city walls were already in place by the time of Sancho's arrival: the recent and ongoing cathedral renovations have revealed that they date back to the 11th century, rather than the 12th as had been previously thought. These city walls have been rebuilt or partially rebuilt at various stages over the centuries, even undergoing substantial renovations as recently as the 1960s. As for the name, eventually the 'c' and the 'nueva' were dropped from 'Nueva Victoria' and for many centuries Vitoria was the town's official name. Around 1200, King Alfonso VIII of Castile took the city and expanded it by constructing three new roads – namely Zapatería, Correría and Herrería – on the west side of the hill, but the town was ravaged by a fire in 1202. Under the reign of then king, Alfonso X, further expansion took place with the 1256 addition, to the east of the hill, of three more significant streets, Cuchillería, Judería and Pintorería. In the centuries that followed, Vitoria enjoyed a period of economic prosperity, thanks to its position on the shortest route between the powerful Kingdom of Castile and its trading partners in northern Europe. This allowed the city to raise duties on goods passing through. In 1443, Vitoria suffered another serious fire, destroying the western part of the city and prompting the use of stone and adobe, rather than wood, in the rebuilding project.

Handsome palaces such as Montehermoso and Escoriaza-Esquivel were constructed for members of the court of Carlos I of Spain (Carlos V of Germany), giving a more elegant aspect to Vitoria. As elsewhere in Spain, the expulsion of the Jewish population in 1492 led to a long period of economic decline lasting for centuries.

The 1813 Battle of Vitoria had repercussions far beyond the town, province and even Spain. The victory over Joseph, Napoleon Bonaparte's brother (the then King of Spain) by allied Spanish, British, Portuguese and German troops resulted in the return of the Spanish crown to Fernando VII, and many historians acknowledge the enormous significance of this battle in the demise of Napoleon himself. Joseph Bonaparte had installed himself in the city, having moved out of hostile Madrid to be in a more welcoming environment nearer to his native France.

Vitoria's longstanding status as a customs post with the right to levy duties was lost to the coast in 1841, dealing a significant blow to the town's economy. To some extent, the subsequent creation of the Banco de Vitoria and the arrival of the railway helped to rejuvenate the prosperity of the city.

Vitoria's experience in the 20th century is not unusual, being a story of industrialisation and rapid expansion, with the city pushing ever outwards to accommodate a burgeoning population. In 1980, the original name of Gasteiz was added once more, giving the city its current double-barrelled designation. Its appointment in the same year as administrative capital of the Basque Autonomous Community (BAC) was a neat way of cooling the simmering rivalry between San Sebastián and Bilbao, the alternative claimants. The city is frequently rated as one of the best places to live in Spain, and is proud of its green credentials and its new-found importance as the seat of local government, parliament and the Prime Minister of the BAC.

GETTING THERE AND AWAY

By road Vitoria-Gasteiz is well connected to Bilbao (50mins) and San Sebastián (1hr 10mins), using the motorway and paying the tolls. With a bit of planning, you can take slower, toll-free routes instead. Madrid is reachable in around 3 hours 45 minutes, again assuming use of the toll roads.

By bus Vitoria's **bus station** is at Plaza Euskaltzaindia [189 B1] (☎ 945 16 16 66), open daily from 06.00 to midnight with half-hourly services to Bilbao (1hr; €6.30), San Sebastián (1hr 20mins; €7), Madrid (4hrs; €35) and other major Spanish cities. There are also good connections to most sizeable towns in Álava. The bus station itself can be reached by tram line 1 or bus number 2, in either case getting off at the Euskal Herria stop. Further information on all buses to, from and around the city can be found on the city website, w vitoria-gasteiz.org, or w autobuseslaunion.com.

By train Vitoria's train station [189 C3] (Plazuela de la Estación 1; w adif.es) is rarely a hive of frenzied activity. There are around nine connections to and from Madrid (Chamartín station, around 4hrs 15mins; €30), Barcelona (5hrs; €30) and seven to Irun (2hrs 30mins; €12) and San Sebastián (1hr 45mins; €11) and six with Pamplona (1hr; €7), plus a few to and from cities in Spain's far west, such as Vigo and La Coruña. There is no direct link to Bilbao.

By air Although Vitoria has dabbled with budget flights to the UK in the past, at the time of writing its small airport catered only for freight traffic, plus a budget passenger route to Cologne/Bonn and a few seasonal passenger flights to the Canary Islands.

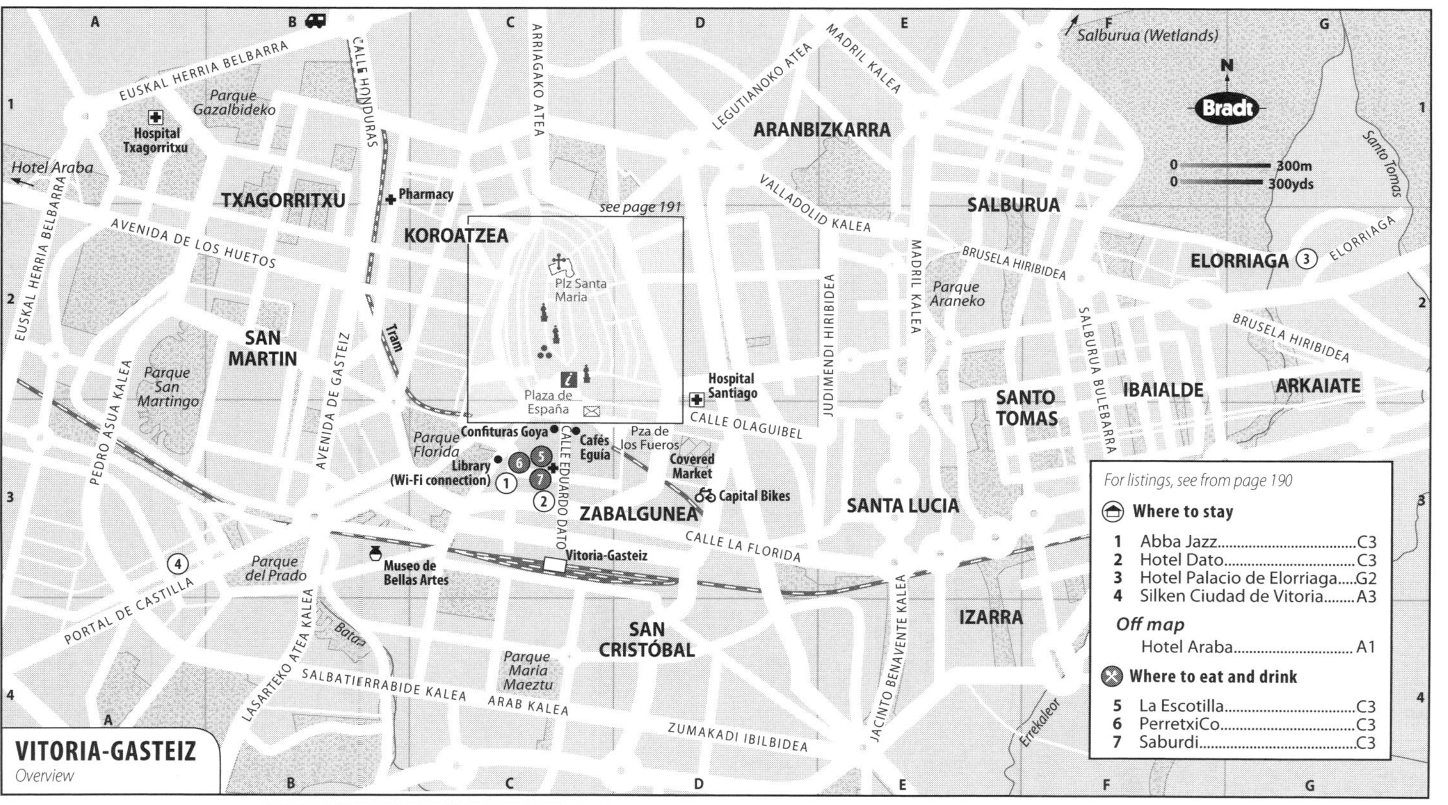
VITORIA-GASTEIZ
Overview
For listings, see from page 190
Where to stay
1 Abba Jazz....C3
2 Hotel Dato....C3
3 Hotel Palacio de Elorriaga....G2
4 Silken Ciudad de Vitoria....A3
Off map
Hotel Araba....A1
Where to eat and drink
5 La Escotilla....C3
6 PerretxiCo....C3
7 Saburdi....C3
Bradt
N
0 300m
0 300yds
Salburua (Wetlands)
Hotel Araba
see page 191
TXAGORRITXU
KOROATZEA
ARANBIZKARRA
SALBURUA
ELORRIAGA
SAN MARTIN
SANTO TOMAS
IBAIALDE
ARKAIATE
SANTA LUCIA
ZABALGUNEA
SAN CRISTÓBAL
IZARRA
EUSKAL HERRIA BELBARRA
CALLE HONDURAS
ARRIAGAKO ATEA
LEGUTIANOKO ATEA
MADRIL KALEA
VALLADOLID KALEA
BRUSELA HIRIBIDEA
ELORRIAGA
Santo Tomas
AVENIDA DE LOS HUETOS
AVENIDA DE GASTEIZ
JUDIMENDI HIRIBIDEA
SALBURUA BULEBARRA
CALLE OLAGUIBEL
CALLE EDUARDO DATO
CALLE LA FLORIDA
PEDRO ASUA KALEA
PORTAL DE CASTILLA
LASARTEKO ATEA KALEA
SALBATIERRABIDE KALEA
ARAB KALEA
ZUMAKADI IBILBIDEA
JACINTO BENAVENTE KALEA
Errekaleor
Batan
Parque Gazalbideko
Hospital Txagorritxu
Pharmacy
Tram
Parque San Martingo
Plz Santa Maria
Plaza de España
Hospital Santiago
Parque Florida
Confituras Goya
Cafés Eguía
Pza de los Fueros
Library (Wi-Fi connection)
Covered Market
Capital Bikes
Parque Araneko
Museo de Bellas Artes
Vitoria-Gasteiz
Parque del Prado
Parque Maria Maeztu

GETTING AROUND

On foot As in Bilbao and San Sebastián, Vitoria is most easily accessed on foot and walking is the preferred method of getting around for most able-bodied inhabitants. The city is generally very well equipped for those of lesser mobility.

By bike To take advantage of the cycle paths in and around town, or to head further afield, try **Capital Bikes** [189 D3] (m 691 11 22 92; e reservas@capitalbikes.es; w capitalbikes.es), a bike-hire company that also hires out electric two-wheelers.

By tram Vitoria's trams run on two lines across the city and, while they are modern and easy to use, they will be of not much interest to those visitors here for only a few days, unless they're arriving or departing by bus (the relevant tram stop for the bus station is Euskal Herria). To buy tickets, tram stops are provided with multilingual ticket machines. Single tickets cost €1.35, though a day pass is available for €4.40. If you are using one of the regular user cards (BAT, Barik, Mugi), you will need to validate your pass before boarding. The service runs on weekdays from 06.15 until 23.00, at least every 15 minutes, but starts a half-hour later at weekends and on holidays.

By bus Vitoria is armed with a good, efficient bus service with ten lines providing an extensive network over the city. Services operate from around 07.00 to 21.30, and on Fridays and Saturdays night buses run from 23.00 until 06.00 the following morning. Tickets can be bought on board and route maps are clearly displayed on the bus shelters. A single journey costs €1.15. Passes for multiple journeys are available, but are likely to be of interest only to those staying for a week or more.

By taxi Visitors wanting a taxi should try **Radio Taxi** (☎ 945 27 35 00).

TOURIST INFORMATION The city's tourist information office (Plaza de España 1; ☎ 945 16 15 98; e turismo@vitoria-gasteiz.org; w vitoria-gasteiz.org/turismo; ⊙ Oct–Jun 10.00–19.00 Mon–Sat, 11.00–14.00 Sun & holidays, Jul–Sep 10.00–20.00 daily) is spacious and has helpful, multilingual staff who can provide copious information both on the city and Álava province. For walkers, the office has a book of ten walks, available in English (€6). This includes river and forest strolls, two walks in the Salburua wetlands (page 199) and a guided hike around the complete 30km circuit of the Green Belt.

Guided walking tours With 24 hours' advance notice, the city's tourist office (see above) can organise guided tours in English, which operate with a minimum of four people and last around 1½ hours (€5). Much, much more expensive – unless you are in a large group – are private tours, details of which are held by the tourist office. Contact them in advance for any kind of tour.

WHERE TO STAY Vitoria's range of accommodation is improving but would still certainly benefit from a couple of top-quality characterful hotels.

Upmarket

Silken Ciudad de Vitoria [189 A3] (149 rooms) Portal de Castilla 8; ☎ 945 14 11 00; e silken@hoteles-silken.com; w hoteles-silken.com. Probably the best of the chain hotels in town, a 4-star located near the train station. Rooms have AC, heating & flat-screen TV; Wi-Fi attracts an extra charge. The hotel has a gym, plus spa (sauna,

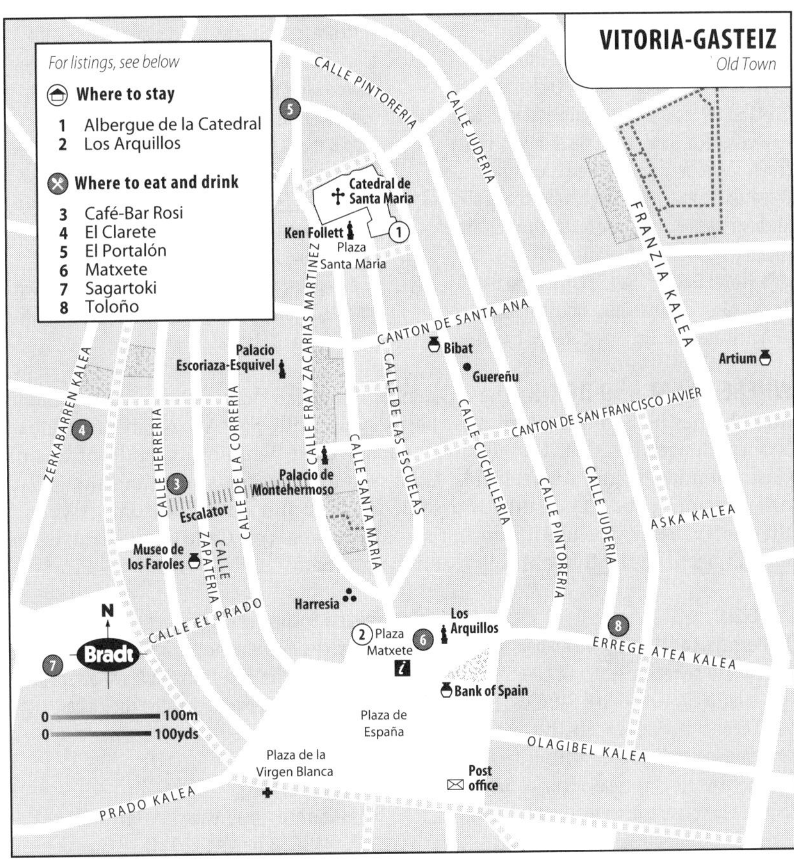

massage & hot tub, at extra cost). Parking is also available at an extra charge. Good room deals are available, but you need to factor in those extras. Excellent b/fast, or to save money, take it in the hotel café instead. **€€€€**

Mid range

Los Arquillos [map, above] (8 rooms) Los Arquillos 1; 945 15 12 59; e via website; w lacasadelosarquillos.com. A perfect, central location, under the historic arches, a few steps from the Old Town & overlooking the sometimes boisterous square. Some rooms are more spacious than others, all are modern & smart. Free Wi-Fi, heating, TV. **€€€**

Budget

Abba Jazz [189 C3] (25 rooms) Calle Florida 7; 945 10 13 46; m 629 22 65 89; e abbajazz@abbahoteles.com; w abbajazzvitoriahotel.com. A small, renovated hotel, part of a chain, but still with a homely feel. A short walk to the main squares, Old Town & train station. Comfortable rooms, TV & free Wi-Fi. Decent b/fast available. Private parking by arrangement (extra cost). **€€**

Hotel Palacio de Elorriaga [189 G2] (21 rooms) Elorriaga 15; 945 26 36 16; e info@hotelpalacioelorriaga.com; w hotelpalacioelorriaga.com. In a town that lacks a boutique hotel, this comes the closest. In a 16th-century building located a bit outside the city centre, the rooms are a little dark, but rooms come with heating, hydro-massage showers, TV & free Wi-Fi. Parking is also free, b/fast is only a little extra cost. **€€**

Hotel Araba [189 A1] (20 rooms) Av de los Huetos 17; 945 22 26 69; e araba@restaurantearaba.com; w hotelaraba.com. Newish, small & popular hotel with private parking. Rooms have AC, free Wi-Fi, TV & minibar. **€€**

Shoestring

Albergue de la Catedral [map, page 191] (17 rooms & dormitories) Cuchillería 87; 945 27 59 55; e info@alberguecatedral.com; w alberguecatedral.com. Dbls & dorms, plus a family room. Very central & excellent prices. Clean & sparse, popular with bargain-hunters & pilgrims. Kitchen, washing machine (extra charge), use of computer terminal & free Wi-Fi. **€**

Hotel Dato [189 C3] (14 rooms) Dato 28; 945 14 72 30; e info@hoteldato.com; w hoteldato.com. Don't be deterred by the ornate entrance, complete with reclining statues, & the glitzy interior. You may think you're in an antiques shop, replete with chandeliers & cornices, and in a way you are, as the owner's father ran such a shop & many items were transferred here when it closed. A central, budget option, with decent bathrooms, TV, free Wi-Fi & central heating from old-fashioned radiators. Some street-facing rooms have galleried balconies, but the 07.00 street-sweeper may double up as your alarm clock. Good off-season rates. Parking nearby is €12 per day. **€**

WHERE TO EAT AND DRINK The city's inhabitants can dine with the best of them, though they will often admit that keeping up with San Sebastián and Bilbao is a challenge. In 2014, they definitely achieved it, winning the title of Spain's Gastronomic Capital. At weekends, all ages are out on the streets and the *pintxo pote* scheme (page 61) assures you some low-cost fun on a Thursday. A young, alternative, noisy vibe fills the air in the Old Town bars on Calle Cuchillería, in the section between the Bibat Museum and the cathedral.

Pintxos

PerretxiCo [189 C3] San Antonio 3; 945 13 72 21; w perretxico.es; 08.00–midnight Mon–Thu, 09.00–01.30 Fri & Sat; 09.00–midnight Sun. Cheerful service, as befits a bar that knows it's providing something excellent. National awards have been won by the creations made here & they continue to deliver *pintxos* to a fine standard, but also do meals, including various menus & b/fasts. Midday menu is a good-value deal.

Saburdi [189 C3] Dato 32; 945 14 70 16; w saburdi.com; 11.00–midnight Sun, 08.00–midnight Mon–Thu, 08.00–01.00 Fri & Sat. Very central, this has a good – perhaps the city's best – selection of tasty, aesthetically appealing savouries. If that leaves you hungry, there's a restaurant, too, open at noon, with a well-priced *menú del día*.

Sagartoki [map, page 191] Prado 18; 945 28 86 76; w sagartoki.com; 10.00–midnight Mon–Fri, 09.00–01.00 Sat & Sun. Another multiple competition winner. This is the place to order a *huevo frito*. A croquette conceals a taste of fried egg & chips & they recommend that you eat it in 1 bite. More familiar, less innovative *pintxos* are also available.

Toloño [map, page 191] Cuesta San Francisco 3; w tolonobar.com; 09.00–midnight Mon–Thu, 09.00–04.00 Fri & Sat, 10.30–15.30 Sun. An 'Irish' doesn't sound even vaguely Spanish or Basque, yet this one – a swirly, cream-&-mushroom affair, served in a glass – won the 'Best Pintxo in Álava' award in 2008. Delicate & decorative, the choice here is absolutely exquisite.

Restaurants

El Clarete [map, page 191] Cercas Bajas 18; 945 26 38 74; 13.30–15.30 Mon–Sat, 21.00–23.00 Thu–Sat. One of the highlights of the restaurant scene in Vitoria, it offers a tasting menu which might consist of 8 or 9 (small) dishes, each expertly elaborated. Midweek lunchtime menus are much cheaper. **€€€€**

El Portalón [map, page 191] Correría 151; 945 14 27 55; w restauranteelportalon.com; 11.00–15.30 & 20.30–23.00 Mon–Thu, 09.00–23.00 Fri–Sun. It may not have a Michelin star, but nowhere in town will match this 15th-century building for its beautiful interior. Spread across 6 dining rooms, some reserved for functions, & with a proper wine cellar. Downstairs is usually *pintxos* only &, while you pay a premium, the quality merits it. Upstairs, the menu promises & delivers high-quality favourites, with prices to match. Set menus, viewable on the website, need to be pre-ordered. **€€€€**

Matxete [map, page 191] Plaza del Matxete 4–5; 945 13 18 21; w matxete.com; noon–23.00 Tue–Sat, noon–18.00 Sun. Get yourself an outside table on a sunny day, order up a grilled fish or a sirloin steak & all's well with the world. One of the town's best *pinxtos*, for food & setting. €€€

La Escotilla [189 C3] San Prudencio 5; 945 00 26 27; w laescotilla.es; noon–midnight Tue–Sat, noon–17.00 Sun. Under the same ownership as the PerretxiCo (see opposite), this fish-only restaurant is bedecked in maritime paraphernalia, brightly lit & undoubtedly *the* place for the fruits of the ocean in Vitoria. Choose from a number of menus. €€–€€€

Café-Bar Rosi [map, page 191] Herrería 44; 945 25 02 48; 13.00–15.30 Sun–Wed, 13.00–15.30 & 21.00–23.00 Thu–Sat. A compact restaurant with a great culinary reputation. The goat's cheese salad, which sometimes appears on the *menú del día*, comes particularly recommended. €€

Saburdi [189 C3] See *Pintxos*, opposite. €€

SHOPPING Vitoria has its own branch of El Corte Inglés department store, but if you want to seek out some local specialities, Dato, Correría and Cuchillería are the three streets to stroll down, virtually unhindered by traffic, while more mainstream outlets inhabit Independencia and General Álava. Mindful of the occasional rain shower, Vitoria has covered its smart, modern **market** (09.00–14.00 & 17.00–20.00 Mon–Thu, 09.00–14.00 & 17.00–20.30 Fri, 08.00–15.00 Sat), located in the Plaza Santa Bárbara and attracting over 40,000 shoppers every week. Thursday and Saturday mornings are the best time to visit, as local producers bring organic products to town, including delicious bread, oil, cheese and pastries – all to be sold on the upstairs terrace. Look out for the 'Eusko Label' on some products, guaranteeing that what you get is local and free from anything artificial. With advance notice, you can also enjoy some wine-tasting here, at a stall run by **Eguren Ugarte** (page 217) and hosted by an English-speaker. On one side of the market building, there are a number of gastro-bars, which do brisk business (08.00–23.00 Mon–Thu, 08.00–01.00 Fri & Sat, 09.30–23.00 Sun). Generally, the city shops open from 10.00 to 13.30 and again from 17.00 to 20.00 from Monday to Saturday, perhaps closing an hour earlier on Saturday evening. Nearly all shops are closed on Sundays.

Cafés Eguía [189 C3] Dato 7; 10.00–14.00 & 16.30–20.30 Mon–Sat. Founded in the late 19th century, this is a a tiny outlet with a big reputation for its coffee, tea, *turrón*, nuts & plenty more goodies.

Confituras Goya [189 C3] Dato 6 (& other branches around town); w confiturasgoya.es; 09.30–14.00 & 16.30–20.00 Mon–Sat, 09.30–14.30 Sun. Other than the name, there is no connection with the famous painter, but you can't help thinking that if he'd turned his hand to confectionery, he might have created some of what's on offer here. Founded in the late 19th century, this tiny outlet has a good reputation for its coffee, tea, *turrón*, truffles & special cakes. It is also renowned for its *Vasquitos* & *Neskitas* ('Little Basque Boys' & 'Little Basque Girls') brand of chocolates, often bought as gifts.

Guereñu [map, page 191] Cuchillería 41; w guerenu.net; 11.00–14.00 & 17.00–20.00 Tue–Fri, 11.00–14.30 Sat, Sun & holidays. Opposite the Museum of Playing Cards, this is one of the few souvenir shops to be found in Vitoria. As well as the usual key rings & fridge magnets, it also sells decorative playing cards. There's another branch at Plaza General Loma 5.

OTHER PRACTICALITIES

Post office [map, page 191] The main post office can be found at Calle Postas 9 (08.30–20.30 Mon–Fri, 09.30–13.00 Sat).

Internet/Wi-Fi As more people access Wi-Fi, Vitoria's internet cafés have mostly closed. It's not hard to locate a café with Wi-Fi and nearly every hotel offers this service. The **Casa de Cultura** (public library) [189 C3] (Paseo de la Florida 9;

🕘 09.00–14.00 & 16.00–20.00 Mon–Fri, 09.00–14.00 Sat) offers internet access to all.

Hospital Vitoria's main hospital is the Hospital Santiago [189 D2] (Olaguibel 29; ☎945 00 76 00) and there is also the Hospital Txagorritxu [189 A1] (José Achotégui; ☎945 00 70 00).

Pharmacies There are many pharmacies in town, of which **Farmacia Virgen Blanca** [map, page 191] in the square of the same name is open every day of the year (🕘 09.00–22.00). **Zulueta Hernández** [189 C3] (Dato 24; ☎945 23 16 30) and **Farmacia Esparza Marin** [189 B1] (Cruz Blanca 8; ☎ 945 24 53 61) are also both centrally located.

FESTIVALS

San Prudencio San Prudencio is the main saint of the province of Álava. His four-day festival begins on 27 April with La Retreta, more of a whimper than a bang, involving the slightly repetitive playing of live music in the Plaza de España accompanied by some nifty folk dancing. As well as the on-stage band, trumpeters blow their hardest from the balconies on the north side of the square and the crowd applaud politely. At midnight, however, the noise level and excitement are increased by a notch or two, as the Tamborrada cuts loose in the Plaza de la Provincia. Dressed in the distinctive clothes of their own gastronomic society (see box, page 60), each society's band beats their drums and strolls the streets of the Old Town and town centre until about 03.00. On 28 April the city's inhabitants – or at least those who are not suffering too much from the previous evening – make a pilgrimage of sorts to the Basílica de Armentia in the park of the same name, where a mass is held, followed by a short performance of the traditional Basque dance, the *aurresku*, a tribute to the mayor of the town and other officialdom. All around the basilica are hundreds of food and drink stalls, with festive specialities such as *caracoles* (snails), *talos* (similar to Mexican tortillas) with spicy sausage and cheese, and *rosquillas* (doughnut-shaped, sugar-coated biscuits), all washed down with cider. For interested visitors, the festival is also a great chance to see some of the Basque traditional sports, with competitions in *aizkolari* (log-chopping) and *harri jazotzea* (stone-lifting). Before and after San Prudencio, a variety of more mainstream sports take place around town. A full programme is published by the municipality and available on the Álava Tourist Board website (**w** alavaturismo.eus).

Not to put a literal damper on the festivities, locals refer to San Prudencio as the 'Pissing Saint', as they say it always rains when it's his festival. (Author's note: I have been twice and it was bright and sunny.)

Virgen Blanca The celebration of the Virgen Blanca ('White Virgin'), held between 4 and 9 August, has acquired a recent adornment, created by a group of friends in 1957. It centres around Celedón, a man from Zalduondo village, 25km to the west of Vitoria. He became much loved for his jovial commitment to fiestas, and is commemorated with a statue in front of the church of San Miguel. The new 'tradition', which has become enormously popular, sees a life-size replica of Celedón holding an open umbrella descend on a diagonal rope from the tower of San Miguel church at 18.00 on 4 August every year, travelling across the packed square to be received into a balcony on the opposite side. He is then replaced by a man dressed as him, who emerges to exhort the assembled masses to join in the fun that will ensue over the next few days of the festival. This 'real' Celedón then has to make his way over the crowd in a display of body-surfing, back up to San Miguel church. Needless to say, the square is awash with alcohol, *cava* in particular being sprayed everywhere, and on hot days the firemen spray the crowd with their hoses to cool everything down. If you're jammed into the square, don't expect to stay dry.

Also on 4 August, the Lamp Procession sets off at 22.00 (see also page 196), moving through the city centre in an impressive show of light and glass, all borne aloft by the members of the *cofradía* of the Virgen Blanca. As for the rest of the festival, the Plaza de los Fueros, designed by Chillida, holds nightly concerts, and elsewhere there are countless events and activities as the city cuts loose. On 9 August Celedón returns to the tower to bid farewell until the following year.

WHAT TO SEE AND DO Getting to know Vitoria is very straightforward. The compact Old Town can be covered in half a day, with sights outside of the immediate centre occupying a further half-day. If you want to really discover some of the green spaces, in particular Salburua, two or three days in the city will suffice.

Old Town If you're a bit disenchanted by Vitoria's rather built-up, bland outskirts, a walk around its quaint, compact Old Town and a visit to a few bars inside or outside the old city walls will lift your spirits immeasurably. Many visitors are delighted by what Vitoria's *almendra* (almond-shaped centre) has to offer. The Old Town sights can easily be visited by using the map on page 191, starting your exploration at the Plaza Matxete, working roughly anticlockwise and ending back at the adjacent Plaza de España. Accordingly, the sights are listed below in that order. Note that admission to museums is free on the first Saturday of the month.

Plaza Matxete (Machete Square) Delightfully named, but with a truly gruesome history, this was the venue for the hangings, garottings and beheadings of criminals and those subject to the persecutions of the Spanish Inquisition, all usually attended by a healthy crowd. The machete itself, however, a replica of which can be seen behind glass on the wall of the square, was used in a solemn ceremony during the Middle Ages as a threat to the local ombudsman, who had to swear to carry out his functions on pain of being beheaded. (An effective strategy, as there is no historical reference to the threat ever having to be carried out.)

Los Arquillos (St Michael's Arches) Constructed over a ten-year period at the end of the 18th century, as Vitoria sought to expand out of its almond-shaped Old Town, these two balconies were designed by Justo Antonio de Olaguibel, the architect also responsible for the Plaza de España. The impressive arched edifices were devised to overcome the problem of the slope of the hill between the Old Town and what was to be the new town, and are visited even today by curious architectural students. They overlook the abandoned Banco de España, soon to open as a memorial to victims of terrorism. Here, you can also say 'hello' to the statue of Celedón (see opposite), standing guard just along from the balconies and waiting for his big day.

Bibat (Archaeology Museum/Museum of Playing Cards) (Cuchillería 5; ☎ 945 20 37 00; 🕘 10.00–14.00 & 16.00–18.30 Tue–Sat, 11.00–14.00 Sun; admission free; wheelchair accessible) The Basque meaning of 'Bibat' is 'Two in One', a reference to the fact that this former palace and its modern neighbour houses both the Archaeology Museum and the rather more unusual Museum of

Playing Cards. With remarkable harmony, your entrance fee admits you to both, and your English-language audio guide takes you through the exhibits of each. A Vitorian resident, Heraclio Fournier González, set up a printing enterprise in the 19th century and redesigned the Spanish playing card in a format that is still in use today. The company is still based in Álava and continues to churn out more than 15 million packs of cards every year. Heraclio's descendant, Félix Alfaro Fournier, founded the museum and gathered together the current collections. The displays of card-making equipment and playing cards from all around the globe, from all different ages, pay homage to his ancestor. Rather unusually, to light up some of the display cabinets, you have to swing your leg across underneath them. The adjoining Archaeology Museum is mainly notable for the modern building, rather than the exhibits themselves, which nevertheless include some remains found during the renovation of the cathedral (see below) and pieces brought in from important sites such as Iruña-Veleia and La Hoya (pages 210 and 223 respectively). The Museum of Playing Cards is in the 16th-century Renaissance Palace, contrasting with its ultra-modern, architect-designed Archaeology counterpart next door.

Catedral de Santa María (Plaza Burullería; ☎ 945 25 51 35; e visitas@catedralvitoria.com; w catedralvitoria.com; visits (by guided tour only) from €8.50; bookings can be made by email or phone, advance notice needed, usually at least 1 day for an English-language visit) Closed in 1994 because of its dangerous structural condition (it was falling down due to drainage problems affecting the foundations), this 13th-century building was reopened for worship again in 2014. Initial excavations first revealed human remains and the remnants of wooden huts, showing that Gasteiz had been there since at least the 8th century. 'Open for repairs' is its humorous catchphrase. Despite a rather impressive Gothic portal, it is the renovation works themselves that constitute the most fascinating part of the guided tour, for which a hard hat is duly provided. Renovation started in 2000, but if you dare to wonder why it is taking so long, your guide's explanations and a sight of the renovated foundations and the tower will quickly hush your enquiries. (And no, they don't know when it will be finished.)

Even if you are not a fan of churches, this is a rare opportunity to see one under renovation and to understand – by the means of a series of models – the changing shape of the town over the ages. The views of the city from the tower allow you to appreciate the almond shape of the original town layout and to observe the modern city and its surroundings. When the works are done, the cathedral will contain interesting exhibition spaces featuring the city and its history. A small museum is now housed in the crypt and is also worth a visit.

Ken Follett statue Wales's famous novelist studied the cathedral and drew inspiration from it for his novel, *World Without End*. As a reward for raising the profile of the city, Ken has been rewarded with his very own statue, slap-bang outside the cathedral's ticket office.

Museo de los Faroles (Lantern Museum) (Zapateria 35; w cofradiavirgenblanca.com; ⏲ 11.00–13.00 Mon–Sat; closed 31 Jul–15 Aug; €2). Every August, the contents of this small museum are emptied through a 9m-high wooden door to take part in two religious processions that herald the festival of the Virgen Blanca (page 194). If you are not in town for these (at 22.00 on 4 August and 08.00 the following day), then for a few hours each day the beautiful *faroles* (lanterns) are now visitable the rest of the year in this small museum, thanks to the efforts of a small team of dedicated volunteers.

City walls The most visible remaining part of the city walls, heavily restored, can be seen on Calle Fray Zacarías Martínez, just south of the cathedral, or further down the same street at the **Harresia** at its far southern end (🕘 spring/summer 10.00–22.00, autumn/winter 10.00–20.00, daily; admission free). Restored parts of the old 11th-century city wall can be encountered in many places around the Old Town, but at this spot you can see the 19th-century ice house, and how the walls have recently been restored with reconstruction using Canadian cedar, which when aged will blend in nicely with the stone. Press a button on the panel in front of the wall and an audio guide with English-language option springs into life with some additional information. A guided tour with the tourist office allows you deeper access to the walls.

Palacio Escoriaza-Esquivel Another 16th-century palace, this family-owned building cannot usually be visited, although guided tours can be organised at Easter, peak times in summer and on public holidays – ask at the tourist office for details (page 190).

Nevertheless, the exterior tells a love story of its former residents. In an age when marriages were nearly always arranged, Fernando d'Escoriaza and Victoria Esquivel married for love and the carvings of them, to the right and left above the front door, each proffering a rose and staring lovelorn across the doorway at each other, shows that they were not ashamed of the fact. Fernando was a doctor to Henry VIII of England and a founder of the Royal College of Physicians in London.

Palacio de Montehermoso (🕘 11.00–14.00 & 18.00–21.00 Tue–Sat, 11.00–14.00 Sun & holidays) Another useful reinvention of a 16th-century palace, this handsome specimen is now used as the Basque House, which opened in 2014 and aims to promote the Basque language through cultural events and houses temporary exhibitions relating to elements of Basque culture. The temporary exhibitions are hosted downstairs in what was at one time the city's 19th-century water tank, and they keep shorter hours than the palace itself. This building was once the house of the Marquesa María Pilar, who allowed Joseph Bonaparte, Napoleon's brother and King of Spain from 1808, to stay when Madrid became unsafe for him (mind you, she was his lover). He stayed here right until the French lost the Battle of Vitoria (page 16), then scarpered to France with María in tow, before unceremoniously dumping her. The palace gardens have been restored as part of Vitoria's green initiative.

Outside the Old Town Immediately beyond the confines of the Old Town, Vitoria's spacious squares and green delights begin to reveal themselves.

Plaza de España Formerly known as the Plaza Nueva (and some still refer to it as such), this 18th-century square had its name changed in 1936 as a demonstration of support for the new Nationalist regime. Originally, it was created for bullfighting and other such events, and is claimed to be the most symmetrical Neoclassical square in Spain, each side being exactly 61m in length. Bullfighting ceased here in 1815 when a bull jumped into the crowd and gored seven spectators. One side now comprises council buildings, while the other three contain 48 private residences. At noon a piece of music called *La paloma* (*The Dove*) by local composer Sebastián Iradier is played in the square, and at 18.00 you can hear Beethoven's *Battle Symphony*, or Opus 91, composed to commemorate the Battle of Vitoria. During the Spanish Civil War, a German pilot from the notorious Condor Legion accidentally crashed his plane into the square, killing two people: local legend has it that he was trying to throw a rose into the square to a local woman he had fallen in love with, but misjudged his approach. (Interflora had yet to be invented.) Nowadays, everything here is much less eventful ... well, except at festival times.

Plaza de la Virgen Blanca Vitoria's very own 'White Virgin' adorns the front of the Iglesia de San Miguel (Church of St Michael) and overlooks the delightful square that bears her name. Intermittent fountains erupt straight from the ground around the square, capable of catching the unaware stroller with an unwelcome jet of water. In the middle of the square is the statue to the 1813 Battle of Vitoria, when Napoleon's troops suffered a sound beating at the hands of Spanish and other troops aided by the Duke of Wellington. The city's award of 'Green Capital' in 2012 is marked by a bright green 'hedge' which spells out the name Vitoria-Gasteiz in giant letters. This is a favourite spot for getting your photo taken, so join the queue.

Parque Florida [189 C3] The bandstand at the centre of this beautiful park, just south of the city centre, is the venue for music in summer, accompanied by dancing senior citizens. At Christmas, life-size nativity figures are placed around the sides. Originally it was designed as a small botanical garden by the side of Santa Clara Convent, but expanded once the convent was demolished. The styling influences are both French and English, but in one corner you'll also find a Japanese garden, known as the Secret Water Garden.

Artium (Museum of Contemporary Basque Art) (Francia 24; ☎ 945 20 90 20; w artium.org; ⌚ 11.00–14.00 & 17.00–20.00 Tue–Fri, 11.00–20.00 Sat & Sun; €5, except for Wed, when you 'give what you want') An important addition to Vitoria's attractions, Artium, most of which is underground, majors on contemporary art from the Basque Country and elsewhere in Spain. Foreign visitors will recognise familiar names such as Picasso, and there is a ceramic mural by Miró on permanent display next to the ticket desk. Also in the entrance lobby is the stunning *Un pedazo de cielo cristalizado* (*A Piece of Crystallised Sky*) by Javier Pérez, involving over 15,000 glass bulbs hanging like teardrops from the ceiling. A motor-generated movement every 2 minutes vibrates them, rattling them together to give the sound of a giant wind-chime. The work was bought by an Álavan firm and 'given' to the provincial council in lieu of them paying their taxes! Those with a penchant for Basque contemporary figures can find works by stalwarts such as Oteiza and Chillida outside the museum, but it is not the big names that are the real attraction here. Exhibits drawn from the museum's collection of nearly 3,000 pieces rotate every year and there is good use of film and other media to give variety to the contents. Innovation and a sense of humour are ever-present and some exhibits are interactive, inviting comment or participation from visitors.

Museo de Bellas Artes (Fine Arts Museum) [189 B3] (Fray Francisco de Vitoria 8; ☎ 945 18 19 18; ⌚ 10.00–14.00 & 16.00–18.30 Tue–Sat, 11.00–14.00 Sun & public holidays; admission free, audio guide included) Stepping back in time a bit from the exhibits in the Artium (see above), here you'll discover Spanish works from the 18th and 19th centuries, plus more modern Basque art from 1850 to

above left Estella is an important staging-post for pilgrims on the Camino Francés, and the riches that have flowed from their journey down the ages have resulted in the town's 11 churches (L/D) page 272

above right Olite's Palacio Real seems drawn straight from a fairytale; the castle was built in the 14th–15th centuries and was once a seat of the Kings of Navarre (Q/S) page 282

below With geological features straight out of the Wild West, it's no surprise that Navarre's Bardenas Reales semi-desert is a favourite for film sets (MS) page 289

above Beachfront Biarritz still retains all of its Belle Époque elegance (SS) page 299

below left At a painstakingly slow pace, the vintage train takes passengers up La Rhune, a distinctive mountain at the very western end of the Pyrenees (MS) page 330

below right Espelette is famous for its peppers, which can often be seen hanging out to dry (MS) page 338

above Boasting handsome buildings, specialist shops and riverside restaurants, Bayonne battles hard to provide competition for Biarritz along the coast (LA/S) page 311

right The Porte de Notre Dame in Saint-Jean-Pied-de-Port is for many the start of their pilgrimage to Santiago de Compostela in northwest Spain (P/S) page 348

below La Villa Arnaga's gardens in Cambo-les-Bains are laid out like a mini Versailles (FJGO/S) page 339

top left *Pelota*, a furiously fast sport, appears in some 22 variations on both sides of the border and is hugely popular in the Basque Country: nearly every village has its own *frontón*, or *pelota* court (B) page 36

above right Balmaseda is renowned for its 'Living passion' re-enactment during Easter week (MS) page 105

above left Basque sports often involve a show of great strength and endurance, such as *aizkolari* (log-chopping) (B) page 37

below A test of stamina: Basque coastal villages compete in summer competitions, rowing traditional boats called *traineras* (p/S) page 37

top left Festivals reinforce the region's strong culture. Here *gigantes* (giants) face off with excited children in Ituren, Navarre (MS) page 250

top right Traditional dances, here in Bilbao, liven up many Basque summer festivals (B) page 32

above left Cheese-making has a long tradition in the Basque Country, with prize-winning cheeses changing hands for vast sums. Here, fine cheeses at Ordizia's 500-year-old market (MS) page 157

above right Sweet-toothed visitors will be spoilt in the Basque Country: cakes are a matter of regional pride, and the exact recipe is often the subject of fierce dispute (MS) page 56

below The *joaldunak,* a fixture at festivals in northern Navarre, are said to drive away evil spirits (MS) page 247

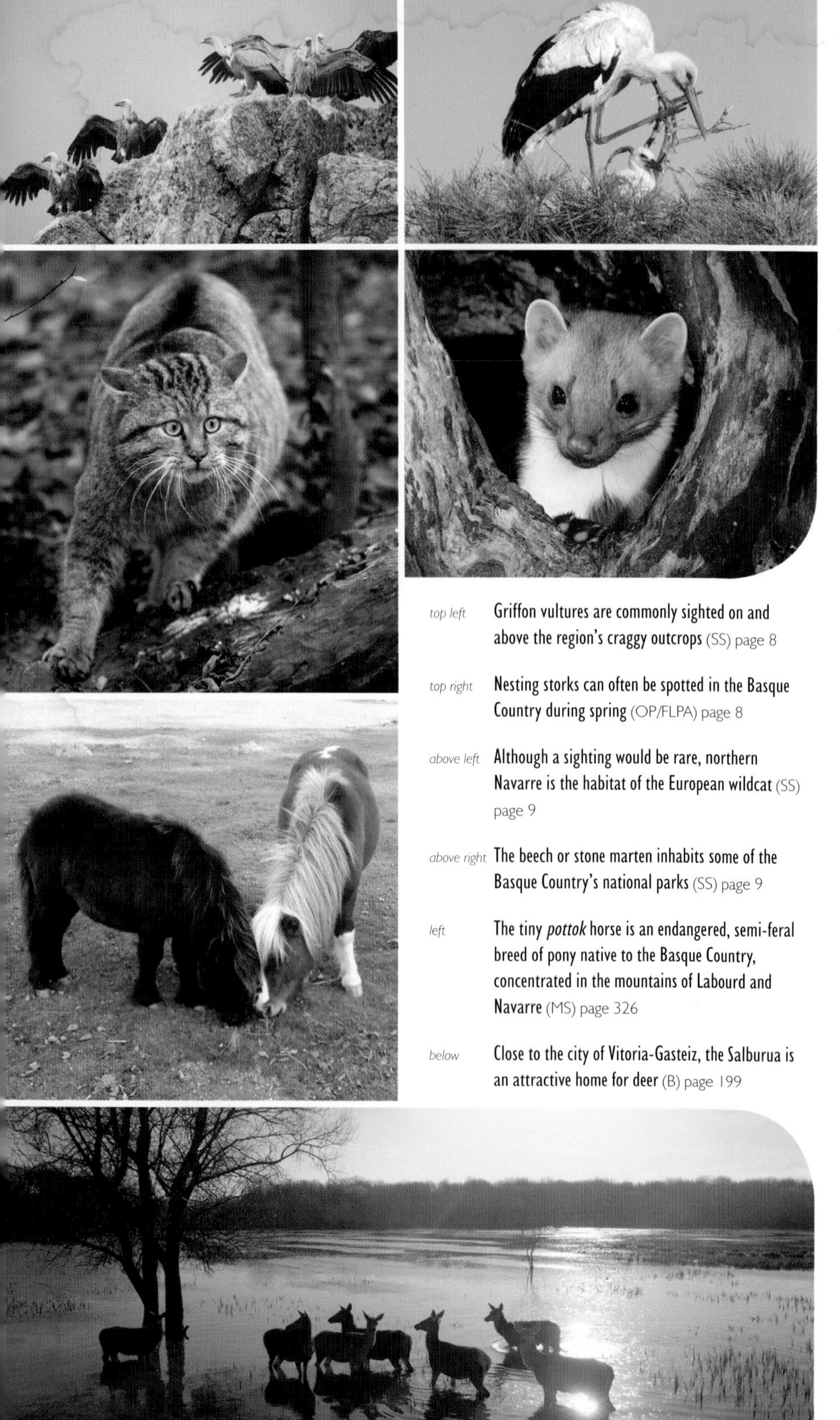

top left Griffon vultures are commonly sighted on and above the region's craggy outcrops (SS) page 8

top right Nesting storks can often be spotted in the Basque Country during spring (OP/FLPA) page 8

above left Although a sighting would be rare, northern Navarre is the habitat of the European wildcat (SS) page 9

above right The beech or stone marten inhabits some of the Basque Country's national parks (SS) page 9

left The tiny *pottok* horse is an endangered, semi-feral breed of pony native to the Basque Country, concentrated in the mountains of Labourd and Navarre (MS) page 326

below Close to the city of Vitoria-Gasteiz, the Salburua is an attractive home for deer (B) page 199

Land of the
BASQUES

1950, including space given over to celebrated local landscape artist Fernando de Amárica. Ignacio Díaz Olano is another son of Álava given prominence here, with his *Vuelta de la romería del Calvario* (*Return of the Calvary Procession*) being the most striking. Some of the displays are housed in a 20th-century Neo-Renaissance palace, the interior of which is in itself beautiful with its polished floors, galleries and wood-panelled walls. Pick up some English-language information with your ticket and the audio guide, although the latter gives commentary on only about 20 of the works.

Ataria, Centro de Interpretación de los Humedales de Salburua (Salburua Wetlands Learning Centre) [189 F1] (Paseo de la Biosfera 4; ☎945 25 47 59; w ataria.es; ⌚ summer 11.00–14.00 & 16.00–20.00 Tue–Sun, winter 11.00–14.00 & 16.00–19.00 Tue–Sun, closed Mon; admission free, but passport/ ID card needed if you're borrowing a bike or binoculars; bus 3 to Portal de Zurbano) Continuing with Vitoria's 'green' theme, this excellent site provides good opportunities for bird-spotting, with a learning centre and two hides from which to observe some of the more than a hundred species that have been recorded in these wetlands. There are two circuits around the lakes, one of 3.8km and one of 5km, but the hides themselves are on the longer route. Visitors can choose to walk or cycle around the park, which in summer has been known to attract over a thousand people daily. Usually it is much, much quieter. There is limited information available in English, but there is a map and the major attractions are (obviously) the birds and other wildlife, viewing of which is helped by the free loan of binoculars from the reception desk and the presence of a webcam in the reception, allowing you to zoom in and out over the wetlands. For restless youngsters, there's also a children's play area indoors.

The highlight, certainly for amateurs, will be the 40 or so stork nests, some of which are very close to one of the hides. Among the other permanent residents of Salburua are European green and black woodpeckers, thriving on the insect life in an area of dead trees which resulted from storm damage around five years ago. Ospreys are occasional visitors. You can also see marsh harriers, red kites, great crested grebe and grey heron, all of which are permanent residents, together with migrators such as black kites, purple heron, greylag geese and great, cattle and little egrets. A pair of tufted ducks bred here in 2014. The park also has a population of deer, foxes and European mink, and 50% of the Basque Country's 46 amphibian species are present.

Threats are posed by non-indigenous species such as the American crab, which eat the same food as the residents and spread diseases. Some visitors abuse the park's attributes to dispose of unwanted pets such as turtles and exotic fish in the wetlands, posing further threats to the native species.

EAST OF VITORIA: LLANADA ALAVESA

If the green spaces of Álava's capital are not enough for you, the plain to the east of town runs for around 30km until it reaches the border with neighbouring Navarre. The population is sparse here, in a region where agriculture has lost some of its importance and the main road (the A-1/E5-E80 eastward towards Navarre, westward to distant Madrid) is thundered upon by trucks and lined with factories and distribution centres. For those who persevere, the principal town of Salvatierra-Agurain is a pleasant, ramparted place and this quiet region also presents a chance to do some excellent walking – perhaps sampling a piece of the Camino de Santiago in reverse – or to see some peculiar church paintings in the otherwise unremarkable villages of Alaiza and Gazeo. A few kilometres east of Vitoria, the waters of the Embalse de Ullíbarri-Gamboa provide a popular summer playground for the city's inhabitants.

GETTING THERE AND AWAY Despite the public transport options detailed below, a car is advisable to get around this sparsely populated area, allowing you to see the highlights on a day's outing from Vitoria.

By car Salvatierra-Agurain is a mere 25km from Vitoria, quickly reached on the busy A1/E5-E80 motorway.

By bus To and from Vitoria, there are 12 buses daily connecting Salvatierra on weekdays, reducing to nine on Saturdays and six on Sundays (25mins; €2.50). Service to Pamplona is six times daily, five at weekends (75mins; €8.50). Full details of these and other connections can be found on the bus company's website, w autobuseslaunion.com/en.

By train On the main line between Vitoria (15mins; €3.50) and Pamplona (55mins; €5.20), Salvatierra connects to both with around six trains each day (w renfe.com).

THERE'S NO COASTLINE, BUT ÁLAVA HAS AN ISLAND

Look closely at the map of Álava and you'll notice that just south of Vitoria lies an area called the Condado de Trevino, surrounded completely by Álava, but belonging not to it but to somewhere else. The clues to its ownership lie in the prefixes to the road numbers that dissect this misshapen region of some 260km^2: the 'BU' preceding the minor roads shows that we are actually in the province of Burgos, while the numbers of the major routes begin with 'CL', showing that we are now also in the autonomous community of Castilla-León. But why? When Álava fell to powerful Castile in 1200, Trevino became annexed to the conqueror, rather than remaining subject to the *fueros* laws of the Basque Country. Despite several petitions to have the municipality of Trevino reincorporated into Álava, with the most recent one being in 1936, and flying in the face of the will of the region's inhabitants (a clear majority voting in 1998 in favour of rejoining Álava), nothing has changed and Trevino remains firmly part of Burgos province, within Castilla-León's autonomous community. But the people have voted, to some extent, with their feet. Since 1930, the then population of some 4,000 has more than halved, with those leaving the 'island' of Trevino heading mainly for Vitoria, which is very much in Álava province, and very much in the Basque Autonomous Community. So Trevino remains stranded.

Head east of Pamplona and you'll find Los Bastanes and the Petilla de Aragón, a mini archipelago of two 'islands' of Navarre isolated in the middle of the autonomous community of Aragón; cross west of Bilbao through the Las Encartaciones region (page 101) and you will stumble inadvertently into the Valle de Villaverde, which is part of Cantabria, but completely surrounded by Bizkaia province. Northern Spain's troubled history is at times quite literally all around.

TOURIST INFORMATION The local tourist office (Calle Mayor 8, Salvatierra; ☎ 945 30 29 31; w agurain.com; ⏰ Jul & Aug & Easter week 10.00–14.00 & 16.00–20.00) is in Salvatierra. Little English is spoken and the town's website is only in Spanish or Basque.

WHERE TO STAY

Argomaniz Parador (44 rooms) El Parador 14, Argomaniz; ☎ 945 29 32 00; e argomaniz@parador.es; w parador.es. Around 12km east of Vitoria (turn off the A-1 on to the A-3108) & housed in an old palace, the elevated position of this state-owned *parador* gives it views down to the Embalse de Ullíbarri-Gamboa (page 202) & over the mountain ranges to the south. Rooms have AC, TV & Wi-Fi. Former guests include Napoleon. **€€€**

WHERE TO EAT AND DRINK You can find good traditional Basque cooking at **Umandi** (Andoni Urrestarazu 4, Araia; ☎ 945 31 46 15; ⏰ 10.00–16.00 daily, also 20.30–22.30 Fri–Sun; **€€**), which has excellent midday menus and English-speaking staff. Try the *goxua*, an Alavese speciality, for dessert.

WHAT TO SEE AND DO Visitors to the area might head straight along the A-1 motorway to Salvatierra and its impressive fortified walls, before taking a walk through the enchanting woods to the San Adrián tunnel on the border with Gipuzkoa and then visiting La Leze cave. On a sunny day, an alternative excursion from Vitoria would be a picnic and perhaps a walk or cycle along the shores of the Embalse de Ullíbarri-Gamboa reservoir, only a few minutes' drive from the capital. If you want to visit the churches at Alaiza and Gazeo, you can get the latest information at Salvatierra's tourist office.

Salvatierra-Agurain The principal town of this quiet region is surrounded by industry, but nevertheless has impressive fortified walls that were given an equally impressive makeover in 2007. Down the main street, the Calle Nagusia, a number of information panels in English provide information on the history of the town and the tradesmen who lived here. Founded in 1256 as Agurain, its name later being changed to Salvatierra. Now the two are united to give it some double-barrelled grandeur.

La Leze (Signposted off the A-3012, just east of Ilarduia) Simply meaning 'the cave' in Basque, this more or less does what it says on the tin. You can't actually enter it without specialist equipment, but there is a year-round waterfall gushing from its mouth and it is a popular picnic area. (If you don't like crowds, avoid sunny Sundays, otherwise it's a peaceful place.) Locals say that the pond below the waterfall is ice-cold all year round. On ledges high up on the cliffs above is a population of common vultures, resident throughout the year. Between April and September, Egyptian vultures come here to breed, there are resident red- and yellow-billed choughs, and common kestrels are not an unusual sighting, either.

Churches If you want to visit the following two churches, each in the centre of their respective villages (Alaiza and Gaceo), your best bet is to contact the tourist office in Salvatierra-Agurain in advance (see above). Otherwise, in theory, you can visit on Saturdays or Sundays, as follows. On Saturdays you arrive in Alaiza at 11.30 for your visit, where a guide will be waiting (English-speaking, if your luck is in), then drive to Gaceo to visit at 12.30. On Sundays you can arrive in Gaceo at 13.30 and drive to Alaiza at 14.00. The cost is €3 to see two churches, or €2 to see only one. It's all a bit haphazard ... so, contact the tourist office!

Iglesia de Alaiza (Alaiza Church) If you're coming here on a weekday (page 201), there *may* be a different way of organising a visit. Approaching the village from the north via the A-4140, you can take the chance of asking for the key from the first farmhouse on the right as you enter the village. Once inside the church, the primitive paintings high up on the wall are unusual in that they look like the work of an eight-year-old. Discovered only 30 years ago when the altarpiece was moved to its present position, the artwork in this church (Nuestra Señora de la Asunción) is actually believed to be the primitive effort of the English soldiers of Edward of Woodstock ('The Black Prince') who came to help Pedro I ('the Cruel') in a dispute he was having with his stepfather. The paintings depict a battle and include a rather comical drawing of a soldier being carted off on a stretcher. The church itself dates from 1366.

Iglesia de Gazeo (Gazeo Church) Modest from the outside, the interior of the church, also known as San Martín de Tours, is remarkable for its wall paintings, which were discovered only in 1967 when the altarpiece was removed and the white walls were scrubbed, revealing artwork which bears no relation to anything else seen in the area. The style is quite unusual, as is the subject matter: one picture shows Jesus being swallowed by a creature said to represent Hell. The church is of 13th-century construction, restored in the latter half of the 20th century.

Embalse de Ullíbarri-Gamboa/Parque Provincial de Garaio (Information centre: ⌚ Jun–Aug 09.30–20.30 Mon–Fri, 09.30–21.30 Sat, Sun & holidays, Sep–May 09.00–15.30 daily; bicycle hire: ⌚ Jun–Aug 11.00–19.00 daily, Mar–May, Sep & Oct 10.00–14.00 Sat, Sun & holidays only; €2 per day or part-day) Situated just to the northeast of Vitoria, the two reservoirs here not only supply around half of the water for the Basque Autonomous Community, but also provide the citizens of Álava with a chance to get wet and have fun without having to trek up to the coast. Swimming is permitted, but as well as the beaches which can be found on the eastern shores of the larger reservoir (Embalse de Ullíbarri), there are also great birdwatching opportunities with an ornithological park (Parque Ornitológico de Mendixur) at its southern tip and cheap-as-chips bikes to hire which can whizz you around the entire circumference or, by cheating and using a couple of bridges, cover just the shorter, southern circuit. True, this is no substitute for the beaches of San Sebastián or Hondarribia, but try telling that to the throngs of happy Álavans who mob the place in July and August. Out of season, it is a delightful place, especially if you get there early to see the morning mist rising from the water's surface as aquatic avian species dive for their breakfast.

To best access the site, take the A-1 motorway east of Vitoria, exiting at the turn-off for Mendixur (Mendijur) and heading north on the A-3012. The Parque Provincial de Garaio is signposted off to the left. Taking the turn-off, you can choose to visit the birds at Mendixur, again signposted left, or continue straight on to Garaio, on the way to which you can stop at the information centre which has details of walks, birds and is also the place to hire bicycles. With the emphasis at Garaio firmly on nature, you will find no cafés or restaurants here: bring your own supplies, otherwise you can rejoin the A-3012 and continue north, taking the A-3014 to Marieta or Landa, both of which have facilities. Garaio has the best beaches, though Landa comes a close second and you can also hire kayaks there. At Mendixur there are two short walks which lead to bird observatories, and the area is a protected Ramsar Wetland Site. The western side of Ullíbarri is a bit less attractive and the road only stays close to the shore for part of the way.

SOUTHEAST OF VITORIA: LA MONTAÑA ALAVESA

Occupying nearly 500km^2 in Álava's southeastern corner, and with forests of beech and oak, rocky outcrops and cliffs, together with unspoiled villages virtually devoid of any major industrial development, La Montaña Alavesa is an area where the inhabitants see little in the way of foreign visitors. Not that there are many inhabitants, with no major towns and a tiny population spread across nearly 50 villages and hamlets. Here you can sit down in a village restaurant for a hearty lunch alongside workers from the nearby farms. Despite the region's name, the mountains in its interior are not that high, certainly not rivalling the Pyrenees and with nothing much more than 1,100m, although the Sierra de Cantabria, which separates the area from Rioja Alavesa to the south, tops out at over 1,400m. The tourist infrastructure is primitive in this land of eye-catching landscapes, but if you are a no-frills traveller, then La Montaña Alavesa and its modest tangible attractions could be to your taste, especially for walkers, birders and cyclists. Prices will be popular too, being noticeably lower than most other places in the Basque Country.

WHERE TO STAY Mercifully devoid of large, impersonal hotels, your choice is limited to small, owner-managed establishments, *casas rurales* or *agroturismos*. For more options try the Montaña Alavesa tourist website, **w** montanaalavesa.com.

Hotel Los Roturos Herrería 10, Maeztu; 945 41 02 50; **e** info@hotellosroturos.es; **w** hotellosroturos.es. A well-cared-for hotel, with spacious dbl & family rooms. Traditional décor, but rooms have TV & there's a large communal living room, too. B/fast included & there's a bar & good restaurant downstairs. **€€**

Casa Rural Izki (8 rooms) Carretera Vitoria–Estella, Maeztu; 945 41 03 88. Cheap & cheerful, a little money buys you a clean bed for the night in a room with TV & private bathroom. Restaurant downstairs. **€**

WHERE TO EAT AND DRINK

Los Roturos (see above) 13.00–16.00 & 21.00–23.00 Mon–Sat, closed Sun evening. *Menús del día* are served day & evening at excellent prices – especially Mon–Thu – & are of good quality. A warm welcome from the staff guarantees an overall memorable experience. **€€**

Obenkun Plaza Juegabolos 2, San Vicente de Araña (Done Bikendi Arana); 945 40 61 23; 09.00–17.00 Mon, Tue & Thu, 09.00–17.00 & 19.00–01.00 Fri, 09.00–01.00 Sat, 09.00–15.30 Sun. A solid rural establishment where rugged farmers tuck into rustic, meaty cuisine straight from the land. The Idiazábal cheese with bread is simple but delicious: ask at the bar if you want to poke your nose in at the tiny *quesería* (cheese factory) round the corner. Vegetarians will struggle here, but others can take advantage of bargain *menús del día*. **€€**

WHAT TO SEE AND DO Practically, you really need a car or bike to navigate around a region as rural as this, because the villages are not big enough to merit a frequent bus service. Covering the short distances required is slowed down only by the narrowness of the roads; the proximity of Vitoria (roughly 30km away) means that a day trip from there to Montaña Alavesa is entirely feasible. If you wanted to explore further, Maeztu or Santa Cruz de Campezo would be the central choices for an overnight stay in this slightly odd-shaped area.

Santa Teodosia Ermita (Hermitage) Set at the top of a hill, on the unnumbered road between Roitegui and San Vicente de Arana, this hermitage is closed except for Sundays, when in the late morning the locals meet for cheese and bread and a general get-together. Everyone is invited to join them and you can combine it with a short, waymarked, circular walk (Ruta Circular de la Montana, 3km) which departs from right outside the hermitage.

Parque Natural de Izki This beautiful park, rich with Pyrenean oak (*Quercus pyrenaica*) and wildlife, offers plentiful walking and good cycling opportunities. There are two information centres: the converted railway carriages at Antoñana and the Parketxea (park learning centre) in the village of Korres (Corres). The former is on the Vitoria–Estella road and the latter is, ironically, the only building which doesn't blend in with the otherwise attractive old village.

Vasco-Navarro Greenway Learning Centre, Antoñana (☎ 945 40 54 24; ⌚ Mar–Jun & Sep 10.30–14.30 & 16.30–19.00 Sat, 10.30–15.30 Sun; Jul & Aug 10.30–14.30 & 16.30–20.00 daily, but may open at other times by contacting the tourist office) The old train line between Estella in Navarre and Vitoria-Gasteiz was constructed at the end of the 19th century, using capital raised in England. After a series of setbacks, it finally opened its first section in 1919, but closed on the last day of 1967. It has now been converted into an award-winning Vía Verde (Greenway), providing over 70km of safe, flattish cycling along the old railway line. You can hire bikes (child-seats available) and helmets (€8/1 adults/children) at this centre

WALK TO THE SAN ADRIÁN TUNNEL

This is a linear walk to the San Adrián tunnel and its small chapel, which ushers the Camino de Santiago into Álava from neighbouring Gipuzkoa (6.4km; 2hrs). It has some steep sections but easy underfoot. In times of heavy rain or low cloud or mist, care needs to be taken at the start and end due to a number of natural holes just off the path. Park your car where the road ends in Zumarraundi. Note that on the outward leg, you will at times be 'following' the yellow arrows of the Camino de Santiago, but backwards – ie: they will be pointing in the opposite direction on your outward leg.

After exiting the A-1 motorway at the Araia turn-off, follow the A-3020 into Araia for nearly 4km, passing the 'Partetxea' sign on your right – this is a learning centre and hydro-electric station where you can get information, if you speak Spanish. A hundred metres after the centre, you reach a T-junction at which you turn left and continue for 800m, keeping right, and then 100m further on, just after some apartment blocks, take a *very* sharp right (signposted 'piscinas'). Follow this road for a kilometre, passing the swimming pool on your right, continue for a further kilometre to a T-junction and then turn right, signposted to Zumarraundi, and continue to the car park at the end of the road.

At the opposite end of the car park to where you entered it, take the wide path that leads up into the wood. After 50m you will see the yellow and white waymarking that will accompany you on this walk. Be on the lookout for the deep natural holes that characterise the beginning and end of the walk: take the hand of any small children! The path becomes increasingly steep and is studded with tree roots. After a few hundred metres, the ground flattens out briefly in a clearing where there are further waymarks. You reach a waterfall, which can occasionally dry up in high summer. Notice also the round, flat area where charcoal was formerly made. Keep to the right of the waterfall, continuing to follow the waymarks.

and the staff will provide you with a map and advice, though it's difficult to get lost. Heading east will take you into Navarre, while west leads you towards Vitoria. You can even choose to cycle one-way and return (with the bike, of course) on the bus. In either direction, you'll pass beautiful countryside, rocky crags and the old train stations, some restored, some abandoned. The centre itself has a short, English-language video about the railway's history and it also doubles as a modest tourist information centre.

Parketxea (Park Learning Centre), Korres In the heart of the village, the displays inside this centre are only in Spanish and Basque, divided up into sections covering geology, nature and ethnography, but there is a 20-minute video in English about the park and some staff are English-speaking.

A number of walks start from here, and the staff helpfully provide maps and translations so you can work out where you are heading.

For birders, the species often seen in this area include many raptors such as the griffon vulture (*Gyps fulvus*), peregrine falcon (*Falco peregrinus*), Egyptian vulture (*Neophron percnopterus*), golden eagle (*Aquila chrysaetos*), short-toed snake eagle (*Circaetus gallicus*) and common buzzard (*Buteo buteo*). European funds have been invested in the park to try to recover the populations of some of the more threatened species such as the Bechstein bat (*Myotis bechsteinii*) and the lesser-spotted woodpecker (*Dryobates minor*).

Some 100m beyond the first charcoal pit, keep on to the right towards a further waymark on a tree. When the path reaches a junction, you will see the yellow arrows for the Camino de Santiago to the left, but at this point you go to the right (note this point carefully for on your way back – this is where you will stop following the yellow arrows!), continuing upwards. You are now following the *calzada* stone road, a medieval traders' route originally built to reach France. When you reach a wooden marker bearing both the yellow Camino de Santiago arrow and the orange arrow of the Camino Ignaciano, you ignore the wide path that bears to the left ahead, instead taking a sharp, 90-degree right turn (directly opposite the marker) to follow a narrower path that leads uphill. After a further 20m, you will see a further yellow arrow, then quickly reach a wide road where you turn right. After 100m the path turns up to the right and you take this, continuing at this point to follow the yellow arrows. When the ground levels out, you follow the signpost for Otzuarte and Sandrati. Further on, keep to the left, now following the wooden sign for San Adrián. Pass under the power lines, now descending and following the yellow arrows, which are of course pointing the other way. You should still be following the distinctive stone road of the *calzada*, which soon turns sharply right and descends. Off to your right, you will see a mountain spring where you can take water, but your path continues as before, still on the stone road, still descending. After 200m, the road emerges into a wide clearing. A sign again directs you to Otzuarte and ahead to the right you can see the narrow entrance that conceals the entrance to the tunnel of San Adrián and the chapel inside. Here, on three Sundays in June, villagers from both Álava and Gipuzkoa meet in the tunnel, bringing food provided by their local councils.

Your return route is the same as the outward leg.

Golf Izki Golf (Urturi; ☎ 945 37 82 62; **e** izkigolf@izkigolf.com; **w** izkigolf.com) is a full-sized 18-hole course, well-tended, nicely contoured and in a beautiful setting. For weekdays there should be no need to reserve in advance, and even on Saturdays they say that no pre-booking is necessary for afternoon play. Despite what seem rather high green fees (€70/50 weekends/weekdays), there are special offers every month that can discount the price substantially. Clubs can be hired, but not shoes. Buggies are available and there are full clubhouse facilities, including a well-regarded restaurant. A handicap certificate is required, but the requirement might be overlooked on weekdays.

Cycling Traffic volume is low, making cycling a pleasure. The area's tourist office website (**w** montanaalavesa.com) details 15 routes of varying length and difficulty, though currently only in Spanish. Bikes and helmets can be hired at the golf course (see above; **e** izki@btteuskadi.net; 🕘 summer 08.30–20.00, daylight hours in winter; €10 per day), but advance booking is required, especially as they only have two bikes! The Vasco-Navarro Greenway Learning Centre in Antoñana (page 204) is a bit cheaper and has considerably more two-wheelers.

WEST AND NORTH OF VITORIA

Ten municipalities make up the sparsely populated and relatively unvisited *comarca* of Añana, snuggled in the southwest corner of Álava. Covering nearly 700km^2, it occupies nearly a quarter of the province and, being so close to Vitoria, its highlights could be visited in a day or two. Quiet and with a few flagship sights, it is an unspoilt area with mountains on every horizon and ideal for those seeking peace and relaxation.

Apart from the fascinating Salinas de Añana salt pans, the tourist infrastructure could fairly be described as fledgling, but the slightly forlorn village of Sobrón is proof that in days long gone by the region attracted more visitors, and could do again. For now, Añana is a pleasant region dozing peacefully, while the surrounding landscape is a joy for walking.

An overnight stay would make for a more relaxing experience than a day trip, with (Salinas de) Añana village itself being the most central point of the region, though it is neither the *comarca*'s capital (that honour going to unexceptional Rivabellosa) nor the most populous settlement (Nanclares de la Oca). On day one, the visitor could take a tour of the salt pans, before driving the short distance east to Trespuentes to visit the beautiful botanic gardens of Santa Catalina and the Roman site at Iruña-Veleia; the following day could be spent with a trip to the Torre Palacio de los Varona before going for a leisurely walk in the Parque Natural de Valderejo or around Caranca.

GETTING THERE AND AWAY Buses do connect this area with Vitoria, but a car is a necessity if you are going to visit the region's highlights with any ease. Exiting the capital to the west will see you in Salinas de Añana in 30 minutes, while even Lalastra and the Parque Natural de Valderejo, at the *comarca's* western extremity, is little over an hour's distance.

TOURIST INFORMATION There is a tourist office in Salinas de Añana (Plaza Miguel Díaz de Tuesta; ☎ 945 35 13 86; **w** ananaturismo.com; 🕘 Dec–Feb 10.30–14.30 Sat & Sun, Mar, Apr & Sep–Nov 10.30–14.30 Tue–Sun, May–Aug & Easter week 09.45–14.30 & 15.45–19.00 daily).

WHERE TO STAY

Madera y Sal Casa Rural (3 rooms, 2 apts) San Cristóbal 1–3, Salinas de Añana; 945 35 11 75; m 600 54 95 29; e maderaysal@gmail.com; w maderaysal.com. At the top of the village (drive up through the main square) & opened in late 2014, the English-speaking & charming owners have created a little gem with super-stylish & fully functional apartments, plus rooms that can cater for couples or families. The apartments have kitchen facilities, TV & – a winter delight – wood-burning stoves. Bathrooms are ultra-modern. Garden space with barbecue & a small outdoor jacuzzi. Sometimes requires a 2-night minimum stay. **€€**

Natura Sobrón (6 rooms) Barrio Sobrón Alta 1, Sobrón; m 676 26 02 50; e naturasobron@gmail.com; w naturasobron.com. In the upper part of Sobrón, lofty isolation in a peaceful surrounding is the key here (not a single bar adorns the village). Pleasant rooms, b/fast is available. The owner is a teacher of the Basque traditional musical instrument, the *txalaparta*. **€€**

Ulle Gorri (5 rooms, plus house rentable for groups) Leku 2, Untza-Apregindana; m 647 71 28 06; e contact@ullegorri.com; w thelandofthebasques.com; see ad, 2nd colour section. Beautifully isolated in lush, gentle countryside, this former farmhouse is enthusiastically run & offers the possibilities for guided walks in the local area, plus bespoke programmes of tours & activities in the wider Basque Country. Great views over to the western sierras. **€€**

Camping Angosto Villanañe; 945 35 32 71; e info@camping-angosto.com; w camping-angosto.com; 27 Feb–9 Dec. One of Álava's few camping sites, Angosto has tent pitches & bungalows to rent. Bar/restaurant, shop, children's playground, sauna, free Wi-Fi. In high season, it has an outdoor heated pool (Easter–Oct) & entertainment. **€**

WHERE TO EAT AND DRINK

La Casa del Patrón San Martín 2, Murguia; 945 46 25 28; w casadelpatron.com; lunch & dinner daily, winter closed Mon. A busy bar, with huge outdoor space & buzzing with excited chatter. Food is elaborate at w/end, lower-priced & less fancy during the week. **€€–€€€**

Asador Arcena Carretera de Bóveda 1, San Millán de San Zadornil; 947 35 32 30. On the main A-4336, this restaurant is (whisper it) in Burgos province, but you have to pass through on the way to Valderejo, & the chance to dine *chez* the heavy metal-loving owner should not be passed by. Thankfully, the music is turned down, while the food quality is good. **€€**

Camping Angosto (see above) Campsite restaurants rarely feature in top dining choices, but if you want a lively atmosphere & maybe w/end live music, an evening here will not disappoint. The food is just fine, too. W/end reservation recommended. **€€**

WHAT TO SEE AND DO

Valle Salado (Salt Pans) (Calle Real 42, Salinas de Añana; 945 35 11 11; e reservas@vallesalado.eus; w vallesalado.eus; Easter–mid-Oct 09.45–14.30 & 15.45–19.30, daily; Mar & mid-Oct–Nov 10.30–14.30 Mon–Fri, 09.45–14.30 & 15.30–17.30 Sat & Sun, Dec–Feb 10.30–14.30 daily; visit only by guided tour, €8/6 adults/students & other concessions; English-language tours available; advanced booking, which can be done online, is advised) Salt has been produced here for around 6,000 years, and the same production method has been used for over 2,000 years. At the beginning of the 20th century over a thousand people worked here, but by the end of it there was only one. A programme of restoration has been under way since 2001, replacing or rebuilding the wooden structures that support the salt pans and seeking to increase the salt production. An additional initiative involves archaeological work being undertaken, seeking to find out more about the site's history. A non-profit foundation organises the work, but at present salt and ticket sales cover only 40% of the costs. The salty water itself is still owned by the villagers, as a result of rights granted by Alfonso I in the 12th century when the village was

PARQUE NATURAL DE VALDEREJO CIRCULAR WALK FROM LALASTRA

Distance: 12.9km; time: 4hrs; difficulty: easy underfoot, one sharp ascent, not advisable in heavy rain or low cloud. Refreshments in Lalastra at beginning and end. Parking in Lalastra, can be busy on Sundays and holidays. This is a beautiful walk, visiting an abandoned village and deep gorges with craggy cliffs and peaceful forest scenery. Lalastra village itself has a learning centre and a few points of interest (see opposite).

From the car park, continue on foot into the village, passing the restaurant and the church. Two points of interest at the latter: note the wooden rack which was formerly used for shoeing the oxen, at one time important beasts in agriculture. Next, note the *bolera*, the bowling alley, still in use. If you fancy a game, ask for the bowls at the Casa del Parque. To start the walk, take the path which starts directly opposite the gate for the Casa del Parque, signposted Senda Purón Desfiladero (PR A-8), descending then climbing slightly to reveal a large, roundish valley surrounded by craggy escarpments. Shortly afterwards you continue to follow the sign for Senda Purón and Ribera PR A-8. When you reach another sign (Ribera 3.3km) you will see the abandoned village of Villamardones on the other side of the valley. After you've walked a total of around 1km, the path enters a forest: ignore paths off to the left and right and continue ahead for Senda Purón and Ribera. Further on, you reach another fork, where you take the right-hand path and continue downward, heading for Ribera. After 100m, take a narrow path down to the right (Senda Purón). Down through the forest, you reach a T-junction, where you turn right following (for now) the 'yellow dot' waymarking. You cross a stream (signposted Arroyo Polledo) and soon a high cliff will appear in front of you, often a nesting place for vultures. The path continues downward with the stream on your right. You pass through a gate and soon see the clifftop church of the abandoned village of Ribera. After 100m, turn right and cross the stream, continuing up to the right to visit the church, which has a few wall paintings. Now retrace your steps briefly, but instead of crossing the stream, now follow the sign for Senda Purón, indicated as being 15 minutes away. You pass the picnic spot on your right, crossing through a gate to now reach a wide meadow, at the end of which you go through another gate, continuing in the same direction. The path soon descends, and you go down

enclosed inside fortified walls. So, why is there salt here? Two hundred million years ago the area was covered by ocean, but once the waters retreated then salt deposits were left, in particular a bubble of salt 3km deep. Now the site contains both fresh and salt water springs. Amazingly, the salt is not washed after it has been collected, but the impurities are simply picked out by hand.

The guided tour details the production method and the site restoration programme and ends at a foot spa, where you can dip your feet. Displayed in some of the salt pans you will also see the names of some of the Basque Country's top restaurants and chefs who use and thus promote the Añana salt. Occasionally there are salt 'tastings' organised here as the foundation mixes the salt with garlic, cayenne pepper and curry powder to increase their product range. There is a small shop beside the ticket desk, where you can buy the flavoured salts.

Further down the road to the west, there is a public, salt-water swimming pool, open in summer and popular with locals and visitors.

some steps and find yourself in an impressive gorge, with cliffs to your right and water rushing below to your left. (Optional diversion: soon you'll see steep steps leading down to the water. Swimming is prohibited here, but you might fancy a foot-bath before you continue.)

You continue through the gorge, crossing a couple of bridges with a few waterfalls to admire. The path veers gently to the left and the noise of the water recedes. Around 2km after leaving Ribera, take the path off to your left, signposted Senda Santa Ana and Ribera, now 3.6km away, leading you sharply uphill. This path zigzags upwards, with occasional red and white waymarking. As you climb, the mountains of Burgos are visible in the near distance. After 20 minutes of hard climbing you come to a T-junction, where you turn left, still ascending. When you reach a sign for Villafría de San Zadornil, 2.6km, you ignore a path to the left and continue for 50m until you reach a clearing, where you follow the sign for Senda Santa Ana and Ribera, 2.5km. At the end of the clearing, go through a gate (now waymarked with a yellow dot) and continue to a second post, similarly marked, and descend through a wood. After a short while you reach a five-way junction, where you take the second left. (Note: logging activity can disrupt the waymarking here, so your direction is broadly at 10 o'clock from the path which leads you to the five-way; you should pick up the round yellow dot waymarking within a couple of hundred metres.) The waymarks take you soon to a wide meadow, where you continue to follow them down the meadow's left-hand side, with a wood on your left. You descend a fairly narrow path, again waymarked, until the wood ends, where you cross briefly to your right and follow a narrow path with a line of trees on either side, descending and waymarked. You will soon see the familiar church of Ribera ahead of you (memorise its location!). At the bottom of the valley, you cross a stream and climb up the grassy hill in the same direction, heading roughly for the church, which is now out of sight. You soon join a muddy road, continuing to your left. The church now reappears and you reach a wooden sign announcing that you are reaching Ribera. You have the option of taking a long route back, following a sign for Lalastra (6.3km), but our walk proceeds by first continuing a few metres to the bridge and then following the sign for Senda Purón and Lalastra 3.6km, retracing the path which brought us from Lalastra to Ribera on the first part of the walk.

Jardín Botánico de Santa Catalina, Trespuentes (From Vitoria, exit the AP-1/E-5 motorway at Junction 343, then take the A-3302 north, then the A-4358 that leads to Trespuentes, following the Jardín Botánico signs; m 688 89 70 48; ⌚ May–Sep 10.00–14.00 Mon–Fri, 10.00–20.00 Sat, Sun & holidays, 7 Mar–30 Apr & 28 Sep–8 Dec 10.00–14.00 Tue–Fri, 11.00–15.00 Sat, Sun & holidays, closed 8 Dec–Feb; €3/1.50/free adults/students & seniors/under 10s; guided tours might be available in English, if you can give a couple of days' notice) Opened to the public in 2003, this site has the attraction of being a botanical garden set in the mountains of the Sierra de Badaya, but is given additional interest by the ruins of the Santa Catalina Monastery. The park gathers together both indigenous species and imports from all five continents – over a thousand species in total. Indigenous species include the Montpellier maple (*Acer monspessulanum*) whose leaves turn red in autumn and which is the symbol chosen to represent the park, as well as the holm oak, which was always a useful source for making charcoal. The park is divided into three distinct zones, with the diverse conditions allowing a wide range of vegetation to flourish. On the south-facing slopes, for example, visitors will find cacti and yuccas, plus other species from Latin America. There's an example of the world's oldest and perhaps most resilient tree species, the gingko (*Gingko biloba*), which famously survived the atomic blast at Hiroshima. Most species are labelled in Spanish, with the Latin names also given.

There is a social purpose to the park, too, with a non-profit association managing the project, and prisoners from the nearby jail being employed to look after and rehabilitate the garden during the week. Lack of funds has slowed the development of the project, which includes the proposed addition of various themed gardens.

At the top of the park you reach the captivating ruins of the monastery of Santa Catalina, originally built as a family tower-house in the 13th century. In 1407, the tower-house was gifted to a religious order, but after 60 years they abandoned it and it was taken over by the self-sufficient Augustinians, who maintained it for four centuries until in 1835 it became a victim of the laws of Ecclesiastical Confiscation, through which monastic properties were taken and given to the people. When the first Carlist War began in 1836, the monastery was burned down and the Augustinians left, first (legend has it) burying a golden bell, whereabouts unknown. Now the structure has been made safe for visitors and those with a head for heights can ascend the metal stairs for spectacular views across the plain to Vitoria-Gasteiz.

Next to the ticket office there is a small cabin used for exhibitions, such as local artwork, plus a temporary display and a short, Spanish-only video. There are also toilets and a coffee machine.

Iruña-Veleia, Trespuentes (Signposted off the A-4358 road, between Villodas & Trespuentes; m 618 53 93 53; ⌚ Easter week & May–mid-Sep 11.00–14.00 & 16.00–19.00 Tue–Sat, 11.00–14.00 Sun & holidays, mid-Sep–30 Apr 11.00–15.00 Tue–Sat, 11.00–20.00 Sun & hols; admission free) The Basque Country's most prestigious Roman remains, on the old route between Astorga and Bordeaux, the

CIRCULAR FOREST WALK FROM CARANCA TO IRON AGE FORTIFICATIONS

Distance: 5.5km; time: 2hrs; difficulty: easy underfoot, some sharp ascents, can be muddy in places. No refreshments en route. If coming from the south (Villanañe) you will find parking on the left in the centre of Caranca. This is a short walk through pine and mixed forest on wide tracks, with no traffic, great mountain views and a chance to see the Castros de Lastra, the ruins of a hill fort dating from the Iron Age.

From Caranca village centre, retrace your route down the road towards Villanañe, passing the 42km marker then turning sharp left down a road to the bridge, visible below, which you cross and turn right, continuing on a grassy track, keeping a renovated house and the river to your right to reach a metal gate. Pass through the gate and take the fork to the left (you will return on the right-hand fork) which ascends immediately. After 200m, ignore a path to the left and continue to the right, always ascending. The attractive village of Caranca is behind and below. Reaching a three-way crossing, turn sharp left and continue upwards on a wide path flanked with trees and foliage. After around 400m, the path flattens and you will have superb views of the mountains to your right. At a three-way crossing,

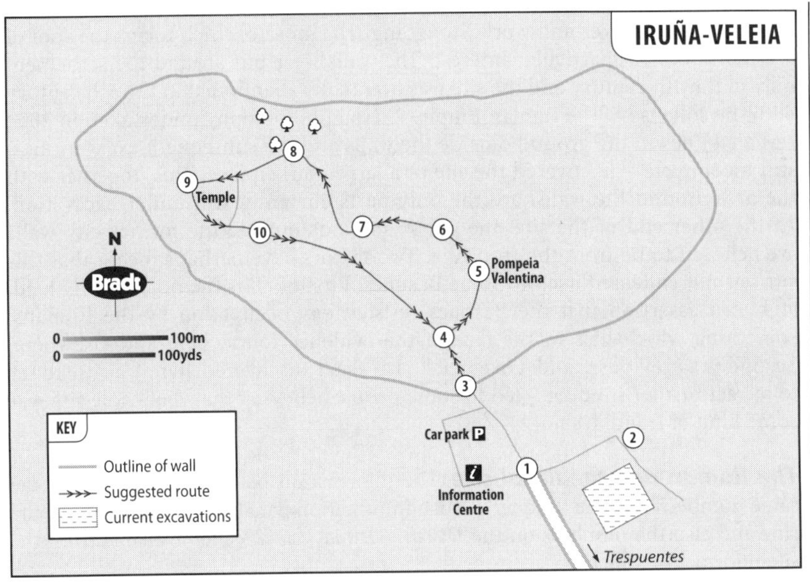

superb strategic position of this site was the attraction for the Romans when they first built here in the 1st century AD, but settlement of some sort can be traced back at least to the Iron Age, around 1000BC.

For the English-speaking visitor, the office has a leaflet with very limited information, but using the map above and the notes below allows you to visit the site on your own. If you want a guided tour, then normally these only operate with a minimum of ten people (and will be in Spanish), but if you ring a few days in advance, you might be lucky … or they might bend the rules. Sporadic excavations since the 19th century, using different techniques, have meant a lack of continuity, but with only 5% of the supposed site actually excavated, there is

we take a sharp left, marked by a sign for Los Castros de Lastra. Soon you reach a further sign, behind which are the largely unexcavated remains of the settlement, which were discovered in 1870 along with remains from the first and second Iron Ages. There are also traces of 20th-century charcoal manufacture. After your visit, retrace your steps 100m or so back to the three-way crossing with the sign, then turn left, continuing in the same direction as before you diverted to the remains. The path starts to descend and soon you reach a barbed-wire fence. Although it has a gate, do not cross to the other side – instead turn right immediately *before* it, on to a wide path which immediately starts to descend. Soon you pass (except in dry periods) two ponds, then a small clearing, before reaching a second, larger clearing where you take the right-hand path of the three, which continues to descend through the woods. (Note: this section can be muddy in rainy times.) Soon the path runs parallel to the river, which you can hear below you to the left. You keep on this path until you reach the metal gate which you passed through at the start of the walk, go through it, turn left when you reach the bridge and climb back to the road to reach Caranca village.

still much to discover and work is ongoing. The mosaic which forms the roof of a water tank is of particular interest. The walls were put around the settlement only in the 4th century and the site was eventually abandoned in the 5th century with the collapse of the Roman Empire. Aerial photography undertaken in 2004 revealed lines in the ground outside the walls and the subsequent excavations – still incomplete – uncovered the site of a large marketplace. This, together with the area around the walls, are the only parts currently still under excavation. At the other end of the site, the grassy mounds outside the former city walls are believed to be from the Iron Age. Two factors have perhaps meant that this site has not endeared itself to some Basques. First of all is the occasionally held, stubborn assertion that the Basques resisted *any* occupation by the Romans, something which flies in the face of the evidence found here and elsewhere. Secondly, a previous scandal over a faked artefact 'discovered' here – a ruse to try to attract further funding – led to some people believing that the whole site was some kind of fraud. It's not.

The Roman and medieval site The information below is ordered with the same numbering as the Basque/Spanish information panels positioned around the site, and also the numbers on the *Discover Iruña-Veleia* leaflet available from the site information office.

1 **The urban centre** The slopes to the east and south of the hill of Iruña were densely urbanised during the first few centuries AD. Archaeological digs since 2010 have permitted the documentation of the existence of various constructions erected on a series of parallel terraces, designed to 'level off' the slope in the ground.

Among those buildings was highlighted one particularly large edifice, at the side of the road that entered the city. Of an irregular, quadrangular floor plan, it was composed of a central patio, on to which opened various smaller rooms. The theories assert that this was a public market (*macellum* in Latin), which functioned in a similar manner to a traditional trading square. Inside, several shops were situated along with various other rooms (for example, the remains of a small sanctuary, richly decorated with marble squares, has been identified).

2 **From Astorga to Bordeaux: the Via Veleia** Veleia occupied a position of great strategic importance in the extreme west of the Llanada region. Through here passed the Roman road (*calzada*) which connected Astorga with Burdeos (Bordeaux), and which was known as the Iter XXXIV. This important communication route was a public way, the property of the Roman state, and it was furnished with supply and relay stations to ease communications and facilitate merchant traffic. At the place where you are now standing, the road entered into the city, becoming transformed into an urban street, with gated walkways that permitted access into the neighbouring buildings.

3 **The walls** The walls are the most prominent part of the Veleia ruins. Their construction seems to correspond with the end of the 3rd or the beginning of the 4th century, being built to repel the incursions of Frankish and Germanic tribes. Despite their more than 1,200m of circumference, they only served to protect a small part of the city, the so-called *oppidum*, as most of the population continued to live outside its limits until at least the 5th century. It is estimated that the maximum height of the wall would have reached 12m. The front

constituted one of the most monumental sections, with walls more than 5m thick and imposing circular towers flanking its entrance gate. The external wall used huge masonry blocks recycled from previous buildings. In other sections, stone of an inferior quality was used, necessitating the simplification of the design of the defensive fortification (with towers of a square floor plan) although still retaining the large dimensions.

4 **The interior face of the wall** This sector was excavated in 1975 by J C Elorza, following renewed archaeological interest in walled cities. The cylindrical sections of column in the wall confirm the recycling of previously used materials and the haste with which it was constructed. The function of the other buildings that adjoined the wall, built directly on to the natural rock, is unknown.

5 **The house of Pompeia Valentina** The name Pompeia Valentina appears inscribed on a ceramic fragment recovered during the excavation of this house, which started in 1996 and is not yet complete. It was a house (*domus*) of the type typically occupied by the powerful families of the time. The principal façade had a central entrance (*fauces*) with two side-rooms for commercial usage (*tabernae*). The house was organised with a patio (*atrium*), around which were arranged the rest of the rooms: the main room (*tablinum*) where the head of the household would receive his clients, the bedrooms (*cubicula*), the dining room (*triclinium*) and the kitchen (*culina*). The atrium, decorated with mosaic flooring, features an opening up above (*compluvium*) to ventilate and illuminate the other rooms and permit the gathering of rainwater in an underground cistern. This house was built in the 1st century, and modified later on, with the addition of new rooms organised around a large flag-stoned patio surrounded by columns.

6 **The house of the 'Rosetones' mosaic** This house shows a similar structure to that of Pompeia Valentina, but its original floor plan is somewhat concealed by significant modifications carried out in the late Romanic period. It takes its name from the motifs of the mosaic that decorates the floor of the lower atrium where the cistern is found. The partial rupture of the flooring allows us to appreciate the technical details of its construction, tiny pieces of stone of various colours (*teselae*) encrusted in a layer of mortar, making up the pattern outlined above.

7 **The cisterns** The excavations by Gratiniano Nieto, in 1950, documented at this spot three underground cisterns from the 1st century AD, which were radically remodelled in the 3rd century, following a fire. Later excavations identified a further cistern from this later period. The structure is quadrangular, with two pillars to support the floor. The inside was plastered to prevent water leaks. When it fell into disuse in the 5th century, it gradually became full of debris, including some human skulls!

8 **The Priory of the Knights of St John of Jerusalem, Rhodes and Malta** In the Middle Ages, the members of this order – having taken over the terrain in the late 13th/early 14th century – erected various buildings on the Roman ruins in order to establish a priory in an area which is now a small wood. According to available written sources, they repaired the walls of the old fortifications and erected the priory house, which included various other buildings and a

church. In its current state, the ruins are totally concealed by vegetation and you can barely make out a few walled sections. In the 19th century, Ricardo Becerro de Bengoa visited the ruins and discovered the carving illustrated on the information panel.

9 **The 'cistern' that turned out to be a temple** The discovery at the start of the 20th century of these significant ruins led the discoverer, Jaime Verástegui, to believe initially that they were a huge water tank for the distribution of water. His finding of a series of shafts and a large-dimension capital indicated the indisputable existence of a large building of a public character, with the characteristic architectural décor of official buildings. Very probably what we are actually looking at is a temple, which by its location was one of the most important sacred buildings of the city. In later times, additions were made to the temple structure to give it a defensive function.

10 **Constructions attached to the city wall** The excavation works by Gratiniano Nieto in this zone, carried out in the 1950s, made possible the discovery of a number of diverse constructions from the late Roman period, adjoining the city wall, but which cannot be successfully interpreted. It is interesting to approach the inward-facing side of the wall of the *oppidum* to observe the various works.

Torre Palacio de los Varona (Villanañe; 945 35 30 35 or 945 35 30 40; Sep–Jun 11.00–14.00 Sat, Sun & public holidays only, Easter, Jul & Aug 11.00–14.00 & 16.00–19.00 Tue–Sat, 11.00–14.00 Sun & hols; €5, guided tours are obligatory & available in English – advance notice is required) Signposted and easily visible from the main road as you approach Villanañe, this medieval tower-house and its adjacent church dominate the wide, flat plain in which they stand. The guided tours will take you through the reason for the unusual origin of the family's 'female' surname and history, including the fact that the current Señor Varona still lives in an apartment upstairs, having struck a deal with the public authorities who now run the tower. Completely renovated (including a lift for the less mobile), the 14th/15th-century building and the mainly 19th-century furniture make for a pleasant hour's visit.

Sobrón Off the A-2122, a 2.5km drive up the steep, rough but easily passable A-4324 takes you to a dead end. Your route is flanked on one side by steep cliffs, and on the other by tremendous views over the neighbouring forested mountains. At the top is 'upper' Sobrón, a soporific hamlet with a *casa rural* but without so much as a bar. In the valley bottom you can see the reservoir which lies behind the lower part of Sobrón village, once a favourite in the Franco years as a spa settlement renowned for its water quality, now a rather sorry row of decaying, closed hotels and cafés, with one restaurant option left for a drink or simple *menu del día*. Locals say the spa, the Balneario de Sobrón, closed when the owner was killed by his pet bear. More cheerfully, here you will now find **Aventura Sobrón** (686 98 38 61; e info@aventurasobron.com; w aventurasobron.com), an outdoor activity park featuring horseriding, bike trails, paintballing, archery, kayaking, SUP (stand-up paddleboard) and the only *via ferrata* in Euskadi.

Salto de Nervión A waterfall without water does not sound much of a visitor attraction, but the spectacular views from the *mirador* (viewpoint) here make a strong argument to the contrary. The viewpoint is actually in Burgos province, but the valley over which it looks is very definitely Basque, so it belongs in this book. After times of heavy rain, or even better after snow-melt, the water here plummets over 220m, making it Spain's highest waterfall, but for most of the year it is dry, with the waters remaining subterranean, before starting their journey to Bilbao and turning into the Nervión River en route. To get there, zig-zag up the A-2625 south of the town of Orduña, cross the summit and turn left shortly afterwards to find the car park. There is a short walk to reach the viewpoint, spectacularly poised above the Valle de Delica. From the vertiginous cliff-edge, look out for the vultures colonising the rock ledges below you.

Cascada de Goiuri/Gojuli (waterfall) Not as high nor as frequently visited as the Salto de Nervión, the Goiuri waterfall is still capable of taking the breath away as its waters plunge 100m down a sheer rock face to the gorge floor. Signposted, the official viewpoint lies on the A-2521 Vitoria–Orduña road, though a second one on the other side of the waterfall also offers spectacular views. (Caution: there is no guardrail at this second one and it's a straight drop, so not ideal for children.) Apart from in July and August, there should be a worthwhile fall of water.

Euskal Buztingintzako Museoa (Museo de Alfarería Vasca, Pottery Museum) (Ollerias, Elosu; 945 45 51 45; w euskalzeramika.com; 10.00–13.00 & 16.00–19.00 Mon–Fri, 10.00–14.00 Sat) Built in 1711, this pottery passed through the hands of seven generations of the Ortiz de Zárate family before the last of these handed over to its current driving force, Blanka Gómez de Segura. This inspirational woman had to fight hard to acquire the clay-throwing skills which were reserved traditionally for men. She reopened the pottery as a museum in 1993, and is now assisted by English-speaking staff. The old kiln (last fired-up in 1958, when the creation of the nearby reservoir led to flooding and the pottery's closure) forms part of the building; gorse was originally used to fuel the kiln and fire the pots. For health reasons, toxic lead in the glaze was replaced by tin imported from Cornwall in England, a 'backload' cargo returning in the ships that left Bizkaia for Britain filled with iron ore. Nowadays, the pottery produced here is commissioned by some of the Basque Country's top restaurants, but prices at the factory shop are reasonable and the pieces are attractive. School visits are encouraged to foster interest in the tradition; visitors are given a guided tour and can see Blanka in action, throwing her clay.

Walking The Añana region is a walker's dream, particularly for those who head to the Parque Velderejo, where there are nine walking routes waymarked in a compact area of hills and gorges, a distinct topography that assists with orientation. The problem, as elsewhere in the Basque Country, is that not much of the information is in English, and budgetary pressures mean that this issue may not be resolved very soon. The walks on pages 208 and 210 give you an introduction but, if you speak Spanish or are a skilled navigator, there is huge potential here. At Lalastra, in the Parque Velderejo, there is a small museum, learning centre and a Casa del Parque (park centre) with information on wildlife and the ecosystem (in Spanish only).

LA RIOJA ALAVESA (ARABAKO ERRIOXA)

The Sierra Cantabria rudely divides Álava from west to east, and south of the mountain range you're in a region that's a world apart from the rest of the Basque Country. Everywhere is covered in vines and you don't have to guess how people make their living in the Rioja Alavesa. Here, there are more hectares of vineyard than there are inhabitants and you can taste, drink, buy – even bathe in – their liquid products. The Romans can take the credit for bringing viniculture to the area, but it's only since the 1970s that the production of wine here has become truly commercially focused. Now, wine tourism is very firmly established too and, as well as visitors from other parts of Spain, Americans, Australians, British, Germans and many others flock here to indulge, tasting the wines in *bodegas* that range from medieval caves to architect-designed eccentricities. While the vine dominates, cereals and olives are also grown, though the latter's importance is less than it was a hundred years ago.

As well as the agricultural landscape, the small towns that punctuate it are attractive, too: Laguardia (Biazteri) is the jewel, its strategic, lofty location at one time making it 'the Guardian of Navarre', as it watched out for armies approaching from Castile. Now, its pedestrianised Old Town oozes charm and points of interest, with over 250 caves lurking beneath its narrow streets. The southern border of Álava is defined by the River Ebro, beyond which lies the province of La Rioja. In terms of wine, rather than administration, Rioja is a geographical denomination, meaning that Rioja wine comes from this part of Álava, a small part of Navarre and a tiny patch of Burgos, as well as La Rioja province itself. Unlike the areas of southern Álava on the north side of the mountains, Rioja Alavesa has a clear peg on which to hang its tourism hat and most visitors are here to quaff the products of the grape. Harvesting takes place by hand in October, with an influx of grape-pickers into the area from eastern Europe, North Africa and especially from Portugal for three weeks of frenzied activity.

GETTING THERE AND AWAY

By car Although the most direct route from the north is via the AP-68 motorway and then the A-124/LR-132, a more scenic route for those with time to spare – and one that avoids road tolls – would be to enter the region on the A-126 then the A-2126, crossing the Sierra Cantabria at the Bernedo Pass for a stunning first sight of Rioja Alavesa.

By bus Laguardia connects around 20 times per day with Logroño on weekdays (30mins; €1.80), less frequently at weekends; with Vitoria-Gasteiz 11-times daily (1hr; €6.10), less often at weekends; and twice with Bilbao (w cuadrabuslineas.com; 1hr 40mins; €8.30). There are 11 buses to and from Labastida (Bastida) to Vitoria daily (50mins; €4.25). Apart from the Bilbao buses, all details of fares and timetables can be found at w araba.eus/alavabus.

By train The nearest train station to Rioja Alavesa is Logroño, which is 18km and 25 minutes away, while the major railway junction of Miranda del Ebro is some 40km and 40 minutes away (both distance and time from Laguardia).

TOURIST INFORMATION

Apart from at the tourist offices detailed below, you can also find more information on w rutadelvinoderiojaalavesa.com/en.

Elciego (Zieko) Calle Norte 26; 945 60 66 32; e info@elciego.es; w elciego.es; summer 10.00–14.00 & 16.00–19.00 daily, 10.00–14.00 Tue–Sun rest of year

Labastida Plaza de la Paz; 945 33 10 15; e turismo@labastida-bastida.org; w labastida-bastida.org; May–Oct 10.00–14.00 Tue–Thu, 10.00–14.00 & 15.00–19.00 Fri, 09.00–14.00 &

15.00–18.00 Sat, 09.00–14.00 Sun, mid-Mar–end Apr, Nov & Dec 10.00–14.00 & 15.00–19.00 Fri & Sat, 09.00–14.00 Sun

Laguardia Calle Mayor 52; 945 60 08 45; e turismo@laguardia-alava.com; w laguardia-alava.com; 10.00–14.00 & 16.00–19.00 Mon–Fri, 10.00–14.00 & 17.00–19.00 Sat, 10.45–14.00 Sun. Multilingual staff & a touch screen providing info on hotels, restaurants & *bodegas*.

WHERE TO STAY

When visiting the region, most people stay in Laguardia and the places to stay here are shown on the map on page 221. Places to stay in Labastida are shown on the map on page 186.

Hotel Hospedería Los Parajes (18 rooms) Calle Mayor 46–48, Laguardia; 945 62 11 30; e info@hospederiadelosparajes.com; w hospederiadelosparajes.com. Right on the main square, classy rooms with soundproofed windows, the hotel sports a jacuzzi & spa, labyrinthine basement & an old *calado* (wine cave) converted to an atmospheric bar. Free Wi-Fi. **€€€€**

Hotel Viura (33 rooms, 4 suites) Calle Mayor, Villabuena de Álava; 945 60 90 00; e info@hotelviura.com; w hotelviura.com; closed Jan–mid-Feb. A boxy, Cubist's dream, designed by the owners in conjunction with a local lady architect. Rooms are standard or deluxe, all spacious & arty. Interior décor is ultra-modern, each floor's corridors painted by a different artist. The restaurant has a wine cellar which diners can visit to make their choice & a roof terrace to enjoy the sun. Small gym, massage room, no pool, but guests can use the adjacent (seasonal) municipal one. Free Wi-Fi. **€€€€**

Wine Oil Spa Villa de Laguardia (84 rooms) Paseo San Raimundo 15, Laguardia; 945 60 05 60; e reservas@hotelvilladelaguardia.com; w hotelvilladelaguardia.com. Gym, spa treatments & a 'spa circuit' (extra cost) just out of town on the road to Logroño. There is also free Wi-Fi, gardens, outdoor pool & bike rental. **€€€–€€€€**

Hotel Castillo del Collado (10 rooms) Paseo del Collado 1, Laguardia; 945 62 12 00; e hotel@hotelcollado.com; w hotelcollado.com. A charming old-world family hotel, a few mins' walk from the Plaza Mayor. Rooms with TV & AC all have their own personality & are decorated with conservative taste. Some have spa-baths, all have interesting names: 'Love and Madness' is the one for romantic couples, surely. **€€€**

Eguren Ugarte (21 rooms) On the A-121 at km61, Paganos, Laguardia; 945 60 07 66; e info@egurenugarte.com; w egurenugarte.com. A large complex set in its own gardens, with different classes of rooms, all smart. Ask for a room with a view. TV, AC & free Wi-Fi. Restaurant & winery attached. B/fast inc. **€€€**

Posada Mayor de Migueloa (8 rooms) Mayor 20, Laguardia; 945 60 01 87; e reservas@mayordemigueloa.com; w mayordemigueloa.com. A charming, atmospheric, well-managed hotel, in a 400-year-old mansion house, with old tiled floors & period furniture. Wine bar, 2 restaurants, wine tours/tastings. **€€€**

Casa Rural Osante (7 rooms) Calle Frontin 10, Labastida; m 649 42 64 07; e info@osante.com.es; w osante.com.es. Large converted house with a huge public area. Suitable for those with lesser mobility, including lift. Rooms have TV, free Wi-Fi – ask for one on the 3rd floor for the best view. Excellent b/fast. **€€**

Casa Rural Rojanda (5 rooms) Manuel Iradier 8, Elciego; 945 60 61 90; e info@casarojanda.com; w casarojanda.com. Tasteful rooms in a renovated old house. Wi-Fi. The family also has a *bodega* next door & can organise winery trips. B/fast inc. **€€**

Hostal Biazteri (9 rooms) Calle Mayor 72, Laguardia; 945 60 00 26; e reservas@biazteri.com; w biazteri.com. Very good-value small *hostal* close to the centre of Laguardia. All rooms have TV, free Wi-Fi & bathroom. Quadruple rooms are also available. **€€**

Solar de Quintano (4 apts) Varajuela 7, Labastida; m 646 49 23 52; e solardequintano@gmail.com; w solardequintano.com. Fully equipped self-catering apartments set in a gorgeous 18th-century building, built by one of the region's wine pioneers & located in lower Labastida. Varying in size, they can sleep up to 6 guests. The apartments have free Wi-Fi, TV & heating, garden, washing-machines & parking. B/fast is a nominal €2. **€€**

WHERE TO EAT AND DRINK All establishments in Laguardia are marked on the map on page 221.

Eguren Ugarte (page 217) Elegant dining in a modern winery. The service & food are top class & the setting tranquil. Bag a seat with a mountain view. €€€€

Los Parajes (page 217) In a heavily chandeliered dining room, fine cuisine & a very long wine list. Steamed hake makes a change from the usual grilled & the *nouvelle* touches are unpretentious. €€€€

Amelibia La Barbacana Errepidea 14, Laguardia; 945 62 12 07; w restauranteamelibia.com; 13.00–15.30 Wed–Mon, 21.00–22.30 Fri & Sat only. With pleasant views down over the vines, friendly service & a light, bright interior, this is a good place to sample some inventive cuisine. For dessert, the *canutillos rellenos* (custard horns with rum & hot chocolate) are recommended. €€€–€€€€

Biazteri (page 217) 13.00–16.00 & 21.00–22.30 daily. 3 renovated dining rooms, 1 with a glass floor section allowing you to see the cave where the grapes were crushed by foot. Traditional Basque cuisine at decent prices & children's menus. €€€

Posada Mayor de Migueloa (page 217). There are 2 choices here: a formal, intimate upstairs dining-room or the downstairs, less formal cafeteria style with less fancy food. €€€

Jatorrena Florida 10, Labastida; 945 33 10 50; w jatorrena.com; lunch & dinner daily. Excellent food, though the dining room lacks much character. Try *chuletillas al sarmiento* (lamb chops cooked over vine wood), which are a local speciality. €€

SHOPPING Laguardia is replete with wine shops and has a good selection of other small boutiques for poking around in as you stroll the narrow alleyways. **Pepita Uva** (Calle Mayor 29, Laguardia; 945 60 02 18; w pepitauva.com; 10.00–14.30 & 16.00–20.00 daily) prides itself on its small selection of local wines, with daily tastings, bilingual (Spanish/English) children's books, handmade jewellery, pottery, scarves and olive oil.

FESTIVALS In both Laguardia and Labastida, the end of the grape harvest is celebrated with a festival in the first week of November. San Juan and San Pedro are celebrated in **Laguardia** on 24 and 29 June respectively, with bull-running down the Calle Mayor and dancing in the town centre. In the tourist office, the two *gigantes* (giant figures) of Doña Blanca de Navarra and Sancho el Sabio stand waiting to be wheeled out on the saints' days to take part in the festivities. Dozens of pipe bands descend on Laguardia on either the second or third weekend in May (it varies from year to year) from all over the world for the Gaiteros ('Pipers' Festival'). Strolling from street to street, stopping for refreshments, the pipers then amass for a communal dinner and bagpiping through the night. There's no sleep to be had in town this weekend.

Labastida celebrates its medieval origins with a weekend festival in July, and on December 24 and 25 also hosts the 'Shepherds' Dance'. On a Sunday in June, there's the 'Bodegas a Pie de Calle', when representatives from the local wineries set out stalls and sell tickets to let the townsfolk taste their wares. More raucous is the San Gines festival, 40 days after Easter, when a huge wine battle takes place.

Each year a different town in the region hosts the celebration of a harvest festival in mid-September and the Entorno a la Mesa in July; the latter one focuses on local Basque products, with children's activities, showcooking, etc.

WHAT TO SEE AND DO For most travellers to Rioja Alavesa, the compact quaintness, atmospheric streets and sheer choice of accommodation, wineries and restaurants of **Laguardia** will single it out as the ideal centre for exploring both the town itself and the surrounding area. Some visitors may have set their sights on particular architect-designed hotels, which will lure them elsewhere, and **Labastida** maintains a certain charm and authentic feel which can sometimes be temporarily lost in high-season Laguardia. Labastida's 16th-century church is said to have the best organ in the Basque Country, though it's only played on special occasions. Take the short climb to the Ermita Fortaleza de Santo Cristo in Labastida to enjoy a great view of the castles that are spread across neighbouring La Rioja. The beautiful, solid limestone architecture of some of the towns and *bodegas* in Álava is a contrast to that of the northern Basque provinces. Peaceful Elciego village is a particularly neat and tidy example.

Tour guides and organised trips With plenty of wine-related activities, it's no surprise to find organised tours ready to take you with them to the vineyard. Gastronomic trips, as well as more general interest and active trips, are also on offer.

Los Cazaventuras ☎676 92 57 46; e info@cazaventuras.com; w riojaalavesaturismo.com. Organises a wide range of wine- & sport-related activities in the Basque Country & elsewhere.
Pepita Uva Calle Mayor 29, Laguardia; ☎945 60 02 18; e info@pepitauva.com; w pepitauva.com. Organises excellent, well-informed tours of Laguardia & fun trips for children.
Thabuca Wine Tours Mayor 4, Labastida; ☎945 33 10 60; e info@thabuca.com; w thabuca.com. Wine, food & cultural tours in the Basque Country & La Rioja.

Bodega visits With dozens of wineries to visit in Rioja Alavesa, the choice is bewildering. If you are here just for the wine, then no doubt you will avail yourself of more than just the ones mentioned below. Fans of modern architecture might want to visit the Calatrava-designed Ysios winery, though arguably the best view of its exterior can be seen from the Torre Abacial in Laguardia (page 222). The even more famous Marqués de Riscal winery is located in Elciego, but note that it is the hotel, not the neighbouring winery, that is the emblematic work of Frank Gehry. Other wineries of architectural interest are Bodegas Baigorri in Samaniego and Bodegas Viña Real in Laserna – both boast stunning interiors. A full list of wineries open for visits can be found at w rutadelvinoderiojaalavesa.com, or ask at the tourist offices in Laguardia or Labastida. Remember that many of the wineries are small, family concerns with few staff, and for all visits, especially off-season if you want a guided English-language one, contact your selected winery in advance to make a reservation.

Bodegas Campillo Carretera de Logroño, Laguardia; ☎945 60 08 26; e info@bodegascampillo.es; w bodegascampillo.com; tours available between 10.00 & 18.00 Mon–Sat; €10. The first architect-designed winery in the region, & part of the well-known Faustino group, nevertheless the production of the 8 wines is small (700,000 bottles) & the visit to the vineyards & the handsome winery is homely but comprehensive, starting out in the vineyard & ending in the tasting room. Only 8% of their wines are exported. A new young wine, 'El Niño' ('The Boy') is increasingly popular. They also supply the official wine for the Guggenheim. Adapted for wheelchairs.
Bodegas Carlos San Pedro Pérez de Viñaspre Páganos 44, Laguardia; m 647 72 04 45 or 605 03 30 43; e info@bodegascarlossanpedro.com; w bodegascarlossanpedro.com; ⏲ year-round daily; €9/7/5 with 3/2/1 wine tastings. A great chance to see the old caves while taking an English-language tour – contact them for exact times of these. Wine produced here is in tiny quantities & therefore only sold from the shop up above. Located right in the town centre. You can have a wine-label custom-made from one of your photos & stuck to a bottle.
Bodegas Ostatu Carretera de Vitoria 1, Samaniego; ☎945 60 91 33; e communicacion@

ostatu.com; **w** ostatu.com; ⌚ 09.00–14.00 & 15.00–18.00 Mon–Fri, 10.00–18.00 Sat, 10.30–13.30 Sun & hols; €12, including a bottle to take away. 3 brothers, 1 sister, 10 different wines. This family business is in a modern winery but the tasting is in the adjacent 18th-century former inn on the main A-124 road. Small production, friendly reception for visitors.

Bodegas Remírez de Ganuza Constitución 1, Samaniego; 945 60 90 22; **e** visits@ramirezdeganuza.com; **w** remirezdeganuza.com; ⌚ Book in advance; €30 including taste of 3 wines. A slightly exclusive winery, this would best suit those knowledgeable about the subject. The winery is only around 30 years old; the founder is something of an inventor, as will be clear from your tour. Only brand-new barrels are used. Production of red dominates, only Joven, Reservas & Grand Reservas, no Crianza. Whites are also made in small quantities. A maximum of 150,000 bottles are made annually from their 70ha.

Bodegas Tierra Labastida El Olmo 16, Labastida; 945 33 12 57; **m** 605 67 23 13; **e** info@tierrayvino.com; **w** tierrayvino.com; ⌚ year-round, but phone in advance for visit; €10, including 2 tastings. Signposted 'Bodega Agricola Labastida' off the main road, this is run by the Fernández Gómez brothers & located in 4 houses & a yard at the top of the town. Far from the big, architect-designed wineries, the production of reds, whites & rosés is small, & your tour will take you into a network of caves dating back over 600 years. The tasting room has a window with superb views up to the Toloño mountain range.

Bodegas Ysios Camino de la Hoya, Laguardia 945 60 06 40; **e** visitas.ysios@pernod-ricard.com; **w** ysios.com; tours 11.00, 13.00 & 16.00 Mon–Fri, 11.00, 13.00 & 16.00 Sat, 11.00 & 13.00 Sun. Note: English-language tours are only Sat at 16.00; €15, including visit to winery (1½hrs) & tasting of 2 wines. Owned by a global drinks conglomerate, this winery lacks much intimacy, but a tour will let you enjoy a close-up of the renowned Santiago Calatrava architecture. The building blends in surprisingly well with the stunning backdrop of the Sierra de Cantabria mountain range.

Contino For contact details, see *Viña Real*, below. After it featured in an episode of American reality show *Bacholerette* this picture-postcard vineyard was suddenly deluged with phone calls from the USA. Viewers wanted to get married here, or simply take lunch out in its pretty gardens. Like Rachel in the TV show, you are guaranteed to fall in love . . . at least with the venue, if not with each other. 6 wines – all 'single vineyard' – are produced from its 62ha of vineyards, but in poor years they will not produce at all if quality cannot be guaranteed.

Marqués de Riscal Torrea 1, Elciego 945 18 08 88; **e** reservas.marquesderiscal@luxurycollection.com; **w** marquesderiscal.com. Tours take place daily, but times vary. €16/8 adults/children, including winery visit & tasting of 2 wines. Visits are available in several languages, including English. A well-known name in Spanish wine & a chance to see the outside (at least) of the designer hotel in Elciego: Guggenheim comes to the countryside.

Viña Real Carretera Logroño-Laguardia, km4.8; 945 62 52 55 or 941 30 48 09; **e** visitas@cvne.com; **w** cvne.com; €15, visit & tasting with 5 wines; €50 visit plus lunch; wine-tasting courses also available, €20. Fully adapted for those with sight or mobility restrictions. A hilltop winery whose principle is to operate only with gravity, something which the French architect had to consider carefully in his radical design. From a distance, the winery looks like a spaceship; once inside, it could be the setting for a James Bond film, with its singular shape & impressive overhead crane system. Harvest time would be an interesting time to visit, to see the machinery in full flow. Oak barrels sourced from Hungary are now used in addition to the more traditional French & American, as DNA has shown that they are related to French oak!

Laguardia and around

See page 217 for accommodation and restaurant listings.

Calle Mayor The narrow main street of this beautiful hilltop town is loaded with charm, filled with attractive buildings, mouthwatering bakeries and delicatessens, plus a collection of wine and gift shops. Low, studded doors and solid limestone buildings create an old-world atmosphere, and the almost complete pedestrianisation

of the thoroughfare gives you time to browse at leisure.

Iglesia Santa María de los Reyes (Calle Mayor (northern end); for visit times, consult the tourist office (945 60 08 45); tours last 30mins; €3 – buy ticket at the tourist office or the church itself) Guided visits in English are by advance booking with the tourist office, preferably with a few days' notice. Normally you need a group of 15, but on weekdays they will organise it with less. In any event, the visit is largely visual, with the Gothic stone doorway from the 14th century and the 17th-century polychromes being the highlights. The visit starts with a talk about the doorway, undertaken in darkness and with the statues of the apostles being spotlighted as they are discussed. The church construction began in the 12th century but was not finished until the 16th century, explaining the mix of architectural styles. An English-language handout is available.

Puerta de San Juan Situated on the eastern side of the walls, the Spanish inscription on the tile outside of this gate and Gothic watchtower translates as: 'Peace to those who arrive, health to those who reside, good luck to those who depart.'

Plaza Mayor and Reloj Carillón (clock) Laguardia's Plaza Mayor isn't particularly big, yet it still finds space for two town halls, one new and the old one which bears the double-eagled crest of Carlos I. The clock high on the wall draws a good crowd of tourists at noon, 14.00, 17.00 and 20.00 (Jun–Sep also at 13.00 & 22.00), when the striking of the hour prompts the appearance of figures in Basque traditional costume to perform a little dance. Bizarrely, the crowd often applaud the inanimate dancers! From Easter until October, a band gathers under the arches on Sundays at 20.00, striking up a few classical numbers before retiring to a bar for a drink or two, after which they return, then retire, then return …

Villa Lucía Centro Temático del Vino (Thematic Wine Centre) (Carretera de Logroño, Laguardia; ☎ 945 60 00 32; e museo@villa-lucia.com; w villa-lucia.com; 🕘 Tue–Sun (morning only on Sun); email or phone well in advance, or turn up on the day & show yourself around; from €7 to €11.50, including tasting) An entertaining, award-winning 4D film (in English), a chance to test your sense of smell in relation to wine – guessing between vanilla and cinnamon, or shoe leather for example – plus a tour of the museum, with information in English, makes this a worthwhile excursion, easily walkable from Laguardia.

'Barbacana' Estanque Celtibérico (Celtoiberian pond) (Western end of Calle Mayor, Laguardia; 🕘 visits Tue–Sun, for detailed times, consult tourist office (page 216); €4) While digging up the ground for a much-needed new car park, workmen discovered a 2,000-year-old water tank, the preservation of which demanded an abrupt halt to proceedings. Now converted into a learning centre, you can visit this interesting presentation about man and water. There's a film, normally shown in Spanish, but if you can wait, they will put it on in English.

Viajeros *(Koko Rico sculpture)* As you glance to the right, approaching the Santa María Church up the Calle Mayor, you might think a shoe sale is taking place. But no: the 'footwear' on display is the 2004 work of Vitoria-born sculptor, Koko Rico. The sculpture is entitled *Viajeros* (*Travellers*) and is inspired by the footwear of the Camino de Santiago pilgrims who pass through the town.

Torre Abacial (Abbot's Tower) (🕘 visits Tue–Sun, for detailed times consult tourist office (page 216); €1) At the north end of the town, this 13th-century tower with its 112 steps is highly recommended, and is worth a visit just for the views it affords over the town and the vineyards. From here, you can see the distinctive architecture of the distant Marqués de Riscal and close-by Ysios wineries (page 220), the classic almond shape of Laguardia town, the Lagunas de Laguardia, the Sierra Cantabria range and the distant, higher mountains of La Rioja. You can also ring the bell at the top of the tower, and there are some souvenirs on sale.

Lagunas de Laguardia Just east and south of Laguardia, a wetland area of four 'lakes' provides a 10km circular walking route and the chance for some birdwatching. One lake, the Prao de la Paul, has a bird observatory and is manmade, while the others are natural. All four rely on rainwater; in high summer, some almost dry out, leaving shining deposits of salt. The area attracts many migratory species from September to June, and storks, grey heron and grebes are not uncommon. The Laguardia tourist office has a leaflet with a map, but you can easily access the area on your own by foot, heading briefly out of Laguardia towards Logroño on the A-124, before turning left at the sign. The path is waymarked and the walk is flat.

Trujal Coop 'La Equidad' (Olive oil mill & tour) (Moreda de Álava; ☎ 945 60 16 02; e info@euskadi.coop; visits by appointment only, reserve in advance; €20) The relative decline of olive trees in the area is down to money, as the planting of vines became more lucrative. Now, around 500,000kg of olives are harvested each year from four presses, here and in the nearby area. Mid to late spring sees the flowering of the trees, yet only 2% of flowers turn into fruit. The trees are the *arroniz* variety, resistant to the frosts that could damage more delicate varieties. In past times, rich families owned the village presses and took a healthy part of the production for themselves, leading to the creation of the co-operative press. This small plant offers the chance to find out about the working of the old machinery (still operational, but not in use for production), and the process of production. You also visit the olive groves, discovering that the trees here yield only around one-third of those in southern Spain. The second weekend in March is when the new season's oil is ready to be celebrated with the village's festival.

Dolmens For those interested in prehistory, a quick drive around the area surrounding Laguardia will be satisfying. Two dolmens, La Hechcera and Los Llanos, both lie signposted off the road from Laguardia to Bernedo and could be visited as part of a short drive to the top of the pass (see below), while a third, La Hoya, is just to the west of Laguardia, once again clearly signposted. The first two are unattended and can be visited at leisure. At La Hoya (🕘 Apr–Sep 11.00–14.00 & 16.00–19.00 Tue–Fri, 11.00–15.00 Sat, 10.00–14.00 Sun, Oct–Mar 11.00–15.00 Tue–Sat, 10.00–14.00 Sun; admission free) there is some limited information about the former inhabitants who dwelt here from 1500BC to 250BC. Some of the findings here are on display in the Vitoria Archaeology Museum (page 195). In total, there are eight dolmens in this area.

Labraza Crowded in July and August, this tiny village east of Laguardia is home to only 65 residents in winter, 100 in summer. You will find one bar (🕘 15.30–21.00 Mon–Fri, 12.30–15.00 & 17.30–close Sat & Sun) – you'll have to hunt for it down by the *pelota* court – and no restaurants. Totally unspoilt, but not without recognition, Labraza won the award for 'World Walled Town of the Year' in 2008–09, and property prices are high.

Mountain drive to Bernedo Pass For the best view of Rioja Alavesa (and, depending on the weather, of La Rioja, Navarre and Burgos), a short drive east of Laguardia up the A-3228 takes you swiftly up to 1,000m of altitude. You briefly enter Navarre after passing through Kripan village, and the landscape changes almost at once: trees appear as the vines vanish. If you continue over the pass, the rest of Álava reveals its carpet of forest, a huge contrast to the vineyards you've left behind.

BASQUE COUNTRY ONLINE

For additional online content, articles, photos and more on the Basque Country, why not visit w bradtguides.com/basque?

SEND US YOUR SNAPS!

We'd love to follow your adventures using our *Basque Country* guide – why not send us your photos and stories via Twitter (@BradtGuides) and Instagram (@bradtguides)? Alternatively, you can upload your photos directly to the gallery on the Basque destination page via our website (**w** bradtguides.com/basque).

Part Three

NAVARRE

FOLLOW BRADT

For the latest news, special offers and competitions, subscribe to the Bradt newsletter via the website **w** bradtguides.com and follow Bradt on:

BradtTravelGuides
@BradtGuides
@bradtguides
bradtguides
bradtguides

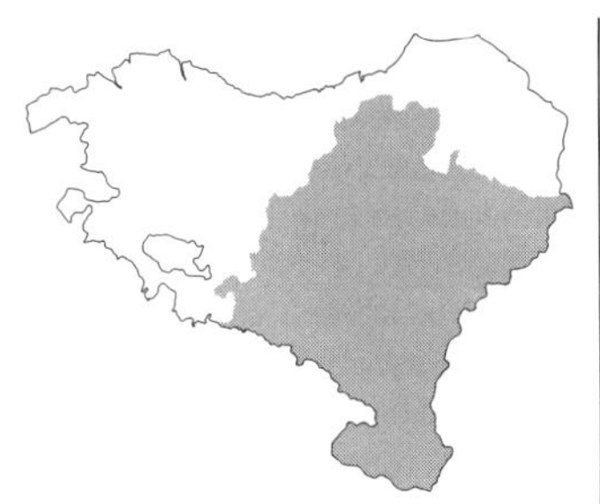

Navarre (Nafarroa)

Today's Navarre occupies territory of nearly 10,500km^2, more than the entire area taken up by those six other 'Basque provinces' lying south and north of the Pyrenees, yet with a population of roughly 640,000, representing only around one-fifth of the total. As half of those live in the wider metropolitan area of Pamplona, the rest of Navarre is characterised by wide open spaces, from the high peaks and sleepy valleys of the north, the fertile central plains, to the semi-desert and agricultural terrains of the south. Sparsely populated, economically Navarre cannot quite compete with the industrial strength of the Basque Autonomous Community, but it still enjoys relative wealth and low unemployment compared with the rest of Spain.

In tourism terms, while Pamplona is famous worldwide for the frenzied bull-running and world-class party of its San Fermín festival, many of Navarre's highlights still await discovery by visitors from abroad. Slowly, however, it is emerging from obscurity, aided and abetted by the increasing number of pilgrims walking the Camino Francés route of the Camino de Santiago, entering northern Navarre at Roncesvalles and exiting stage left in western Navarre beyond Viana. By its nature, however, such tourism is transient and – sticking to a set path – it ignores any delight or distraction that does not fall exactly on the well-trodden route. Pilgrims also cross Navarre from the east, via the Monasterio de Leyre, and also along the little-used Camino del Baztán, a lesser northern entry point. So what can Navarre offer its guests? Everything from entrenched Basque culture, deep-rooted in the valleys of the north and immovable from its Pyrenean heartland, to boisterous Pamplona, rich in history, down through vineyards to its Mediterranean-influenced south. Everything from solid Basque farmhouses, scattered through peaceful villages and tranquil, wooded valleys, to Roman remains, medieval towns, hilltop settlements and the fairy-tale palace of Olite. And once you think you've seen it all, the extraordinary semi-desert of Bardenas Reales awaits.

HISTORY

'Navarre *is* the Basque Country' claims a Basque nationalist saying, seeking to conveniently incorporate the province into a mindset that unites it with the other six Basque-speaking ones. If only things could be tidied up so neatly: the claim is only an aspiration for Basque nationalists, not a reality. Navarre's history and demography is way too complex for that, and making such a claim in the southern, Spanish-speaking reaches of Navarre will almost certainly result in disagreement, and probably hostility.

Navarre is one of Spain's 17 autonomous communities. While Basque culture, identity and language may hold sway in the province's mountainous north, the overwhelming majority of the inhabitants of Navarre speak Spanish as their first language and maintain a strong regional identity that defines itself as Navarrese. Little more than 10% of Navarre's inhabitants are fluent speakers of the Basque language. Recalling a time long passed into history, it still calls itself 'the Kingdom of Navarre'.

In pre-Roman times Navarre's territory was occupied by the Vascones who inhabited both the southern slopes of the western Pyrenees and some of the Atlantic coastline. The Romans' conquest of the whole territory in the 1st century brought roads, as well as improvements to agriculture, including vineyards. After the decline of the Roman Empire, the regions around the western Pyrenees remained at least partially outside the control of first the Visigoths, and then the Moors who had invaded from the south, but in the 8th century the Franks of Charlemagne destroyed the defensive walls of Pamplona. In revenge, the Basques routed his returning troops at the legendary Battle of Roncesvalles, in 778. Soon after, a Moorish governor was installed in Pamplona by the Emirate of Córdoba, but the Franks took control again in the early 9th century and Franks and Moors battled for control until the crowning of Íñigo Arista in 824. This was the start of the Kingdom of Pamplona (later, the Kingdom of Navarre), a period that holds the key to the importance Navarre retains in Basque nationalist mentality. Why? At the very height of its powers in the early 11th century, under Sancho III 'the Great', the area of this kingdom included what are now the three Basque provinces of Bizkaia, Gipuzkoa and Álava as well as significant other lands in the north of Spain, extending from eastern Galicia to the west to the then county of Barcelona. Importantly, it also included land to the north of the Pyrenees. In this short period under Sancho III's reign (1004–35), the seven Basque provinces were 'united' under one power for the only time in their history, hence embedding the notion of a Basque nation. Of course, far from everyone in this territory was Basque, nor is it clear if there was any sense of collective 'Basque' consciousness present in this huge territory. On Sancho's death, his territories were divided among his successors, and by 1200 the three Basque provinces had been lost again, conquered by Castile, never to be recovered and thus depriving Navarre of any coastline. In 1234, through a lack of successors, the throne of Navarre passed to the House of Champagne, meaning that the kings of France were now also to be the Kings of Navarre and that Paris's power stretched all the way down to the River Ebro. But although Navarre's allegiances moved closer to France during this time, it continued to survive as an independent kingdom for another 300 years, its territory including Basse-Navarre, north of the Pyrenees.

Much of Navarre's importance in the development of the Camino de Santiago can also be traced to the period in which Sancho III held sway, as he sought to offer safe passage to pilgrims passing through Roncesvalles, down through Pamplona and continuing south and west along what is now known as the principal pilgrim route, the Camino Francés. With the pilgrims came foreign ideas and influences that can still be witnessed today in the Romanesque and Gothic church architecture of the towns between Pamplona and Logroño in neighbouring La Rioja.

Fifteenth-century Spain was marked by a series of disputes over succession, with Ferdinand the Catholic eyeing Navarre from nearby Castile. Annexation to the Castilian crown duly took place in 1515, three years after the invasion by troops loyal to Ferdinand, yet a degree of Navarrese autonomy was still precariously preserved, including the maintenance of the *fueros*, those precious local laws, right through until the 19th century. Despite Castile's invasion, the area north of the

Pyrenees proved too troublesome to govern from the south and was abandoned by the Spanish Castilians. Navarre continued to exist, therefore, as a much-reduced, separate kingdom, comprising Basse-Navarre and neighbouring Béarn, until in 1620 these were absorbed into France.

Following defeat in the First Carlist War in 1839, during which the Basques and some parts of Navarre fought to preserve their *fueros* in the face of an increased Spanish movement towards centralisation and the suppression of regional powers, the subsequent peace deal theoretically preserved some of Navarre's autonomy. In return, Navarre had to accept status as a mere province of Spain, but in practice that vestigial claim to any regional autonomy was ignored. The two subsequent Carlist Wars later in the 19th century ended with the same result, namely defeat, further weakening the autonomy of northern Spanish provinces such as Navarre. One grave economic consequence of the Carlist defeats brought the forced relocation of the custom border from its position on the River Ebro north to a new location at the Pyrenees, resulting in economic crisis in Navarre and driving many inhabitants to emigrate to the Americas.

Navarre opposed Spain's Second Republic in 1931, paving the way for the province's overall pro-Franco stance in the Civil War. However, the Basques occupying the valleys of northern Navarre were fiercely opposed to the dictator and suffered atrocities as a result. Taking Navarre as a whole, its perceived loyalty to Franco's nationalists allowed it to enjoy some privileges even under the ensuing dictatorship. After Franco's death, and the period of transition to democracy in Spain, Navarre negotiated its own autonomy with the Spanish Government, allowing it to collect its own taxes within a set framework, but it declined the opportunity to become joined to the Basque Autonomous Community, much to the disappointment and disgust of Basque nationalists.

Today, the Comunidad Foral de Navarra enjoys the same autonomy as the Basque Autonomous Community, the two having more wide-ranging powers than any of the other autonomous communities in Spain.

NORTHERN NAVARRE

The northern part of landlocked Navarre nudges up to the western Pyrenees, which divide Spain from France. Bordered on its western frontier by Álava and to the northwest by Gipuzkoa, to the east lies Aragón. Two distinct geographical areas occupy what might be described as northern Navarre, namely the Cuenca de Pamplona (Basin of Pamplona), and the Pirineos de Navarra (Navarran Pyrenees). Pamplona is Navarre's capital, its only true city, centrally positioned to act as a meeting-point between the mountains to the north and the flatter terrain to the south; between the Basque heartlands of the Pyrenees and the more Mediterranean ambience of 'Spanish' Navarre. West and northwest of Pamplona stand a series of high sierras, craggy and karstic – Urbasa, Andía and Aralar – while directly north and to the northeast the landscape is scored by beautifully green and forested valleys – Bidasoa, Baztán, Aezkoa, Salazar and Roncal/Belagua – ushering you up to the highest peaks that Navarre can offer. In Navarre's extreme northeast towers the high point of La Mesa de los Tres Reyes, at 2,424m providing spectacular backdrops for battle-hardened cyclist and resolute walker alike. Those valleys of Bidasoa and Baztán in particular retain a strong Basque identity. West of Pamplona, the mellow landscape is interrupted again by the spectacular, rugged gorges of Arbayún and Lumbier.

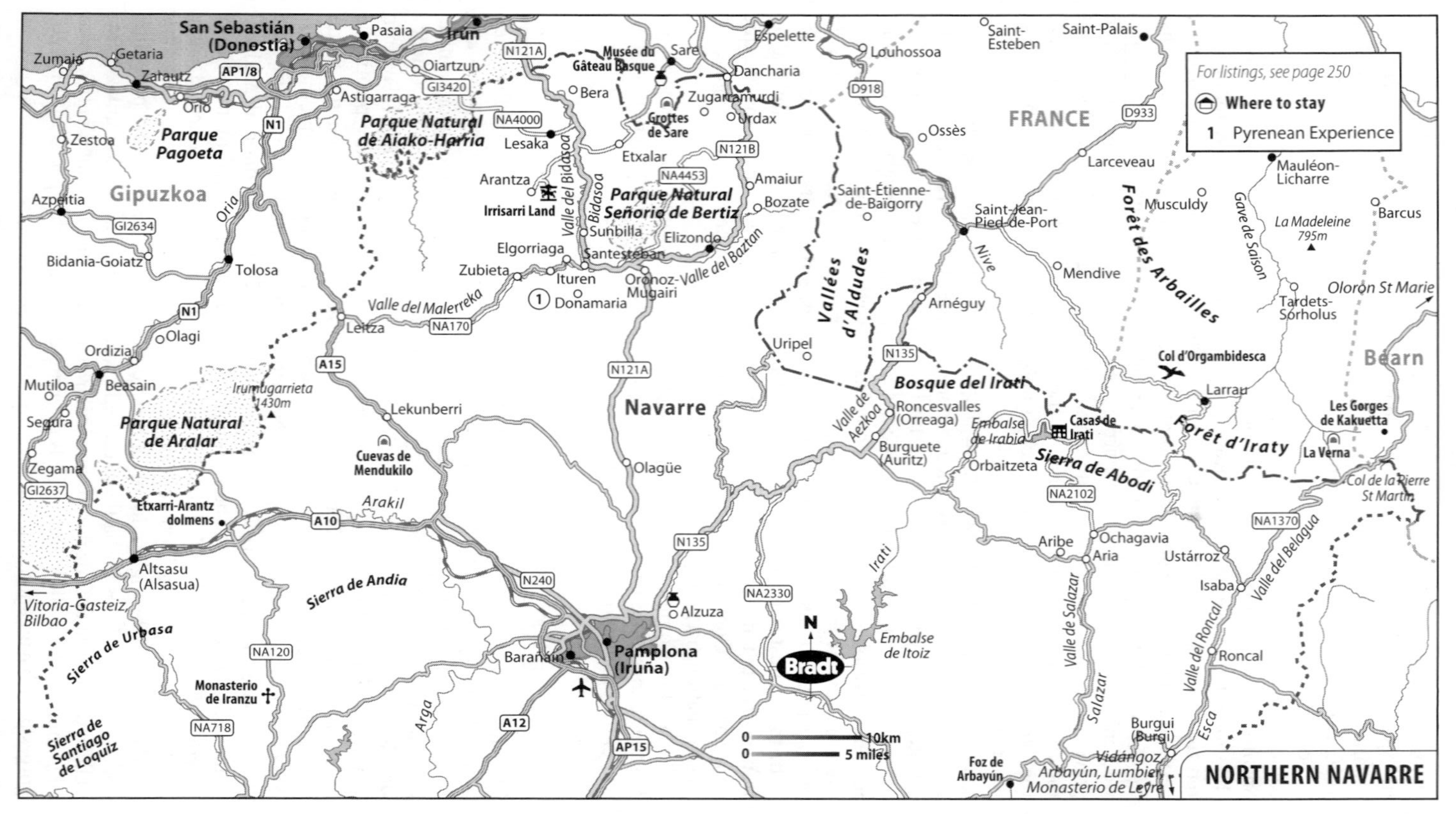
NORTHERN NAVARRE
For listings, see page 250
Where to stay
1 Pyrenean Experience
FRANCE
Navarre
Gipuzkoa
Béarn
San Sebastián (Donostia)
Pasaia
Irun
Zumaia
Getaria
Zarautz
Orio
Oiartzun
Astigarraga
Zestoa
Parque Pagoeta
Azpeitia
Bidania-Goiatz
Oria
Tolosa
Parque Natural de Aiako-Harria
Musée du Gâteau Basque
Sare
Bera
Lesaka
Espelette
Dancharia
Zugarramurdi
Urdax
Grottes de Sare
Etxalar
Louhossoa
Saint-Esteben
Saint-Palais
Ossès
Larceveau
Mauléon-Licharre
Arantza
Irrisarri Land
Valle del Bidasoa
Bidasoa
Parque Natural Señorío de Bertiz
Amaiur
Bozate
Sunbilla
Elizondo
Valle del Baztan
Elgorriaga
Santesteban
Zubieta
Ituren
Oronoz-Mugairi
Donamaria
Valle del Malerreka
Leitza
Saint-Étienne-de-Baïgorry
Saint-Jean-Pied-de-Port
Nive
Mendive
Musculdy
Forêt des Arbailles
Gave de Saison
La Madeleine 795m
Barcus
Tardets-Sorholus
Oloron St Marie
Vallées d'Aldudes
Arnéguy
Uripel
Col d'Orgambidesca
Larrau
Les Gorges de Kakuetta
La Verna
Olagi
Ordizia
Beasain
Mutiloa
Segura
Zegama
Irumugarrieta 1430m
Parque Natural de Aralar
Lekunberri
Cuevas de Mendukilo
Bosque del Irati
Valle de Aezkoa
Roncesvalles (Orreaga)
Burguete (Auritz)
Embalse de Irabia
Casas de Irati
Forêt d'Iraty
Sierra de Abodi
Orbaitzeta
Olagüe
Col de la Pierre St Martin
Etxarri-Arantz dolmens
Arakil
Altsasu (Alsasua)
Vitoria-Gasteiz, Bilbao
Sierra de Andia
Sierra de Urbasa
Aribe
Ochagavia
Aria
Ustárroz
Isaba
Valle del Belagua
Irati
Alzuza
Embalse de Itoiz
Pamplona (Iruña)
Barañain
Monasterio de Iranzu
Arga
Sierra de Santiago de Loquiz
Valle de Salazar
Salazar
Valle del Roncal
Roncal
Esca
Burgui (Burgi)
Vidángoz
Arbayún, Lumbier, Monasterio de Leyre
Foz de Arbayún
N
Bradt
0 10km
0 5 miles
AP1/8
N1
GI3420
N121A
NA4000
GI2634
NA170
A15
GI2637
A10
N240
NA120
NA718
A12
AP15
N121B
NA4453
D918
D933
N135
NA2330
NA2102
NA1370

PAMPLONA (IRUÑA) Pamplona is the only major conurbation in Navarre and thus unrivalled as the capital of the autonomous community. The city marches to at least two distinct beats. Its fast-forward setting shows itself during the nine days in July when it is overwhelmed by the frenzied festival of San Fermín, an internationally acclaimed party throwing together delirious locals with hardcore visitors to take part in – or more wisely, to watch – the bull-running that has become the city's hallmark. How important is the festival? The digital clock at the end of Calle Estafeta, which counts down to the start of the festival (and is reset immediately after it finishes) gives you the answer. Marching to an altogether different pace, pilgrims descend slowly into town from Roncesvalles, largely between April and September, to enjoy the big city facilities quite frequently denied to them en route to Santiago. For the rest of the year, Pamplona returns to its normal self, a pleasant place to live and visit. Recently, it has claimed the title of having the 'most green space per inhabitant' of any city in Spain, though Vitoria-Gasteiz (page 185) might raise an eyebrow at that accolade. Certainly, from the Parque Taconera, populated by deer and peacocks, to the Japanese-themed Parque Yamaguchi, the sculpture park in the *ciudadela* and the peacefulness of the Parque Media Luna, there are plenty of open parklands to enjoy.

Getting there and away

By car From Madrid, Pamplona is 4 hours' car drive to the northeast, while from Barcelona the journey takes 4½ hours. Driving east to the city from Vitoria or Bilbao takes 1 hour or 1 hour 45 minutes respectively, and San Sebastián is an hour's drive to the north. Parking in the city is mainly in underground lots, including one right beneath the super-central Plaza de Castillo, where 24 hours costs around €18. (If you're parking up there for three days or more, visit the attendant's office once you've parked: generous discounts are available on request.) Away from the immediate centre, parking charges are a bit lower and the map issued by the tourist office kindly indicates the free car parks, most of which will then require a bus ride or at least 10 minutes' walk to access the Old Town.

By bus Deserving a nomination for 'world's best-concealed transport hub', Pamplona's **bus station** [233 D8] is large, busy but well-hidden underground. Buses run to most of the main towns around Navarre and to many long-distance destinations such as Madrid (w plmautocares.com; 7-times daily; 6hrs; €22.19), Logroño (w laestellesa.com; 5-times daily; 90–100mins; €9.10), Vitoria-Gasteiz (w www.autobuseslaunion.com; 7-times daily; 85–100mins; €8.95), Bilbao (w www.autobuseselaunion.com; 6-times daily; 2hrs; €14.95), and San Sebastián (w conda.es; 14-times daily; 1hr; €7.80). Some companies have a staffed office here, but tickets can also be obtained via ticket machines (with English-language option) in the forecourt. The bus station is open 06.30–23.00 every day, save for Christmas and New Year's days, and full details of all bus services can be found on the website (w estaciondeautobusesdepamplona.com, Spanish/Basque only).

By train Pamplona's train station [232 A3] lies outside of the immediate city centre, but is easily accessible from the bus station and other places around town via the frequent bus Line 9. There are around nine trains daily each to Madrid (3–6hrs; €45) and six to Barcelona (4hrs; €40), four daily trains to San Sebastián (1hr 45mins; €11) and Vitoria-Gasteiz (1hr; €6). Within Navarre, there are a dozen or so trains to Tudela (1hr; €10), while many Madrid-bound trains stop at Tafalla (25mins; €6). There is no direct service to Bilbao, but there are trains to Zaragoza, Burgos, Vigo and La Coruña and many places in-between.

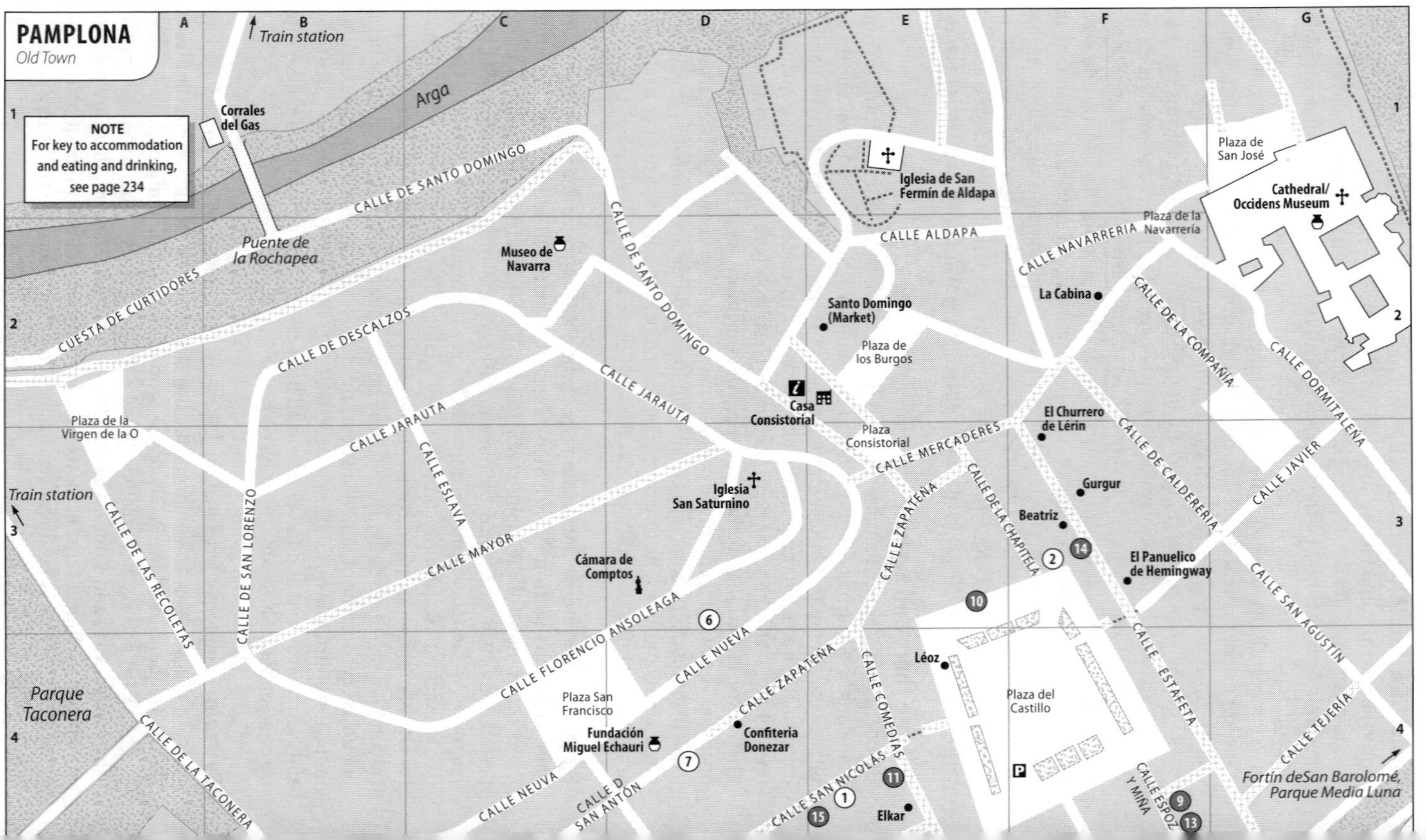

PAMPLONA
Old Town
NOTE
For key to accommodation and eating and drinking, see page 234
A
B
C
D
E
F
G
1
2
3
4
Train station
Train station
Corrales del Gas
Arga
Puente de la Rochapea
CALLE DE SANTO DOMINGO
CUESTA DE CURTIDORES
Museo de Navarra
CALLE DE DESCALZOS
Plaza de la Virgen de la O
CALLE JARAUTA
CALLE ESLAVA
CALLE DE SAN LORENZO
CALLE DE LAS RECOLETAS
Parque Taconera
CALLE DE LA TACONERA
CALLE MAYOR
Cámara de Comptos
CALLE FLORENCIO ANSOLEAGA
CALLE NUEVA
Plaza San Francisco
Fundación Miguel Echauri
CALLE D SAN ANTÓN
CALLE ZAPATEÑA
Confiteria Donezar
Iglesia San Saturnino
Iglesia de San Fermín de Aldapa
CALLE ALDAPA
Santo Domingo (Market)
Plaza de los Burgos
Casa Consistorial
Plaza Consistorial
CALLE MERCADERES
CALLE DE LA CHAPITELA
CALLE COMEDIAS
CALLE SAN NICOLÁS
Léoz
Elkar
Plaza del Castillo
CALLE NAVARRERÍA
Plaza de la Navarrería
La Cabina
El Churrero de Lérin
Gurgur
Beatriz
El Panuelico de Hemingway
CALLE ESTAFETA
CALLE ESPOZ Y MIÑA
CALLE DE LA COMPAÑÍA
CALLE DE CALDERERÍA
CALLE JAVIER
CALLE DORMITALEÑA
CALLE SAN AGUSTÍN
CALLE TEJERÍA
Plaza de San José
Cathedral/ Occidens Museum
Fortín deSan Barolomé, Parque Media Luna
1
2
6
7
9
10
11
13
14
15

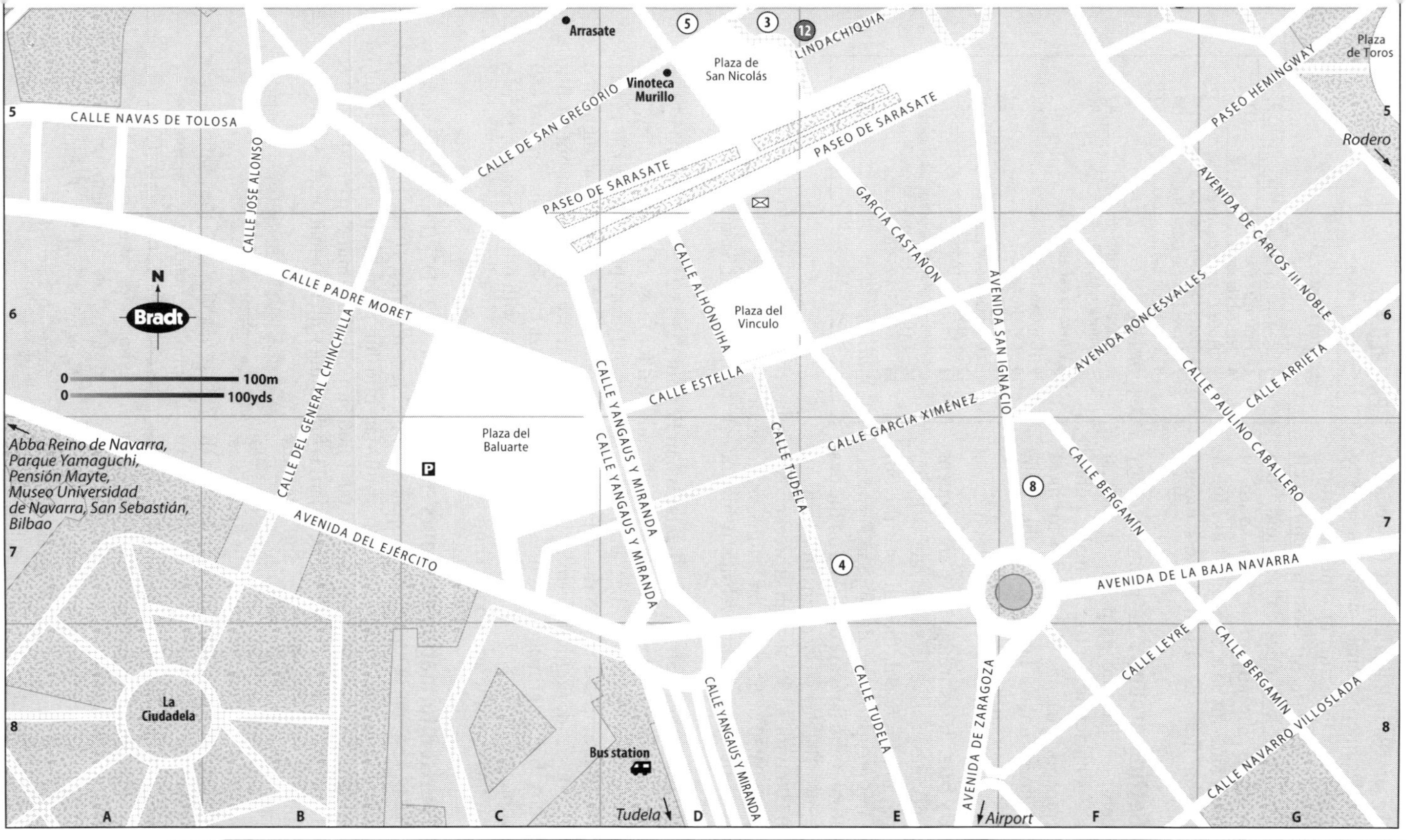
Arrasate
Vinoteca Murillo
Plaza de San Nicolás
LINDACHIQUIA
Plaza de Toros
PASEO HEMINGWAY
Rodero
CALLE NAVAS DE TOLOSA
CALLE DE SAN GREGORIO
PASEO DE SARASATE
PASEO DE SARASATE
CALLE JOSE ALONSO
GARCIA CASTAÑON
AVENIDA DE CARLOS III NOBLE
CALLE ALHÓNDIHA
Plaza del Vinculo
AVENIDA SAN IGNACIO
AVENIDA RONCESVALLES
N
Bradt
0 100m
0 100yds
CALLE PADRE MORET
CALLE ESTELLA
CALLE GARCÍA XIMÉNEZ
CALLE ARRIETA
CALLE PAULINO CABALLERO
CALLE DEL GENERAL CHINCHILLA
Plaza del Baluarte
CALLE YANGAUS Y MIRANDA
CALLE YANGAUS Y MIRANDA
CALLE TUDELA
CALLE BERGAMÍN
Abba Reino de Navarra, Parque Yamaguchi, Pensión Mayte, Museo Universidad de Navarra, San Sebastián, Bilbao
AVENIDA DEL EJÉRCITO
AVENIDA DE LA BAJA NAVARRA
CALLE LEYRE
CALLE BERGAMÍN
La Ciudadela
Bus station
CALLE YANGAUS Y MIRANDA
CALLE TUDELA
AVENIDA DE ZARAGOZA
CALLE NAVARRO VILLOSLADA
Tudela
Airport
A B C D E F G
5 6 7 8

By air Pamplona's airport (w aena.es) carries international traffic, but only to and from Frankfurt at time of writing, although Iberia/Air Nostrum connect it directly at least once daily to and from Madrid. The airport is 5km south of town and can be accessed by bus Line A leaving from the bus and train stations.

Getting around The immediate city centre is flat and its points of interest are sufficiently central to make public transport virtually unnecessary for most visitors, unless heading to the train station or airport.

By bus Buses around town are frequent and inexpensive (a single fare is €1.35, payable on board, though even the bus fares go up to €1.60 during San Fermín). Routes and fares are displayed on the bus stops. The day service runs from around 07.00 until 22.30, though at weekends a night service takes over from about 23.30 until 03.30 or later still on Saturdays, depending on the route. All bus information is on the municipality website (w infotuc.es), though only in Basque and Spanish.

PAMPLONA *Old Town*

For listings, see opposite

Where to stay

1	Casa Otano	E4
2	Gran Hotel la Perla	F3
3	Hostal Bearán	D5
4	Hostal Navarra	E7
5	Hotel Castillo de Javier	D5
6	Hotel Maisonnave	D3
7	Hotel Palacio Guendulain	D4
8	Hotel Yoldi	F7
	Off map	
	Abba Reino de Navarra	A7
	Pensión Mayte	A7

Where to eat and drink

9	Bar Gaucho	F4
10	Café Iruña	E3
11	Café Roch	E4
	Casa Otano	(see 1)
12	Catachu	E5
13	Europa	F4
	Hotel Yoldi Restaurant	(see 8)
14	La Cocina de Álex Múgica	F3
15	La Mandarra de la Ramos	E4
	Off map	
	Rodero	G5

By taxi The local taxi firm **Teletaxis San Fermín** (☎ 948 23 23 00 or 948 35 13 35; w taxipamplona.com) has some vehicles adapted for those of lesser mobility. Taxis can usually be found at the train and bus stations and many places in the city centre. As an example, a trip to the airport will cost around €12. Fares rise at night and, of course, during San Fermín. For pilgrims who arrive in Pamplona but wish to start their pilgrimage at Roncesvalles, an eight-seater taxi should cost around €60, though €100 to St-Jean. If you want to share the cost with others, you can register on their website and hope to find fellow pilgrims.

Tourist information and tours The tourist office [232 D2] (Plaza Consistorial; ☎ 948 42 07 00; w turismodepamplona.com; ⌚ Jan–mid-Mar 10.00–14.00 & 15.00–17.00 Mon–Sat, 10.00–14.00 Sun, mid-Mar–mid-Jun & mid-Sep–end Dec 10.00–14.00 & 15.00–19.00 Mon–Sat, 10.00–14.00 Sun, mid-Jun–mid-Sep 09.00–14.00 & 15.00–20.00 daily; closed 1st week Jan) is brimming with information about the city and the rest of the province, and this is the place to buy maps for hiking and biking, as well as finding bus and train timetables. The multilingual staff are keen to help. If you're staying a while, you can get hold of a seven-day Pamplona-Iruña Card for €1, giving you access to museums, events and shopping discounts.

If you fancy getting to know the city in a short time, an English-speaking, well-informed and entertaining guide can be

LOCAL HOLIDAYS

In addition to the national public holidays, Pamplona celebrates San Fermín for a whopping nine days from 6 July, San Saturnino on 29 November and San Francisco Javier on 3 December.

provided by **Novotur Guías** (m 629 66 16 04; e novotur@novotur.com; w novotur.com). They also organise tours in wider Navarre and beyond, as well as renting out balconies during San Fermín (see box, page 239).

Where to stay For most of the year, the accommodation trade is steady and prices are very reasonable in the Navarrese capital, but come San Fermín time, you can forget turning up without an advance booking. Even with that, you'll be paying a huge premium, as prices triple or worse. Even if you don't get gored by a bull, you might get severely wounded in the wallet by a few nights' stay. The prices below refer to high season outside the San Fermín period. If you haven't booked before arriving in town, the tourist office has a full list of accommodation, or you could just browse Calle San Nicolás, which is a good – but sometimes noisy – street on which to seek out economical accommodation.

Upmarket

Gran Hotel la Perla [232 F3] (44 rooms) Plaza de Castillo 1; 948 22 30 00; e informacion@granhotellaperla.com; w granhotellaperla.com. A hotel with a history of illustrious clients: since 1881 it has hosted King Juan Carlos I, Woody Allen, Charlie Chaplin & Julio Iglesias, but it is best associated with Ernest Hemingway. Free Wi-Fi, excellent soundproofing, AC & TV with international channels are what you would expect at this price, but it also respects its own history – note the old wooden lift in the lobby. All rooms have balconies. **€€€€**

Mid range

Hotel Maisonnave [232 D3] (147 rooms) Calle Nueva 20; 948 22 26 00; e informacion@hotelmaisonnave.es; w hotelmaisonnave.es. Renovated completely in 2013, this is a modern, high-class, privately owned hotel with great views out over the city & mountain surroundings. Tasteful artworks adorn the walls. Rooms, with TV (international channels), free Wi-Fi, AC & bath or shower, are spacious & bright. Buffet b/fasts are hearty. Suites are also available. Guests have free access to the gym & sauna. **€€€**

Hotel Palacio Guendulain [232 D4] (23 rooms, 2 suites) Zapatería 53; 948 22 55 22; e info@palacioguendulain.com; w palacioguendulain.com. A beautifully renovated palace with heavy wooden doors & an impressive collection of artwork. A handsome 18th-century carriage waits in the lobby, & in the interior courtyard you'll find a collection of vintage cars, but the in-room facilities are indisputably modern: AC, TV, free Wi-Fi. **€€€**

Budget

Abba Reino de Navarra [233 A7] (88 rooms) Acella 1; 902 15 31 63; e abbahoteles@abbahoteles.com; w abbahoteles.com. Decent 4-star opposite Yamaguchi Park & part of a well-known Spanish chain. Free Wi-Fi, satellite TV, AC. Hotel has restaurant & café-bar. Town centre is 20mins' walk away. Parking on-site at extra charge. English spoken. **€€**

Hotel Castillo de Javier [233 D5] (18 rooms) San Nicolás 50–52; 948 20 30 40; w hotelcastillodejavier.com. One of the cheaper hotels with AC, a 1-star featuring renovated, smart rooms with TV & free Wi-Fi & pleasant management. Very central, disabled access. **€€**

Hotel Yoldi [233 F7] (50 rooms) Av San Ignacio 1; 948 22 48 00; w hotelyoldi.com. A pleasant hotel, easy walking distance to the centre & handy for the bus station. Rooms have AC, TV with international channels, free Wi-Fi, minibar. Buffet b/fasts are good, but there's also a popular café downstairs if you want something more modest & cheaper. Expresses itself as 'gay-friendly', & has a floor of the hotel exclusively for women. A decent place for the money. **€€**

Shoestring

Casa Otano [232 E4] (30 rooms) San Nicolás 5; 948 22 70 36; e casaotano@yahoo.es; w casaotano.com. Ask in the bar downstairs or restaurant upstairs. Basic choice, though with heating, TV, free Wi-Fi &, despite the low price, private bathrooms. Special rates for pilgrims. **€**

Hostal Bearán [233 D5] (17 rooms) San Nicolás 25; 948 22 34 28; w bearanpamplona.com. Comfortable, basic rooms in a central location, family-run. AC, heating, TV, free Wi-Fi.

A good central choice at this price, though late-night revelry might keep you awake. €

Hostal Navarra [233 E7] (15 rooms) Tudela 9; 948 22 51 64; w hostalnavarra.com. Very close to the bus station & a short walk to the centre. Upstairs, with no lift. Rooms are compact & pleasant, with TV & free Wi-Fi, some with balconies. €

Pensión Mayte [233 A7] (4 rooms) Av Pío XII 32, 5 Centro; m 686 47 99 66; w pensionmayte.com. A 15min walk out of town, though on a bus route, this converted apartment is a steal, with heating, free Wi-Fi, TV in spacious rooms, some with balcony. Note that some rooms share a bathroom. Don't turn up on spec, as it's often unattended – ring first. €

Where to eat and drink

A lunchtime, weekday trawl around the centre will reveal plenty of restaurants offering three-course menus for very reasonable amounts. At the other end of the scale the city's two Michelin-starred establishments are the **Europa** [233 F5] (w heuropa.com; €€€€€) and the more *nouvelle* **Rodero** [233 G5] (w restauranterodero.com; €€€€€). For some fun, Calle Estafeta is the bull-running street, but also the place to head the rest of the year for the bars, *pintxos* and late-night atmosphere. Calle San Nicolás is another lively, late-night option which runs it a close second, no bull.

Restaurants

Casa Otano [232 E4] (page 235) Mon–Sat lunch & dinner, Sun lunch only. The hotel rooms may be cheap, but this pleasant upstairs dining room has a touch of class about it, & with 100 years of history thrown in for good measure. The *menu del día* costs more than elsewhere on the street, especially at the w/end, but the variety & quality really shines without breaking the bank. €€€

Hotel Yoldi Restaurant [233 F7] (page 235) 08.00–22.30 daily. The burgers here are sublime & good value. €€

Catachu [233 E5] Calle Indachiquia 16; 948 22 60 28; w catachu.com; 13.00–17.00 & 20.00–midnight Sun–Thu, 13.00–midnight Fri & Sat. Down an unpromising side street 2mins from the Plaza del Castillo, this is a great-value, midweek lunchtime favourite that delivers no-nonsense *menus del día* with a wide choice of starters & main courses. The quirky room is decorated with old TVs & gramophones from the 1960s. Don't turn up before 13.00. W/end & evening menus are pricier, but still good value. €

Pintxos

Bar Gaucho [232 F4] Espoz y Mina 7; 948 22 50 73. With nearly 50 years behind it, Bar Gaucho's walls sport awards for 'best *pintxo*', & it's hard to argue with their motto: 'Great Navarran cuisine in miniature'. *Huevo trufado* (truffled egg) is one of the specialities in this popular watering-hole. A little on the expensive side, & service can sometimes be found wanting.

Café Iruña [232 E3] Plaza del Castillo 44; w cafeiruna.com; 08.00–23.00 Mon–Thu, 09.00–01.00 Fri & Sat, 09.00–23.00 Sun. As the oldest café in town, this place deserves respect, its opening in 1888 coinciding with the arrival in Pamplona of electric lights. A spacious, ornate interior, fancy columns & chequer-board floor ensures a bar counter packed with tourists & pilgrims, but there's plenty of tables to choose from. The food doesn't quite match the décor or the history, but for such a tourist magnet it is good value. A must-visit, if only for a coffee, b/fast & the surroundings. Through a connecting door you'll find a wood-panelled bar, El Rincón de Hemingway, open from lunchtime. You can guess the identity of its most famous former client.

Café Roch [232 E4] Comedias 6. The second-oldest café in town, Roch has not weathered its 120 years quite as well as the beautiful Café Iruña (see above). Tiny & scruffy, it nevertheless has a delightful, Bohemian ambience of its own. *Croquetas* (croquettes), or *fritos*, especially those stuffed with Roquefort cheese, are the pick of the *pintxos* here.

La Mandarra de la Ramos [232 E4] San Nicolás 9; 948 21 26 54; w lamandarradelaramos.com; 10.00–midnight Mon–Thu, 10.00–01.00 Fri & Sat, 11.00–midnight Sun. An impressive display of hams is suspended above possibly the most photogenic display of *pintxos* in town. This lively bar also does lunch menus – salads, *cazuelas*, hamburgers, *chuletón* – almost everything.

La Cocina de Álex Múgica [232 F3] Estafeta 24; 948 51 01 25; w alexmugica.com; noon–

16.00 & 19.00–22.30 Tue–Sat, noon–16.00 Sun. An upmarket bar that has won numerous awards for its culinary creations & is thronged with important-looking locals. *Txangurro* (spider-crab) in mushroom cream is a regular treat, but the best nibbles change according to the time of year, so ask for the seasonal specials.

Nightlife Some of Calle Estafeta's bars change into nightspots late on Friday and Saturday nights, and that and the Calle San Nicolás are definitely the places to head for.

Shopping There are branches of all the usual chain stores to the south of the Plaza del Castillo and more interesting shops in the streets of the Old Town in general.

Beatriz [232 F3] Estafeta 22; 🕘 09.00–14.00 & 16.00–20.00 Mon–Fri, 09.00–14.00 Sat. Just opposite Gurgur is a very modest-looking bakery, but the queue will tell you that the *garroticos* (tiny chocolate croissants) are well worth the wait.
Confitería Donezar [232 D4] Zapatería 47; w donezar.com; 🕘 09.30–13.45 & 16.30–20.00 Mon–Fri, 09.30–13.45 Sat. Still uniting the many diverse, traditional skills of the confectioner from days gone by, this place makes candles & of course delicious confectionery (*turrón rojo* – red turrón – is the house favourite). Dried fruits & honey are also on sale.
El Pañuelico de Hemingway [232 F3] Estafeta 41; 📞 948 22 91 17. It goes without saying that Hemingway never visited this place & equally certain that he would not have approved. Tacky souvenirs abound … but at the back, you can have your photo taken 'running' with some replica bulls against a realistic backdrop of Pamplona's streets. The result is surprisingly good, but surely won't convince your friends that you had the *cojones* to do the real thing.
Elkar [232 E4] Calle Comedias 16; 🕘 09.30–13.30 & 16.30–20.00 Mon–Fri, 09.30–13.30 & 17.00–20.00 Sat. Well-known Basque bookshop chain with travel books together with some English-language titles.
Gurgur [232 F3] Estafeta 21; 📞 948 20 79 92; w gurgurestafeta.com; 🕘 daily. In a city that is not shy about commercialising itself (especially tacky San Fermín-related souvenirs), this is a breath of fresh air, with genuine edible goodies from around Navarre. Fill your bag with wines & artisanal beers, jars of artichokes & asparagus, Elizondo's chocolates, cheese from Roncal & elsewhere, Tafalla chorizos, plus jams, honey, confectionery, wines & *patxarán*.
La Cabina [232 F2] Calle Curia 17; 📞 948 21 08 69; w lacabinamuebles.com; 🕘 09.00–21.00 daily. A great little shop stuffed with tasteful, retro furniture, with an emphasis on lighting. Prices are reasonable, too.
Pan Artesano Arrasate [233 C5] San Antón 23; w arrasate.es/panaderia. A bakery justly popular for its variety of breads, but your reason to visit is to try their speciality, the *lazos de hojaldre*, tasty pastries unique to the shop. Look out for other branches around town.
Vinoteca Murillo [233 D5] San Miguel 16–18; 📞 948 22 10 15; w vinotecamurillo.es; 🕘 09.30–13.45 & 17.00–20.00 Mon–Fri, 09.30–14.00 Sat. In this age-old, dusty-smelling emporium, you'll find a great selection of local & other wines, from bargain bottles to something special & expensive. Liqueurs & spirits, too, in a business that's nearly 130 years old.

Other practicalities

Post office [233 D5] Pamplona's main post office is located at Paseo de Sarasate 9 (🕘 08.30–20.30 Mon–Fri, 09.30–13.00 Sat).

Markets Pamplona has two markets, which are both pretty standard in the sense that each sells pristine fresh fish, meat, cheese, fruit and vegetables. The more central one, the **Mercado de Santo Domingo**, is located behind the Casa Consistorial [232 E2] (🕘 08.00–14.30 Mon–Thu, 08.00–14.30 & 16.30–20.00 Fri, 08.00–14.30 Sat). The other, slightly larger, market is less central, situated on the corner of Calle de Amaya and Calle Felipe Gorriti (🕘 09.00–14.30 Mon–Thu & Sat, 09.00–14.30 & 17.00–20.00 Fri & holidays).

Newspapers English-language papers are thin on the ground, but **Léoz** [232 E4] (Plaza del Castillo 38) and the newsagents in the subterranean bus station can usually oblige, perhaps only with the Sunday editions or a *Financial Times*.

Internet You can help yourself to free municipal Wi-Fi at various spots around town, including in the Plaza del Castillo, Plaza Consistorial, some of the city parks and the bus station.

What to see and do

Catedral de Pamplona/Occidens (Pamplona Cathedral/Occidens Museum) [232 G1–2] (Plaza Santa María; ☎ 948 21 25 94; w catedraldepamplona.com; ⏲ museum: last week Mar–3rd week Oct 10.30–19.00 (last ticket sold 18.00) Mon–Sat, last week Oct–3rd week Mar 10.30–17.00 (last ticket sold 16.00) Mon–Sat, closed Sun; €5/4/3/free adults/seniors/under 13s & pilgrims/under 7s; note that you can often enter the cathedral – not the museum – for free before 10.30, & if you visit on your birthday, tickets are free, too!) Boasting the largest working bell in Spain (yes, the one in Toledo is broken!) Pamplona's cathedral has inspired mixed reactions. Victor Hugo described the building as being 'a beautiful lady … with donkey ears' referring to the two towers that dominate the city-centre skyline. The façade is 18th-century Neoclassical, it having replaced the previous frontage which collapsed, though much of what is behind dates back to the 14th and 15th centuries. The sundial, up to the right as you face the entrance, is entirely useless: in 1942, General Franco insisted on changing Spain's time zone to fall in line with Nazi Germany, meaning that any pre-Franco sundials are an hour out – and 2 hours off when the clocks change every year. Inside, the 11th-century Virgin is known as 'Holy Mary of the Adopted Child', recognising the 16th-century theft of the original baby Jesus and its subsequent replacement. The cathedral has one of only three Gothic kitchens in the world (the others being in Avignon and Sintra), but the problem is that the kitchen is actually 1m *higher* than the cathedral, an architectural faux pas and pure sacrilege, as clearly nothing should be higher than the cathedral … unless (as has been suggested) the architect was trying to suggest that the bishop cared more for food than for prayer. A plan of the cathedral in English is included in the entrance price. Times of masses are generally 09.30 and 19.30 Monday–Saturday, 10.00, noon and 19.30 Sunday.

The **Occidens** museum is not just an exhibition of religious artwork but is themed around the conflicts and challenges which Christianity has faced over the centuries, for example from other religions or materialism, and how it has chosen to react to them through its artwork. Worthwhile. On the floor is a useful timeline, which guides you around the displays.

Plaza de la Naverrería [232 F2] This square is also known locally as the Plaza de los Australianos, as it is a favoured spot for worse-for-wear Antipodeans to hurl themselves from the tall fountain during the hedonistic festival of San Fermín. They rely on their equally inebriated friends catching them before they hit the ground. Sadly, it doesn't always result in a happy ending.

Plaza del Castillo [232 F4] The principal square of the city and also the site of the former castle – hence the name – is a wide, pleasant space, very popular as a meeting-place, but a real mongrel of architectural styles. No houses were actually constructed here until the 18th century, and they then appeared in a somewhat random fashion. As a family grew in size, so another floor would be added to accommodate the new arrivals, perhaps with a different style. In one corner is the

Gran Hotel La Perla (page 235), where Hemingway installed his wife during his visits, while he partied elsewhere, explaining why in *The Sun Also Rises* he prefers to talk about another hotel, the Montoya (whose real name was the Quintana), now no longer in existence. On the same side of the square as La Perla is the oldest café, Café Iruña (page 236). On the opposite side is the building of the Government of Navarre, its chunky walls still bearing some of the bullet holes from the Civil War.

Museo Universidad de Navarra (University of Navarre Museum) [233 A7] (Campus Universitario; ☎ 948 42 57 00; w museo.unav.edu; ⏲ 10.00–20.00 Tue–Sat,

SAN FERMÍN'S BULL-RUNNINGS

Watching on the streets is free of charge, though you have to be in position in good time and enjoy the throng. Hiring a balcony is considerably pricier, running to around €30–150, but normally including some form of breakfast or other sustenance (see El Churrero de Lerín, *page 241, for example). Tickets to watch proceedings in the bullring are relatively cheap – see* w *feriadeltoro.com for advance booking.*

One of the world's great festivals, San Fermín takes place annually from 6 to 14 July. Ostensibly a day to celebrate the patron saint of Navarre, it now combines strict rituals with unbridled excess. Although it attracts people from all over the world, some of Pamplona's own inhabitants now exit the city during the festivities, seeking some respite from the hordes.

At exactly noon on 6 July, the beginning of the festivities is heralded by the launch of the *chupinazo* rocket from the balcony of the Casa Consistorial (City Hall) (page 242), the honour of setting it off usually granted to a local politician or celebrity. Watching from below, some 12,000 festival-goers, dressed in white and waving their red neckerchiefs, pack the square, while many more throng the surrounding streets. With *cava* being sprayed everywhere, no-one stays dry, whatever the weather, and the crush makes it inadvisable for attendance by small children, the elderly or infirm. For those who don't number among the 'lucky' ones to get into the square, large screens are set up around town and there is always the option of renting a much-coveted balcony to watch proceedings in safety.

7 July sees a procession take place at 10.00, with the image of San Fermín himself paraded through the Old Town streets. But it is the running of the bulls that defines San Fermín. Although the first bull-running in Pamplona dates back to the late 14th century, the use of the term *encierro* to describe racing of man and bull was only coined in 1856. The striking of the clock at the Iglesia de San Saturnino signals the start of each morning's fun; rockets are then launched, first from the Santo Domingo corral to announce the beginning of the run, then another to tell everyone that the bulls are on the street, then again to signal their arrival in the Plaza de Toros. Finally, a fourth is released when the day's event is complete. The run is measured at exactly 848.6m and the free tourist office booklet on the festival carefully analyses each section of it for would-be participants, highlighting the relative dangers and describing the route as if it was a Formula 1 circuit. Dangers there certainly are, accentuated by the amount of alcohol that has been imbibed by some of the runners, and there are several deaths every year. Pamplona's bull-runnings are certainly the most famous in Spain, though they are not unique. A quick view of the many videos available on the internet should be sufficient to deter all but the most brave/foolish.

noon–14.00 Sun; €4.50/3/free adults/students, seniors and disabled/accompanied under 17s) A fairly new museum (though really more of an art and photography gallery, with cinema and theatre, too) based on the campus to the south of the centre, the exhibits here are a mix of permanent and (usually) innovative temporary displays. Art by Rothko, Kandinski and Picasso mixes with locals such as Chillida and Oteiza among the modest collection of permanently resident pieces here. It's perhaps worth asking at the tourist office as to what temporary exhibitions are current before you trek out here (or take the bus, lines 1 or 5). There is English-language information (by way of handout) to enhance your experience. Guided tours are given daily at noon and 18.00, at no extra charge, but only in Spanish. The website is translated into English. There is also a restaurant and café.

Fundación Miguel Echauri (Miguel Echauri Foundation) [232 D4] (San Antón 6; 948 22 03 24; w fundacionmiguelechauri.blogspot.com.es; gallery noon–19.00 Mon–Fri, house visits noon–13.00 & 19.00–20.00 Mon–Fri; free admission to gallery & house, donations welcome) In a former family house from the 17th century, here you'll find a downstairs gallery displaying either the works of Echauri, sometimes spoken of as Spain's greatest living artist and now in his 90s, or else showing the visiting exhibitions of other notables. You can also visit the house's upper floors, with beautiful period furniture and much more of Echauri's impressive and distinctive work, which uses limited colours and relies heavily on subtleties of shadow and light. The artist, a charming man who celebrated his 88th birthday in 2015, may even be present to greet you. A family member still resides in a private part of the house.

Museo de Navarra (Museum of Navarre) [232 C2] (Santo Domingo 47; 848 42 89 26; w navarra.es; 09.30–14.00 & 17.00–19.00 Tue–Sat, 11.00–14.00 Sun & holidays; €2/free adults/children, free to all on Sat pm & Sun; English-language information is via returnable laminated handouts from the ticket office) The former hospital of Our Lady of Mercy displays religious art, while the remainder of the ground floor hosts temporary exhibitions and the other floors take you through chronologically from prehistory to Romanisation, the Middle Ages and right up to the present day, with the top floor being dedicated to contemporary Navarran art. The star of the show is Goya's 1804 portrait of the Marqués de San Adrián, but the collection of Roman capitals is impressive too, and a Spanish-Muslim ivory chest from the monastery of San Salvador de Leyre, crafted in 1005, also draws visitors' attention. The works of Pamplona's very own 19th-century artist, Javier Ciga Echandi, are also exhibited here.

Fortín de San Bartolomé (Learning Centre for Pamplona's Fortifications) [232 G4] (Calle Arrieta, behind the Plaza de Toros; 948 21 15 54; w murallasdepamplona.com; summer 11.00–14.00 & 17.00–19.00 Tue–Sun, winter 10.00–14.00 & 16.00–18.00 Tue–Sun; €3/1.50/free adults/students/under 12s) If you're interested in the city walls, this must be your first stop, with a number of well-presented short films (available in English) explaining the development and significance of the city's fortifications over the centuries. Pamplona's walls are indeed remarkably well preserved and demand much more attention than they get from mere bull-obsessed visitors. As in many towns, the walls eventually had to give way for city expansion, but in Pamplona's case there is still plenty to admire: the tourist office can provide a 5km walking route for those who want the full fortification experience.

Iglesia San Saturnino (Church of San Saturnino) [232 D3] (Calle San Saturnino; 09.15–noon & 18.00–19.30 Mon–Sat, 10.00–13.30 & 18.30–19.30,

PAMPLONA WALK

A short urban walk that traces the steps of the bull-running, mainly along pedestrianised streets and with no bovine threat whatsoever – as long as you avoid San Fermín.

You start your walk just across the Arga River at the so-called ***Corrales del Gas*** (Gas Corrals), where the running bulls and fighting bulls are kept during San Fermín. At one time this was the site of the 19th-century gas factory built to supply the city's street lighting, hence the name. From here you walk up **Calle de Santo Domingo**, which eventually leads you to the **Casa Consistorial** (City Hall), but for now note on your left the Santo Domingo **holding pen** from where the bulls are released each day during the festival. One tradition is the *encierrillo*, or 'little bull-running', which takes place each evening during San Fermín, and involves the transfer of the bulls from the Gas Corrals to the Santo Domingo pen, ready for the next day's proper bull-running. (For the *encierrillo*, there are no human runners and it is watched in silence, by those who have obtained the necessary pass, obtainable ten days in advance from the City Hall.)

At the top of the hill, you reach the Casa Consistorial (page 242), the starting point for the whole festival and one of Pamplona's truly iconic buildings. You are also now on the **Camino de Santiago**, albeit walking it – briefly – in reverse. Crossing the square, you enter the **Calle Mercaderes** and turn right into **Calle Estafeta**. The corner of these two streets is a wonderful viewpoint during the bull-runnings, though preferably from the safety of one of the sought-after balconies up above, as the sharp right-hand turn inevitably results in falling runners and tumbling bulls.

As you turn into Calle Estafeta, treat yourself to a stop at number 5, **El Churrero de Lerín**, a small café that serves up delicious hot chocolate and *churros* – a classic Spanish combination. Here, unless you choose to run with the bulls, you can organise your San Fermín viewing – a great vantage point comes to €70 per person for an hour's briefing and a further hour or two on one of their six balconies, with chocolate and *churros* included. Make sure you book well in advance (**m** 620 53 13 06; **e** contact@el2delaestafeta.com; **w** el2delaestafeta.com), as it's highly popular. Further on, at number 41, you could pop into **El Pañuelico de Hemingway** for some tacky bull-related souvenirs (or some spoof photography – page 237).

At the end of Estafeta, your walk finishes at the ramp that leads into the **Plaza de Toros**, the third-biggest bullring in the world after Mexico City and Madrid. Constructed in 1923, it holds nearly 20,000 spectators. All of the money raised here goes to a charity for the elderly, which may or may not soften your objections to bullfighting. Note to the left of the ramp the bust of **Ernest Hemingway**, who was much revered for the international profile he brought to Pamplona through his nine visits to the city. He drew inspiration from Pamplona, while partying fairly hard and also finding time to indulge in fishing trips on the rivers flowing down from the Pyrenees. Sadly, his last visit to Pamplona left him disillusioned by the commercialisation and debauchery that had taken over San Fermín. Now, more than 50 years on from his death, you can only wonder what he would make of it today.

Sun & holidays) Named after the principal saint of the town, this is actually two churches in the same building, one Baroque, one Gothic. On the floor, in the Gothic part, some of the wooden numbered burial places carry the letter 'D', which indicates that the deceased made a donation in the belief they would be delivered more swiftly to heaven; where there are *two* 'D's, they were clearly on the fast track. Outside the church, you can see the location of the well where the city's patron, San Saturnino, baptised the first Christians in the city in the 4th century. He also baptised the much more celebrated San Fermín, who is the patron saint of Navarre, not the city. From the church's south tower, the bells ring out during the San Fermín festival to signal the start of the daily bull-running.

Cámara de Comptos (Chamber of Accounts) [232 D3] (Florencio Ansoleaga 10; w camaradecomptos.org) The oldest building in the city centre, the Chamber of Accounts dates back to the 13th century and is now a national monument. Despite the presence of a security guard it can be briefly visited, with an English-language leaflet and wall panel. As well as the solid Gothic styling, you can admire the peaceful garden with its central well. For 300 years from 1524 this was where taxes were collected and coins minted. Prior to that, the building was a nobleman's palace and it has also served time as the seat of Navarre's Monuments Commission. Since the 1990s it has reverted to its fiscal function.

Casa Consistorial (City Hall) [232 E2] (Plaza Casa Consistorial) One of Pamplona's most ornate and famous buildings, this was purpose-built in the 18th century and is best known for its balcony where, at noon on 6 July, the San Fermín fiesta gets under way (see box, page 239). Outside the festival period, the building provides an attractive backdrop for the selfies of passing pilgrims.

Iglesia de San Fermín de Aldapa [232 E1] (Calle Dos de Mayo/Calle Aldapa) Unless it's 25 September, this early 18th-century church is nothing truly special. But on that day, a rocket is launched to mark the start of the San Fermín Chiquito (Little San Fermín), a festival *without* the madness of the bull-running but with plenty of entertainment, including dance, concerts, communal meals, *pelota* competitions and child-friendly fun.

Ciudadela (Citadel) [233 A8] (Main entrance off Av del Ejército, opposite Calle General Chinchilla; admission free) In the southern flatlands of Pamplona sits the citadel, constructed in the 17th century in the shape of a five-pointed star. In 1808, the supposedly impregnable construction was conquered by French troops who, it is said, lured the inhabitants to open the gates by inviting them to take part in a snowball fight. Still in use for military purposes up until the 1960s, it is now in happier service as a park, a peaceful oasis for citizens, and on occasions it also hosts concerts. As you enter the main gate, there is a multilingual touch-screen information point on your left. Local artists now use some of the structures of the citadel as galleries to exhibit their work in the evenings (🕘 usually open 18.00–20.00) and there are sculptures permanently on display outside in the grassy areas. The Fortín de San Bartolomé Learning Centre has excellent information on the history of Pamplona's fortifications (page 240).

AROUND PAMPLONA

Museo Oteiza (Jorge Oteiza Museum) (Calle de la Cuesta, Alzuza; 📞 948 33 20 74; e info@museooteiza.org; w museooteiza.org; 🕘 Jul & Aug 11.00–19.00 Tue–

Sat, 11.00–15.00 Sun, Sep–Jun 10.00–15.00 Tue–Fri, 11.00–19.00 Sat, 11.00–15.00 Sun & holidays; €4/2/free adults/students, seniors & disabled/under 18s) Some 9km northeast of Pamplona, off the NA-150, this space-age building designed with input from Jorge Oteiza himself incorporates the sculptor's former house, where he lived from 1975. A native of Orio in Gipuzkoa (page 175), he nevertheless chose to gift this museum, which opened in 2003, to Navarre. The display panels are in Spanish, French and Basque only, though an English-language leaflet gives some limited information.

Although he is known for his sculpture, Oteiza decreased his output in the 1970s, concentrating more time on the study of mythology, engaging in drawing and producing the tiny experimental chalk creations that can be seen on the ground floor. Those who have visited the sanctuary at Aránzazu (page 162) will recognise a model of the controversial '14 Apostles' sculpture that adorns the doorway of that revered place, and many of the pieces on display here are experimental works carried out while Oteiza was formulating his plans for the work he undertook there.

NORTHWEST NAVARRE

Valle del Bidasoa (Bidasoa Valley) From the north, the busy N-121A burrows deep into Navarre's interior, leaving the San Sebastián–Biarritz motorway just south of Irun/Hendaye and following the course of the Bidasoa River upstream as far as Doneztebe/Sanesteban before proceeding further south to Pamplona. After a mere 10km, you have already left Gipuzkoa behind in favour of Navarre. The road is flanked with high walls of pine and chestnut, but the goods traffic thundering north and south makes the journey at times feel merely like a means to an end. For relief, there are a few welcome side tracks which allow you to temporarily escape the haulage frenzy. If approaching Navarre from San Sebastián, an alternative route which avoids the main road is the GI-3420 from Oiartzun which winds up past Arditurri, transforms itself on the Navarran side into the NA-4000 and spits you out again at Lesaka. If you are accessing directly from France, then the narrow D-4 brings you into Navarre over the Collado de Ibardin, at which point it becomes the NA-1310 and deposits you at Bera. In truth, neither Lesaka nor Bera are particularly worth a stop, although the rather industrial outskirts of the former mask an admittedly attractive town centre.

For some real tranquillity, a lunch stop at **Etxalar**, just a few kilometres along the NA-4400 and east of the N-121A, is the preferred option (page 244). The village itself is very picturesque in a truly macho fashion, with its massive stone houses looking totally out of scale, particularly imperious in this compact setting and all well looked-after. Indeed, Etxalar has bagged itself awards granted for the 'Beautification and Improvement of Spanish Towns'.

On the other (western) side of the carriageway, the NA-4420 is a dead end, but before the road runs out, **Arantza** is a quiet place for lunch, with a choice of three restaurants. Before reaching there, a sign to the left takes you to the intriguingly named **Irrisarri Land** (Igantzi; 948 92 89 22; e info@irrisarriland.es; w irrisarriland.com), which turns out to be an activity park, so a suitable diversion for families. Here, a canopy circuit, bike park, guided trail, kids' kart-circuit and horseriding are all on the menu. It also has two restaurants, and even accommodation available in its hotel or cabins, should you fancy staying longer. Back on the main road, a little further south the village of **Sunbilla** offers a chance to take a break down by the river.

Perhaps the most pleasant way to travel the Bidasoa Valley is on two wheels, along its Vía Verde (see box, page 255).

Where to eat and drink Just on the right past the car park as you enter Etxalar from the west is **Bar La Basque** (Iñarreta 3; ☎ 948 63 51 53; €€), serving a huge *menu del día* for a cheap price in an atmospheric, authentic setting.

Valle del Baztan (Baztan Valley) and around Although it lacks much of a population, the Baztan Valley is overflowing in most other ways. Spoiled by gorgeous landscapes, surrounded by stunning views, rich in folklore and steeped in tradition and witchcraft, this is an area that rewards the visitor who can linger among its 15 neat and tidy villages or attend one of its unforgettable festivals. In financial terms, this is also a wealthy area, arising from the granting of noble titles and land rights to peasants and shepherds way back in medieval times. From the border with France, the valley begins at Dancharia with the inevitable array of frontier shops and petrol stations, geared towards border-crossing bargain-hunters, but quickly turns into unspoiled rural bliss. Pastoral farming and low-impact rural tourism sustain the local population, much of whose first language is Euskara. The road that runs up the valley, the N-121B, is scenic enough, twisting and turning upwards, offering eyefuls of greenery and great valley views, peppered only by the pristine white farmhouses. The high point by car is Puerto de Otxando (602m). If you want an even more remote option, you could veer southwest from the summit down the NA-4453 and end up in Oronoz-Mugairi, ready to visit the Parque Natural Señorío de Bértiz (page 249).

Approaching from the French border, the points of interest in the Baztan Valley are covered below, from north to south.

Tourist information The tourist office (Calle Braulio Iriarte 38, Elizondo; ☎ 948 58 15 17; w baztan.eus; ⏲ Jul & Aug daily, other months Fri–Sun) is at the southern end of the valley, and the office shares its space with the Ethnographic Museum, which to date has no English-language information.

Zugarramurdi Witches, witches and more witches. This village makes its living by sorcery, or rather from the curious visitors who come to see its witches' cave and excellent witches' museum. Zugarramurdi has a dark history, the scene of a literal witch-hunt by zealots in a time when the infamous Spanish Inquisition was carrying out purges. Village folk were denounced by the dozen, carted off to Logroño for trial and burnt at the stake. Visit the museum first, followed by the caves, to learn more. The village itself is well signposted west off the main road, and is a pretty place with a few restaurants and bars. Its tiny population might address you in French, Spanish or Basque – it's a linguistic lottery in these border villages. For parking in high season, follow the signs through the village.

Museo de las Brujas (Witches' Museum) (Calle Behitiko Karrika; ☎ 948 59 90 04; ⏲ 11.00–18.00 Wed–Fri, 11.00–19.00 Sat & Sun, 15 Jul–15 Sep 11.00–19.30 Tue–Sun, closed 1st fortnight Jan; €4.50/2/free adults/under 12s/under 6s, a small discount is available if you visit both museum & caves) If you have previously consigned thoughts of witches to Halloween night, broomsticks and pointy hats, a visit here should remind you that there was (and maybe still is) a whole more serious side to witchcraft. There are four short videos which the staff will put on in English; the ground-floor auditorium houses the first of these, which is thought-provoking and may lead you to conclude that you were a witch simply 'if someone said you were'. It cleverly contrasts the witch-hunts of medieval times with the persecution of scientists in Hitler's Germany and Stalin's Soviet Union. Apart from the videos, English-language information is given via a (returnable!) tablet computer, with which you follow the numbered displays in Spanish and Basque. An excellent museum.

Cueva de las Brujas (Witches' Cave) (948 59 93 05; summer 11.00–19.00 Tue–Sun, winter 11.00–18.00 Tue–Fri, 11.00–19.00 Sat & Sun; €4/2 adults/children) Further down the same road as the museum which you should visit first. The ticket to this attraction provides an English-language leaflet and lets you wander through a long moss-covered cave, more of a tunnel really, as well as accessing a viewpoint that allows you a view back over the pretty village with its whitewashed houses tumbling down the hillside.

THE MYSTERY OF THE AGOTES

The man behind the counter in Bozate shifts uncomfortably and his eyes drop before he answers my question.

'And are the Agotes still discriminated against?' was my enquiry.

'No, not now,' he replies, but his response lacks certainty and when I leave a few moments later it's with the feeling that he has held something back, adding further to the many mysteries surrounding the Agote people.

A newspaper article in 2008 purported to interview the 'last living Cagot' (as the Agotes are known north of the Pyrenees), but ancestry can't simply be obliterated overnight and their descendants are still said by some to be identifiable. Records mention the Agotes/Cagots as long ago as the 13th century, but the references fail to shine any light on their origins. Facts are sparse, theories are plentiful: they were lepers; they were descendants of the Visigoths; of criminals; deserters from the army; Cathar refugees from Occitania in southwest France or Moorish escapees left over after the *reconquista* of Spain. One thing is certain: for eight centuries, despite speaking the local language and seeking to practise the same religion as their neighbours, the Agotes were subject to terrible discrimination. And there, no doubt linked to the first mystery, lies the second: no-one has any idea why.

But discrimination against them was real and the traces can still be seen today. More than 60 Pyrenean churches still have the side-door reserved for the Agotes, who were forbidden from entering through the main door to worship. Examples of such doors can be seen at La Bastide-Clairence and Saint-Etienne-de-Baïgorry – pages 341 and 346 respectively. In the streets they were not allowed to walk barefoot, leading to rumours that they were web-footed. Restricted to working as carpenters and stonemasons, and later as metalworkers, they were not allowed to commune with non-Agotes, and had to live in separate parts of town. They were forced to dress differently, even having at times to wear a goose's foot to distinguish them.

Despite a papal edict in 1514 that they were to be treated more kindly, the discrimination continued until the early 20th century. In 1715 Juan de Goyeneche founded the town of Nuevo Baztán near Madrid, built by Agotes brought from Navarre and intended to provide the marginalised people with houses and jobs, but the experiment was of limited success and the factories created to employ them had ceased to function by the end of the 18th century.

Bozate is recognised as having been the last enclave of the Agotes. It seems that the mystery will never be resolved.

Urdax (Urdazubi) Urdax village lies in a wide, flat-bottomed valley signposted off the N-121B a few kilometres further south of Zugarramurdi. With all its handsome buildings on the same level, it contrasts nicely with its hilly neighbour and, being at the end of a dead-end road, it retains its calm outside its lively fiestas. For those interested in Basque art, a visit to the monastery is recommended.

Where to stay and eat

Hotel Irigoienea (10 rooms) Signposted to the left, just 1km before entering Urdax village from the north; 948 59 92 67; e reservas@irigoienea.com; w irigoienea.com. A beautifully presented & restored house oriented firmly towards adult guests. Rooms are all different, though all the same price, & have TV, heating & free Wi-Fi throughout. A communal lounge, garden & terrace offer valley views. Casual evening meal available on request. **€€**

Mikelen Borda Calle Landibar, Dancharia; 948 59 90 45; 09.00–19.00 (meals noon–15.30) Tue–Sun. In a typically imposing 19th-century Basque building, this *venta* offers veal, seafood paella & pigeon (in season) among its specialities. Its shop sells sangria & rosé wine among its liquid delicacies. **€€€**

What to see and do The village centre is home to the **Monasterio de Urdax** (948 59 90 31; w otxondo-urdax.com; summer 11.00–19.00 daily, winter 14.00–18.30 Wed–Fri, 11.00–19.00 Sat & Sun; museum €5/3 adults/under 16s; exhibition prices vary) The cloister of the Urdax Monastery, which dominates the village centre, provides a splendid setting for a permanent exhibition of Basque art. Although the exhibits change regularly, the dozen or so artists do not. The artists are either Basque or have a strong connection to the region, perhaps being descendants of those who emigrated to South America or other parts of the globe, but who draw their inspiration from Basque culture. Each has his or her profile and style explained in English on helpful display panels and, if you have the budget, some of the works, which range from abstract paintings to bronze sculptures, may be for sale.

The **Cuevas de Urdax (Urdax Caves)** (signposted right off the road, 1km before entering the village; 948 59 92 41; w cuevasurdax.com; Jul & Aug 10.30–noon & 16.30–18.00 daily, Mar–Jun & Sep–Dec 11.15–13.15 & 16.15 Tue–Sun, Jan & Feb 11.15 & 15.15 Sat & Sun; €6/3 adults/under 14s) are open by guided visit only, so you'll need to call in advance if you want an English speaker. Visits take 40 minutes, with light and sound to enhance your viewing of the stalactites and stalagmites.

Amaiur (Maia) Continuing up the valley, in summer this attractive settlement off the main road is available for guided visits in Spanish only (10.00–14.00 & 17.30–22.00 w/ends & Easter week only; tours from €3, including a *talo* snack). The renovated, fully operational village mill and apple press form part of the tour, which can be extended to include the village and its castle. The village is famed for its *talos*, similar to a filled Mexican corn tortilla, with the flour being made at the mill. Even if you don't want a tour, the tasty *talos* are worth a diversion anyway. But the greater claim to fame for Amaiur is that it was Navarre's last stronghold of resistance in 1522 against the Spanish invaders from Castile. If you talk to a local, it won't be long before they tell you about it, and the monument on the hill to the north of town, in memory of those who died in the conflict, emphasises the significance of this episode of history. If you trek up to the monument – a walk of only 10 minutes from the village centre – you'll find that an archaeological dig is gradually unearthing the remains of Amaiur's castle. English-language display panels guide you around and the visit is free.

THE *JOALDUNAK* OF ITUREN

Georgina Howard, proprietor of Pyrenean Experience,
w *pyreneanexperience.com*

Ituren and Zubieta are two small Basque hamlets set deep within the medieval landscapes of the Navarran Pyrenees. Even deeper within the village psyche lie the pagan rituals of the *joaldunak* or 'bell-wearers' – key players in rituals that have been passed on from father to son since pre-Christian times and which have become an icon of Basque culture. Ask, and the locals will recount the excitement they felt as children, waking to the atavistic dirge of the bells and the mournful wail of the horn as the troupe of *joaldunak* marched through the village, blessing their homes in the sleet and the snow. They will remember peering out through lace curtains in the early morning twilight and discerning huge sheepskin-clad forms with grave faces and colourful conical hats. They'll recall the flicker of horse-hair whips and lace petticoats.

Although today the *joaldunak* are known popularly as the protagonists of the Ituren and Zubieta 'carnivals', anthropologists argue that their origins go back to the winter ceremonies of pre-Indo-European times and are among the oldest 'carnival' rites in Europe. Even during Franco's times, when all expressions of Basque culture and identity were forbidden, these rituals continued clandestinely behind closed doors. Today, these winter ceremonies are the high point of the year. The villagers don masks and dress as demons, monsters and beasts arriving in grotesquely decorated carts, and whipping up a staged frenzy of horror and aggression in the village square. They taunt and tease the *joaldunak* before finally scattering in their wake.

Unsurprisingly, the symbolism behind these pagan rituals represents the differences between good and evil. The *joaldunak* represent the benign forces of the spring; the sunshine and light, and the fertility and health of future crops which they bless with their horse-hair whips. The rhythmic toll of their bells, in chasing away the villagers, purges the village of the evil spirits of darkness; of wolves, bears, witches and disease.

The unusual attire of the *joaldunak* is also said to represent fertility, marrying elements of masculinity and femininity. The blue workman's trousers, the sheep's skins and the cockerel's feather, set high upon a tall conical hat, represent the masculine side of human nature, while the lace petticoats and the bright-coloured ribbons flowing from their hats (said once to have been the ribbons from infants' swaddling clothes) are said to signify femininity.

The winter celebrations of Zubieta and Ituren are held on the first Monday and Tuesday after the final Sunday in January, a date brought forward in more recent times as many men traditionally left for logging jobs in the higher Pyrenees in the early spring. However, the *joaldunak* do appear at other moments – during the village fiestas in the summer – and on special days during the months of September and October when they pay their respects to their ancestors, visiting their farms and joining the locals at an immense banquet in the village square.

In the past only single men were allowed to be *joaldunak*, an honour taken with great solemnity and pride. However, today the troupe of *joaldunak* has accepted married men and even the occasional women, an interesting token of equality which is not always common among other Basque ceremonies and dances in the area.

BASQUE SMUGGLERS OF THE ATLANTIC PYRENEES

Georgina Howard, proprietor of Pyrenean Experience,
w *pyreneanexperience.com*

It was a silent trade, carried out at the dead of moonless nights, and in complete secrecy, lest the *mugalari* (bordermen) and their families be silenced once and for all. Only now are the adventures of these Basque smugglers of the Pyrenees – sometimes heroic, sometimes terrifying, sometimes even comical – coming to light.

First, it should be said that the majority of Basque smugglers in the past century were considered local heroes and that their packets of clandestine goods were more likely to contain lace or ladies' tights than drugs, coffee, radios, car tyres, copper, etc – those essential goods that helped breathe life into a starving and deprived Spain during Franco's regime.

Other smugglers focused on moving livestock over the borders, often taking horses over the mountains from Spain into France, and bringing back large herds of calves, swimming back with them across the Bidasoa River when the waters were low (and when the Guardia Civil were nowhere to be seen). Koikili Fagoaga Oiartzabel from Lesaka, who now describes himself as an 'unemployed smuggler', started his smuggling career when he was only 11 years old. He points out a certain white rock in the river, just south of Lesaka Bridge. If the rock jutted out of the water, he says, then the waters were low enough to allow a safe crossing: the time was then right to head out over the border to pick up the next herd of calves.

However, the *mugalari* with the most dangerous jobs of all were those who helped to move people over the borders. At different points in history, political refugees, soldiers or Jews escaping oppressive regimes all benefited from the smugglers' activities. Between 1941 and 1945 Basque smugglers offered an invaluable lifeline to the COMET network, a resistance network masterminded by Belgian woman Andrée de Jongh and running from Belgium and Holland down through Nazi-occupied France and out over the Basque Pyrenees into Spain, helping hundreds of Allied pilots and soldiers, who were stranded on French soil, to safety. Escorting them over the Bidasoa and Baztán rivers, Basque smugglers and their families were instrumental in their rescue.

Bozate To the east off the NA-121B, sleepy Bozate has two points of interest. First, it was a settlement for the mysterious Agote people (see box, page 245), and secondly it is the home of an outdoor sculpture exposition, dedicated to the memory of those same people.

Where to stay and eat Turn off the NA-121B towards Bozate, then left again after 100m, for **Señorío de Ursua** (19 rooms; Barrio Ordoki, Arizkun; ☎ 948 45 35 00; **e** info@hotelurua.com; **w** hotelursua.com; **€€€**). Featuring a small spa, this old-style hotel is set in solitude away from the main road, and has an outdoor area for summer dining. All rooms have TV and free Wi-Fi, and some have a lounge. When booking, it is worth checking whether breakfast and the spa are included as offers vary. It is also worth looking at their special offers.

What to see and do The **Santxotena Parque-Museo** (on the NA-2600, Bozate; ☎ 945 39 66 64; **e** tlafragua@santxotena.org; **w** santxotena.org; ⏲ mid-Jul–end Aug 11.00–14.00 & 16.30–19.30 Mon–Sat, 11.00–14.00 Sun, other months same times w/ends only; €4.50/2 adults/children) is a park of Basque

There were many reasons why the Basque Pyrenees became a favoured crossing place into Spain. First, the Basque people have always viewed the border as a mere technicality, at times working to their advantage and at other times definitely not. The Basques have occupied these lands since the Stone Age (some theories even date their presence back to the time of Cro-Magnon man) and they have extended families on both sides of the 'official' French–Spanish border. Their in-depth knowledge of these misty, mountainous landscapes, their inscrutable Basque language, their bravery and code of honour, enabled them to set up a formidable network over the border while their isolated farmhouses in hidden, heavily wooded valleys offered good (but not always infallible) hideaways for their charges. The landscapes of the Atlantic Pyrenees themselves were almost co-conspirators, the hostile mountain passes and almost impenetrable labyrinth of shepherding paths providing the perfect stage for clandestine night-time crossings or *gaulan* (night work), as it was known in Basque.

With a twinkle in his eye, Koikili recounts some of the ruses of his former trade. His father bought his mother a Vespa and dressed her up in tight jeans, sending her off to the border to distract the eye of the Guardia Civil while he got on with his illegal business. Trucks were hidden in bracken stacks and tree trunks were hollowed out to accommodate smuggled vehicle tyres. There was the priest who used to cycle backwards and forwards over the border, and although the Guardia Civil had a hunch that he was smuggling, whenever they stopped him and searched his bicycle, they could find nothing. In the end they gave up, while the man of the cloth continued to make a healthy trade … smuggling bicycles! Or the truck that passed over the border full of right shoes that were duly confiscated by the authorities, who auctioned them off as seemingly worthless at a ridiculously low price. Naturally, as the smuggler bought back his lorry load of *right* shoes, his business partner was bringing in another lorry load of *left* shoes over a mountain pass further down the valley!

Basque ingenuity at its best.

sculptures, all outside, where you can wander at leisure, admiring and touching if you choose.

Oronoz-Mugairi Southwest of Bozate, via the N-121B, Oronoz-Mugairi is an unexceptional village, but is the jumping-off point for one of the region's most-visited parks.

Parque Natural Señorio de Bertiz First referenced as long ago as 1392 and for a long time private, this estate (signposted off the main road, Oronoz-Mugairi; ☎ 948 59 24 21; **w** parquedebertiz.es; 🕘 Apr–Sep 10.30–19.30 daily, Oct 10.30–18.00 daily, rest of the year opening hours change each month so check website) was bequeathed to the public authorities and then declared a natural park in 1984. Now it contains a hundred-year-old botanical garden with many exotic species and is crossed by waymarked walking circuits from 2.5km to 22km in length. The paths are good and easy to follow. Much of the park is tree-covered, with beech and oak to the fore: the palace, once a stately family home, sometimes shows temporary exhibitions. Information in English is available from the cabin at the park entrance.

Malerreka Valley As the southern end of the Baztán Valley turns from being on a north–south trajectory and orients itself towards the west, beyond the town of Santesteban/Doneztebe, it becomes the valley sometimes referred to as Malerreka, sometimes just seen as an extension of the Baztán. This is a true paradise for walkers, nature fans and lovers of authentic rural culture. Here you'll also find the villages of Ituren and Zubieta, the two places in the Basque Country from which emanate the enigmatic *joaldunak* (see box, page 247).

Where to stay

Pyrenean Experience [map, page 230] (5 rooms) Iaulin Borda, Ameztia, Ituren; m 650 71 37 59; e info@pyreneanexperience.com; w pyreneanexperience.com; see ad, 2nd colour section. Highly recommended renovated & extended Basque farmhouse, located in the wilds, overlooking a stunning valley & imposing mountains. Operates as a B&B (all rooms are en suite), but is also available to rent as a whole house. English-speaking Georgina is part of the local community & runs guided & self-guided walking holidays & Spanish immersion courses, along with opportunities to meet interesting local characters. Free Wi-Fi. Min 3-night stay. **€€**

Tresanea (9 apts & suites) Konzeju karrika 11, Ituren; 948 45 02 87; e info@tresanea.com; w tresanea.com. Modern stylish interior in an old building, with beautiful rooms. TV, mountain views. Terrace, common room, free Wi-Fi, bar & restaurant downstairs. Rates vary according to day of week, use of kitchen, so check the website in advance. Min 2-night stay at certain times. **€€**

ITUREN VILLAGE CIRCULAR WALK

Distance: 4km; time: 1hr 15mins; difficulty: easy, occasionally muddy underfoot, with some moderate ascent. Possibility of refreshments and water en route. Parking usually available in Ituren, by the plaza.

From Ituren Plaza, take the turn between the *ostatua* (bar) and a large building that runs along the side of the *frontón* (*pelota* court) and continue walking down this pretty village street between houses and vegetable gardens until the very end, where you turn left and out on to the main road. Note the intricate carvings of the 17th-century Palacio de Sagardia (Apple Manor House) before you leave the square, and then the pattern of a *joaldunak* (see box, page 247) on the door of the house at this end of the street. Cross the road and turn right and then left just before the sophisticated pink hotel and bar of Tresenea. When you meet the road running along the back of the hotel turn right and follow it out to the final chalet on your left, where you take a left around the perimeter of the chalet, ending up at the old village washing stones and a fountain (*ituria* in Basque, from where the village of Ituren gets its name). At one time, this wash house would have offered one of the only social gathering places for the women.

Turn right at this wash house and follow a grassy path through the field, slowly curling up left towards a small gate (**caution required here**: there is a sharp drop into the stream immediately beyond the gate!) and an entrance into a walled-off grove of trees. Go through the gate and then straight ahead (although you can make a short detour to look at the 18th-century tile kiln just to your right: this would have been a place of industry several hundred years ago). Leaving the tile kiln to your right, follow the path opposite the gate up the side of the stream, soon crossing it as the path bears left and climbs to a wider path. Continue along this path with views of the fields and the backs of the houses of Ituren to your left. The path reaches a cemented road where you walk downhill

Where to eat and drink

Donamaria'ko Benta Barrio de la Venta, Donamaria; 948 45 07 08; w donamariako.com; hours vary. Serving excellent traditional set menus with a few well-chosen creative touches, the service here is cheerful but efficient. An interesting 19th-century building provides the setting, with a garden out the back running down to the river. Pig cheeks, duck *confit* & hake spring rolls are regular contributors to the excellent-value menus, available in English. €€€

Tresanea (see opposite) 17.00–21.00 Mon, 18.00–midnight Fri, noon–midnight Sat & Sun, Jul & Aug same hours, but daily. Well-respected restaurant, popular & good value with local fare & good *pintxos*, too, in pleasant surroundings. €€

What to see and do This is an area made for absorbing the rich culture of village and valley, ideal for those seeking peace and quiet and the gentle discovery of local life through walking or cycling.

Walking Options abound for those who want a short walk through well-kept, peaceful hamlets or more strenuous hikes with a bit of 'up and down'. Two sample walks are given below and on page 253, but there are many more, too.

Cycling For those seeking some strenuous cycling activity, the valley floor and surrounding hills can provide the full range of challenges. A Vía Verde (Greenway)

to reach a large house with impressive wrought-iron railings (not surprisingly, the local blacksmith's house) to your right. When this road joins another road, turn left downhill, but just before you arrive at the main road turn sharp right to follow the road, first cobbled, then paved, uphill. After around 300m, take a path of flagstones leading off to the left. Soon you'll see the 17th-century church (Iglesia de San Martín de Tours). Climb up the steps to this church, heading through the gate into the garden and grounds, pausing to look at the 17th-century tombstones with their coats of arms under the porticos (notice one that has a spectacular coat of arms containing an engraving of a mermaid-like figure called a *lamia*). Continue out the back gate of the church, now take a right down the road towards the hamlet of Aurtiz. When you join the area of the houses, at a distinctive fountain in the wall to your right (built in 2008), turn sharp left downhill into the village until you reach the *ostatua* (bar). Here you turn left again, passing the *pelota* court on your right and then a wood yard on your left before joining the main road.

Turn left, very briefly walking along the main road (**caution: this is a blind bend!**) and, at the gap in the crash barriers, take the right-hand track downhill towards a spectacular arched bridge spanning the river. Cross the bridge and turn left along a path, soon paved, through the woods, which leads up and away from the river and out into the hamlet of Latsaga. Continue on the path which soon becomes a road, through the middle of a number of immense Basque houses (dating from the 17th to 19th centuries) and noting the impressive vegetable gardens and distinctive cobbled 'door mats' outside.

Continue through this hamlet until you come out at a square with a fountain on your right, then continue out to the main road and bear left, downhill, past a newish wooden chalet, towards some flats on your right and the bridge which takes you back to Ituren Plaza.

along a disused railway track offers an easier option. Best contactable through Jorge in the Ameztia Taberna (bar) opposite, **Ameztia Taberna Bike Hire** (Ameztia 9, Santesteban; 948 45 00 28; e info@ameztia.com; w ameztia.com; 08.00–13.00 daily, bikes can be returned outside the centre's opening hours) provides bike hire which includes mountain-style bikes, insurance, rain cape, helmet and puncture repair kit (the last three returnable, please) for €20 per day (€60 per week). Bikes of all sizes, including children's, are available, as well as baby seats. They can also provide a dozen or so route maps of varying difficulty, including one for the flat Vía Verde (see box, page 255) that leads along the old railway track to Behobia near Hendaye on the coast (42km). Maps and info are in Spanish.

For those with their own bikes, the route maps can be bought (€2 each) at the bar. The centre also has a repair shop and showers, plus 20 good-value, basic but modern rooms upstairs (**€**), and a dining room where bike-hire clients are given priority. Jorge's wife speaks a little English.

Spa After a day of walking or cycling, a bit of relaxation in the spa at the **Hotel Balneario Elgorriaga** (Calle Erroltaldea, Elgorriaga; 948 45 60 45; e reservas@balnearioelgorriaga.com; w sanvirilahoteles.com; **€€€**) could be just the answer to aching limbs. On offer are jacuzzi, sauna and a range of massages. Open to non-residents, with a full range of facilities, it has a pleasant bar and a decent restaurant, as well.

Zubieta Old Mill (On the NA-170 between Ituren & Zubieta; Jan–Jun & Sep–Dec 11.00–14.00 Wed–Sun, Jul 11.00–14.00 daily, Aug 11.00–14.00 & 17.00–20.00 daily; €3/1.50/free adults/children, students & seniors/under 8s) Here you can visit a well-preserved and operational corn mill dating from 1785, plus a small eco-museum. Although the written information is in Spanish and Basque only, there is a 10-minute film in English about milling, but also focusing on the surrounding area, its villages and traditions. A *very* small shop sells a few local products and – as the manager is an excellent musician – some Basque music CDs.

THE VALLEYS OF THE NORTHEAST There are several roads from Pamplona up to Roncesvalles and the valleys of northeast Navarre, but starting out on the NA-150 as far as Urroz-Villa and then turning north on to the NA-2330 allows you a gentle climb as the road endlessly criss-crosses the Erro River, occasionally flanked by cliffs or lined by trees. Traffic is light, though the route is popular with cyclists. Once you turn east on to the NA-135, the Camino de Santiago replaces the river as your roadside companion and the cyclists make way for weary pilgrims.

Roncesvalles (Orreaga) From whichever side of the Pyrenees the pilgrims choose to start their trek towards Santiago de Compostela, Roncesvalles will be of great significance. Nestled at the foot of the Pyrenees, this village with a permanent population of just 33 welcomes those who started their pilgrimage from across the mountains at Saint-Jean-Pied-de-Port, most of them exhausted after what might just prove to be the toughest day of the roughly four weeks it will take them to reach their Galician goal. For others, perhaps arriving by bus or taxi from Pamplona or Saint-Jean, Roncesvalles represents the start of the very first stage, a comparatively gentle downhill stroll through heavily forested slopes, perhaps after a hearty lunch at one of the village's restaurants. In high summer, the flood of pilgrims is augmented by tour buses full of casual visitors, who come to visit the museum, church and cloister, and have a drink or lunch before disappearing again. Of no

CIRCULAR WALK FROM ELGORRIAGA: THE 'MUSHROOM' WALK

Distance: 5.5km; time: 2hrs; difficulty: mainly easy, occasionally muddy underfoot, with around 40mins of sharp ascent at the start. Possibility of water en route, refreshments at beginning and end. Parking usually available opposite the Hilarion restaurant, Calle San Pedro, in Elgorriaga.

The walk starts by taking the narrow alleyway up the side of the Hilarion restaurant. Continue up this path, passing after 100m a renovated wash house. At some picnic tables, turn sharp right and continue upwards into the trees on a cemented path, alongside a stream. You reach a stone cross on your right. The path soon turns into a dirt track, and you continue uphill to reach a road where you turn right. At the next large information panel ('*Pehudi-Pinar*'), you turn left uphill on a rough track. The track becomes grassy and zigzags up the hill. Ignore the first right (a grassy turn) and any forestry tracks leading off to the left into the pines. Reaching a road, take the 'Elgorriaga' signposted path to the left of the distinctive lime-kiln and climb the 115 steps up to the path's next junction with the road, where you turn left on to the road, reaching a long, striking *borda* that houses a bread oven. At the *borda*, take the road that bends sharply round to the right and continue uphill on a cement road for around 200m before veering off to the left (again indicated by the now-familiar mushroom sign) and climbing slightly up to a wide clearing where there are some Neolithic dolmens. Ignore the path that leads up to the summit on your right, cross the clearing and (again) follow the mushroom sign, taking you down a path with tall pines on your right and deciduous vegetation to your left. The path soon veers round to the left and you will have magnificent views down the valley to your right and to distant mountains before the path leads you down to a picnic area with tables, shade and a barbecue. Passing with the picnic tables on your left, you immediately pick up the signage again and take a narrow path that flanks another *borda* and heads out above a field towards a pine plantation. The path takes you along the top of this plantation, at the end of which the path divides. Here you will have views down to the Malerreka Valley, while above you on the hill is yet another *borda* and further dolmens. Now you leave the main path which heads down into the pines, instead taking a narrower, fern-lined path to the right. The path widens and becomes rocky, leading steeply downhill. At the next intersection of paths, at an information panel on charcoal-making, again follow the mushroom markings, continuing straight ahead and walking gently downhill. Continue as the rough track opens up on to a brief cemented section, then continues downhill until you see – on your left – a small *borda*, somewhat hidden among the trees. Before you reach this, take a right, signposted for Elgorriaga. Soon you see on your right another distinctive *borda*, in a grove of trees in the middle of a field. Very shortly, the path divides again, and you take the left-hand option, still heading downhill until you emerge at an intersection of paths with a stone cross ahead of you. Here you take the path on the extreme left, that is, between the cross and the information panel, seemingly leaving the main track and, with a barbed-wire fence immediately on your left, and a deep valley also on your left, you head downhill again. Always keeping to the left-hand path, keep heading down until you reach a road where you turn left and head back towards Elgorriaga. At a T-junction, you turn briefly right to reach the main road, then left along it, reaching the Hilarion restaurant after 150m.

significance to the bus passengers, but ominously for the walkers, the sobering sign at the end of the village reads: 'Santiago de Compostela 790km'. Ouch! If you're here to start a pilgrimage, before leaving town you can stock up on maps, rain-capes and all sorts of other *camino*-branded artefacts that you will (and some that you won't) need on the journey. Welcome to the pilgrims' route.

Roncesvalles is also the site of a famous battle … well, probably. It is generally believed that it was near here in the year 778 that Roland, the nephew of Charlemagne, got a hiding from the Vascones (Basques) as he returned across the Pyrenees from Spain. However, the actual site of the battle is unknown, with some historians even believing it took place as far away as Catalonia! Nevertheless, it's at Roncesvalles that you'll find a monument to the confrontation. By the car park, there's also a sculpture called *La Muerte de Roldán* (*The Death of Roland*), just to emphasise the victory.

Getting there and away In summer, **buses** connect with Pamplona, usually twice daily, between Monday and Saturday (Autocares Artieda; w autocaresartieda.com; 70mins; €4.65). From September to June, the service reduces to once per day, again with no Sunday service. In high season, buses from Pamplona can become full very quickly and the bus company advises turning up at Pamplona bus station to buy your ticket at least 2 hours ahead of schedule. No online or telephone bookings are allowed.

Tourist information The tourist office (Antiguo Molino; 948 76 03 01; w roncesvalles.es; Jan–Mar & mid-Oct–Dec 10.00–14.00 Sun–Thu, 10.00–17.00 Sat & Sun, Jul 10.00–14.00 & 15.00–18.00 Mon–Sat, 10.00–14.00 Sun, Aug 10.00–14.00 & 15.30–18.30 Mon–Sat, 10.00–14.00 Sun, other months 10.00–17.00 Mon–Sat, 10.00–14.00 Sun) is oriented towards the pilgrims but the multilingual and friendly staff dole out information about other subjects, too.

Where to stay and eat Being a *bona fide* pilgrim holding a *credencial* (page 66) will entitle you to share a dormitory but, assuming that you are not on your way to Santiago, you can avoid the snorers and communal sleeping spaces and buy a piece of solitude in somewhere more upmarket. Dining-wise, you can save your euros by choosing the pilgrims' menus available, or trade up a notch.

Hotel Roncesvalles (16 rooms, 24 apts); 948 76 01 05; Apr–Sep. A new hotel in an old building, with singles, doubles, triples & also apartments which can accommodate up to 4 guests. TV, free Wi-Fi. Restaurant. Transfers to St-Jean are offered for pilgrims. **€€**

La Posada (20 rooms) Carretera de Francia; 948 79 03 22; e laposada@roncesvalles.es; mid-Mar–mid-Dec. The bar's a bit dingy, but it's busy enough & most choose the outdoor tables for a drink. The restaurant's good (€€), open to all & the beds are comfortable. A special menu is available for pilgrims, but if you want to partake, it's necessary to get a ticket for 1 of the 2 evening sittings. **€€**

Casa Sabina (4 rooms) 948 76 00 12; e casasabina@roncesvalles.es; w casasabina.roncesvalles.es; restaurant 08.00–22.00 Sun–Thu, 08.00–23.00 Fri & Sat. Beside the tourist office, this is a favourite place to stretch legs out under the wooden tables. There are a few well-priced sandwiches & cakes along the bar, a budget pilgrims' menu (available to all, midday & evening), plus a more upmarket version with decent choices (€–€€). The rooms have TV, AC & private bath. **€**

What to see and do The whole village of Roncesvalles belongs to the church. The **Museo de Roncesvalles (Roncesvalles Museum)** (Apr–Oct 10.00–14.00 &

VÍA VERDE: SANTESTEBAN TO BERA

A straightforward cycle up a former railway line, alongside the Bidasoa River, this trail actually forms a tiny part of the 'Eurovélo 1' route from Norway to Sagres in Portugal. Almost completely flat, the route is linear and well signposted. The section described here should take around 4 hours of actual cycling time (return journey), for someone of moderate fitness. A rough map is available from Ameztia Taberna Bike Hire (page 239). Take a torch to assist you through the tunnels: there are tunnel lights, but occasionally they don't work.

Starting from Santesteban, this trail allows you to cover as much or as little of this well-established Vía Verde as you wish or can manage, before turning back and retracing your route. Depending on your fitness and motivation, you could cover the entire route to Behobia, and then come back the same day (84km), or hire your bike for longer and stay overnight. The description below covers the route as far as Bera and back to Santesteban (46km round trip).

From the Ameztia Bike Centre it's a mere 100m to the bridge where you pick up the Vía Verde sign. With the river on your left, continue until you reach a park, crossing it in its entirety and then turning left. At the park's exit, you'll find a Vía Verde information board, after which you cross the river and shortly afterwards turn right on to the old railway track, now concreted. The river will now stay on your right-hand side for the entire journey to Bera. The first section of the track, to Sunbilla, provides good opportunities to spot both heron and kingfishers going about their business as the Bidasoa River proceeds towards the sea. Originally, the railway line that ran along the northern section of this route carried minerals extracted from the locality, having been established by the British company 'Bidasoa Railway and Mines' in the late 19th century. It was later extended south to Elizondo and converted into a passenger line, but closed when it was no longer profitable.

Sunbilla, after 5km, provides the first opportunity to grab a coffee. Down by the river – which has temporarily veered off to your right at this point, though not far – the village has commemorated the achievements of one of its champion woodchoppers with an impressive statue by the river bridge.

Back on the route, you soon reach a long tunnel, one of several on the way. Some of these tunnels are short, some have permanent lighting, while others need to be activated by a switch on the wall. Sometimes, the lights don't work, so dismounting is advisable, as is the carrying of a small torch – the light from your mobile phone is not really enough. Although there is no danger in the tunnels, stepping in a puddle could spoil your day out. After Sunbilla, there are no cafés until Puente de Lesaka, where the Vía Verde crosses the main road, and Bera (23km from your starting point), which is a good place for lunch. Take time in Bera to see the bridge over the river, with its commemoration of a British soldier and his gallant comrades from the 2nd Battalion of the 95th Rifle Brigade who died defending the town against the French in 1813.

This Vía Verde is an excellent route for those who are not hardcore cyclists, being largely on tarmac, concrete or wide, unmade track. Families would find it especially suitable, and you will encounter only the occasional vehicle. The only slight downside is the noise from the busy NA-121A road, which occasionally crosses overhead and slightly mars the tranquillity.

15.30–19.00 daily, Nov & Mar 10.00–14.00 & 15.00–18.00 daily, Dec–Feb 10.00–14.30 closed Wed; last entry 75mins before closing time; €5 for museum, church & cloister) can only be visited as part of a guided tour in Spanish, but English-speakers can use the translated audio guide script. A project to alter the whole layout of the museum, scheduled to take place in 2017, has halted owing to a lack of funds. Exhibits include paintings, books preserved from the 13th century and carved images. The **cloister** and **church** are open the same times as the museum.

Burguete (Auritz) The neat houses of Burguete form themselves into a village that would be of little extra consequence over and above its location on the pilgrims' route if it were not for its one-time patronage by Ernest Hemingway. Just a few kilometres south of Roncesvalles, it was here that the great American writer liked to fish for trout, aided and abetted – it is said – by a case of beer, maybe two, and a few of his Bohemian cronies. He describes the village in *The Sun Also Rises*. On an information board by the side of the Hostal Burguete, you can read about his connections with Navarre, which begin in this very spot, for this was the *hostal* he stayed in, back in 1923. If you need some 'proof', the current owner may lift the lid on the piano that rests quietly against one wall of the dining room and show you Hemingway's signature, scratched on the inside.

Where to stay Try to book room number 23 at the **Hostal Burguete** (20 rooms; San Nicolás 71; 948 76 00 05; e info@hotelburguete.com; w hotelburguete.com; 1 Apr–10 Dec; **€**) – that's the one in which Hemingway wrote much of *The Sun Also Rises*. The owner insists he charges nothing extra for this room, but he says it with a smile which suggests otherwise. Anyway, you'll have TV and free Wi-Fi, luxuries unknown to Ernest. Otherwise, the rooms are fairly basic, but fine. The hotel also has a bar and restaurant (**€€**).

Valle de Aezkoa East of Roncesvalles is the Aezkoa Valley, which borders on the western side of one of Europe's most important woodlands, the huge Irati beech forest (better accessed from the NA-2012), and is also known for its abandoned munitions factory. Look out for the stone *horreos*. Looking like miniature houses, these are in fact granary stores, built as protection from the weather and rodents. Fifteen of Navarre's specimens are to be found in this area, particularly in Aribe, Aria and Orbaitzeta. There is a **tourist office** on the main NA-140 in Aribe (948 76 43 76; Jul–Oct 10.30–13.30 & 16.30–18.30 Tue–Sat, 10.00–14.00 Sun).

Fábrica de Orbaitzeta From Aribe, the NA-2030 twists up a narrow valley, heavily wooded until you reach the disused weapons factory 5km beyond the village of Orbaitzeta itself. The factory is a ruin, a relic from the 18th century. Although some of them are a bit weathered, multilingual signboards nevertheless explain how iron ore was brought down from the nearby hills, while water power from the mountains was harnessed to help in the production. Above the ruined factory stand the houses of the one-time workers, together with the 'palace' that housed the factory bosses, as well as a church now used to shelter the farm animals of a local resident. The palace is undergoing a painfully slow restoration, funds being drip-fed by the provincial government to (hopefully, eventually) produce a museum and a café. For the time being, there are no refreshments, though excellent sheep's cheese can be bought from one of the houses. Several waymarked walks begin from here. Although it is not clear from some otherwise reputable maps, the road itself continues beyond the factory and after 7km takes you up and over into

France. The summit is prone to low cloud, but the road is perfectly passable in dry weather without a 4×4. Beware of snow in winter, however.

Between the factory and the village of Orbaitzeta to its south, you can take the turning to find one of the access points for the **Irati Forest** (page 258). After a couple of kilometres you reach an information kiosk (Easter & mid-May–Nov daily), where the entrance fee of €5 per vehicle is reduced to €2 if you've spent €15 or more in the local shops – keep your receipt! You can pick up advice on walks and continue up to the reservoir. There are no bikes to hire here and swimming is not permitted. Essentially, this is an area for walkers.

Valle de Salazar Retrace your route from Orbaitzeta and, rejoining the NA-140 at Aribe a little further eastward, you will pass through Abaurrea Alta, at 1,039m the highest village in Navarre, before the route takes you seamlessly out of the Valle de Aezkoa and into the Valle de Salazar, the road precariously switch-backing and waltzing you downward past the picturesque village of Jaurietta and on to Ochagavia. At times, these north Navarran settlements appear to have been recently spring-cleaned, such is their admirable neatness and well-tended appearance. In summary, this is a beautiful drive.

Ochagavia (Ostagabia) At an altitude of over 750m, Ochagavia is a pretty village adorned by handsome houses, shod with cobbled streets and set on the banks of no fewer than three rivers. In the beautiful landscape of the northern part of the Salazar Valley, this is a good base for exploring the nearby Irati Forest.

Getting there and away One **bus** (w alsa.es; 90mins; €9.15) runs between Ochagavia and Pamplona, though not always daily. Consult the website for availability.

Tourist information The tourist office (Labaria 21; 948 89 06 41; w cinirati.es; Jul & Aug 10.00–14.00 & 16.30–19.30 Mon–Sat, 10.00–14.00 Sun, Sep–Jun 10.00–17.00 Mon–Thu, 10.00–14.00 & 16.30–19.30 Fri & Sat, 10.00–14.00 Sun) also doubles up as the **Centro de Interpretación de la Naturaleza** (Nature Learning Centre; €1.50) for those interested in the area's rich flora and fauna. Information at the office is in Spanish only.

Where to stay Accommodation in this region is noticeably inexpensive. The Salazar area is teeming with *casas rurales*, many of which are grouped together in an umbrella organisation. Note that as elsewhere in Navarre, many of these can only be rented as a whole house, but where individual rooms are available, they provide very good-value accommodation indeed. See also w roncal-salazar.com (Spanish only). All local accommodation is listed on the wall outside the tourist office – handy if you haven't booked and the office is shut.

Hotel Rural Auñamendi (13 rooms) Urratia 23; 948 89 01 89; e info@hotelruralaunamendi.com; w hotelruralaunamendi.com. Recently updated, this upmarket place on the square has a popular bar & restaurant. Rooms have TV, free Wi-Fi & heating, & some have a balcony. Family & reduced-mobility rooms also available. B/fast inc. **€€€**

Casa Rural Martinezker (4 rooms) Irigoyen 5; 948 89 02 11. The town has several discreet *casas rurales* in its narrow, cobbled streets. Some only rent the whole house, but this one offers individual rooms at a good price. The entrance is dark & foreboding, the owner bright & welcoming. Communal lounge with TV, & a shared kitchen if you want to cook. The 4 rooms share 2 bathrooms. A bargain option. **€**

Where to eat and drink

Asador Kixkia Urrutia 59; 948 89 05 17; m 686 38 74 07; w kixkia.com; Jul–Oct lunch & dinner daily, Nov closed Mon & Tue, other months lunchtimes only Thu, lunch & dinner Fri–Sun & holidays. A traditional cider-house, with set menus but also offering fish & meat main courses. Opening hours are a tad flexible, but the locals rave about the meat quality. Worth phoning ahead to reserve. €€€

Auñamendi (page 257) 13.00–16.00 & 20.30–22.30 daily. Bar snacks, sandwiches, *raciones* & *pintxos* are available outside the above hours. A *menu del día* competes for your appetite with a more elaborate restaurant menu based on game & fish specialities. There is free Wi-Fi in the bar. €€€

What to see and do Just 500m along the NA-140 east of Ochagavia and 4km up a winding road (NA-2013) lies the **Santuario de Muskilda** (Mar & Apr 11.00–14.00 & 16.00–19.00 Sat & Sun, May & Jun 16.00–19.00 Mon–Fri, 11.00–14.00 & 16.00–20.00 Sat & Sun, Jul & Aug 11.00–14.00 & 16.00–19.00 daily; admission free, donations welcome), a quaint hermitage that is more notable for its location than its architectural wonder, though its restoration has been meticulous and imbues it with some charm. But it's the views that take the breath away here, down into the valleys and across to the Pyrenees, which often harbour pockets of snow as late as June. The highest peaks visible from here are Anie (2,507m, but it's actually across the border in Béarn) and Navarre's highest point, the Mesa de los Tres Reyes (Table of the Three Kings, 2,424m). On 8 September every year a group of dancers gather to perform their traditional dance at this hermitage, having danced the previous day in Ochagavia – a 300-year-old tradition.

Sierra de Abodi/Embalse de Irabia A little to the northwest of Ochagavia, a 20km diversion on the NA-2012 will lead you ultimately to a dead end. Its twists and turns ensure that you enjoy spectacular views in nearly every direction before the tarmac finally runs out at the Casas de Irati. (Some maps show a through-road for cars that would theoretically take you across the top of the reservoir and link up with the Aezkoa Valley, but this is not possible.) Your drive affords you close contact with the beautiful Irati Forest, where Ernest Hemingway went to 'lose himself in the woods', taking time out from his carousing and bull-running in Pamplona. The route reaches its high point at the Tapla Pass (1,365m), at which there is a *mirador* marking out the Pyrenean peaks in the middle distance. Don't be fooled by the restaurant advertising hoarding, though – it's still another 10km away, at Casas de

WALKING THE PYRENEES – A WARNING

The high Pyrenees make for tremendous walking country through unspoilt and untamed nature. For experienced walkers, the dangers are obvious in a region where the weather can change suddenly, brewing up violent storms from seemingly nowhere. One peculiarity is that in high summer – especially July and August – a perfectly sunny morning can and often does turn into an afternoon of thunder and lightning. At this time of year, locals advise visitors to do their walking early in the day. Snow patches can be seen all year round, though their permanence or otherwise alters from year to year. Impenetrable mists can descend suddenly, and the thick forests can make orientation difficult. Unfortunately, walking maps provided by tourist offices can prove inadequate, so your best guide may be someone who has actually walked your intended route (and recently).

CIRCULAR WALK: THE 'CAMINO DEL ZEMETO' FROM BELAGUA REFUGE

Distance: 4.3km; time: 1hr 45mins; difficulty: easy, occasionally muddy under foot, with a moderate ascent at the end. No water en route, no refreshments at beginning or end. Ample free parking. Griffon vulture sightings are a near certainty and you might also encounter deer on this walk. The views of the Pyrenees and down to the valley are incredible. Best done in the morning – check the weather forecast in advance.

The starting point is the car park at the derelict Belagua refuge, 17km north of Isaba, situated down to the right of the NA-137 road as it heads up the valley towards France. From the information board nearest to the refuge, drop down to the wooden signpost ('Camino Zemeto') that is visible from the car park. With the car park now behind you, turn left and follow the well-trodden grassy path, heading towards a thick pine forest. About 100m before you reach the trees, the path veers off to the left, continuing to descend slightly and following some short wooden posts with blue waymarking. You cross the course of a partially underground stream and the path now leads diagonally to a large, flat pasture, formerly a lake. A taller wooden post carrying the red and white GR waymarking takes you round to the right, heading towards a narrow exit from the pasture area a few hundred metres away and partially concealed by some conifers. You soon pick up, once again, the short wooden posts with blue markings. The exit from the pasture now descends down a usually dry stream-bed, rocky in places but not steep. After 200m, and before entering a dense tree tunnel, you turn right, along the front of a cliff-face on your right and dense forest below to your left. You should spot the occasional blue waymarking to reassure you. After 400m you reach a clearing, where you can take a brief diversion to the viewpoint, signposted *'mirador'* off to your left. The diversion adds only 10 minutes' walking time to your trip, and is worth it for the views of the wide Belagua Valley and the road leading back to Isaba. Now retrace your steps to the three-way signpost and continue in the same direction as before (signed RI-S4 Zemeto). The path climbs moderately to reach a large clearing. Straight ahead you will see the huge structure of another abandoned refuge, far away in the distance, which – for the time being – you head towards. Now descend out of the pasture, soon entering some trees. After a little while you will reach a partial clearing with, at the far end, a large tree with the red and blue waymarking. At the tree, do **not** go straight ahead, but instead turn sharp right across a stream-bed, following a path that descends gently through the forested hillside. (Important: if you find yourself descending steeply through the trees, you have made a mistake and need to retrace your steps!) After 75m or so, you cross another stream-bed and pick up the blue waymarking once more and continue along the side of the hill. The path soon rises slightly to the right, but very quickly levels out again and continues along the shoulder. Soon you escape the trees and you continue across the meadow, ascending slightly. Seeing the road above you, you now have a steep climb to reach it. The return route along the road takes no more than 10 minutes and outside of July and August there are usually more cows on the tarmac than cars.

Irati. Note that there is an entrance fee of €5 to access the forest, though this reduces to €2 if you have spent at least €15 in the local shops – keep your receipt!

At the end of the road is the **Casas de Irati Mountain Biking Centre** (w irati.org; ⌚ Easter–start Dec, subject to weather, 10.00–18.00 daily), which also houses a bar/restaurant. The centre hires out bikes with helmet for 3 or 6 hours (€10/15) and issues a free route map, including 16 circular waymarked trails of between 2km and 60km and of varying difficulty. The information is in Spanish, Basque and French only. A number of walks can also be done from here, including one that visits the nearby Virgen de las Nieves (Virgin of the Snows) hermitage or the El Cubo or Itsuosin waterfalls.

Valle de Roncal/Valle de Belagua Coming from Salazar, your transition into the Valle de Roncal is marked by the summit of the Portillo de Lazar (1,129m), with its parking, picnic site and viewpoint out on to the Pyrenean summits to the east. Roncal's northern section is accurately referred to by locals as Belagua, a wide and beautiful flat-bottomed glacial valley that stretches up to the border with France. This is the easternmost of the northern Navarrese valleys and the home of the mountain of Mesa de los Tres Reyes (Table of the Three Kings), a reference to its position at the meeting-point of Spain, France and the former kingdom of Navarre. An area that has traditionally relied on livestock rearing and forestry, Roncal is now waking up to the rich tourism potential offered by mountains, gastronomy and traditional culture, but so far it remains completely unspoiled. Many will know it for its renowned Roncal cheese, made from sheep's milk. This stunning, richly forested valley is made up of the seven villages of Uztárroz, Isaba, Urzainqui, Roncal, Burgui and, off the main road, Garde and Vidángoz. The lower valley carries the considerable waters of the Esca River, as they plough through spectacular gorges as they escape Navarre for neighbouring Aragón. In former times the torrent was harnessed as a transport medium to carry wooden rafts of cargo down to join the much larger River Ebro to the south.

Getting there and away One bus (La Tafallesa; ☎ 902 42 22 42; 2hrs; €10) per day connects the Roncal Valley with Pamplona, leaving Uztárroz and calling at Isaba, Urzainqui, Roncal and Burgui.

Uztárroz A pretty, pass-through town, though you might be tempted to visit the tiny Ekia cheese factory, which houses the **Museo del Queso (Kabila Enea, or Cheese Museum)** (on the main NA-140, just north of Uztárroz; ☎ 948 89 32 36; ⌚ 10.00–13.00 & 16.00–18.00 Tue–Sat, noon–14.00 Sun; admission free). This offers a chance to buy a few local products (wine, *patxaran*, fruit liqueurs, natural cider, not forgetting cheese) rather than anything else, but with free entrance you can poke about upstairs for a few minutes among the cheese moulds, old photos, cowbells and cheese-making equipment. There is no information in English. Cheese-making takes place from December to July. Like Idiazábal cheese from the Basque Autonomous Community, Roncal cheese is hard, nutty and chewy, using only milk from the *latxa* sheep. Roncal was the first Spanish cheese to gain a PDO (Protected Designation of Origin) demarcation, in 1981.

Isaba (Izaba) For a sleepy valley town, Isaba harbours a lot of very good accommodation options, especially in season, and restaurant choices are now improving. Park your car at the car park at the north end of town because, off the main road, the streets are cobbled and very narrow. Despite the promising signposts, both the tourist office and the Casa de Memoria museum remain closed. On the main street you'll find two banks and a bakery.

Where to stay

Hostal Lola (21 rooms) Mendigatxa 17; ☎ 948 89 30 12; e info@hostal-lola.com; w hostal-lola.com. Totally refurbished, with a boutique feeling. All rooms are different but all have TV & free Wi-Fi. Some with a balcony – worthwhile given the views to the rugged mountains. There's even a suite, if you want to splurge. **€€**

Hostal Rural Ezkaurre (12 rooms) Garagardoia; m 699 56 78 29; e info@hostalezkaurreisaba.com; w hostalezkaurreisaba.com. Simple rooms with TV & heating, Wi-Fi & private bathrooms. Located 100m up from the free public car park at the north of town. Pleasant terrace for outdoor b/fasts (extra cost) looks up the valley. Top-floor lounge. Free Wi-Fi. **€€**

Where to eat and drink Isaba is not overwhelmed with good restaurants, but **Lola** (Mendigatxa 17; ☎ 948 89 30 12; €€€) is one of the better ones, set in a pleasant dining room with service on the formal side. Set menus are good value, sometimes featuring local trout.

Shopping Located at the town end of the car park, in the northern part of the town, is **Ezkiaga** (☎ 948 89 34 94; ⌚ summer 10.00–13.00 & 16.00–19.00 daily, winter 16.00–19.00 Fri & Sat only). You won't find too many shops in Isaba, of any kind, but here they sell some decent local products such as gifts carved from local wood, liqueurs, cheese, chocolate, postcards and souvenirs.

What to see and do Travelling further afield, a drive all the way up the Roncal and Belagua valleys to the north, maybe with a **walk** (see box, page 259) included if the weather is favourable, would be an excellent way to occupy a day and provide you with great Pyrenean vistas. As you might expect with the Pyrenean rocky landscape all around, raptors are everywhere, but there are many other species, too.

Roncal (Erronkari) Roncal village shares its name with the valley. As well as its cheese, Roncal is also known – well, at least among opera-lovers – as being the birthplace of Julián Gayarre, a renowned tenor from the 19th century. Whether you've heard of him or not, he will be loved in his home village in perpetuity, having paid for their *frontón* and council building. In return, they look after his museum and aficionados could also visit his monument, and even his mausoleum which is a kilometre out of town.

Tourist information Situated on the main road in the village centre, the spacious tourist office (Calle Gayarre; ☎ 948 47 52 56 or 948 47 53 17; w vallederoncal.es; ⌚ mid-Jun–mid-Sep 10.00–14.00 & 17.00–20.00 Mon–Sat, 10.00–14.00 Sun, mid-Sep–mid-Jun 10.00–14.00 Sun–Thu, 10.00–14.00 & 16.30–19.30 Fri & Sat) offers brochures and sells a few local products. Three floors of the building are dedicated to explaining the wildlife and communities within the valley.

Where to stay One block back from the road, on the opposite side from the tourist office, is **Casa Tetxe** (4 rooms; Barrio Iriondoa 6; m 628 44 73 22; e casatetxe@tetxe.es; w tetxe.es; **€€**), a small, beautifully renovated *casa rural*. It's a little bit dark inside, but provides a warm welcome. All rooms have private bath and heating, and there's a communal TV area. Breakfast and dinner can be supplied on request, but a minimum of three or even five nights' booking is required at certain times.

PEACE, THANKS TO THREE COWS

On Bastille Day 2015, the Tour de France cycle race made a rare visit to the Col de la Pierre Saint Martin, 1,600m above sea level. An estimated 800 motorhomes lined the route to the summit and all the commercial pomp and circumstance of the world's greatest cycle race descended (or rather, ascended) on the region. The summit is actually in the province of Béarn, not Navarre, but the previous day had witnessed another event, of much greater significance – one that has been celebrated almost continuously for over 630 years, with only a short interruption for World War II.

The Pax Avant, the Junte de Roncal, the Tres Vacas ... many names are used to refer to the annual reaffirmation every 13 July of a peace treaty first signed in 1375 and still in force today. For two years running, disputes between the Pyrenean shepherds from the Baretous Valley in Béarn and those from the Valle de Roncal in Navarre over rights to a high-altitude water source had led to around 300 deaths. It was decided to put the matter before the Bishop of Jaca. His judgement determined that it was the Spanish who held the rights, but also that the Béarnais could continue to use the source, providing they paid the sum of three cows per year for the privilege. And since 1375, this payment has been honoured, accompanied by a solemn ceremony of the Pax Avant ('future peace') at the Col de la Pierre Saint Martin.

And so it is that the mayors of six Béarnais villages and those from four in the Roncal Valley put on their finest ceremonial costumes and meet in amicable spirit at this high Pyrenean altitude to place their hands, one upon the other, on the marker stone (the 'Borne 262') and repeat the words '*pax avant*' three times over. Prior to this endorsement of the ancient treaty, priests from both sides of the mountains preside over an open-air mass, attended by around 1,500 people. After the treaty has been reaffirmed, 15 cows are herded into a corral for a vet from Navarre to make his selection, a process which involves shepherds demonstrating much *macho* grabbing of the reluctant beasts' heads, allowing their teeth to be inspected and the selection to be made.

The formal part of the ceremony complete, the crowds can retire to the temporary mountain-top bars or take part in the communal lunch organised in a large tent nearby. An enthusiastic group of Béarn singers perform traditional songs and there are guided walks around the summit, with insights into the life of the shepherds, the history of the treaty and some rum tales of the smuggling which went on until the creation of the European Community removed the incentives for such activities. This mountain ceremony is hugely significant, but it has an element of fun, too. And, unlike the Tour de France, it was back again the following year.

Where to eat and drink A renovated mill, 50m along from the tourist office, now houses **Errota Barrio** (Iriartea 37; 948 47 51 04; 13.30–15.30 Tue–Sun, 21.30–23.00 Fri & Sat only; €€), which serves simple *menus del día* (no à la carte) and slightly fancier fare at the weekend. There is a lively bar, with some good bottled beers available.

What to see and do Situated inside the tourist office building, the **Centro de Interpretación de la Naturaleza de Roncal** (Calle Gayarre; 948 47 52 56;

w vallederoncal.es; ⌚ same hours as the tourist office – see page 261; €1.20) is an excellent place to get an introduction to the natural attractions of the Roncal Valley. The exhibits consist of a number of high-quality audio-visual presentations and touch-screen information panels, all accessible by means of a swipe card programmed to provide the information in English. You can learn all about birds and even bears: although the indigenous mammals have died out, some imported specimens from Slovenia still inhabit the high slopes, though seeing one is extremely unlikely. In fact, it is thought that only one bear, of Slovenian parentage, now actually lives in the valley. Information about local history, economic activity and traditions is also provided. The complete visit here takes around 40 minutes.

The other attraction in Roncal is the **Casa-Museo Julián Gayarre** (☎ 948 47 51 80; w juliangayarre.com; ⌚ Apr–Sep 11.30–13.30 & 17.00–19.00 Tue–Sat, 11.30–13.30 Sun, Oct–Mar 11.30–13.30 & 16.00–18.00 Sat, 11.30–13.30 Sun; €2). A former shepherd, shop assistant and blacksmith, Julián Gayarre went on to become one of the 19th century's most revered tenors, and Pamplona's theatre is named after him. Born in Roncal in 1844 to parents of modest means, his career led him to perform in all the world's great opera houses, from Rome to Paris and New York to Covent Garden. The museum displays are spread over three floors, with the ground floor giving a timeline of his life, linked to contemporary events in Spain and the wider world. Here are also photographs, documents, musical scores and some curios collected by Gayarre on his travels. Although there are no recordings of his singing, his reputation is evidenced by the prestige of the operas that he performed and the venues in which he performed them. The first-floor displays are mainly costumes used in his shows, newspaper cuttings and gifts he received.

On the second floor, two period rooms are preserved; this house was built in 1879 on Gayarre's instructions, on the same spot as the house of his birth. Although the information panels are in Spanish, information in English is provided by an illustrated leaflet.

Burgui (Burgi) The annual Día de la Almadia (Day of the Raft) is held on the Esca River in Burgui on the first weekend of May and commemorates this former mode of transport, with traditionally dressed rafters racing downstream, while onshore activities include music, dance and food. If visiting in March, you may stumble across the local men constructing the rafts down by the river. Continuing south from Burgui brings more spectacular gorge scenery, but soon the road takes you out of Navarre and into Huesca province in Aragón. Eventually you reach the Embalse de Yesa reservoir.

Vidángoz (Bidangoze) Away from the main road that threads itself through the Roncal Valley, this is a charming village which every August commemorates the day of its patron, St Augustine, in an unusual way. Residents light their torches from a giant bonfire and await the descent of Maruxa the witch, riding her broomstick and suspended on a cable. Dancing around the bonfire ensues, followed by five days of festivities, before Maruxa ascends again to signal the end of the fun.

Arbayún, Lumbier (Irumberri) and the Monasterio de Leyre A few kilometres south of Burgui, and before the southern end of the Roncal Valley, the NA-137 exits Navarre and enters Huesca province. To remain in Navarre, take the NA-214, which leads west out of Burgui towards Navascués and invites you to enjoy dramatic landscapes much different in character from the Pyrenean heights, still less than an hour away. (If arriving directly from Pamplona, the journey to Lumbier, using the A-21 motorway, takes little more than 30 minutes.) Justly famous for the

Arbayún, Lumbier and other lesser gorges, this is an area which deserves a visit, preferably taking in both of the major gorges and also incorporating a trip to enjoy the tranquillity of the Monasterio de Leyre. The two deep limestone gorges with their sheer rock faces, lush vegetation and ubiquitous birdlife have been created by the rivers Salazar and Irati in the northern foothills of the Sierra de Leyre. Although similar in terms of geology, the visits to each produce very different experiences, with Arbayún being seen from above and Lumbier viewed almost from water level. Lumbier itself is a pleasant, quiet medieval town with narrow streets and balconied houses fronted by imposing wooden doors, and the area around the town is characterised by a wide valley with wheat fields and vines in scenery with Mediterranean overtones. Deciduous and common-pine woodlands occupy the higher areas of the Sierra de Leyre, whose highest peak, Arangoiti (1,353m) overlooks the Monasterio de Leyre and the waters of the Embalse de Yesa reservoir on the sierra's southern side.

Tourist information The tourist office in Lumbier's Plaza Mayor (✆ 948 88 08 74; w focesdenavarra.com; ⏲ Jul & Aug 10.00–14.00 & 16.30–19.30 daily, other months 10.00–14.00 Fri–Sun only, Easter week daily) is well worth a visit to enhance your 'gorges' experience (see below). You can pick up walking maps in English here.

What to see and do The **Centro de Interpretación de las Foces (Gorges Interpretation Centre)** (inside the tourist office & with the same opening times; admission free) has laminated information sheets in English for a self-guided tour. The ground floor of this exhibition is given up to basic ethnographic displays, explaining the importance of vines and cereals to the area. On the first floor there is more information about Navarre's gorges, almost all of which are found in the Pyrenean and pre-Pyrenean regions. Most of the rocks in the Aois and Lumbier basins are sedimentary, the limestone being created from plants and the bones of animals which lived in the sea which once covered the region. Although wind-resistant, the limestone is gradually eroded by rain and river water, which dissolve it and result in the type of erosion known as karstic. This produces the many caverns and cavities found in the mountains of Leyre. If you intend to visit the gorges, there are some English-language leaflets available, which contain minute-scale maps. Two short films, one available in English, the other with subtitles, can also be seen here. One, shot in the Lumbier, shows – somewhat comically, in semi-cartoon fashion – a year in the life of a baby vulture, while the other concerns itself with the geology.

Seen from above, the **Foz de Arbayún (Arbayún Gorge)** (*mirador* (viewpoint) signposted off the NA-178, east of Lumbier town; free access at any time) is perhaps the most dramatic of all Navarre's gorges, a site to make you gawp from the strategically placed *mirador*. Indeed, Arbayún styles itself as 'La Reina de las

HORSERIDING

The **Club Hípico Arbayún** (clearly signposted in Usún; m 608 86 57 86 or 630 74 72 40; e info@clubhipicoarbayun.com; w clubhipicoarbayun.blogspot.com) is based in a beautiful rural setting at the foot of the Arbayún Gorge. Prices are very reasonable, with a half-day trip costing €35. Shorter and longer trips, including overnight excursions, are available, though English-speaking staff are not always available, so it's best to enquire before booking. Given the language barrier, enquiries are best done by email. Some trips are only suitable for intermediate or advanced riders.

LINEAR WALK TO THE NACEDERO DE UREDERRA

Unusually, this is a walk you have to reserve online, due to its popularity! Only 450 tickets (no charge) are available each day, with a view to protecting the environment (w nacederourederra.es; ⌚ 09.30–17.30). Distance: 5.3km; time: 2hrs 45mins; difficulty: easy/moderate, occasionally muddy and slippery underfoot, with a couple of moderate ascents. Bar/restaurant at beginning and end. Parking and the starting point is around 18km north of Estella at Baquedano (€4.50 when attended – but often not on w/days). If it all sounds too much trouble, you can search w turismo.navarra.es, where you will find some details of other walks and mountain biking routes in this area.

Starting in the Valle de Amescoa, this is a well-trodden path that leads to the *nacedero* (literally 'birthplace') of the Urederra River as it first sees daylight, emerging from the karstic massif courtesy of a beautiful waterfall beneath the looming rock faces of the Sierra de Urbasa. Baquedano, where you park your car, is a typically neat northern Navarran village and, if you time your walk correctly, there is a pleasant and well-priced bar/restaurant (page 270) at which you could dine on your return.

From the car park entrance, simply follow the wooden signs marked Urederra into Boquedano village. Continuing, make sure you keep left and walk in front of the newish *frontón* (*pelota* court). Before leaving the village, the concrete road passes the restaurant and soon you reach a fork in the road, where you take the left-hand fork, descending. Stay on this path, ignoring a fork to the right. Leave a picnic area to your right. There's a rich mix of trees on this walk, with oak, beech, maple, hawthorn and hazel to the fore. If you're lucky, you may also see some of the birdlife, such as Egyptian vultures, falcons, choughs and swifts. Note that fishing and camping are prohibited. Reaching an information board, in theory you can take either of the two forks, reserving the other for your return journey, but the right-hand fork is sometimes closed due to minor rockfalls. If that's the case it should be signed but, if in doubt, take the left-hand one. Assuming you take the left-hand (lower) one, you will reach an information hut and pass through a wooden gate, after which the path begins to climb. The river soon comes into view to your left and, at a clearing, the first, small waterfall appears. The path continues up by some chunky wooden handrails to another viewpoint, above the falls. Continuing, you reach an area optimistically signed 'Las Arenas' (The Sands). There is no sand here, but the brave are welcome to try the icy cold waters if they fancy a dip. You continue upwards and, on reaching a narrow wooden bridge, the sign (in Spanish) advises you that it can carry no more than eight people – so count carefully. After crossing a second bridge, you soon reach the source of the river, gushing from the rocks above and plunging around 20m into the river. The volume of water depends on the season, but it's always beautiful.

Your return is by the same route, or – subject to the advice given earlier – by the alternative route you ignored on the way up.

Foces Navarras' (Queen of the Navarre Gorges). Immodest, perhaps, but it's hard to dispute. The Salazar River, having risen in the Irati Forest, ends just south of the gorge after its 34km journey. Over time it has gouged its way through the limestone, creating vertical rock walls that extend for over 5km and reach – in places – a height of nearly 200m. Designated as a nature reserve and an area of special protection for birds, the dense vegetation of the valley floor is home to boar, deer and wildcat, though it would be a near miracle to spot any from the viewpoint. On rock ledges and riding the thermals are peregrine falcons, golden eagles, Egyptian vultures and over 220 breeding pairs of griffon vulture, while lower down the food chain are wallcreeper, Alpine swift and red-billed chough among the many recorded avian species. The *mirador* has a few information boards in English explaining the geology and fauna, but (depending on your direction of travel) you can obtain more information before or after your visit by stopping at the Gorges Interpretation Centre in Lumbier town (page 264). A pair of binoculars will greatly enhance your visit. It is also possible to swim in the river by accessing the gorge via Usún village, which is also off the NA-178, further west. If you decide to enter the gorge this way, the walk from the small car park at Usún is around 1.5km, with the chance of also visiting a hermitage a further 500m down the track.

Signposted off the NA-178, just west of Lumbier town, is the **Foz de Lumbier (Lumbier Gorge)** (free access, car park attendant present 09.00–20.00 to collect the €2; an English-language leaflet explains about the gorges, former railway & birdlife). It provides a different experience from Arbayún, as you enter the Lumbier Gorge at ground level through a longish former railway tunnel (torch advisable!), at the end of which you can take a swim in the river (freezing cold, even in August, according to the car park attendant). The walk up the old railway line is 1km on the flat, through a second tunnel and then turn around and come back. An alternative 5.5km circular walk begins off to the left, just before entering the tunnel, but offers no top-down views of the gorge and its latter section returns along the railway anyway so, unless you want the extra exercise, there's no great advantage. Birdlife is abundant in the Lumbier

MORE THAN JUST A HOUSE: *BASERRI*, THE BASQUE FARMSTEAD

David Elexgaray/Murray Stewart

The imposing, half-timbered, red-shuttered *baserri* (Basque farmhouse) is a distinctive feature of the countryside throughout the Basque Country and northern Navarre. For centuries, it was a productive and largely self-sufficient agricultural unit, representing a well-established social order that defined the relationships of the *baserri*'s inhabitants.

The law specified the succession and role of each family member, establishing that custodianship (not ownership) of the property, together with ultimate household authority, was passed down to just one heir or heiress, usually the eldest. This beneficiary would be duty-bound to manage the property, providing for those who remained living in the farmhouse and preserving and improving it for the next generation. With the passing of the property, the beneficiary's siblings would have to choose between moving out or 'staying put' under this fraternal authority. This law of succession has played a significant part in Basque history, 'encouraging' nose-out-of-joint Basque siblings to emigrate to the New Worlds, enter religious orders or marry into the families of nearby farms.

Curious, too, is the inseparable relationship between the property and the family name. Many Basque surnames refer to the location or type of *baserri* in which the bearer lives, hence the proliferation of names beginning with Etxe- (Basque for 'house'). Thus, 'Etxeverry' – 'new house' – is a common surname. An English lady living in northern Navarre recounts how, despite her 17 years of residence, the

Gorge, with vultures and other raptors soaring high and perching on the cliffs. Smaller species dart around lower down. There is a water fountain before entering the tunnel, and a barbecue and picnic area, but no café or refreshments on-site.

Monasterio San Salvador de Leyre (Yesa, on the NA-2113 off the A-21; 948 88 41 50; e visitas@monasteriodeleyre.com; w monasteriodeleyre.com; Mar–Jun, Sep & Oct 10.15–19.00, Jul & Aug 10.00–19.00, Nov–Feb 10.30–18.00, all daily, closed 24 & 25 Dec & 1 & 6 Jan; €3.20/1.70/free adults/under 12s/under 6s; guided visits available, but very expensive unless you're in a large group) Driving up to the monastery, you can enjoy views down to the Embalse de Yesa, only a tiny part of which lies inside Navarre (the rest is in Huesca province, Aragón). Some locals swim there in summer, though at the time of writing it was undergoing works to increase its capacity. The monastery itself is in a beautiful setting, and here you have a chance to speak to the monks and tour the crypt and the church. A small shop sells the herb liqueur concocted on-site by the 18 resident Benedictine monks. The acoustics in the church are tremendous, something you can sample via the Gregorian chanting at the monks' liturgies, should your visit coincide. Everyone is proud of the new organ, too, with its 2,750 pipes, and which arrived courtesy of EU money after the monks complained about the sound quality of the previous incumbent. Organ concerts and recitals take place through the year, with details to be found on the website.

Where to stay and eat

Villa Clementina [map, page 271] (9 rooms) Asunción 9, Murillo de Lónguida; 948 10 29 22; e info@hotelvillaclementina.com; w hotelvillaclementina.com. On the NA-150, 14km north of Lumbier, a 19th-century building that stands out with its unusual brick construction,

neighbours were still oblivious to her actual surname. They had christened her with a new Basque surname which translated as 'from the linen-making house', referring to the activity which had formerly taken place in her *baserri*.

The *baserri* façade is typically oriented at a 90° angle from east to south, maximising the sunlight, leaving the back portion for stables and storage, and giving the front living quarters protection from the north winds. Each self-sufficient farmhouse had an outdoor oven, a vegetable garden next to the house, as well as an orchard, pastures and a small wood for construction and heating. It would often have three storeys, with animals traditionally kept on the ground floor, thus helping to heat the living quarters above. (A Basque lady told me how, when visiting a neighbour, she commented that the house was a little warm. The neighbour responded by letting her cows out to graze!)

Ox blood was often used to colour the shutters, lime plaster being employed for the white walls. Timber somewhat disappeared from the construction after the 17th century, being replaced by stone. Visitors will note the distinctive lintel-stones which carry the name of the builder and the year of construction, as well as the *armarriak*, a stone on the front wall bearing the family name and coat of arms.

Twentieth-century industrialisation brought seismic changes to the Basque rural way of life. People moved to the cities, to work in factories and embrace consumerism. Still the *baserri* decorates the Basque landscape, but many are now successfully converted into guesthouses (*casas rurales*) and serving the tourist sector.

passed down through the generations & now run as a smart boutique hotel by the present charming owners. B/fast (extra cost) can be taken outside in summer. AC, free Wi-Fi. Dinner available on request (guests only). The nearest restaurant is 4km away. **€€€€**

Hotel Monasterio de Leyre (32 rooms) Yesa; 948 88 41 00; e hotel@monasteriodeleyre.com; w monasteriodeleyre.com; 1 Mar–9 Dec. Situated within the monastery building itself & offering comfortable rooms with free Wi-Fi & private bath. Singles, doubles & triples; only family rooms have TV. Bar & good-value restaurant on-site, with local specialities to the fore, including *pochas* (beans) & trout (€€). Booking essential in Easter week, & advisable in Jul & Aug. **€€**

NAVARRE'S WESTERN SIERRAS: ANDÍA, URBASA AND ARALAR

The landscape to the west and northwest of Pamplona distinguishes itself through the three mountain ranges, the high sierras of Andía, Urbasa and Aralar. While nowhere near reaching the heights of the Pyrenees, the highest peaks of this area still claim an altitude of over 1,400m. A road bisects each of the sierras from south to north, but the rugged terrain prevents many routes running through them from east to west. As a result, much of the territory is largely inaccessible by vehicle. Only the busy A-10, which carries endless volumes of traffic from Navarre to Vitoria-Gasteiz, squeezes itself westward through the one gap in the ranges, running north of Andía and Urbasa and south of Aralar. Aralar, the northernmost of the three sierras, spills into neighbouring Gipuzkoa province, with its highest peak (Irumugarrieta, 1,430m) marking the boundary and sitting equidistant between the two roads which connect Navarre with its western provincial neighbour.

To explore this area, you could drive south to north on the NA-120, taking in the Iranzu Monastery, then continue northwards and explore the Sierra Aralar and complete the loop back down through the Sierra de Urbasa on the NA-718. Alternatively, you could shorten the circuit after driving the NA-120, excluding Aralar by briefly following the A-10 westward until taking the turn-off at Alsasua and heading south on the NA-718, which crosses the beautiful Sierra de Urbasa on its way to Estella-Lizarra (page 272).

TOURIST INFORMATION Visitors to the area will find useful information, translated into English, at w tierrasdeiranzu.com. This site includes a variety of walking and cycling routes.

SIERRA DE ANDÍA

What to see and do

Monasterio de Iranzu (On the NA-7135, turn off the NA-120 at Abárzuza; 948 52 00 12; May–Sep 10.00–14.00 & 16.00–20.00 daily, Oct–Apr 10.00–14.00 & 16.00–18.00 Tue–Sun, closed Mon; €2.50/2/1.50 adults/seniors/children) For a monastery setting, Iranzu is close to perfection. In a wide valley, surrounded by fields of grazing sheep and impressive rock faces, only five monks from the Theatine Order now live here and benefit from the tranquillity. Worldwide, the total number of members of this order is less than 200.

Until 1839 the Cistercians occupied this monastery, until the infamous Confiscation Laws deprived them of their property and forced them out. For over a hundred years, the monastery lay empty and abandoned until restoration began in 1942. The Cistercian church is from the late 12th century, with the cloister being both Cistercian and Gothic (13th century). There is a seasonal tourist information centre here (Jul & Aug).

Mirador del Puerto de Lizarraga (viewpoint) If driving the NA-120 between Abárzuza and Lizarraga, after exiting the tunnel which carves through the mountain, look out for this viewpoint, from where you can admire the lush Ergoyena Valley below.

SIERRA DE ARALAR

Tourist information In a former train station, the tourist office at Lekunberri (Plazaola 21; ☎ 948 50 72 04; e oit.lekunberri@navarra.es; w plazaola.org; 🕘 summer months 10.00–14.00 & 16.00–19.00 Mon–Sat, 10.00–14.00 Sun, see website for other months) has an adjacent café and provides routes for walking, as well as bike hire (€20 per day, €15 half-day) and routes. A Vía Verde of some 50km follows the route of a former rail track, passing nearby – see the website for details.

What to see and do

Etxarri-Aranatz dolmens (Follow signposts off the NA-120 north of Etxarri-Aranatz for the camping site – the walk begins from there) Aralar is stuffed with prehistory, with no fewer than 44 dolmens and a solitary *menhir* in the territory. From the camping car park, two walks – one whole day (15km) and one half-day (10km) – let you explore the ancient stones. A signboard in the car park gives you directions and the routes are waymarked. The longer one takes you to ten different dolmens, while the shorter one lets you visit two.

Cuevas de Mendukilo (5km south of Lecumberri, direction Astitz; ☎ 948 39 60 95; w mendukilo.com; 🕘 visit schedule on website, advance enquiry recommended; €8/6 adults/children & seniors) Since 2005 three caves have been open here for 90-minute-long visits. They were previously used by shepherds for shelter. At present there are no tours in English. As an alternative to visiting them, continue your circuit by briefly following the A-10 westward, then taking the turn-off at Alsasua and heading south on the NA-718.

SIERRA DE URBASA Taking the road south to Estella is a joy, carving through the dense population of trees with daunting rock faces sometimes overhanging the road. The NA-718, to give this route its correct name, begins life at the junction with the Pamplona–Vitoria motorway and weaves its magic up and downhill for nearly 40km until it reaches the town of Estella. Ignoring Alsasua (which does, however, have good accommodation – see page 273), a town necessarily defined by quarrying activity, a huge cement works and some well-frequented truck-stops, this is a wonderful journey flanked on either side by the Sierra de Urbasa. First you follow the switchbacks spiralling you up the hill through thick forest. Then you arrive, not at first at the expected twisting, steep descent, but rather at a large plateau, a flat green pastureland with roaming horses, sheep and itinerant donkeys. Completely unheralded, apart from a couple of cattle-grids, the various beasts demand cautious driving. At 927m you cross the pass, the Puerto de Urbasa, and that much-anticipated descent does indeed begin, but not before you've caught your breath at the wondrous scenery below. After descending, you reach Baquedano, where you might wish to divert for a walk (see box, page 265) or simply continue on, noting the Sierra de Santiago de Lóquiz as its craggy rock faces demand your attention to the west.

Where to stay and eat Apart from the options immediately overleaf, Estella (page 272) makes a great base for those staying or touring in this area.

Hotel Lemik (7 rooms) Plaza de los Fueros 12, Alsasua; 948 56 43 71; e info@hotellemik.com; w hotellemik.com. A small, central, family-run hotel with on-site caféteria (see below). Chic, modern rooms are brightly furnished. Wi-Fi, TV lounge, good-value b/fast. **€€**

Hotel Palacio Dos Olivas (17 rooms) Plaza Luis Balerdi 2, Galdeano; 948 54 05 45; e recepcion@palaciodosolivos.com; w palaciodosolivos.com. Just off the NA-718, a few km north of Estella, is this beautifully renovated 13th-century palace. The building dominates the village & enjoys great views to the surrounding sierras & valley below. There is a cider-house/restaurant, available to non-residents (with advanced reservation), champagne bar, reading lounge, outdoor terrace, hot tub (extra charge) & gardens. Rooms vary but are spacious & modern, with TV, heating, some with hydro-massage bath, but no AC (unnecessary, says the owner). B/fast inc. **€€**

Bar-Restaurante Urederra La Fuente 15, Baquedano; 948 53 90 95. Recommended as a place to eat before or after the walk to the Nacedero de Urederra (see box, page 265). Booking advisable at w/ends & holidays. *Menus del día* only. **€€**

Lemik (see above) With a terrace overlooking the square, this place offers *pintxos*, & on Fri & Sat evenings, salads, hamburgers plus a limited selection of more local main dishes & desserts. Options for children, too. **€€**

SOUTHERN NAVARRE: LA ZONA MEDIA AND LA RIBERA

Southern Navarre's trick is to seem both large and small at the same time. Large, because the horizons are always immense, the roads empty outside of July and August; small, because the driving distances are always shorter than you might think from the map, and the towns and villages, when you reach them, are nearly always sleepy and compact.

Heading southwest of Pamplona, it is the settlements lining the Camino de Santiago which form the spine of the western Zona Media (Middle Zone) region before it reaches the border with the next-door province, La Rioja. Directly south of the capital, Olite, with its iconic palace, is the jewel; while to the east, empty terrain is punctured by the intrusion of yet another pilgrims' route that has crossed the Pyrenees at Jaca, in Aragón, to enter Navarre on its eastern border. As you move even further from north to south through La Zona Media and on to La Ribera, the southernmost bulge of Navarre, the vines and vegetables replace the Pyrenean pines, the people carrying umbrellas in summer are protecting themselves from the sun, not the rain, and drivers have to be prepared to apply their brakes to make way for shepherds and their canine assistants, nonchalantly guiding their sheep and goats down the main road. La Ribera's main natural attraction is undoubtedly the Bardenas Reales, the semi-desert masquerading as a mini Arizona. The Basque culture gradually thins out the further south you progress, and encountering Euskara as a language in the streets becomes increasingly rare. The river waters are no longer on their way to the Atlantic, but are heading firmly for the far-off Mediterranean, from which both the climate and the ambience now take their cue.

WEST OF PAMPLONA: THE CAMINO DE SANTIAGO

Puente la Reina (Gares) Just a day's walk (or 20 minutes' drive) to the southwest of Pamplona, Puente la Reina is significant as the place where two pilgrim routes meet, as the Camino Aragonés joins the Camino Francés, merging into one for the remainder of the long journey to Santiago de Compostela. Puente la Reina owes its prosperity, if not its very existence, to the pilgrims, with the town's charter being granted in 1122 to allow it to cash in on those passing through. Today, nearly 900 years on, it's much the same story. Puente la Reina is a linear town, and following the pilgrims along the town's Rúa Mayor from northeast to southwest will introduce you

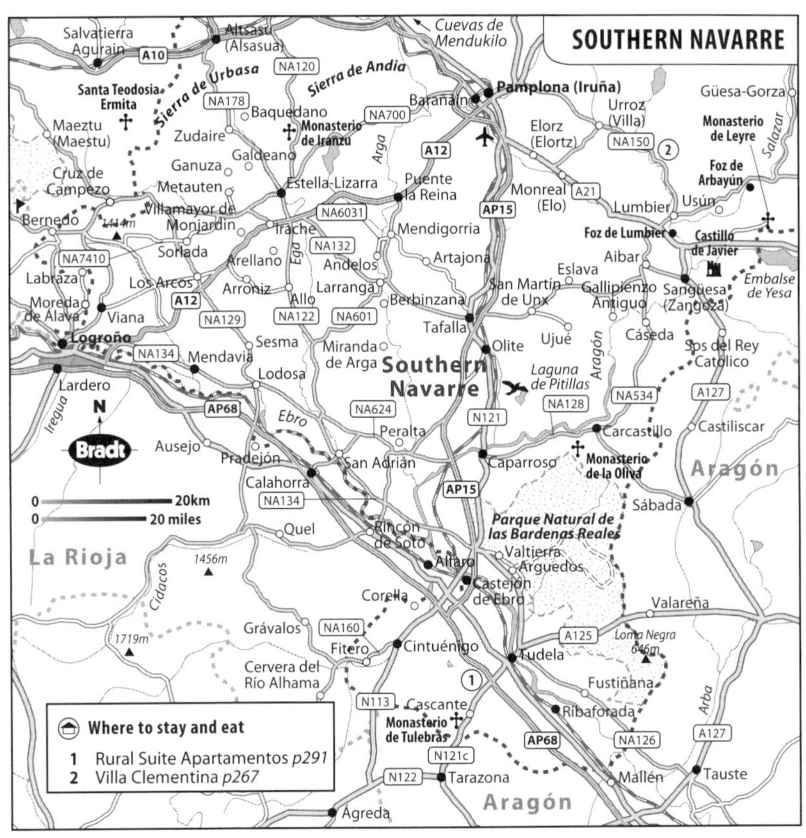

to virtually everything you need to see here: 12th-century churches, solid houses adorned with heavy doors, wrought-iron balconies bursting with geraniums. The main street ends with the river and the bridge. This Puente Románico with its seven arches spanning the Arga is undoubtedly the emblem of the town. At 110m long, it is generally considered to be one of the finest pieces of the Camino's architecture. It was built in the 11th century to assist the pilgrims, helping them to avoid greedy ferry operators who until then had fleeced them for the river crossing, but it is not clear exactly which queen ('*la Reina*' of the town's name) ordered its construction. The candidates are Doña Mayor, wife of Sancho el Mayor, or Doña Estefanía, wife of King García Sánchez III, so take your pick.

As well as the famous bridge, the Rúa Mayor is distinguished by the **Iglesia del Crucifijo** at the north end and by the **Iglesia de Santiago**, towards its midpoint. The former church is from Templar times, while the latter is a hotchpotch of Romanesque, 17th- and 18th-century constructions.

Reaching the end of the street, at the town end of the bridge is the **Casa del Vínculo**, a 17th-century warehouse once used to store wheat and other crops. It was enlarged at the start of the 18th century, part of it being converted into a prison and also to accommodate administration buildings. This purpose endured until the mid-20th century but, fully restored in 2004, it is now used for cultural events as well as housing the **tourist office** (Casa del Vínculo, by the bridge; 948 34 13 01; **w** puentelareina-gares.es; 10.00–14.00 & 16.00–19.00 Tue–Sat, 11.00–14.00 Sun & hols).

Where to stay

Albergue Jakue Irunbidea 948 34 10 17; e info@hoteljakue.com; w jakue.com. A hostel aimed at pilgrims, but no need to be one, or even to share a dormitory – or a bathroom – in this well-rated, central, budget option. Garden, terrace, free parking, shared lounge & Wi-Fi. **€€**

Hotel el Cerco (10 rooms) Rodrigo Ximenez de Rada 36; 948 34 12 69; e info@elcerco.es; w elcerco.es. A small, family-run hotel, beautifully fashioned out of a 12th-century tower. It's all tasteful stone, wood beams and subtle lighting. Rooms have TV, free Wi-Fi and AC. Friendly staff & management. **€€**

Estella-Lizarra Estella kicks a lot of life into the dawdling Camino, its narrow streets echoing with a bit of a buzz and its sprawling layout managing to project a feeling of size far beyond its 14,000 inhabitants. For visitors who are not Santiago-bound, or those who are but need a day's rest, here's a town with enough to detain you for a day. Being only 21km from Puente la Reina, this is logically the next staging-post for those pilgrims but, although they're here in their numbers, the town is big enough to comfortably absorb them and still carry on with its daily business. As long ago as the 12th century, Estella was already a rich place, its wealth deriving primarily from the right granted to hold a market, bestowing on it an importance that carried weight not only in the immediate surrounding region but also beyond.

The second source of its wealth came, of course, from the passing pilgrims, and the riches that flowed enabled the building of no fewer than 11 churches, many of which remain today. Today, some locals will tell you that there are two Estellas of interest to the visitor, one on either side of the river. Slap-bang in the centre of town, the large Plaza de los Fueros comes alive in late afternoon, a stereotypically Spanish focal point full of kids kicking footballs, practising cartwheels and playing tag as soon as the school day is done; their watching parents chat animatedly at the plaza's cafés.

But across the River Ega, lined up along the tranquil Calle de la Rúa, are a number of places of historical interest, directly on the pilgrim route but perhaps ignored by those weary walkers obsessed with the singular purpose of finding a bed for the night. And it's equally easy for those already in the town centre to never traverse the bridge and see those churches, museums and palaces across the water. The stream of pilgrims means that hotel accommodation can fill up quickly as pilgrims seek solace from dormitories and snorers. For cyclists seeking a flat route, the Vía Verde de Ferrocarril (Greenway) runs along the old train line from here all the way to Vitoria-Gasteiz. For the more serious two-wheeled fanatic, the hard grind up the valleys to the north of town, between the sierras of Urbasa and Andía, will pose a far more serious challenge.

Getting there and away At least a dozen **buses** daily depart from the Plaza Coronación to Pamplona (50mins; €4.25), and around nine to Logroño (1hr; €4.75). You can also connect to San Sebastián, as well as Hendaya/Irun, Calahorra and a few other destinations with lesser frequency, including Madrid (5hrs; €25). See w laestellesa.com for full timetables and fares. Weekend frequencies are heavily reduced.

Tourist information The official tourist office (Plaza San Martin; 948 55 63 01; w estellaturismo.com; Jun–end Aug 10.00–15.00 & 16.00–18.00 Mon–Sat, 10.00–14.00 Sun, Sep–Jun 10.00–17.00 Mon–Sat, 10.00–14.00 Sun) is sensibly positioned on the Camino de Santiago, with helpful English-speaking staff. English-language

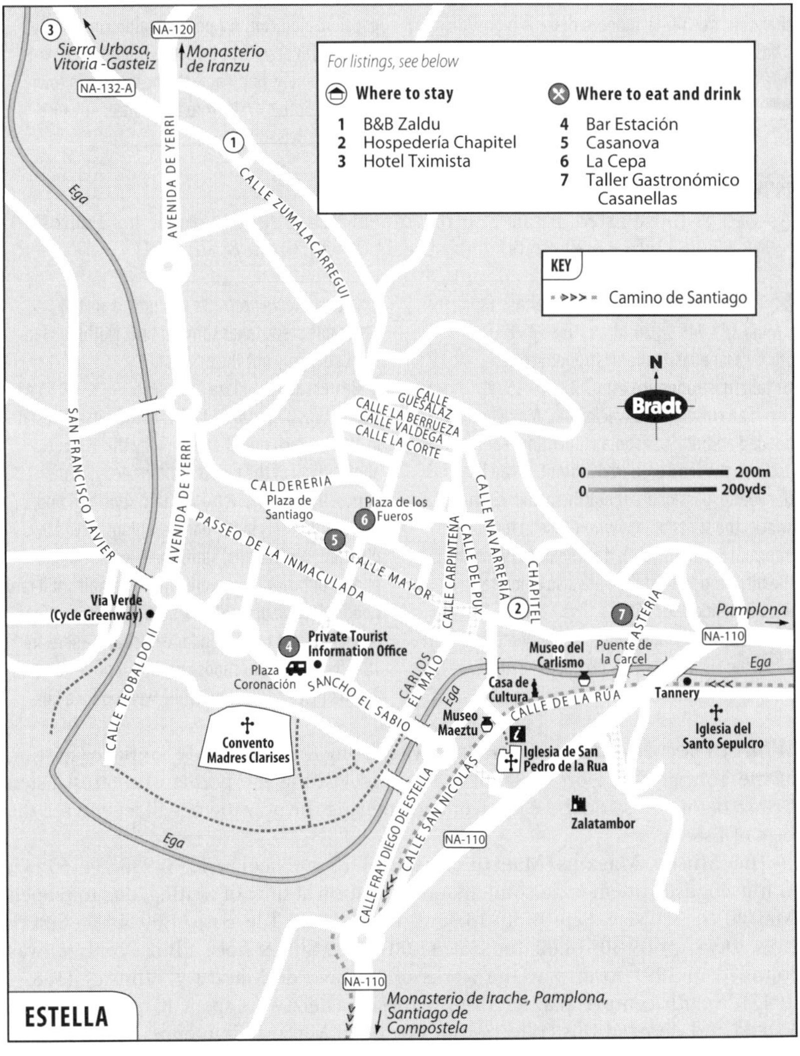

ESTELLA

For listings, see below

Where to stay
1 B&B Zaldu
2 Hospedería Chapitel
3 Hotel Tximista

Where to eat and drink
4 Bar Estación
5 Casanova
6 La Cepa
7 Taller Gastronómico Casanellas

KEY
Camino de Santiago

Sierra Urbasa, Vitoria -Gasteiz
NA-120
Monasterio de Iranzu
NA-132-A
Avenida de Yerri
Calle Zumalacárregui
Ega
San Francisco Javier
Calle Gueşalaz
Calle La Berrueza
Calle Valdega
Calle La Corte
Caldereria
Plaza de Santiago
Plaza de los Fueros
Passeo de la Inmaculada
Calle Mayor
Calle Carpintería
Calle del Puy
Calle Navarrería
Chapitel
Asteria
Pamplona
NA-110
Via Verde (Cycle Greenway)
Calle Teobaldo II
Private Tourist Information Office
Plaza Coronación
Sancho el Sabio
Carlos el Malo
Museo del Carlismo
Puente de la Carcel
Casa de Cultura
Calle de la Rúa
Tannery
Museo Maeztu
Iglesia del Santo Sepulcro
Iglesia de San Pedro de la Rua
Convento Madres Clarises
Calle San Nicolás
Calle Fray Diego de Estella
Zalatambor
Monasterio de Irache, Pamplona, Santiago de Compostela
200m
200yds
Bradt

guided visits to the town can sometimes be arranged, advance notice is required. Be aware that a private 'tourist information office' is located in the old train station building on the Plaza Coronación; it partners up with selected local entreprises, so its information may be prone to commercial influences.

 *Where to stay* *Map, above*

Hospedería Chapitel (14 rooms) Chapitel 1; 948 55 10 90; e contacto@hospederiachapitel.com; w hospederiachapitel.com. The best address in the town centre, where to stay if you're a pilgrim deluxe. You'll pay a bit extra for the pleasure, but it still remains a good price/quality balance, set in a 17th-century building in the town's old quarter. Rooms enjoy AC, TV, free Wi-Fi & a private balcony. Advance booking essential in summer. **€€€**

Hotel Tximista (29 rooms) Zaldu 15; 948 55 58 70; e info@hoteltximista.com; w sanvirilahoteles.com. To the northwest of town, an unusual former flour mill by the river houses a good, mid-range option. AC, TV with international channels, free Wi-Fi, modern décor & high-quality b/fast justify the price. If you book the pilgrim rate, b/fast comes free. €€€

B&B Zaldu (4 rooms) Travesía Pío Baroja 1; 948 55 22 63; m 636 11 69 43; e info@pensionzaldu.com; w pensionzaldu.com. Some rooms with private bath, some shared. Free Wi-Fi. Small, homely, popular & the best value in town, though 15mins' walk from the centre. Advance booking advisable. €

Where to eat and drink *Map, page 273*

As well as those listed, locals also recommend **La Cepa** (Plaza de los Fueros 15; 948 55 00 32; 13.00–16.00 daily, also 21.00–22.30 Sat & Sun; €€).

Taller Gastronómico Casanellas Espoz y Mina 3; 948 98 26 11; m 638 91 28 38; e casanellas@tallergastronomico.es; w tallergastronomico.es; 13.30–15.00 Tue–Sat, closed last 3 weeks Aug. A much-needed addition to Estella's lunchtime eating options, the food prepared in front of you by the young, passionate (English-speaking) chefs knocks the spots off anywhere else in town. Informal & delightful. 1-day cooking courses in the ultra-modern kitchen are also of interest. Recommended. €€€

Casanova Fray Wenceslao de Oñate 7; 948 55 28 09; 13.00–15.30 & 19.15–22.00 Tue–Fri. A solid, unsophisticated menu with generous portions: the *menestra de verduras*, a sort of vegetable stew, takes some eating. Nothing's fancy here, certainly not the prices. €€

Bar Estación Plaza Coronación 1; 948 55 43 16; 06.30–23.00 daily. The station itself closed in 1967, which might explain why this is a cut above many of the world's (often seedy) station bars. A handsome, Neo-Romanic-style building, lively with locals in the early evening, served by pleasant, professional staff. There are a few old photos of how things were when the trains still ran. Good selection of *tortillas* & *bocadillos*, with a few fancier *pintxos* too. If you fancy a cuppa, there are 18 different teas to choose from, but no restaurant. A good place to kill time while waiting for a bus.

What to see and do A 'contraflow' walk along the Camino de Santiago, starting at the Tourist Office on Calle de la Rúa and visiting the points of interest listed below, before crossing the Ega River and entering the new town, will let you see the best of Estella.

The **Museo Maeztu (Maeztu Museum)** (San Nicolás 1; 948 54 60 37; w museogustavodemaeztu.com; under renovation at time of writing, due to reopen Mar 2019; May–Sep 09.30–13.30 & 16.00–19.00 Tue–Sat, 11.00–14.00 Sun & hols, Oct–Apr 09.30–14.00 Tue–Sat, 11.00–14.00 Sun & hols; admission free) was founded in 1991 to display the works of Gustavo de Maeztu y Whitney (1887–1947), a 20th-century painter from Vitoria-Gasteiz who spent his final years in Estella and donated this collection to the town. Maeztu's influences include Goya and Velázquez, among many others. English-language information is available at the reception. Located in the former Palacio de los Reyes de Navarra (Palace of the Kings of Navarre), which dates from the 12th century, the ground floor was where the incumbent King of Navarre would press the flesh with his subjects, when he wasn't waving to them regally from the first-floor balconies. On one of the capitals outside is a depiction of the battle between Roland – commonly assumed to be Charlemagne's nephew – and Ferragut, a Saracen giant.

Estella's main church is the **Iglesia de San Pedro de la Rúa (Church of St Peter)** (Calle de la Rúa; 10.00–13.30 & 18.00–20.00 Mon–Sat, 10.00–13.30 Sun; admission free), with a 13th-century arched door and interior influences ranging from Romanesque and Gothic to Baroque. From the tourist office opposite the church entrance, make sure you pick up a city map and guide, in English, for in-depth architectural details. A signboard on the steps also provides information. The demolition of the town's Zalatambor Castle in 1572 resulted in damage to the church's roof and cloister. Inside the church there is a poignant poem addressed to visiting pilgrims, its translation into no fewer than seven languages reflecting the diverse nationalities of the walkers: 'You are blessed, pilgrim, if your rucksack becomes emptier and emptier of clutter, while your heart struggles to find room to hang on to so many emotions.'

As some of the town's other churches have closed across the years, their altarpieces, paintings and sculptures have been transferred to San Pedro, and its recent restoration has given it true splendour. The cloister is sometimes used as a venue for a local artist to display his work and is dominated by a giant hundred-year-old *Abies pinsapo* (Spanish fir) tree. If you exit the rear of San Pedro, you will observe how Estella is positioned in a natural basin, surrounded by rocks.

Further along the Calle de la Rúa, at number 6, is the **Casa de Cultura (House of Culture)**, formerly the palace of Fray Diego de Estella, who was a confidant to King Felipe II. Although not really a visitor attraction, you are welcome to poke your head in for a look at the courtyard. Further on, on the other side, you can see up above to the right the remains, high on the rock, of **Zalatambor**, the castle of Estella. Originally part of Navarre's defence against troublesome Castile, the castle was abandoned and then destroyed in the 16th century, not by marauding armies but by the locals when they determined that it had outlived its use as a defensive structure. The creation of the *ciudadela* in Pamplona (page 242) had lessened the importance of Estella as a fortress, so the good citizens of the town simply blew up their own castle and used the rocks in other construction projects in the area.

Also in Calle de la Rúa is the attractively restored 12th-century **Palacio del Gobernador (Governor's Palace)**, now home to the **Museo del Carlismo (Carlism Museum)** (Calle de la Rúa 27–29; ☎ 948 55 21 11; w museodelcarlismo.navarra.es; ⏲ 10.00–14.00 & 16.00–19.00 Tue–Sat, 11.00–14.00 Sun & holidays; €2/1/free adults/students/children, pilgrims & over 65s; free to all Sat pm & Sun). Bought as a ruin by the town council in 2000, this handsome early 17th-century palace has been renovated to its elegant glory and put to use to record an important movement in European history. Carlism can be seen as part of an 18th/19th-century European Counter-Revolutionary movement, which was particularly strong in Navarre, Catalonia and the Basque Country, determined to protect religion and reject the revolutionary movements of the time. In Spain, the Carlist Wars concerned both an ideological struggle and a dispute over the right to the throne. The story of Carlism is told here through interactive displays, but for English speakers a returnable booklet can be collected from reception along with your ticket, giving direct English translations of all the museum's wall panels. Occasional temporary exhibitions here seek to explore aspects of Carlism in greater depth.

Next, the bridge across the river to your left is the arched **Puente de la Carcel**, a 20th-century reconstruction of a previous medieval one. At your feet, note the gold markings embedded in the road surface (Calle de la Rúa has now become Rúa Curtidores (Tanners' Street)). These tiny, golden maps of Spain tell you that this is the road to Jerusalem, or the Camino a Cultura Judía. Next on your right is the **Iglesia del Santa Sepulcro (Church of the Holy Sepulchre)**, built in the 12th century, but which has been closed since the end of the 19th. On the left and plastered with adverts for pilgrim accommodation is the old **tannery**, which is currently closed but is well preserved inside. There are plans to turn it into a museum and exhibition space. Above you to the right are the walls of the old **Jewish quarter**; unusually, the Jews had a quarter away from the town itself, with its own walls. The Jews' tenure in this part of town was short-lived, less than 50 years. By 1135 they had abandoned the area, relocating elsewhere in town, and shortly afterwards the synagogue was given to the Bishop of Pamplona to be replaced by a church. Continuing your walk, now you retrace your steps, cross the 'medieval' bridge over the river and proceed into the 'new' town. You will soon enter the parish of **San Miguel**; in the Middle Ages, each parish of the town would have had its own church, town council and walls. The long **Calle Mayor** is the venue at the start of August for Estella's own *encierro*, though it's the cows, not bulls, who run here. Looking down the **Calle Gaiteros**, you will see the City Hall. Estella's **food market** takes place every Thursday in the **Plaza de los Fueros**, and has done for hundreds of years.

Around Estella To the north of town rise the high limestone sierras of Urbasa and Andía (page 268), part of the Basque mountains that lie between the Cantabrian range and the western Pyrenees. Continuing to the southwest of Estella, the Camino pilgrims reach Ayegui and then the settlement of Irache with its monastery, winery, wine museum and curious free wine fountain, all clustered together.

Bodegas Irache Museo del Vino (wine museum and winery) (Ayegui, off NA-1110; ☎ 948 55 519 32; w irache.com; ⏲ museum: 10.00–14.00 & 16.00–18.00 Sat & Sun only; guided tours of the winery are by appointment only, €7 or €12, depending on option chosen) Although this winery has been producing wines since 1891, the art of viniculture in the area stretches back to at least the 12th century. The museum has a collection of winemaking equipment, but has information only in Spanish and is of somewhat limited interest. Downstairs, you'll find the Cava Centenaria, a cellar that was created as far back as the First Carlist War and stores a private collection of barrels of the best wines, some dating back to 1933. Naturally, you can buy wine here, of better quality than the free stuff available at the famous fountain next door. The Irache label is the winery's premier product, though cheaper wines are available, too.

Monasterio de Irache (Irache Monastery) (Address as per Bodegas Irache (see above); ⏲ winter 10.00–13.15 & 16.00–18.00 Wed–Sun, summer 10.00–13.15 & 16.00–19.00 Tue–Sun; admission free) Perhaps worth a visit if you are combining it with a museum and wine fountain trip (see above and below), this was the site of Navarre's very first pilgrim hospital, built in the 11th century. The Romanesque church is of 12th-century construction. For over 250 years, until 1824, there was also a university here and it has also served as a military hospital in times gone by. A crucial lack of monks has meant that the monastery has now been uninhabited since 1985.

Bodegas Irache Fuente del Vino (wine fountain) (⏲ 08.00–20.00 daily; admission free) As the pilgrims pass by the Bodegas Irache, they are in for a treat. In the true spirit of the Camino, this *bodega* offers them free and unlimited wine from a tap fixed to a wall outside. Helpfully, there's a water fountain too, but unsurprisingly it's largely ignored. There's even a webcam here now, allowing you to go online and see which of your fellow pilgrims have been drinking the most. On a hot day, many of the pilgrims soon regret having emptied the water from their bottles and replacing it with wine.

Villamayor de Monjardín An attractive town glued to a hillside, nevertheless Villamayor has but one tick-box attraction. Catching the eye of those travelling on the A-12 road, the building that dominates the town looks like a monastery but turns out to be the substantial, decidedly non-monastic building of the **Bodega Castillo de Monjardín** (☎ 948 53 74 12; w monjardin.es; ⌚ 09.00–19.00 Mon–Fri, 11.00–14.00 Sat), a young winery whose signature product is its Chardonnay. With notice, it can organise winery visits and tastings, and it also has a restaurant. Above the well-preserved town, the less well-preserved remains of a medieval fortress perch on the hilltop, but are not really worth a visit unless you're in the mood for a steep hike.

Villa de las Musas: Museo Arqueológico de Arellano (Arellano Archaeological Museum/Roman Villa) (Signposted & accessed between Arroniz & Allo, off the NA-6340, between km3 & km4; ☎ 948 74 12 73; w guiartenavarra.com; ⌚ Oct–Mar 10.00–14.00 & 15.00–18.00 Fri & Sat, 10.00–14.00 Sun, Apr–Jul 10.00–14.00 & 15.00–19.00 Fri & Sat, 10.00–14.00 Sun, Aug 10.00–14.00 & 16.00–20.00 Wed–Sat, 10.00–14.00 Sun; €3/1 adults/children & seniors) In rolling countryside amid olive groves and fields of cereal, the sheer compactness of this Roman villa has allowed a roof to be put over it to protect it from the elements. Archaeological digs have determined construction dates for the various rooms as being between the 1st and 5th centuries AD. Known as the 'Villa of the Muses' due to a mosaic depicting nine goddesses, there are also remains of a wine cellar, *fumarium* (smoke chamber, used to artificially age the wine) and press room, all showing that much of the villa was dedicated to producing wine. The mosaic was only discovered during vine-planting in 1882; what you see here is a replica, with the original now stored in the National Archaeology Museum in Madrid.

Los Arcos Another logical stop on the Camino, being 21km southwest of Estella, Los Arcos is dutifully awash with bars and restaurants offering 'pilgrim menus'. Little remains of the town's medieval history, save for two gates that once formed part of the city walls, together with its huge church, the **Iglesia de Santa María (Church of Our Lady)**, which is one of Navarre's biggest. Fiesta time here is the third week in August, with bull-running and bullfights.

Sorlada Off the pilgrims' route – but retaining associations with it – is Sorlada's impressive hilltop **Basílica de San Gregorio Ostiense** (off the NA-7410; ⌚ closed for renovation at time of writing, but normally 11.30–13.30 & 16.15–19.00 Sat, occasionally Sun; admission free, but donation expected). This 17th/18th-century Baroque basilica was built in tribute to the bishop who saved (and, it is said, continues to save) the area's agricultural produce from plague and pestilence. Arriving in the 11th century by mule all the way from his Bishopric in Ostia near Rome, Gregory had been nominated by the then Pope to find a solution to the disease that had wreaked havoc to the crops around Sorlada. After his arrival, the plague disappeared and murals in the church illustrate the story. Gregory died in 1144, but is thought to have been one of the Camino de Santiago's first pilgrims. He lives on in the popular phrase 'Travelling more than the head of St Gregory', said to hark back to the tradition of 'borrowing' the saint's skull and carrying it through the fields of neighbouring towns and villages, with water being poured through it to ensure a healthy harvest, free from disease.

If you want to see all the images of the Virgins from the most important churches in Navarre, there is an exhibition, hidden away behind a low door inside the church. Upstairs in the neighbouring building is a permanent exhibition of models of all the key cathedrals along the Camino de Santiago. Made out of plastic and illuminated, they are hardly beautiful, but they are most certainly unique. Outside, the views from the hill are excellent, reaching to the mountains of Codés, Lóquiz and Andía, weather permitting. In May, pilgrimages are made here from the nearby valleys. From the car park, a short walk will lead you to some stone towers, believed to be half-finished sculptures whose origin is unknown.

Viana On a hill 18km from Los Arcos, Viana is the last significant stop on the Camino in Navarre and allows pilgrims to see ahead of them the city of Logroño, the capital of the autonomous community of La Rioja and famed for its lively bar culture, less than 10km away. Not many will choose, therefore, to stay the night in Viana, which is characterised by one long street running along a ridge before it descends to the flat plain that ushers visitors into La Rioja. For those who do choose to linger, there is one of the few civil Gothic buildings in Navarre, the **Casa de Cultura**, formerly a pilgrims' hospital. The **Ayuntamiento (council building)** in the Plaza de los Fueros displays some elegance, this time Baroque, while the **Iglesia de Santa María de la Asunción (Church of Our Lady of the Assumption)** is a 13th-century Gothic edifice with many subsequent modifications across the centuries. For pilgrims, Viana is a stiff climb up, then a climb down again; for others, it is a town of only moderate interest.

Roughly 3km southwest of Viana and squeezed into Navarre just before the La Rioja border is the **Embalse de las Cañas** (w www.lagunadeviana.es), a reservoir that is also a nature reserve and area of special protection for birds.

SOUTH OF PAMPLONA: OLITE AND THE CENTRAL ZONA MEDIA Directly south of the Navarrese capital, the topography can seem a bit mundane compared with the mountains to the north or gorges to the east. Flatlands are, however, ripe for human habitation and history fans will be delighted to discover remains of prehistoric, Roman and more recent occupation to liven up the landscape. At the end of a short drive southward, the town of Olite ranks as the 'must-visit' of this central part of Navarre. La Zona Media is the transitional region between the mountain regions of the north and the fertile plains of the south, containing 11 towns, including Olite, Artajona, Mendigorria, Ujué, Pitillas and Berbinzana, all of which hold some interest for visitors.

Andelos Roman Site and Archaeology Museum (Signposted off the NA-601 – take the NA-6031 south of Mendigorria; t 948 74 12 73; w guiartenavarra.com; summer 10.00–14.00 & 15.00–19.00 Fri & Sat only (Wed–Sat in Aug), 10.00–14.00 Sun, winter (Sep–Mar) 10.00–14.00 & 15.00–18.00 Fri & Sat, 10.00–14.00 Sun & holidays; €2/1/free adults/under 13s & seniors/under 6s) Amid the gently rolling wheat/barley fields close to Mendigorria you'll find one of Navarre's most important archaeological sites, the Roman town of Andelos. Milestones unearthed here demonstrate that Andelos was at the significant road junction between Jaca, Pamplona and Logroño, which makes sense of what otherwise might be a puzzlingly isolated location. In fact, the site at Andelos is split into three distinct parts: the museum and town, the water reservoir and, some 3km away, the impressive remains of a dam. The last two are accessible at any time, without charge, while a nominal entrance fee admits you to the small museum and main site, but more importantly gets you the English-language leaflet that gives an impression of the Roman town (the display panels are only in Spanish). Andelos's most intriguing feature is the intricate water supply system created by the Romans, which involved the dam, an aqueduct, reservoir and water tower. Remains of a laundry, porched street and baths are also visible, as well as some traces of a medieval settlement that occupied the site in the 14th century, before being abandoned after the Great

Plague. Once you've seen the main site, museum and nearby water reservoir, it's best to take the car down the stony track to the dam, not walk as the information leaflet suggests, unless you're in the mood for the 6km return trip. It's worth the car journey, however: a raised wooden platform gives you a better view and you may have the place to yourself, except for a few croaking frogs who make their presence known from inside the *arquetas* (water reservoirs).

Cerco de Artajona (Artajona; w reinodeartajona.com; free access, free admission; there is a tourist office within the site ☎ 670 48 19 65; ⏲ Jul & Aug 10.00–14.00 & 16.00–19.00 daily, other months less frequently, through which guided visits to the church can be arranged)) Almost *too* well restored, the hilltop Cerco de Artajona is still a hugely imposing, medieval French-style fortress town, once a key location in the defence of Navarre. Construction of the original town began in 1085, though the fortifications currently visible are from the 13th century: the town has been destroyed and rebuilt many times throughout Navarre's turbulent history. Nine of its original 14 towers are still intact, their square bulk dominating the 700m circumference. The San Saturnino fortress-church within the site replaced an earlier Romanesque church, but opens only for guided tours. Some information panels around the site are in English, though in truth there is not too much to see once you've breached the fortress walls and enjoyed the spectacular views. At night-time the site is occasionally floodlit, but there are no set dates – check the website. Just 500m along the road to the north of town lies the large building of the Ermita de Nuestra Señora de Jerusalén, a hermitage that is not open to visitors.

Dólmenes de Artajona (Signposted off the NA-6020, north of Artajona; free access) Near to Artajona, though a bit off the beaten track, are these two dolmens, some of the most southerly in Navarre and dating from between 3000BC and 1800BC. The nearest dolmen, the Portillo de Eneriz, is a mere 40m from the parking spaces, clearly signed, but to get to the second, La Miña de Farangotea, you need to walk along the wide path (signposted) for 500m, before turning left where indicated up a narrow track for 250m through the pine forest, heading towards the wind turbines until you reach the sign and dolmen. It's a pleasant walk, but you won't see anything at La Miña that you haven't already seen at the Portillo. There are information boards at the site, in Spanish only.

'Las Eretas' Berbinzana (Iron Age settlement and museum) (Berbinzana; ☎ 948 72 21 76; w eretas.es; ⏲ Jul & Aug 10.00–14.00 & 17.00–19.30 Fri & Sat, 10.00–14.00 Sun & holidays, Apr–Jun, Sep & Oct 10.00–14.00 & 17.00–19.30 Sat, 10.00–14.00 Sun, Nov–Mar 10.00–14.00 & 16.00–18.00 Sat, 10.00–14.00 Sun; €4/2/free adults/seniors & children/over 75s, under 7s & disabled) Discovered only in 1991, this settlement nevertheless dates back over 2,600 years. It is estimated that only one-fifth of the site has been excavated to date. Originally there would have been only a fortification with walls and towers here, with the nearby River Arga offering additional protection. The stronghold was then converted into a small village of perhaps 150–200 people, with houses and a central street. The outdoor exhibit shows the original foundations of several structures, plus a reconstructed house and tower. A leaflet in English is provided with your ticket, but make sure you are also given the (returnable) booklet which has translations of all the wall panels in the museum, which are in Spanish and Basque. Topics covered include death rituals, agriculture, trade and currency. There is also a short film about the Iron Age in general, as well as about the Berbinzana settlement, available in English.

Olite (Erriberri) Once of enormous importance for strategic reasons, Olite was one of the chosen seats of the Kings of Navarre, owing its medieval prosperity to the privileges granted to it by King García Ramírez in the year 1147. The foundation of the town probably stretches back to AD621, but a walled Roman settlement was undoubtedly sited here long before then. Now the town's significance derives from tourism and wine production, the latter encouraged by the Mediterranean climate and evidenced by the many *bodegas* in and around town, many of which can be visited. And as for alcohol-free tourism, Olite has the Palacio Real, an outstanding French Gothic-style monument dating from the 14th and 15th centuries and restored to great glory over a 40-year period starting in the 1930s. Ask an eight-year-old child to draw a palace and they might come up with something like this, all towers and pointy turrets. But despite its notable visitor attractions, Olite remains largely unspoilt, with its narrow medieval streets, noble houses and ample squares almost totally free of the souvenir shops that can be found in myriad places of lesser interest.

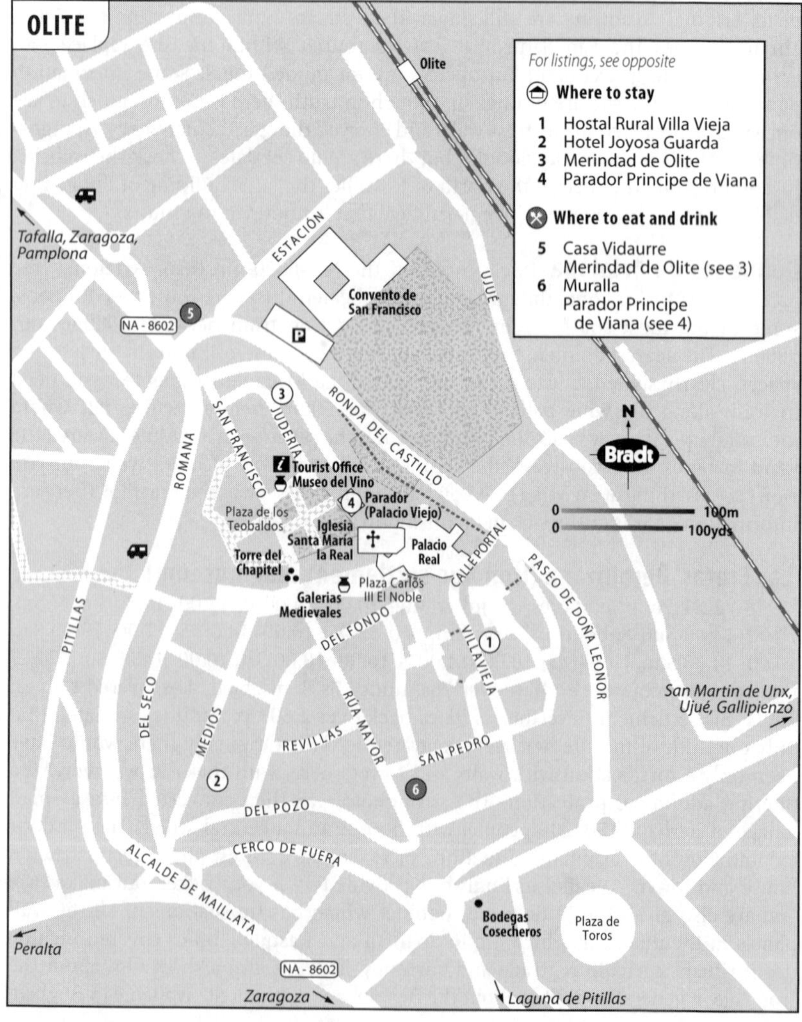

Culturally, the second half of August is Olite's time to let its hair down, with its medieval festival awash with sorcerers, jugglers, musicians, knights and troubadours, as well as a popular market. With little time taken to draw breath, the first part of September then sees the town turn its attention to celebrating the grape harvest. Outside of festival times, many of those quaint streets remain quiet, with everyday life centred on the two squares, the Plaza de Carlos III el Noble, formerly the venue for bullfights, and the Plaza de los Teobaldos, named in honour of the Kings of Navarre who bore that name ('Thibaut'). The square-side bars can be packed to the rafters, especially on sunny Sunday lunchtimes. Another Olite claim to fame is at number 5, Rúa Mayor, where a plaque commemorates the birthplace of Spanish composer Jesús García Leoz, who wrote the soundtrack to the 1953 comedy film *Bienvenido, Mr Marshall!*

Getting there and away

By train Many trains pass through Olite, but not all of them stop. Pamplona (40mins; €4) can be reached three times per day and in the other direction three trains depart for Zaragoza (1hr 40mins; €11.35). There are two trains to Vitoria-Gasteiz (2hrs; €10.45) and one direct service to Burgos (4hrs; €22). You can also travel by rail to Tudela (40mins, €5.20), Tafalla (5mins; €2.15) and the major rail junction of Miranda del Ebro in La Rioja (3hrs 30mins; €17). Five minutes' walk from the town centre, Olite's train station is otherwise a hive of inactivity, unmanned, so you buy your ticket on the train.

By bus Around 15 buses depart for Pamplona each day, stopping in Tafalla, with the company La Tafallesa (948 70 09 79). On Saturdays, the number reduces to 11 and dwindles on Sundays to six. Journey time is around 45 minutes, tickets are €3.50.

Parking If arriving by car, the best option to park is in front or at the side of the convent, where it is free and unlimited [map, opposite].

Tourist information (Plaza de los Teobaldos 10; 948 74 17 03; Easter week & May–mid-Oct 10.00–14.00 & 16.00–19.00 Mon–Sat, 10.00–14.00 Sun, mid-Oct–Apr 10.00–14.00 Sun–Thu, 10.00–14.00 & 15.00–18.00 Fri & Sat) Visitors can pick up a map with detailed information, in English, about the town's main points of interest. The building also houses the Wine Museum (page 283).

Where to stay *Map, opposite*

Parador Principe de Viana (43 rooms) Plaza de los Theobaldos 2; 948 74 00 00; w paradores-spain.com. Housed in the former palace, a grand old 3-star establishment which welcomes you with watchful suits of armour in its entrance hall. Definitely the smartest & most expensive place in town, but super-central & not overpriced. AC, satellite TV, free Wi-Fi. **€€€**

Hostal Rural Villa Vieja (11 rooms) Villavieja 11; 948 74 17 00; e info@hostalvillavieja.com; w hostalvillavieja.com. A newish *hostal* in the Old Town, with free Wi-Fi, heating, TV with cable channels & free public parking close by. Two rooms have a 'palace' view; some have hydro-massage baths; one is adapted for those of lesser mobility. A pleasant welcome, a good choice without any pretensions. Good b/fast, at extra cost. **€€**

Hotel Joyosa Guarda (24 rooms) Rúa de Medios 21; 948 74 13 03; e hotellajoyosaguarda@gmail.com; w lajoyosaguarda.com. Sharing its name with the watchtower in the Palacio Real, in a quiet street close to the centre. Modern interior within an 18th-century mansion house. Spacious tiled reception, with parking (extra charge), a lovely courtyard for b/fast & a restaurant on-site. Some rooms have a balcony, & all are to a high level with AC & TV. Some suites have fancy showers, but the spacious standard bathrooms will satisfy most guests. Free Wi-Fi. **€€**

Merindad de Olite (10 rooms) Rúa de la Judería 11; 948 74 07 35; e reservas@hotelmerindaddeolite.com; w hotelmerindaddeolite.com. Some rooms are compact, with TV & AC, some with bath, some with shower. Free Wi-Fi. While they're simply furnished, the reception is fancier & more ornate. Management keep it all spick & span. The building has parts of the old city incorporated into its structure. Close to the centre, but not too close to the noise. Good b/fast (extra cost). **€€**

Where to eat and drink *Map, page 280*

The places to *tapear* (yes, we've almost moved too far south for *pintxos*) are centred on the two main squares. But if you want somewhere a bit quieter to dine …

Parador Principe de Viana (page 281) lunch & dinner daily. Slightly pricier menus than elsewhere in town, but the food quality, elegant setting & service make it all justifiable. If 'fancy' isn't your thing, they have a popular cafeteria, too. €€€€

Merindad de Olite (see above) 13.00–16.00 & 20.00–23.00 Wed–Mon, closed Tue. There's no sign of tapas on the counter, but don't fret: look at the blackboard, they'll produce them fresh and deliver them to your table. In the restaurant, you can choose your wine from the excellent shop at the back, with just a modest extra charge for drinking it with your meal. Luis, the owner, welcomes his foreign clients with translated menus and by opening early, by Spanish standards, at 20.00 in the evening. The food's good, too. €€€

Muralla Rúa Mayor 31; 948 74 15 10; 13.00–16.00 & 20.00–23.00 daily. A simple dining room with upstairs restaurant & small courtyard, serving well-priced *menus del día*, tapas & sandwiches. Bar downstairs. €€

Casa Vidaurre Calle de la Estación 3; 948 74 05 79; 07.30–15.00 & 16.30–22.00 Tue–Sun. An excellent bakery, a smart café & the most popular place for the local seniors to catch up on gossip on a Sun afternoon. Superb collection of cakes, pastries, scrumptious biscuits & some true local specialities. Early opening & cheap b/fast, busy at w/ends. Free Wi-Fi. €

What to see and do

Palacio Real (Royal Palace) (Plaza de Carlos III; 948 74 12 73; w guiartenavarra.com; Jul & Aug 10.00–20.00 daily, Apr–Jun & Sep 10.00–19.00, Oct–Mar 10.00–18.00 daily; €3.50/2 adults/children; audio guide €2 extra, for which an ID card or passport must be deposited; guided visits in Spanish only, except for groups – pre-booking required) This national monument looks exactly like a palace should. If you spotted a damsel in distress begging from one of the towers, it would be only a minor surprise. Note that, next door, what is now known as the 'Old Castle' was built by Sancho VII ('The Strong') and is now the upmarket *parador* hotel, with only very few parts of the 11th–13th-century construction remaining within. As for the 'new' castle, it actually dates from the 14th and 15th centuries. Be sure to pick up the informative English-language pamphlet with your ticket, as the audio guide – with commentary by a fictitious lady-in-waiting from the era of King Carlos – may annoy some visitors. The only disappointment is that the palace is devoid of any furniture or fittings, for when Carlos III was in his pomp, not only were there beautiful tiled walls and sumptuous carpets, but also exotic birds and a small zoo with giraffes, wolves and camels. After Navarre succumbed and became part of Castile in 1512, the palace ceased to be the permanent Royal Court and all the tapestries, furniture and jewellery inside gradually disappeared. In 1813, the palace suffered further, being torched by the Navarrese to prevent it falling into French hands during the Peninsular War, with restoration work not starting until

1937. An exhibition halfway up one of the towers shows the state of disrepair before renovation began.

Museo del Vino (Wine Museum) (Inside the tourist office & with the same hours – page 281; €3.50/2 adults/children & seniors, combined tickets also available with the palace) The building that houses the tourist office has three floors dedicated to the most important product of the local area – wine. All the information panels and touch screens are thankfully in English, starting with the 2,000-year-old history of Navarran viniculture, introduced by the Romans. Disastrously, the 19th-century plague of phyloxera destroyed nearly all of Navarre's 50,000ha of vines. In the museum, there is a detailed calendar of what needs to be done, and when, in the vineyards, as well as an explanation of the various grapes grown in Navarre, of which tempranillo and garnacha (Grenache) are by far the most common. Each of these varieties accounts for around one-third of the production. Navarre has two DOs (designation of origin), one of which is DO Navarra and the other DO Calificada Rioja. A map shows the many areas of the province in which wine can be produced. (For more on Navarran wines, see box, page 58.)

By pulling out some handy wooden drawers, you can pick out (or not!) some of the aromas commonly found in wine, and there are also tips on matching wines to your chosen food.

Galerías Medievales (Medieval Galleries) (Underground, Plaza de Carlos III; ⌚ 11.00–13.00 Tue–Fri, 11.00–14.00 & 17.00–19.00 Sat, Sun & hols; €1.50) The permanent displays comment on matters such as spices, ecclesiastical clothes and shoes, and there is a recreation of a medieval pharmacy. The English-language information here is very basic.

Torre del Chapitel (Chapitel Tower) (Plaza de Carlos III) Also known as the Torre del Reloj (clocktower), this remnant from medieval times lies on the northern side of the Plaza de Carlos III, which marks the divide between the old Roman town and the expanded, medieval one. Although handsome to look at, it is viewable from the outside only.

Iglesia de Santa María la Real (Church of Mary Queen of Heaven) (Plaza de Carlos III; ⌚ 11.00–13.30 & 16.00–18.00 Mon–Wed, 10.00–13.30 & 16.00–17.00 Thu, 10.30–13.30 & 16.00–19.00 Fri–Sun; €1.50/free adults/under 12s) Right next to the palace is this fine Gothic specimen, built between the 12th and 14th centuries. Its façade is particularly renowned, with French-influenced sculpture similar to that found at the church of San Saturnino in Artajona (page 279). Inside, marvel at the detailed altarpiece.

Bodega visit It would be remiss not to sample the wines while you're here, so if a glass or two in the cafés is not enough, then you might fancy a visit to one of the many *bodegas* in and around town. None, surely, will be more entertaining and informative than an hour spent with Octavio González at the **Bodegas Cosecheros** (Plaza San Antón 1; ☎ 948 74 00 67; w bodegacosecheros.com; ⌚ 09.00–14.00 & 16.00–19.00 Mon–Fri, 10.00–14.00 & 16.00–19.00 Sat & hols, 10.00–14.00 Sun; guided visits are officially at noon & 18.00, but use your charm at other times & you might be lucky; free, or €3 if you want cheese! 'I don't do boring tours,' English-speaking Octavio says and, as a natural entertainer, he is absolutely right. The *bodega* is a co-operative and boasts an *ovum*, one of only two egg-shaped, oak barrels in Spain. Octavio sells only to bars and restaurants, so you won't find these wines on the supermarket shelves. A visit includes tastings of white, rosé and sweet Muscat and you'll learn all about Leonardo da Vinci and the 'Golden Number' in relation to the 'star of the show', yes, that egg-shaped barrel. Bizarre, but fascinating. If you visit in October, you might be able to see the frothing as the wine ferments naturally. There is no minimum number of visitors required, and Octavio is usually present at the *bodega*.

The tourist office carries an up-to-date list of all local winery tours, with times and prices. Two who offer visits in English are **Ochoa** (948 74 00 06; w bodegasochoa.com) and **Marco Real** (948 71 21 93; w familiabelasco.com), though phoning in advance is essential.

EAST OF PAMPLONA: LEYRE, SANGÜESA AND THE EASTERN ZONA MEDIA If you thought you'd left behind those blessed pilgrims on the Camino Francés, then the area of Navarre around the border with Aragón will quickly dispel the thought. The Embalse de Yesa reservoir sits on that border, with Navarre able to claim only a tiny proportion of its waters within its territory. Along its northern shores runs the road, while the pilgrim route skirts the southern side, with the next stop being Sangüesa. The standout visitor site here is the Monasterio de Leyre to the north (page 267), set in an area of tranquillity, but a few lesser attractions – plus the possibility of combining a tour with trips to the spectacular gorges of Lumbier and Arbayún (page 263) – make exploration of Navarre's eastern borders a worthwhile detour before the visitor continues south to the region of La Ribera.

Castillo de Javier (On the NA-5410, halfway between the Monasterio de Leyre & Sangüesa; 948 88 40 36; w javier.es; Mar–Oct 10.00–18.30 daily, Nov 10.00–17.30 daily, Dec–Feb 10.00–16.00 daily; €2.75/1.25/free adults/under 12s/under 6s; audio guides €4.25, including entrance price) The Castillo de Javier was originally built in the 10th century but partially demolished in 1516. A long restoration to the fabric of the building began in the 1950s, with the interior being revamped as recently as 2005. Francisco Javier, who has the honour of being Navarre's co-patron saint (along with San Fermín), was born at the castle in 1506 and spent his childhood here. In truth, the castle and its surroundings (two hotels, a café, souvenir shops, a huge billboard of Saint Francis and a lurid, giant metallic 'J' in front of the castle) have a bit of a sanitised air to them, while the interior, full of models depicting the phases of the saint's life, weapons, period furniture from the 17th and 18th centuries, religious art – mainly from the 17th century – carries something of the atmosphere of a renovated hotel.

Walking There is a tourist office here, not always open, but its outside wall sports a helpful map showing four different signposted walks that all begin from the castle. Of these, the **Paseo del Papa – Peña del Adiós** (circular; 13km; 3hrs 30mins) leaves from just beyond the castle. Its first half runs high above the River Aragón, with opportunities to see cormorants below and usually hordes of vultures above. The scenic views end rudely with a couple of factories belching out smoke, but you soon turn your back on these as you turn for home through gentle, hilly countryside.

Sangüesa (Zangoza) Standing on the Aragón River, and being a major town on the less-travelled branch of the Camino de Santiago that crosses the Pyrenees at Somport, Sangüesa is a medieval town with one major attraction – the Iglesia de

Santa María la Real church – for those interested in religious art. For more minor attractions, a stroll along the streets of Calle Mayor and Alfonso el Batallador will introduce you to noble houses from across the centuries. To the north of town is Rocaforte, the hilltop location chosen as the site for the area's original settlement in an era when defence against Muslim invaders was more important than welcoming in Christian pilgrims. When the pilgrims arrived, the new town (Sangüesa la Nueva) was spawned down below. At the same latitude as Rocaforte, the waters of the Irati River flow into the Aragón River. Sangüesa switches to festival mode on 11 September, when a week of bull-running and livestock fairs takes place. On 6 January, an allegorical play called *Misterio de los Reyes* (*Mystery of the Three Kings*) is enacted by the townsfolk.

Tourist information The tourist office (Calle Mayor 2; ☎ 948 87 14 11; w sanguesaturismo.com; ⌚ Jul–mid-Oct 10.00–14.00 & 16.00–19.00 Tue–Sat, 10.00–14.00 Sun; mid-Oct–Jun 10.00–14.00 Sun–Thu, 10.00–17.00 Fri & Sat) is situated close to the metal bridge that crosses the Aragón River.

Iglesia de Santa María la Real (Church of Our Lady Queen of Heaven) (Opposite the tourist office; m 620 11 05 81; e info@sanguesaturismo.com; ⌚ Sep–Jun 11.00–13.45 & 16.00–18.15 Tue–Fri; admission free during mass, otherwise €2.30/2/free adults/seniors & pilgrims/under 12s, including sound & light show) For fans of Romanesque architecture and religious art, this church, a national monument since 1889, is a must-see. Constructed from the 12th century onward, its splendid façade accommodates Old and New Testament scenes, the Day of Judgement and a motley collection of monsters and figures from medieval times. Inside, the worthwhile sound and light show is only in Spanish, but English-language information is provided with your entrance ticket.

Walk around town Along the Calle Mayor, you can admire the houses of noble families such as those of Añués (15th century) and Iñiguez Abarca (18th century), as well as the splendid town hall (1570), which has a beautiful gallery of porches. In the adjoining Calle Alfonso el Batallador, you'll find the Palacio Vallesantoro – now Sangüesa's Casa de Cultura (cultural centre) – with beautiful wooden eaves.

Gallipienzo Antiguo Abandoned by man, reclaimed by nature, then reclaimed again by humans: that could be Gallipienzo Antiguo's story in another decade or so. In the 1950s, much of the population of Gallipienzo was relocated to the new town of Gallipienzo Nuevo, a few kilometres away, lower in altitude and with the then luxury of running water and vehicle accessibility. If you choose to visit the Old Town, you'll quickly understand how life could be tough here, with few facilities and narrow streets that could accommodate a slender wheelbarrow and not much more. Now, the descendants of those who moved are returning to reclaim their ancestors' properties and renovate them. Down below, towards the river, a hotel project is now complete, giving you the chance to linger. Otherwise, there is but one *casa rural* and the delightful Bar los Buitres (The Vultures' Bar), the ambience of which captures magnificently the time warp of the village. Pull the door-string to get in, but don't expect to find a draught beer or any other sophistication here, though it does have a pleasant, sunny terrace. Climb to the village's *mirador* but, for the best photos of the town, continue to follow the path with the 'bird logo', taking you to an observation point that looks out over the Aragón River far below. Here some mainly Spanish-language panels provide information about the local wild herbs such as thyme and rosemary, the former importance of rafting as a method of transport and also introduce you to some of the bird species resident nearby. These include low mountain inhabitants such as the red-legged partridge (*Alectoris rufa*) and short-toed snake eagle (*Circaetus gallicus*), with the latter capable of catching 2m-long serpents; river-dwellers such as the common kingfisher (*Alcedo atthis*); and raptors such as the peregrine falcon (*Falco peregrinus*) and the endangered Bonelli's eagle (*Aquila fasciata*), while high above an Egyptian vulture (*alimoche* in Spanish, *Neophron percnopterus*) or griffon vulture (*Gyps fulvus*) may soar obligingly. It's good to realise that the village bar is named after the birds, rather than in honour of any estate agents who might be tempted to transform the place into a chic venue for second homes, given half a chance. A few hand-painted '*Se vende*' ('For sale') signs already adorn the walls of ruined houses, healthy fig-trees pushing through the spaces where windows once were. Does the town have a future? For now, back in Los Buitres, six elderly gents sip their glasses of red wine, while animatedly discussing the quality of the olives and peppers they're sharing from a huge ceramic bowl. According to the notice at the village entrance, Gallipienzo sits '*a medio camino el valle y el cielo*' – 'halfway between valley and sky'. But *cielo* also means 'heaven', and Gallipienzo Antiguo seems, for now at least, much closer to heaven than it is to the valley.

Where to stay and eat

Heredad Beragu (9 rooms) Calle El Abrigo, Gallipienzo Antiguo; 948 05 01 09; e info@heredadberaguhotel.com; w heredadberaguhotel.com. After 7 years of renovation, this beautiful adults-only establishment finally opened fairly recently, delighting everyone lucky enough to stay here. Dripping with taste, it could adorn the cover of any style magazine. Each room is different, each a fantastic adaptation of this old stone building. 1 room is suitable for those of lesser mobility. Free Wi-Fi, communal terrace & garden. The dining room looks down to the river & across to the wooded slopes beyond. Bar, & evening meals, for hotel guests only. **€€–€€€€**

San Martín de Unx This crossroads town makes a good place to have lunch or stop over. The town celebrates a lively rosé wine festival in June. With all the *bodegas* lined up along the main road, it's certainly a town well equipped to host it.

Where to stay and eat

Casa San Pedro (4 rooms) On the NA-5310 from San Martín de Unx to Ujué; 948 73 82 57; m 699 51 02 57; e linda@casapedro.net; w casapedro.net. This is a long-established place run by Linda from Sunderland & Pedro from Gipuzkoa. Uses solar power. Rooms have showers, a small swimming pool provides welcome relief on hot days. There's a bar & restaurant too, with good-value *menus del día* served inside or outside (€€). Dormitory beds also available. Internet access. Good-value, friendly option. **€**

Casa Tomás 13 de Septiembre 1; 948 73 80 34; w asadorcasatomas.com; 13.00–15.30 Wed–Sun, 21.30–23.00 Sat only. A small but lively bar gives way to a huge & handsome dining room, all wooden beams & bare stone. A long way from the sea, but the hake is top-drawer, the meat excellent & the sumptuous desserts all homemade. Limited evening opening, but a good lunchtime stopover. The price reflects the quality. **€€€**

What to see and do

San Martín de Tours Church (m 669 41 22 03; 11.00–13.00 & 16.30–18.30 Sat, Sun & hols, at other times, call the above number; €2) Two Romanesque churches provide the architectural highlights in this town of only 400 inhabitants, but of the two it's the cute 12th-century San Martín de Tours that steals the show with its crypt accessed down a spiral staircase. The exterior is distinctive for its capitals showing various battles between animals and soldiers, as well as of San Martín and Samson. Inside, as well as the crypt, the sheer simplicity of the chapel is the most striking feature. To find it, take the disconcertingly narrow street that climbs from the main road, starting at the side of the Gothic church of Santa María del Popolo, and pray for somewhere to park. Alternatively, as it is only 600m uphill from the town, you could walk.

Festival The town is renowned for its orange-tinged, *clarete* (rosé wine), *garrapiñadas* (almonds with a honey coating) and (at festival time) its *fricafea*, made from a carnivore-friendly blend of trotters, tripe and blood and which forms the gastronomic centrepiece of the *romería* (pilgrimage) that takes place annually on the Saturday nearest to 27 April.

Ujué (Uxue) Everyone can choose their own favourite hilltop settlement from many worthy contenders in Navarre, but if you were voting purely on panoramic views, Ujué would take a lot of beating. No enemy could approach this town unannounced, given its 360° views. Understandably, this was once an important fortress for the Kings of Navarre. The town attracts its share of tourists to visit its Iglesia Fortaleza (fortified church, free access in daylight hours), enjoying the vistas and sampling its two gastronomic specialities: almonds and wine.

Where to eat and drink Ujué is *very* popular at weekend lunchtimes, so booking is advisable. There are just four restaurants of which the **Meson las Migas** (948 73 90 44; w mesonlasmigas.es; mid-Jul–end Aug lunchtimes only daily, other months Sat, Sun & hols only; €€€), and the **Meson las Torres** (948 73 90 52; w mesonlastorres.com; Fri–Wed lunchtimes only; €€€) are the picks for views. At the entrance to the town you'll find **Urrutia** (year-round 10.00–18.00 Thu–Tue, meal service 13.30–15.30; €€), a simpler and cheaper affair, a bakery with a bar and shop but also serving meals. It has a great range of local specialities on sale, including *tortas txantxigorri* which oddly combine sugar with pork sausage in a giant, unpronounceable biscuit! A good place to find organic wines, too.

Eslava This pretty piled-up town catches the eye as you drive along the N-132 between San Martin de Unx and Sangüesa, but it's a photo opportunity only. On the opposite side of the road, between kilometres 56 and 57, look out for the sign for **Santa Criz**. Following this side road for a couple of kilometres takes you to the car park for this newly excavated Roman town (open access at all times; admission free). Climb the path from the parking area to find a surprising collection of capitols, columns and a few explanatory signboards (Spanish and Basque only). The sheer mid-countryside location is perhaps the biggest surprise. There are plans for a museum here.

Laguna de Pitillas (Signposted off the NA-5330, 13km south of Olite; m 619 46 34 50; free access to the *laguna* at any time; observatory: May 11.00–14.00 & 17.00–19.00, Jun–Sep 11.00–14.00, Sat & Sun only, occasionally at w/ends & holidays in other months; admission free; outside, near the car park, there's a signboard with a map, while inside the information centre you can get free guidance on suggested walks around the lake; binoculars & telescopes can be borrowed free of charge when the observatory is open) An enormous variety of birdlife has been recorded here, with residents at this natural lake including grey heron, little and cattle egret and common pochard, as well as raptors such as the golden eagle, marsh harrier, peregrine falcon and Eurasian sparrowhawk. Bitterns, stilts and lapwings are also populous here. Nesting season is from around March to June, when many species take advantage of the reed beds that surround the waters. Summer visitors spotted to date include the booted eagle, short-toed eagle, Bailon's crake and little bustard, but there are many, many others, too. Over 40 species of passage migrants have been observed, and over 100 species in total, making this one of Navarre's best wetland sites, with something of interest at any time of year. It is a nature reserve, an Area of Special Protection for birds and a Ramsar Wetland of International Importance. Covered by reeds and bulrushes, the water here is never more than 3m deep. On dry land, you would be lucky to spot the badgers, weasels, foxes or wild boar which nevertheless frequent the area around the *laguna*.

LA RIBERA: BARDENAS REALES AND TUDELA

La Ribera, the southern prong of Navarre, is comprised of both the province's agricultural heartland and the semi-desert of the Bardenas Reales. Thanks to the influence of the mighty River Ebro and the horticultural skills introduced by the Moors, La Ribera produces a variety of crops and vegetables, but the farming land sits in stark contrast to the arid Bardenas Reales, which extends over 42,000ha, making it the biggest of Navarre's three natural parks. Those hankering after astounding scenery need look no farther. If you've arrived from the north of the province, it's astonishing to realise that the Pyrenees are only an hour away from this desert. For fans of manmade history, the pickings of La Ribera are a bit slimmer, yet the Monasterio de la Oliva with its Cistercian church and Gothic cloister competes with Tudela's religious art and architecture for visitors' attention.

MONASTERIO DE LA OLIVA (Off the NA-128, 2km west of Carcastillo; ☎ 948 72 50 06; **w** monasteriodelaoliva.org; ⌚ 09.30–noon & 15.30–18.00 Mon–Sat, 09.30–11.30 & 16.00–18.00 Sun & hols; €2.50) Still home to some two-dozen Cistercian monks, the tranquil setting conceals the centuries of history that have passed by and through the Monasterio de la Oliva. La Oliva is one of three remaining monasteries in the south. Various buildings make up the complex here: the huge Santa María church was built in the 12th and 13th centuries, and the monastery itself was named – according to legend – after a heroic Navarrese king who died after battle with the Moors beside an olive tree which then became the site for the monastery. Also here are the 12th-century cloister, refectory, kitchen and a particularly impressive 16th-century staircase. A combination of the 19th-century wars and the infamous Laws of Confiscation (which deprived the Church of its properties) led to the ruination and abandonment of the site until it was restored in the 20th century. Once again, it became a working monastery. The tall cypress trees, trimmed lawn and twittering of birdlife in the gardens all add to the peaceful ambience. On 23 March and 23 September, the light shining through the church's central round window rests directly on the altar. The well-stocked shop sells the wines still produced from the monastery's own vineyards, ranging from rosés to aged *reservas*. The monks also find time to produce honey, olive oil and even rice, which can be seen growing in the paddy fields to the west.

If the silence grabs you, you can stay overnight at the monastery hostel, or even for up to seven nights, or choose to respectfully attend the monks' chanted liturgies, the schedule for which starts at a faith-testing 04.30 with Lauds, and continues with the Eucharist (07.00), Terce (08.15), Sext (12.45), None (15.10), Vespers (18.30) and Salve (20.30). More information on all aspects of the monastery are available on the website, but the English-language translation is decidedly shaky.

LAS BARDENAS REALES [map, below] Navarre's film-star semi-desert, the Bardenas Reales, was first designated a natural park in 1999 and then as a biosphere reserve a year later. The **Centro de Información de Bardenas Reales de Navarra** (accessed from the NA-8712 near Arguedas; ☎ 948 83 03 08; w bardenasreales.es; ⏰ summer 09.00–14.00 & 16.00–19.00, winter 09.00–14.00 & 15.00–17.00 daily, Holy Week 09.00–19.00 daily; free admission to the centre & park) is the place to pick up a leaflet in English with a useful map of the area, find out about park conditions and (importantly) visit the toilets. Usefully, there is a vending machine

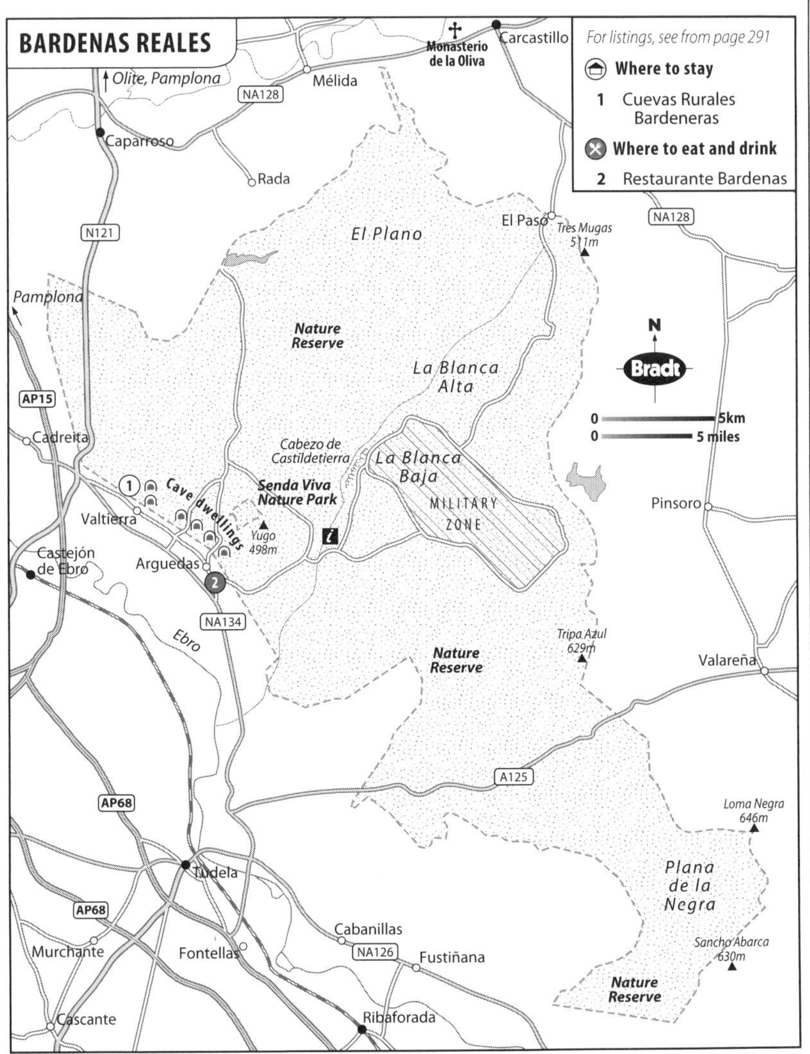

selling water, but there are no other refreshments, so don't forget to arrive well stocked as temperatures in midsummer can be punitively hot.

The **Bardenas Reales Parque Natural y Reserva de la Biosfera** (🕘 08.00–1hr before sunset) is genuinely extraordinary in many ways. The wonders of the landscape are self-evident once you are inside the park, but other peculiarities are not so obvious. First of all, the area is owned by 20 nearby communities, as well as by the nearby Monasterio de la Oliva (page 288), and the distant valleys of Roncal and Salazar in the Pyrenees. Rights of perpetual pasturage were granted by the king in centuries long gone, giving the territory its *Real* (Royal) title. Every year from 18 September, shepherds bring their flocks of sheep down the *cañadas reales* (drovers' routes) from those valleys to avoid the Pyrenean winter, and stay until April or May. Some small waterholes have been created to supply the flocks, while the shepherds live in the nearby towns. Secondly, this heavily protected area has a military base and firing range in its very middle. Every day in clear weather, Spanish air force jets arrive from Zaragoza, screaming down from above, dropping dummy bombs and occasionally live ammunition on to targets said by locals to be neatly arranged to represent Middle Eastern airbases. Needless to say, many locals want the base removed from this beautiful, rugged location, but the Government pays the communities richly for its presence and there seems little chance of the situation altering anytime soon. For first-time visitors, the planes are an additional attraction in themselves, perhaps the closest many people will (hopefully) ever come to being in a war zone. Curiously, Bardenas Reales's incredible scenery attracts a mere 50,000 visitors annually to marvel at how nature has sculpted the landscape over a period of millions of years. Many locals will exclaim that this is still a little-known natural wonder, under the radar even of many Spaniards. Indeed, the French account for over half the visitors.

Despite its relatively low profile, ornithologists outside Spain *are* aware of the region, turning up to enjoy the many bird species that live here. Raptors such as the golden eagle (*Aguila chrysaetos*) and black kite (*milano negro* in Spanish, *Milvus migrans*) can be seen, often at ground level, but it is smaller species like the Dupont's lark (*Chersophilus duponti*) that have the birdwatchers drooling. The Balcón de Pilatos, just southeast of the information centre (page 289), is recognised as one of the best sites in the park for avian followers.

But it's not just birds and soldiers who reside here, not quite. One doughty local shepherd, aged well into his 80s, lives here all year round, only a few hundred metres from the military base, the only civilian inhabitant in the park. At the Cabezo de las Cortinas viewpoint you can climb the 240 steps up the rock to look down at the glistening military targets in the near distance, as well as the stunning rock formations, of course. But the most striking feature of the park is the Castildetierra, the poster boy of many a Navarran tourist board brochure. This table-shaped hill has been sculpted by the winds and occasionally by rain to leave a twisted spike that stands alone. The park has provided a scenic backdrop for several well-known movies, including the James Bond film *The World is Not Enough* and the Ridley Scott-directed *The Counselor*.

In April and May, the Bardena Blanca (White Bardena) temporarily loses its *blanca*, turning green with some colourful flowers. In high summer, there is a risk of short thunderstorms here, the rain turning some of the tracks to mud, so it is vital to stay on the official roads that are clearly marked on the map issued at the information centre. After rain, the desert colours change, bringing out the ochres of the rock formations. At the first viewpoint after the information centre, if you stand behind the larger of the two information panels (Spanish only) you can sometimes get a view of the Pyrenean peaks to the north.

To the south of the central Bardena Blanca, accessible from the NA-125 that joins Tudela to the province of Zaragoza in the east, is the area known as the Bardena Negra (Black Bardena). In this zone the rock is of more durable limestone, formed from bones and shells of creatures who lived in the sea that once covered the area. Here there is less erosion and more vegetation, juniper, oak and hawthorn, among which live wild boar, marten and badger. To the north, in the third distinct area known as El Plano, the waters originating in Yesa have been harboured into the reservoir called Embalse de El Ferial, and the park is penetrated in three places by drovers' routes from the Valle de Roncal and the sierras of Urbasa and Andía.

Guided tours of the park **Activa Experience** (948 85 04 48; e info@activaexperience.com; w bardenasrealesnavarra.com), a local firm based south of Bardenas, provide English-speaking guides to the Bardenas. Whether you want to horse-ride, quad-bike, cycle or walk, Activa can show you the best of Bardenas with a bit of advance notice. Gastronomy, astronomy and wine-related tours are also available, and the company has its own upmarket motel. Although other guides *are* available, it is not easy to find an English speaker. **David Espino** (m 670 82 44 90; e david@laveredadelcierzo.com; w laveredadelcierzo.com) speaks a little English and very good French, but he may be able to find you a better English speaker. **Trip Navarra** (m 688 98 87 47; e info@tripnavarra.com; w tripnavarra.com) also offer a variety of English-language tours in Navarre, half and full day, some of which include Bardenas Reales.

Cave dwellings Dug out of the rock in the 19th century by locals of Valtierra and neighbouring Arguedas, these 400 former cave dwellings are today a curiosity for visitors and a memory of a local lifestyle of not so long ago. The former inhabitants couldn't afford to build houses, but after generations cooped up inside these primitive dwellings, over 1,000 people finally vacated their caves in 1961 to live in General Franco's new, affordable housing down the road. To see them up close, look for the signs that read Paseo del Bordón at the southern end of Arguedas town. Park near the spaces reserved for motorhomes, the pathway is obvious.

Where to stay and eat nearby With no food inside the park, you'll have to divert into nearby Arguedas or Valtierra for sustenance. No worries, as the former boasts 15 bars and five restaurants for its 2,400 inhabitants and many visitors!

Cuevas Rurales Bardeneras [map, page 289] (8 caves) Palomares 46, Valtierra; 948 84 32 25; m 661 84 67 57; e lasbardeneras@gmail.com; w bardeneras.com. Staying in a cave might sound a little unappealing, but what if it had a kitchen, TV, BBQ, free Wi-Fi, garden & terrace? Some of the former cave dwellings have been converted into hotel accommodation. Best suited to families (they accommodate 4–8), you can't argue with the quality of the interiors. 4×4 excursions can be arranged to nearby Bardenas Reales, as well as horseriding, guided walks, etc. English spoken. From mid-Jul to end Aug, there is a 4-night min stay, & a 2-night min the rest of the year. **€€€€** (*4 people*)

Rural Suite Apartamentos [map, page 271] (9 apts) On the N-121C, 5km south of Tudela; 948 85 04 48; e info@ruralsuite.com; w ruralsuite.com. Set out in motel fashion, with a café & restaurant on-site. All apartments are ultra-modern, with TV, AC, kitchen & free Wi-Fi. The bonus is the communal jacuzzi outside. Staff are efficient & helpful. The hotel also organises quad-bike rides & other tours to the Bardenas Reales. **€€€**

Restaurante Bardenas [map, page 289] Calle Real 96, Arguedas; 948 83 01 45; 13.00–16.00 Tue–Sun, plus 20.30–23.00 Fri & Sat. Probably the pick of the Arguedas eating options, with a great-value lunch menu. **€€**

TUDELA If you've just spent a few days in the Navarran Pyrenees, got used to the empty roads that took you south to Olite, and marvelled at the parched wasteland of the Bardenas Reales, then the build-up of trucks on your way to Tudela followed by the sight of nine-storey apartment blocks rising out of almost nowhere can come as a bit of a shock. Although nowhere near the size of Pamplona, Tudela's 35,000 population entitles it to comfortably claim the status of Navarre's second-largest town. Size, of course, isn't everything and the town now has none of the importance that it enjoyed for the 300 years following its creation as a 'new city' by the Muslims in the early 9th century. During those years the Muslim, Jewish and Christian population coexisted in relative harmony, and this is still a source of pride for the townspeople. After the reconquest of Tudela by the King of Aragón, Alfonso I 'El Batallador' in 1119, the defeated Muslims were moved outside the city boundary, but were allowed to maintain their administrative infrastructure. In 1170, the town's Jewish quarter was also moved, relocated on the orders of Sancho VI 'El Sabio' from its location near the current cathedral to an area adjoining the castle walls. With a few hiccups, the coexistence of religions continued and the town even resisted, albeit temporarily, the first thrusts of the Spanish Inquisition. Navarre's Jewish population lasted fractionally longer than its counterparts in Aragón or Castile, but the inevitable expulsion finally took place in 1498, leading to either exile or forced conversion. Less than 20 years later the Muslims were also expelled. Nevertheless, today's Tudela still enjoys something of an ethnic mix, at least by Navarre's standards, and has a couple of historical attractions tucked into its Old Town that are worth a visit. Another claim to fame in these agricultural flatlands is that, in a region of

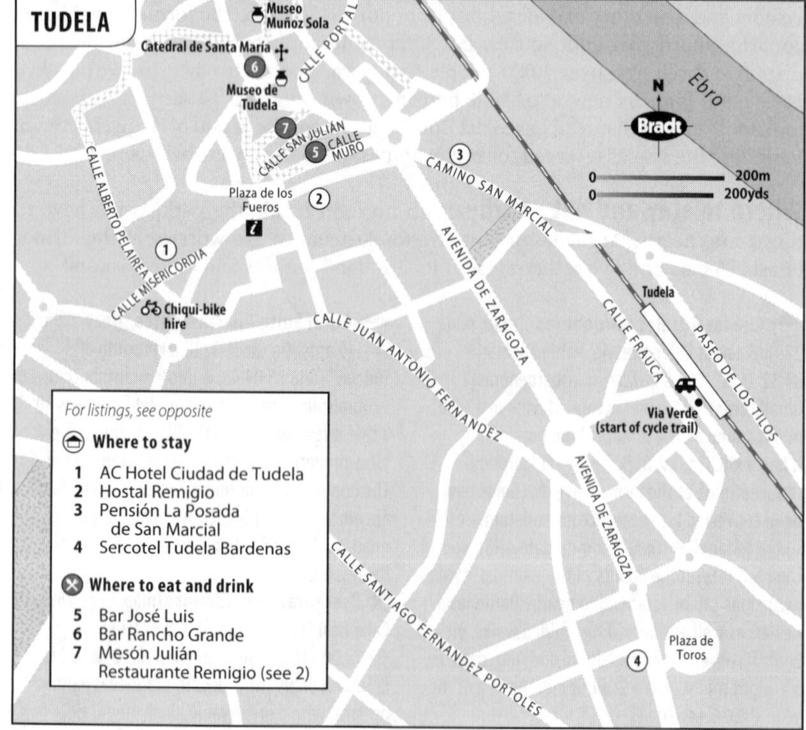

meat-eaters, Tudela is justly renowned across Spain for the superb quality of its vegetables. The town recognises its history with a medieval market, the Mercado Medieval Tres Culturas, in mid-September; at the end of July, Tudela's week-long party in honour of Santa Ana takes place; and in May the area's renowned vegetables are honoured.

Getting there and away

By train Tudela's railway and bus stations sit conveniently side by side to the east of the centre. For once in Navarre, the train can rival the bus for frequency and convenience, with around ten trains daily to Barcelona (3hrs; €35), a dozen to Madrid (2hrs 30mins; €40), a dozen to Pamplona (1hr 10mins; €12), ten to Zaragoza (1hr; €6), and at least one service daily to Logroño, Vitoria-Gasteiz, Vigo, Burgos and Gijón. Bilbao is connected twice daily (3hrs 15mins; €20). Weekend services are a little less frequent.

By bus Nine buses depart for Pamplona daily (1hr 15mins; €8.30), with fewer on Sundays. There are also nine buses daily to Zaragoza (1hr 15mins; €7.25). Other long-distance destinations are Logroño, Barcelona, Madrid and even Alicante, while local buses serve Cascante, Falces and Peralta, among others.

Getting around Tudela is small and the points of interest are close together, but there is an urban bus service, should you feel the need. Details, in Spanish only, are on the tourist office website (see below); the service is much reduced at weekends. Line 2 takes you to and from the bus/train stations.

Tourist information Located in the main town square, the tourist office (Plaza de Fueros; ☎ 948 84 80 58; w tudela.es; ⌚ 10.00–14.00 & 16.00–19.00 Mon–Sat, 10.00–14.00 Sun & holidays) now shares space with the town administration services. Take a ticket and wait your turn, or help yourself to the brochures. Staff are helpful, and the opening hours are the longest in Navarre.

Where to stay *Map, opposite*

AC Hotel Ciudad de Tudela (42 rooms) Misericordia; ☎ 948 40 24 40; w marriott.co.uk. The upmarket option, a chain hotel in a renovated mansion, with spacious rooms, equipped with Wi-Fi, AC, TV. Fitness room. For those who need their mod cons, pleasant English-speaking staff. On-site parking costs extra. **€€€**

Hostal Remigio (35 rooms) Gaztambide Carrera 4; ☎ 948 82 08 50; e info@hostalremigio.com; w hostalremigio.com. Very central, run by the lovely Carmen for more years than she'll admit. A marble staircase & polished banisters lead you up to rooms which, while nothing fancy, have AC, free Wi-Fi, TV, heating & private bath. B/fast is reasonably priced. **€€**

Sercotel Tudela Bardenas (47 rooms) Av Zaragoza 60; ☎ 948 41 07 78; e hotel@tudelabardenas.com; w tudelabardenas.com. In a town with no boutique hotels, a chain option which often offers good deals. A bit out of the town centre (10mins' walk), this is a perfectly decent & inexpensive option, if a bit soulless. It has a gym, restaurant & a Scottish pub, of all things. Ask for one of the renovated rooms. AC, free Wi-Fi, TV with international channels. Suitable for those with lesser mobility. **€€**

Pensión La Posada de San Marcial (4 rooms) San Marcial 13; m 638 76 27 82 or 659 77 90 69; e info@laposadadesanmarcial.es; w laposadadesanmarcial.es. Trust the address: it *is* there, but at first you seem to be entering a car park to find it. Shared bathroom, so if you can handle that, this is good value. Rooms have a fan, Wi-Fi is free & there's a shared kitchen, too. Dining is on the outdoor terrace, though the view's not beautiful. They also have an apartment for rent. Parking is €5 per day. No credit cards. **€**

Where to eat and drink *Map, page 292*

Mesón Julián Calle de la Merced 9; 948 82 20 28; w mesonjulian.com; 13.15–16.00 Wed–Sun, 21.15–23.00 Fri & Sat only, closed Tue. A choice of set menus – so arrive hungry – feature upmarket meat & fish dishes, creatively presented. Check out the daily menu. Pricier than some, but worth the extra cost. €€€

Bar Rancho Grande Calle de la Rúa 6; 948 82 27 80; 08.00–01.00 Thu–Tue. A place for *pintxos*, with pork & pig parts to the fore. Salads & main dishes also available, though it's a bar rather than restaurant. Set in the heart of an area of town that comes alive on Thu evenings. The ambience lasts through the w/end, inc Sun. For diners, portions are generous. A good place to enjoy the area's fine vegetables. €€

Restaurante Remigio (page 293) 13.00–16.00 Thu– Tue, also 21.00–23.00 Thu–Sat, Mon & Tue, closed all day Wed & Sun evenings. A handsome, wood-panelled dining room, old-fashioned service & a wide choice. It is well loved by management & customers alike. You can eat a bit cheaper elsewhere, but the price/quality ratio here is excellent. Recommended for lunch. €€

Bar José Luis Calle del Muro 23; 948 82 00 91; 10.00–23.00 daily. Great for creative *pintxos*, including vegetarian options. Has some outside seating, a modern interior, but service varies from gruff to charming (tending towards the former), & the place can get very busy . . . but their snacks are good.

What to see and do

Museo de Tudela (Tudela Museum) (Roso 2; 948 40 21 61; w museodetudela.com; 10.00–13.30 & 16.00–19.00 Mon–Fri, 10.00–13.30 Sat; €4/3/2/free adults/students & seniors/under 12s/under 6s, entrance is combined with the cathedral (see below)) Housed in the mainly 15th-century building known as the 'Dean's Palace', Tudela's museum was fully restored at the end of the 20th century following a period of abandonment and neglect. The contents are big on religious iconography and there's a room devoted to archaeological findings ranging from prehistory through the Iron Age to Roman rule and more recent times. Of particular interest is the reproduction of *La Manta*, a 17th-century canvas used to display the names of those Jews who converted to Christianity.

Catedral de Santa María (Cathedral of Our Lady) (See Museo de Tudela above for hours & entrance fee; visit is a combined one – get your ticket from the museum next door) Built on the site of Tudela's Grand Mosque after the town's reconquest, the Santa María la Blanca church became the cathedral in 1783. Construction began in the 12th century, so Romanesque features are visible in its architecture. There are three entrances, with the ceiling around the south (Virgin's) door being noteworthy for its Mudéjar (Moorish-influenced) paintings. A plan and information leaflet in English, detailing all the different artistic and architectural styles to be found here, is provided for visitors. For the 12th-century cloister, be sure to pick up the separate information leaflet which helps to identify the scenes depicted on the 42 remaining capitals.

Museo Muñoz Sola (Plaza Vieja 2; 948 40 26 40; 10.30–13.30 & 17.30–20.30 Tue–Sat, 10.30–13.30 Sun; €1) Tudela artist César Muñoz Sola (1921–2000) collected 19th- & 20th-century works during his lifetime as well as producing his own portraits, landscapes and still-lifes. All are displayed here in this three-storey palace house. There are often temporary exhibitions here, too.

Plaza de los Fueros At first sight, this 17th-century plaza is not the most attractive of squares. To see the best of it, you need to raise your eyes slightly to take in the brightly painted bullfighting scenes and coats of arms. The former acknowledge the original purpose of the plaza's construction, namely bullfighting, which had previously taken place in the square next to the cathedral.

Cycling Starting out from the side of the bus station, where there is a rough map, the **Vía Verde Tarazonica** is a Greenway route that runs south for 22km along a former railway line to Tarazona in nearby Aragón. Rolling through agricultural land with the Moncayo mountains to the south, six of the former stations provide appropriate resting places. The railway itself closed in 1970. The tourist office has a list of companies that rent bikes, including **Chiqui-Bike** (Misericordia 1; 948 82 52 01; m 629 32 20 31; w chiquibike.com; €20 per day).

CASCANTE Situated some 12km southwest of Tudela, Cascante traces its origins back to Celto-Iberian times. Its Basílica del Romero in the higher reaches of the town, the adjoining park (Parque del Romero), offering views out over the valley, and the series of 18th-century arches that connect the basilica with the lower town are worth a look, and other visitors may be lured here by the Centro Termolúdico (see below) for its water-based activities. Otherwise, there is a little museum open weekends only in July/August, and from the second Saturday in September the town celebrates its heritage with a week-long Roman celebration. The nearby Laguna de Lor is popular with birdwatchers, but most people in the area will be on their way to the Monasterio de Tulebras.

Where to eat and drink With a well-reputed cook, the **Taberna de Tulebras** (Carretera Tudela 1, Tulebras, 3km south of Cascante; 948 85 15 92; 13.00–17.00 daily; €€€) is a decent place to avail yourself of a cheap lunchtime *menú del día*, right next to the monastery. The price rises at the weekend, but the quality and choice do, too.

Shopping

Aceite Queiles Carretera Tudela–Tarazona N-121C at km12; 948 41 06 50; w haciendaqueiles.com. Organic olive oil factory on the main road just south of Cascante. Opening hours are not fixed, but if you're passing & want to buy some olive oil, this is the place. Some of their trees are reckoned to be over 1,000 years old, including one directly in front of the building, marked with a stone plaque.

Hermanos Orta Artesania On the N-121C, at the northern entrance to Cascante; 948 85 15 54; m 606 29 41 37; w artesaniaorta.com. A family-run business with a shop on the main road & a workshop out the back, a place to get genuine olive-wood gifts such as kitchen utensils, bowls & some more expensive carved faces & figurines. If the shop's not open, ring the mobile & the owner will be there in 5mins – he promises!

What to see and do

Centro Termolúdico de Cascante (Av Fundación Fuentes Dutor; 948 84 45 38; w termoludicocascante.es; 10.00–22.00 Mon–Fri, 10.00–20.00 Sat & Sun, check website for full opening hours; €17/13/8 adults/seniors & under 18s/under 14s) Not pretty, nor subtle, but if you need some spa time then here are indoor and outdoor pools, steam baths, jacuzzi and a gym. Many activities, classes and treatments are available (extra charges apply). The centre also offers a number of walking and mountain bike routes, starting and finishing at the centre. Restaurant and terrace bar.

Monasterio de Tulebras (Tulebras Monastery) (Tulebras, 3km south of Cascante; w monasteriodetulebras.com; May–Sep 11.00–13.30 & 16.00–18.00

Tue–Sun, Oct–Apr 16.00–18.00 Sat & Sun only; admission free, but a donation will be welcomed; no English spoken) Tulebras's claim to fame is to be the first Spanish monastery to house Cistercian nuns, founded as it was in 1157; Fitero (see below) was the very first to have monks, in 1140. Now there is a small museum of sacred art, open to the public and displaying the monastery's collection, much of which is 16th-century Renaissance. An English-language leaflet details the contents of the three exhibition rooms, which as well as paintings contain some 17th- and 18th-century silverware. The upheavals of the 19th century took their toll on Tulebras, with the monastery being thoroughly sacked by Napoleonic troops in November 1808. All the monastic property, including lands, was confiscated by law in 1837, though the nuns were permitted to stay in residence.

Collect your leaflet at reception and one of the resident 21 nuns will show you around. A monastery shop sells wine, jams, candles, olive oil and insect repellent.

FITERO Close to the border with La Rioja, Fitero is home to the first Cistercian monastery to be built in the whole of Spain.

Tourist information As well as dispensing information, the tourist office (Calle de la Iglesia 8; ☎ 948 77 66 00; **w** fitero.es; ⏱ hours vary) can organise guided visits to the monastery, with a minimum of three people.

Where to stay Recently renovated, **La Hospedería del Monasterio** (5 apts; Garijos 2; Fitero; ☎ 948 08 87 81; **e** info@lahospederiadelmonasterio.com; **w** lahospederiadelmonasterio.com; **€€**) features heating and TV in the modern, tasteful, self-catering apartments. There is free Wi-Fi in the communal areas and a patio with barbecue.

What to see and do

Monasterio Santa María (Monastery of Our Lady) (Plaza de la Iglesia 12; ☎ 948 77 66 00; **w** https://turismofitero.com; ⏱ self-guided visits 11.00–13.30 & 16.30–18.30 Tue–Sat, 11.00–13.30 Sun; €2; guided visits in Spanish 11.30, 13.15 & 18.00 Mon–Sat, noon Sun; €3) The oldest Cistercian monastery in Navarre, founded in 1140 by St Raymond, an unusual saint who spent a lot of effort raising a military force of over 20,000 soldier-monks to fight off the Moors. On display inside are Arabic chests, an enamel reliquary and some jewellery boxes from medieval times.

Balneario de Fitero (Calle Extramuros, 2km from Fitero; ☎ 948 77 61 00; **w** balneariodefitero.es) This spa resort has two hotels, tennis, table tennis, a *frontón*, swimming pools and all the therapeutic treatments you can shake a walking stick at. The whole complex is plug-ugly and out of step with its surroundings, but if you need a treatment, you need a treatment.

BASQUE COUNTRY ONLINE

For additional online content, articles, photos and more on the Basque Country, why not visit **w** bradtguides.com/basque?

Part Four

THE FRENCH BASQUE COUNTRY

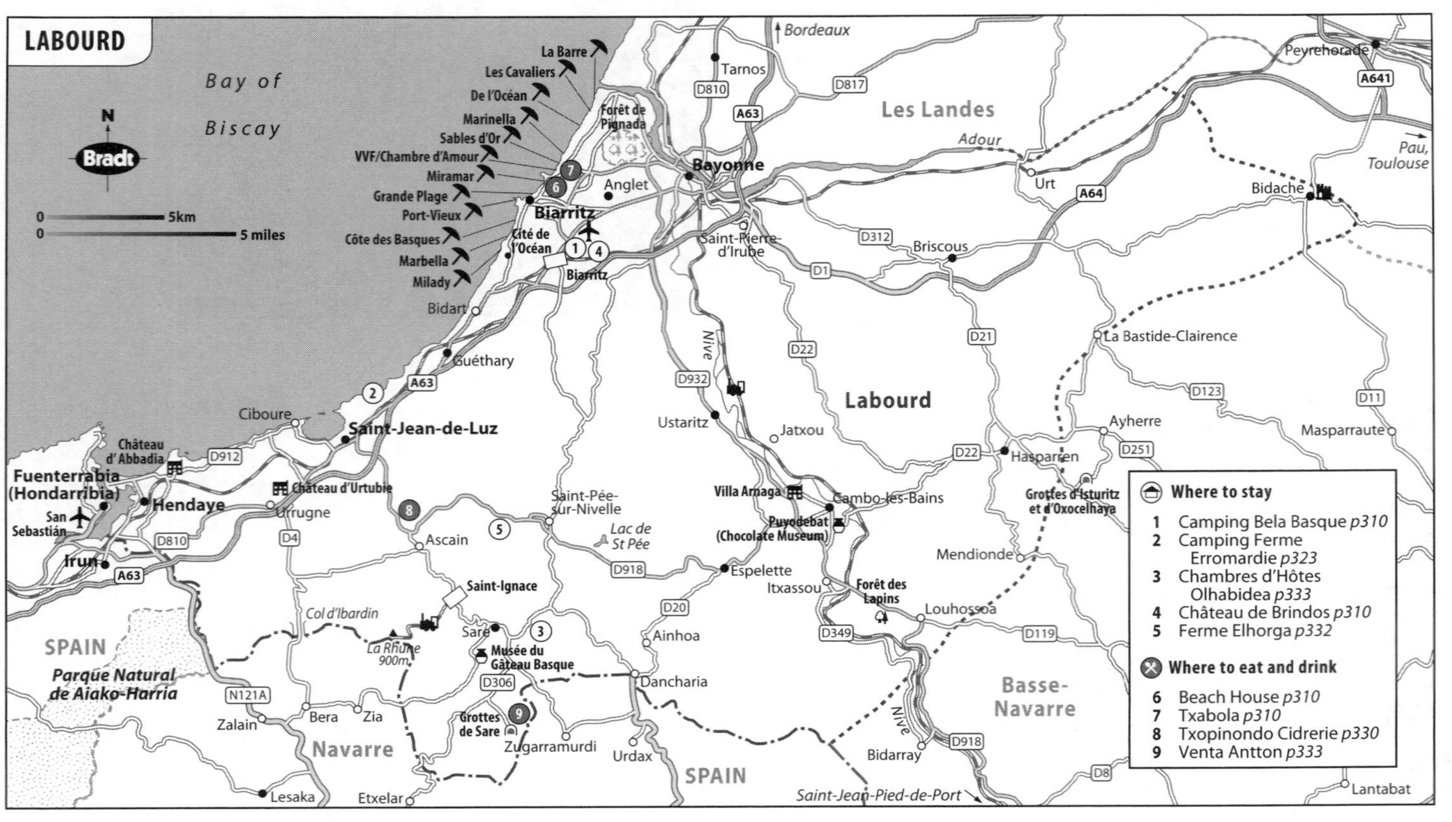
LABOURD
Bay of Biscay
N
Bradt
0 5km
0 5 miles
La Barre
Les Cavaliers
De l'Océan
Marinella
Sables d'Or
VVF/Chambre d'Amour
Miramar
Grande Plage
Port-Vieux
Côte des Basques
Marbella
Milady
Forêt de Pignada
Cité de l'Océan
Biarritz
Anglet
Bayonne
Tarnos
Bordeaux
Les Landes
Adour
Urt
Bidache
Peyrehorade
Pau, Toulouse
Saint-Pierre-d'Irube
Briscous
Bidart
Guéthary
Ciboure
Saint-Jean-de-Luz
Château d'Abbadia
Fuenterrabia (Hondarribia)
Hendaye
San Sebastián
Irun
Château d'Urtubie
Urrugne
Ascain
Saint-Pée-sur-Nivelle
Lac de St Pée
Saint-Ignace
Col d'Ibardin
La Rhune 900m
Sare
Musée du Gâteau Basque
Grottes de Sare
Zugarramurdi
Urdax
Dancharia
Ainhoa
Espelette
Itxassou
Ustaritz
Jatxou
Nive
Labourd
Villa Arnaga
Puyodebat (Chocolate Museum)
Cambo-les-Bains
Forêt des Lapins
Louhossoa
Bidarray
Mendionde
Hasparren
Grottes d'Isturitz et d'Oxocelhaya
Ayherre
La Bastide-Clairence
Masparraute
Lantabat
Basse-Navarre
Navarre
SPAIN
Parque Natural de Aiako-Harria
Zalain
Bera
Zia
Lesaka
Etxelar
Saint-Jean-Pied-de-Port
A63
A64
A641
D810
D817
D312
D1
D21
D22
D932
D918
D20
D349
D119
D306
D4
D912
D123
D251
D11
D8
N121A
Where to stay
1 Camping Bela Basque p310
2 Camping Ferme Erromardie p323
3 Chambres d'Hôtes Olhabidea p333
4 Château de Brindos p310
5 Ferme Elhorga p332
Where to eat and drink
6 Beach House p310
7 Txabola p310
8 Txopinondo Cidrerie p330
9 Venta Antton p333

Biarritz, the French Basque Coast and Inland Labourd

A town with international cachet, a well-known coast, and an often ignored interior: in some ways Labourd (Lapurdi) mirrors its Spanish coastal counterparts of Gipuzkoa and Bizkaia. Like San Sebastián, Biarritz has enjoyed a maritime history of whaling and trading with the countries of northern Europe, royal patronage in the 19th century and a contemporary focus on tourism, based on beaches and surf. But the French Basque Country differs from its Spanish Basque neighbours in that here there are no real cities, only Labourd's modestly proportioned towns of Bayonne and Biarritz. There is little industry here, and few scars on the landscape. Away from the coast are rolling Pyrenean foothills, a verdant richness. Also inland awaits a collection of oh-so-pretty villages, with sizeable, handsome villas of distinctive Basque architecture and the occasional culinary quirk, including Itxassou black cherries and the beaming red pepper of Espelette. The culture, meanwhile, is also different, a somewhat diluted brand of Basque, albeit occasionally more commercialised than over the border. History has had its say, with Celtic, Norman and English influences prominent in Labourd over the centuries, and the centralisation that followed the French Revolution did its best to weaken the region's Basque identity and language. Nowadays, you'll hear little Euskara spoken in the streets, and you're more likely to see the Basque flag on a souvenir T-shirt than flying from a balcony. Few of the girls sport the pudding-bowl Basque haircut, and there are very few banners demanding that ETA prisoners be returned home. Many inhabitants are as comfortable with being French as they are with being Basque, that's true, but their identity remains strong. You're definitely still in the Basque Country.

BIARRITZ (MIARRITZE)

British visitors may find Biarritz reminiscent of an English south coast resort in its 19th-century prime. Just add a pier, and you'd need only the smallest helping of imagination to complete the pretty picture. Often mentioned in the same breath as French seaside icons such as Cannes or Saint-Tropez, the town's very name still conjures up an image of glitz and glamour, even though the Belle Époque came to an end over a hundred years ago. The one-time patronage of the ruling classes – Emperor Napoleon III and his wife Eugenie chose to spend their Septembers here – is also a thing of the past. But make no mistake, Biarritz is no faded glory, no tarnished gem, no museum piece. With its elegant period villas, stylish hotels and well-trimmed green spaces, this is a town that has looked after itself. The celebrities that once graced the town might have moved on, but if they ever chose to come back, then Biarritz would be ready to welcome them with style. In the meantime, surfers bring their own vibe to town, mastering the waves and the equally difficult art of riding scooters while clutching their giant boards. The town undulates, stretching itself out along its many beaches, its sandy and rocky shore. A stroll out to the promontory of Le Rocher de la Vierge is a good way to get some perspective on the town and the coastline to north and south. From this natural intrusion into the sea, the visitor can admire the straight-as-a-die coastline as it unfolds down to the border with Spain. The elongated Plage Côte des Basques, awash with waves and surfers, takes the immediate attention; beyond, and inland, the distinctive shape of La Rhune mountain stands guard, just as the coast prepares to make a right-turn around the corner, westward into Spain. To the north, the seascape begins with the quaint Port des Pêcheurs, the fishermen's harbour, and continues with the city sands of the Grande Plage and Plage Miramar until another headland, carrying the lighthouse, protrudes into the Atlantic rollers. Below the lighthouse lies Anglet with its beaches, then the mouth of the Adour River and with it the limits of the Basque lands. As far as the eye can see – and that's usually quite far – the vista beyond is now of the uninterrupted sands that fringe the coastline of the neighbouring department of Les Landes.

GETTING THERE AND AWAY

By air For details of international flights to Biarritz Airport (now Aéroport de Biarritz Pays Basque), see page 45. It is very close to the centre, and the airport bus reaches the Mairie (town hall) in 15 minutes, calling at several other stops around town (Chronoplus line 14; **w** chronoplus.eu; €1) with departures every 20 minutes between 07.00 and 20.30. The same line serves both Bayonne (30mins) and Anglet (15mins). Chronoplus buses also go directly to Bidart, while Transports 64 operate to Saint-Jean-de-Luz and Hendaye (**w** transports64.fr).

By bus The inexpensive and frequent bus service means that Biarritz links nicely to most of the towns up and down the Basque Atlantic Coast. There are also regular services to San Sebastián (45mins; €7) with both Conda (**w** conda.es) and Pesa (**w** pesa.net).

By train Biarritz's train station is 3km south of the town centre, reachable by bus from the Mairie and other stops (Chronoplus line 8; 15mins; €1). A dozen or more trains run daily to Bayonne, Saint-Jean-de-Luz and, finally, Hendaye, from where you can change for Spanish destinations. There are also trains to Paris (5½hrs) among other French cities.

THE TRAM BUS

Intended to ease congestion along the coast, linking Bayonne, Anglet and Biarritz, it remains to be seen whether a heavy investment in digging up the road between the three towns to insert rails in the tarmac will succeed or not. Many locals are sceptical, doubtful if the high-season bottlenecks are indeed likely to disappear. After all, there is already a really good bus service. Time will tell, but the installation works are certainly likely to continue to disrupt through (at least) most of 2019.

THE GOLDEN AGE: I'M A CELEBRITY, GET ME INTO HERE

Biarritz had already been declared by 18th-century doctors to have curative seawaters when Emperor Napoleon III endorsed it as his preferred summer residence in 1854. Members of Napoleon's court, the industrial bourgeoisie and other movers and shakers flocked to the town between 1854 and 1870. The arrival of the railway in 1855 to nearby Bayonne had connected the area with Bordeaux and Paris, accelerating the development of Biarritz as a chic resort. But it was already on the radar of the British. After Napoleon's brother Joseph was ousted from his tenuous position as King of Spain, in 1813–14 the Duke of Wellington's soldiers occupied the area, sending home glowing reports about its delights. English-style tea shops appeared together with tennis courts built by hoteliers eager to make the British upper class feel at home. A British club was established near the lighthouse and a golf course was built. By 1896 over a thousand British tourists were making their way here every year, and in the years that followed notable visitors included Gladstone, Winston Churchill and Charlie Chaplin. Edward VII, crowned in 1901, was nicknamed the 'King of Britain and Biarritz' by the locals, such was his patronage. Queen Victoria was a visitor too, as was the future George VI.

GETTING AROUND

On foot The combination of relentless, high-season sun and Biarritz's topographical ups and downs mean that walking, while the best way to see everything, can become tiring very quickly in summer. The town is compact but, if you become weary, the free *navette* is the answer (see below).

Parking City-centre car parking on the street costs around €1.20–1.60 per hour, with parking also available in underground car parks at around €12 per 24 hours. There is free car parking at the train station, by the lighthouse and at a few other on-street venues in town.

By bus Letting the bus driver do the work manoeuvring around town is a good idea in July and August. The streets are narrow, often one-way, the traffic heavy and parking hard to find. The eight lines of the Chronoplus bus network (0559 52 59 52; w chronoplus.eu) are cheap, smart and efficient and will take you from Bidart to Bayonne, and all around Biarritz's major points of interest. A ticket costs €1, which lasts for 1 hour, allowing changes of bus where necessary. You can also buy a 24-hour ticket for €2 which allows unlimited travel on both the Chronoplus and Transport 64 networks, letting you go further afield. Tickets are bought on board.

Even better, a free *navette* (half-size bus) tootles on three lines around the town centre every 15 minutes from Monday to Saturday (daily in high season) reaching all of Biarritz's major points of interest.

Taxis Taxis can be picked up at various points or called in advance (0559 03 18 18), but not flagged down in the street.

By scooter/electric bike/bicycle High-season parking woes and slowly throbbing four-wheeled traffic make the use of two wheels a practical alternative

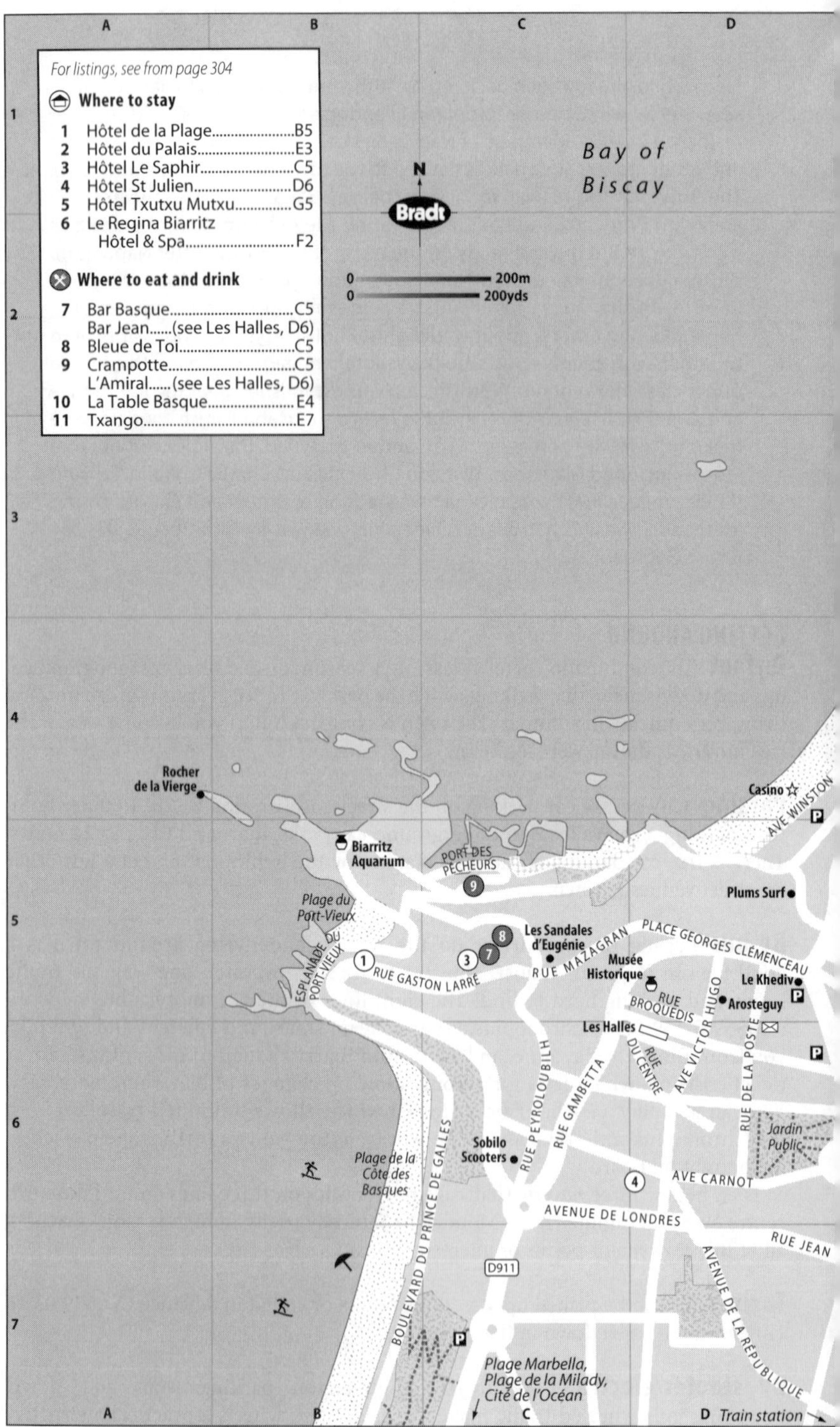
For listings, see from page 304
Where to stay
1 Hôtel de la Plage....B5
2 Hôtel du Palais....E3
3 Hôtel Le Saphir....C5
4 Hôtel St Julien....D6
5 Hôtel Txutxu Mutxu....G5
6 Le Regina Biarritz Hôtel & Spa....F2
Where to eat and drink
7 Bar Basque....C5
Bar Jean......(see Les Halles, D6)
8 Bleue de Toi....C5
9 Crampotte....C5
L'Amiral......(see Les Halles, D6)
10 La Table Basque....E4
11 Txango....E7
Bay of Biscay
Bradt
0 200m
0 200yds
Rocher de la Vierge
Biarritz Aquarium
Port des Pecheurs
Plage du Port-Vieux
Esplanade du Port-Vieux
Rue Gaston Larré
Les Sandales d'Eugénie
Rue Mazagran
Place Georges Clémenceau
Musée Historique
Rue Broquedis
Les Halles
Rue du Centre
Ave Victor Hugo
Rue de la Poste
Casino
Ave Winston
Plums Surf
Le Khediv
Arosteguy
Jardin Public
Rue Peyroloubilh
Rue Gambetta
Sobilo Scooters
Ave Carnot
Avenue de Londres
Rue Jean
Avenue de la République
Plage de la Côte des Basques
Boulevard du Prince de Galles
D911
Plage Marbella, Plage de la Milady, Cité de l'Océan
Train station

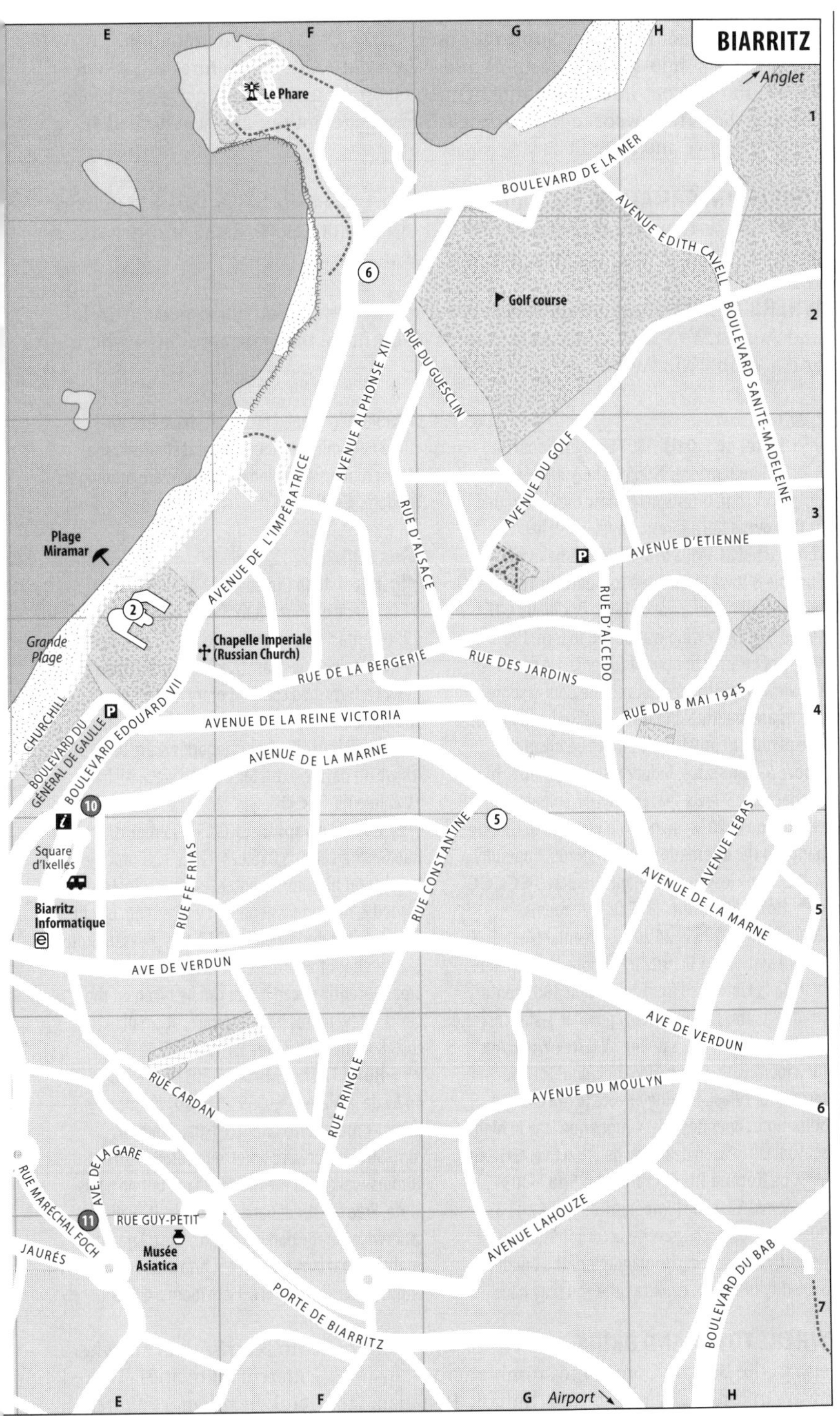

Biarritz, the French Basque Coast and Inland Labourd BIARRITZ (MIARRITZE) 7

around town. For rental, try **Sobilo Scooters** [302 C6] (24 Rue Peyroloubilh; ☎ 0559 24 94 47; w sobilo-scooters.com; ⏰ mid-May–mid-Oct), which hires out scooters for around €16 per hour, including helmet; electric bikes are €42 per day; bicycles €18 per day. Their website has an English-language option, and you'll need ID, a driver's licence and a credit card.

TOURIST INFORMATION The tourist office is at 1 Square d'Ixelles [303 E5] (☎ 0559 22 37 10; w tourisme.biarritz.fr; ⏰ Jul & Aug 09.00–19.00 daily, at other times 09.00–18.00 Mon–Fri), and has free Wi-Fi available.

WHERE TO STAY Bank on booking early for your stay in Biarritz, especially in July and August. You should also expect to pay a bit more than you would elsewhere – and a lot more in August.

Luxury

Hôtel du Palais [303 E3] (153 rooms) 1 Av de l'Impératrice; ☎ 0559 41 64 00; w hotel-du-palais.com. Guests here know they've landed at the town's top address. Napoleon III had this constructed as a villa in 1854 for his beloved Eugenie & it was converted to a hotel in 1893, being rebuilt after a fire of 1903. Originally a 'U' shape, the extra wing was added to form the shape of an 'E', in honour of Eugenie. Oozing class, the views from the restaurant, the pool & some rooms are breathtaking. This is classed as a Palais, one of only 13 hotels in France to be given this 'above 5-star' status. Indoor & outdoor pools, huge sundeck & a 5-level spa. Free Wi-Fi. Following renovation in 2018, ownership was due to change hands to the international Hyatt group, hopefully without any loss to its elegant character. **€€€€€**

Hôtel St Julien [302 D6] (20 rooms) 20 Av Carnot; ☎ 0559 24 20 39; e contact@hotel-saint-julien-biarritz.fr; w hotel-saint-julien-biarritz.fr. Converted from an elegant 19th-century residence, this is a deservedly popular 3-star choice. Heating, discreet AC, satellite TV & free Wi-Fi. Ask for a room with a view. Elegant lounge, outside terrace for b/fast. Parking on-site (extra charge). Sometimes operates a 3-/4-night min stay in high season. Off-season deals can be attractive. **€€€€€**

Le Regina Biarritz Hôtel & Spa [303 F2] (65 rooms) 52 Av de l'Impératrice; ☎ 0559 41 33 00; e H2050@accor.com; w accorhotels.com. Recently renovated, the grandeur of the building & quality of service evoke a time you may have thought had slipped by. Rooms have free Wi-Fi, cable TV & minibar. Top-drawer restaurant, spa, steam room, swimming pool. Prices are thoroughly modern. **€€€€€**

Mid range

Hôtel de la Plage [302 B5] (23 rooms) 3 Esplanade du Port-Vieux; ☎ 0559 23 95 19; e contact@hoteldelaplage-biarritz.com; w hoteldelaplage-biarritz.com. Unpretentious, newly refurbished contemporary hotel looking straight down on to the Plage du Port-Vieux. Rooms fall into different categories & are bright. It's worth paying extra for a beach view. All have TV & free Wi-Fi. **€€€**

Hôtel Le Saphir [302 C5] (15 rooms) 3 Rue Gaston Larre; ☎ 0559 24 12 23; e contact@hotel-lesaphir.com; w hotel-lesaphir.com. Family-owned & run, professional but welcoming. Bright & tastefully refurbished in 2013, this pleasant hotel is 200m back from the seafront in the Port-Vieux area. Decently priced b/fast can be taken on the patio. A few rooms have a terrace, at small extra cost, & all have TV & free Wi-Fi. **€€€**

Hôtel Txutxu Mutxu [303 G5] (14 rooms) 44 Av de la Marne; ☎ 0559 24 85 90; e contact@txutxu-mutxu.com; w hotel-txutxu-mutxu.com. Straightforward hotel, renovated in 2015, 10mins' walk from the Grande Plage but on a bus route. Free on-street parking outside, if available, otherwise garage parking at extra cost. Friendly, English-speaking staff, decent b/fast served in bright salon. Free Wi-Fi & TV in rooms. **€€€**

WHERE TO EAT AND DRINK The visitor will find it easier in Biarritz than anywhere else in the Basque Country to stumble across cuisine of different ethnicities. Tucked away in the back streets are Indian, Peruvian, Thai and Brazilian restaurants, to name but a few. Of course, some of the surf brigade demand to be fuelled up on burgers and pizza. Apart from those listed below, there are numerous popular places to eat on the Rue des Halles, beside the market hall. The atmosphere buzzes there. Down by the Vieux Port, the waterfront restaurants are more frequented by tourists than locals.

Bar Jean [302 D6] 5 Rue des Halles; 0559 24 80 38; 08.30–02.00 Thu–Mon, 09.00–13.00 Wed. A frenzy of activity, tables outside & in are sought after in this lively place. Hands-on management of a hard-working team of young waiting staff, together with *pintxos* & meat & fish dishes which pay homage to the Basque Country south of the Pyrenees. €€€

Crampotte [302 C5] 30 Port des Pêcheurs; 0535 46 91 22; noon–14.00 & 19.00–22.00 daily. In the well-hidden fishermen's harbour, a tiny place with outdoor tables only, it finds much favour for its fresh fish & location. There are vegetarian options. On the downside, opening hours seem a bit erratic, perhaps determined by the weather. €€€

L'Amiral [302 D6] 9 Rue des Halles; 0533 47 51 31; 10.00–15.00 & 18.30–02.00 daily. One of the many places on Rue des Halles, good seafood options, *cassolettes* & small dishes in another people-watching hotspot. A bit quieter than Bar Jean (see above), so take your pick. Service can be patchy in high season. €€€

Txango [303 E7] 5 Av de la Gare; 0559 51 24 98; 12.15–14.00 & 19.30–22.30 Tue–Sat. Innovative cuisine, beautifully presented. Vegetarian options available. The midweek menu is good value. €€€

La Table Basque [303 E4] 4 Av de la Marne; 0559 22 23 52; w restaurant-ltb-biarritz.com; noon–13.15 & 19.15–21.15 Thu–Mon. Good, hearty fare served by smiling, hard-working staff. Daily specials plus Basque standards guaranteed to send customers home happy. Not elaborate, but definitely good value. €€

Bleue de Toi [302 C5] 30 Rue Mazagran; 0559 24 37 08; 10.00–23.00 daily. For a light lunch of delicious, savoury crêpes, this is a good choice with little chance of breaking the bank. Some outside tables, friendly service. €

Bar Basque [302 C5] 1 Rue du Port-Vieux; 0553 47 54 96; w bar-basque.fr; 18.00–02.00 daily. A low-key, relaxed ambience in this pub with shaded outdoor terrace & a decent selection of quality *pintxos*. Mellow evening music changes as the place gets livelier. At the apex of 2 streets running up from the beach, it's good for people-watching while sipping a house cocktail.

SHOPPING In keeping with a resort of some *élan*, Biarritz has a great selection of high-class shops with lots of fashion outlets, souvenir shops and browsing options. Mouth-watering patisseries are to the fore and the market is definitely worth a visit, especially for self-caterers.

Les Sandales d'Eugénie [302 C5] 18 Rue Mazagran; m 0559 24 22 51; 10.00–13.00 & 15.00–18.30 Tue–Sat. The place to buy a pair of espadrilles, just right for beach or town wear.

Maison Arostéguy [302 D5] 5 Av Victor Hugo; 0559 24 00 52; w arosteguy.com; Sep–Jun 09.30–13.00 & 15.30–19.00 Tue–Sat, Jul & Aug 09.30–19.30 Mon–Sat. Fine cheeses & wines, some of the best *gâteaux Basques*, plus loads of other treats.

Les Halles (Market) [302 C6] Quartier des Halles; 07.30–13.30 daily, mid-Jul–mid-Aug also 18.00–21.00 daily. The renovated building conceals over 100 stalls brimming with the freshest & best fish, vegetables, cheese & meat. Not to be missed.

OTHER PRACTICALITIES

Internet/Wi-Fi You can access free Wi-Fi at the tourist office. Municipal Wi-Fi is also available at several places around the centre. Many cafés can also indulge you in exchange for the price of a cup of coffee. If you are without device, Biarritz Informatique [303 E5] (5 Av de Verdun; 09.30–19.30 Mon–Sat, Jul & Aug 15.00–

19.00 Sun) is one of the rare remaining cybercafés, and also scans, copies & faxes as well as repairing computers.

Newspapers A few newsagents sell international press, including Le Khédiv [302 D5], located at the corner of Place Clémenceau/Rue Maréchal Foch.

Communications The **post office** [302 D6] can be found at 17 Rue de la Poste (🕘 10.00–18.00 Mon–Fri, 09.30–13.30 Sat).

SURFING Unlike many of the Basque Country's mysteries, the history of Basque surfing is short, sweet and straightforward. American scriptwriter Peter Viertel turned up here in 1957, bringing his surfboards with him, and surfing on the Basque coast was suddenly on its way to acquiring its current international reputation. From its tiny beginnings, it's now a hugely important visitor attraction in Biarritz and beyond.

Plums École de Surf [303 E4] 9 Rue des Gardères; 📞 0559 24 10 79; **e** plums@wanadoo.fr; **w** plums-surf.com; 🕘 Apr–Nov. English-speaking surf school, a family business now run by the sons of one of Biarritz's surf pioneers in the 1960s. Insurance & equipment included with all courses, which take place on the Grande Plage. 5 90min lessons (in a group) cost €190.

Hastea Surf School [302 B6] Plage de la Côte des Basques; **m** 0681 93 98 66; **e** ecoledesurf.hastea@gmail.com; **w** hastea.com. Established over 20 years, multilingual school offering a full range of courses & equipment hire. €180 for 5 90min lessons, including insurance & equipment.

FESTIVALS Often a host venue for international surfing competitions, Biarritz can find other ways to party, too. Every month sees a celebration of some sort, be it cultural, sporting or gastronomic. A useful website, **w** biarritz-evenement.fr, will help you plan your trip to coincide. A few of the major annual festivals are:

Festival des Arts de la Rue (Street Art Festival) Four days in May during which the streets are full of dancers, actors, jugglers and music.

Les Casetas de Biarritz The town's restaurants decamp temporarily to stalls set up at the Plage de la Côte des Basques, showcasing their cuisine over a five-day period in June. Meandering musical groups add to the fun.

Nuit Féerique (Fireworks) 15 August (Feast of the Assumption) sees an explosion of fireworks in the night skies above the Grande Plage.

Le Temps d'Aimer la Danse September brings nine days of dance spectaculars, with international acts gracing the streets as well as the town's theatres, and also a chance for you to show off your best moves.

Biarritz en Lumières From mid-December to the start of January the façades of some of the town's most illustrious buildings are illuminated.

WHAT TO SEE AND DO A great morning walk and means of familiarising yourself with the town would be to promenade the coastline from the Le Phare (lighthouse) at the northern end of Biarritz, down past the Hôtel du Palais, along the back of the Grande Plage, past the Ports des Pêcheurs and out to the Rocher de la Vierge promontory. This route is a favourite for joggers, but there's no obligation to hurry.

After visiting the Aquarium and the Plage du Port-Vieux, head directly inland to find the town centre before visiting the Musée Historique and the Musée Asiatica. Save the long walk down the Plage de la Côte des Basques and inland on to the Cité de l'Océan for the afternoon, or a different day.

Le Phare (Lighthouse) [303 F1] (🕘 Jul & Aug 10.00–13.30 & 14.00–19.00 daily, May–Jun & Sep 14.00–18.00, Oct–Mar 14.00–17.00 Sat–Sun only; €2) To ensure that you see beautiful Biarritz from every angle, a walk up to the lighthouse is essential, whether you actually climb the 73m tower or not. From the hill on which it stands, the views to the south over beaches, mountains and as far as Spain make the effort worthwhile. On the way from the town centre, you also pass the grandiose Hôtel du Palais (page 304) and, opposite its entrance, the church built to satisfy visiting Russian nobility in the 19th century. Continuing up the Avenue de l'Impératrice, note the motley but magnificent collection of mansions that bear testament to the town's glorious past: at number 18, the British-styled Villa Cyrano; at number 15, the Neo-Gothic aspect of La Roche Ronde. Just before reaching the lighthouse at 7 Rue d'Haitzart is the Villa Etchepherdia, in unmistakable neo-Basque style. Once in front of the lighthouse, note the propeller of the Frans Hals, a ship that ran aground on the Plage Miramar in 1996. The long-serving manageress of the Hôtel du Palais still tells of the staff's mounting fright as the ship broke its tow-line and approached the hotel. It was refloated after a month of head-scratching logistics. Be sure to walk all the way around the compact gardens behind the lighthouse, giving you further vistas down on to neighbouring Anglet's beaches and all the way north up to the department of Les Landes.

Biarritz Aquarium [302 B5] (Esplanade du Rocher de la Vierge; ☎ 0559 22 75 40; w aquariumbiarritz.com; 🕘 09.30–20.00 daily, 09.30–midnight Jul &Aug, closed last 3 weeks of Jan & sometimes Mon Nov–Mar; €14.90/11.0/10.50 adults/under 17s/under 13s, tickets can be bought in advance, online) Fairly standard aquarium housed in a beautiful Art Deco building constructed in 1933. The information panels on the wall are only useful if you speak French. Nevertheless, this is essentially a visual experience. Highlights, especially for children, will be the somersaulting seals, sharks, green and loggerhead turtles and, in tank number 9 upstairs, the macabre-looking green moray eel (*Gymnothorax funebris*) and his ugly companion the goldentail moray eel (*Gymnothorax miliaris*), two evil-looking, serpentine creatures with vicious teeth. The middle floors contain exhibits to do with the Basque Country's fishing and whaling traditions. On the roof is an open-air pool, but don't bring your swimsuit – it's reserved for the seals, who alternate between sunbathing and swimming, depending on the weather. The view from the roof is excellent. As dictated modern-museum-style, your exit is via the museum shop.

Le Rocher de la Vierge [302 A4] A must-do in Biarritz, a simple walk out along the manmade promontory to the Virgin's statue affords you superb views down over the jagged rocks and along the coast in both directions. On the approach, local artists sometimes display their work.

Musée Historique (Historical Museum) [302 D5] (Rue Broquedis; ☎ 0559 24 86 28; 🕘 Jul & Aug 10.00–12.30 & 14.00–18.30 daily, Sep–Jun 10.30–13.00 & 14.30–18.30 daily; €4) Housed in the former St Andrew's Anglican Church, the memorial in the porch notes the visit of Queen Victoria in 1889. King Edward VII also attended the Sunday service here during his frequent visits to town. The small museum's exhibits are centred on four key themes: the sea, Biarritz and the Empire,

Biarritz and the world and Biarritz in the 20th century. Much is made of Biarritz's illustrious visitors, both foreign and domestic, across the ages and the evolution of the town from fishing village to seaside resort is well documented. The museum underwent a renovation in 2018.

Musée Asiatica (Asian Art Museum) [303 E7] (1 Rue Guy-Petit; ☎ 0559 22 78 78; w museeasiatica.com; ⌚ 14.00–18.30 Mon–Fri, 14.00–19.00 Sat & Sun, Jul, Aug & school holidays 10.30–18.30 Mon–Fri; €10/€8/free adults/students & adolescents/child (under 8), plus €5 extra for English-language audio guide, or ask for the translated booklet, which has the same text as the audio) A private collection of over 1,000 pieces of art and artefacts, gathered from China, India, Nepal and Tibet by passionate local researcher and collector Michel Postel. The visit starts in the basement with works from ancient India, organised chronologically and according to region (north, east, central and south). Some extraordinary wood and stone carvings are on display, particularly a 13th-century piece from the temple at Konarak, which apparently represented a year's work for its master carver and his pupil. A truly magnificent 18th/19th-century teak door from Gujarat also catches the eye. The exhibition continues through China, Nepal and Tibet, with additional laminated information in English for those who want to know more. Although the art is magnificent, it is likely to be of most interest to enthusiasts or experts, and there is certainly very little to entertain children.

La Cité de l'Océan (City of the Ocean) [302 C7] (1 Av de la Plage, Milady; ☎ 0559 22 75 40; w citedelocean.com; ⌚ 10.00–19.00 daily, 10.00–22.00 Jul & Aug, sometimes closed Mon in winter; check website, as times change each month; €12.50/9.90/8.50 adults/under 17s/under 13s) Only six years old, this is a state-of-the-art museum designed to complement the Biarritz Aquarium. Far from traditional, it contains mainly interactive exhibits and short 3D films – shown at specified times – on subjects such as global warming, the birth of the oceans, how tsunamis occur, the mechanics of wave energy and creatures of the deep. The final display is a clever explanation of four 'mysteries of the sea', including the Bermuda Triangle. Nearly all the exhibits have English-language audio options, and the films – with audio in French only – are largely a visual experience. New in 2015 was a 3D surfing simulator, allowing you to try out Biarritz's favourite sport without any need to squeeze into a wetsuit or enter the ocean. Although there are a number of interactive games to entertain children, the staff advise that the museum is not recommended for the under 7s.

Beaches All beaches are supervised in season, but check what the locals are doing before taking the plunge; the waves are often big and the coast is rocky in places. Apart from Marbella beach, there are surf schools on every beach. The beaches below are listed from north to south.

Grande Plage/Plage Miramar [303 D3/D4] Right in the town centre, this sandy stretch is very scenic and will surely feature in your holiday photos, but it is not really top choice for paddling or surfing. There's a seasonal children's club and, if the sea doesn't take your fancy, there is a municipal swimming pool inside the casino building.

Plage du Port-Vieux [302 B5] A tiny beach and the winter venue for the brave (or foolish) 'Ours Blancs' ('White Bears') swimming club, whose members take to the water every day, even in December. They've been doing it since the club's foundation in 1929. For the rest of us, the waters here are usually calm, even though there are big breakers on either side of the narrow cove. The water is never crystal clear, but it is safe for paddling or swimming most of the time.

Plage de la Côte des Basques [302 B6] From the promenade above this lengthy strip of sand, south of the centre, the hundreds of heads bobbing in the waves will tell you that this is the surfers' beach. The surfer schools occupy the southern end from April to October, and this famous beach hosts many surfing competitions. Swimming is forbidden at high tide due to lack of access.

Plage Marbella and Plage de la Milady [302 C7] From town, it's not possible to walk all the way down the coast to these two, situated well to the south: you'd have to cut inland at some point, or take the *navette*. Both beaches have full facilities and are very popular. Milady offers direct sea access for those with lesser mobility.

ANGLET (ANGELU)

The huge number of trees that define the hinterland immediately beyond the coast have led to Anglet's epithet of 'Le Poumon Vert' ('Green Lung'). Anglet, the 'A' in the 'BAB' (Bayonne–Anglet–Biarritz) conglomeration that merges the three towns seamlessly into one, may not have the administrative importance of Bayonne or the international reputation of glamour-puss Biarritz, but still has its own identity despite being wedged between the two. The Forêt de Pignada is over 250ha of beautiful forest, mainly pine, created in the 17th century to stabilise the fragile sands of the coast. Now it is crossed by cycle tracks and paths, loved by the locals who can be seen exercising here at almost any time of day. With 4.5km of sands spread across no fewer than 11 beaches and waves big enough to host surfing competitions, Anglet has plenty of seaside joy to offer, too. To make you feel welcome, the town provides free parking, free bikes, two tourist offices and prices a bit lower than Biarritz. Overall, Anglet feels more like a down-to-earth French seaside resort than Biarritz, with the wide boardwalk around the Sables d'Or beach backed with endless bars, restaurants and beachwear shops. If you want to endear yourselves to the locals, make sure you firmly pronounce the 't' at the end of the town's name, whatever your French teacher may have told you at school.

GETTING THERE AND AROUND

By car Although the parking is free and plentiful in off-season, in summer it still struggles to cope. If staying outside the town, arrive early or use the bus.

By bus The frequent Chronoplus (☎ 0559 52 59 52; w chronoplus.eu) service connects Anglet with both Biarritz and Bayonne, as well as the airport and Bayonne train station. In July and August, a free *navette* shuttles frequently between Anglet town centre, set back from the coast, and some of the car parks (Minerva, Quintaou, Cinq Cantons and Stella Maris) and the beaches of La Madrague, Les Corsaires and Sables d'Or.

TOURIST INFORMATION The Cinq Cantons office is at 1 Avenue de la Chambre d'Amour (☎ 0559 03 77 01; w anglet-tourisme.com; ⌚ Sep–Jun 09.00–12.30 & 14.00–18.00 Mon–Fri, 09.00–12.30 Sat, Jul & Aug 09.00–19.00 Mon–Fri); this is the office for the town and for borrowing bikes for free. The Chambre d'Amour office (Av des Dauphins; ⌚ Jul & Aug 10.00–19.00 daily, closed Nov–Easter, enquire for other months) is the 'seaside' office, offering helpful information about all of the activities available, including downloadable brochures on accommodation, events and tide tables.

WHERE TO STAY As should befit a town with so many beaches, and visitors with so many different holiday plans, Anglet's accommodation ought to stretch from surfer-friendly campsites through self-catering apartments to top-range hotels, but is somewhat lacking in the last category. The tourist office site lets you book online, but a few of the best choices are listed below. Many surfers use the campsites down the coast at Bidart, then take the bus to their chosen beach.

Château de Brindos [map, page 298] (22 rooms & 7 suites) 1 Allée du Château; 0559 23 89 80; e info@chateaudebrindos.com; w chateaudebrindos.com. Rated for its beautiful interior, rich parkland & private lake, this is Anglet's plushest address, equipped with a gastronomic restaurant, located well away from the town, but only 2mins' taxi ride from the airport. The grounds are lush, full of trees & twittering birdlife, the huge lake stuffed with carp. A seasonal outdoor pool, sauna & fitness facility provide the activities. Rooms have AC & satellite TV, plus terrace, balcony or access to the garden. Free Wi-Fi, elegant & high-end restaurant. The best hotel around, the highest cost – by a stretch. And the suites, some with large sun terrace, are sumptuous, but a further step up in price. **€€€€**

Chambres d'Hôtes d'Emilie (3 rooms) 164 Bd des Plages; m 0616 95 38 44; e milielerecouvreux@hotmail.com. Charming B&B with big garden, located in the Chiberta district. Free Wi-Fi, ping-pong. B/fast inc. **€€**

Chambres d'Hôtes La Musica (3 rooms) 4 Rue Thalie; m 0674 31 72 65; w maisonlamusica.fr. This small B&B has welcoming hosts. Rooms all have private bath & free Wi-Fi. Use of fridge & garden. Free parking. Guests can hire mountain bikes. No credit cards accepted. 2 nights' min (5 nights' min Jul & Aug). B/fast inc. **€€**

Camping Bela Basque [map, page 298] 2 Allée Etchécopar; 0559 23 03 00; w camping-belabasque.com. Chalets for hire, pitches for tents & caravans. Swimming pool & children's pool, water slide, Wi-Fi (extra charge), some shade. Located very near to the airport & public buses to Anglet's centre & the beaches pass 400m from the campsite entrance. **€**

WHERE TO EAT AND DRINK

Txabola [map, page 298] 34 Av des Dauphins; 0559 03 87 86. A pleasant terrace for sunny days, good food & very close to the seaside tourist office – perfect after a day on the beach. Vegetarian options available. **€€€**

Beach House [map, page 298] 26 Av des Dauphins; 0559 15 27 17; w beachhouseanglet.com; noon–14.00 & 19.30–22.00 Wed–Sat, 11.30–15.00 Sun, Jul & Aug daily. Everything from small sharing dishes through to salads, mains & desserts. W/end booking is advisable. **€€**

OTHER PRACTICALITIES Anglet's post office is at 7 Rue du 8 Mai (08.45–18.00 Mon–Fri, 08.45–noon Sat).

SHOPPING The town has a number of markets, including the brand-new indoor **Halles des Cinq Cantons** (year-round 08.00–14.00 Tue–Sat, also 16.00–20.00 Fri & Sat). The **Marché de Quintaou** (Esplanade de Quintaou) happens every Thursday and Sunday, and is the place for self-caterers to stock up with local cheeses and delicacies. It's a morning-only affair, so if you turn up after 13.00 you've missed the action. **Les Puces de Quintaou** (Esplanade de Quintaou), Anglet's flea market, takes place every fourth Saturday of the month (third Saturday in December) from 08.00 to 18.00. The **Brocantes** (antiques/collectables fair) (Pl des Cinq Cantons) is held every first Sunday of the month, mornings only.

WHAT TO SEE AND DO

Beaches Everyone will find their own favourite beach here, depending on their taste and purpose. The improbably named Petite Chambre d'Amour (Little Chamber of Love) might attract romantics and also has facilities for the disabled, though its scenic beauty is marred slightly by the huge holiday complex, looking for all the world like some futuristic spy lair, that rudely nudges up to the promenade. All is redeemed by the beautiful sands and the lighthouse above. Youngsters and the young at heart might choose the Marinella, while Cavaliers is the place for international surfing competitions. La Barre is too quiet for those chasing the waves, so more suited to families with young children. Sables d'Or is popular for beach volleyball. The tourist office website gives full details of all Anglet's beaches, with a clever interactive map letting you highlight those with your desired facilities.

Walking/cycling The **Forêt du Pignada** is a lovely splurge of pine trees, presenting opportunities for walking, picnicking or cycling. Bus number 5 connects from here to Anglet's beaches and to Bayonne. As well as the free bikes available from the tourist office, you can also obtain more upmarket bikes privately from **Les Roues de Lilou** (☎ 0981 96 44 11; m 0688 34 30 23; w lesrouesdelilou.com), which offers off-road bikes for adults and children, electric bikes and guided tours.

Golf Anglet has a course that welcomes visitors with or without a handicap certificate, although the latter pay more, at Golf Chiberta (104 Bd des Plages; ☎ 0559 52 51 10; w golfchiberta.com). Booking a few weeks in advance is required, as many competitions are hosted here. A high-season round can cost a stiff €85, but special offers mean that playing late in the day can halve that price. It also offers the much cheaper *Impératrice* course, perfect for beginners, plus a pro shop and full facilities.

Surfing/bodyboards/stand-up paddles Most beaches have surf schools, though shifting sand banks mean that the schools choose their beach accordingly. Summer is popular, though experts prefer the bigger waves of April, May, September and October. The schools open April–October, but might give private lessons to experienced surfers outside that time period.

Rainbow École de Surf Plage de la Petite Chambre d'Amour; ☎ 0559 03 54 67 (shop); m 0618 22 37 82; e contact@rainbow-surfshop.com; w ecoledesurf-rainbow.com. Offering surf lessons at all levels, including taster sessions from €34, plus equipment rental of surfboards, stand-up paddles & body boards.

BAYONNE (BAIONA)

Those visitors prepared to prise themselves from the nearby beaches of Biarritz or Anglet will find that Bayonne is full of its own, slightly inland delights. Its centre almost completely pedestrianised, with many handsome buildings, specialist shops and riverside restaurants, this is a town that defies you to rush. There has been much investment in careful renovation, with great success. Bayonne is composed of several distinct quarters, of which Grand-Bayonne and Petit-Bayonne – kept apart by the Nive River – are likely to be of most interest to visitors. Across the Adour – the Nive's bigger, wider sibling – St-Esprit still feels like the separate town it once was, before being absorbed into Bayonne in 1857. Once the Jewish quarter, it is now perhaps most notable as the site of the train station and exudes a Bohemian ambience; a walk down the Rue Sainte Catherine will unveil a few quirky shops and low-cost

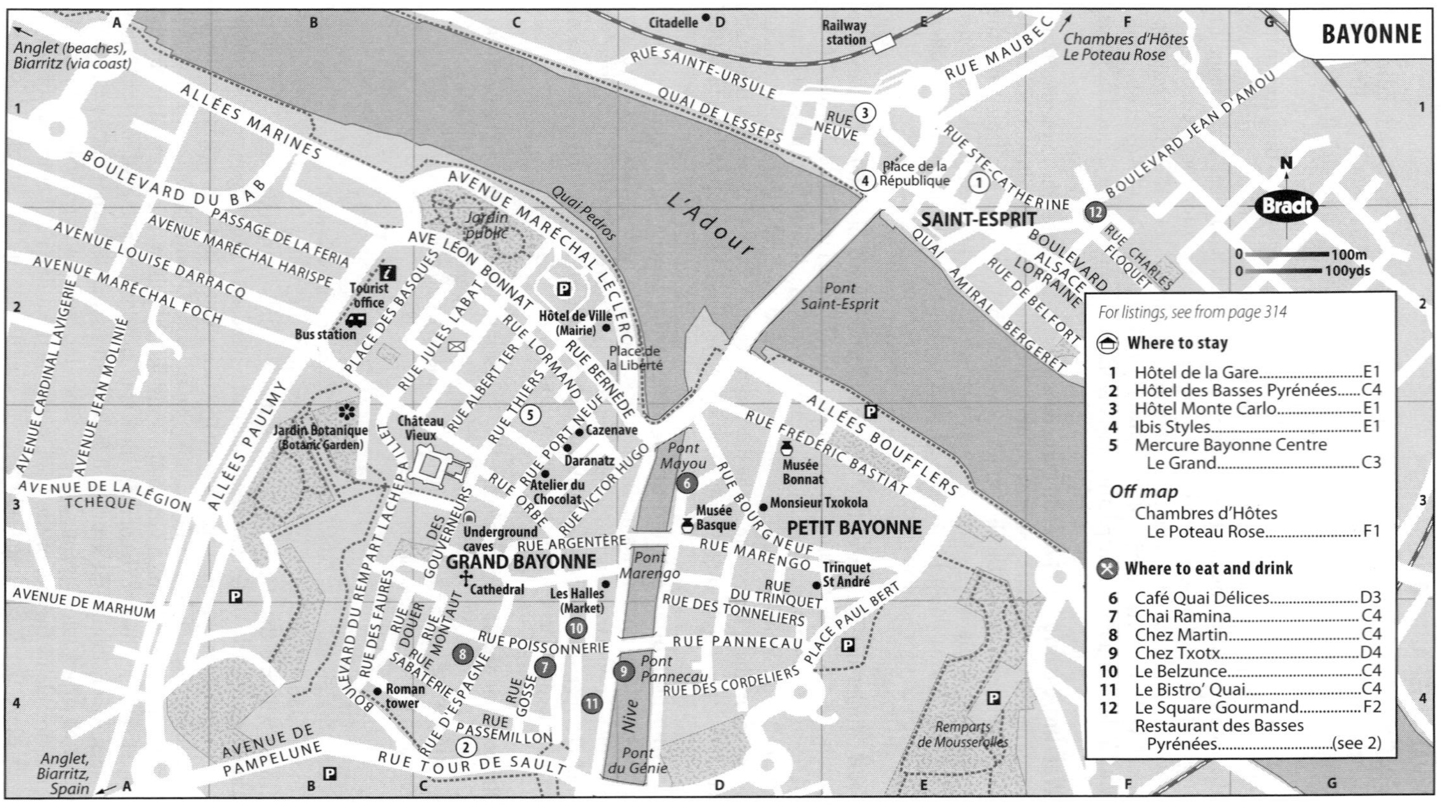
BAYONNE
For listings, see from page 314
Where to stay
1 Hôtel de la Gare....E1
2 Hôtel des Basses Pyrénées....C4
3 Hôtel Monte Carlo....E1
4 Ibis Styles....E1
5 Mercure Bayonne Centre Le Grand....C3
Off map
Chambres d'Hôtes Le Poteau Rose....F1
Where to eat and drink
6 Café Quai Délices....D3
7 Chai Ramina....C4
8 Chez Martin....C4
9 Chez Txotx....D4
10 Le Belzunce....C4
11 Le Bistro' Quai....C4
12 Le Square Gourmand....F2
Restaurant des Basses Pyrénées....(see 2)
Bradt
N
0 100m
0 100yds
Anglet (beaches), Biarritz (via coast)
Anglet, Biarritz, Spain
Chambres d'Hôtes Le Poteau Rose
Citadelle
Railway station
L'Adour
Nive
SAINT-ESPRIT
GRAND BAYONNE
PETIT BAYONNE
ALLÉES MARINES
BOULEVARD DU BAB
PASSAGE DE LA FERIA
AVENUE MARÉCHAL HARISPE
AVENUE LOUISE DARRACQ
AVENUE MARÉCHAL FOCH
AVENUE CARDINAL LAVIGERIE
AVENUE JEAN MOLINIÉ
AVENUE DE LA LÉGION TCHÈQUE
AVENUE DE MARHUM
ALLÉES PAULMY
AVENUE DE PAMPELUNE
RUE TOUR DE SAULT
RUE SAINTE-URSULE
QUAI DE LESSEPS
RUE NEUVE
RUE MAUBEC
RUE STE-CATHERINE
BOULEVARD JEAN D'AMOU
Place de la République
QUAI AMIRAL BERGERET
BOULEVARD ALSACE LORRAINE
RUE DE BELFORT
RUE CHARLES FLOQUET
Pont Saint-Esprit
Quai Pedros
AVENUE MARÉCHAL LECLERC
Jardin public
AVE LÉON BONNAT
PLACE DES BASQUES
RUE JULES LABAT
RUE ALBERT 1ER
RUE THIERS
RUE LORMAND
RUE BERNÈDE
Hôtel de Ville (Mairie)
Place de la Liberté
Tourist office
Bus station
Jardin Botanique (Botanic Garden)
Château Vieux
RUE PORT NEUF
Cazenave
Daranatz
Atelier du Chocolat
RUE ORBE
RUE VICTOR HUGO
DES GOUVERNEURS
Underground caves
RUE ARGENTÈRE
Cathedral
Les Halles (Market)
BOULEVARD DU REMPART LACHEPAILLET
RUE DES FAURES
RUE DOUER
RUE MONTAUT
RUE SABATERIE
RUE D'ESPAGNE
Roman tower
RUE POISSONNERIE
RUE GOSSE
RUE PASSEMILLON
Pont Mayou
Pont Marengo
Pont Pannecau
Pont du Génie
ALLÉES BOUFFLERS
RUE FRÉDÉRIC BASTIAT
Musée Bonnat
Monsieur Txokola
Musée Basque
RUE BOURGNEUF
RUE MARENGO
Trinquet St André
RUE DU TRINQUET
RUE DES TONNELIERS
RUE PANNECAU
PLACE PAUL BERT
RUE DES CORDELIERS
Remparts de Mousserolles

restaurants. Halfway down, the wall is decorated with some old photos of the Bayonne of yesteryear. Towering above St-Esprit, usually with the French flag fluttering in the wind, is the 17th-century *citadelle*, home to French special military forces and not open to visitors. Bayonne actually sits on the confluence of the narrow Nive and the ample Adour, the latter surprisingly wide as it prepares to meet the ocean.

Bayonne battles hard to avoid playing second fiddle to its hedonistic seaside neighbour, Biarritz, and, for those prepared to dwell here for a day or two, it succeeds. Its claims to fame are ham, chocolate and the bayonet, the last of which takes its name from the town. From the bookshop windows and the T-shirt designs, it is clear that rugby is also a big part of the common culture here. Horrifyingly, in 2015 a proposal was made to merge Bayonne's team with that of local rivals Biarritz – a short-lived threat to the pride and separate identities of both towns. Biarritz may have turned its head towards tourists, but Bayonne can offer plenty of history to its visitors. Among its citizens, a strong Basque spirit and a determination to enjoy life burn brightly.

HISTORY Bayonne's history is lively to say the least. Once a Roman garrison town, the evidence of Roman occupation can still be seen in the vestiges of the city walls. All too accessible at times, the city suffered, being razed by both Vikings and Normans before the marriage of Henry II to Eleanor of Aquitaine put the town under English control in the 12th century, a situation that endured for nearly 300 years. Bayonne flourished during this time, developing as a port and enjoying commercial significance under English rule before being reclaimed by the French in the 15th century. With the Adour silting up and changing course, Bayonne's maritime importance was threatened, but in 1578 a huge project was undertaken to ensure that the town remained located on its river and thus with access to the sea. Although the fragility of the river never allowed it to become a true transatlantic port, nevertheless the town benefited enormously from years of whaling, fishing and as a home for corsairs. Eventually, its fortunes declined as its importance as a military town began to take precedence over its commercial significance, with the famed military engineer Vauban building the *citadelle* and strengthening its walls. Bayonne took a blow when Pau (in Béarn) was made the departmental administrative capital after the French Revolution, but the arrival of the railway in the mid-19th century brought some renewed prosperity as it carried noble passengers down to newly fashionable Biarritz.

Bayonne owes its reputation for chocolate to the Jews. Arriving in town in the 15th century to escape the Spanish Inquisition, they were not permitted to live in the town of Bayonne, instead being housed across the Adour in the St-Esprit *quartier*, which falls outside the town boundary.

Bayonne provided harbour for Spanish Basques fleeing Franco's dictatorships after the Civil War and was also favoured as a refuge by a number of ETA members in the 1980s.

GETTING THERE AND AWAY

By car Bayonne is well signposted off the A63/E5/E70 motorway, which is the main north to south artery just inland from the coast. Running parallel to this is the D-810 road which gives access to Anglet, Biarritz and all the coastal towns down to the Spanish border.

By bus Bayonne's frequent and inexpensive buses pick up and drop off mainly in the bus station/car park next to the tourist office in the Place des Basques [312 B2]. Some of the services also call at the train station and various points around town. Long-distance destinations served from Bayonne include San Sebastián with Pesa (w pesa.com) or Ouibus with the latter also serving Pau, Tarbes and Toulouse (w ouibus.com). Regional options down the coast include Biarritz, Saint-Jean-de-Luz, Hendaye and places in-between. Inland you can reach Espelette, Cambo-les-Bain, Hasparren, Tardets and Labastide-Clairence. All information for these routes is available on the network website (w transports64.fr).

There are also buses which head north into the Les Landes region for Dax and other towns, and these also leave from the Place des Basques.

By air For more information on getting to Bayonne by air, see page 300.

By train Trains depart about 16 times daily to Hendaye (35mins; €8) and points in-between, including Biarritz and Saint-Jean-de-Luz. (Note that for Biarritz, the bus is a better option, as it drops you nearer the beaches and town centre.) Bayonne's train service also connects seven-times daily with Bordeaux, and as often with Toulouse. There are also services to Tarbes and Paris. The inland service to Saint-Jean-Pied-de-Port (60mins; €10.10) is frequently under repair, but a bus replacement service takes its place.

GETTING AROUND

By bus A free *navette* (half-sized bus) operates from most of the town's car parks from 07.30 to 19.30, Monday to Saturday, dropping off passengers at various points in the town centre.

By taxi Taxis are usually to be found by the station or the tourist office, or can be summoned on 0559 59 48 48.

TOURIST INFORMATION AND TOURS The tourist office [312 B2] (Pl des Basques; 0559 46 09 00; w bayonne-tourisme.com; Nov–Feb 09.00–18.00 Mon–Fri, 10.00–13.00 & 14.00–18.00 Sat, Mar–Jun, Sep & Oct 09.00–18.30 Mon–Fri, 10.00–13.00 & 14.00–18.00 Sat, Jul & Aug 09.00–19.00 Mon–Sat, 10.00–13.00 Sun) is the place to get information and pick up the Bayonne Citypass, which gives you unlimited transport on the Chronoplus bus network around Bayonne, Biarritz and Anglet, entrance to Bayonne's museums and discounts in shops and restaurants. It also entitles you to a city tour. The pass costs €12/16/20 for one/three/seven days respectively.

Even without a Citypass you can take the 2-hour guided tour; it costs €7, with tickets available from the tourist office.

WHERE TO STAY

Upmarket

Chambres d'Hôtes Le Poteau Rose [312 F1] (4 rooms) 51 Av Louis de Foix; w lepoteaurose.com. On the main D-810, a couple of miles north of town, this is a trendy artist's place whose décor reflects the owner's talents. Bikes for hire & DVDs can be borrowed. On-site parking is free. Only some rooms have Wi-Fi (free). TV & private bath. B/fast inc. **€€€€**

Hôtel des Basses Pyrénées [312 C4] (27 rooms) 12 Rue Tour de Sault; 0559 25 70 88; e contact@hoteldesbassepyrenees.com; w hotel-bassespyrenees-bayonne.com. Renovated over a 3-year period & reopened in mid-2015, this is a beautiful 16th-century building now put to good use as a stylish hotel/restaurant/bar & one of the top addresses in town. Gentle colour tones induce calm. TV & free Wi-Fi. Outdoor tables in the peaceful square & pleasant lounge with soft chairs & satellite TV. **€€€€**

Mercure Bayonne Centre Le Grand Hotel [312 C3] 21 Rue Thiers; 0559 59 62 00; e ha0y1@accor.com; w legrandhotelbayonne.com. Some rooms have been upgraded but not all. Ensure you get a 'supérieure' one when booking – it's worth paying extra, but perhaps not for the top 'prestige' category. Free Wi-Fi. **€€–€€€€**

Mid range

Ibis Styles [312 E1] (45 rooms) 1 Pl de la République. A chain hotel, yes … but a great location close to the station & in a building with some character. Get a river view if you can. Rooms have TV, heating & free Wi-Fi. Unusually for France, b/fast is included. Public parking is free after 19.00. English spoken. **€€€**

Budget

Hôtel de la Gare [312 E1] (19 rooms) 8 bis Rue Sainte Catherine; w hoteldelagare-bayonne.fr. Some rooms have shared toilet, some shared bathroom – be careful when booking. Free Wi-Fi & TV. 400m from train station & free public car parking close by. Restaurant on-site & b/fast available. **€€**

Shoestring

Hôtel Monte Carlo [312 E1] (16 rooms) 1 Rue Sainte Ursule; 0559 55 02 68; e montecarlo@numericable.fr. A budget option next to the station in St-Esprit, with rooms varying from small sgls to family rooms, all at low prices. Popular with pilgrims heading to Saint-Jean. TV & free Wi-Fi, but not all rooms have private bath/toilet. Friendly management. Restaurant & bar downstairs. **€**

WHERE TO EAT AND DRINK

Restaurants Both sides of the Nive are lined with restaurants, and this is definitely the place to be on a summer evening. Choose between sunny side or shade. Alternatively, the area around the cathedral has a number of popular haunts.

Chez Martin [312 C4] 29 Rue d'Espagne; 0559 55 84 41; Wed–Sat, Jul & Aug Mon–Sat. A tiny place set on one of the main pedestrian streets. Grab an outside table to enjoy thoughtful, cared-for cuisine with artistic presentation. **€€€**

Le Belzunce [312 C4] 6 Rue Salie; 0559 25 56 60; w lebelzunce.allcommerces.com; *salon de thé* 09.00–19.00 Mon–Thu, 09.00–22.30 Fri & Sat, restaurant hours noon–14.30 Mon–Sat, also 19.00–22.30 Fri & Sat only. Named after a brave 15th-century knight who slayed a dragon on the banks of the Nive, saving the town from disasters. A well-established team produce daily specials to supplement favourites such as *risotto de gambas* (prawn risotto) or *magret de canard au miel* (duck in honey). Be sure to pop your head into all of the dining rooms to admire the arches & stone staircases. **€€€**

Restaurant des Basses Pyrénées [312 C4] 1 Pl des Victoires; 0559 25 70 88; noon–14.30 & 19.30–22.00 Tue–Sat. Part of the hotel (see opposite). A short, bistro-style menu, high on quality. Outside tables in the square allow good people-watching opportunities. Professional service is attentive but not obtrusive. **€€€**

Café Quai Délices [312 D3] 46 Quai des Corsaires; 0559 64 95 85; w café-delices-bayonne.fr; 09.00–midnight daily. A relaxing place on the banks of the Nive, more a café/tearoom than bar, serving crepes, waffles, desserts, homemade cakes, as well as meals which include vegan/vegetarian options. Friendly management, mellow music. Free Wi-Fi. **€€**

Le Bistro' Quai [312 C4] 27 Amiral Jaureguiberry; 0559 56 91 36; noon–14.00 & 19.00–22.00 daily. One of many quayside choices, an obliging hostess offers good-value, good-quality fare in a relaxed setting. Some outside tables. **€€**

Le Square Gourmand [312 F2] 2 Bd Jean d'Amou; m 0689 35 47 15; noon–14.00 Mon–Fri, also 20.00–22.00 Thu & Fri. In the St-Esprit district, this is a great option for those on a budget. A few hundred metres away from the station & light years away from the nearby fast-food options. There are 2 or 3 dishes on offer daily, super-fresh, large portions, with good side salads. Vegetarians will be happily accommodated. **€**

Bars and nightlife Outside of festival times, much of the late-night bar scene centres on Petit-Bayonne and Rues Cordeliers and Pannecau, the liveliest spots for the young set. These days, the activity in nearby Rue des Tonneliers ('Barrel-makers

A CIRCULAR WALK AROUND GRAND BAYONNE

45mins; easy, flat

Start by walking up the **Rue d'Espagne**, leaving the cathedral behind you to the right. Up until 1913, this street was the major artery between Paris, via Bordeaux, and Madrid, hence its name. Now it's happily pedestrianised, guaranteeing stress-free strolling for all among its quirky shops and lively cafés. Note how many of the shops in this street sport a small plaque that details the changing use of their premises since 1900, a project painstakingly researched by a local restaurateur. Towards its southern end, turn right into narrow Rue Vielle Boucherie and continue to the end of the street. Standing at the junction of the **Rue Douer** (barrel-makers), **Rue Vielle Boucherie** (butchers) and **Rue des Faures** (blacksmiths) provides a beautiful perspective of old Bayonne, each street representing the site of these three old guilds. The spires of the cathedral towering behind add to the view. Turn around, with the cathedral in the distance behind you, and walk through the gap in the Roman wall. You are now next to one of the town's remaining round, 4th-century **Roman towers**, one of five left of the original 30 that defended the town. Turn right on to Boulevard du Rempart Lachepaillet, keeping the houses on your right. Across the road to your left are the remains of later fortifications, as Bayonne over centuries was constantly reinforcing itself against threats, perceived and actual. Turn right on to Rue des Prébendés and continue to the end, heading for the substantial outside wall of the cathedral's **Gothic cloister**, one of France's largest. Turn right, then left on to Rue de Luc, keeping the cloister on your left, then turn left again on to Rue d'Espagne and left again along the third side of the cathedral, built in the period of English control between the 13th and 15th centuries. A previous Romanesque cathedral burnt down, though not much is known about it. On reaching the fourth side of the cathedral, note how there are no statues above the main door: in 1793, the otherwise good citizens of Bayonne destroyed them, fed up with the Church's estimated 60% land ownership and the high taxes they levied on the poor.

Now take the **Rue des Gouverneurs,** quickly reaching the **Château Vieux** on your left, dating from the 11th century and being renovated in 2018. The plaque on the wall tells you that one-time visitors include **Le Prince Noir** (Black Prince)

Street') is more focused on drinking the contents of barrels than making them, attracting its share of revellers as a result.

Chai Ramina [312 C4] 11 Rue Poissonnerie; 09.00–20.00 Sun–Thu, 09.00–02.00 Fri & Sat. Lots of rugby-related artefacts hanging from the ceiling, plus a whole load of other random junk. Standing room only (there's only a few bar stools!), so the crowd spills noisily on to the pavement.

Chez Txotx [312 D4] 47 Quai Jaureguiberry; 11.00–02.00 daily. Cider-house, wine bar, tapas bar & restaurant. Lively atmosphere.

SHOPPING

Market

Les Halles [312 C3] 07.00–13.30 Mon–Fri, 06.00–13.30 Sat, 08.00–13.30 Sun. On the banks of the Nive, Bayonne's well-manicured indoor market is exclusively food, with fresh fish, meat, cheese, fruit & vegetables & local products. It also houses a couple of cafés, with outdoor tables to enjoy the sun.

and royalty such as **Louis XI** and **Louis XIV**. Now it is used for military purposes, meaning that it is not open for visiting. Opposite you will see the excavations under way to expose some of the 130 14th-century **Gothic underground caves** that exist beneath this part of town. The plan was to create a learning centre, though the project has hit some difficulties with unsettling the foundations of neighbouring buildings. As no construction was allowed outside the city walls until 1907, many solutions were sought to create extra space for the inhabitants, the caves being one of them. Caves also helped to protect personal property from the ever-present fire risk. Just past the Château Vieux, turn right on to Rue Orbe, then left on to **Rue Pont-Neuf.** This is a chance to indulge in one of Bayonne's specialities (see below), but the street also reveals houses from various centuries, as well as a chance to see some real treasures that are not visible from the street, but nevertheless open to the public. Number 42 dates back to 1690, while 38 was built in the 18th century. Push open the door to number 32 and walk to the end of the corridor: looking up will let you see the stunning 19th-century spiral staircase, well worth a photo. If stopping at **Cazenave** for some hot chocolate, be sure to ask for the key to the toilets (whether you need to go or not) as this will give you access to another staircase, equally beautiful but different in style. After sating yourself on house façades, staircases and chocolate, you reach the end of **Rue Pont-Neuf**, arriving at the **Place de la Liberté**, site of the **Hôtel de Ville** (town hall). Turn right and then second right up **Rue Victor Hugo.** Many French towns have a street named in honour of the illustrious poet, of course, but Bayonne's connection with him is somewhat unusual. Visiting here at the age of nine, he fell in love with a girl slightly older than himself. It is said that he returned, decades later, to find her, but without success. At number 7, look up to see a wall plaque in honour of **Frédéric Bastiat**, a name that may not be known to you. This native of Bayonne, born in this very house, was a free-market economist, often quoted by and said to have inspired the thinking of **Margaret Thatcher** and **Ronald Reagan**. At the end of the street you come to a five-way street junction, which once served as Bayonne's financial hub, a meeting place for moneylenders and traders. If you walk up **Rue Argenterie** for 100m, you will reach your starting point.

Chocolate The town has plenty of opportunities for satisfying the sweetest-toothed visitor: hounded out of the Iberian Peninsula by the Spanish Inquisition, it was the Jews who brought their chocolate-making secrets to Bayonne, and the tradition remains. A trip down the Rue de Port-Neuf [312 C3] and its half-dozen outlets will be enough to satisfy most addicts. Chocolate here is a high-quality product; mouth-watering it may be, but prices can be eye-watering.

Atelier du Chocolat [312 C3] 37 Rue du Port-Neuf; ⌚ 09.30–19.15 Mon–Sat. Using another local speciality, the owner invented chocolate flavoured with Espelette peppers (see box, page 338). An acquired taste, but there are plenty less forceful flavours to enjoy. Chocolate with an incredible 97% cocoa is for hardcore fans, though. There's also a workshop at a separate location with tastings and guided visits, but in French only.

Cazenave [312 C3] 19 Rue du Port-Neuf; w chocolats-bayonne-cazenave.fr; ⌚ 09.00–noon & 14.00–19.00 Tue–Sat, Jul & Aug also Mon, same hours. The oldest *chocolaterie* in town. Its hot chocolate served with Chantilly makes a great holiday treat. Check out the impressive stained-glass windows too.

Daranatz [312 C3] 15 Rue du Port-Neuf; w chocolat-bayonne-daranatz.fr; ⌚ 09.15–19.00

Tue–Sat, 10.00–19.00 Mon. With over 125 years' experience, this family business crafts innumerable tastes & colours. Some excellent gift ideas.

Monsieur Txokola [312 D3] 11 Rue Jacques Laffitte; ☏ 967 65 66 94; w monsieurtxokola.fr; ⏱ 10.00–18.00 Tue–Sat. Monsieur Txokola makes his own chocolate in town, using carefully selected cocoa beans. His products are crafted with local techniques to create high-end chocolate.

Ham Bayonne ham is justly famous and the town has its own 'ham fair' during Easter weekend. **Pierre Ibaïalde** (41 Rue des Cordeliers; ☏ 0559 25 65 30; w pierre-ibaialde.com; ⏱ opening times vary from week to week – see the website) is a well-known shop which also offers free guided visits with a jolly character, and there's a tasting at the end. The tours are only in French but, if your language is up to it, it comes highly recommended.

OTHER PRACTICALITIES The **post office** [312 C2] is on Rue de la Nouvelle Poste (⏱ 08.30–18.00 Mon, Tue, Thu & Fri). Free public **toilets** are to be found by the tourist office and in front of the train station.

FESTIVALS AND EVENTS

Bayonne Festival To get a full-on taste of Bayonne, no holds barred, a couple of days of the town's main festival at the end of July is the answer. In fact, the festival lasts for a mighty five nights and four days in total, a mixture of apparent anarchy and strict formula. The dress code is not obligatory, but if you're clad in white, preferably with a red scarf or even a beret, you will feel much more part of the fun. Proceedings commence on the Wednesday evening in the Place de la Liberté, with the mayor handing the city keys (not the real ones, obviously) over to his citizens. Bayonne's festival was unashamedly inspired by Pamplona's more internationally famous San Fermín, and is a similar cocktail of music, bull-running, bullfights, dancing, food and alcohol. It can get wild, that's for sure. There's even a junior bull-running, with youngsters between the ages of six and 12 being chased by cardboard bulls. So that the residents of Bidart and Biarritz don't miss out, there is a network of night buses that run to around 04.00 on festival days, allowing you to stay somewhere where you might get a night's sleep but still take part. The Bayonne bars take a break between 03.00 and 09.00, menu options at the restaurants are restricted to let them cope with the volumes of festival-goers, hotels get booked up quickly and prices rise. Controversially, from 2018 you will have to pay to take part: as many residents flee town during the festivities, they have decided that they should not pay for all of the considerable costs (especially security) of staging this popular annual event.

Music Festival On 21 June the whole of France celebrates the Fête de la Musique, now an international event. Bayonne takes it very seriously indeed, with the 2015 version showcasing everything from tea dances to punk rock in 17 venues across town. St-Esprit's multi-cultural spirit is celebrated with African dancing and singing from Mali and Guinea. Add in some impromptu singalongs in bars, a dash of rock and reggae, male voice choirs performing on the streets and the skirl of the Gascon bagpipes belting out *The Fields of Athenry* and you'll get an idea of what to expect.

Bullfighting 'Bayonne and the Basque Country are proud of their bullfighting culture!' scream the posters that advertise these August and September events. Bullfights take place in the town's 10,000-seat bullring (Rue Alfred Bouland).

WELSH CONNECTIONS

Bayonne owes its emergence as a rugby power before World War I to a Welshman. Harry Owen Roe introduced a fast, running game to the town. Roe was born near Aberavon and played at outside-half for Penarth, but was recruited by a visiting team from Bayonne as their player-coach and moved to the town. He became a stalwart of the team and was responsible for an expansive style that brought Bayonne the French championship in 1913. Such is the respect he gained that he has a Bayonne street named after him, fittingly close to where the town's stadium is located.

It's not to everyone's taste, but the running of bulls in Bayonne is recorded as far back as the 13th century. Full details are available from the tourist office.

WHAT TO SEE AND DO

Musée Basque et de l'Histoire de Bayonne (Museum of Basque Culture and the History of Bayonne) [312 D3] (Maison Dagourette, 37 Quai des Corsaires; ☏ 0559 59 08 98; w museebasque.com; 🕘 Apr–Sep 10.00–18.30 Tue–Sun, Oct–Mar 10.30–18.00; €7.50/free adults/under 26s, free to all on 1st Sun of the month) A pleasant, well-laid-out ethnographic museum, covering many aspects of Basque culture and providing insight into the town and region's history. The building itself, a renovated 16th-century house, is over 400 years old, while the museum is a near-centenarian. Information in English is provided by a returnable laminated booklet, whose contents faithfully translate all the wall panels.

Musée Bonnat (Bonnat Museum) [312 D3] (5 Rue Jacques Lafitte; w museebonnat.bayonne.fr) Closed for renovations – which seem interminable – this museum previously housed an impressive collection of works by Rubens, Degas, Goya and El Greco. It *may* reopen by the end of 2019.

Cathédrale Sainte-Marie (Bayonne Cathedral) [312 C3] (🕘 Cathedral: 08.00–12.30 & 15.00–19.00 Mon–Sat, 08.00–12.30 & 15.30–20.00 Sun, no admission during services; Cloister: 09.00–12.30 & 14.00–17.00 (18.00 in summer) daily; admission free) Situated on a pilgrimage route to Santiago de Compostela, to which it owes its UNESCO World Heritage Site status, construction of Bayonne's cathedral began in 1258 during the period of English control over the city. Replacing a Romanesque predecessor destroyed by fire, the current incumbent's architectural influences are drawn from French cathedrals such as Reims. The spires were not completed until the 19th century, when the whole cathedral was subject to a major restoration by Emile Boeswillwald. Inside, there is a seven-bay nave, in the upper part of which can be seen glass showing the Creation, as well as the Nativity and New Testament scenes. Some helpful, English-language signboards provide information on some of the paintings and windows. Dating from 1531, the window in the second chapel on the north side shows the story of the Canaanite Woman. The cloister is from the 13th to 14th centuries, and is one of the largest in France. It can be visited from the Place Pasteur.

Le Trinquet St André [312 D3] (Rue des Tonneliers; m 0688 86 81 91; €10/2 adults/children) Claiming to be the world's oldest indoor *pelota* court, Le Trinquet St André hosts demos every Thursday afternoon at 16.00 from October to June. Further information is available from the tourist office.

BIDART (BIDARTE)

Bidart describes itself as 'the Basque village by the seaside' – its size gives it a different feel from the bigger resorts of Biarritz to the north or Saint-Jean-de-Luz to the south. Six beaches await the visitor, each with its own surf school, snack bars and restaurants, showers and toilets.

TOURIST INFORMATION The tourist office (Rue Erretegia; **w** bidarttourisme.com; ⌚ Jul & Aug 09.00–19.00 Mon–Sat, 09.00–13.00 Sun & holidays, low season 09.00–12.30 & 14.00–17.00 Mon–Fri, 09.00–13.00 Sat & holidays) offers free information and Wi-Fi.

WHERE TO STAY AND EAT

Hôtel Itsas Mendia (15 rooms) 11 Av de la Grande Plage; 0559 54 90 23; **e** info@hotelbidart.com; **w** hotelbidart.com. An elegant 1920s villa now serves as a chic, stylishly furnished boutique hotel. Rooms have free Wi-Fi, TV & AC. Some have a balcony or view to the sea, & the beach is a 5min walk. Seasonal, heated swimming pool, free parking. €€€€

L'Antre 6 Av de la Grande Plage; 0559 47 78 92; ⌚ 19.30–22.00 Wed–Sun, noon–13.30 Sun. French-Australian run, this 2014 newcomer is carving out a reputation for creative dishes based on local products. Constantly changing menus are displayed on blackboards in a classy dining room. €€€

Venta Gaxuxa Av de la Grande Plage, Pl de la Mairie; 0559 54 88 70; **w** ventagaxuxa.com; ⌚ noon–14.00 & 19.00–22.00 Thu–Tue. 'More of a house than a restaurant' is the claim of this place, which has generous portions based on local products such as beef & *boudin* (black pudding). *Pintxos* are also available here. €€€

GUÉTHARY (GETARIA)

A comparatively quiet place on the coast, off-season Guéthary retains vestiges of its sleepier, 19th-century pre-railway days. It's all too easy to miss the turn-off for the town from the main road. Coming here by train drops you a few steps from the centre, next to the restaurants, the handsome late 19th-century second homes and the tiny fishing harbour below. The town shares its long, attractive beach, the Plage de Parlementia, with neighbouring Bidart, 3km to the northeast, and is home to a surf school or two. Other than that, Guéthary is a tranquil choice for a Sunday lunch.

TOURIST INFORMATION The tourist office is at 74 Rue du Comté du Swiecinski (0559 26 56 60; **w** guethary-tourisme.com; ⌚ Jan–Mar & Oct–Dec 09.00–12.30 & 14.00–17.30 Mon–Fri, Apr–Jun & Sep as above, plus 09.00–12.30 Sat, Jul & Aug 09.00–12.30 & 14.00–18.30 Mon–Sat, 10.00–13.00 Sun).

WHERE TO EAT AND DRINK Restaurants cluster around the train station, but a few steps further towards the seafront will take you to **Heteroclito** (Chemin de la Plage; **m** 0559 54 98 92; ⌚ Apr–Oct 11.00–01.00 daily; €€€), a pleasant terrace bar/restaurant. The ambience is funky and alternative, the welcome warm and the food choices sometimes spicy.

SAINT-JEAN-DE-LUZ AND CIBOURE

With its beautiful protected bay and curvaceous beach, Saint-Jean-de-Luz (Donibane) wraps itself around the ocean and tempts its many visitors to enjoy the sea in an oasis of calm, far from the fierce waves found elsewhere on the coast. But it was not always so. The three long breakwaters that now protect the beach

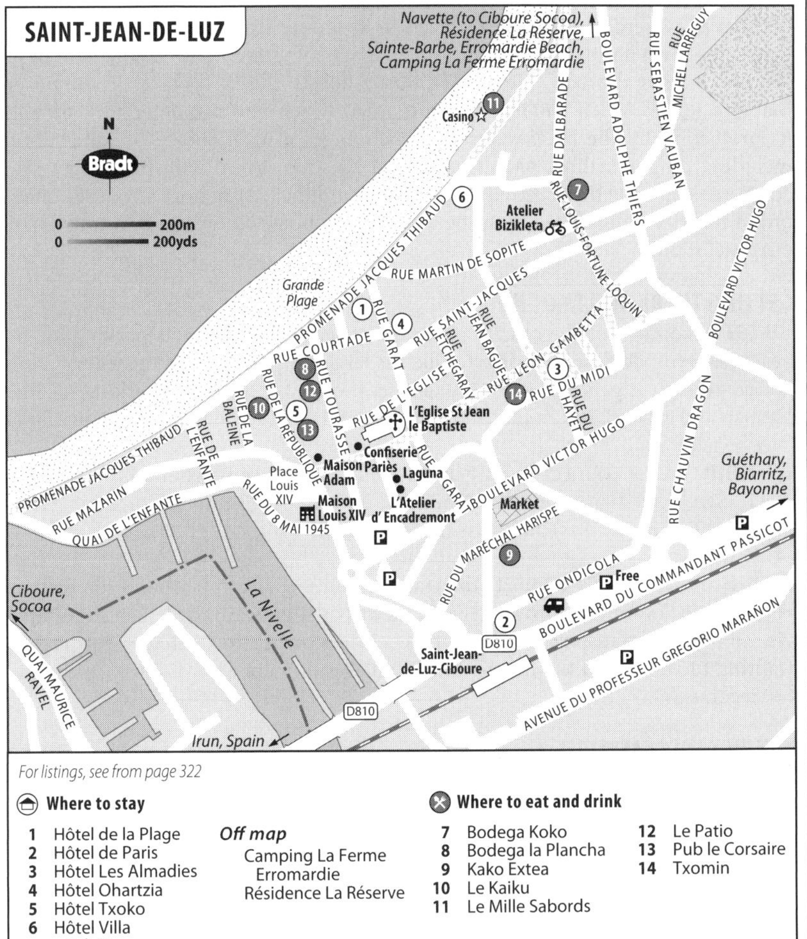

serve as reminders of a time when the town was plagued by flooding from the sea, particularly in the 17th and 18th centuries. In 1782 some 40 houses and a convent were swept away. At one time, the silting up of the port led to the ruination of the maritime trade that provided the backbone of the town's prosperity, and two-thirds of the population had left by the time of the French Revolution in 1789. Napoleon III's decision to beef up the sea defences led to a thriving fishing trade in sardine and tuna, reviving the town's economy and population. In 1843, Saint-Jean decided to establish itself as a resort, with the objective of attracting guests from overseas. The town soon became fashionable, gambling was authorised and in 1912 it was classified as a 'thermal seasonal station'. At its height, it attracted the Prince of Wales, the Prince of Bavaria and various Russian grand dukes among its visitors. The current casino building dates from 1928 and dominates the main beach. In its 21st-century incarnation, away from the shore, Saint-Jean's painted shutters, characteristic street signs and narrow streets make for a delightful ambience, replete with charming restaurants and shops full of delicacies and tasteful souvenirs. With no waves on the Grande Plage, the surfer crowd has to decamp elsewhere and Saint-Jean revels in its family atmosphere. Away from the ocean, the town has two golf courses and a thalassotherapy centre to further tempt visitors. Across the bay, Ciboure (Ziburu) boasts the birthplace of composer Maurice Ravel. Much smaller, it has its own beach and a quieter feel, though its protection by the breakwater also encourages a wide choice of watersports including dinghy sailing, paddleboard and all sorts of fun with inflatables. The companies offering these activities cluster around the leisure port. Ciboure's once-proud fort, though a listed building, is currently boarded up and awaiting a new purpose in life.

GETTING THERE AND AROUND

By car Like most of the coastal towns, Saint-Jean charges for its parking by the beaches. If you don't mind a short walk, the large car park behind the train station is free, though it gets full early. Otherwise, there's free on-street parking on Rue Vauban and around. But in July and August you'll need some luck to find anything.

By train Trains connect Saint-Jean to Hendaye (15mins, from where you can reach San Sebastián); Biarritz (15mins), Bayonne (30mins), Bordeaux (2hrs 30mins), Toulouse (4hrs) and Paris (5hrs 30mins).

By bus From directly opposite the train station, buses can be found for Biarritz and Bayonne (40mins/1hr respectively), as well as southward to Hendaye (40mins) via Ciboure (w transports64.com). Ticket prices are €2 for a single. For anyone wanting to venture to the nearby inland villages, a mere €1 will buy you a ticket (w hegobus.fr).

TOURIST INFORMATION The tourist office is at 20 Boulevard Victor Hugo (☎ 0559 26 03 16; w saint-jean-de-luz.com; ⏲ 09.00–12.30 & 14.00–18.00 Mon–Sat, 10.00–13.00 Sun except Nov–Mar).

WHERE TO STAY *Map, page 321*

A dozen or so campsites lie to the north of the town, near the exposed beaches popular with surfers, but in the centre itself hotel prices remain on the high side, with plenty of good mid-range choices, but no real budget options.

Hôtel de la Plage (22 rooms, 6 suites) 48 Promenade Jacques Thibaud; ☎ 0559 51 03 44; w hoteldelaplage.com. Spitting distance to the beach, with 6 new suites & excellent rooms. Try for a room overlooking the beach & bay – worth the extra cost – & fall asleep to the sound of the waves. TV & free Wi-Fi. Restaurant on-site. **€€€€**

Hôtel Villa Bel-Air (20 rooms) 60 Promenade Jacques Thibaud; ☎ 0559 26 04 86; e inforesabelair@orange.fr; w hotel-bel-air.com. No renovation here, but if you like to take a trip back in time, this is a place of character, now in its 4th generation of family ownership. Rooms vary from those with sea view, those with terrace, those with balcony & those wwwith none of the above. A step away from the beach. **€€€€**

Résidence La Réserve (44 apts) 1 Av Gaetan de Bernoville, Point Saint Barbe; ☎ 0559 51 32 00; e info@hotel-lareserve.com; w hotel-lareserve.com. A family option for those who don't mind being a 20min walk from town. Recently renovated, with seasonal swimming pool, tennis, table-tennis, sauna & restaurant. Apartments for up to 7 guests also available. Free Wi-Fi. **€€€€**

Hôtel les Almadies (7 rooms) 58 Rue Gambetta; ☎ 0559 85 34 48; e hotel.lesalamadies@wanadoo.fr; w hotel-les-almadies.com. Small & looked-after town-centre hotel with a welcoming host. Ask for a balcony room, if available. TV, free Wi-Fi. Parking is €10 per day. **€€€**

Hôtel Ohartzia (15 rooms) 28 Rue Garat; 0559 26 00 06; e hotel.ohartzia@wanadoo.fr; w hotel-ohartzia.com. A few steps from the Grand Plage, this is a brightly renovated hotel with a delightful garden at the rear & welcoming staff. Decent-sized rooms, TV, free Wi-Fi. There's no AC, so ask for a fan if it's hot. €€€

Hôtel Txoko (9 rooms) 20 Rue de la République; 0559 85 10 45; w hotel-txoko.com. AC, satellite TV & free Wi-Fi. Quaint but comfortable, fully renovated & close to the beach & centre. More luxurious & expensive rooms, some with terrace, are also available. €€€

Hôtel de Paris (28 rooms) 1 Bd du Commandant Passicot; 0559 85 20 20; e contact@hoteldeparis-stjeandeluz.com; w hoteldeparis-stjeandeluz.com. Away from the seafront & close to train & bus stations, so the price is a shaving lower. Recently renovated, rooms have AC, TV & free Wi-Fi. This hotel has no great character, but brightly painted & well soundproofed from the main road. €€

Camping Ferme Erromardie [map, page 298] 40 Chemin Erromardie, 2km north of town; 0559 26 34 26; e contact@camping-erromardie.com; w camping-erromardie.com; 15 Mar–30 Sep. This is a large site with bar, restaurant, covered & heated swimming pool & entertainment. A good variety of mobile homes with attractive Jun & Sep prices. Tent pitches, too. €

WHERE TO EAT AND DRINK *Map, page 321*

Le Kaiku 17 Rue de la République; 0559 26 13 20; w kaiku.fr; 12.30–14.30 & 19.30–22.30 Thu–Mon. In a 16th-century building, the oldest in town, Kaiku's celebrated chef weaves modern French magic with an occasional Asian tinge, artistically presented. €€€€

Kako Etxea 18 Rue Harispe, Place des Halles; 0559 85 10 70; noon–14.15 & 19.30–22.00 Tue–Sat, Jul & Aug daily. Right next to the market, with excellent Basque artwork in the interior & outside tables for sunny days. Fish of the day is fresh as can be, & locally produced cherry ice cream rounds off your meal. Local Irouléguy wine by the glass. €€€

Le Patio 33 Rue Tourasse; 0559 85 10 47; Jul & Aug midday & evening daily, low season closed Wed. Punches above its weight in quality & presentation. You can dine on tables out front, in the cool interior, or the sunny rear courtyard. The menu is excellent value. €€€

Bodega Koko 19 Rue Loquin; m 0648 36 19 01; 11.00–15.00 & 19.00–22.30 daily in season, off-season Wed–Sun. The short menu might deter you, but the ambience, food & service rate highly. The *assiette mixte* of tapas is almost too decorative to eat. €€

Bodega la Plancha 31 Rue Tourasse; 0559 26 97 42; Sep–Jun Fri–Tue, Jul & Aug daily. Bullfighting posters remind you that you are close to Spain. Set in one of the less busy St Jean streets, great food at good prices. Varied evening menus are top value. €€

Le Mille Sabords 9 Passage de la Pergola; 0559 51 03 56; mid-Jun–mid-Sep daily, other months Wed–Mon. Located within the seafront casino building, the name translates as 'Blistering Barnacles'. A mix of Basque & Breton influences, help yourself to delicious savoury & sweet *galettes*, very filling & a good alternative to a midday 3-course meal. €

Pub le Corsaire 16 Rue de la République; 0559 26 10 74; 18.00–23.00 daily. A 'pub' with a huge list of beers from across the world, some chic style & eclectic music. The nautically themed bar counter is beautifully carved. Don't be deterred by the 'house rules' on the menu – it's a relaxed place.

Txomin 54 Rue Gambetta. The best artisan ice cream in town. Closed in the morning as they're making the stuff, but in the afternoon they open the doors & make people very happy.

SHOPPING For those who like to browse, window-shop or even make a purchase, the town centre is flat and physically undemanding. Head for Rue Gambetta, plus a few of its side streets. In this compact area you'll encounter lots of delicatessens and gift shops, a truly great place for shoppers to spend an hour or two.

Confiserie Pariès 9 Rue Gambetta. Everyone has a view on who makes the best *gâteau Basque* (Basque cake, filled with cream or cherry jam), & Pariès is definitely on the list. With 120 years of experience, their offerings are truly delicious.

Laguna 2 Rue St Jean; 0559 26 15 98; **m** 0650 68 43 38; **w** encadrementpaysbasque.com; ⌚ Jul & Aug 10.00–12.30 & 15.00–19.00 daily, other months same hours Mon–Sat. A tiny shop full of Basque antiques, including pottery from the now-closed pottery at Ciboure. Not cheap, but the place to pick up something unique with distinctive Basque styling.

L'Atelier d'Encadrement 4 Rue St Jean; ⌚ as *Laguna*, above. Next door to the antiques shop above & run by the owner's wife, a shop with stylised Basque artwork, sometimes giving in-house exhibitions.

Maison Adam Pl Louis XIV; **w** maisonadam.fr. A small chain that excels in many delicacies, but the real speciality here is the *macaron*, made according to a recipe passed down through the family since the 17th century.

OTHER PRACTICALITIES

Boat trips Two boats – the ***Nivelle V*** and ***Samatheo II*** – provide a number of **fishing trips** (**m** 0609 73 61 81; **w** croisiere-saintjeandeluz.com; ⌚ operates Apr–mid-Oct, coastal cruise at 16.00 daily), as well as excursions along the coast – though only with French commentary. Prices depend on the length and type of trip, but a 45-minute coastal cruise is €10/7 for adults/children. In addition, you can take ***Le Passeur* to Socoa and Ciboure** (⌚ Apr–Sep, departs noon, 14.40, 15.40, 16.40 & 17.40 Mon–Fri, plus extra trips at 11.00 & 18.40 at w/ends; €2.80 one-way), which departs from the centre of the Grande Plage and the harbour in Saint-Jean.

Cycle hire Bikes are available from **Atelier Bizikleta** (21 Rue Sopite; **m** 0663 14 24 40; ⌚ Jul & Aug 09.30–12.30 & 14.00–19.00 daily, other months 10.00–noon & 14.00–18.00 Tue–Sat) at reasonable prices (mountain bike €13 per day). They also have two wheels of all varieties: mountain bikes, road bikes, retro bikes and even electric bikes. The owner can advise on routes.

WHAT TO SEE AND DO Saint-Jean-de-Luz is a classy, leisurely resort for a swim, a stroll and excellent shopping but also has some points of historic interest. It is crying out for a good museum to present its history, which is surely more exciting than most. The ride around town on board Le Petit Train (tourist train) does not really cut the mustard: some enjoy the English-language audio guide, but for others the soundtrack of (annoying) music may detract from the experience.

Grande Plage Saint-Jean's beach is beautifully clean, very child friendly, with small waves and lifeguards on duty in high season, making it one of the safest places to bathe on the French Basque coast. Deckchairs, beach tents and sun umbrellas can be hired in summer. Out of town to the north, the waves get bigger and the beaches become more surf-friendly. In high season, a cheap bus (€1; **w** hegobus.fr) runs from the town north to the surfing beaches of **Erromardie** and **Lafitenia**.

L'Église Saint Jean le Baptiste (Church of St John the Baptist) (Rue Gambetta; ⌚ 09.00–18.00 daily; admission free) On the site of its 12th-century predecessor, this church dates from the latter part of the 17th century and achieved fame when Louis XIV was married here to María Teresa of Spain in 1660. The wedding was part of a treaty signed in 1659 between France and Spain, ending years of warfare. The church was still not complete at the time; indeed, it was unable to accommodate all the royal court for the ceremony. Visitors will be struck by the amount of woodwork in the interior, the result of the local shipbuilders turning their carpentry skills to its construction. Particularly impressive are the three-tiered oak galleries on either side, which until the 1960s were strictly 'men only'. Women were relegated to the chairs on the floor of the nave, on top of the tombstones, as they were considered to be the 'guardians of the dead'. Although unusual to visitors, such galleries and gender segregation are characteristic of Labourd's churches.

Maison Louis XIV (Louis XIV House) (Pl Louis XIV; ☎ 0559 26 27 58; w www.maison-louis-xiv.fr; ⌚ Jun–Sep 11.00–15.00 & 16.00–17.00, closed Tue; guided visits in French, 40mins, €6/3.80 adults/students & children) This 17th-century house has been in the same family since 1643, so furniture and crockery have stayed put.

Les Halles Marché (market) (Bd Victor Hugo) A lively, morning-only (⌚ 07.00–13.00 daily), food-only affair that takes place inside Les Halles, but swells in size on Tuesday and Friday, when producers and growers from the surrounding area set up stalls and join in the fun. The larger version also repeats on Saturdays in July and August.

Walking The *sentier du littoral* (coastal path) runs 25km along the coast from Hendaye to Bidart, passing through Saint-Jean. Forming part of it, a great short walk that affords you the best views down over the town and its three breakwaters starts from the northern end of the promenade and wends its way gently up to the Sainte-Barbe headland. At the top is an orientation table that points across the bay to Ciboure and its 17th-century fort, La Rhune mountain and other places of interest. Contrast the calm waters of the protected bay with the relentless waves breaking on the ocean side of the breakwaters. A bit beyond the summit you begin to see the spectacular karstic rock formations for which the Basque coast is famous, as well as some of the military defences erected by the Germans in World War II. If you wish, you can continue along to Erromardie beach, where there are restaurants in season, or even beyond. In July and August the inexpensive bus will bring you back to town.

URRUGNE (URRUÑA) AND AROUND

Urrugne is located inland, just southeast of Saint-Jean-de-Luz. Without any outstanding features, the village itself doesn't really merit a detour, but the nearby Château d'Urtubie is a worthwhile attraction.

CHÂTEAU D'URTUBIE (signposted off the D-810 just north of Urrugne; ☎ 0559 54 31 15; w chateaudurtubie.net; ⌚ mid-Jul–end Aug 10.30–18.30 daily, Apr–Oct 10.30–12.30 & 14.00–18.30 daily; €8.50/5 adults/children (castle & gardens)) In the same family since 1341, this is a historic monument that lists French kings and the Duke of Wellington among its former guests. Over the centuries it has undergone many modifications and enlargements, receiving its first bathroom only in the 19th century! The interior is richly decorated with 16th-century Flemish tapestries, solid wooden Basque furniture and more delicate Spanish and English pieces from various eras. Among the curiosities are a massive wooden fireplace and a china cup with a special lip designed to prevent gentlemen getting froth in their moustaches. The surrounding gardens date from 1745 but were refashioned as an English garden in the 19th century. They are pleasant and dominated by two very impressive magnolia trees. There are herb plantations, too. The outbuildings provide venues for temporary exhibitions, often horticultural in nature, and you can visit the tiny chapel with its distinctive upside-down hull-shaped roof, created by Ciboure's marine carpenters. There is a shop, too, and a hotel on-site. Information is provided by an English-language leaflet and some laminated sheets, and if you're lucky there may be an English-speaking guide on duty.

COL D'IBARDIN Directly south of Urrugne, the D-4 and then the D-404 leads you inland to the Col d'Ibardin and over the Pyrenees into Spain. You are unlikely to have the road to yourself, and certainly not during daylight hours. Smugglers no longer cart illicit wares over the mountains in either direction, but the price variance between the two countries ensures that there's a steady stream of French traffic looking for a cheap lunch at a *venta* (roadside inn and shop), of which there are plenty at the summit. No-one drives this narrow, twisting road for the views: instead, it's a question of filling the car boot with cheap booze and tobacco and the tank with fuel. You can buy all manner of souvenirs, have lunch and do your weekly grocery shop here. There is even a shop that will sell you a *pottok* horse. It can all seem faintly obscene but, if we lived here, we'd surely be doing the same.

HENDAYE (HENDAIA)

The last town in France, or the first town in France, depending on which direction you're approaching from, Hendaye's resort quarter stretches itself out along the sand while the main part of town is on the east bank of the Bidasoa River. On the other bank lies Hondarribia and Spain. Inevitably, Hendaye's close proximity to France's Iberian neighbour has shaped its history and put it in the front line of many a conflict, but nowadays Basques from either side shuttle happily across the estuary on the *navette*, the French to enjoy a cheaper lunch and the Spanish to sunbathe on Hendaye's long beach (voted among France's Top Ten in 2018) or to surf the breakers. Ever keen to improve its welcome for visitors, in 2018 the town revamped its seafront, creating a cycleway and enlarging its pedestrian-only spaces. Compared with Saint-Jean-de-Luz, Hendaye has a more 'common' feel about it; its hotels are less expensive and its restaurant choice is more orientated towards fast food. Fuel, perhaps, for its seasonal surfy population.

GETTING THERE AND AWAY

By air The airport at San Sebastián may be a mere stone's throw away across the river from Hendaye, but as it receives domestic Spanish flights only, this is of little use to most foreign visitors. A bus service links the town with Biarritz airport, with around 15 buses per day, journey time 65 minutes (**w** transports64.fr).

By train From Hendaye's train station (Bd du Général de Gaulle) Euskotren runs a frequent service to San Sebastián. The French SNCF (**w** sncf.fr) network will take you to all stations in France, including Paris (6hrs).

By bus A regular service, line 816, links Hendaye with all of the significant towns up the Atlantic coast to Biarritz as well as its airport (**w** transports64.fr). In Hendaye, the bus stops at the Boulevard de la Mer (seafront), town centre and train station.

By boat Hopping across to Hondarribia in the Spanish Basque Country is easily achieved with the **Navette Maritime**, which leaves from Hendaye's leisure port.

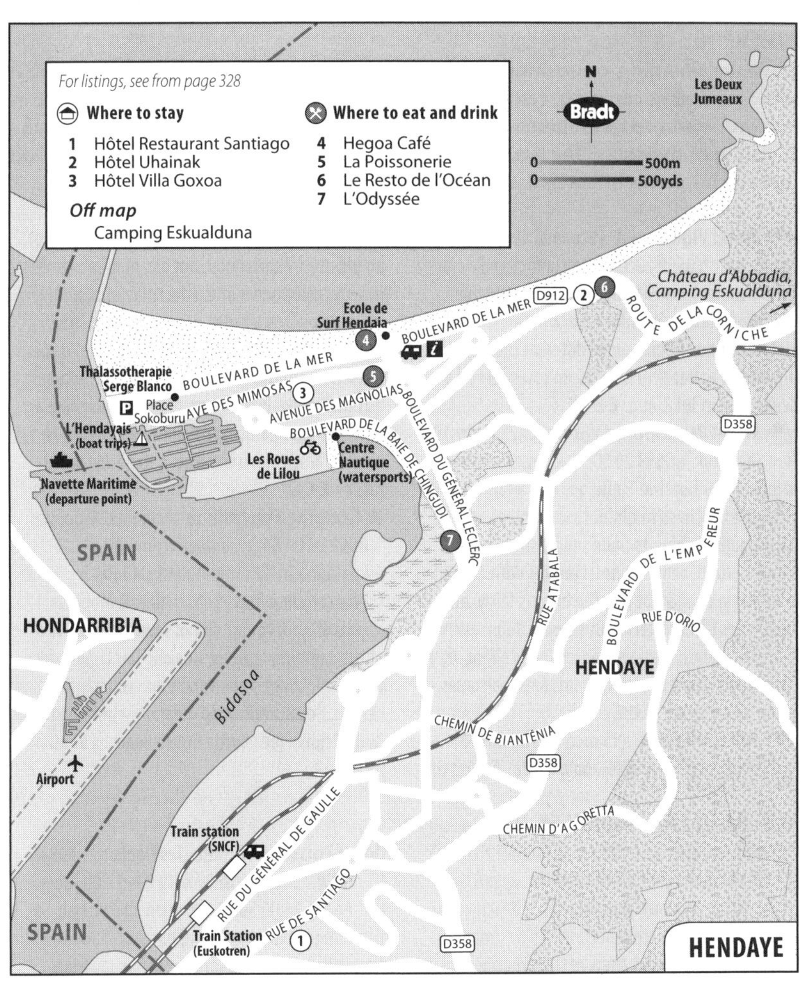

Boats run every 15 minutes between 10.00 and 01.00 between July and mid-September and every half-hour between 10.00 and 19.00 at other times of the year (€1.90 single).

GETTING AROUND Hendaye is flat and unless your accommodation demands otherwise, you can reach all points of interest on foot. Bikes can be hired (page 329). A bus takes passengers to and from the campsites in summer.

TOURIST INFORMATION AND TOURS The **tourist office** is at 67 Boulevard de la Mer (☎ 0559 20 00 34; w hendaye-tourisme.fr; ⌚ Jul & Aug 09.00–19.00 Mon–Sat, 10.00–13.00 & 15.00–18.00 Sun & holidays, Sep–Jun 09.00–12.30 & 14.00–18.30 Mon–Fri, 10.00–noon holidays). There are a number of **free Wi-Fi spots** around town, including the tourist office, the Place de la République, Place Sokoburu and the Centre Nautique. **Guided tours** (€4) are available in high season, one of the town and one of the beach area, on Tuesday and Thursday, but only in French. Ask at the tourist office.

WHERE TO STAY *Map, page 327*

If you're planning on visiting in July or August, advanced booking is essential whether you're camping, renting an apartment or staying in a hotel. Hendaye is not over-endowed with hotels, as many visitors choose to rent an apartment for the duration of their stay. The tourist office can be contacted by email and will help you arrange bookings of hotels and apartments.

Hôtel Villa Goxoa (9 rooms) Av des Magnolias; 0559 20 32 43; e contact@villa-goxoa.com; w hotel-hendaye.com. Handy for the beach, only a few blocks back from the front. Helpful owner. Rooms are in different categories, all with TV & free Wi-Fi. No AC, so you'll rely on a sea breeze in Jul & Aug. **€€€€**

Hôtel Restaurant Santiago (25 rooms) 15 Rue Santiago; 0559 20 00 94; e hotel.santiago@infonie.fr; w hotel-le-santiago.com. A fair way from the beach, so might not suit families with little people itching to build sandcastles, but this ultra-modern, compact hotel tempts with a small swimming pool & hot tub. The hotel is fairly new & the owner is characterful. Bus stop is 100m away. Staff are friendly & the restaurant is excellent. AC & satellite TV channels, most rooms have balconies, some have terrace. **€€€**

Hôtel Uhainak (15 rooms) 3 Bd de la Mer; 0559 20 33 63; w hotel-uhainak.com. Facing the distinctive Les Jumeaux rocks, this has the feel of an old-style beach hotel, but recent improvements have transformed it into a decent & comparatively good-value 3-star hotel. Private car park (free, pre-booking required) or garage (payable) across the road from the beach. The main town action is a 10min walk along the promenade, but there are places to eat nearby (see below). Room 6, with balcony & sea view, is the best, though a touch pricier. **€€€**

Camping Eskualduna Chemin d'Asporotz; 0559 20 04 64; e contact@camping-eskualduna.fr; w camping-eskualduna.fr; for camping May–Sep, chalets & mobile homes all year round. Out of town with the rest of the camping options, this one has chalets for those who want something more substantial than canvas. Restaurant, shop, heated swimming pool & kids' club. Free shuttle bus to beaches in Jul & Aug. **€**

WHERE TO EAT AND DRINK *Map, page 327*

Hegoa Café 2 Bd de la Mer; 0559 20 64 82; 08.30–midnight daily, closed Jan. At the side of the old casino, pick your table for a beach view & tuck in to some excellent fresh fish or succulent meat. To finish, try out a few of their special desserts. **€€€**

L'Odyssée 24 Bd de la Baie de Chingoudy; 0559 48 01 04; noon–15.00 & 19.00–22.30 Tue–Sun, also Mon afternoons in Jul & Aug. Good value, especially at lunchtime, & efficient, pleasant service. Away from the beachfront, it overlooks the port. **€€€**

La Poissonerie 9 Rue les Figuiers; 0983 03 40 79; noon–14.00 & 19.00–22.00 Tue–Sat, noon–14.00 Sun, shop open all day. Half fishmonger, half restaurant, but both halves serve fantastic fresh fish bought the same day from Saint-Jean-de-Luz. Opening hours can be a bit unreliable in low season. **€€**

Le Resto de l'Océan 1 Bd de la Mer; 0559 15 94 57. At the east end of the beach, a simple place with fresh fish & excellent mussels. Choose a table away from the main road, in sun or in shade, and be served straightforward fare by friendly, helpful staff. **€€**

OTHER PRACTICALITIES

Boat trips From next to where the *navette* berths, in mid and high season there's a variety of trips around the estuary and along the beaches, explaining points of interest. ***L'Hendayais II*** (Port Sokoburu; m 0650 67 03 44; w hendayais.com; Jun–Oct; €10–35, according to trip length) is a small boat that hosts trips varying in length from 45 minutes to see the coast to 4-hour fishing expeditions. Check that your captain for the day speaks English before you book – not all of them do.

Spa/Thalassotherapy Off-season, a good option might be the **Thalossothérapie Serge Blanco** (125 Bd de la Mer; 0559 51 35 35; w thalassoblanco.com; 09.00–20.30 daily, closed Dec), where you can use the excellent facilities in this huge complex owned by the former rugby player Serge Blanco. It has pools, saunas, jacuzzis, massages, a gym and a steam room.

Walking Hendaye is the starting point for the 15km-long Chemin de la Baie, which would take you west into Spain if you were to walk its entire length. The route follows the beach before winding through Hendaye's Old Town, passing some cannons pointing out towards Hondarribia and Spain. It is waymarked with information panels. If you want to take a shortcut, the *navette* across the bay comes in handy. In the other direction, the Chemin Littoral goes all the way up the coast, a total of 25km, until it reaches Bidart.

Watersports The Bay of Chingoudy (or Txingudi) is tucked away down the Bidasoa River estuary. It is a calm, protected environment to learn to sail, stand-up paddleboard or engage in a bit of gentle kayaking. The **Centre Nautique** (Bd de la Baie de Txingudi; 0540 39 85 43; e centre-nautique@itsasoko-haizea.org; w centrenautique.hendaye.com) offers kayaks, sailing lessons, yacht hire, stand-up paddle lessons and hire in high season.

Surfing Hendaye calls itself *la piste verte* ('Green Run') for surfers – an admission that it may not be the best for experts, but it is a great place for learners. The area in front of the old casino is home to the surf shops and it is here that the waves are most suited to beginners. September and October are the best months, but Hendaye surfs all year round. Note that at the north end of the beach, near Les Deux Jumeaux (Two Twins) rocks, there are a lot of sharp rocks, which are invisible at high tide. The staff at the **École de Surf Hendaia** (2 Bd de la Mer (in the old casino building); 0559 55 20 28; e info@ecoledesurf-hendaye.com; w ecoledesurf-hendaye.com) speak English and have a good reputation.

Cycle hire **Roues de Lilou** (1 Rue des Orangers; m 603 77 11 35; w lesrouesdelilou.com; beside the Centre Nautique; Apr–Sep, not always manned, so call ahead to reserve) offers bikes for off and on road, plus electric ones, with prices from around €15 per day.

WHAT TO SEE AND DO

Château d'Abaddia (Route de la Corniche; 0559 20 04 51; w chateau-abbadia.com; see website for full details, note the narrow window for self-guided tours; self-guided tour €6.60/3.20 adults/children, guided tour (French only) €9.50/4.50 adults/children, family tickets €22) Scientist Antoine d'Abaddie lived in Ethiopia for 11 years, creating the country's first ever map and hunting in vain for the source of the River Nile. Of Irish-Basque parentage, he was a keen astronomer and his Neo-Gothic castle contains an observatory that was internationally renowned and operated until the 1970s. D'Abaddie bequeathed his château to the Academy of Sciences in 1896. Don't be deterred by the two fearsome (stone) crocodiles at the entrance. After ten years of restoration, the castle is well worth a visit, having been designed by Violet-le-Duc, who in the 19th century was also responsible for the renovation of Notre Dame in Paris and the citadel in Carcassonne, perhaps explaining why this edifice has distinct medieval touches. Construction took nearly 20 years, although it is not quite complete, as Napoleon III promised to lay the last stone but died in exile in 1873 without being able to keep his pledge. The interior is richly decorated with silk wall hangings, magnificently carved fireplaces, polished furniture and engraved quotes in Basque, French, German, Geez (an Ethiopian language) and English, denoting the scientist's outlook on life. In the circular lounge, note the shamrock patterns that hint at d'Abbadie's Irish origins and the verses inscribed on the ceiling beams, penned by the British poet Buchanan. Surely the most impressive space is the main stairwell, adorned with African-themed art, though the galleried library is also beautiful. For visitors, a booklet in English contains comprehensive information, which provides enough detail to let you undertake a self-guided visit (guided tours are generally only in French, or occasionally Spanish).

Le P'tit Train d'Hendaye (€6/4/free adults/under 12s/under 4s) Commentary is available in four languages, including English. A classic tootle around town – details are available from the tourist office.

INLAND LABOURD

ASCAIN (AZKAINE) AND LA RHUNE (LARRUN) Away from the sought-after coast, the more rural Basque ambience quickly takes hold. The village of Ascain and its inhabitants look to the mountains and pastures for their livelihood, and this pleasant countryside is the main lure for visitors to this area, too. Yet the beaches of Saint-Jean-de-Luz are less than 6km away. Ascain is a handy centre for walkers and a jumping-off point for those wanting to take the recommended train ride to the top of La Rhune.

Tourist information The tourist office can be found on Rue Oletako Bidea 23; ☎ 0559 54 00 84; e ascain@psjl.fr; ⏱ Jul & Aug 09.00–12.30 & 14.00–18.30 Mon–Sat, 09.30–12.30 Sun & holidays, other months 09.00–12.30 & 14.00–17.30 Mon–Fri).

Where to eat and drink Combine your lunch with a free visit to a cider-house at **Txopinondo Cidrerie** [map, page 298] (Chemin de la Cidrerie, off the N-918 between Ascain & Saint-Jean-de-Luz; ☎ 0559 54 62 34; w txopinondo.com; ⏱ restaurant: Jul–Sep & public holidays 12.30–13.30 & 19.30–21.30 daily, other months lunch only Thu–Sun, cider-house/shop: Apr–Oct 10.30–noon & 15.00–19.00, Nov–Mar 15.00–19.00; €€€), where you can taste the many apple-related products, including spirits, apple juice and cider, enjoy a hearty beef chop for lunch or take part in the ritual Basque *txotx*.

What to see and do

La Rhune Although not exactly high in Pyrenean terms, at a trifling 905m, La Rhune somehow dominates the skyline for many miles around, visible from all directions. And it has something going for it that none of the bigger summits can offer: you can get to the top without any effort at all, using the **Train de La Rhune** (Col de St Ignace, Sare; ☎ 0559 54 20 26; w rhune.com; ⏱ mid-Mar–early Nov 09.30–11.30 & 14.00–16.00, mid-Jul–31 Aug 08.20–17.30 daily, departs every 40mins; single €16/9, return €19/12 adults/children). An infrequent bus service operates from Saint-Jean-de-Luz (w hegobus.fr), taking only 20 minutes and avoiding parking problems that occur in high season. Since 1924 this emblematic train has hurtled up the slopes of La Rhune at a leisurely 9km per hour, using a rack

WALK: FROM LA RHUNE TO THE STATION AT SAINTE- IGNACE

A walk of just over 5km with no dangers in good weather, but steep and on rocky and muddy paths most of the way. Not advisable during or after rain. Not suitable for those with weak knees. Refreshments at the beginning and end.

To reach the start of the walk, take the train to the summit of La Rhune or walk the 3 hours to get to the top. From the top, cross the railway track just below the summit station and follow the yellow waymarking – at times painted on to the previous 'green arrow' waymarking – down a steep, rocky path that heads downward at a 45° angle to the track. Progress is slow and care is required as you zigzag down what becomes a shallow stream-bed if it has been rainy. After 45 minutes of steep descent, you reach a clearing between two woods, with the sea directly in front of you. Look out carefully for the yellow waymarking at this point. As the clearing widens, you will see the Bidasoa estuary with the two towns of Hondarribia and Hendaye off to the left. At the end of the woods, you veer right on the path following the signpost that says 'Retour Petit Train Gare Col Sainte-Ignace, 1hr 20mins, 3.4km'. You have now descended from your starting altitude of 925m down to 574m. Your waymarking of yellow stripes and green arrows is now briefly accompanied by the red and white of the GR route. The path soon descends briefly into a wood, veering right and then heading across a wide clearing, with a wooden corral on your left and towards a craggy hill directly in front of you. At the end of the clearing, you cross a stream and turn left, following the sign for 'Sentier du train de la Rhune', now marked as 2.8km away. The path climbs briefly and then runs across the shoulder of the hill. You soon reach a corral made of flat stones, formerly used as a place of strategic defence by Napoleonic soldiers in the early 19th century. The path descends, becoming rocky again and steep. Soon you'll see the roof of the large engine shed for the trains, and once the path takes you down to it you cross the track in front of it, turn right on to a concrete path and arrive back at the car park and the station shortly.

and pinion system to get traction on slopes that average 18%. La Cremaillerie de la Rhune, to give it its official name, has never had any purpose other than leisure, being conceived and built as a tourist train following an idea hatched by three local businessmen in the early 20th century. It takes just over 30 minutes to cover the 4.2km to the summit, the slow grind up to the top starting through pine forest and fern, before giving way to views over a wide valley on the inland side. The view from the top, if you are blessed by the weather, is a stunning 360° panorama of the seven Basque-speaking provinces. You can choose to travel by train one-way and hike the other, or simply return on the train, perhaps after a bit of shopping or dining at the many *ventas* (shops) that await you at the top. For walkers, there is the opportunity to meet up with the *pottok* horses, sheep and perhaps see some of the vultures overhead. The waymarked walk takes 3 hours for the ascent, leaving from directly behind the station, 2½ hours for the descent (see box, above, plus full details and advice on the website).

Note that in high season, public holidays and weekends in May/June/September, the crowds can detract somewhat from the experience. It's best to book online, or arrive early and be prepared to queue. There may be no wind at ground level, but the summit is exposed and is no place for flimsy summer dresses or loose-fitting caps!

ST-PÉE-SUR-NIVELLE (SENPERE) A pleasant place for an overnight stop or as a base for touring the area, though crowded in high season, when the campsites and hotels fill up. The nearby lake has a sandy beach should you hanker after a swim. St-Pée's claim to Basque fame is the invention of the *chistera*, the basket used to catch and propel the ball in some variants of *pelota*. You can hardly ignore this fact, having been confronted by a giant version of it on the roundabout just before you enter town on the N-918 from Ascain.

Tourist information The tourist office is on the Place du Fronton (☎ 0559 54 11 69; e saintpeesurnivelle@psjl.fr; w saint-pee-sur-nivelle.com; ⏱ Jul & Aug 09.00–12.30 & 14.00–18.30 Mon–Sat, 09.00–12.30 Sun & holidays); the building is also home to the small Ecomusée Pilotari.

Where to stay nearby A mere 2km from St-Pée, **Ferme Elhorga** [map, page 298] (5 rooms & 2 gîtes; Chemin d'Elhorga; ☎ 0559 85 18 35; e contact@elhorga.com; w elhorga.com; ⏱ closed mid-Nov–towards end Mar; **€€€€–€€€€€**) is a beautifully decorated, fully renovated 17th-century farm that appears to have stepped straight from a home interiors magazine. Gorgeous rooms have ample space, bright colours and use of a tasteful common lounge area, kitchen (with washing machine), decent-sized outdoor heated swimming pool and hot tub. There is free Wi-Fi and the owners speak English.

What to see and do

Ecomusée Pilotari (see *Tourist information*, above; €5/2.50 adults/children) This museum is dedicated to *pelota*, your 45-minute visit including a video on a giant screen introducing you to some of the different forms of the game. If you want to see a live game, there are often demonstrations in the town's smart *trinquet* (indoor court), particularly on summer evenings. The tourist office will have details.

Lac de Saint-Pée-sur-Nivelle Just 2km out of town, this artificial lake is a godsend in summer for locals and visitors to the town. Here you can swim, hire pedalos, kayaks and stand-up paddleboards, or build sandcastles on the manmade beach. The walk around the perimeter is about 3km. Full facilities are available, including toilets and restaurants/bars, but be warned that in high summer it gets rammed. High-season facilities are available for the disabled.

SARE (SARA) Sare can trumpet its inclusion on the official list of 'Plus Beaux Villages de France' (most beautiful villages in France) and its eye-pleasing array of timbered residences, standing proudly since the 16th century, are all the evidence it needs to justify its inclusion. Unsurprisingly, Sare attracts visitors in numbers in July and August, but is an off-season delight, its centre dominated by a huge *fronton* that doubles as a car park. Take a drink of water from the unusual 'wind-up' fountain in the main square and note the monument to the local hero of the French Resistance, who listed a British Military Cross among his decorations.

Tourist information The tourist office is on Herriko Etxea (☎ 0559 54 20 14; e sare@psjl.fr; w sare.fr; ⏱ Oct–Mar 09.00–12.30 & 14.00–17.30 Mon–Fri; Apr–

Jun & Sep 09.30–12.30 & 14.00–17.30 Mon–Fri, 09.00–12.30 Sat, Jul & Aug 09.00–12.30 & 14.00–18.30 Mon–Sat, 09.00–12.30 Sun & holidays).

Where to stay

Hôtel Arraya (16 rooms) Pl de Sare (main square); 0559 54 27 04; e hotel@arraya.com; w arraya.com; closed Nov–Mar. Rather than admire those 16th-century dwellings from the outside, take your chance to get inside & stay in one. Once an inn for travellers on the Camino de Santiago & now a family-run hotel passed down through 3 generations, it's all beautifully refurbished, with wooden beams & staircases, modernised but with the character fully retained. Individually styled rooms (in 3 different categories) have AC, satellite TV & free Wi-Fi. Some have private balconies. There is a lift, terrace & a garden. Management are charming, professional & speak English. If intending to dine in the gastronomic restaurant, HB can make sense. **€€€€**

Chambres d'Hôtes Olhabidea [map, page 298] (5 rooms) On the D-4, 2km from Sare towards St-Pée; 0559 54 21 85; e fagoagaj@gmail.com; w olhabidea.fr. This 16th-century farmhouse, set in beautiful gardens, is dripping with olde worlde character & has been owned by the same family for over a century. Rooms are large & comfortable, & the communal areas spacious – the large fireplace is a winter godsend. Charming hosts, b/fast inc. Advanced reservation essential. **€€**

Where to eat and drink

Restaurant Arraya (see above) noon–14.00 & 19.30–21.00 daily, closed Nov–Mar, all day Mon, & lunch Thu except 7 Jul–8 Sep. In an elegant dining room or out on the terrace, service is discreet & formal, the food is beautifully prepared. A place where dining from the *menu* rather than à la carte makes economic sense. **€€€€**

Venta Antton [map, page 298] Istilarteko Borda (beyond the caves); 00 34 948 59 91 61; 11 Jul–31 Aug daily, other months w/ends only. So close to the border that it's got a Spanish phone number & the car park & restaurant are in different countries (says the waitress). Large stone tables & hearty mountain fare; catch the ambience of the smugglers' heyday in a beautiful setting with great views. **€€€**

What to see and do

Grottes de Sare (Sare Caves) (6km south of Sare, off the D-306; 0559 54 21 88; w grottesdesare.fr; daily, see website for full details; €8.50/4.50 adults/children) Guided visits (compulsory) are in French, and in summer in Spanish and English, with accompanying melodic piped music featuring the *txalaparta*, the instrument used by Basque shepherds. English-speaking visitors are provided with a returnable information booklet.

The Sare Caves were inhabited in prehistoric times, but more recently provided refuge during the Carlist wars in the 19th century and during World War II. Ten varieties of bat have been recorded in the caves, which stretch for nearly a kilometre. The hour-long visit includes entrance to the small museum, which has some information in English. Also on-site is a café, restaurant (summer only) and souvenir shop.

Le Musée du Gâteau Basque (Maison Harenea, Quartier Lehinbiscaye, on the D-406, 2km south of Sare; m 0671 58 06 69; w legateaubasque.com; mid-Apr–end Oct, see website for times of guided visits; €8.50/6.50 adults/children) Perhaps more of a chance to relax and enjoy the delicious *gâteau Basque* than to learn much about its history, but you can watch the famous cake being made. You can also take the longer and more pricey *atelier* (workshop) tour and learn to make your own cake, of course. There is a restaurant on-site, lunchtimes only.

AINHOA Ainhoa is a photographer's dream – a pretty Basque village *par excellence*. The Rue Principale is a perfect parade of 17th- and 18th-century houses, with fierce red shutters and heavily studded doors. Add in a *fronton* and a church that are so close that they look inseparable and some carefully concealed, understated souvenir shops, and the formula for one of France's most beautiful villages is complete. For lazy visitors, everything happens on the Rue Principale. For the energetic, a number of good, waymarked walks begin from the far end of town, including a little-frequented stretch of the Camino de Santiago – the Voie de Bastan – which crosses into Spain shortly after leaving the village. The village has a number of translated information panels, enlightening visitors about the *fronton*, the church and the history of some of the houses. At the end of the village, there is a *lavoir* where the women once washed their clothes and caught up on gossip. Local records state that Napoleon III and his wife Eugenie stopped there for a drink in 1858, though ironically there is now a notice that states that the water is not drinkable!

Tourist information The tourist office is at Le Bourg (off the Rue Principale) (0559 29 93 99; e ainhoa@psjl.fr; w ainhoa.fr; Nov–Mar 09.00–12.30 & 14.00–17.30 Mon–Fri, Apr–Jun, Sep & Oct 09.00–12.30 & 14.00–17.30 Mon–Fri, 09.00–12.30 Sat, Jul & Aug 09.00–12.30 & 14.00–18.30 Mon–Sat, 10.00–12.30 Sun). It is also the home of the Maison du Patrimoine, which has a 25-minute film (watchable in English) about the town's history.

Where to stay The best address in town is **Ithurria** (28 rooms; Rue Principale; 0559 29 92 11; e hotel@ithurria.com; w ithurria.com; **€€€€**). Although the rooms are not exceptional, the public spaces (garden, terrace, swimming pool and sauna) more than compensate. There is AC, free Wi-Fi, international TV channels and some rooms have a balcony. There are two restaurants – one top-end (**€€€€**) and one bistro, which is a lunchtime-only option, but kinder on the wallet (**€€**). Both restaurants open daily in July and August; in other months they close Wednesday and Thursday.

Shopping Ainhoa's shops are low key: nothing gaudy is allowed here in case it despoils the homogenous street frontage. It is a good place for souvenir shopping. One highlight is **Les Pains d'Épice de Ainhoa** (0559 29 34 17; w pain-epice.net), a speciality shop at the far end of the main street, where *pain d'épice* has been made for over 20 years. Here, hidden away, you can try five different flavours of this delicious gingerbread, as if you were tasting fine wines. Particularly good are those flavoured with Earl Grey tea or *anise*.

ESPELETTE (EZPELETA) If red peppers ever take over the world then it will look something like this. True, the town has a nicely restored castle, a church and a host of attractive residences all kept prim and proper, ready to please the flood of visitors who come to enjoy its attractions at weekends and in high summer, but for once it is not the red of the window shutters that catches the eye. Espelette doesn't want you to admire its buildings, it wants you to buy its peppers. Everywhere in town the spicy red thing dominates. You can buy them on their own, made into mustard, flavouring the artisanal beer; you can eat them *in situ* in the town's restaurants, where they play a leading role in the staple dishes; you can be photographed in front of the rows and rows of them hanging out to dry, or in front of a giant replica of one. As well as the peppers, there are plenty of other

WOOD PIGEON HELL, WOOD PIGEON HEAVEN

Should you be strolling in the forests around Sare, you may well stumble across trees with what look like tree-houses built in them. No, the schoolboys of the region have not engaged in a frenzy of high-quality carpentry; instead, these are *palombières*, strategically placed hides which allow hunters to pick off migrating pigeons on their way south in late autumn. The previous method of chasing them into nets has been replaced to some extent by the rifle, but this tradition has shown little sign of abating. *L'enfer des palombes* – 'wood pigeon hell' – is the gruesome nickname for Sare. But for gastronomes, October is more 'wood pigeon heaven', as the plump birds start to appear on the restaurant menus.

Basque souvenirs on offer here, something of a shock if you've just arrived from the Spanish side where Basqueness has not – as yet – been overly commercialised. Here, on the contrary, you can buy a variety of witty Basque T-shirts, French Basque liqueurs, Basque berets, a Basque calendar ... Basqueness meets tourism head on.

Tourist information The tourist office is situated on Rue Karrika Nagusia (☎ 0559 93 95 02; w espelette.fr; ⌚ Nov–Mar 09.00–12.30 & 14.00–17.00 Mon–Fri, Jul & Aug 09.00–12.30 & 14.00–18.30 Mon–Fri, 09.30–12.30 & 14.00–18.00 Sat, 09.00–13.00 Sun).

Where to stay and eat

Hôtel Restaurant Euzkadi (27 rooms) 285 Karrika Nagusia; ☎ 0559 93 91 88; e hotel.euzkadi@wanadoo.fr; w hotel-restaurant-euzkadi.com. In the heart of the village, a pleasant 3-star with accompanying restaurant (⌚ closed summer Mon, winter Mon & Tue; €€–€€€), family-owned & run for 5 generations. Heated pool, free Wi-Fi. **€€**

Shopping Here's how to 'monetise' the Basque brand. As well as the peppers, you can buy any manner of Basque paraphernalia, such as T-shirts, berets, CDs and linen. All in a short stroll through this compact village.

Arrobio Situated between the *fronton* & the church; m 0616 90 07 22; ⌚ Jul & Aug 08.00–18.00 daily, other months 08.00–18.00 Mon–Fri. A Basque brewery & an organic one, too. Opened in 2017, this bar/shop/brewery produces no fewer than 10 different beers, all organic ... but thankfully only 1 containing pepper. You can sample a couple of them on draught, buy any of them in bottles, but there is no brewery visit or English-language information.

Atelier du Piment Chemin de l'Église; ☎ 0559 93 90 21; w atelier-du-piment-espelette.fr; ⌚ Apr–Oct 09.00–20.00 daily, Nov–Mar 09.30–18.00 daily. A chance to buy *anything*, as long as it contains pepper. Visits are free, though explanations in English are a little hard to come by. Still, no translation is required for the tasting, so you can nibble at pepper sausage, sip pepper-spiced Armagnac & enjoy chocolate with pepper. The shop also sells local wine (admittedly, no pepper) & a variety of other Basque products. A 10min walk from the centre.

Markets Local producers descend in their dozens throughout the year for the Wed morning market. In Jul & Aug this is replicated on a smaller scale by an additional market on Sat.

Parfums et Senteurs du Pays Basque (Christian Louis) 443 Karrika Nagusia; w christianlouisparfums.com, w parfumsonline.com. Master Parfumier Christian may have his 'laboratory' in Labastide-Clairence, but it's in his shop in Espelette that you are most likely to find him, in summer at least. Whether you're interested in perfume or not, if the man is in residence then a visit here will be entertaining. Suspend any disbelief as he introduces you to his 'signature scent': wolf! You've probably never smelt a wolf, but the earthy overtones of the perfume thrust under your nose by M. Louis are quite convincing. He or one of his assistants will try to match you to a scent that suits you, but there's no hard sell & it's fun to watch as your host buzzes around his shop, flattering & amazing his would-be customers. Christian is one of only 13 recognised 'Nez' (noses) in France, honoured for his sense of smell. Be warned: such 'expertise' comes at a cost.

What to see and do The town itself is small, but makes for a good wander at any time of day, particularly at weekends when there is a lively buzz to the place. This is a super spot for souvenir hunting.

Etxea, le Centre d'interpretation de l'AOP Piment d'Espelette (Pepper Interpretation Centre) 455 Irazabaleko Bidea; ☎ 0559 22 56 76; ⏲ Mar–Jun, Oct & Nov 10.00–13.00 & 14.00–17.00 Mon–Fri, Jul–Sep 10.00–13.00 & 14.00–17.30 Mon, 10.00–18.30 Tue–Fri, 10.00–13.00 & 14.00–17.00 Sat; admission free) Brand new for 2017, this small interpretation centre is supported by the 188 local producers of the fiery red beast. Well, not that fiery: a series of quirky posters demonstrate that the Espelette pepper is pretty harmless when compared with its global siblings. You can smell the powdered pepper of several producers and guess which one smells of tomato, toast, hay and so on. A short film is available, though

'BIXTA EDER' OR 'PANORAMIQUE' CIRCULAR WALK FROM AINHOA

Distance: 8km; time: 3hrs; difficulty: moderate, with some steep inclines, some sections on tarmac roads but with virtually no traffic. Refreshments at beginning and end (Ainhoa). Parking is in the village's car parks. Waymarking changes from red and white to yellow and white and back again, but the route is clearly signed 'Bixta Eder' throughout.

From beautiful Ainhoa village (page 334) walk south from the tourist office down the main street until the road bends sharply left. At this point, cross the road, leaving it to descend to the bottom car park before following the red/white (and at this point, also yellow) waymarking up a tarmacked road. At the top of the rise, where the road forks, take the left-hand branch, following signs for Bixta Eder and Voie du Baztan, descending through chestnut, oak and hazelnut trees. The tarmacked road climbs again steeply. Shortly across to the right you'll see the distinctive peak of La Rhune (page 330) with its slightly incongruous collection of *ventas* (shops) visible on the summit. When the road plateaus at a house, keep following signs for Bixta Eder, keeping left at a fork. Shortly afterwards, at a house called Arbonakoborda, take the left at a T-junction. Descend down to a main road which you cross, and descend (again) down a steep road, leaving the tarmac after 200 metres and continuing on a rough road down to a stream which you cross on a narrow stone bridge. Continue upwards, ignore a road off to the left, then after 50m turn sharply left (waymarked) to ascend across a meadow before entering through a gap in the ferns. Shortly afterwards, you join a rough track which continues to rise and soon leads to a tarmacked road where you turn left, again continuing to ascend. Behind you again is La Rhune. Cross a cattle-grid and turn immediately left, following signs for Bixta Eder. You rise steeply on a grassy

only in French, but the helpful staff speak English and a leaflet available in English gives information and recipes.

Espelette's dedication to the pepper goes into overdrive during its Fête du Piment (Pepper Festival), which takes place during the last weekend in October. As well as a solemn mass in church to bless the spicy speciality, the town celebrates with performances by Basque choirs, dancing from Soule and hundreds of stalls, most of which promote the edible delicacies of the wider area. One highlight is the procession of *cofreries* (associations) of the producers of wines, mushrooms, ham, *gâteaux Basques* and, of course, peppers. The members of the *cofreries* are all beautifully bedecked in colourful capes and carry banners, while the parade is accompanied with music from a marching band, all brass and drums. You can book a ticket on the day to enjoy a meal at communal trestle tables, make some new friends and dine on lamb, *axoa* (the local veal speciality), local cheese and *gâteau Basque*. Shop around the various options and you can have a mini banquet for around €20 before watching the dancing or the *pelota* tournament. All in all, a great day out although, to avoid the inevitable parking nightmares, try to get into town by 09.00. Details appear on the town's website as the festival approaches.

CAMBO-LES-BAINS (KANBO) 'Les Bains' at the end of a French place name signifies a place with curative waters and for many years Cambo-les-Bains enjoyed its reputation as a resort for the recuperation of those suffering from tuberculosis. Thankfully for France, that's a disease largely consigned to history and, although

path with the summit of a small hill ahead. (For reference, soon you will see – and maybe hear – a large quarry behind you). On a happier note, on a clear day you will see the French Atlantic coast. At the top of the climb, you reach a fence where you turn left, continuing with the fence to your right and gorse bushes to your left. Where the fence turns sharply right, continue walking in the same direction as before, across a grassy meadow that narrows and turns into a ridge. At the end of the ridge, you descend steeply towards a white stone shepherd's shelter. The path eventually dips to the left of the shelter and rises again to join a wider track which you follow, leaving the shepherd's shelter behind you. Continue until you reach another signpost for Bixta Eder, which indicates that you now have 1 hour left of your walk. You now leave the wide path in favour of a grassy uphill track, flanked by telephone poles and then a fence. The path becomes rocky and continues steadily upwards. After 300m you turn sharply left (signposted) for Bixta Eder ('Panoramique') along a narrow path that runs along the side of the hill, soon arcing left and with La Rhune temporarily straight in front of you. Down to your left, on the opposite hillside, is the white shepherd's building you passed earlier. After a further 10 minutes, you cross a small pasture with one large and a few small beech trees and the path begins to descend. Down to your left you will soon see three large crosses and the stelae – head towards these. Take time to admire these handsomely carved stones, as well as the chapel and, down below, the neatness of the village of Ainhoa. The tiny *pottok* horses also favour this spot for their grazing, unruffled by the presence of walkers and those who choose to visit by car. The easiest route down to your starting point now is simply to follow the road, visible below as it winds its way back to the village, passing a series of roadside crosses on the way and with red and white waymarking to further assist.

THE ESPELETTE PEPPER

While the manner in which Espelette's pepper seems to have taken over the whole town may raise a smile or two among visitors, this is a spice that is to be treated with solemnity. For a start, it enjoys an Appellation d'Origine Protégée (AOP) denomination, the only spice in France to do so, guaranteeing its quality and place of origin. The progress of each year's crop is treated not much differently from that of a fine wine, being carefully monitored and scrutinised. No-one quite knows where these little red treasures came from, but it is probable that they were brought back from Mexico in the 17th century by a returning émigré, who found that the climate and growing conditions here in Espelette were similar to those of its place of origin. Before it took such a prominent part in the cuisine of the area, the pepper was used for its medicinal qualities and for conserving meat and other foodstuffs. Although it is Espelette which is most closely associated with the pepper, in fact ten villages are covered by the AOC. When the pepper turns red, it is harvest time, which can be any time from August to the end of November. And of course, there's a Festival of the Pepper, well worth a visit, held over the last weekend of October.

Cambo still has a steady trade in *curistes* (people seeking convalescence from respiratory and rheumatic problems), it has turned its hand to providing a base for tourists of a more general nature. The gardens of the Villa Arnaga are the big visitor attraction in town. South of Cambo, the D-918 road runs for much of its journey parallel to the river and the railway.

Tourist information The tourist office is at 3 Avenue de la Mairie (0559 29 70 75; w cambolesbains.com; Nov–Feb 10.00–12.30 & 14.00–17.30 Mon–Fri, 09.00–13.00 Sat, Mar–Jun & Oct 10.00–12.30 & 14.00–18.00 Mon–Sat, Jul–Sep 09.00–18.30 Mon–Sat, 09.00–13.00 Sun).

Where to stay and eat

Hotel du Trinquet (12 rooms) Rue du Trinquet; 0559 29 73 38; e sarl.du.trinquet@wanadoo.fr; w hotel-trinquet-cambo.net. 'Trinquet' is an indoor *pelota* court & sure enough, if you peer through the door in reception, you will see the players doing battle. The hotel was fully renovated in 2017 & the rooms are modern & smart. Efficient management, a café, large TVs, AC/heating & free Wi-Fi. A good choice. **€€–€€€**

Hostellerie du Parc (11 rooms) Av de la Mairie, Cambo-les-Bains; 0559 93 54 54; e hostellerieparc@orange.fr; w hotel-parc-cambo.com. A solid choice in an old-style French hotel. Not your thing if you like chic, modern furnishings, but if you want a warm welcome by hard-working, English-speaking owners at a good price, a few steps from the centre, this fits the bill. The restaurant is reserved for hotel guests' dinners. Price discounts for longer stays. Free Wi-Fi & access to computer. **€€**

Hôtel Ursula (15 rooms) Route du Bas Cambo, Cambo-les-Bains; 0559 29 88 88; e infos@hotel-ursula.com; w hotel-ursula.fr. In a 17th-century farmhouse, a smart renovated hotel featuring some rooms with terrace, all with AC, satellite TV & private bathroom. Free Wi-Fi & parking. B/fast sometimes included out of high season. **€€**

Au Déjeuner sur l'Herbe 17 Pl Duhalde, Cambo-les-Bains; 0559 42 67 17; noon–19.00 Sun–Fri. A lunchtime choice for a light meal, early evening meal or take-away. Quirky & colourful with the emphasis on a selection of delicious homemade tarts, both savoury & sweet. Tables inside or out. Owners speak English. €

What to see and do

La Villa Arnaga (Av du Docteur Camino; ☎ 0559 29 83 92; w arnaga.com; ⏲ Apr–Jun, Sep & Oct 09.30–12.30 & 14.00–18.00, Jul & Aug 10.00–19.00 daily, Nov–Mar closed; €8.30/4/2.50/free adults/under 18s/under 11s/under 7s; self-guided or guided tours, the latter in French) This handsome early 20th-century villa with exterior styling inspired by the traditional Basque farmhouse was once the home of Edmond Rostand, famous in France as the writer of the play *Cyrano de Bergerac*. The gardens are equally magnificent, particularly for the contrast between the clean, geometric lines of the French garden at the front and the more 'free-form' curved styling of the English garden at the rear. After Rostand's death, the property was sold by the family and plans were drawn up to convert the English garden into another French one, but these were thankfully abandoned. The gardens display their best colours in spring or early summer. After overwork and stress led him to contract pneumonia in 1900, Rostand abandoned his urban lifestyle in Paris and moved to Cambo-les-Bains to convalesce, following advice from his physician. Settled into his new environment, the poet and writer decided to have this huge villa built and engaged some renowned contemporaries to decorate the interior (obviously, writing paid well in those days). The results, beautifully preserved, are 18 rooms whose varied styles draw on influences from England, China and the Roman Empire, with panelling and furniture in lemon wood. Given the number of glowing references throughout the house to Rostand's elegant wife, it comes as something of a shock at the end of your tour to find out that the couple separated in 1914, after she was involved in a torrid love affair with a young musician.

Chocolaterie-Musée Puyodebat (Av de Navarre; ☎ 0559 59 48 42; w chocolats-puyodebat.com; ⏲ Apr–Oct 14.00–19.00 Mon–Sat; visit with tasting €7/3.50 adults/children) Unless you speak French, this will appeal more as a shop and a tasting opportunity than a museum, given that there is no information available in English. On the wall, the story is recounted of how an angel guided a mysterious ship to the Basque Country, bearing chocolate moulds and beans, and taught the Basques his chocolate-making secrets. The truth, of course, is less romantic, with the recipes being brought by Iberian Jews fleeing the Inquisition. The self-guided tour around this modern facility will show you a variety of chocolate machinery, chocolate labels and boxes, a collection of over 350 key rings related to chocolate, and a chance to peer through the laboratory window where the *chocolatiers* work their magic. If you're lucky, they may be working on something spectacular, such as a fancy piece designed for a shop window display. In the shop, the chocolate is delicious, but – as elsewhere in the region – it does not come cheap.

ITXASSOU Another well-kept little village with over 1,500 inhabitants, Itxassou is steeped in rural tranquillity. Famous for its cherries, it is awash with colourful blossoms around the end of March and celebrates the ripening of the fruit towards the end of May or beginning of June. A shop opposite the *fronton* sells jam and other regional products. A number of well-waymarked walks from 1 to 8 hours in duration start from the village and are shown on a panel in the car park below the Hôtel Agian.

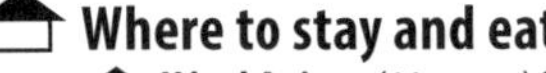

Where to stay and eat

Hôtel Agian (11 rooms) Pl du Fronton; ☎ 0559 29 75 21; e reservation@hotelrestaurantfronton.com; w hotel-agian.com. Adjacent to the Hôtel du Fronton & under the same ownership, sharing the pool, bar & restaurant. The Agian was brand new in 2015 & is adults only. Free Wi-Fi & parking. Rooms adapted for those of lesser mobility. **€€**

Hôtel du Fronton (23 rooms) Pl du Fronton; 0559 29 75 10; e reservation@hotelrestaurantfronton.com; w hotelrestaurantfronton.com. This well-kept hotel has been in the same family for 4 generations. Rooms were all given a thorough revamp in 2018, so everything's new. Some have a bath, some a shower. Seasonal outdoor pool. Free Wi-Fi & parking. **€€**

Restaurant Le Fronton See *Hôtel du Fronton* (above); 12.30–14.00 & 19.30–21.00 daily. With a choice of 2 menus, the Hôtel du Fronton's restaurant serves up quality cuisine on a beautifully located terrace, with views to the hills in the near distance. A young, professional team are kept on their toes by a fearsome (but friendly) manageress. **€€€€**

What to see and do

La Forêt des Lapins (Forest of Rabbits) (Chemin Argorreta, Itxassou, signposted off the D-918 between the 35km & 36km markers; 0559 93 30 09; e olivierlaforetdeslapins@hotmail.fr; w laforetdeslapins.net; 15 Jun–30 Sep 10.15–18.30 daily, other months 14.00–17.30 daily; €7/5/4/1 adults/students/children/infants, though presentation of a Bradt guide might encourage a discount) This rabbit reserve, set in woodland high on a hill, is home to over 80 species. The owner is, needless to say, a rabbit fanatic and has run this quirky homage to the bunnies for 15 years.

The setting for the Forest of Rabbits is truly rural, with the hutches dotted around a hilly forest. The largest rabbit weighs over 10kg, and there are some Indian pigs to see too: apparently they help to keep the snakes away. Guided tours at 15.00 in high season are in French, but guides can speak some English.

NORTHERN LABOURD

Away from the coast and the Pyrenees, Labourd flattens out as it extends north before it reaches its border with Les Landes. It is strange to think that this was once the historic boundary of Navarre, France and Béarn. Two towns merit a detour if you're in the area.

BIDACHE (BIDAXUNE) As you approach Bidache from the east or west you will notice the ruins of the **castle** to the north. This was the castle of the dukes of Gramont, which was largely destroyed by fire in 1796. Indeed, the castle has had a troubled history since first being mentioned in the records in 1329. Only three towers of the original medieval castle remain, the rest having been razed to the ground by the troops of Carlos I of Spain (Carlos V of Germany) in 1523. Important restoration works were undertaken in the 17th century, following the fashionable architectural styles of Louis XIII, including the creation of gardens and terraces. At the start of the 18th century the monumental entrance door was installed. In 1793, the castle and its dependencies were confiscated by the state and it then served briefly as a military hospital, but was empty again by the time of the fire. At the time of writing, the castle is under renovation, the pace of which is hampered by financial constraints, but you can usually visit the outside: the **tourist office** (1 Pl du Fronton; 0559 56 03 49; Sep–Jun 09.00–noon & 14.00–18.00 Tue–Sat (Nov–Jan Wed, Fri & Sat only), Jul & Aug 10.00–12.30 & 14.00–18.30 Tue–Sat, 14.00–18.30 Mon, 14.30–18.30 Sun) can advise of the latest situation, although it may be several years before the renovation progresses. During the high season in July and August, there are firework displays, horse shows and concerts at the castle. Guided visits, in French, take place between April and October (€5/2.50 adults/under 13s). Contact the tourist office for the schedule.

LA BASTIDE-CLAIRENCE (BASTIDA) One of several hundred *bastides* (fortified towns) built in France, this is now registered as another of France's most beautiful villages. Such fortified towns were created in the 13th century, offering protection to those who lived there, and many newcomers came from Gascony to settle here. This one was created by the King of Navarre, whose territory extended this far north in the 14th century, as he sought access to the sea after the route through Gipuzkoa was denied. In the 17th century the town became home to a population of Sephardi Jews from Spain; La Bastide-Clairence was one of the few places that welcomed them. The town, now with less than a thousand inhabitants, is smart and very well cared for. Discreetly hidden behind the arches and around the side streets you'll find a number of **artisanal shops**, making it a pleasant place for a couple of hours' visit. Between mid-July and mid-September a **Tuesday farmers' market** takes place in the main square, between 08.30 and 13.00, often with a musical accompaniment. The **tourist office** is at 5 Place des Arceaux (📞 0559 29 65 05; w labastideclairence.com).

Where to eat and drink Across the Joyeuse River to the north of town is **Iduki Ostatua** (Pont de Port; m 0629 30 19 07; w restaurant-pays-basque.fr; 🕘 May–Aug lunch & dinner daily, other months phone to enquire; €€€), an authentic restaurant that leans towards the meaty side of things with its solidly Basque menus, topped off with deliciously flavoured sorbets to cleanse the palette. Food is served on the terrace or inside, where the dining room features the owner's Basque artworks.

Handicrafts In much the same way as the Navarrese royalty once invited people to settle here in the 13th century, La Bastide has in recent times encouraged artisans and artists to set up workshops in town, most of them based in the main square. If you are interested in finding a high-quality souvenir, you can choose from woodwork, leather bags, metalwork, picture frames, pottery or textiles. The tourist office website carries full details of all of them; a couple are listed below, but there are also potters, jewellers and painters. If you're making a special trip to the workshops it's worth phoning ahead, as many of the artists spend the off-season elsewhere, at shows or exhibitions.

Garralda Pl des Arceaux; 📞 0559 70 14 64; w artisanat-garralda.com. Mainly animal-themed crafts using a variety of materials & made with a sense of humour.

Les Sacs à M'Alice Rue Notre Dame; 📞 0547 02 20 85; w lessacsamalice.com. Bags & purses crafted from leather in a variety of colours.

UPDATES WEBSITE

You can post your comments and recommendations, and read feedback and updates from other readers online at w bradtupdates.com/basque.

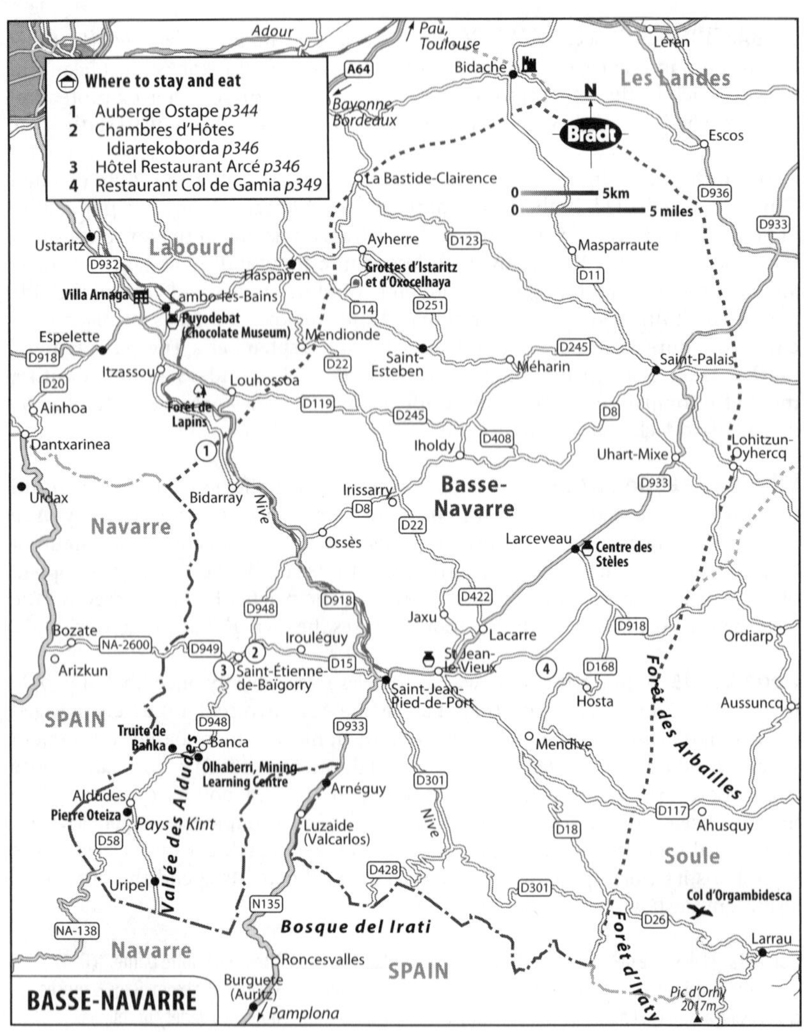

Where to stay and eat
1 Auberge Ostape p344
2 Chambres d'Hôtes Idiartekoborda p346
3 Hôtel Restaurant Arcé p346
4 Restaurant Col de Gamia p349
BASSE-NAVARRE
Basse-Navarre
Labourd
Les Landes
Navarre
SPAIN
Soule
Adour
Nive
Pau, Toulouse
Bayonne, Bordeaux
Pamplona
Bidache
Léren
Escos
La Bastide-Clairence
Ayherre
Masparraute
Ustaritz
Hasparren
Grottes d'Istaritz et d'Oxocelhaya
Villa Arnaga
Cambo-les-Bains
Puyodebat (Chocolate Museum)
Espelette
Mendionde
Saint-Esteben
Méharin
Saint-Palais
Itzassou
Louhossoa
Forêt de Lapins
Ainhoa
Dantxarinea
Urdax
Iholdy
Uhart-Mixe
Lohitzun-Oyhercq
Bidarray
Irissarry
Ossès
Larceveau
Centre des Stèles
Jaxu
Lacarre
Ordiarp
Bozate
Arizkun
Irouléguy
Saint-Étienne-de-Baïgorry
St Jean-le-Vieux
Saint-Jean-Pied-de-Port
Hosta
Aussuncq
Truite de Banka
Banca
Olhaberri, Mining Learning Centre
Mendive
Forêt des Arbailles
Aldudes
Pierre Oteiza
Pays Kint
Vallée des Aldudes
Arnéguy
Luzaide (Valcarlos)
Ahusquy
Uripel
Bosque del Irati
Col d'Orgambidesca
Forêt d'Iraty
Larrau
Roncesvalles
Burguete (Auritz)
Pic d'Orhy 2017m
0 5km
0 5 miles
N
Bradt
A64
D936
D933
D123
D932
D11
D14
D251
D245
D918
D22
D20
D119
D8
D408
D422
D948
D949
NA-2600
D15
D168
D301
D117
D18
D428
N135
NA-138
D26

8

Basse-Navarre (Behe Nafarroa)

The Pyrenees might neatly divide Basse-Navarre from Navarre in Spain, but the presence of the high mountains has not prevented the dominion over this small region being batted back and forward between France and Spain like a ping-pong ball. The clue is really in the name, for it references Basse-Navarre's long association with the Kingdom of Navarre and previously the Kingdom of Pamplona. Now, Basse-Navarre is a quiet place with a small population that declined steadily after the end of the 19th century before experiencing a revival in the last 30 years. It may be affected by influences from Béarn to the northeast and Landes to the north, but stumbling across a game of *pelota* or a cluster of imposing, red-shuttered farmhouses will remind you that the Basque spirit is alive and kicking here. Scattered among characteristic valleys, with hills all around, Basse-Navarre provides a focal point for visitors in the shape of Saint-Jean-Pied-de-Port, an attractive town of no great size but one of huge importance as a jumping-off point for pilgrims, bracing themselves for the big push up and over the high mountains and into Spanish Navarre. On its way to Bayonne and the coast, the River Nive bowls its way down the mountains and across the region's southern reaches. Elsewhere, a tiny acreage of vineyards in and around Irouléguy produces the French Basque Country's only recognised quality wine and the valleys themselves make for ideal excursions by car, studded sporadically with small-scale tourist attractions based firmly on nature and natural products. Among these, look out for Ossau-Iraty cheese and the renowned ham from the Aldudes Valley.

Three communes today make up what was once the distinct Basque province of Basse-Navarre, before it became merely part of the department of Pyrénées-Atlantiques. In the south, **Uhart-Cize** accounts for half of the area's landmass, borders Spain and includes the best scenery and areas of greatest interest for the visitor. **Uhart-Mixe** lies to the north and east, with Saint-Palais being its most significant settlement. Tiny **Saint Martin d'Arberoue** is wedged between the two, sharing its short western border with Labourd, criss-crossed by narrow country roads and with the caves of Isturitz and Oxocelhaya as its main tourist attractions.

HISTORY

At the end of the first millennium, these lands were part of the Duchy of Vasconia (Gascony), although the then-independent Kingdom of Navarre already had a territorial foothold in the region, at times controlling some of the rugged valleys of what is now Basse-Navarre, such as Baigorri and Ossès, at times conceding it to Gascony. The subsequent centuries were a succession of territorial wrestling matches, with either Gascony or Navarre enjoying dominance over the terrain at first. But when troops loyal to Ferdinand II of Aragón invaded Navarre at the start of the 16th century, Saint-Jean-Pied-de-Port was also seized by his Spanish forces, then changed hands frequently as Navarre fought back. Although recaptured by the troops of Carlos I of Spain, pro-Navarre local lords resisted strongly and, with the whole of Navarre south of the Pyrenees now lost to the Spanish, Navarre clung on to the northern territory until again it was invaded in 1525, only to be reconquered once more two years later by Esteban d'Albret. Soon, the Spanish deemed this *ultrapuertos* ('beyond the mountain passes') region of Navarre to be too difficult to subdue and govern and gave up the chase, choosing instead to sign a treaty with France and thus establish peaceful relations (for a while at least).

Despite the seat of power of the reduced Kingdom of Navarre moving eastward to Pau in neighbouring Béarn, at first the traditional laws of Navarre were respected and upheld, but by the time of Louis XIII of France that respect was diminishing and the Kingdom of Navarre merged with that of France in 1620. France was on the move towards centralisation, which would culminate in the French Revolution in 1789 and the subsequent suppression of regional identities and languages. Along with the rest of the French Basque provinces, Basse-Navarre would be submerged into the then newly created – and now defunct – *département* of Basses-Pyrénées.

UHART-CIZE COMMUNE

BIDARRAY (BIDARRAI) *Fronton*, bar, church: the classic ingredients that make up a Basque village. All three of these lie within a few yards of each other, the heart of languid Bidarray being found perched high on a plateau, while down by the river and main road a few houses and rafting companies complete the community. The church façade even assumes the same shape as the *fronton*, but that's no real surprise, as the church wall in many villages was often pressed into service as an essential part of the early *pelota* court. This pretty village is on both the long-distance GR10 path and the Sentier des Contrabandiers (smugglers' route), making it popular with walkers.

Where to stay and eat

Auberge Ostape [map, page 342] (22 rooms/suites) Domaine Chahatoenia, on the west side of the Nive River, 2km north of Bidarray; 0559 37 91 91; e contact@ostape.com; w ostape.com. A very high-end, 5-star hideaway, carrying an air of exclusivity, with a superb location atop a hill, giving great views. Reception is housed in a 17th-century manor house, while suites are arranged across a number of buildings in the 45ha site. Golf buggies whisk guests up to the restaurant & around the terrain. Suites are large, with all amenities: swimming pool, sauna, hammam, fitness room, jacuzzi. The owner is a Porsche fanatic & there is a private Porsche museum on site, visitable by guests. **€€€€€**

Hotel Barberaenea (9 rooms) Pl de l'Église, Bidarray; 0559 37 74 86; e hotel@barberaenea.fr; w hotel-bidarray.com. Run by the same family for 140 years, this old-style place has wooden beams & staircases, & simple rooms.

THE BEST *GÂTEAU BASQUE*?

Everyone has their own opinion, and a discussion with a local about the beloved *Gâteau Basque* can sometimes seem like a discussion about a fine wine. Bidarray's version of this local delicacy can be obtained from the well-marked building halfway up the hill between the river and the upper village. Try the *myrtille and vanilla* flavour. Irresistible.

Some have shared bathrooms; others have private facilities. Either way, they are great value. Family rooms sleeping up to 6 are also available. Free Wi-Fi. B/fast is served on the terrace & there is a traditional restaurant. **€–€€**

What to see and do Mainly from April to October, but sometimes year-round, the waters of the Nive are suitable for rafting and canoeing. **Ur Ederra Rafting** (on the D-918, south of Louhoassoa at km44; 0559 37 78 01; m 0681 28 46 99; e contact@rafting-pays-basque.com; w rafting-pays-basque.com; year-round; €30 for 1 adult, 2hrs 30mins, discounts for groups/families, advance reservation required), a long-established firm, provides helmets, neoprene suits and life jackets for its accompanied trips in inflatable rafts, or for unaccompanied journeys in smaller craft such as kayaks. An ability to swim is essential. There are a few similar enterprises dotted along the river, such as **Ur Bizia** (0559 37 72 37; m 0607 85 04 38; e ur-bizia@wanadoo.fr; w ur-bizia.com) and **Arteka** (0559 37 71 34; e infos@arteka-eh.com; w arteka-eh.com).

OSSÈS (ORTZAIZE) On the main road that bypasses Ossès village on its way towards Saint-Jean-Pied-de-Port, a number of artisans have formed a 'craft village', though any images of quaintness should be dismissed as the 'village' is cut in half by the road. Nevertheless, in an area not renowned for its souvenirs, here you'll find an outlet for Mauléon's famous espadrilles, adjoining a compact **learning centre/museum** (Apr 14.00–19.00 Tue–Sat, May, Jun & mid-Sep–end Oct 10.00–13.00 & 14.00–19.00 Mon–Sat, Jul & Aug daily; admission free, information in French only). There is also a metalworker, a carpenter and at the **Poterie Goicoechea** (Route de Saint-Jean-Pied-de-Port (D-918); 0559 37 71 30; w poterie-goicoechea.com; 08.30–12.30 & 14.00–18.30 Mon–Fri, 10.30–12.30 & 14.00–18.30 Sat) generations of the same family have fashioned innovative creations using clay from Navarre. Many of the pieces would struggle to fit in the average car boot, but they are attractive and innovative. Nearby is a branch of **Arnabar** (w arnabar-foie-gras.com; 09.00–12.30 & 14.00–18.00 Mon–Sat), a firm which farms ducks in the vicinity and – as the shop assistant describes it – 'transforms' them into duck *foie gras* and other products. Local wines and other goodies are also on sale.

For those of an active and equine bent, the **Ferme Équestre Les Collines** (Aihce; 0559 37 75 08; w fermelescollines.com) offers a chance to explore the lovely scenery around Ossès on horseback. A ride with Eugene Ondars or his daughters makes a wonderful experience. They have a busy calendar of two- or three-day riding excursions between May and November, heading further afield to places such as the Vallée d'Aldudes or even to the coast but, if you want a shorter trip, they can usually fit you in. Prices are very reasonable, from €22 for 2 hours to €50 for a full day's trip. Eugene speaks enough English to get you riding and teach you about the vultures, wild boar and red squirrels that inhabit the valleys. To find it, take the road (Subi Aldia) off the D-8 in the centre of Ossès village and follow it for 1.2km.

IROULÉGUY (IRULEGI) This town produces the only wine from the French Basque region to carry the AOC certificate, although its output is small, with between 500,000 and 600,000 litres of wine made annually, the grapes provided by a mere 220ha of vineyards. Wine culture here goes all the way back to the 12th century, when vines were planted in the area by the monks from the abbey at Roncesvalles. The limited quantity means that you'll struggle to find these wines outside France – all the more reason to try them here. Having almost disappeared at the start of the 20th century, the vineyards were revived after World War II. Their AOC denomination was proudly gained in 1970 and Irouléguy wines have since won international competitions. The lack of flat terrain means that most of the vineyards are terraced, easily visible around Irouléguy village and the other ten communities entitled to use the name. For the whites, Courbu, Gros Manseng and Petit Manseng grapes are used, while Cabernet Franc, Cabernet Sauvignon and Tannat are predominant in the reds.

The **Cave d'Irouléguy** (Route de Saint-Jean-Pied-de-Port; 0559 37 41 33; w cave-irouleguy.com; Apr–Sep 09.00–noon & 14.00–18.30 daily, Oct–Mar 09.00–noon & 14.00–18.00 Mon–Sat) is the shop of the co-operative, created in 1952 and selling wines by most, though not all, of Irouléguy's producers. Ask at the counter and they'll crank up two English-language videos with information about the region's wine. You can then taste and buy it. Artisanal beer, cider, honey and other local products are also on sale here.

SAINT-ÉTIENNE-DE-BAÏGORRY (BAIGORRI) A mere photo stop for many, this scenic town is now home to only 1,600 inhabitants, having suffered from large-scale emigration to the USA since the mid-19th century. It boasts a beautiful 'Roman' bridge (actually from the 17th century) over the Nive des Aldudes River, and lies at the head of the lush Aldudes Valley, which leads to the Spanish border a few kilometres away. Directly west, the twisting D-949 crosses the border even more rapidly, over the Col d'Ispéguy, and connects with the Baztán Valley in Navarre.

Saint-Étienne's **church** is typically Basque inside, with its wooden balconies, but it is also noteworthy for the separate door to the right of the main entrance, through which the Cagots (Agotes; see box, page 245) were grudgingly allowed to enter.

Tourist information The tourist office (Pl de la Mairie; 0559 37 47 28; w baigorry.fr; Sep–9 Jul 09.00–noon & 14.00–18.00 Mon–Fri, 10 Jul–Aug 09.00–13.00 & 14.00–19.00 Mon–Fri; 09.00–noon & 14.00–18.00 Sat, 10.00–13.00 Sun) can furnish you with walking routes, if your French is up to scratch.

Where to stay and eat

Hôtel Restaurant Arcé [map, page 342] (16 rooms, 4 suites) Saint-Étienne-de-Baïgorry; 0559 37 40 14; e reservations@hotel-arce.com; w hotel-arce.com; see ad, page 353. In the same family for 150 years, a beautifully located hotel by the gently flowing river. Rooms combine modernity with tradition, free Wi-Fi, TV in the rooms. Renowned restaurant (see below). Heated swimming pool (weather-dependent), tennis, *pétanque*. For walkers, the Sentier des Contrabandiers (smugglers' route) passes by the door. Popular with anglophone clientele & English spoken. **€€€€**

Chambres d'Hôtes Idiartekoborda [map, page 342] (5 rooms) Route de Belexi, nr Saint-Étienne-de-Baïgorry; 0559 37 46 29; w idiartekoborda.com; mid-Mar–mid-Nov. Surely with one of the best locations anywhere in the Basque Country, English-speaking Sandrine's mountain hideaway overlooks the valley in all its magnificence. Follow the signpost from the roundabout at the southern end of town, keep your nerve as the single-track road winds upwards for 2.5km then turn left (signposted). You will be rewarded for your efforts, especially if you fight hard to get a room with a valley view. Prices are good in low season & reduce if staying more than 1 night. English spoken. **€€€–€€€€**

Hôtel Restaurant Arcé (see above) noon–13.45 & 19.30–20.45 Tue–Sun, also closed mid-Sep–mid-Jul Wed & Thu lunch. Advance reservations obligatory. High-end cuisine, lovingly prepared & presented. Focus is on local products: trout from the nearby rivers, Pierre Oteiza sausage (page 347). Outdoor tables overlook river. €€€€

Bar Brasserie du Fronton Pl Fronton; 0559 37 48 00; closed Tue eve. In the square in the centre of town, this is a good place for a light lunch, with delicious, simple fare at low prices. Check out the *plat du jour* (dish of the day), but the *Salade Baïgorri*, with local ham & hot goat's cheese, is also recommended. €

What to see and do

Chocolaterie Laia (Rue de l'Église, Saint-Étienne-de-Baïgorry; 0559 37 51 43; w laia.fr; Easter–Sep 09.00–12.15 & 14.00–19.00 Tue–Sat) With everything made on the premises, this is a great place to stop on your way up the Aldudes Valley for a delicious hot chocolate when the weather's cold, or a homemade ice cream when it's hot.

Festival des Forces Basques If you didn't witness the array of macho Basque sports on the southern side of the divide, make sure you're in Saint-Étienne on the first Sunday in July or August for a bit of wood-chopping or stone-lifting.

VALLÉE DES ALDUDES (ALDUDE) If you thought that the Nive Valley was remote, the beautiful Aldudes takes isolation to another level as the road south of Saint-Étienne-de-Baïgorry narrows and the habitation thins. This is a beautiful drive, or cycle if you have the legs, with a few points of interest along the way. Two kilometres beyond Banca, carved in the grass high on the hill, is the word 'Kintoa', the Basque name for Pays de Quint.

What to see and do

Olhaberri (Mining Learning Centre) (on the D-948, in the centre of Banca; 0559 37 71 10; e contact@olhaberri.com; w olhaberri.fr; 09.00–18.00 Mon–Wed, 09.00–19.00 Fri & Sat, 09.00–13.00 Sun, closed Thu; hours can vary so phoning ahead is advisable; admission free) It is somewhat surprising to find that mining for both copper and latterly iron ore took place in such a remote valley, stretching back as far as the 4th century. After centuries of inactivity, mining was revived in the 18th century, once again for copper. This reached its peak in the 1750s. With copper reserves dwindling and the cost of extraction increasing, in 1825 a large forge was built in Banca, at the site of the copper foundry, and interest switched from copper to iron. The remains of the iron forge lie by the side of the main road, a few hundred metres south of Banca. The learning centre currently only has information in French, though translations – including into English – are promised. There is a café on-site.

Truite de Banka (Trout Farm) (signposted off the main road, Banca; 0559 37 45 97; w truitedebanka.com; 08.30–12.30 & 14.00–18.00 Mon–Sat; self-guided visit, admission free) You can walk around the farm, a family concern that has been running for 50 years, based on the site of a 17th-century mill, making the most of the clean waters of the Nive des Aldudes. The explanatory panels are in French, but the owner's son, Peio, speaks good English, and a short film is available in English. A small boutique sells you products, including handbags and trouser belts made from trout skins!

Pierre Oteiza (Route Urepel, situated between Uripel & Aldudes; 0559 37 56 11; w pierreoteiza.com; 10.00–18.30 daily, except Sun in Jan; admission free) The Basque pig, distinctive with its black head and hindquarters, came close to extinction in the 1980s, when numbers sank to mere dozens. Now, thanks to the efforts of local producers headed by Pierre Oteiza, numbers of these fine specimens have swelled again, reaching over 5,500 animals that are looked after by over 80 breeders. The pigs are fed chestnuts, acorns and herbs, giving the ham a distinctive, delicate flavour. By the age of 14 months, the average pig weighs around 160kg. Visitors can see the animals, which are reared outdoors, at any time of year, either in what they call the '*maternité*' where the mothers look after their litters – usually eight to ten piglets – which appear twice per year, or up in the hills behind as part of a signposted walking route, the Sentier de Decouverte de Porc Basque (2.5km; 1hr). The information is all in French, but children will love seeing the pigs and can take a donkey ride, too. Samples of local cheeses and dried sausages are offered to every visitor.

There is a shop, restaurant and bar on-site. The Oteiza products are sold in further shops in Bayonne, Biarritz, Saint-Jean-Pied-de-Port, Saint-Jean-de-Luz, Bordeaux and Paris.

SAINT-JEAN-PIED-DE-PORT (DONIBANE GARAZI) The 'foot of the pass' by name, this is truly 'pilgrim central' for those who are brave enough to want their first day of the Camino de Santiago to be a long struggle over the Pyrenees. The railway reached here in 1898, and today nearly 60,000 pilgrims arrive here every year, amid much excitement and trepidation. But Saint-Jean has been a destination for pilgrims for hundreds of years. For those not on their way to Santiago de Compostela, this town of a mere 1,700 still generates an ambience of its own and is an ideal base for visiting the region.

Getting there and away

By train Four trains per day connect Saint-Jean with Bayonne (€10.10; 75mins), but the line is frequently being repaired and a bus replacement service comes into operation to get you to Saint-Jean. The train journey along the banks of the River Nive is a scenic one and when running calls at Cambo, Ossès and Arossa.

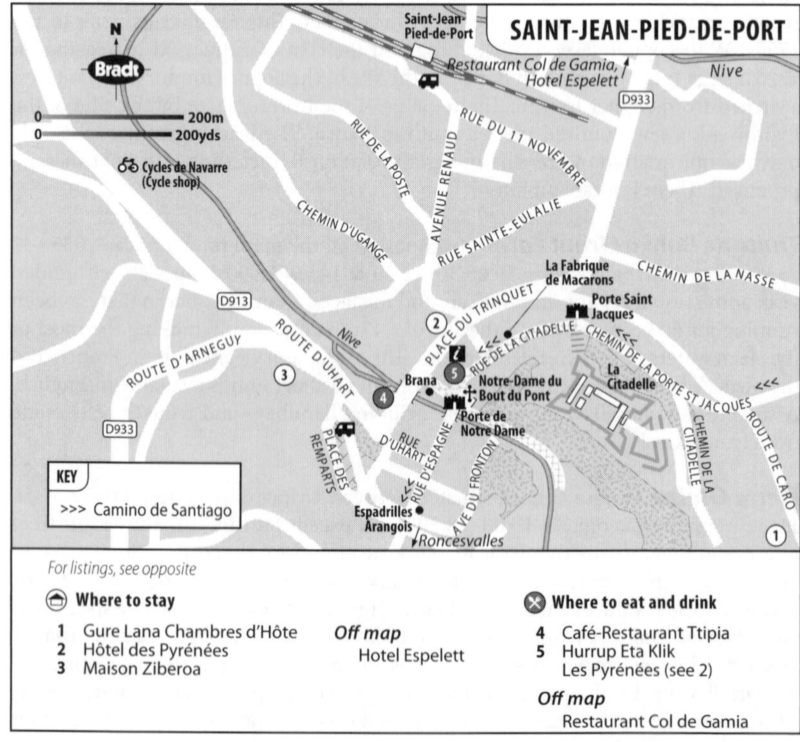

By car Coming from the north, Saint-Jean can be reached in an hour from either Biarritz or Bayonne, on the D-932 and then the D-918. Arriving from the south, the journey from Pamplona is 1 hour 40 minutes accessing the NA-135 through Roncesvalles, before crossing the border and continuing on the D-933.

Tourist information The tourist office (Pl Charles de Gaulle 14; 0559 37 03 57; e saint.jean.pied.de.port@wanadoo.fr; w saintjeanpieddeport-paysbasque-tourisme.com; mid-Jul–end Aug 09.00–19.00 Mon–Sat, 10.00–13.00 & 14.00–19.00 Sun, other months 09.00–noon & 14.00–18.00 Mon–Fri) offers a multilingual service and can organise guided tours of the town (French only). Books of walks and cycle routes are also available, as is free Wi-Fi and internet access.

Where to stay in and around Saint-Jean *Map, opposite*

Hôtel des Pyrénées (18 rooms) Pl Charles de Gaulle 19; 0559 37 01 01; e hotel.pyrenees@wanadoo.fr; w hotel-les-pyrenees.com. In a town heavily geared towards walkers, the non-pilgrim will find this to be a decent choice. Seasonal swimming pool & children's pool. Rooms are comfortable, without exuding luxury, & some have both bath & shower. Immaculately dressed staff are formal but friendly. Free Wi-Fi, AC & TV with international channels. Parking is €10 extra per day. Refreshingly, the room price does not vary according to season. **€€€€–€€€€€**

Gure Lana Chambres d'Hôte (4 rooms) Route de Caro 8; 0524 34 14 97; e reservation@bedandbreakfast-gurelana.com; w bedandbreakfast-gurelana.com. An excellent choice, in perfect peace just a few mins' easy walk from Saint-Jean's centre. Spacious rooms, communal lounge with TV, free Wi-Fi, free parking, very good b/fast (included in the price), but best of all are the genial hosts – fluent English speakers – who welcome you as a family member, without intruding. **€€**

Maison Ziberoa (4 rooms) Route d'Arneguy 3; 0559 37 75 25; m 0661 23 59 44; e maisonziberoa@ziberoa.com; w ziberoa.com. Just a few mins' walk from Saint-Jean, a lovely beamed & wooden-floored 18th-century house with a slightly alternative feel, a charming & kind hostess, a communal lounge & free Wi-Fi throughout. A family room is available. Public parking is free & very close by. B/fast inc; dinners available with notice (extra cost). **€€**

Hotel Espelett (20 rooms) Larceveau; 0559 37 81 91. Nothing fancy, this hotel on the main road north of Saint-Jean is a retro throwback to French hotels of the 1970s, with not a hint of renovation. The clean, spacious rooms would suit budget travellers, but not the choosy. Bargain family rooms are available. The truly enormous restaurant (€) downstairs serves rustic fare that is good value but unexceptional. **€**

Where to eat and drink *Map, opposite, unless otherwise stated*

The highly transient nature of the visitor to Saint-Jean keeps the price of meals down, meaning you can always find a cheap menu in town without much effort, but perhaps the overall quality suffers a bit, too. 'Pilgrims' menus' are usually available to all comers – no need to prove your credentials – but don't expect *haute cuisine* if you choose that option.

Les Pyrénées (see above) Jul–mid-Sep 12.15–13.45 & 19.45–21.00, Nov–Mar closed Mon & Tue, other months closed Mon. This hotel restaurant has renowned chef Philippe Arrambide at its helm, & a Michelin star, so you can treat yourself to some fine cuisine. A cut above anything else in town, it has prices to match. Locals who are in the know will gladly endorse the many official accolades it has received. **€€€€€**

Restaurant Col de Gamia [map, page 342] Route Quart Sarrasquet, Bussunarits; 0559 37 13 48; w restaurant-gamia.fr. Come here for the view (stunning) & the food (excellent). Remote hilltop location 20mins' drive from Saint-Jean, but worth the detour. Gastronomic menu available, but you can eat on a budget too. **€€€**

Café-Restaurant Ttipia Pl Floquet; 0559 37 11 96; w cafettipia.com; 07.30–

23.30 Thu–Tue. Unless you have cash to burn at Les Pyrénées (page 349), then this is probably the next-best option. The outside terrace is by the main road, making it ideal for pilgrim-watching. The food consists of good-quality Basque standards. €€

Hurrup Eta Klik Rue de la Citadelle 3; 0559 37 09 18; high season daily. It calls itself a *cidrerie*, but shares little in character with the raucous cider-houses you'll find elsewhere in the Basque Country. Instead, tourists & pilgrims munch happily on the outside terrace, the latter (and some of the former) taking advantage of the cheap menu. Quality is good & prices are reasonable. Vegetarian-friendly. €€

Shopping A walk along the Rue de la Citadelle, Rue d'Espagne and Rue de l'Église will be enough to satisfy your need for souvenirs, locally produced products and hiking supplies. Every Monday morning local producers display their wares at a market in the Place des Remparts.

Brana 6 Rue de l'Église. A well-known local winemaker & distiller, this is the place to look for Irouléguy wines, as well as spirits & *eaux de vie*.

Espadrilles Arangois 42 Rue d'Espagne; 0559 37 11 09; Jun–Sep 09.30–19.00 daily, other months 09.30–12.30 & 14.00–19.00 Mon–Sat. Hand-sewn regional footwear.

La Fabrique de Macarons 25 Rue de la Citadelle; w www.lafabriquedemacarons.fr; 10.00–13.00 & 14.00–19.00 daily. Promises *macarons* according to grandmother's recipe. Grandma knew what she was doing: choose from flavours including almond, chocolate, coconut or even the insidious Espelette pepper (see box, page 338).

Activities

Walking You could soak up the pilgrim spirit and start out on the Camino de Santiago, simply following the *very* steep ascent out of Saint-Jean to Orisson and then returning (15km round trip). Orisson has a café and excellent views. In addition, the tourist office has a number of walking routes available for a nominal charge, but they are in French only. A stroll along the banks of the Nive is also a pleasant diversion.

Cycling On the outskirts of town, **Cycles de Navarre** (Route de Bayonne; 0547 86 90 13; e cyclesdenavarre.64@gmail.com; 09.00–noon & 14.00–19.00 Mon–Fri) has both mountain bikes and the increasingly popular electric bikes available. A day's hire costs €13 (including helmet and puncture repair kit); electric bikes are €40. A passport/ID card is required as deposit. The tourist office has some suggested cycling routes.

What to see and do The best way of seeing Saint-Jean-Pied-de-Port is to make your way up to the citadel to get your bearings, then meander back down the Rue de la Citadelle, cross the river and enter Rue d'Espagne. Together, these places form the nub of the Old Town.

La Citadelle After nearby Saint-Jean-le-Vieux (then called Saint-Jean-de-Cize) was destroyed by Richard the Lionheart in 1177, a new, more strategic site was sought and Saint-Jean-Pied-de-Port was selected, with its outlook towards the Pyrenees and Spain. A *chatelain* was installed by the Kings of Navarre to guard their interests, collect taxes and ensure that Navarrese laws were enforced in the region. Much more recently, during the Spanish Civil War, children from the Bilbao area were given refuge here in Saint-Jean's citadel. At first, they were viewed with suspicion by the locals, branded as 'children of communists', but gradually the refugees built relationships with local children. Seventy years after their first arrival, some of them returned as elderly men and women, and were temporarily reunited with their one-time hosts.

At present the building on the site of the old citadel is a college and usually not open for visits, but a walk to the top of the hill is recommended for the views over the town and across the mountains to Spain. An orientation table gives assistance.

Rue de la Citadelle From the **Porte St Jacques**, where pilgrims enter the town, the Rue de la Citadelle leads down to the town centre. Note how at **number 29** the letter 'n' is engraved backwards in the word '*année*', as the manual workers of the era were obviously unable to read or write. At number 39, you'll see the ***Accueil des Pelerins***, the welcome office for pilgrims. Usually the up-to-date statistics for the numbers of pilgrims passing through town are posted on the wall here, broken down by nationality. The French, Spanish and Italians are top of the list, together with those from the United States. The rapid rise of Americans is maybe due in part to the film *The Way* with Martin Sheen, while Koreans also now arrive in droves following a book published in that language. In 2017, a total of over 56,000 pilgrims from over 100 countries passed through, demonstrating the importance of the Camino de Santiago to the town. Peak numbers are in May, explained by the walkers' desire to reach Santiago before the high heat of July and August. At **number 32**, you'll see the house with the oldest date ascribed to any building in town – 1510. Above the **Porte de Notre Dame**, the figure of St John the Baptist, the town's patron saint, looms large. On the other side is the Virgin and child. Diverting briefly down **Rue de l'Église**, the lintel of one of the houses to your left is inscribed '*1796 4 eme AR*' or 'fourth year after the Republic', a reference of course to the French Revolution and the subsequent creation of the Republic in 1793. Notice also the **stone plaque** that claims that '*Ici ont veçu les ancêtres de Saint Francis Xavier*' ('the ancestors of Saint Francis Xavier lived in this house'), though subsequent archive-digging has shown that their residence was actually a different one, a few metres away. This street is where Saint-Jean's market once took place.

Once through the Porte de Notre Dame, you cross the **River Nive**, a picturesque watercourse and the venue for many pre-pilgrimage photo shoots. The road then seamlessly becomes the **Rue d'Espagne**, once the home of artisans and tradesmen. At **number 30**, for example, you can see the lintel to the right bearing the symbols of some keys, indicating that the blacksmith once lived and worked there.

NEAR SAINT-JEAN-PIED-DE-PORT

Saint-Jean-le-Vieux Roman site Discovered only in 1965, this site is the remains of a settlement that once lay on the important Roman road between Bordeaux and Astorga. Fragments of amphorae and coins are on display in the small museum, while outside are the remains of Roman baths. Formerly Saint-Jean-de-Cize, the town changed its name to Saint-Jean-le-Vieux when the region's capital town was relocated to Saint-Jean-Pied-de-Port. To visit, best to ask in the Saint-Jean tourist office (page 349), as opening times are sporadic and a bit limited. Upstairs, next to the *mairie*, there is a tiny new **museum** (🕘 09.00–noon & 14.00–17.00 Mon–Fri, 09.00–noon Sat, admission free), with some related exhibits.

Larceveau Otherwise no more than a drive-through village, tiny Larceveau harbours one unusual point of interest. The **Centre des Stèles** (on the D-918; 🕘 09.00–19.00 daily; admission free, to access the centre, ask the staff at the *pharmacie*, opposite the Restaurant Espelett, for an electronic swipe card – the visit is effectively self-service) is by the Larceveau village church, about 100m down from the hotel. Information is provided in English, by translated display panels and also by press-button audio with an English option. With over 100 *steles* (stelae) on display, the centre makes for an interesting visit for anyone curious about these distinctive solid-stone funerary slabs and the great importance attached to death and funerary rites in Basque culture. The *steles* were gathered together into this centre, which opened in 2007, to protect them from the damage and decay they were suffering elsewhere in the Basque Country.

SAINT MARTIN DE ARBEROUE (DONAMARTIRI) COMMUNE

The scenery becomes less rugged away from the mountains, but below ground this region still has some sites of interest in the form of two caves. **Les Grottes d'Isturitz et d'Oxocelhaya (Caves of Isturitz and Oxocelhaya)** (Saint Martin d'Arberoue; 0559 29 64 72; e reservation@grottes-isturitz.com; w grottes-isturitz.com; 15 Mar–15 Nov daily; Mar–May, Oct & Nov, visits hourly 14.00–17.00 (last visit), Jul & Aug visits hourly between 10.00 & 18.00 (last visit), Jun & Sep visits at 10.30, 11.30 & hourly between 14.00 & 17.00; €11/8.50/4.50/free adults/students/under 14s/under 7s, family tickets €32) Two caves for the price of one, this is a place of interest for fans of both prehistory and geology. Visits are by guided tour only for safety reasons, and are in French, but most of the guides speak English and are more than willing to answer questions. Both the museum and the caves are accompanied by information sheets in English, though it's advisable to bring a torch to let you read them during your visit. The temperature of the caves is always around 14°C, so an extra layer is advised. For geologists and casual visitors alike, the formations of stalactites and stalagmites are breathtaking, while evidence of human habitation ('Aurignacian man') in the Isturitz cave stretches back over 80,000 years. Researchers have identified specific areas of the caves where animal carcasses were prepared and another where animal skins were turned into clothes. Jewellery was also made here. The later Upper Palaeolithic period was a particularly active time, and visitors can see rock carvings of various animals, including deer, wolverines and fish. Many of the tools and bones found during research are now kept in the National Archaeology Museum near Paris, though the on-site museum has some exhibits. At various points in more recent history, the caves have come under threat: in the 14th century a castle was built on top of the caves and in 1895 permission was granted to mine the hills for phosphates, resulting in the partial destruction of potentially interesting archaeological evidence. Subsequently, this was thwarted by legal action and digging began in 1913, uncovering the carved pillar in Istaritz. Oxocelhaya was discovered in 1929 and the caves were then opened to visitors. Although experts have been aware of the caves for a long time, academic interest in them was heightened in 1999, with the discovery that some of the findings here dated back 40,000 years, when the first *Homo sapiens* arrived in western Europe. Research is still ongoing.

UHART-MIXE COMMUNE

SAINT-PALAIS Once a capital of Basse-Navarre, Saint-Palais is now the main town in the commune of Uhart-Mixe, a hub of agricultural and commercial activity. Only 33km from Saint-Jean, it is a stopping point for pilgrims who started their journey much, much earlier, perhaps on the route from Vézelay, hundreds of kilometres to the north. A small town of only 1,800 inhabitants, it is probably only worth a diversion should you be around the area in the third weekend in August, when a championship of *force Basque* (traditional Basque sports) takes place, with the full menu of wood-chopping, stone-lifting and so on, accompanied by much music, dancing and good humour.

Practicalities The **tourist office** is at 14 Place Charles de Gaulle (℡ 0559 65 71 78; w saintpalais-tourisme.com; ⌚ Jul & Aug 09.30–12.30 & 14.00–18.30 Mon–Sat, 10.00–12.30 Sun, Sep–Jun 09.30–12.30 & 14.00–18.30 Tue–Sat).

Where to stay and eat

Hôtel de la Paix (27 rooms; 33 Rue du Jeu de Paume; ℡ 0559 65 73 15; e contact@hotellapaix.com; w hotellapaix.com. In this centrally located hotel, the rooms all have TV & free Wi-Fi. Free parking is available close by. **€€€**

Le Trinquet Saint-Palais/Le Bouchon Basque 31 Rue du Jeu-de-Paume; ℡ 0559 65 73 13; w lebouchonbasque.com. This family-run restaurant was once a hotel, but now merely focuses on serving seasonal food, such as flambéed pigeon in October. €€€

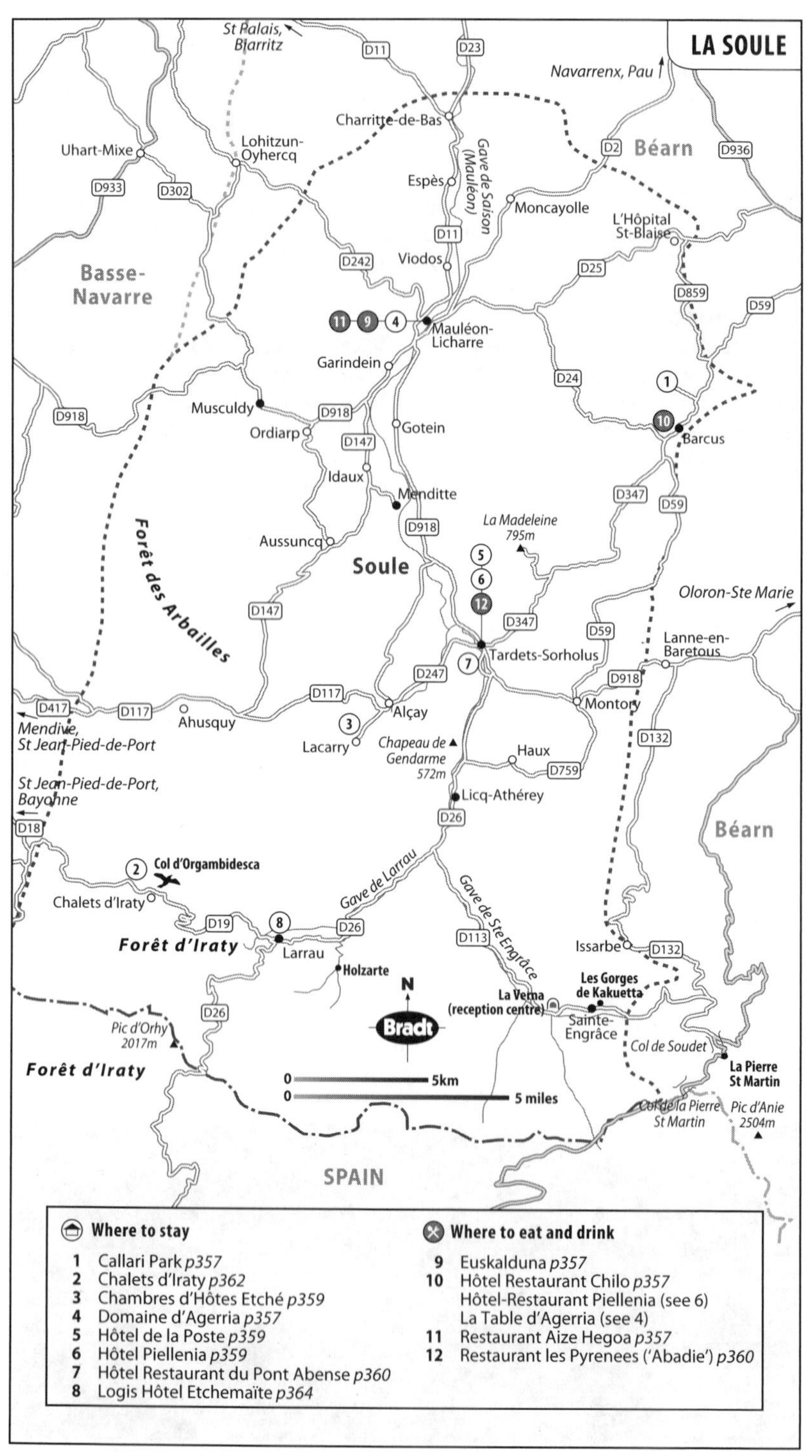
LA SOULE
St Palais, Biarritz
Navarrenx, Pau
D11
D23
Charritte-de-Bas
Uhart-Mixe
Lohitzun-Oyhercq
D933
D302
Espès
Gave de Saison (Mauléon)
D2
Béarn
D936
Moncayolle
L'Hôpital St-Blaise
D11
D242
Viodos
D25
Basse-Navarre
D859
D59
11
9
4
Mauléon-Licharre
Garindein
D24
1
D918
Musculdy
D918
10
Barcus
Ordiarp
Gotein
D147
Idaux
Menditte
D347
D59
Forêt des Arbailles
D918
La Madeleine 795m
Aussuncq
5
6
Soule
12
Oloron-Ste Marie
D147
D347
D59
Lanne-en-Baretous
Tardets-Sorholus
7
D247
D918
D417
D117
D117
Montory
Ahusquy
Alçay
Mendive, St Jean-Pied-de-Port
3
Lacarry
Chapeau de Gendarme 572m
D132
Haux
D759
St Jean-Pied-de-Port, Bayonne
Licq-Athérey
D18
D26
Béarn
2
Col d'Orgambidesca
Gave de Larrau
Gave de SteEngrâce
Chalets d'Iraty
D19
8
D26
D113
Issarbe
D132
Forêt d'Iraty
Larrau
Holzarte
N
Les Gorges de Kakuetta
La Verna (reception centre)
D26
Bradt
Sainte-Engrâce
Pic d'Orhy 2017m
Col de Soudet
La Pierre St Martin
Forêt d'Iraty
0
5km
0
5 miles
Col de la Pierre St Martin
Pic d'Anie 2504m
SPAIN
Where to stay
1 Callari Park p357
2 Chalets d'Iraty p362
3 Chambres d'Hôtes Etché p359
4 Domaine d'Agerria p357
5 Hôtel de la Poste p359
6 Hôtel Piellenia p359
7 Hôtel Restaurant du Pont Abense p360
8 Logis Hôtel Etchemaïte p364
Where to eat and drink
9 Euskalduna p357
10 Hôtel Restaurant Chilo p357
Hôtel-Restaurant Piellenia (see 6)
La Table d'Agerria (see 4)
11 Restaurant Aize Hegoa p357
12 Restaurant les Pyrenees ('Abadie') p360

9

La Soule (Xiberoa)

The most sparsely populated of the seven Basque 'provinces' and the smallest in area, landlocked Soule, also known as Xiberoa, finds itself somewhat forgotten and struggling to advertise itself to potential visitors. No motorways touch its territory, with only one major road artery traversing it north to south and several minor ones cutting through on the west to east axes. Crossable in either direction in an hour's car journey, you could almost blink and miss it. Soule's geography builds from the north, its lowlands turning to hilly midlands which then usher in the full-blown mountains of the Pyrenees, the source of the one major waterway, the Gave de Saison.

Of course, Soule is no longer a real province, nor even – as it once was – a viscounty. Instead, it is merely a small part of the French *département* of Pyrénées-Atlantiques. It is boundaried to its east and north by Béarn, which, while still part of the same *département*, is definitely not Basque. To the west of Soule you'll find the region of Basse-Navarre and to its south, across the range of mountains, lie Navarre and Spain.

Sleepy Soule is far removed in terms of character and number of visitors from the glitzy coastal delights of Biarritz and its neighbours, and the main trail of pilgrims marching down through Basse-Navarre towards Saint-Jean-Pied-de-Port passes by to the north. Here, the Souletine houses are generally smaller, more subdued, and with fewer of the blood-red shutters seen elsewhere in the Basque Country, but still distinctive with their sombre grey roof-lines. This markedly different architecture has more in common with Béarn than with Soule's neighbours of Labourd to the west or Navarre to the south. Also characteristic here are the ubiquitous *trinitaires*, churches with three-pointed belltowers.

Don't be fooled, however, by these 'on-the-surface' peculiarities. Perhaps aided by its isolation, the Basque identity and spirit is surprisingly undiluted in Soule, every village has its *frontón* and Soule even has its own version of *pelota*, known as *rebot*, with five players to a team. It is a landscape of huge caves, impressive gorges, low-lying cloud, lush forests of oak and chestnut, not forgetting the brooding mountains, so it comes as no surprise that Soule harbours a wealth of legends (see box, page 363).

Without any real show-stopping tourist draws, Soule will appeal to those who like to immerse themselves in a genuine rural or mountain culture, dine well but simply, stay in no-frills accommodation, enjoy the outdoors by walking, cycling or taking car tours on narrow roads while watching the unspoilt scenery unfold in front of them. Soule will feel comfortable to visitors who are unperturbed at giving way to a herd of sheep or the occasional eyelash-fluttering blonde Aquitaine cow who refuses to relinquish her preferred position in the middle of the tarmac. A few days exploring the quiet towns, southern gorges and heavily forested landscapes will satisfy all but the most ardent pleasure-seeker.

HISTORY

Evidence has been discovered of settlement in the area during the Neolithic period, although written acknowledgement of Soule as a distinct entity dates back only as far as the 7th century AD. During the Roman tenure of Aquitaine, Soule's isolation and numerically insignificant population made it of little interest to the occupiers. In the Middle Ages, the King of Navarre, Sancho VI, appointed the first Viscount of Soule in 1023 and the territory was administered through a succession of viscounts for 200 years, with the seat of control being the *château-fort* of Mauléon (page 357). With Aquitaine passing into English hands in 1152, the days of Navarre's control were numbered, but it was not until 1261 that Soule's last viscount was forced to give up Mauléon to the English, with Prince Edward arriving in person with his army to ensure the surrender of the chateau. In 1295, the deposed viscount took it back again, but relinquished it once more a mere eight years later. English rule lasted until the mid-15th century, with the role of the viscount being replaced by a tax-collecting Lord of Soule, supported by a group of compliant captains. The French ousted the English for good in 1449 and from then on Soule recognised French royalty. In 1589, the crowning of Henry IV as King of France and Navarre resulted in the three French Basque provinces being under common control. In 1792, following the French Revolution, the Basses-Pyrénées was created as a *département* despite strong opposition, absorbing Soule along with the other French Basque provinces as well as Béarn. In more recent times, and despite the manufacture of espadrilles providing some temporary rejuvenation of Soule's economy in the late 19th century, the region's already tiny population has been slowly dwindling: figures show that only 14,500 now reside here, down from 25,000 at the beginning of the 20th century.

GETTING THERE AND AROUND

BY ROAD A car is essential to visit the best of what Soule has to offer, unless you have endless time and patience to plan journeys by buses and then wait for them to arrive. In addition, accessing the best views requires you to take narrow, mountain roads that are not frequented by buses. Nevertheless, if you are determined to use public transport, **Transports64** (w transports64.fr) operates a cheap bus service from Bayonne at least twice daily (twice on Saturday, no Sunday service) to Tardets-Sorholus (1hr 45mins; €2) calling at a dozen Soule destinations including Mauléon-Licharre en route. There is no rail network in Soule, but a bus service from Mauléon serves the train station at Oloron-Sainte-Marie, in Béarn, three times per day, except Sundays (50mins; €2).

BY BIKE If you are a very fit traveller, cycling offers a wonderful alternative. Quiet roads are compensation for the often hilly terrain. Bike hire is available from the tourist office at Tardets-Sorholus (which also has electric bikes) or the outlets below and there are suggested itineraries for road and mountain bikes on the website of the Bearn/Pays Basque Tourist Board (w tourisme64.com). One circular route (80km) which avoids the high Pyrenees follows the '*Le Tour de Soule*' circuit from Mauléon – Moncayolle – l'Hôpital St Blaise – Barcus – Montory – Haux – Lichans-Sunhar – Tardets-Sorholus – Alçay – Camou-Cihigue – Aussurucq – Ordiarp – Mauléon.

Chalets d'Iraty On the D-19; 0559 28 51 29; e info@chalets-iraty.com; w chalets-iraty.com. Has (a very few) bikes for rental – at a starting height of 1,300m, but also offers electric bikes.

Cycles Poppe Zone Industrielle de la Gare, Mauléon-Licharre; 0559 28 13 62; e cycles.poppe@wanadoo.fr; Tue–Sat am; €13 per day

MAULÉON-LICHARRE (MAULE-LEXTARRE)

Once two separate towns, Mauléon and Licharre eventually hitched themselves together in 1842 and the double-barrelled result is now both the capital of Soule and the region's largest town, gathering together the necessary commercial enterprises to service the surrounding villages and farms. A dose of perspective is required at this point, for its population is still a mere 3,500, although this represents a quarter of Soule's thinly spread inhabitants. Mauléon-Licharre's combined urban area is nowadays distinguished by two imposing buildings – a fort and a palace – and one emblematic product – the espadrille. Sadly, the making of the famous footwear only employs around 120 people, a fraction of the workers involved during the town's glory days in the 19th century. Nevertheless, it still accounts for around 70% of the production in France, the factories now concentrating more on the higher-end fashion market and leaving the cheaper mass-manufacture to the labour forces of the Far East. Elsewhere, the town contents itself with the production of cheese and *gâteaux Basques*, as well as a couple of industrial estates.

TOURIST INFORMATION The tourist office is at 10 Rue J B Heugas (0559 28 02 37; w soule-paysbasque.com; Sep–Jun 09.30–12.30 & 14.00–18.00 Mon–Sat, Jul & Aug 09.30–13.00 & 14.00–19.00 Mon–Sat, 10.00–12.30 Sun). As well as dispensing information and promoting the region (don't be surprised if the lady behind the counter is wearing espadrilles), the building also houses the Maison du Patrimoine with some permanent French-language displays on Soule's heritage.

WHERE TO STAY *Map, page 354*

Callari Park Chambre d'Hôtes (3 rooms) Chemin Lohidoy, Barcus; 0524 34 16 38; e info@callaripark.com; w callaripark.com. For those seeking escape, this hilltop retreat 15km east of Mauléon is well away from habitation & should fit the bill. The views are well worth the detour. Seasonal swimming pool. Rooms are renovated, with AC. English owners provide English-style b/fast (included in the price) & evening meals at a good price. **€€**

Domaine d'Agerria (17 rooms) 3 Rue du Frère Alban, Mauléon-Licharre; 0559 19 19 19; e contact@domaine-agerria.com; w domaine-agerria.com. A newcomer, perched on a hill looking down over town & across to the castle, this former monastery has been smartly renovated. A good option, in a town with no hotels. Rooms have AC & free Wi-Fi. Super terrace with great views. **€€**

WHERE TO EAT AND DRINK *Map, page 354*

Hôtel Restaurant Chilo Le Bourg, Barcus; 0559 28 90 79; e resa@hotel-chilo.com; w hotel-chilo.com; lunch & evening Tue–Sat, lunch only Sun, Oct–Apr closed Tue. 15km east of Mauléon, a deservedly reputed restaurant, not cheap but with fine cuisine. Lunchtime is good value, but service can be a bit formal. **€€€**

Restaurant Aize Hegoa 30 Bd Gambetta, Mauléon-Licharre; 0559 28 27 96; w aizehegoa.eus; noon–14.30 & 19.30–23.00 Tue–Sun. Mauléon may not win any prizes for its restaurants, but this place has recently moved upmarket. A choice of menus, food is reliably fresh. **€€€**

Euskalduna 4 Rue Pasteur, Mauléon-Licharre; 0559 28 23 35; 11.45–14.00 Tue–Fri, also 19.15–23.30 Wed & Thu, 19.15–02.00 Fri & Sat. A welcome newcomer to town, bright décor, welcoming smiles & excellent food. **€€**

La Table d'Agerria (see above) noon–13.30 & 19.30–21.00 Tue–Fri, 19.30–21.30 Sat, noon–13.30 Sun. A modern dining room with decent food at prices that are surprisingly low for a smart establishment. Sunny days make the outdoor terrace a must for lunch. **€€**

SHOPPING If you want to buy a pair of French-made espadrilles, in the footwear's capital, you have three choices. But if you want to know more about their history, the museum in Ossès (page 345) is the best option.

Atelier Don Quichosse Zone Artisanale; ☎ 0559 28 28 18; w donquichosse.com; ⏲ 09.00–noon & 14.00–17.00. Shop only, no longer does factory visits.

Atelier Prodiso Zone Artisanale; ☎ 0559 28 28 48; w espadrilles-mauleon.fr; ⏲ 09.00–noon & 14.00–18.00 Mon–Fri. Shop only.

Megam Espasoule 52 Bd Gambetta; ☎ 0559 28 13 89; w espasoule.com; ⏲ 09.00–17.00 Mon–Thu, 09.00–noon Fri. Guided visits may be available during the above hours (€9 including a pair of espadrilles). If no tour is available, you can content yourself with browsing the shelves.

WHAT TO SEE AND DO

Château-Fort (⏲ Easter w/end, 11 Apr–10 May daily, then mid-May–mid-Jun Sat & Sun only, mid-Jun–Sep 10.00–13.00 & 15.00–18.00 (Jul & Aug till 19.00) daily; €3/2 adults/children) There's no problem finding this sturdy 13th-century building, standing high over the town like a proud father. Squat and intimidating, its strategic importance is obvious, particularly when you consider how close it is to both Béarn and Navarre. As a result of the château's prominence, Soule's history has been inextricably determined by the answer to the question: 'Who controls the castle?' It was attacked 13 times between the 13th century and the 17th century, being destroyed, rebuilt, demolished, strengthened, converted to a prison (after the French Revolution) and then finally abandoned. With a permanent exhibition inside, an access bridge, dungeon, cannons, towers and a courtyard, it certainly deserves a visit. There's also an excellent panorama of the town.

Château d'Andurain de Maytie (⏲ Jul–Sep; guided visits at 11.00, 15.00, 16.15 & 17.30 daily, closed Sun morning & Thu; €6/free adults/under 18s) An entirely different type of 'castle' lies within the walls of this building, once situated in the middle of the countryside but now at the town's very centre. Remarkably, the family still live in part of this 16th-century castle and your tour includes a visit to their rather elegant living room. Even more remarkable are the two ornate, Italian-style chimneys, as well as the 17m-high wooden roof structure, probably built by ship's carpenters. (In the loft you can also see the hatch leading to the roof void where the servants were locked in every night by the head valet to stop them escaping.) Both chimneys and the roof are protected by French law as being of great historical interest. When Soule's peasants revolted in 1661, appalled at the aristocracy's creeping acquisition of common farming land, some damage – visibly, the removal of coats of arms from the fireplaces – was incurred. The eclectic furnishings within the castle include pottery from Italy and China, plus some chunky 17th-century wooden Basque *kutxas* (chests). In a separate room, visitors can marvel at some old books from the 16th and 17th centuries, including an original French dictionary from 1690 and a copy of another 14th-century dictionary, translated into no fewer than nine languages, including English. Visits are only possible by guided tours, which are conducted in French, though visitors will be given an English-language handout to assist them.

L'HÔPITAL SAINT-BLAISE (L'OSPITALE PIA)

Once a major stopover on the Route d'Arles branch of the Camino de Santiago, all that remains of the facilities created for pilgrims in the Middle Ages is the church, now listed as a UNESCO World Heritage Site. In medieval times, a hospital was built, and a small village grew up to serve the thousands of pilgrims passing through from the east on their way to Santiago de Compostela. Now, the pilgrim traffic is hugely reduced on what has become a lesser route and the permanent residents of the quaint village, with its attractive houses dating from the 16th and 17th centuries, number a mere 80.

ÉGLISE DE L'HÔPITAL SAINT-BLAISE (CHURCH) (0559 66 07 21; w hopital-saint-blaise.fr; 1 Apr–11 Nov 10.00–19.00 daily; no official entrance fee, but donation expected; audio guide in English provided; from Apr to Nov, a sound & light show takes place at 11.00, 17.00 & 18.30, €5/2.50 adults/children) Dating from the 12th century, this Roman-style church is renowned for its eight-sided tower and its original preserved woodwork. The influence of Muslim architecture can be seen in the eight-pointed star decorating the dome. Although the architects' identity is unknown, it is possible they came from Spain, influenced by the Moors who occupied that country. Along with the pilgrims came ideas passed back and forward along the routes. Additional evidence of the influences brought across the Pyrenees can be seen in the narrow windows, closed off by stone frames, a feature almost unknown in France but common in Spain at the time. The interior is generally fairly sparse, with limited décor. More ornate, Baroque features were added in the 18th and 19th centuries. The large wooden pews above the nave were – as traditional in the Basque Country – reserved for the menfolk. Cornices sculpted from oak are the original ones from the 12th century. Saint-Blaise, known to the Spanish as San Blas, was an Armenian bishop martyred by beheading at the beginning of the 4th century. He was renowned for his healing of illness, especially throat infections, and is also the patron saint of wool-combers.

TARDETS-SORHOLUS (ATHARRATZE)

Given the relative dearth of accommodation options elsewhere, Tardets's plum-central location makes it a good base for excursions anywhere in Soule. Sainte-Engrâce is a mere 17km to the south, Mauléon only 13km to the north, and a variety of drives start from here (see box, page 361). The town's lively centre is composed of a rather anarchic square into which five roads pour cars and delivery vans, all gently jostling for parking spaces. Here's where you'll find the tourist office, restaurants and hotels.

TOURIST INFORMATION The tourist office is on Place Centrale (0559 28 51 28; e office-tourisme-tardets@wanadoo.fr; w soule-paysbasque.com; 09.00–12.30 & 14.00–19.00 Mon–Sat). It has a bright interior and shares space with the Basque 'Myths and Legends' exhibition upstairs, which has audio exclusively in Basque (see box, page 363).

WHERE TO STAY *Map, page 354*

Hôtel de la Poste (4 rooms) Le Bourg, Tardets; 0559 28 51 30; e contact@hotel-poste-tardets.com; w hotel-poste-tardets.com. Renovated rooms in an old building, with large outside terrace, just off the main square. Ground-floor bar, popular with elderly men chewing the fat. Rooms have TV & free Wi-Fi. **€€**

Hôtel Piellenia (11 rooms) Pl Centrale, Tardets; 0559 28 53 49; e jb@hotel-piellenia.fr; w hotel-piellenia.fr. A hotel that retains some quirky charm of yesteryear. The 17th-century building is right in the main square. Some rooms have a balcony, all have free Wi-Fi. A low-price option, but value for your money & pleasant management. **€€**

Chambres d'Hôtes Etché (3 rooms) Lacarry, 6km southwest of Tardets; 0559 28 55 14; e etchegoyen.louise@orange.fr. Charming Louise speaks barely a word of English, but the linguistic obstacle is worth hurdling to stay in one of her 3 lovely rooms. The house, situated in a quiet valley west of Tardets, has a garden & a small swimming pool. Free Wi-Fi. Price, as with all *chambres d'hôtes*, including b/fast. May specify a 2–3-night min stay in high season. €

Hôtel Restaurant du Pont Abense (6 rooms) Abense le Haut; 0559 28 54 60; e contact@hotelrestaurant-pontabense.com; w hotelrestaurant-pontabense.com. 2-star hotel, just south of Tardets. Good value. Free Wi-Fi. €

WHERE TO EAT AND DRINK *Map, page 354*

Hôtel-Restaurant Piellenia (page 359) The huge dining room speaks of a time gone by, but you can eat in the more compact bar area, or on the outside terrace. The walls display some delightful photos of the town in the early 20th century, devoid of cars but with couples dancing in the square. Food choices are good, nothing elaborate: the *tartine Basque* looks like an English cooked b/fast on a pastry nest, but is delicious. Good quality, pleasant service. €€

Restaurant les Pyrénées ('Abadie') Pl Centrale, Tardets; 0559 28 50 63; Wed–Mon. High-end, reputed chef, serving specialities such as omelette with *foie gras* being the speciality. Traditional fare, traditional dining room. €€

SAINTE-ENGRÂCE (SANTA GRAZI)

Soule's southernmost habitation cowers below the mountain peaks, yet is itself at a height of over 600m. Not quite at the end of the world, though certainly at the extreme eastern edge of the Basque Country in France, Saint-Engrâce's 200 residents owe their picturesque, Romanesque church to the Monastery of Leyre in Navarre, which founded it in 1085 together with a hospital for pilgrims. Wild nature

SWALLOWS AND ESPADRILLES

Mentioned by Pliny the Younger as long ago as the year AD100, the espadrille in the 18th century was still manufactured at home, or perhaps occasionally made by a village craftsman, using materials such as hemp and linen which were easily available in the locality. Fast-forward to the late 19th century, and the process became industrialised, with materials such as cotton, rubber and jute being imported from the colonies of the European powers, particularly from the Indian subcontinent. When Mauléon became one of the first towns in France to receive electricity, it was an ideal place for industrial-scale production of espadrilles, spawning what was then one of France's biggest factories with over a thousand employees. The footwear was particularly popular among the miners of northern France, but Basque emigrants created additional demand, ordering them for delivery to their new homes in Brazil and Venezuela. Customers on both sides of the Pyrenees would receive a pair of espadrilles every week with their pay-packet, dance in them, work in them all week, then receive another pair the following week – in effect, disposable footwear. Many of the factory workers employed in Mauléon in the espadrille 'season' were actually Spanish women. Nicknamed '*Hirondelles*' (swallows), they migrated every year from the south, from towns such as Salvatierra or Fago, crossing the Pyrenees on foot to work for a few months for 15 or 16 hours per day in the Mauléon factories. Carrying a little wooden seat to rest on during their mountainous ascent, and with their few possessions wrapped in a handkerchief, they dressed in traditional costume and made for quite a sight. The Licharre quarter, in the upper part of town, was the home for these migrant workers and their children, who also worked in the factories.

dwarfs the village, which is set in a savage limestone environment of canyons, caves, wooded mountainsides and underground rivers. Two sites of natural interest, Grotte La Verna and Les Gorges de Kakuetta, are nearby and, if that does not satisfy you, there is a 7-hour walk to reach the Gorges d'Ehujarré, starting from the church, an altogether more remote experience recommended only for hardened trekkers.

GROTTE LA VERNA (Reception centre on the D-113, Sainte-Engrâce; **m** 0637 88 29 05; **e** contact@laverna.fr; **w** laverna.fr; ⌚ Jul & Aug 09.00–13.00 & 13.30–19.30 daily, May, Jun, Sep & Oct 09.00–13.00 & 13.30–17.30 Wed–Sun, Apr

SOULE'S BEST SCENERY: SOME CAR JOURNEYS

FROM L'HÔPITAL SAINT-BLAISE Beyond L'Hôpital to the east, take the D-859 then D-59 down a narrow, sometimes single-track road towards Barcus. The route goes through rich forest, with at first the sharp peak of Pic d'Anie (Béarn) fixing your gaze, before the road turns west and runs parallel with the mountain range. At the Croix Agueret (altitude 500m), you can pull in and admire the distant layers of Pyrenean peaks to the south. This route will also give you a close-up of some of the Souletine architecture that styles the houses and you should also keep an eye open for the tall wooden ladders reaching up into the roadside foliage, accessing what look like tree-houses: these are the *palombières*, used by avid hunters for trapping pigeons in season.

FROM TARDETS TO THE COL DE LA PIERRE SAINT-MARTIN (BÉARN) Taking the D-918 to Montory, continue east on the same road and turn right on to the D-632, which runs flat through a Béarnaise valley at first before beginning a twisting ascent towards the Spanish border. The road is narrow, with many hairpins, surrounded by banks of lush fern and tall trees. In times of bad weather, visibility in the mountains can be reduced to almost zero; and in winter … well, the snow-poles are not there for nothing. Watch out for herds of sheep and obstinate blond Aquitaine cows, who roam the grass and tarmac, even at 1,600m above sea level. On reaching Issarbe, you'll be rewarded by a café and some great views, and then you can continue onward to the Col de Soudet and the Col de la Pierre Saint-Martin, the latter the site of a curious annual festival (see box, page 262). Unless you're crossing to Spain, you can return via Sainte-Engrâce, perhaps visiting the beautiful Gorges de Kakuetta or the La Verna cave (see above).

FROM TARDETS TO AHUSQUY With one of the best viewpoints in La Soule, Ahusquy with its *frontón* – one of the cutest in the whole Basque Country – is recommended for a lunchtime visit. From Tardets, take the D-247 then D-117, or from Mauléon the D-918 then D-147. Have lunch at the **Auberge Ahusquy** ✆ 0559 28 57 95; ⌚ Jun–Nov, lunch & evenings; **€€**). If the stuffed bear (not on the menu, thankfully) in the bar doesn't give it away, then the stag's head in the dining room will. Yes, this is a true mountain *auberge*, and if the shepherds who once frequented it are now a bit thin on the ground, the place still has atmosphere and good food in generous portions to satisfy the families who swamp it on summer Sundays. Advanced booking advisable, no credit cards.

& Nov 10.00–13.00 & 13.30–16.00; €17/11 adults/children (1hr trip), €22/16 (1hr 30mins) or €27/21 (2hrs), prices include return transport to the cave) Over 430km of tunnels have been uncovered so far in this Pyrenean karstic terrain, with more being revealed each year. Thirteen underground rivers have been recorded in the area, and one of them flows into La Verna, the largest visitable cave in the world, with underground waterfalls and spectacular rock formations. Only discovered in 1953, this enormous cave has a maximum height of nearly 200m and a diameter of 250m; the Eiffel Tower could fit inside it.

Warm clothes and decent footwear are recommended. There is little light inside, but the dimensions are breathtaking. Some guides speak excellent English – ask when booking. A variety of trips are available, but reservation at least one day in advance is required. Trips involve taking a bus up into the mountains to access the cave and vary in length from an hour to a whole day. The shortest option is accessible to all. Age restrictions apply depending on trip length.

LES GORGES DE KAKUETTA (On the D-113, Sainte-Engrâce; ⌚ 15 Mar–15 Nov 08.00–nightfall daily, though always subject to weather conditions – in times of rain or imminent storms the site is closed due to risk of rockfall; €5/4; hard hats available, walking boots advised) A 3km round trip along a narrow, beautiful gorge, rich with plant life and often with vultures soaring overhead. You walk beneath cliffs that range between 30m and 350m in height, passing waterfalls and ending in the Grotte des Lacs (Cave of Lakes), which features stalactites and stalagmites. Most of the route is on a raised wooden boardwalk 10–20m above the water, but the latter part is on rock that can be slippery. Despite handrails, this is not suitable for those of limited mobility or unsteady on their feet. Good footwear is required. There is a café and shop on-site.

LA MADELEINE Just 7km northeast of Tardets is the summit of La Madeleine, topped off with its little chapel and very popular on sunny days with families taking a picnic. A single-track road whisks you to the top, with marvellous views to enjoy with your sandwiches.

SOULE'S SOUTHWEST

Entering Soule on a clear day along the D-18 from the west, via Mendive, the perfectly pointed cone of Le Pic de Béhorléguy guides you as the road begins to twist upwards in a series of hairpins. Make good use of the viewpoints, of which there are a few, to enjoy the endless views south over the Pyrenees into Spain. Care is required when driving this route, as not only are there sharp drop-offs and bends, but both horses and cows are wont to appear in the middle of the tarmac. There is a bar with a small learning centre on pastoralism at **Chalet de Iraty-Cize**; all panels are in French but the bar staff on duty may speak English and will help where possible. You then turn left, continuing upwards, passing two tiny lakes before reaching the **Chalets d'Iraty** at 1,327m.

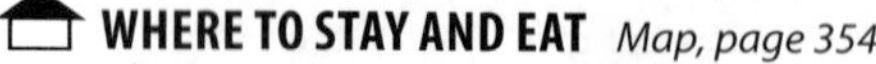

WHERE TO STAY AND EAT *Map, page 354*

Chalets d'Iraty (39 chalets) On the D-19; ☎0559 28 51 29; e info@chalets-iraty.com; w chalets-iraty.com; ⌚ year-round, though subject to weather conditions. At this altitude, it's surprising to find a host of chalets in the forest, nicely separated out & as discreet as you could reasonably expect, with tennis courts, shop, communal bar & restaurant (which has Wi-Fi). Horseriding is available Jul & Aug. Visitors have the opportunity to enjoy the mountain location while ensuring that development does not ruin the precious setting. To some extent this aim is successful, though it will not be to every

CREATURES AND LEGENDS IN THE FRENCH BASQUE COUNTRY

In a savage land of isolated farmhouses, craggy mountains, deep dark caves, swirling low clouds, dense oak and beech forests, legends and myths breed and distort. Like the Basque language and cuisine, stories vary from valley to valley, community to community, and are tweaked further as they are passed from the mouth of one generation to the ear of the next. Here are some of the characters you might 'meet' (or probably not) during your visit.

The **laminak** are among the most frequently appearing characters in the mythology of the Basques. A lamina (the singular of the species) is often portrayed as a female of stunning beauty, completely normal in shape, except for her webbed feet. Or her chicken's feet. Or even her mermaid-like fishtail. Sometimes, however, a lamina can be male, a goblin-like creature. Whichever gender, they live in caves or underground, venturing out only at night due to a fear of sunlight. By daybreak, they return to their dark abodes. Fairly standard stuff, you may be thinking. But the real oddity of a lamina is the nature of their night-time activity, 'moonlighting' quite literally as construction workers. In Soule they are credited with building churches and houses, but most famously the bridge over the Gave de Saison at Licq-Athery. Legend has it that the laminak agreed with the villagers to build the bridge, receiving as payment the village's most beautiful girl. All went well, until the beloved of the maiden took exception. With one stone left to complete the construction, the young man woke up a cockerel which promptly heralded (incorrectly) the daybreak. Off the laminak scarpered to avoid the pending daylight, the bridge was left minus the stone – as indeed it still is – and the young damsel was saved.

The **basajaun** is another popular and not particularly frightening figure who crops up in the legends of the Basques. Very definitely male, he is huge and hairy, often referred to as 'the Basque *yeti*', and is another creature with a strange passion for building things. In the basajaun's case, though, it is megaliths that he chooses to construct. His female companion is a **basandere**, and their habitat is the thick forests of the Basque mountains. Far from being a purveyor of mischief, the basajaun is renowned for his wisdom, busying himself keeping guard over the flocks of the mountain shepherds, as well as giving them lessons in agriculture and tool-making. Unlikely as this may sound, some have theorised that the myth of the basajaun has a base in reality, stemming from the Neanderthals who once inhabited the forests alongside *Homo sapiens* for centuries, before disappearing. Indeed, evidence of Neanderthal settlements has been discovered near Aussurucq, for example. Skilled hunters and known megalith-builders, perhaps the links with the Neanderthals show that basajaun is more than just a myth.

And finally, a real bad guy. **Herensüge** was a seven-headed serpent who dwelt in a cave near Ahusquy and dined on the livestock which grazed the mountain pastureland. His cunning technique was to use his strong breath to inhale the animals, leaving the shepherds in despair at their dwindling flocks. The local count was asked to help and duly sent his son, who ingeniously filled the skin of a slaughtered bull with gunpowder and matches, with inevitable results when the serpent emerged from his cave and couldn't resist the apparently tempting feast in front of him. He disappeared in a ball of flame and was never seen again. Unfortunately, the count's son died of fright on the spot.

nature lover's taste. There is a huge range of chalets available, sleeping 2–29, & prices vary according to capacity & view (forest, mountain, valley – or all 3). Isolated location would suit those content with self-catering, hiking & biking. All chalets have kitchens & a lounge area with wood-burning stove. Normally rented weekly (€410), but can be hired off-season for a 2-night min stay. Between 15 Nov & 15 Apr your vehicle must be fitted with snow chains. **€€**

Logis Hôtel Etchemaïte (17 rooms) Bourg, Larrau; 0559 28 61 45; e contact@hotel-etchemaite.fr; w hotel-etchemaite.fr. A good choice, try for a room with a balcony. TV, free Wi-Fi. Decent b/fast. Bar & restaurant. **€€**

OUTDOOR ACTIVITIES

Horseriding Jul & Aug only, bookable through Chalets d'Iraty (page 362). Rides from €16 per hour.

VTT Centre (mountain bike hire) At Chalets d'Iraty (page 362). As well as hiring bikes & helmets, the Chalets d'Iraty office has details of a number of mountain bike routes available, ranging from 2km to 50km, from easy to difficult.

Walking The Chalets d'Iraty office issues a leaflet detailing (in French) a number of walks ranging from 2.4km to 18km. Some, but not all, of the walks are waymarked, & some should be only attempted in good weather: remember, you're over 1,300m above sea level.

LARRAINE (LARRAU) Watched over by the Pic d'Orhy, the westernmost 2,000m summit in the Pyrenees, the village of Larraine has a couple of accommodation options and a bar, and is well placed for the walk to see the spectacular gorges of Holzarte.

La Passerelle de Holzarte (Accessed off the D-26 at Logibar – parking available) Starting from the parking at Logibar, allow 2 hours for the return trip, a linear walk taking you above the gorges of Holzarte and Olhadubia with a chance to traverse the 67m-long suspension bridge that crosses 150m above the ravine below. The walk is waymarked, following the GR10 path. After reaching the bridge, you can return by the same route or choose to complete a longer circuit (5hrs) by continuing to follow the GR10 along the Olhadubia Gorge until reaching a second bridge, then leaving the GR10 and walking along the opposite side of the gorge, following the violet-coloured waymarking.

SEND US YOUR SNAPS!

We'd love to follow your adventures using our *Basque Country* guide – why not send us your photos and stories via Twitter (@BradtGuides) and Instagram (@bradtguides)? Alternatively, you can upload your photos directly to the gallery on the Basque destination page via our website (w bradtguides.com/basque).

Appendix 1

LANGUAGE

BASQUE It's impossible in the space available to teach you to speak Basque, and in truth you are unlikely to be in a situation where you will actually *need* to speak it to get by. Certainly, no-one will expect you to speak it, though a few words learned before your stay and repeated during it will bring a look of surprise and a smile. Assuming, of course, that you make a half-decent attempt at pronouncing them correctly. Here are a few tips.

Pronunciation

- Certain consonants (eg: c, q, v, w and y) appear in the Basque language only in respect of foreign words or place names that have been imported into Basque.
- The letter 'h' is silent, except for in certain words in certain dialects.
- The following letters or combinations have different pronunciations from their English-language equivalents:
  - 'x' is pronounced as 'sh' as in the English 'mash'
  - 'tx' – which is common in Basque – is pronounced as the English-language sound 'ch' as in 'church'
  - 'tz' has no exact English equivalent; pronounce it as the 'ts' in 'boots'
  - '-in' carries the pronunciation as if it has a 'y' after the 'n' and therefore a word such as *zikina* (dirty) is pronounced 'zikinya'
  - '-il' as in *botila* (bottle) is similar, so would be pronounced 'botilya'

Stress Although the rules on stress are not hard and fast in Basque, generally words with three syllables or more will have the emphasis placed on the second syllable. A word with only two syllables will carry the stress on the first syllable.

Word order In a positive sentence, the word order is different from that in English (or Spanish or French) and is subject–object–verb (stem + auxiliary). Thus:

Ander etxera etorri da	Ander has come home (literally: Ander to home come has)

In the negative equivalent, the order changes:

Ander ez da etxera etorri	Ander has not come home (literally: Ander not has to come home)

Miscellaneous

- To make a noun into a plural, add 'ak', or simply a 'k' if the base word ends in an 'a'
- The article 'the' is shown at the end of the noun, as part of the word:

  liburu book *liberua* the book
- The article 'a' or 'an' also comes after the noun, but is a separate word:

  liburu book *liberu bat* a book

SPANISH (CASTILIAN) Spanish is spoken throughout the three provinces of the Basque Autonomous Community and Navarre. Occasionally, *very* occasionally, foreigners may encounter a Basque diehard who is reluctant to speak Spanish, but in such cases, if they speak

English, they will be happy to do so. For the most part, Spanish is pronounced as it is written, which makes it a relatively easy language to learn. Anyone who has watched a Spanish TV chat show will know that Spanish is spoken very quickly and often by two (or more) people at once: understanding what is being said is usually the biggest challenge for non-natives.

Pronunciation Generally, the mastery of a few key different pronunciations will allow you to speak Spanish and be understood, even if you don't quite have the vocabulary to understand it yourself. The letters, or letter combinations, which are significantly different in their pronunciation from their English-language equivalents are as follows.

- 'c' is soft before an 'e' or an 'i', but otherwise is hard and is then pronounced like the English 'k'
- 'g' is a hard sound (as in the English word 'gallop') but where it precedes an 'e' or 'i' in Spanish then it takes on a sound similar to the 'ch' in the English word 'loch'
- 'i' is the equivalent sound to an English double 'e'
- 'j' is pronounced as a breathy 'h', thus *jabalí* ('wild boar') is pronounced as if written 'habalee'
- 'll' is pronounced like an English 'y' sound. Thus *tortilla* ('omelette') is pronounced as if written 'torteeya'
- 'n' is pronounced the same as in English, but if accented ('ñ') then it is pronounced as if followed by a 'y'. *Mañana* ('tomorrow') is thus pronounced as if written 'manyana'
- 'qu' is pronounced the same as a 'k' in English
- 'r' is rolled, as if there were two or three letters 'r' in the word. Where a word contains a double 'r', it is rolled even more
- 'u' is a long sound, as in the English word 'fool'. The short English-language 'u' sound, as in 'hurry', is unknown in Spanish
- 'v' is an oddity, pronounced more like a 'b'. *Ventana* ('window') is thus pronounced as if written 'bentana'
- 'x' is pronounced as in English, when it precedes a vowel; when it precedes a consonant (fairly rare in Castilian) it takes the sound of an English 's'
- 'z' is pronounced somewhere between a 'c' and a 'th'. *Zanahoria* ('carrot') is pronounced as 'thanahorria'

Stress If in doubt, place the stress on the penultimate syllable. If the word ends in a vowel, an 'n' or an 's' then the stress should be placed on the penultimate syllable; otherwise, place the stress on the final syllable. If the word contains an accent, place the stress on the 'accented' syllable.

Word order Word order is flexible, to some extent, in Spanish. Sticking to the noun–verb–object structure (eg: The book is expensive – *El libro es caro*) is the best bet for novices.

Miscellaneous All nouns in Spanish are either masculine or feminine, and if they end in a vowel then it is either 'o' or 'a' respectively. Any adjective applied to the noun takes the same ending. A noun ending in a vowel will have an 's' added to it to form its plural; if it ends in a consonant, then 'es' is added at the end. The same applies to any accompanying adjective.

FRENCH There is probably some truth in the Anglo-Saxon belief that the French are very reluctant to speak English, so a few words of French will certainly be helpful in the French Basque Country. Given the low proportion of the inhabitants who speak Basque, French will certainly be more useful north of the border. Although France is full of regional accents, the French in the Basque Country is fairly standard and easy to understand for foreigners who speak French.

Pronunciation The use of accents (´ ` ˆ) can be intimidating to some, but the last two of these are actually redundant from a punctuation perspective. The acute as used on the é is worth noting, as it indicates that the letter must be fully pronounced: eg: *(je) donne* – (I) give, as opposed to *(J'ai) donné* – (I have) given.

- 'ç' when accented is pronounced as an English 's' sound, otherwise (without the accent) it is pronounced as the English 'k' sound

- 'ch' is pronounced the same as 'sh' in English
- 'e' is usually pronounced like the English 'e' as in the English word 'bet'
- 'é' is pronounced like the letter 'a' as in the English word 'day'
- 'g' is pronounced as a hard English 'g' as in glove; if it is before an 'e', 'i' or 'y' it is pronounced the same as the 's' as in the English word 'treasure'
- 'h' is not pronounced
- 'i' is pronounced the same as a double 'e' in English, except where it is at the start of a word
- 'j' is pronounced the same as the 's' in the English word 'treasure'
- 'qu' is pronounced like an English 'k'
- 'r' is a 'rolled' sound
- 'u' is a long sound, pronounced the same as the 'ew' in the English word 'few'
- 'w' is pronounced like an English 'v'

In addition to the single vowel sounds in the above list, French contains a number of vowel combinations, or vowel/consonant combinations, the pronunciation of which is not immediately obvious. The most common of these are:

- 'ai'/'ay'/'ais'/'ait'/'aient' are all pronounced 'a' as in the English word 'date' or can all be pronounced 'eh' as in the English word 'bet'
- 'ail' is pronounced the same as the 'ie' sound in the English word 'lie'
- 'au' is pronounced 'o' as in the English word 'donut'
- 'eu' is pronounced as a short 'u' sound, as might be found in the English word 'burn'
- 'oi' is pronounced like the English sound 'wah'
- 'ille' is pronounced either like the English word 'eel' or like the sound 'yu' in the word 'yuppy'
- 'ou' is pronounced like a double 'o' as in the English word 'shoot'
- 'ui' is pronounced like the English word 'wee'

Stress The bad news is that the subject of stress in the French language is hugely complex, as emphasis depends on the specific context in which the word is used, rather than the word itself; the good news is that, although complex, it is not important in the French language. For the average holidaymaker, a lack of knowledge of where to place the stress is not a great barrier to being understood.

Word order Although many variations to word order are possible in French, sticking to the noun–verb–object structure (eg: The book is expensive – *Le livre est cher*) is the best bet for novices.

Miscellaneous All nouns in French are either masculine or feminine. Adjectives ending in consonants will generally have an 'e' added when describing a feminine noun (*noir* (black) becomes *noire*, while *prochain* (next) changes to *prochaine*). There are of course many exceptions to this rule. A noun will have an 's' added to it to form its plural, as will any adjective that describes it.

VOCABULARY AND PHRASES

Essentials

English	Basque	Spanish	French
Good morning	*Egun on*	*Buenos días*	*Bonjour*
Good afternoon/ evening	*Arratsalde on*	*Buenas tardes*	*Bonsoir*
Hello	*Kaixo*	*Hola*	*Salut*
Goodbye	*Agur!*	*Adiós*	*Au revoir*
My name is …	*… naiz*	*Me llamo …*	*Je m'appelle …*
What is your name?	*Zein da aure izena?*	*¿Cómo te llamas?*	*Comment tu t'appelles?*
I am …	*NI – naiz*	*Yo soy …*	*Je viens d'…*
… from England	*Ingalaterrakoa*	*… de Inglaterra*	*Angleterre*
… from Scotland	*Eskoziakoa*	*… de Escocia*	*Écosse*
… from Wales	*Galeskoa*	*… de Gales*	*Pays de Galles*

English	Basque	Spanish	French
… from Ireland	*Irlandakoa*	*… de Irlanda*	*Irlande*
… from the United States	*Estatu Batuetakoa*	*… de los Estados Unidos*	*États-Unis*
… from Canada	*Kanadakoa*	*… de Canada*	*Canade*
… from Australia	*Australiakoa*	*… de Australia*	*Australie*
… from New Zealand	*Zelanda Berrikoa*	*… de Nueva Zelanda*	*Nouvelle Zélande*
How are you?	*Zer moduz?*	*¿Cómo estás?*	*Ça va?*
Pleased to meet you (m/f)	*Urte askotarako*	*Encantado/encantada*	*Enchanté/enchantée*
Thank you	*Eskerrik asko*	*Gracias*	*Merci*
Please	*Mesedez*	*Por favor*	*S'il vous plaît*
Sorry!	*Barkatu*	*¡Disculpe!*	*Excusez-moi*
You're welcome (don't mention it)	*Ez horregatik*	*De nada*	*De rien*
Cheers	*Topa!*	*¡Salud!*	*Santé*
Yes	*Bai*	*Sí*	*Oui*
No	*Ez*	*No*	*Non*
I don't understand	*Ez dut ulertzen*	*No entiendo*	*Je ne comprends pas*
Could you speak slower?	*Astiroago hitz egin dezakezu?*	*¿Podría hablar más despacio?*	*Pouvez-vous parler plus lentement, s'il vous plaît.*

Questions

How?	*Nola?*	*¿Cómo?*	*Comment?*
What?	*Zer?*	*¿Qué?*	*Quoi?*
Where?	*Non?*	*¿Dónde?*	*Où?*
What is it?	*Zer da?*	*¿Qué es?*	*C'est quoi, ça?*
Which?	*Zein?*	*¿Cuál?*	*Lequel/Laquelle?*
When?	*Noiz?*	*¿Cuándo?*	*Quand?*
Why?	*Zergatik?*	*¿Por qué?*	*Pourquoi?*
Who?	*Nor?*	*¿Quién?*	*Qui?*
How much?	*Zenbat?*	*¿Cuánto?*	*Combien?*

Numbers

1	*bat*	*uno*	*un*
2	*bi*	*dos*	*deux*
3	*hiru*	*tres*	*trois*
4	*lau*	*cuatro*	*quatre*
5	*bost*	*cinco*	*cinq*
6	*sei*	*seis*	*six*
7	*zazpi*	*siete*	*sept*
8	*zortzi*	*ocho*	*huit*
9	*bederatzi*	*nueve*	*neuf*
10	*hamar*	*diez*	*dix*
11	*hamaika*	*once*	*onze*
12	*hamabi*	*doce*	*douze*
13	*hamahiru*	*trece*	*treize*
14	*hamalau*	*catorce*	*quatorze*
15	*hamabost*	*quince*	*quinze*
16	*hamasei*	*dieciséis*	*seize*
17	*hamazazpi*	*diecisiete*	*dix-sept*
18	*hamazortzi*	*dieciocho*	*dix-huit*
19	*hemeretzi*	*diecinueve*	*dix-neuf*
20	*hogei*	*veinte*	*vingt*
21	*hogeita bat*	*veintiuno*	*vingt et un*
30	*hogeita hamar*	*treinta*	*trente*

English	Basque	Spanish	French
40	*berrogei*	*cuarenta*	*quarante*
50	*berrogeita hamar*	*cincuenta*	*cinquante*
60	*hirurogei*	*sesenta*	*soixante*
70	*hirurogeita hamar*	*setenta*	*soixante-dix*
80	*laurogei*	*ochenta*	*quatre-vingts*
90	*laurogeita hamar*	*noventa*	*quatre-vingts dix*
100	*ehun*	*cien*	*cent*
1000	*mila*	*mil*	*mille*

Time

What time is it?	*Zer ordu da?*	*¿Qué hora es?*	*Quelle heure est-il?*
It's … in the morning/ afternoon/at night	*Goizeko/arratsaldeko/ gaueko …-ak dira*	*Son las … de la mañana/de la tarde/de la noche*	*C'est … du matin/de l'après-midi/du soir*
today	*gaur*	*hoy*	*aujourd'hui*
tonight	*gaur gauean*	*esta noche*	*ce soir*
tomorrow	*bihar*	*mañana*	*demain*
yesterday	*atzo*	*ayer*	*hier*
morning	*goiza*	*mañana*	*matin*
afternoon	*arratsaldea*	*tarde*	*après-midi*
evening	*iluntzea*	*anochecer*	*le soir*

Days

Monday	*astelehena*	*lunes*	*lundi*
Tuesday	*asteartea*	*martes*	*mardi*
Wednesday	*asteazkena*	*miércoles*	*mercredi*
Thursday	*osteguna*	*jueves*	*jeudi*
Friday	*ostirala*	*viernes*	*vendredi*
Saturday	*larunbata*	*sábado*	*samedi*
Sunday	*igandea*	*domingo*	*dimanche*

Months

January	*urtarrila*	*enero*	*janvier*
February	*otsaila*	*febrero*	*fevrier*
March	*martxoa*	*mars*	*mars*
April	*apirila*	*abril*	*avril*
May	*maiatza*	*mayo*	*mai*
June	*ekaina*	*junio*	*juin*
July	*uztaila*	*julio*	*juillet*
August	*abuztua*	*agosto*	*août*
September	*iraila*	*septiembre*	*septembre*
October	*urria*	*octubre*	*octobre*
November	*azaroa*	*noviembre*	*novembre*
December	*abendua*	*diciembre*	*décembre*

Getting around – public transport

A (return) ticket to … please	*… (joan-etorriko) txartel bat, mesedez*	*Un ticket de ida y vuelta, por favor*	*Un billet (aller et retour) à … s'il vous plaît*
I want to go to	*… ra joan nahi dut*	*Quiero ir a …*	*Je voudrais aller à …*
How much is it?	*Zenbat da?*	*¿Cuánto cuesta?*	*Ça fait combien?*
What time is the train/bus to …?	*Ze ordutan da trena/ autobusa … ra joateko?*	*¿A qué hora es el tren/ autobús para ir a …?*	*À quelle heure départ le train/le bus vers …?*
ticket office	*txartel leihatila*	*Taquilla*	*bureau de vente*
timetable	*ordutegia*	*Horario*	*horaire*

English	Basque	Spanish	French
from	*... (e)tik*	*desde ...*	*de*
to	*... (e)ra*	*hasta ...*	*à*
airport	*aireportu*	*aeropuerto*	*aéroport*
port	*portua*	*puerto*	*port*
bus	*autobusa*	*autobús*	*bus*
bus station	*autobus geltokia*	*estación de autobuses*	*gare routière*
plane	*hegazkina*	*avión*	*avion*
train	*trena*	*tren*	*train*
train station	*tren geltokia*	*estación de tren*	*gare*
boat	*(itsas) ontzia*	*barco*	*bateau*
ferry	*Ferry-a*	*ferry*	*ferry-boat*
car	*autoa*	*coche*	*voiture*
taxi	*taxia*	*taxi*	*taxi*
motorbike	*motoa*	*moto*	*moto*
bicycle	*bizikleta*	*bicicleta*	*bicyclette*
here	*hemen*	*aquí*	*ici*
there	*hor*	*ahí*	*là*
bon voyage!	*bide on!*	*¡buen viaje!*	*bon voyage!*

Private transport

Where is the service station?	*Non dago hurrengo zerbitzugunea?*	*¿Dónde está la próxima estación de servicio?*	*Où est la station-service?*
Full, please	*Beteta, mesedez*	*Lleno, por favor*	*Le plein, s'il vous plaît*
Ten euros of unleaded, please	*Hamar euro berun gabe, mesedez*	*Diez euros sin plomo, por favor*	*Dix euros sans plombe, s'il vous plaît*
diesel	*diesela*	*gasóleo*	*gazole*
How can I get to ...?	*Nola joan naiteke ...*	*¿Cómo puedo ir a ...?*	*Comment j'arrive à ...?*
I have broken down	*Matxuratu egin zait*	*Se me ha estropeado*	*Je suis en panne*

Road signs

give way	*pasatzen utzi*	*ceda el paso*	*cédez le passage*
danger	*arriskua*	*peligro*	*danger*
diversion	*saihesbidea*	*desvío*	*déviation*
entry	*sarrera*	*paso*	*entrée*
one-way	*noranzko bakarra*	*de sentido único*	*sens unique*
entrance	*sarrera*	*entrada*	*entrée*
toll	*bidesaria*	*peaje*	*péage*
no entry	*ez sartu*	*prohibido el paso*	*défense d'entrer*
exit	*irteera*	*salida*	*sortie*

Directions

Where is it?	*Non dago?*	*¿Dónde está?*	*Où est ...?*
go straight ahead	*jarraitu zuzen aurrera*	*siga adelante, todo recto*	*Procédez tout droit*
turn left	*ezkerretara biratu*	*gire a la izquierda*	*Tournez à gauche*
turn right	*eskuinetara biratu*	*gire a la derecha*	*Tournez à droite*
... at the traffic lights	*semaforoan*	*en el semáforo*	*... aux feux*
... at the roundabout	*biribilean*	*en la rotonda*	*... au rond-point*
north	*iparra*	*norte*	*nord*
south	*hegoa*	*sur*	*sud*
east	*ekialdea*	*este*	*est*
west	*mendebaldea*	*oeste*	*ouest*
behind	*atzean*	*atrás*	*derrière*
in front of	*aurrean*	*delante*	*devant*
near	*hurbil*	*cerca*	*près*
opposite	*aurrez-aurre*	*enfrente*	*en face de*

Street signs

English	Basque	Spanish	French
entrance	*sarrera*	*entrada*	*entrée*
exit	*irteera*	*salida*	*sortie*
open	*irekita*	*abierto*	*ouvert*
closed	*itxita*	*cerrado*	*fermé*
toilets	*komunak*	*servicios*	*toilettes*
information	*informazioa*	*información*	*information*

Accommodation

Where is a cheap/ good hotel?	*Non aurki dezaket hotel merkeren/ onen bat?*	*¿Dónde puedo encontrar un hotel barato/bueno?*	*Où se trouve un hôtel à bon prix/ bon hotel?*
Do you have any rooms available?	*Gela librerik ba al duzu?*	*¿Tiene habitaciones disponibles?*	*Avez-vous des chambres disponibles?*
How much is it per night?	*Zenbat da gaueko?*	*¿Cuánto es por noche?*	*Ça coûte combien la nuit?*
I'd like …	*… nahi nuke*	*querría …*	*Je voudrais …*
… a single room	*… gela bakun bat*	*una habitación individual*	*… une chambre individuelle*
… a double room	*… gela bikoitz bat*	*una habitación doble*	*… une chambre double*
… a room with two beds	*… gela bat bi oherekin*	*una habitación con dos camas*	*… une chambre avec deux lits*
… a room with a bathroom	*… gela bat bainugelarekin*	*una habitación con baño*	*… une chambre avec une salle de bain*
… a dormitory bed	*… gela bat literekin*	*una habitación con literas*	*… un lit en dortoir*
Is there free Wi-Fi?	*Wi-Fi-rik ba al dago?*	*¿Hay Wi-Fi gratuito?*	*Il y a du Wi-Fi gratuit?*
What is the Wi-Fi password?	*Zein da Wi-Fi-rako pasahitza?*	*¿Cuál es la contraseña para el Wi-Fi?*	*C'est quoi, le mot de passe pour le Wi-Fi?*
Is breakfast included?	*Gosaria ere barne dago?*	*¿Está incluido el desayuno?*	*Est-ce que le petit déjeuner est inclus?*
How much is breakfast?	*Zenbat balio du gosariak?*	*¿Cuánto cuesta el desayuno?*	*Ça coûte combien, le petit déjeuner?*

Food

What time do you open?	*Zer ordutan zabaltzen duzu?*	*¿A qué hora abren?*	*À quelle heure le restaurant est ouvert?*
Do you have a table for … people?	*… entzako mahaia, mesedez*	*¿Tiene mesa para … personas?*	*Vous avez une table à … personnes?*
… a children's menu?	*umeentzako menua*	*un menú infantil?*	*… un menu enfants?*
I am a vegetarian	*Begetarianoa naiz*	*Soy vegetariano*	*Je suis végétarien*
Please may I have the bill	*Kontua, mesedez*	*La cuenta, por favor*	*L'addition, s'il vous plaît*

Basics

bread	*ogia*	*pan*	*pain*
butter	*gurina*	*mantequilla*	*beurre*
cheese	*gazta*	*queso*	*fromage*
oil	*olioa*	*aceite*	*huile*
pepper	*piperbeltza*	*pimienta negra*	*poivre noir*
salt	*gatza*	*sal*	*sel*
sugar	*azukrea*	*azúcar*	*sucre*

Fruit

English	Basque	Spanish	French
apples	*sagarrak*	*manzanas*	*pommes*
bananas	*platanoak*	*plátanos*	*bananes*
cherries	*gereziak*	*cerezas*	*cerises*
grapes	*mahatsak*	*uvas*	*raisins*
lemon	*limoia*	*limón*	*citron*
melon	*meloia*	*melón*	*melon*
nectarine	*nektarina*	*nectarina*	*nectarine*
orange	*laranja*	*naranja*	*orange*
peach	*muxika*	*melocotón*	*pêche*
pear	*udarea*	*pera*	*poire*

Vegetables

carrot	*azenarioa*	*zanahoria*	*carotte*
garlic	*baratxuria*	*ajo*	*ail*
onion	*tipula*	*cebolla*	*oignon*
pepper	*piperra*	*pimiento*	*poivron*
potatoes	*patatak*	*patatas*	*pommes de terre*

Fish

anchovies	*antxoak*	*anchoas*	*anchois*
cod	*bakailaoa*	*bacalao*	*morue*
(baby) squid	*txipiroia*	*chipirón*	*seiche*
hake	*legatza*	*merluza*	*merlu*
monkfish	*itsas zapoa*	*rape*	*lotte*
sea bream	*bisigua*	*besugo*	*dorade*
squid	*txibia*	*calamar*	*calamar*

Meat

beef	*behi okela*	*carne de vaca*	*bœuf*
chicken	*oilaskoa*	*pollo*	*poulet*
lamb	*bildoskia*	*cordero*	*agneau*
pork	*txerria*	*cerdo*	*porc*

Drinks

beer	*garagardoa*	*cerveza*	*bière*
coffee	*kafea*	*café*	*café*
fruit juice	*zukua*	*zumo*	*jus de fruits*
milk	*esnea*	*leche*	*lait*
tea	*tea*	*té*	*thé*
water	*ura*	*agua*	*eau*
wine (red)	*ardo beltza*	*vino tinto*	*vin rouge*
wine (white)	*ardo zuria*	*vino blanco*	*vin blanc*

Shopping

I'd like to buy …	*… erostea gustatuko litzaidake*	*Me gustaría comprar …*	*Je voudrais acheter …*
How much is it?	*Zenbat da?*	*¿Cuánto es?*	*C'est combien?*
I don't like it	*Ez zait gustatzen*	*No me gusta*	*Je ne l'aime pas*
I'm just looking	*Begiratzen nabil bakarrik*	*Sólo estoy mirando*	*Je regarde*
It's too expensive	*Garestiegia da*	*Es demasiado caro*	*C'est trop cher*
I'll take it	*Hartuko dut*	*Me lo llevo*	*Je vais le prendre*
Please may I have …	*Mesedez, izan dezaket …*	*Por favor, podría tener …*	*Puis-je avoir*

English	Basque	Spanish	French
The bill, please	*Kontua, mesedez*	*La cuenta por favor*	*L'addition, s'il-vous-plaît*
Do you accept …?	*Onartzen duzu …?*	*¿Acepta usted …?*	*Acceptez-vous …*
credit card	*txartela*	*tarjeta*	*carte de crédit*
more	*gehiago*	*más*	*plus*
less	*gutxiago*	*menos*	*moins*
smaller	*txikiagoa*	*más pequeño*	*plus petit*
bigger	*handiagoa*	*más grande*	*plus grand*

Communications

I'm looking for …	*… -ren bila nabil*	*Estoy buscando …*	*Je cherche …*
bank	*banketxea*	*banco*	*banque*
internet café	*internet kafea*	*internet café*	*café internet*
post office	*postetxea*	*correos*	*bureau de poste*
tourist office	*turismo bulegoa*	*oficina de turismo*	*office de tourisme*

Health

diarrhoea	*beherakoa*	*diarrea*	*diarrhée*
nausea	*goragalea*	*náusea*	*nausée*
doctor	*medikua*	*médico*	*médecin*
prescription	*preskripzioa*	*prescripción*	*ordonnance*
pharmacy	*farmazia*	*farmacia*	*pharmacie*
painkiller	*analgesikoa*	*analgésico*	*antidouleur*
antibiotic	*antibiotikoa*	*antibiótico*	*antibiotique*
antiseptic	*antiseptikoa*	*antiséptico*	*antiseptique*
tampon	*tanpoia*	*tampón*	*tampon*
condom	*kondoia*	*preservativo*	*préservatif*
contraceptive	*antisorgailua*	*anticonceptivo*	*contraceptif*
sunblock	*eguzkitako krema*	*protector solar*	*écran total*
I am asthmatic	*Asmatikoa naiz*	*Soy asmático*	*Je suis asthmatique*
I am epileptic	*Epileptikoa naiz*	*Soy epiléptico*	*Je suis épileptique*
I am diabetic	*Diabetikoa naiz*	*Soy diabético*	*Je suis diabétique*
I'm allergic to …	*… eri alergikoa naiz*	*Soy alérgico a …*	*Je suis allergique à*
penicillin	*penizilina*	*penicilina*	*pénicilline*
nuts	*fruitu lehorrak*	*frutos secos*	*noix*
bees	*erleak*	*abejas*	*abeilles*

Travel with children

Is there a …?	*ba al dago …?*	*¿Hay algún/alguna …?*	*Y-a-t'il …?*
… baby changing room?	*… umeak aldatzeko gelarik?*	*¿… cambiador de bebés?*	*… une pièce pour changer le bébé?*
… a children's menu?	*… umeentzako menurik?*	*¿… menú infantil?*	*… un menu enfants?*
Do you have …?	*Ba al daukazu …?*	*¿Tiene usted …?*	*Est-ce-que vous avez …?*
… infant milk formula?	*… esne-formularik?*	*… leche de fórmula?*	*… du lait maternisé*
nappy	*fardela*	*pañal*	*couche*
potty	*txizontzi*	*orinal*	*pot de bébé*
babysitter	*ume zaintzailea*	*niñera*	*babysitter*
high chair	*trona*	*trona*	*chaise haute*
Are children allowed?	*Umeak onartzen dira?*	*¿Están permitidos los niños?*	*Est-ce que les enfants sont acceptés?*

Other

my/mine	*nire/nirea*	*mío*	*le mien*
ours/yours	*gureak/zuenak*	*nuestro/vuestro*	*le nôtre/le vôtre*
and/some/but	*eta/batzuk/baina*	*y/algunos/pero*	*et/de or de la or du/ mais*

English	Basque	Spanish	French
this/that	*hau/hura*	*esto/aquello*	*celui-ci/celui-là*
cheap	*merkea*	*barato*	*bon marché*
expensive	*garestia*	*caro*	*cher*
beautiful/ugly	*polita/itsusia*	*bonito/feo*	*beau/laide*
old/new	*zaharra/berria*	*viejo/nuevo*	*vieux/nouveau*
good/bad	*ongi, ona/txarra*	*bien, bueno/malo*	*bon/mauvais*
early/late	*goiz/berandu*	*pronto/tarde*	*tôt/tard*
hot/cold	*beroa/hotza*	*caliente/frío*	*chaud/froid*
difficult/easy	*zaila/erraza*	*difícil/fácil*	*difficile/facile*
boring/interesting	*aspergarria/ interesgarria*	*aburrido/interesante*	*ennuyeux/ intéressant*

Emergency

English	Basque	Spanish	French
Help!	*Lagundu!*	*¡Socorro!*	*Au secours!*
Call a doctor!	*Deitu medikuari!*	*¡Llamad a un médico!*	*Appelez un médecin!*
There's been an accident	*Istripu bat egon da*	*Ha habido un accidente*	*Il y a eu un accident*
I'm lost	*Galdu egin naiz*	*Me he perdido*	*Je suis perdu*
Go away!	*Alde hemendik!*	*¡Vete!*	*Allez-vous en!*
police	*polizia*	*policía*	*police*
fire	*sua*	*fuego*	*feu*
ambulance	*anbulantzia*	*ambulancia*	*ambulance*
thief	*lapurra*	*ladrón*	*voleur*
hospital	*ospitalea*	*hospital*	*hôpital*
I'm not feeling well	*Ez naiz ondo aurkitzen*	*No me encuentro bien*	*Je ne me sens pas bien*
I'm injured	*Zaurituta nago*	*Estoy herido*	*Je suis blessé*

Appendix 2

FURTHER INFORMATION

BOOKS

History and general background

Chislett, William *Spain – What Everyone Needs to Know About Spain* Oxford University Press, 2013. For those wanting a concise, functional history of Spain, with some useful contributions on the Basques.

Douglas, William and Zulaika, Joseba *Basque Culture: Anthropological Perspectives* Center for Basque Studies, University of Nevada, Reno, 2007. Recommended for those who want to delve deep into issues surrounding Basque culture and history, a textbook-style publication.

Kurlansky, Mark *The Basque History of the World* Jonathan Cape, 1999. Interesting and thought-provoking reading before, during or after a visit.

Watson, Cameron *Modern Basque History: Eighteenth Century to the Present* Center for Basque Studies, University of Nevada, Reno, 2003.

Woodworth, Paddy *The Basque Country: A Cultural History* Signal Books, 2007. Highly readable book that sheds light on aspects of Basque culture, the relationship between north and south, Navarre, Bilbao's rejuvenation and much more.

Food

Sevilla, María José *Life and Food in the Basque Country* Weidenfeld & Nicholson, 1989. An entertaining insight into Basque culinary traditions – and with recipes, too.

Basque literature

Atxaga, Bernardo *The Accordionist's Son* Harvill Secker, 2003. A novel by the most celebrated of Basque writers explores the effects of the Civil War.

Olaziregi, Mari Jose *Strange Language: An Anthology of Basque Short Stories* Parthian Books, 2008. A good introduction to a number of modern Basque writers, with some poignant stories.

Uribe, Kirmen *Bilbao–New York–Bilbao* Seren Discoveries, 2008. Winner of the Spanish National Literature Prize.

Walking

Cooper, Philip *The Basque Country of France and Spain: Walks and Car Tours* Sunflower (Landscapes Series), 2010. Good selection of walks across the whole region, but needs to be read in conjunction with updates given on the publisher's website (**w** sunflowerbooks.co.uk).

Topoguide Series *Le Pays Basque à Pied* Fédération Française de la Randonée Pédestre, 2013. In French, but if your language skills are well polished, a useful book of 20 walks with detailed maps, all in the western French Pyrenees.

Camino de Santiago and Camino Ignaciano

Brierley, John *Pilgrim's Guide to the Camino de Santiago* (11th edition) Camino Guides, 2015.

Iriberri, José Luis and Lowney, Chris *Guide to the Camino Ignaciano* Ediciones Mensajero, 2017.

Kelly, Gerald *Walking Guide to the Camino del Baztán* Self-published, 2015.

Whitson, Dave and Perrazoli, Laura *The Northern Caminos: The Norte, Primitivo and Inglés Routes* Cicerone, 2015.

Language (Basque)

Knörr de Santiago, Garikoitz *Kaixo! English–Basque Conversation Guide* Txertoa Argitaletxea, 2010. Decent starting point for anyone bold enough to want to learn Basque.

Buying property

Foster, Anthony I *The Complete Guide to Buying a Property in Spain* (12th Edition) Creative Media Associates Spain, 2016.

Sampson, Mark *Essential Questions to Ask When Buying a House in France, and How to Ask them* Summersdale Publishing, 2014.

Other European travel guides For a full list of Bradt's European guides, see **w** bradtguides.com/shop.

Abraham, Rudolf *Alpe-Adria Trail* Bradt Travel Guides, 2016.

Bird, Angela and Stewart, Murray *The Vendée* Bradt Travel Guides, 2018.

Di Gregorio, Luciano *Italy: Abruzzo* Bradt Travel Guides, 2017.

Facaros, Dana and Pauls, Michael *Northern Italy: Emilia-Romagna* Bradt Travel Guides, 2018.

Phillips, Laurence *Lille* Bradt Travel Guides, 2015.

Rix, Juliet *Malta and Gozo* Bradt Travel Guides, 2019.

Robinson, Alex *Alentejo* Bradt Travel Guides, 2019.

Sayers, David and Stewart, Murray *Azores* Bradt Travel Guides, 2019.

Whitehouse, Rosie *Liguria* Bradt Travel Guides, 2019.

WEBSITES Tourist board websites are listed on page 42.

w **etxepare.eus** This website is that of the Basque Institute, with comprehensive sections on important aspects of Basque culture, including language, literature, music and architecture. For the real enthusiast who wants to probe in detail, everything is well translated into English.

w **ine.es** The site of the Instituto Nacional de Estadística with official economic data on Spain, by region.

w **insee.fr** Provides economic and demographic data on France, by *département*.

w **mundicamino.com** This multilingual and comprehensive site, useful for planning any Camino de Santiago pilgrim adventure.

w **tourisme64.com** Clicking on to the 'Itineraries' link accesses nearly 300 itineraries on foot, by bike (road or all-terrain) and on horseback through the French Basque Country, all translated into English.

Index

Page numbers in **bold** indicate main entries; those in *italics* indicate maps.

INDEX OF ADVERTISERS